W9-AEF-220

The History of
ISRAEL

THE HISTORY OF
ISRAEL

VOLUME II
From the Exile to A.D. 135

GIUSEPPE RICCIOTTI

TRANSLATED BY

CLEMENT DELLA PENTA, O.P., S.T.Lr., Ph.D.
RICHARD T. A. MURPHY, O.P., S.T.D., S.S.D.

THE BRUCE PUBLISHING COMPANY
MILWAUKEE

IMPRIMI POTEST:
> EDWARD L. HUGHES, O.P., S.T.M.,
> *Prior Provincialis*

NIHIL OBSTAT:
> JOHN A. SCHULIEN, S.T.D.,
> *Censor librorum*

IMPRIMATUR:
> ✠ ALBERTUS G. MEYER,
> *Archiepiscopus Milwauchiensis*

Die 27a ianuarii, 1955

Catholic University of America Classification:
Dewey, 933

Library of Congress Catalog Card Number: 54-8619

COPYRIGHT, 1955, THE BRUCE PUBLISHING COMPANY
MADE IN THE UNITED STATES OF AMERICA

INTRODUCTION

In the year 135 of our era, Jerusalem fell. It was a cataclysmic event. Other great cities had fallen in the past, and others would fall in the future, but this was the City of David, and the center of the Jewish religion. With its fall and destruction, a thousand years of both civic and religious tradition ground jarringly to a halt. Well might the world, and all ages, pause to gaze upon this spectacle and ask: What led up to this catastrophe? And what were those glories and traditions which now lie covered under the rubble and ashes of this Holy City?

Almost everyone knows something of the history of the Chosen People, from the time of Abraham on down to the days of David and Solomon. But even among professed teachers of the Bible, relatively few know anything at all about what took place after the glorious days of David and Solomon. This is indeed strange, for it was precisely in this important period that Judaism was developing into the form which it had assumed when the gospel was first preached in Judea. The present volume takes up the story of this "dark period," beginning with the Babylonian Exile (586 B.C.) and ending with the bitter frustration and defeat of A.D. 135.

To read these pages, then, is to march to and fro across Asia Minor, Mesopotamia, Syria, Palestine, and Egypt. It means trudging along ancient roads with warriors from Persia, Greece, and Rome, crossing rivers hitherto unheard of, taking part in decisive battles in places whose names are only vaguely familiar (if at all), and well-nigh breaking one's jaw on unfamiliar and quite unpronounceable names of courtiers, soldiers, prophets, and kings.

Yet all this background, as arduous, wearisome, and difficult to cover as were some of those interminable wars of ancient days, is necessary for serious-minded readers of the Bible. The story quickens with interest when it focuses on such Old Testament highlights as Esdras and

Nehemias, or the Exile and the Return, the Samaritan Schism (of which there are repercussions in the gospel story), and the Diaspora and its growth. Then there is the important phenomenon of Prophetism, and the stirring story of the heroic Machabees, father and sons, balanced on the other end of the scale by the bloody but fascinating story of the ignoble Herods, father and sons. Finally, the story of Rome's intervention in the affairs of the Near East and her eventual rule over it, leads quite naturally to the chapter on Israel's life under the Roman Procurators. That life seemed to flicker and die when Jerusalem fell in the year A.D. 79, but the end was not to come until the last embers of fanatical nationalism, stirred into flame under the leadership of Simeon ben-Kosebha, were definitively stamped out in the year A.D. 135. Having served its purpose in the plan of divine Providence, an era of glorious history comes to a close.

When it first appeared in Europe, Ricciotti's HISTORY was hailed as filling a critical need of long standing. Here in America there has been an even greater need for a work such as this, offering to the average reader a truly enormous amount of well co-ordinated biblical material not easily available elsewhere. Ricciotti has made it clear, however, that he did not intend to produce a biblical encyclopedia, or an historical novel based on biblical events; he proposed to write *a history* in which due importance would be given to those basic facts so indispensable to further investigation and research. Obviously, then, he does not answer all the questions that need answering, but he has traced out a path through many tangled and complicated areas. His successors in this field must widen this path; it is up to them to explore the tempting side-passages which he was prevented from investigating by his iron-clad resolution to deal only with the main issues. We can be grateful that he has done so much; no one is so naïve as to think that nothing has been left to be done.

✿　　✿　　✿

There remains now the pleasant duty of acknowledging the debt of gratitude owed to those who have helped prepare this HISTORY OF ISRAEL for the English-reading public. Considerable help was given by two colleagues who are also Scripture professors: Father Joseph Considine of the Dominican House of Studies in River Forest, Illinois, and Father John Francis McDonnell of St. Rose Priory, Dubuque, Iowa, and cordial thanks are hereby extended to them both. A word of grateful appreciation must also be tendered to The Bruce Publishing Company, whose interest in this work has extended far beyond the mere publication of another book. The willing and persevering co-operation of the two Bruces, William C. and William G., and of Mr. Aloysius Croft, not only explains the high caliber of the Bruce publications in general, but in the case of Ricciotti's HISTORY OF ISRAEL, merits the thanks both of the translators and of the readers who will benefit by it as well.

St. Rose Priory M.
Dubuque, Iowa
Nov. 23, 1954

ABBREVIATIONS

ANET — Ancient Near Eastern Texts (ed. by J. B. Pritchard)

AO — Altorientalische Texte sum A. T.[2] (H. Gressman et al.)

BA — The Biblical Archaeologist

BASOR — Bulletin of the American School of Oriental Research

DBS — Dictionnaire de la Bible (Vigoroux), Supplément

JNES — Journal of Near Eastern Studies

RB — Revue Biblique

CONTENTS

LIST OF MAPS

TABLES

The History of
ISRAEL

THE ACHAEMENIDS

1. At the time of Israel's exile and during the first decades of that exile, Asia enjoyed a seemingly stable political equilibrium which gave promise of long enduring. What had been Assyria had been divided between the two powers which destroyed it. The lands to the east and a great part of those to the north of the Tigris came into the possession of Media so that its territory — comprising the vassal states beyond the eastern bank of the Persian Gulf — extended from this gulf, ran from there to the other side of the Tigris, and reached to Cappadocia in the center of Asia Minor. The regions to the southwest of Media belonged to Babylonia and thus its territory, which began from the northwestern bank of the Persian gulf, consisted of Mesopotamia, Syria, and Palestine, bordering on Egypt to the south, and to the northwest including Cilicia, it extended to Cappadocia.

To the west of Median Cappadocia and Babylonian Cilicia in Asia Minor, meanwhile, the state of Lydia with its capital Sardis had been created, and had extended its dominion over the rest of Asia Minor up to the Aegean Sea. The eastern limits of Lydia, which bordered Median Cappadocia, had given rise to doubts and quarrelings but in the year 585 a treaty between Aliatte, king of Lydia, and Cyaxares, king of Media, fixed the boundary of the two states at the River Halys.

On the other hand, there was no serious rivalry between Media and Babylonia, which countries had divided the territories of Assyria satisfactorily between them. Thus, there was no visible threat to the equilibrium which was created in anterior Asia after the fall of Nineve. There still remained Egypt, the perennial antagonist of every state in anterior Asia, but it was so weak at that time that it was more in a position to be conquered than to conquer. This is borne out by the expedition which, in all likelihood, Nabuchodonosor waged against it in the year 567 (Vol. I, § 42; cf. also §§ 13 ff., 518 ff.).

2. Yet, the unpredictable came to pass and, paradoxically, destroyed that political equilibrium in the short interval of one generation. Cyrus the Great was the factor which upset all calculations.

1

The king of the Medes did not exercise direct dominion over all the territories under him, for over the tribes settled to the south and southeast of the capital, Ecbatana, he exercised only a nominal sovereignty. These tribes, such as the Pasargadae, Maraphans, Maspians, Panthialaeans, etc. (Herodotus, I, 125), wanted their own leaders to govern them, even though they were dependent more or less on Ecbatana. With the passage of time, probably on the occasion of the fall of Assyria, these tribes were obliged to move, and found their way, for the most part from the mountainous region of their native Parsa (Persia), into the valleys of Susiana and, at the same time, strengthened their bonds of ethnic affinity as they regrouped into larger units. The family of the Achaemenids, which had succeeded in creating the modest kingdom of Anzan in the region of Susa, normally subject to Media, belonged to the tribe of the Pasargadae.

In the year 558 the Achaemenid Cambyses was succeeded on the throne by his son Cyrus, who was called the "King of Anzan" by the Babylonian Chronicle of Nabonidus (550 B.C.). In the ninth year of Nabonidus (546), however, the title was changed to that of "King of Persia." The change was the result either of the steps taken by Cyrus from the beginning of his reign, or of what he had accomplished in the sixth year of the reign of Nabonidus.

The petty but enterprising king of Anzan had at once set about uniting another ten tribes or so with his own Pasargadae, and from this fusion there emerged the nation of the Persians. The internal work of nationalization was also tailored to fit a bold political plan, the emancipation of the unified nation from the suzerainty of Media.

The king of Media at that time was Astyages, the son of Cyaxares. If the Greek historians can be believed (excluding of course the fictional *Cyropaedia*), Cyrus and Astyages were related, since, according to the more common tradition, Cyrus' mother, Mandane, was the daughter of Astyages. Whether this be true or not, about the year 553 the vassal "King of Anzan" took up arms against the king of Media and invaded his territory. The struggle was not brief nor was it at first favorable to the insurgent, who was repulsed. The war was then transferred to Persian territory, and in this new sector fortunes changed. In the year 550, perhaps at Pasargadae, the capital of the rebels, the victorious Astyages was defeated, owing largely to the mutiny of some of his troops. He was sent to Cyrus as a prisoner.

Not long after, the capital, Ecbatana, fell to Cyrus, who carried away its treasures to Anzan. The victor, however, inaugurated a new policy which was entirely contrary to the usual procedure in the Orient, for he did not damage the city nor did he savagely mistreat the conquered people. He even treated the prisoner Astyages with consideration. Thus

The Bastions of Sardis.

from the year 550 Cyrus became "King of Persia" and into it the title "King of Media" was absorbed. At one stroke, his dominions were extended from the plateau of Iran to the center of Asia Minor.

3. The disappearance of Media was not displeasing to Nabonidus, monarch of Babylonia. On the contrary, his religious preoccupations inspired him to take advantage of the situation and occupy Harran, which had been a bone of contention between him and Astyages. However, he soon had to change his mind, for all signs indicated that the new king would not be satisfied with the enormous increase in territory and would become ever more threatening. Croesus, king of Lydia, Persia's other neighbor at the extreme edge of Asia Minor, was of like mind. These similar views led to the formation of a league against Cyrus. Besides Nabonidus and Croesus, it included Amasis, Pharaoh of Egypt, and Sparta, a city which was friendly to Croesus, and whose soldiers were famous throughout Asia.

In the year 546 Croesus took the offensive and entered Persian Cappadocia. Cyrus encountered him at Pteria in the spring, pursued him to Lydia, where he inflicted a serious defeat upon him, and then besieged him in the autumn at Sardis. The Babylonians and Egyptians, among Croesus' allies, did not come to his aid; the Spartans were on the point of sending a fleet when the news came that Sardis had fallen. The siege had lasted hardly two weeks. The new tactics of the Persians, which relied chiefly on the extensive use of expert archers and the encircling manoeuvre of cavalry, proved to be very effective and would remain so until confronted by the Greco-Macedonian tactical formation. Although the Babylonian Chronicle of Nabonidus is mutilated at this point,

Persian Archer (Persepolis). (From Herzfeld, *Am Tor von Asien*.)

it seems that Croesus was killed by Cyrus, although a Grecian tradition has it that he was spared.

With the disappearance of Lydia and the extension of Cyrus' kingdom to the Aegean Sea, Xiennes, king of Cilicia, and many Ionian cities of the coast, submitted spontaneously. The other cities, except Miletus, which was granted special concessions, were in turn brought under the obedience of the generals of Cyrus, so that all of Asia Minor was now under Persian domination.

After the conquest of Sardis, Cyrus transferred his activities to the other extremity of his kingdom, where the peoples east of Iran represented a grave threat. By a series of campaigns which were protracted until the year 540, he subdued the territories there up to Sogdiana and stabilized his frontier at the River Iaxertes.

4. Contemplating the tranquillity which prevailed from India on the east to the Mediterranean on the west, the Persian monarch decided that the time had come to square accounts with Babylonia to the south. His timing was perfect, and demonstrates again that he combined a most remarkable gift for strategy with a no less remarkable political intuition. The Babylonian empire at that time was, for all practical purposes, without a head. Nabonidus (Vol. I, § 16)

Persian soldiers with lance and shield.

was not a great success at governing. Led by his religious preoccupations he exerted himself in bringing to Babylon the statues of the divinities most venerated in the various centers of Chaldea, thinking thus to assure divine protection for his city; but the move also aroused the indignation of the devout peoples who were despoiled of their gods. Moreover, for reasons which are not clear but which might be religious ones, in the seventh year of his reign he decided, oddly enough, or was obliged to do so, to remain at Tema, an isolated spot in northern Arabia bordering on the Syrian desert and far from the capital. Thus the venerable cult of the temples of Babylon was interrupted, to the new discontent of the citizens, and the reins of government remained almost entirely in the hands of his son Balthasar (Belshassar), under whom things took a turn for the worse. The restlessness of the native peoples was enormously increased by the ferment of the foreign peoples who had been deported to the country of Nabuchodonosor, and were chafing at their servitude on a foreign soil. There is reason to believe that while affairs were developing spontaneously in Cyrus' favor, he helped the cause along. It seems that Elamite governors favorable to Cyrus succeeded in installing themselves in southern Chaldea about the tenth year of Nabonidus (545). It is certain, moreover, that the region of the Gutians (Vol. 1, § 3), which commanded the northern approach to Babylon, the capital, had not only been disposed favorably and won over to the Persian cause, but even its governor, Gubaru (Ugbaru, i.e., Gobryas), seems to have depended upon the directives of Cyrus. Babylonia, in short, could at this time be compared to a person afflicted with dropsy, in whom dissolution had set in even before death. On its flank the youthful Persia, under the guiding genius of Cyrus, was like a powerful athlete poised for any action.

5. In the year 540 Cyrus opened his campaign. Like his other decisive ones, it was very brief. Little is known about his opening movements, but at the beginning of the month Tishri (September-October), he was already master of the region of the Gutians. When he departed from that region to make his thrust against Babylonia on the south, he was accompanied by Gubaru, to whom he had given command over one of his armies. At the beginning of the month, the Babylonians were defeated at Opis on the Tigris, which was the southern extremity of Gutium and opened on Babylonia. Nabonidus had returned some years since from Tema and resided at Sippar on the Euphrates, a little north of the capital. The fourteenth of the same month, the army of Cyrus took Sippar. In a synchronized manoeuvre the army of Gubaru descended southward and two days later took Babylon on the sixteenth of Tishri, in the year 539.

The Chronicle of Nabonidus has the following concerning the great

Excavation of the impregnable walls of Babel.

event: "The fourteenth [*Tishri*] Sippar was seized without a battle. Nabonidus fled. On the sixteenth, Gobryas, the governor of Gutium and the armed forces of Cyrus, penetrated Babel without a battle. Afterward Nabonidus was taken prisoner in his flight to Babylon. The shieldbearers of Gutium stood guard at the gates of Esagila [*the temple of Babylon:* Vol. I, § 2] until the end of the month. Nothing was taken out of Esagila and its temples; the festivity was not omitted. On the third of Arahshamnu [*the following month: October-November*], Cyrus entered Babel . . . [*lacuna*] . . . were displayed before him. Peace was imposed on the city. Cyrus proclaimed peace to all of Babylon." Nabonidus was sent to Carmania to live quietly; according to Daniel 5:30 (cf. *Cyropaedia*, VII, 5, 30), however, Balthasar was put to death.

That Babylon, so renowned for its impregnable walls, should fall in less than a fortnight is explained by the fact that there must not have been a real siege, as indeed the Chronicle of Nabonidus and Cyrus himself in his Cylinder (line 17) admit. The faction which was opposed to Nabonidus and Balthasar must have flung open the gates of the city. On the other hand, Herodotus, I, 191 (as also the *Cyropaedia*, VII, 5, 15) describes the stratagem by which Cyrus deflected the river which flowed through the city, thus allowing the soldiers to enter it by the nearly dry river bed. They thus surprised the besieged who were celebrating a great feast. It is difficult, however, to harmonize the amount of labor required for this task with the limited time so clearly indicated in the Chronicle of Nabonidus.

6. In this change of government, neither the material city nor its social life suffered much, if at all, for tablet records of ordinary contracts have come to light which are dated to within a few days after the beginning of Cyrus' reign. More striking still for that time was the moderation shown by the victor in so great a triumph, and his mild treatment of the vanquished. If all anterior Asia was surprised in 550 more at the benignity of Cyrus toward the vanquished Astyages than at his victory over the Medes, some sort of explanation can be found in the fact that the two peoples were of similar stock, or in the probable relationship of the two kings. But in the case of Babylonia such an explanation does not apply. The Semites of Mesopotamia would have considered it altogether normal that Cyrus should employ in his conquest the methods which were usual in Babylonian and Assyrian warfare: slaughters, deportations, lootings, and vexations of every description. The Semites found in Cyrus not a Semitic conqueror but something of a benefactor.

Cyrus' Aryan but unsemitic mentality was a factor in this attitude, but certainly not the most dominant, and much less the exclusive one. His political perspicacity made him realize that people may be conquered by the sword, but are won over only by goodness. His ambition was of too high an order to content itself with holding peoples by force. He wanted inward allegiance as well. Many practical reasons, then, were behind his policy.

In the first place, the rapidity of his triumph over Babylonia was due to his policy of appearing as a liberator before whom the doors would swing open. He therefore owed a debt of gratitude to those of the oppressed who had facilitated his triumph, and it was necessary to inaugurate a policy entirely contrary to that which had caused so much harm under Nabonidus. Besides, Babylon was a very rich city and its

The Euphrates near Babel.

Panorama of excavated Babylon.

territories produced all sorts of goods; why destroy the city and pillage the provinces, the usual procedure among the Semites, and one which had been visited upon Ninive seventy years before? Such damage would deprive his empire, supreme from India to the Mediterranean, of its finest and most famous city, and would plunge the population into misery, thus alienating it from him.

7. Besides the natives, there were in the newly conquered empire also foreign peoples deported there by Nabuchodonsor and by others. How should he treat them? Some groups of these people were by this time certainly assimilated and were doing well, but this was not true for most of them. The majority of these considered themselves as plants uprooted from their native soil, and nourished as their fondest hope the possibility of returning to that distant soil to replant their own vines and olive trees; they wished to revive their ancient domestic life under the indispensable protection of their own local and national gods. Their return would certainly mean a great economic gain for those regions which, for the most part, had been abandoned. But would not their departure impoverish the district too much? And how could they be returned to their provinces when the statues of their gods, which were the symbols of their national unity, still remained in Babylonia as if in bondage to Bel, Nebo, Marduk, and the other local gods?

Cyrus was not the kind of man to shrink before the ultimate consequences of his political directives; he applied them also to the field of religion and thereby inaugurated a policy exactly opposite to that of his predecessor in Babylon. Nabonidus was a centralizer, Cyrus a decentralizer; the Babylonian had been a cultural absolutist insisting on a vague kind of monotheism; the Aryan put into effect a practical norm which resembled very much "liberty of conscience" for others but which worked out for him personally as a special kind of polytheism. His peoples were free to worship as they pleased, and could adore their own gods as they wished. For the monarch, who was the proprietor of all his peoples, it was shrewd politics to ally himself with all their cults; it was good psychology for him to sum up in himself all the various religions which were scattered throughout his domain. That way, each of his innumerable subjects could look upon the monarch as his coreligionist.

8. In all likelihood, Cyrus was a believer in Zoroastrianism (§ 84) but since, as a result of his policies, he was favored previously in his undertakings in Lydia by the oracles of the Greek divinities (cf. Herodotus, I, 15, 174), so now in Babylonia he affirmed that the Babylonian god Marduk had called him to the throne of Babel to replace Nabonidus, who was negligent in the service of this god from whom he had mastery of "all the earth" (Cylinder of Cyrus). So too, addressing himself to the Hebrews, he affirmed that it was not Marduk, but Yahweh, God of the Hebrews, who had given him "all the kingdoms of the world" and had commanded him to build the house of Yahweh in Jerusalem (Esdras 1:2; 2 Para. 36:23). Not without reason did Herodotus (I, 135) a little later make the following observation: "Persians more than any others, follow after strange customs." It is common knowledge that in ancient times the foremost of these social customs was religion.

Cyrus, therefore, pursued his policy to its logical consequences. He immediately decreed that the peoples who had been deported to Babylonia could, if they wished, return to their respective provinces. Religious considerations were not to form a barrier to their repatriation. Not only were the statues of the gods and other objects used for worship, which had been transported as booty to Babylonia, to be restored to the repatriated, but similar restitutions were to be made to the various native peoples.

The decree was immediately executed. From the month of Chislev, that is, one month after Cyrus' entry into Babylon, up to the month Adar (March), the statues of the various regions, which not only Nabonidus but others who had preceded him had concentrated in Babylon, were sent from the capital and returned to their ancient worshipers. Together with their gods, the respective peoples slowly made their exodus. Cyrus himself thus tells of this new and important event in the history of mankind: "From . . . [*lacuna*] . . . as far as Ashur and Susa, Agade, Eshnunna, Zamban, Me-Turnu, Der, as well as the region of the Gutians, I returned to (these) sacred cities on the other side of the Tigris, the sanctuaries of which have been in ruins for a long time, the images (gods) which used to live therein, and established for them permanent sanctuaries. I gathered together all their inhabitants and re-established their dwelling-places. And at the command of Marduk, the great lord, I resettled the gods of Sumer and Akkad, whom Nabonidus had brought to Babylon [thus provoking] to anger the lord of the gods, unharmed in their chapels, to the delight of their hearts" (Cylinder of Cyrus). The attitude of the monarch was not the result simply of a liberal mind but also of a certain active participation in the various cults. It has already been noted in the Chronicle of Nabonidus (§ 5) that not only were the temples not damaged in the least in the capture of Babylon and were actually protected by the armed forces of Cyrus, but that later on he himself set about to restore them, so that he could be called in their inscriptions the "builder of Esagila and of Ezida" (for Esagila, cf. § 5; Ezida was the temple of the god Nebus at Borsippa).

He treated the Hebrews who had been deported to Babylonia in the same manner (§ 84 ff.).

9. The empire of Cyrus was so extended after the conquest of Babel, and he was so well thought of by his subjects because of his policies, that he could truthfully say: "I am Cyrus, the King of the world, the great king, the powerful king, king of Babylon, king of Sumer and of Akkad, king of the four rims of the earth . . . whose rule Bel and Nebo have chosen, whose reign has been the delight of their hearts" (Cylinder of Cyrus).

The end of such an extraordinary man was worthy of his career. In the year 529, scarcely ten years after the conquest of Babylon, he died in battle against people (tradition is not certain whether they were Massagetae, Derbices, or Dahae) who threatened the eastern frontiers of his empire. Of the ancient Semitico-Mediterranean civilization only Egypt and Greece were untouched by the Achaemenid scepter; but it was not long before it would descend upon these two also. Egypt, large though its territory, was conquered by it, but tiny Greece was to break it into pieces.

10. Cambyses (529–522), son and successor of Cyrus, will link his name with the realization of a conquest to which his father had given only remote thought — the conquest of Egypt. Under the long

reign of the Pharaoh Amasis (Vol. I, § 42), Egypt had achieved a notable degree of prosperity. The Pharaoh had many Hellenic traits: he had married Ladyce of Cyrene, sent rich offerings to Greek sanctuaries, had conquered Cyprus, and taken part in the futile league with Croesus (§ 3). Evidently, he desired to brace himself on a Greek foundation in the event of a thrust against Persia, which the ancient rivalry and the recent league with Croesus made even more probable.

As a matter of fact, Cambyses adopted as his own his father's plan to unite Africa with Asia by subjugating the empire of the Pharaohs. He was impeded in the beginning by revolts which occurred in the empire after the death of Cyrus, instigated, perhaps, by his younger brother, Smerdis (Bardiya). Striking at the root of the difficulty, he had Smerdis secretly killed, and with his throne thus secured, moved against Egypt.

The success of the expedition was facilitated in this case as in others, by the help of traitors. The Greek mercenaries went over from the service of the Pharaoh to Cambyses, and the Egyptians were defeated at Pelusium on the Delta. Psammetichus III, who had succeeded his recently deceased father Amasis, fled and shut himself up in Memphis. The city was besieged and fell soon after; Psammetichus was later put to death, and Cambyses was recognized as sovereign of Egypt in May, 525 B.C.

11. Besides the empire of the Pharaohs, Cambyses tried also to conquer Carthaginian Libya to the west and Ethiopia to the south. The attempt on Libya by way of the sea never materialized, because the Phoenicians, who manned the fleet in the service of Cambyses, refused to act against their own relatives on the African coasts. An attempt by land, in which an army moved from Thebes where Cambyses resided, failed disastrously, and the sands of the desert swallowed up the army (Vol. I, § 214). The attempt on Ethiopia had little better success. The Persian army advanced considerably beyond the first cataract (Vol. I, § 21), but was unable to deliver a decisive blow against the Ethiopian kingdom, and the terrible difficulties of the march obliged them to retreat.

The failure of these two expeditions and the personal character of Cambyses (Herodotus always portrays him as proud and ill-tempered), together with the more or less latent hostility which he everywhere encountered in Egypt, drove him to assume toward the natives an aggressive bearing entirely different from that of Cyrus in similar circumstances; he went so far as sacrilegiously to slay the sacred bull Apis at Memphis. That he perpetrated sacrileges against temples and sacred objects can hardly be denied, for on this point Greek tradition is clearly confirmed by the testimony of the papyri of Elephantine (§ 166 ff.).

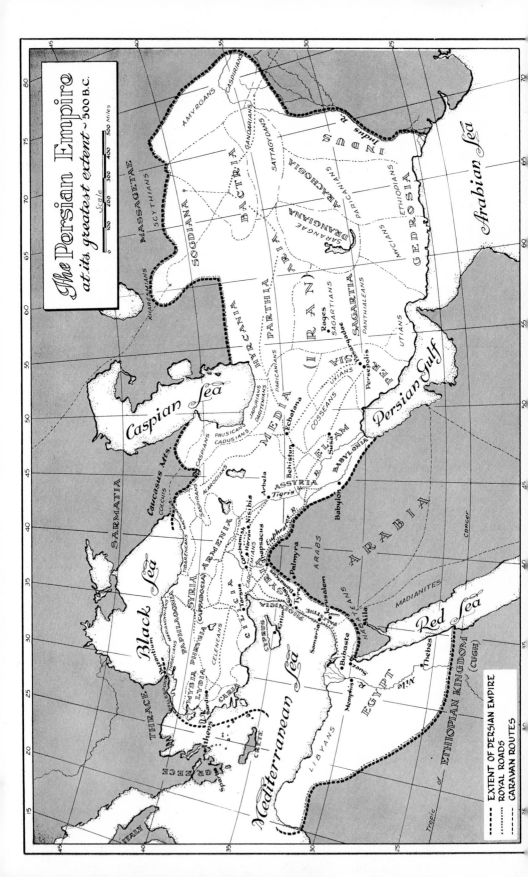

The Persian Empire
at its greatest extent ~500 B.C.

Scale
0 100 200 300 400 500 Miles

EXTENT OF PERSIAN EMPIRE
ROYAL ROADS
CARAVAN ROUTES

Inscription of Darius I at Bisutun (Telephoto). Above, the god
Ahura-Mazdah. (Sarre.)

It seems that, in the beginning, Cambyses also pursued a conciliatory
policy in regard to the native populations, but this was abruptly changed
for one or other of the causes mentioned above.

12. At any rate, Egypt did not rebel. Instead, alarming news came
to Cambyses from Asia, where revolts were breaking out because of
his absence; then came even more serious news, that his brother
Smerdis (§ 10) had been resuscitated. A magician by the name of
Gaumata (the "false Smerdis") exploited his perfect resemblance to
the vanished Smerdis by pretending to be the latter, and was readily
acknowledged as king. Cambyses hurried homeward on hearing this,
but died on the way (the spring of 522 B.C.); whether he was killed
in a conspiracy or was an unwilling suicide is not known.

The impostor Gaumata, however, did not rule for long. His identity
was discovered by the heads of the more authoritative families who had
free access to court, and he was killed with his followers in his residence
at Sikayahunati in Media (the autumn of 522 B.C.). He was succeeded
by one of the aforementioned heads of the Achaemenid family, Darius I,
son of Hystaspes (522–485). As is stated in his famous rock inscription
of Bisutun (Behistun), he was of a younger branch than the dynasty
of Cyrus.

13. When Darius was proclaimed king, revolts broke out everywhere.
In Susiana, the rebel Ashina was quickly vanquished; in Babylonia,
Nidintu-Bel resisted longer, but when Babylon was besieged, he was
overcome and slain (521). It then became the turn of the other
provinces, which were little by little pacified in nineteen battles and
seven years of campaigning, all of which are listed in the inscription

Palace of Darius I at Persepolis. (Sarre.)

of Bisutun. Meanwhile, Darius extended the eastern borders of his empire in the direction of India.

After the expansion toward India and the pacification of the empire, Darius proceeded to a new organization of the empire in order to render his control over such different peoples and such extended territory more effective. Many of the local governments were not suppressed but were allowed to remain, after some modifications. Such were the democratic governments of some Phoenician cities and the ethnarchic-sacerdotal government of Judean Palestine (§ 121). Yet they and all others were subjected to the organization known as the "satrapy." Although limited in various ways, the satrapy, for the most part, included a vast extent of territory as well as peoples diverse in race and civilization. The satrap who was the head was practically "King" and was sometimes designated as such by contemporary documents. But he was an underling "King" subordinated to the "King of Kings" or the "Great King," that is, to the Achaemenid monarch whose representative he was. The tenor of his life was deliberately grandiose and solemn, either for practical reasons or because the satrap was always of noble lineage and, therefore, a member of the royal family or related to it, as in the case of Cyrus the Younger. The satrap's duties were the ordinary administration of civil and military affairs in his satrapy, and the payment to the Great King of a stated tax, as well as a contribution of works or troops in the general interests of the monarchy. The satrap was not left alone; at his side, subordinate to him, were two other regents, the one entrusted with protocol, the other with military affairs. They were in fact, especially the former, two "controls" who reported directly to the court concerning the affairs of the satrapy. Other periodic inspections were made by persons closely related to the Great King, and they always came well escorted by armed forces.

The empire of Darius was divided into twenty satrapies. The most important for the present purpose was the Fifth Satrapy, Abar-Nahara ("Beyond the River," i.e., the Euphrates), which included Syria, Phoenicia, Palestine, and Cyprus. According to Herodotus, III, 89 ff., who reckons in Euboic talents (one of these weighed about 57 lbs.), the total taxes levied on the satrapies came to 14,560 talents; the quota of the whole Fifth Satrapy, not of Judean Palestine alone, was 350 talents (about 20,000 pounds of gold).

It is interesting to recall the judgment which was expressed by the subjects of Darius because of this fiscal arrangement, as it sums up his character as well as that of his predecessors: "It is by reason of this fixing of tribute, and other like ordinances, that the Persians called Darius the huckster, Cambyses the master, and Cyrus the father; for Darius made a petty profit out of everything, Cambyses was harsh and arrogant, Cyrus was merciful and ever wrought for their well-being." It is evident that the speakers here are those whose pocketbooks had been affected, but the fact is historically well founded.

14. Once his immense empire was internally organized, Darius turned his energies to the western frontier, the only one to give him cause for worry. To the north, beyond the Bosporus in the present-day Balkans, the Scythians kept out of his reach and could not be crushed, but the whole Greek world, more to the south, was no less dangerous with its nationalistic and commercial connections on the Mediterranean coasts, chiefly in Asia Minor, and its passionate desire for independence, especially with the sea as a refuge. This last reason was all the more cogent because on this sea the Great King had been obliged to depend exclusively on the doubtfully loyal Phoenician navy or worse yet, on the Ionian navy of Asia Minor.

About the year 516, Darius personally directed the expedition against the Scythians; it was the first time that Asia had assailed Europe. Although his forces were overwhelming — according to Greek tradition there were 800,000 men and 600 boats (the figures are probably exaggerations) — the results of the expedition were so meager, because of the enemy's ability for flight, that it seemed rather a failure. As a result, the spirit of revolt which was nourished in the Ionian cities, and which relied on the support of Greece, the motherland, spread abroad and became stronger. In 499, the revolt broke out at Miletus and with the help of Athens spread to a great part of Asia Minor and Cyprus.

Sardis, the land capital, was burned by the rebels, but Darius set about the reconquest. He retook Cyprus; in the year 494, he defeated the Ionian fleet off the shore of Miletus, and somewhat later the city was reconquered and the revolt brought under control. In the year 492, Mardonius, son-in-law of the Great King, conducted a campaign in Thrace, perhaps in preparation for a land passage to Greece, but his fleet was seriously damaged by a tempest at Mount Athos, and his army was harassed vigorously by the natives of that region.

15. Darius then decided to get at the bottom of the difficulty and extinguish the cause of all these flames by subduing Greece, and thus to punish Athens for having aided the Ionian cities. His fleet traversed the Aegean, subdued the Cyclades, and disembarked at Marathon, where the celebrated battle took place (490 or 491?). It may have been a complete victory for the Athenians and a turning point in the history of mankind, but for the empire of Darius it was only an isolated skirmish whose material losses were hardly noticeable in the immense network of the empire. Aside from its effect on morale, the more serious result of Marathon was that for the first time the tactics of the Persians, which relied chiefly on projectiles (it seems that the cavalry did not take part, § 3), failed; the 6400 dead which the Persians left on the field, as compared to the 192 of the Athenians, were slain in the ferocious hand-to-hand fighting forced upon them by the Greeks, who were incomparably superior to them in this type of combat.

Darius was irritated by the unsuccessful attempt and set about to prepare in great detail a punitive expedition against the victors, which had for its aim the subjugation of Greece, but luckily for that country, he did not live to see its result. He died in the year 485 (or 486), while serious revolts were breaking out in Babylonia and Egypt.

16. His son Xerxes I (485–465), who succeeded him on the throne of the Achaemenids, inherited none of the good qualities which had distinguished his predecessors, but only a love of opulent display which progressively sapped his moral fiber. According to Herodotus, VII, 187, Xerxes was exceptionally tall and handsome, but his magnificent body housed a soul of mean proportions. His comeliness explains to some degree the adulterous and incestuous episodes recorded by Herodotus, IX, 108 ff., and his mania for women which is mirrored in the book of *Esther*.

The revolts were quelled after some time; that of Egypt in 482, that of Babylon, which was particularly grave, provoked the cruel vengeance of Xerxes. The fortifications of Babylon were all dismantled, the temple of Esagila (§ 5) battered down, the most venerated idol of Marduk was carried away, and a great part of the possessions of the natives passed into the hands of the Persians.

As for Greece, Xerxes was willing to forget Marathon and settle down

Athens and its Acropolis.

to enjoy court life, but it was not to be. Goaded by the Greek exiles and by the defeated Persian war leaders who made it a point of honor. Xerxes set out on his famous expedition. It can be summarized by the following facts: July 21 (or August 19) of 480 B.C.: land battle at Thermopylae and naval battle of Artemisium. The Greek allies retreated on land and sea before the onslaught of the Persians, and the Acropolis was besieged. — September 21, 480: the Acropolis was captured. — September 23, 480: naval battle of Salamis. The Persian fleet was defeated and the retreat was begun by land and by sea. — August 27, 479: battle of Plataea. The Persian forces under Mardonius, who had remained in Greece from the year before, were annihilated, and he himself killed; on the same day, off Micale on the Ionian coast facing Samos, the Persian fleet was destroyed by the allies. Thus, the expedition of Xerxes terminated in a complete disaster, which demonstrated the moral inferiority of the gigantic Asiatic empire when faced by the small European states.

This was further confirmed in the year 470 in the battle of Eurymedon on the coasts of Pamphylia, where the Persian army and navy were routed by Cimon. Only after a new defeat inflicted by Cimon upon the Persian fleet at Salamis in Cyprus, was a halt called to the fifty-year-old struggle by the so-called "Peace of Cimon." Persia retained full liberty over Egypt and Cyprus, but her ships were not to pass the roadstead of Phasaelis in Pamphylia (about midway on the southern coast of Asia Minor), nor were the Greek colonies of western Asia Minor anymore to be disturbed.

17. In the year 465, a conspiracy did away with Xerxes and he was succeeded by his son Artaxerxes I Longomanus (465–424). However, he did not begin to exercise his authority until a few months later, when he succeeded in freeing himself of Artabanus, one of the leaders of the conspiracy. Besides this, he had his brother Istaspis for a

competitor until the year 462, when the latter was defeated and
killed. Meanwhile, there broke out in Egypt a serious revolt against
Persian rule instigated by Inarus, son of Psammetichus, who, in the
year 460, with the help of the Athenians, defeated and killed
Achaemenes, brother of Artaxerxes and satrap of Egypt. Megabyzus,
satrap of Syria and brother-in-law of Artaxerxes, was sent to Egypt
and succeeded in quelling the revolt and arresting Inarus. Megabyzus
himself in turn then revolted against his brother-in-law and defeated
him twice, thus obliging him to sue for peace.

Artaxerxes I was only slightly better than his predecessor. He had
a great passion for big game hunting and oftentimes left the affairs
of government to his courtiers or to the favorites of his harem.

18. At his death the court intrigues broke out into bloody conflicts.
Xerxes II, the son of the dead king, ascended to the throne but
occupied it little more than a month, when Sogdianus, another illegitimate son of Artaxerxes, killed him and seized the throne. After about
six months, Sogdianus met the same fate at the hands of another
illegitimate son, Darius II Notus (424–405 [404]). Revolts continued
under him also, among which was that of his brother Arsitis (who was
backed by Artifrius, satrap of Syria) is noteworthy. All, however, were
suppressed. He succeeded in again imposing tribute on the Ionian cities
of Asia Minor, taking advantage of the struggle between Athens and
Sparta. Cyrus the Younger, the son of Darius and satrap of Sardis, furnished every possible aid to Sparta. Darius, for that matter, was himself
a figurehead; the real decisions were made by Parysatis, his wife

Series of reliefs in the hall of Xerxes at Persepolis.

and half-sister and the mother of Cyrus the Younger, one of the most astute and cruellest women ever to sit upon a throne. When he fell ill, Darius shared his throne with his eldest son Arxaces who later succeeded his dead father, taking the name Artaxerxes II (405 [404]).

19. Artaxerxes II Memnon (405 [404]–358) had immediately to cope with the intrigues and then the insurrection of his younger brother Cyrus the Younger, for whom his mother Parysatis desired the throne. Besides the satrapy of Sardis, Cyrus had, through the intervention of his mother, obtained the supreme command of the Persian forces in Asia Minor, and since that time had become a great friend of the Spartans, doubtless with the

Reliefs in the royal palace at Persepolis. Above, the king on his throne.

view of using them as allies in his plans for the future. At the death of his father he repaired to Babylonia and there, it seems, tried to rid himself of his brother, who had ascended the throne. He was arrested, but once liberated and restored to his satrapy through the efforts of his mother, he set about preparing the reconquest by force of arms which resulted in his famous expedition.

Leaving his satrapy with an army which tradition numbered at 100,000 men but which was probably nearer 30,000, the principal nucleus of which was the force of 13,000 Greeks commanded by the Spartan Clearcus, Cyrus advanced boldly toward the heart of the empire and at Cunassa on the Euphrates, about fifty miles from Babylon, engaged in a furious battle with the Persian army led by Tissaphernes and whose center was held by Artaxerxes. The right wing, made up of the Greeks, pushed the enemy back, but Cyrus, in his desire to strike down his brother with his own hand, grew careless, and was transfixed by a deadly Persian arrow (September, 401). The famous Ten Thousand Greeks who survived the battle then began, under the leadership of Xenophon, Clearcus' successor, that extraordinary retreat to the sea toward the north which their leader has described in his famous *Anabasis*. Artaxerxes' crown was saved, but its prestige had been dealt a serious blow by the expedition of Cyrus. Worse yet, the expedition showed that with better preparation and more prudence, it would be possible to lunge at the very heart of the immense empire (for example, Cyrus had blundered seriously in having only 2600 horses to oppose to Artaxerxes' powerful cavalry: § 3). A half century later Alexander would profit from this lesson.

The satrapy of Cyrus passed to Tissaphernes (400), who immediately inaugurated in Asia Minor a policy different from that of his predecessor, and which brought him into conflict with Sparta. The war spread to Athens and other states, and dragged along with alternate changes in fortune after the death of Tissaphernes until 386, when the so-called "Peace of Antalcidas" or "Peace of the King" was concluded. This restored to Persia the possessions lost in the "Peace of Cimon" (§ 16), and was the greatest success the Achaemenids enjoyed in the Mediterranean.

20. In Egypt, on the other hand, things were going badly. The conquest effected by Cambyses (§ 10) had inaugurated Dynasty XXVII, which was entirely Persian. In the repartition of the empire by Darius (§ 13), Egypt was made the Sixth Satrapy and despite the attempt under Artaxerxes I (§ 17), of Inarus and of other younger men, had always remained under the scepter of the Achaemenids. But even before the expedition of Cyrus the Younger and probably as soon as Darius II died (§ 18), upheavals began, and a Lygian prince, Armiteus, succeeded in chasing the representatives of the Great King from the Delta, and constituted by himself (404–398) what Manetho lists as Dynasty XXVIII (Sahidic). An expedition of Artaxerxes was made ready for the reconquest of the lost satrapy, but was delayed first because of the undertaking of Cyrus, and then by the war against Sparta. The successors of Amirteus, Nepherites (398–393), Achoris (392–380), and Psammuthis comprised Dynasty XXIX (Mendesian) which succeeded in preserving its inde-

Royal tomb of the Achaemenids near Persepolis. (Sarre.)

pendence. Between the years 385–383, Achoris had repulsed the attempt of Artaxerxes to reconquer Egypt, thanks to the loyalty of his Athenian servant Cabria. This same Cabria made it possible for a prince of Sebennitais, Nectanebus I (378–361), to secure the throne in the face of other pretenders and to establish Dynasty XXX, which was the last of them all.

During this latter reign (373), Artaxerxes again attempted to recover Egypt. Through the good offices of the Athenians, Cabria was persuaded to withdraw from the country, but this time also, despite some minor success at the beginning, the enterprise failed. Following this, the unfinished business of Egypt became involved with the uprising of western satrapies which from the Euphrates to the Mediterranean were joining the rebellion against the Great King. The secret agreement between the satrapies and Egypt was entirely spontaneous; the Pharaoh Tachos (361–359), who had succeeded Nectanebus at the height of the insurrection, led an expedition in the year 360 to extend the Egyptian dominion beyond Palestine and Phoenicia, as it had been in the classic times of the Pharaohs. Farther to the north were the satrapies which he would help in maintaining their autonomy against the threats of the Great King. Cabria had returned to the paid employ of Tachos and was put at the head of the fleet, and the old Spartan king Agesilaus had been engaged for the occasion. A revolt broke out in Egypt, however, and the throne of the absent Tachos was occupied by Nectanebus II (or better Nectanabus: 358–341), who was supported by Agesilaus.

Without aid from Egypt the revolt of the satrapies was quickly snuffed out by the Great King, thanks more to treason and shrewdness than to war.

21. At the death of Artaxerxes II (358), Artaxerxes III Ochus (358–337) ascended the throne of Persia. Seeing all around him vacillate, his cruel nature asserted itself and he set about safeguarding his crown by the liquidation of the royal family, forestalling in this manner all possible rivals for the throne (it is said that eighty relatives were slain). When the occidental satrapies rose in new rebellion, with the usual promptings from Egypt and the customary help from Greece, Artaxerxes moved against them. At first, he fared badly, but because the rebels were not joined by Greece, and Egypt made no move to help them, he was later victorious.

Convinced that Egypt was the instigator or the helper of every revolt, Artaxerxes III determined to reconquer it. A first attempt made around the year 351 was repulsed at the entrance to the Delta, a setback due principally to the Greek mercenary troops. The failure encouraged, as usual, other uprisings. Phoenicia, Cyprus, and part of Syria rebelled, and it seems that even the Jews of Palestine were involved in the revolt (§ 151). In the year 345, Artaxerxes III moved against Tabnit (Tennes), king of Sidon and head of the league, to whose aid Nectanebus had sent Mentor of Rhodes with 4000 Greek mercenaries in the pay of the Egyptians. The outcome of the affair is not clear. It is certain that Sidon was taken (tradition mentions a surrender of Tabnit, who betrayed the league), and that Mentor then went over to the service of the Great King. With the disbanding of the league, the road to Egypt lay open, and Artaxerxes advanced in that direction. At Pelusium on the Delta opposition was made to him by the Greek mercenaries faithful to Nectanebus, but Mentor, who commanded the Persian army, accomplished more with his cleverness than by force of arms. The Delta was invaded, and the Pharaoh withdrew to Memphis and soon afterward fled to Ethiopia with a great part of his treasures. Egypt had once more become Persian. Artaxerxes

Drachma of
Artaxerxes III.

gave vent to his rage by looting and slaughtering. He also offended the local beliefs by slaughtering the sacred bull Apis, in which act he imitated the ancient example of Cambyses (§ 11).

He did not long survive. The eunuch Bagoas, a subaltern captain in the Egyptian campaign who had later become all-powerful at court, poisoned Artaxerxes (337 B.C.) out of fear of losing his influence, which was then threatened by a court faction.

22. Bagoas also caused the crown prince to be assassinated and put Arsetis on the throne, but neither did he long survive (337–335 B.C.). When he tried to escape the influence of his mentor, Bagoas had him and his sons killed and put his friend, the satrap Darius III Codomanus (335–330), on the throne. Shortly afterward Darius rid himself of Bagoas by making him drink the poison which the latter had prepared for the king.

History oftentimes records that the twilight of great dynasties was graced by worthy representatives, and so it was in the case of Darius III, the last of the Achaemenids. Here was a monarch endowed with many fine qualities. Even the empire, thanks to the successes of Artaxerxes III, stood restored almost as it had been in the times of Cambyses. But conditions had changed from the times of the son of Cyrus. Internally, unity had weakened. In the northern and eastern parts of the empire, vast regions had been occupied by almost savage and practically independent peoples. The western empire had been for more than a century a vast field of struggles and revolts. While peoples of Greek stock who had secured a permanent hold on the coasts of Asia

Ruins of Persepolis. (Sarre.)

Minor had permeated the whole hinterland through a thousand subtle channels, the satraps in the interior were constantly withdrawing from the central authority of the empire. The organization and reciprocal controls instituted by Darius I (§ 13) still existed in theory but had lost all force in actual practice. Various conflicting offices of supervision were often entrusted to the same individual, and too often the periodic inspections which were supposed to be entrusted to the high court officials were either not made or were mere empty formalities. The army had been reduced in everything but numbers to a shadow of what it was in the time of Cyrus. Its fighting spirit had been replaced by love of adventure and money; its armament was obsolete, and it relied greatly on Greek mercenaries who were undeniably superior in the waging of war, but whose loyalty was only what could be expected of a mercenary and a Greek. The family tragedies which had occurred at the death of the last monarchs, and the court intrigues of powerful eunuchs and plotting women had caused the authority of the first Achaemenids to all but disappear.

The Persian empire at that time was like an immense statue; it had a head of gold, but its other members were composed of increasingly inferior materials, and its feet were only clay. The various members, too, were not bound together; they simply rested, one upon the other, with hardly any real contact. A medium sized stone would cause it to crumble at one blow, member upon member.

Again, as in the time of Cyrus the Great (§ 2), occurred the "unpredictable," the paradoxical, and now, as then, it was expressed in and by a single individual. The stone which struck the statue this time was neither too small nor ill-directed, as in the time of Cyrus the Younger (§ 19); it was a gigantic boulder whose like the world had never seen, Alexander the Great.

ALEXANDER —
THE DIADOCHI — HELLENISM

23. Alexander III of Macedonia, called the Great, son of Philip, succeeded his father, assassinated in the summer of 336, when he was twenty years old; only a few months separated his ascent from the elevation of Darius III to the throne of Persia. His most remarkable deeds, accomplished in thirteen years of reign, cannot be explained by any one special formula, but were the result of many factors and exceptional circumstances, not the least of which was his own good fortune. It would be a mistake to overlook the opportuneness of the moment in which he appeared on the stage of history to play his part, and the fitness of the means at his disposal; it would be a more serious mistake to fail to recognize the power of his genius, which enabled him to comprehend and overcome the many and often grave difficulties which threatened his undertakings. Recognition of his exceptional genius was later expressed by such men as Hannibal and Julius Caesar.

The twenty-year-old youth already had much experience in war and politics when he ascended the throne of Macedonia; he also had a grandiose plan inherited in part from his father. His first activity as monarch was dedicated to the sketching out of this plan, and the rest of his life he spent in blocking it in. His plan was to make himself the head of a league of all Hellenes — his own Macedonia was considered Hellenic — and the head of an expedition against the Persian Empire to avenge the losses and offenses which that empire had inflicted on the Hellenic people from the time of Marathon (cf. Diodorus Siculus, XVII, 4, 9; Cicero, *De republ.*, III, 15). Love for the adventures of war and of heroic undertakings undoubtedly contributed to this design of the ardent youth, but there was also an equal portion of nationalism which was unwilling to admit even a purely material superiority of the "Barbarians" over the "Hellenes." It was not for nothing that, under Aristotle's guidance, Alexander had from an early age been an enthusiastic reader of the *Iliad,* and had chosen as his ideal

Alexander the Great (copied from Lisippus?). (Rome, Capitoline Museum.)

Achilles, the hero of the struggle of the Hellenes against the Trojan barbarians of Asia.

Alexander first secured his position on the throne by spilling the blood of many of his kinfolk, according to the Persian custom (§ 21) and then guaranteed the frontiers of Macedonia to the north by his expedition into what are now the Balkans in the spring of the year 335. Next he consolidated the supremacy of his reign over all the Hellenic states by means of a terrible warning, the destruction of Thebes in Boeotia (October, 335). He then left Antipater (§ 27) as regent of the kingdom, and turned his attention to Persia.

24. The expedition began in the spring of 334. Alexander had with him 32,000 men as infantry and 5000 cavalry, and this formed the core of his army. In Asia Minor he quickly reorganized the remnants of the expedition which Philip had previously sent there, and other contingents which had gravitated there from the Ionian cities as they were liberated; 160 ships formed his fleet. The Great King could oppose these forces with unlimited reserves of men and money, and with a goodly number of expert Greek mercenaries attracted by Persian gold. The fleet which was at the disposal of the Great King was in great part Phoenician and in quality was in no way inferior to that of the Greeks, while in quantity it may have been twice as numerous.

The chief stages in the expedition were as follows.

After landing at Abydos in Troas, the battle of Granicus ensued (May–June, 334), and opened to the victorious Alexander the gates of Asia Minor. Most significant is the action of Alexander in condemning to forced labor the 2000 Greek mercenaries of the Persians taken prisoner, as "traitors" to the Hellenic cause.

After all of Asia Minor was conquered, Alexander pushed on to the lower extremity of Cilicia where he encountered Darius himself. The Battle of Issus (November, 335) opened for Alexander the gates both of Mesopotamia to the east, and Syria, Phoenicia, Palestine, and Egypt

Battle of Issus. (Naples, National Museum — Pompeian Museum.)

to the south. Besides an immense booty, the mother, wife, and daughters of Darius also fell into his hands. The victor treated them with the highest respect *non amoris sed humanitatis causa* (Justin, XI, 12, 6). At the following Isthmian games in Greece, the crown of gold was awarded to Alexander as the defender of the liberty of the "Hellenes" against the "Barbarians."

Instead of pursuing the enemy into Mesopotamia, Alexander wisely provided for the protection of his flanks by seizing control of all the regions of the Persian empire which bordered the Mediterranean, and thus nullified the naval superiority of his enemy. For that reason also he descended to the south and took over Syria and Phoenicia. He encountered a serious obstacle in Tyre, but it was assaulted and destroyed after a siege of seven months (August, 332); Gaza, the ancient Philistine city farther down, resisted for only two. To reach Gaza, Alexander had to traverse Judea, but it seems that the inhabitants were not molested. The account of Josephus (*Antiquities*, XI, 8, 4 ff.) states that after the capture of Gaza, Alexander went to Jerusalem and was there received by the people and the high priest Jaddua with honors; that he offered sacrifices in the Temple and granted generous concessions to the people. This is commonly held, however, to be a legend created by later Jewish nationalism in its desire to link together, in some manner, both its capital and its Temple with the conqueror of the world (§ 215). From Gaza, Alexander went down to Egypt and took it without a struggle, and was hailed as the liberator by the Egyptians when they saw that he was solicitous in administering public affairs and

Alexander (detail of the preceding mosaic).

most considerate of their religious institutions. He remained there during the winter of 332–331 B.C. and founded Alexandria (§ 190).

25. The next spring he resumed his campaign, crossed the Euphrates and the Tigris and came up against Darius, who awaited him with an enormous army in a vast plain suitably prepared near the site of ancient Nineve between Arbela and Gaugamela. The battle which followed (October 1, 331) made Alexander the master of all Babylon and of the immense treasures of the Achaemenids. Susa, Persepolis, and Ecbatana fell in succession (in the spring of the year 330), and Darius retreated steadily eastward before the invader. A little later the last of the Achaemenids, who had been deposed from the throne and held prisoner by Bessus, satrap of Bactria, was killed by him at Ecatompilus (July, 330).

With his death the program which Alexander had officially proposed to the "Hellenes" was accomplished: the empire of the "Barbarians" had been smashed. Hence, Alexander gave the Greek troops of the league their liberty, retaining only his Macedonian troops, with whom he continued his expedition to the East. Officially, the prosecution of these conquests was his own personal plan. The empire, although no longer belonging to the "Barbarians," still existed insofar as it had passed over to Alexander, and he considered himself the legitimate successor of Darius III. In fact, when he had the satrap Bessus, the murderer of Darius, in his power, he insisted that he be judged guilty of high treason

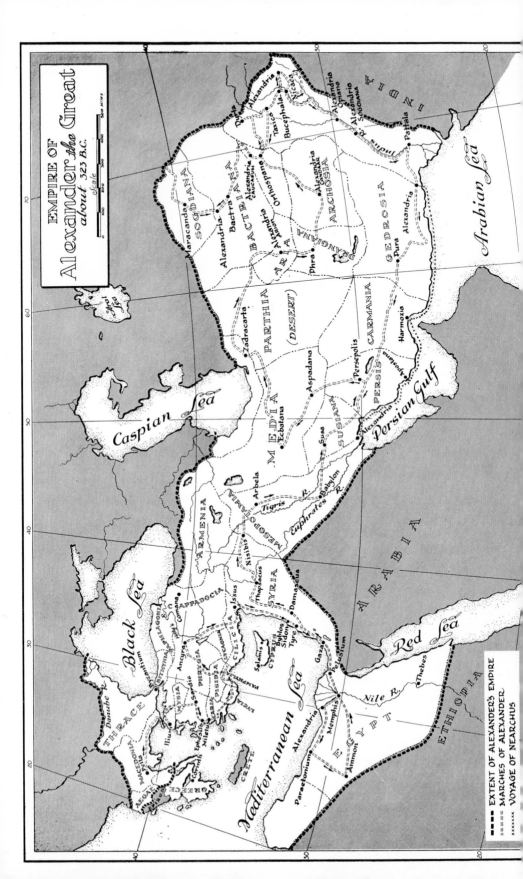

EMPIRE OF
Alexander the Great
about 323 B.C.
Scale

EXTENT OF ALEXANDER'S EMPIRE
MARCHES OF ALEXANDER
VOYAGE OF NEARCHUS

according to Persian law, and at Ecbatana Bessus paid the supreme penalty.

As the successor, therefore, of the Achaemenids, Alexander continued his conquests in the East for six years, and these brought him beyond the Indus, almost to the foot of the Himalayas, whence he returned to Susa in March, 324.

On June 13, 323, the most famous man of destiny the ancient world had ever seen expired, at the age of thirty-three, in Babylonia, from an attack of fever.

Darius III (detail of the preceding mosaic).

*   *   *

26. The Diadochi. At Alexander's death there was general confusion among his most trusted collaborators. The immense empire conquered by him seemed to revolve about his own person, and yet he disappeared from the scene unexpectedly, far from his original kingdom, and without designating a definite successor for his bewildered heirs. His dynasty at that time was represented by Philip Arrhidaeus, his feeble-minded half brother, and by a child soon to be born to his widow Roxana. The child became Alexander IV (329–309). Furthermore, although expressed in a vague sort of manner at the moment of his death, Alexander made known his explicit desire to his officials, who interrogated him about the succession, that his reign be left "to the best" (Arrianus, *Anab.*, VII, 23, 3). This wish of the dying ruler was law, but so too was the hereditary right of the Macedonian dynasty, of which the officials were faithful and devoted subjects. Hence, it was necessary to preserve the unity of the supreme governing body, and with it unity of the whole empire. It would also be advantageous to all in various ways; they could go on together to rule over the territories they had conquered, to defend themselves from the revolts of conquered peoples, and mutually to support one another in the propagation of Hellenism.

But there were other arguments against the maintenance of unity. Macedonia, the cradle of the empire, was too far removed to be a political center of such a vast extent of territory. As Alexander himself had for just such reasons moved his central government to Babylonia,

later experience demonstrated that it was necessary to have direct
contact between the government and the different peoples under it, and
hence decentralized subordinates. But, in the latter case, what would
happen to unity, since Macedonia was too far away and Babylonia no
longer enjoyed the presence of the creator of that unity? To these considerations must be added the personal attitudes, the mutual rivalries,
the excessive ambition of those officials who were descendants of the
feudal lords of Macedonia. These rivalries and ambitions had been kept
in check by the power and splendor of Alexander, but with him out of
the way, they flared up almost at once, and in a manner not likely
to foster unity.

27. Thus began that period which has been and is now called that of
the *Diadochi*, or successors, after which there came the period of the
monarchies, stably constructed out of the fragments of the empire. Of this
complicated period the present work will treat only of the origin of the
two major dynasties connected with the history of Israel.

The succession was settled as follows. There were two kings: the weak-
minded Philip Arrhidaeus, and the newly born Alexander IV. Craterus,
an illustrious official of the dead king, was made regent, and Perdiccas,
capable and powerful coadjutor during the last days of the conqueror,
became "chiliarch" or first minister. The various regions of the empire
were entrusted to the most intimate friends and companions in arms
of the dead warrior. Europe (Macedonia and Greece) was given
to the aged Antipater, governor of Macedonia (§ 23); Ptolemy, son
of Lagus, received Egypt; Antigonus Monophthalmus (Cyclops),
greater Phrygia; Leonatus, Phrygia which borders on the Hellespont;
Thrace was given to Lysimachus, and Eumenes, the secretary of
Alexander, got Cappadocia. Among other lesser assignations, that of
Antiochus' son, Seleucus, to the command over the cavalry, is significant.

Shortly thereafter the war of Lamia broke out between Antipater and
Athens; Leonatus was killed, and soon afterward Antipater, Craterus,
Antigonus, and Ptolemy, jealous of Perdiccas' power, warred against him.
Craterus was killed and Perdiccas also, when he attempted to penetrate
Egypt by way of Pelusium.

28. In view of all these changes, the surviving Diadochi met at Tripara-
disus in Syria (321) and decided upon a new partition of the empire.
Antipater became regent; Antigonus Cyclops was named commander in
chief of the army in Asia; Lysimachus and Ptolemy were confirmed in
Thrace and in Egypt, respectively, and Seleucus was given charge of the
government of Babylonia. Antipater then brought the two kings, the
imbecile and the infant, to Macedonia with him, both to have under his
control the pledges of his power, and for reasons similar to those which

prompted Ptolemy, while Perdiccas still lived, to carry the venerated corpse of Alexander with him into Egypt.

In the year 319 Antipater died, leaving Polysperchon in his place. Cassander, son of Antipater, the generalissimo Antigonus, and Ptolemy, who had extended his dominion into Palestine and Coelesyria in the year 320, banded together against him, with the result that Cassander became master of Macedonia, Antigonus of Asia Minor, and Ptolemy consolidated his conquests up to the Antilibanus. Olympias, the mother of Alexander the Great, rose against Cassander in Macedonia (317), and slew Philip Arrhidaeus, who had been won over to Cassander's cause. A short time later Cassander again gained the upper hand, put Olympias to death, and held the child, Alexander IV, and his mother, Roxana as hostages (316 B.C.).

29. Meanwhile, Antigonus Cyclops had become very powerful in Asia, and because of his threatening attitude, Seleucus abandoned his province of Babylonia and took refuge in Egypt with Ptolemy (316), from whom he always received protection and aid. This provoked new struggles with Antigonus and Polysperchon on one side and Ptolemy, Lysimachus, Cassander, Seleucus, and lesser rulers on the other. Antigonus prevailed at first and occupied the Syro-Palestinian possessions of Ptolemy, but the de-

Demetrius Poliorcetus.

feat which Ptolemy and Seleucus inflicted on Demetrius Poliorcetus, son of Antigonus, near Gaza (spring of the year 312), restored these possessions to Ptolemy and provided Seleucus with an opportunity to re-enter Babylon. Both of them lost these advantages later on, and, in the year 311, a compromise instead of a real peace was reached, granting to Cassander rather than to Polysperchon the "master province" of Europe. Egypt without Syria-Palestine went to Ptolemy, Thrace to Lysimachus, and the rest of Asia to Antigonus. Babylonia actually went to Seleucus, whether he was named in the treaty or not. This state of affairs was of brief duration, until Alexander IV reached his majority. He was the last slender thread upon which the unity of the empire depended, and he remained in Macedonia in the power of Cassander.

The jealous Cassander sundered this thread by having Alexander and his mother Roxana put to death (310 B.C.). Shortly thereafter, Heracles, an illegitimate son of Alexander the Great, was also killed, and thus the official ruling dynasty came to an end. The principal foundation for

a unified empire was thenceforward lacking. Antigonus desired to replace it but, as he relied solely on force, other jealousies and wars came
between him and the remaining Diadochi.

And so it happened that in the year 306, after Demetrius Poliorcetus
won his naval victory over Ptolemy at Salamis in Cyprus, his father
Antigonus Cyclops officially assumed for himself and for his victorious son the title of *basileus*, "king," an evident attempt to designate himself and son the legitimate successors of Alexander over the
whole empire. But the other Diadochi quickly followed suit; Ptolemy,
Cassander, Lysimachus, and Seleucus countered by proclaiming themselves "kings" over the territories under their jurisdiction. With this the
heritage of Alexander the Great was officially dismembered.

30. Antigonus, now turned against Ptolemy, earned the distrust of the
Diadochi. His attempt to penetrate into Egypt was repulsed, and thereafter matters in Greece clamored for his attention (304–302 B.C.).
Lysimachus, meanwhile, began operations in Asia Minor and awaited
the contingents which Seleucus was supposed to draw from Babylonia;
to the south, Ptolemy was advancing and reconquering Syria-Palestine.
When the two armies of Lysimachus and Seleucus were joined, they gave
battle at Ipsus in Lesser Phrygia (summer of the year 301). Eighty years
old, Antigonus Cyclops died in battle, and his army was destroyed.

This event brought to an end the period of the Diadochi. From then
on, the broad lines of the organization which had been given to the
heritage of Alexander the Great remained unaltered. As a result of the
battle of Ipsus the territory of Antigonus was divided among the other
Diadochi kings: Lysimachus obtained Asia Minor on the western side of
the Taurus; Seleucus actually had Armenia, Cappadocia, and upper
Syria, and the right to Coelesyria together with Palestine. Ptolemy of
Egypt, however, claimed the right to these territories, and at the termination of the war reoccupied them both as far as the Libanus and
Damascus (301 B.C.). Seleucus, on his part, was mindful of the aid
Ptolemy had given him in former days (§ 29), and while maintaining
his rights, judged it inopportune to take any definite action.

The warlike incidents which continued for the next twenty years or so
after Ipsus, owing to the adventuresome spirit of Demetrius Poliorcetus,
who had fled from Ipsus, succeeded in substantially confirming the
status quo, and ceased with the battle of Corupedius (281 B.C. [282?]),
when Lysimachus of Thrace was defeated and killed by Seleucus. Parts
of his territory went to Seleucus, while the rest fell to the Celts who were
swarming in from the north.

Hence there remained, besides the kingdom of Macedonia, which lies
beyond the scope of the present work, the kingdom of Seleucus in
Asia, and that of Ptolemy in Egypt (§ 35).

31. Hellenism. So vast and profound were the consequences of Alexander's undertakings that it is extremely difficult to evaluate them even in a sketchy and summary fashion.

Practically the whole of the ancient world felt his impact, politically, but he had scarcely begun his work of organization when he died. So abnormal a state of affairs was bound to be unstable and short-lived. As a matter of fact, the breakup of the empire conquered by Alexander began almost at once, and changed its political aspect.

Other transformations in the cultural and moral spheres also began at the same time. Alexander can be likened to a surging wave of occidental civilization which overflowed all man-made dikes and penetrated deeply into an entirely different civilization. With him came a genuine expansion of "Hellenism," but Greek culture had undoubtedly begun to filter into the Orient long before him (§§ 3, 14 ff.). When the tidal wave receded, many areas of the submerged regions emerged to flourish again, and it is beyond question that the wave of this new civilization here and there took on local color, or simply seeped down into the mire. In any case, in many essentials the face of western Asia was changed by that wave, and the cultural change was not less than the political.

32. Alexander himself had favored the transformation in attempting the absurd fusion of Hellenistic elements, introduced by him, with the various conquered peoples. In this he acted partly from necessity. The territories he had conquered were extensive, and to replace the native administrative personnel by Greco-Macedonians would have called for more men than he could spare. And partly he was moved by political reasons. Seeing that he could not snuff out the cultural centers of the conquered peoples, he tried to win them to himself by inoculating them with Greek culture, and by encouraging their fusion with the Greeks. He himself set the example in the matter of matrimony. First he married Roxana, the daughter of the Bactrian Ossiartis, and then with great solemnity at Susa he espoused the daughter of Darius himself, Statira (another tradition mentions a Barsine [Arrianus, VII, 4, 4] and still another, Arsinoë [Fazio, *Biblioth.*, 68]). Eighty high Macedonian officials and 10,000 soldiers likewise married Asiatic wives; the wives of the former were members of the nobility, the wives of the others were handsomely endowed by Alexander.

Besides this example, a permanent arrangement was set up to encourage the hoped-for intermingling of races. In administrative matters, an Asiatic was usually left in office, surrounded by Greeks who served as his coadjutors and supervisors. The ranks of the army were opened to youths of various districts of Asia; 30,000 youths were instructed in Macedonian tactics and admitted to higher ranks, and some of the more noble (e.g., Ossastres, the brother of Darius) were even allowed to enter the battalion of the "elite," or companions of Alexander.

This policy was even more methodically pursued in the cities. While on his expeditions, Alexander everywhere founded new cities. His Alexandria of Egypt (§ 190) was the most renowned of many "Alexandrias" which arose in various places (as Alexandria of Aria, Sogdiana, Aracosia, the Persian Gulf, etc.), but it was only one of many new cities which had other names. Especially around the eastern limits of the empire facing India there arose a whole chain of cities. They were built for a very definite purpose, being intended as other centers for Hellenic life and culture from which the occidental spirit might be perennially diffused over the surrounding countryside. At the same time, they were to remain in touch with one another, share in the same interests, and be an aid to one another. In short, they were to be, as it were, irrigation ditches in the midst of an arid steppe, or a group of oases in the desert of the "barbarians."

33. These cities were fundamentally Hellenic not only in language and personnel but also in their internal structure. They were peopled by soldiers, merchants, workmen, employees, artists, and adventurers who came from various Hellenic states, and their number was swelled by the local peoples who were willing to assume the spirit and forms of civic life of the conquerors. These cities were shown every favor by the supreme authorities, who looked upon them as the bases of their power. They were usually modeled on the typical Greek *polis* and possessed their *demos*, their *boulē*, and magistrates who were designated and installed democratically. Such was the form of the cell-like Hellenic states which, in turn, lived within and for the larger organism of the empire.

Naturally enough, not only the *polis*, but the life and manners of the Greeks were brought in. Alongside the *bouleuterion* or assembly hall there arose the "gymnasium" for the indispensable athletic exercises; farther along, whenever possible, the necessary theater was built. The altar, much more essential, was set up, or a temple was built for the celebration of Hellenic religious rites. The established pattern of these new cities clearly distinguished them from Asiatic cities, which were built according to other criteria. On the other hand, when an Asiatic city was colonized by occidentals — as often happened — a series of building transformations according to the taste of the newcomers gradually changed the old scene into something recognizably Hellenic.

Thus in all anterior Asia Hellenism became, more or less, something of a necessity, and more often became the "mode." Perhaps it was the aura of superiority which enveloped the conquerors, or it may have been the necessity of getting along with them, but, at any rate, there evolved a *modus vivendi* similar to that which is found in the Belgian Congo in recent times, when a tribe such as the Bantu learns French and becomes Belgianized.

In the various local courts which won the favor of Alexander, Hellenic arts and science began to make headway, and so too Hellenic philosophy and culture. The Greek tongue, which had been widely disseminated by the merchants, enjoyed an ever increasing diffusion throughout the *polis,* the courts, and the various branches of civil and military administration. It began to serve as the international language of anterior Asia, and in this capacity supplanted the Aramaic tongue, just as that had superseded the Babylonian. Later on it became and, in fact, was called the "common" tongue, the *koinē.* Even Berossus, the Babylonian priest who wrote about Babylonia, used it around the year 270.

34. It is to be understood, of course, that this vast spiritual penetration and transformation did not occur suddenly, nor everywhere in the same degree or manner; in many cases local reactions brought about different kinds of syncretism. How profoundly this ferment permeated even regions most remote from Greece can be seen from the example of Bactria alone. In the middle of the third century B.C., this region on the threshold of India became a fundamentally

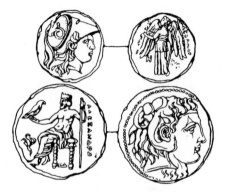

Money of Alexander the Great.

Hellenic but autonomous kingdom (§ 37) and, except for a brief period, was in perfect accord with the kingdom of the Seleucids, who fostered it precisely because it would serve as a barrier for their Hellenism against the "barbarians" of India. It is readily understandable that the Hellenism of that region be permeated by definitely Indian influences, and that as Hellenism declined these became more numerous and active. How potent the expansive force of that peripheral and diluted Hellenism was can be gauged by the commonly admitted fact that some characteristics of the most ancient Buddhistic iconography seem to depend on that contemporary Hellenistic art which penetrated India by way of Bactria. Repercussion of this same art seemed to have been felt as far away as China.

The measures taken for the organization of commerce also led to important results. The monies which Alexander caused to be minted out of the immense hoards of gold found in the treasuries of the Achaemenids (§ 25) became the official coin of the realm. This matter was skillfully handled so that the Macedonian money was equal in value to the

Babylonian; exceptions to this rule quite naturally favored the Greek money. Along with this official issue of money, the money of other Hellenic free cities was given official acceptance.

Alexander also planned to transplant colonies of Asiatics into Greek territories in order to facilitate the mingling of the various nationalities, but this was not carried out because of his death.

The great wave of Hellenism arose during the lifetime of Alexander, but its profound penetration continued during the succeeding centuries in the Asia of the Seleucids, the Egypt of the Ptolemies, and the eastern Mediterranean. Hellenism was checked, and then partially extinguished and partially assimilated by Rome, once she had become mistress of the Mediterranean, of Asia and of Egypt. But this occurred only in the century immediately preceding the coming of Christ.

THE SELEUCIDS—THE LAGIDAE

35. The vicissitudes of Seleucus I Monophthalmus (or Cyclops), called Nicator (312–280 B.C.), founder of the Seleucid dynasty, have already been described. At the death of Alexander the Great he obtained command of the cavalry, after which he took over the governorship of Babylonia (§ 28); this he lost and then regained, assuming the title of "king" (§ 29). He then methodically extended his dominion over the greater part of anterior Asia (§ 30). After the battle of Corupedium his reign extended from the confines of India up to the Mediterranean, although some zones were still contested or independent. Unlike the Ptolemies, who considered themselves successors of Alexander the Great and hence reckoned the beginning of their dynasty from his death (323), the Seleucids did not claim any connection with Alexander for their dynasty, but considered themselves autonomous and independent of the Macedonian conqueror. Thus Apollo was named as the father of their dynasty (as previously Zeus was claimed as the divine father of Alexander), and the origin of their dynasty was determined independently of the death of the Macedonian.

36. The first day of the year 312 B.C. was set as the origin of this dynasty, and since among the Macedonians the first month of the year was the month Dios (September-October), the beginning of the dynasty of the Seleucids dated from the first day of the month Dios of 312 B.C. However, in Babylonia, the beginning of the year came six months later at the vernal equinox in the month of Nisanu (Hebrew, *Nisan:* March-April), and therefore the Babylonians who were included in the kingdom of the Seleucids dated the beginning of the dynasty six months later, that is, the first day of the month Nisanu, 311 B.C. It is quite likely that the Babylonian date was the original calculation, and the Macedonian a later adjustment. This would seem to disprove the hypothesis that the calculation was chosen because of the battle of Gaza (§ 29), with which the fortunes of Seleucus began; the day of Seleucus' entrance into reconquered Babylon is the more probable beginning.

The "Era of the Seleucids," called also the "Era of the Greeks" or the

"Era of the Macedonians," began with this date. It was widely used in the whole Hellenic world, and is even now still used by certain Christian communities of Syria. The two computations, with their six months' difference, remained in use for centuries, although the first day of Dios of 312 B.C. prevailed to some extent. This variation may also explain the apparent disagreement in the chronologies of some ancient documents. It seems that use of this era must have been quickly adopted, for a document of the year 304 B.C. is dated by it.

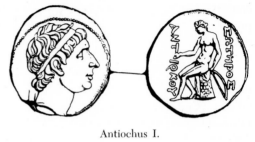

Antiochus I.

Antiochus II.

37. Seleucus survived the victory of Corupedium (§ 30) only a short time; he was murdered in 280 B.C. by Ptolemy Ceraunus, son of Ptolemy I of the house of Lagus, who had been disinherited by his father and had gone over to Seleucus. The capital city of the dynasty, called Antioch in honor of Antiochus, the father of Seleucus, was founded by Seleucus Nicator shortly after the victory of Ipsus. Situated on the Orontes about twelve and a half miles from the Mediterranean, it was in a fine position to dominate Syria and to connect with the rest of the Empire; it was also called Antioch "of Syria" or "of the Orontes" to distinguish it from the other Antiochs which were scattered all over the dominions of the Seleucids, as were the many Alexandrias under Alexander (§ 32).

Antiochus I Soter succeeded his father Seleucus (280–261 B.C.). He had been associated with his father in the government for some fifteen years, and had acquired the administration of the provinces to the east of the Euphrates. The "First Syrian War," which arose out of the Coelesyrian question left unsolved by Seleucus (§ 30), took place during his reign; this territory was to remain a perpetual bone of contention between the Seleucids and the Lagidae. Ptolemy II Philadelphus (§ 53) of the Lagidae not only had continued to occupy the contested territories, but had also ensconced himself in Lycia, Caria, Pamphylia, and the coast of Asia Minor. The war, about which history is ill-informed, was protracted for some years (about 276–272 B.C.) and the outcome was unfavorable to Antiochus. The peace recognized the conquests of Ptolemy II. The following period was, nevertheless, one of prosperity, and Antiochus took advantage of it to intensify the Hellenic colonization of the eastern parts of his kingdom.

His second-born son, Antiochus II Theos, succeeded him (261–246 B.C.). He had assisted his father in governing for some years previous to his accession (the firstborn, Seleucus, had revolted and had been killed). The "Second Syrian War" (about 259–252 B.C.), aided by the intervention of the Greek cities of Asia Minor, occurred during his reign. Antiochus II prevailed and reconquered Pamphylia and Cilicia, and seems to have pressed forward from the region of Coelesyria to Sidon. This time the peace was strengthened by a marriage between the belligerents. Antiochus II repudiated his own wife, Laodice, to espouse Bernice, the daughter of Ptolemy II. Everything now seemed settled, but things became more complicated than before. Antiochus rejoined his first wife Laodice in Asia Minor, and before his death recognized her first-born son, Seleucus, as rightful heir to the throne. Bernice and her little son were slain at Antioch by order of Laodice after the death of her husband. Another war was, thereafter, inevitable.

On the eastern boundaries things went badly. In the year 250 the Greek Diodatus, governor of Bactria, withdrew his country from the dominion of the Seleucids and established, with Sogdiana and Margiana, an independent Hellenic kingdom (§ 34). The Parthians did the same at Astabene in the year 248 and declared themselves independent.

38. Seleucus II Callinicus (247–226 B.C.), son of Laodice and the older brother of Antiochus Hierax, succeeded to the throne. Ptolemy III

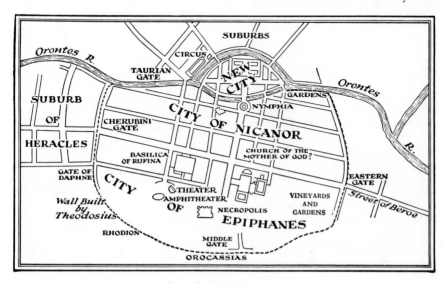

Plan of ancient Antioch.

Antiochus Hierax.

Euergetes had ascended to the throne of the Lagidae almost at the same time and, desirous of avenging his sister, Bernice, initiated the "Third Syrian War," also called the "War of Laodice" because she was the cause of it (c. 246–241 B.C.). This time the victory of the Lagid monarch was complete. The realm of the Seleucids was invaded up to and beyond the Euphrates, and a great part of Asia Minor together with Antioch itself was occupied. Antioch, however, was quickly recaptured by Seleucus, and a little later a peace was agreed upon which confirmed Ptolemy II in his possession of many coastal positions in Asia Minor. The attempts of Seleucus II to recover the lost territory were frustrated by the "fraternal war" which Antiochus Hierax (242?–237 B.C.), waged against him in the hope of becoming independent in Asia Minor with Laodice's support.

The brief reign of Seleucus III Ceraunus (226–223 B.C.), son of Callinicus, accomplished nothing in Asia Minor, where however Gallic invaders were constantly consolidating their gains in the region which was therefore called Galatia.

39. Seleucus III was succeeded by his younger brother Antiochus III the Great (223–187 B.C.), a man fully deserving of the title that was given him in ancient times. Although not without his failings, he displayed an energy and activity which none of the Seleucids had equaled from the very beginning of the dynasty, and had circumstances been more favorable, he would have enjoyed extraordinary success. It was the misfortune of Antiochus III to have to compete with an expanding Rome which, after successfully overcoming the difficult test of the Second Punic War (218–201 B.C.), was now turning her powerful energies to the Orient. Despite the victories won by Rome against Hannibal at Zama (202 B.C.) and against Philip V of Macedonia at

Antiochus III the Great.

Cynoscephalae (197 B.C.), Antiochus III did not accurately evaluate this new power, nor did he comprehend her political game; as a result he fell her victim. The scant attention he paid to the suggestions of his guest, Hannibal, whose strategic and political experience especially in regard to Rome had no equal, must be charged against him.

After quelling revolts in the eastern provinces of his kingdom, and moving to check the uprising of Achaeus in Asia Minor (which was encouraged and helped by Egypt), Antiochus in the year 219 undertook a large expedition against Ptolemy IV Philopator, over the usual question of Coelesyria and related political rivalries. When Seleucia on the Orontes was occupied, he conquered Coelesyria, a good part of Phoenicia including Tyre, Perea, and Samaria, and passed the winter of 218 B.C. at Ptolemais. When he resumed the campaign, however, he was defeated at Raphia (June 22, 217 B.C.) by the Greek army which, re-enforced by 20,000 Egyptians, had at its head the same Philopator, aided by his sister and his future wife Arsinoe III. In the peace which followed, Antiochus had to cede all his conquests except Seleucia.

It was evident that such a peace was only momentary. When Antiochus had reconquered Asia Minor from Achaeus and completed a long and glorious expedition in Bactria, Aracosia, and Carmania as far as India, he resumed in the year 204 his plan to make war on Egypt, and accordingly entered an alliance with Philip V of Macedonia. Invading Coelesyria in the year 202, he pushed on to Gaza which, after a few months of siege, fell before him. In 201 he marched into Asia Minor against Attalus, king of Pergamum, but quickly had to withdraw to Coelesyria where an Egyptian army under Scopas had arrived. Battle was joined near the sources of the Jordan at Panium (Πανεῖον, present-day *Baniyas,* called in the first century after Christ, *Caesarea-Philippi* [§ 368] and then *Neronias* [§ 400]). The name *Panium* was derived from a cavern consecrated to the god Pan and later adorned with statues placed in little niches which can still be seen. The Egyptians were decisively routed, and the possession of Samaria and Judea to the frontiers of the Delta was thus definitely assured to the Seleucids. This decisive battle occurred in the summer of the year 200 (or, according to others, in 198).

In the year 198 Antiochus assured the possession of Syria and of the Ionian cities which had been dependent upon Egypt and, after the battle of Cynoscephalae, went on to annex also some possessions of Macedonia. Although a previous Roman embassy had told him after the battle of Panium that Rome did not oppose his progress, this time Lucius Cornelius Lentulus came to him and ordered him, in the name of the senate, to liberate the occupied Greek cities, and to attempt no more to destroy their independence.

40. The intervention of Rome began to weigh heavily upon him and

Antiochus, although he continued to negotiate, considered making a complete break with her, and went so far as to extend his hospitality to Hannibal (195 B.C.), whose head was sought by Rome. To secure his rear, Antiochus thought to strengthen his hold on Coelesyria and to deprive Rome of a pretext for intervening in favor of Egypt by giving his daughter Cleopatra I, called Syra, to Ptolemy V Epiphanes (194 B.C.). The marriage, however, served only to fan the flames of discord, and it was later contended in the court of the Lagidae that Cleopatra had brought with her, as a dowry, this now contested Coelesyria, and thus new rights to it were claimed. How well founded this claim was, is not clear. It is clear, however, that Coelesyria-Palestine continued to be administered as usual by the Seleucids.

Antiochus entered the inevitable struggle with Rome entirely unprepared, politically and militarily. He neglected to make the alliance with Philip of Macedonia recommended by Hannibal and crossed over to Greece with insufficient forces; there he joined the meager re-enforcements of the Actolians and at Thermopylae attempted to halt the advance of the consul, M. Acilius Glabio. The soldiers of Antiochus, however, unlike those of Leonidas, allowed themselves to be surrounded by the Roman detachment led by M. Porcius Cato. The Syro-Grecian army was completely crushed (191 B.C.). Antiochus retreated to Asia Minor, his fleet lost, and Cornelius Scipio Asiaticus (who had with him as his legate his brother Africanus, the conqueror of Hannibal), went there to meet him. Battle was joined at Magnesia, and Antiochus' army, although greatly superior in numbers, met with disaster (190 B.C.). The conditions of peace dictated by Scipio and later added to by the senate (188 B.C.) were extremely severe: all Asia Minor north of the Taurus was to be evacuated; 15,000 talents, payable in twelve years, were exacted of him; the war elephants were to be surrendered and the fleet reduced to ten ships; limitations were imposed on the right to make war; twenty hostages had to be handed over, and also Hannibal.

Despite this blow and despite the fact that the eastern provinces of of the realm immediately took advantage of the situation to revolt, Antiochus did not lose confidence. He set out against the rebel provinces, with the hope also of garnering money with which to pay the indemnity. He had it in mind to put his hands on the riches guarded in a temple of Bel in Elymais, but there he was killed by the natives who rose to the defense of their sacred place (187 B.C.).

Antiochus III.

41. Seleucus IV Philopator (187–175 B.C.), his son, succeeded to the throne of the shrunken kingdom. In his brief span of government, he was able to do very little amid such adversities. The scanty information about him which history preserves confirms St. Jerome's opinion of him: *"Nihil dignum Syriae et patris gessit imperio, et absque ullis proeliis ingloriosus obiit"* (*In Daniel.*, 11, 20). His chief worry was, of course, the payment of the enormous yearly tribute to Rome according to the terms of the peace. His father had attempted to take the temple riches of Elymais for that purpose; Seleucus IV sought the riches of the Temple of Jerusalem (§ 226). Except for this episode, which can be explained by his solicitude for the supreme welfare of the state, it seems that he was well disposed toward the Jews of Palestine and even granted them subsidies (2 Mach. 3:3). He was slain by his minister, Heliodorus, who perhaps hoped thereby to obtain the regency.

Shortly before his death he had exchanged some of the hostages detained by Rome according to the terms of the peace. His own brother Antiochus IV, son of Antiochus the Great, was one of them; in his place Seleucus obtained permission to send his own son Demetrius. When Antiochus IV was liberated, he began the journey toward Syria, but in Athens news reached him that Seleucus had died. With the help of the armies of the king of Pergamum he then succeeded in taking over the throne, frustrating the ambitious Heliodorus and ignoring the rights of his nephew Demetrius and also of another very young son of the dead king (§ 234).

42. Antiochus IV Epiphanes (175–163 B.C.) was a new kind of king on the throne of the Seleucids, both as man and ruler. He had an acute mind but was extravagant in his habits; he was more ardent than profound in his Hellenism. At first he was a Stoic intellectual, then an Epicurean; he was avid for riches and, at the same time, a prodigal spender; he passionately desired popularity and, at the same time, was cynical in his demeanor. He was the product of the fusion of his own eccentric temperament with the traditions of his Hellenic dynasty, and also with those of the aristocracy of Rome, where he had lived fourteen years as a hostage and had made many friends. The title *Epiphanes* which appeared on his later coins was a divine title of Egyptian provenience: Θεὸς ἐπιφανής, "God manifested," i.e., the Sun god Horus. Even in ancient times the title was changed by a slight alteration to *Epimanus*, "furious" (Polybius, XXVI, 10), and not without reason.

Antiochus IV avoided coming to grips with Rome. Instead he directed all his energies to the realization of the one project permitted him, namely, to infuse the Hellenistic spirit ever more profoundly into his diminished and disintegrated kingdom and so to unify and strengthen it. This project was a compensation for the impossibility of an open struggle with Rome and, at the same time, a necessary preparation for that struggle. There is no doubt that his program was realized in some measure, and that here and there it produced excellent results.

43. After he had begun his program and reorganized the army and his fleet, Antiochus IV again found himself implicated in the question of Coelesyria. Around 173 B.C. Cleopatra I Syra, who ruled in the name of her young son, Ptolemy VI Philometor, died; her policy toward Syria had always been friendly, for she was a Syrian, but the policy ceased with her death. Shortly thereafter Ptolemy VI ascended the throne, and the claims mentioned above (§ 40) were raised in the Lagidae court. Avoiding any concrete threat, Epiphanes moved southward with his army into Palestine as far as Jaffa; but nothing further took place at the moment. In 169 B.C., however, Egypt decided to act and attacked. Epiphanes had prudently assured himself beforehand of Rome's neutrality; indeed, Rome had her hands full with her war against Perseus of Macedonia and must have looked with complacency — in conformity with her policy, "divide and rule" — on the spectacle of the two greatest states of the Mediterranean weakening themselves by war. On receiving an assurance of Rome's neutrality, Antiochus descended against Egypt, routed the army on the frontier, occupied Pelusium, invaded the Delta, and succeeded in taking Ptolemy VI prisoner. But the people of Alexandria were not yet conquered and rose up in revolt, putting on the throne of the Lagidae the younger brother of the prisoner. He later became Ptolemy VII [Euergetes II] Physcon.

Epiphanes then became legitimist and arrayed himself on the side of Ptolemy VI. He obtained satisfactory peace terms and withdrew from Egypt, hoping that the rivalry between the two brothers would work in his favor. Instead, the two brothers, perhaps through the good offices of Cleopatra II, their sister and wife of Ptolemy VI, reached an agreement in the face of the common enemy and established a kind of joint sovereignty or regency, which was afterward employed in Egypt on other occasions.

This turn of affairs angered Antiochus and in 168 B.C., after other negotiations failed, he again invaded the Delta and aimed at Alexandria. His anxiety to be master of Egypt, however, alarmed Rome, just at this time emerging victoriously from her war with Macedonia. Rome vetoed his project. Tradition has preserved for us this famous scene: Popilius Laenas, who had been

Antiochus IV.

his friend in Rome, presented himself to Antiochus, now within a few miles of Alexandria. Before he even replied to the conventional greetings, the Roman communicated to him the demand of the Roman Senate that he retire from Egypt. Antiochus requested time to consider, but Popilius traced a circle with his staff upon the ground around him and replied: Ἐνταῦθα βουλεύου. "Deliberate right here." There could be only one result of such deliberation; Antiochus abandoned Egypt and returned to Syria via Palestine. The fact that just any patrician of Rome could treat an heir of Alexander the Great and of the kings of Persia in such a manner is an eloquent indication of the exact state of affairs.

44. The developments in Palestine and Jerusalem, both before and after the checkmate of Antiochus Epiphanes in Egypt, are of the highest importance for the present work (§ 227 ff.), even though for him they were only of secondary importance and were strictly limited to a small district of his realm.

He realized now that all attempts in the West would be certain to provoke a struggle with Rome, and so he turned to the East, where, however, both his authority and Hellenism were steadily declining as the power of the Parthians increased. Before launching his expedition (165 B.C.) he left his son Antiochus V, who had been associated in the government with him, under the regency of Lysias. He arrived in Armenia, which had rebelled, and subdued it. He continued on to Elymais and there attempted to take possession of the treasures of a temple of the goddess Nana, as his father had done in similar circumstances (§ 40). The opposition of the faithful frustrated his desire, but, unlike his father, he himself was unharmed. It seems quite certain that the similarity of the two episodes caused garbled versions of each to be circulated in Syria and Palestine and brought about a false report of the death of Epiphanes (§ 257, footnote), the report stating that he was killed because he repeated the same sacrilege his father had committed. In reality, however, he fell sick shortly after that episode, probably of consumption and owing to his habitual dissoluteness, and perhaps also manifesting symptoms of paranoia. He actually died between the spring and summer of 163 B.C. at Tabae in Persia. Shortly before he died, perhaps because he distrusted the attitude of Lysias, he named Philip Phrygius, his general, as regent.

45. His son Antiochus V Eupator (163–162 B.C.) made a brief, unimportant appearance on the throne of the Seleucids. Only nine years old, he was merely an instrument controlled by Lysias. He immediately rid himself of Philip, the other regent, by force of arms, but his power was short lived because of an incident which involved Rome. When Cnidus Octavius, the head of a Roman embassy, was stabbed at Laodicea by a nationalistic fanatic (162 B.C.), Lysias hastened to disclaim any

Antiochus V.

responsibility for the deed, and it was plain enough that he had no hand in it. The Roman Senate however made much of the incident, and though it officially denied Demetrius, the aspirant to the throne and hostage in Rome (§ 41), permission to depart, he actually was allowed to escape.

46. When Demetrius I Soter (162–150 B.C.) disembarked at Tripoli in Phoenicia, he quickly won the army over to himself, took possession of the throne, and put Antiochus V and Lysias to death. Demetrius was an energetic youth, but not overly prudent. Despite Rome's suspicious attitude toward him he insisted on asserting his authority by force of arms throughout his realm. He defeated Timarcus, the governor of Babylonia, who had won his independence and had been sustained diplomatically by Rome (§ 264); he intervened with notable success in the revolt of Judea which was becoming ever more vexatious (§ 263 ff.). He had trouble also with Pergamum, Cappadocia, and Egypt, and in his own kingdom his aristocratic and distant manner won him no sympathy.

Any kind of pretender could supplant him. Attalus II, king of Pergamum, presented a pretender in the person of Balas, an obscure youth who seems not to have been related to the Seleucids, but as he greatly resembled Antiochus IV Epiphanes, he pretended to be his son. When he proclaimed himself king and took the name of Alexander at Pergamum, he was immediately recognized by Ptolemy VI of Egypt and by Ariarates of Cappadocia; later on, the Roman Senate also recognized him.

In 153 B.C. Alexander Balas disembarked at Ptolemais in Phoenicia, where he used to good advantage the aid which Egypt furnished him by sea. He exploited the animosity of the local peoples against Demetrius. Demetrius, who had disavowed his previous policy, and Balas then engaged in a struggle to deprive each other of the support of the nationalistic Jews by means of ever greater concessions (§§ 274, 275). Balas won and henceforth Palestine supported him. Demetrius sent his sons Demetrius (II) and Antiochus (VII) to Cnidus for safety and then attacked the army of Balas, but, betrayed by his soldiers and the people, he died in battle during the summer of 150.

47. Alexander I Balas (150–145 B.C.), an inferior type of man and sovereign, was as unfortunate as king as he had been fortunate as pretender. To secure the aid of Egypt he married Cleopatra Thea, the daughter of Ptolemy VI Philometor in Ptolemais (149). The great festivities which accompanied the wedding were calculated to strengthen the bonds of friendship between him and the subject Jews (§ 275); disillusionment was not slow in coming. In 147 Demetrius II, son of Demetrius I, landed at Cilicia with troops led by the Cretan, Lasthenes, with the intention of recapturing the paternal throne. Apollonius, the governor of Coelesyria who had supported Demetrius, was struck down by Jonathan Machabeus who was loyal to Balas (§ 276), but Ptolemy VI also intervened, apparently to help his son-in-law but in reality to retake Coelesyria. After he had fortified his position in Palestine and Phoenicia to suit himself, he arrived with his army at Seleucia and declared himself against Balas and offered his daughter Cleopatra, whom he had taken back, to Demetrius. The armies met near Antioch, and Ptolemy was grievously wounded. The defeated Balas fled to an Arab chieftain, Zabdiel, who promptly killed him and sent his head to Ptolemy (the summer of 145 B.C.). Ptolemy also died of his wounds a few days later, and with him the Egyptian occupation of Palestine came to an end.

48. Demetrius II Nicator [Theos Philadelphos] ascended the throne when he was little more than sixteen years of age. He reigned at two different times. In his first reign (145–138 B.C.) he had two rivals. A general of Balas, Diodotus, afterward called Trypho, took it upon himself to champion the rights of Balas' small son and proclaimed him king; this was Antiochus VI [Theos Epiphanes] Dionysius (145–142 B.C.). When they both entered Antioch, Trypho secured the support of the Machabees (§ 278) and became master of Syria. The rest of the kingdom was left to Demetrius, with Seleucia as the capital. After a short time Trypho himself sought the kingship; obtaining custody of Jonathan Machabeus by treachery, he killed him, and likewise did away with the infant Antiochus VI (142). The surviving Machabeus, Simon, then went over to the side of Demetrius II (§ 280 ff.).

In 140 Demetrius was forced to attend to the eastern provinces of the realm where the Hellenic districts were being overwhelmed by the invasions of the Parthians. After some victories he fell prisoner to the enemy king, Mithridates I, who treated him magnaminously (138). When the other son of Demetrius I, Antiochus VII Sidetes, heard that his brother was a prisoner, he went from Rhodes to Syria to claim the throne for himself. There he won the sympathy of the fickle populace and purchased the friendship of Simon Machabeus (§ 292), and thus quickly obtained the advantage over Trypho, who died in Apamea while besieged there.

49. Antiochus VII Sidetes (138–129 B.C.) became king at the age of twenty years or so and was the last of the Seleucids to govern with any energy. He strengthened his position in Syria and shortly thereafter desired to regulate matters in Judea. He rushed an army there, but meeting with no success, did not then attempt to continue battle. When Simon Machabeus died and was succeeded by John Hyrcanus,

Antiochus VII resumed the campaign and set siege to Jerusalem (134). He made very reasonable terms with the vanquished (§ 295 ff.); in fact, because of the great respect he manifested toward the religion of the Jews (it did not threaten his political plans), the Jews bestowed upon him the title *eusebes,* "pious" (Josephus, *Antiquities,* XIII, 8, 2).

In 130 B.C. Antiochus VII organized an expedition against the Parthians who were holding his brother Demetrius II prisoner (§ 48) and were making deeper raids on the eastern provinces of his realm. At first he enjoyed such success that the Parthians freed Demetrius, but when later on he was obliged to battle under unfavorable conditions with Phraates II of the dynasty of the Arsacidae, he was defeated and killed (129).

50. The liberated Demetrius II returned to the throne of Syria and thus reigned for the second time (129–125 B.C.). It was an unimportant reign. From Egypt, Ptolemy VII Physcon, although related to Demetrius through Cleopatra Thea (§ 47), set up a pretender to oppose him, so as further to weaken his authority. Ptolemy hoped by this to be free to meddle in Syria-Palestine. The pretender, Alexander Zabinas, was said to be the son of Alexander Balas. Demetrius was defeated at Damascus and fled to Tyre, where he was killed (125).

Other disturbances followed his death. Cleopatra Thea had her first-born Seleucus V killed (125 B.C.) and recalled her other son, Antiochus VIII, from Athens. The latter entered the struggle against Alexander Zabinas, and with aid furnished by Ptolemy VII Physcon, who had abandoned Zabinas to support his rival, defeated and killed him (123 B.C.).

51. Antiochus VIII Grypus ruled twice. During the early years of his first reign (125–113 B.C.), he held power jointly with his mother, Cleopatra Thea, but when in 121 she tried to poison him, he had her killed and held the throne alone. Later he had a rival in the person of his half brother Antiochus IX Cyzicenus, who rose against him in 114 and succeeded in occupying Antioch and a great part of Syria (113). Grypus counterattacked and reoccupied Antioch, and again took over the kingdom (111–96 B.C.). But Cyzi-

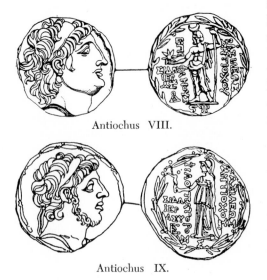

Antiochus VIII.

Antiochus IX.

cenus remaining strong, the fraternal rivalry continued, and the realm remained divided. Antiochus VIII held power in Syria and in the eastern provinces; Antiochus IX (111–95 B.C.) in Coelesyria and Phoenicia, with his capital at Damascus.

And so the rest of the kingdom became ever more disunited. Several cities, among them Tyre and Sidon, proclaimed their independence. Meanwhile this time the competitors, beset by intrigues concocted by their women, and by assassinations, dissipated what was left of the crown's authority, and more and more came to resemble a band of adventurers. It need hardly be mentioned that Hellenism, which was the object of jealous care on the part of the first Seleucids and at the same time their great support, was being progressively diluted at its source. Externally the circle of its influence grew daily less. Rome was advancing inexorably from the Mediterranean and south of the Danube; in the East, the native populations, beginning with the Parthians, spearheaded the Asiatic reaction in the direction of the Mediterranean.

In the year 96 Antiochus VIII was killed in a riot provoked by his favorite, Heracleon, who, as regent of Seleucus VI the son of the slain ruler, took over the throne. Antiochus IX then tried to gain possession of all Syria but he was defeated and lost his life in the attempt (95).

52. These two deaths were followed by a period of anarchy which lasted for twelve years (95–83 B.C.). The armed rivalry was kept alive by the sons of Antiochus VIII and Antiochus IX. The following were the sons of Antiochus VIII: Seleucus VI Epiphanes Nicator, Antiochus XI Epiphanes Philadelphus, Philippus Philadelphus, Demetrius III Eucaerus Philopator Soter, Antiochus XII Dionysius. All were shadow-like sovereigns who reigned briefly. Antiochus X Eusebes (95–83 B.C.), son of Antiochus IX, alone, battled in turn the five sons of Antiochus VIII.

Aretas, an Arab chieftain, took advantage of all this confusion by killing Antiochus XII and taking possession of Coelesyria. Then Tigranes, king of Armenia, saw his chance, and in the year 83 solidly ensconced himself in Syria (§ 308). The Armenian domination continued up to 69 B.C. in which year Licinius Lucullus, who directed the war against Mithridates, king of Pontus, defeated at Tigranocerta the latter's ally, Tigranes, and thus became master of Syria. He then gave it to the last of the Seleucids, Antiochus XIII Asiaticus, son of Antiochus X, who was acceptable to the Romans because at the time of Tigranes' invasion he was in refuge at Rome. Even he had an ephemeral reign. New disturbances arose, and when the question was referred to Pompey, who in the meantime had succeeded Lucullus, Pompey declared that Syria belonged to Rome, which was the conqueror of Tigranes. In conformity with this decision Syria was reduced to a Roman province (65 B.C.) and the kingdom of the Seleucids was ended forever.

53. Next to the Seleucids, the dynasty with which the Hebrews had the most important relations was that of the Ptolemies of Egypt. Established by Ptolemy, son of Lagus (§ 27), it is also called the dynasty of the Lagidae. Although the Seleucids had different names, the Lagidae monarchs all were called "Ptolemy," and the women were usually called "Cleopatra." The complete list of the Lagidae who reigned officially is as follows:

Ptolemy I Soter, as governor		323–305 B.C.
Ptolemy I Soter, as king		305–283 B.C.
Ptolemy II Philadelphus	[285]	283–246 B.C.
Ptolemy III Euergetes I		246–221 B.C.
Ptolemy IV Philopator		221–203 B.C.
Ptolemy V Epiphanes		203–181 B.C.
Ptolemy VI Philometor		181–145 B.C.
Ptolemy VII Euergetes II Physcon .	[169]	145–116 B.C.
Ptolemy VIII Soter II Lathyros		116–108 B.C.
Ptolemy IX Alexander I		108–88 B.C.
Ptolemy VIII (for the second time) . . .		88–80 B.C.
Ptolemy X Alexander II		80 B.C.
Ptolemy XI Auletes		80–51 B.C.
Ptolemy XII ⎫ Cleopatra VII ⎭		51–48 B.C.
Ptolemy XIII ⎫ Cleopatra VII ⎭		47–44 B.C.
Ptolemy XIV Caesar (Caesarion) ⎫ Cleopatra VII ⎭ . . .		44–30 B.C.

The Lagidae effectively controlled Palestine from the battle of Ipsus in 301 B.C. (§ 30), until the battle of Panium in 200 B.C. (§ 39); as a result of the battle, Palestine passed into the control of the Seleucids in the manner already seen (§ 40 ff.). This did not mean that relations between the Lagidae and the Hebrews were entirely broken off. Aside from the fact that the capital Alexandria contained a very powerful and influential Jewish community (§ 190 ff.), there remained in Palestine itself, even after 200, a group of Jews favorable to the Ptolemies who maintained close relations with their fellow countrymen and their sovereigns in Egypt. At any rate, the official political relations between the

Tetradrachma of Ptolemy I.

Lagidae and the Seleucids were
as indicated in our treatment of
the latter.

54. Relations between the
Lagidae and Rome began with
Ptolemy II Philadelphus and
were very courteous; they continued afterward and became
more intimate during the battle
of Panium (§ 39) on which occasion Rome pretended to be
very much interested in the
youthful Ptolemy V Epiphanes.
When Antiochus IV invaded

Money of Cleopatra. (*Enciclopedia
Italiana.*)

Egypt, the action of Popilius Laenas (§ 43) began to reveal Rome's intentions, and to show that she considered Egypt to be under her protection. In fact Ptolemy VI and Ptolemy VII turned to Rome in their struggles; even later, Ptolemy Apion, illegitimate son of Ptolemy VII, willed
Cyrenaica to her. With the decadence of the dynasty of the Lagidae,
Rome held all the reins of government in her hands. Ptolemy XI Auletes
became an "ally" of Rome, but in 58 B.C. Clodius took the island of Cyprus
from him and he did not dare protest; as compensation, however, Auletes
found sanctuary at Rome when a revolt deprived him of his kingdom,
and he was able to regain it with Roman help. He died in the year 51
and left the kingdom jointly to Ptolemy XII and Cleopatra, his children,
who were married to each other. It has been previously pointed out
that marriages between brothers and sisters were very frequent among
the Lagidae and for that matter also among the Achaemenids.

This daughter of Auletes was *the* famous Cleopatra, Cleopatra VII
Thea Philopator. She ascended the throne when only seventeen, and
was endowed with extraordinary energy. She deprived her ten-year-
old brother and husband, and the tutors who surrounded him, of
every vestige of authority. An armed conflict broke out between the
two, during which Ptolemy XII had Pompey the Great assassinated
at the very time the latter sought refuge with him. He hoped by this
to please Julius Caesar. When Caesar took over Alexandria, he reconciled
the two sovereigns, although the reconciliation was not very permanent.
Caesar himself fell victim to the artful charms of Cleopatra and found
himself at war with Ptolemy XII (48–47 B.C.), and, after many hardships, was victorious. Ptolemy was killed. Caesar then established
Cleopatra and her younger brother Ptolemy XIII (he was also her
husband) as rulers of Egypt. In June of the year 47 Cleopatra gave
birth to a boy whom she named Caesar; the Alexandrians in derision

called him "Caesarion." When Cleopatra returned from Rome after the death of Caesar, she got rid of Ptolemy XIII and shared the throne with her three-year-old son Caesarion. Then followed her affair with the triumvir Antony; for her it meant a weaving of grandiose dreams; for him, a matter of blind infatuation. The battle of Actium (September 2, 31 B.C.), however, put an end to the shameful drama, and shortly afterward Cleopatra committed suicide, Caesarion was put to death, and with them terminated the dynasty of the Lagidae. In the year 30 B.C., Egypt was reduced to the status of a Roman province.

THE HISTORY OF ISRAEL

THE EXILE

55. The tempest which had uprooted Israel from the land of its fathers struck it three main blows. The first, by way of warning, was the deportation of the year 597 B.C. (Vol. I, § 530); the second, the destruction of Jerusalem and deportation of the year 586 (Vol. I, § 542), caused the principal damage; the third, completing the destruction, as it were, swept away the turbulent remains and dispersed them in the deportation of the year 582 (Vol. I, § 545).

It is impossible to determine the number of those deported, as was pointed out before, because so much data is missing. One may conjecture that the total number would come to about 30,000, but this is only conjecture. The real number may be quite different, perhaps even larger. The opinion of one modern scholar that only five to ten thousand were involved seems too small an estimate. At any rate, these figures refer only to able-bodied men (leaders, artisans, property owners, etc.) exclusive of women and children who, although they accompanied their menfolk, were ordinarily not counted. The figure would be doubled or tripled if the women and children were included, and the grand total would then be about sixty to eighty thousand.

It must not be imagined that after the third deportation – even considering the many victims of war, massacre, and disease, and the many who fled to neighboring countries or sought refuge in Egypt (Vol. I, § 545) – that the territory of the kingdom of Juda was an abandoned desert. Many who were supposed to go escaped the deportation; many of the lower classes, especially the peasants and shepherds scattered about the countryside or the steppes, were of little concern to the Chaldeans as possible political agitators. Moreover, they were needed to cultivate the soil. Those who were acceptable to the Chaldeans, like Godolias and Jeremias, were left at liberty in the villages which were not so seriously damaged by the war, and were even shown marks of favor. The number of those who remained is also strictly a matter of conjecture; including women and children they may have numbered from thirty to forty thousand.

56. Those Who Remained in the Kingdom of Juda. After the assassination of Godolias (Vol. I, § 546), another governor was of course appointed in his place by the court of Babylon to rule those who remained, but of this we have no documentary evidence. Whether he and his successors were Babylonians, or Jews like Godolias, or whether the territory of Juda was placed in direct dependence upon the governor who had been previously appointed in Samaria after the fall of the kingdom of Israel (Vol. I, § 482), is not known. It is also probable that the new territory acquired by the Babylonian empire, whether it formed a new province by itself or whether it was united with the territory of Samaria, was divided into districts according to the exigencies of the places and peoples, with local rulers to govern them (cf. Neh. 3:15 ff.).

The Chaldeans did not send any of the other subjugated peoples into the new territory (Vol. I, § 545), but sizable groups of surrounding peoples must have penetrated there in the first years of the Chaldean reign, occasionally in the following years, and during the succeeding Persian domination. Moab and Ammon on the east must have infiltrated but slightly; from the south, however, Edom must have sent an alarming number of people (Ezech. 25:12 ff.; 35:10; 36:5, etc.) who settled throughout the whole Negeb (Vol. I, § 65) as far as Hebron, and this section was henceforth called Idumaea. The people of Edom were forced to expand northward because, farther to the south, the Nabatean Arab tribes were dislodging them from their previous settlements. As a result, those clans of Calebites, Qenites, etc., which had previously fused with the Hebrews in the more southern part of Palestine (Vol. I, § 291) were also driven farther north toward Bethlehem.

57. Living conditions for the Hebrews who remained in the homeland, especially in the first years after the catastrophe, were certainly very difficult.

First of all, the capital and the larger villages had suffered very heavy damage. This has given rise to exaggerations in the past; some have imagined that after 586 B.C. Jerusalem was actually razed to the ground and was left as a desert. Today the tendency is to exaggerate on the other side. Some hold that, except for a few villages, the dwellings scattered throughout the territory did not suffer, and that in Jerusalem only some of the larger buildings were burned and some sections of the walls demolished. Some even claim that the Temple of Jerusalem was still standing after the fire which burned only the inflammable materials on the inside, so that only its interior was ruined. This exaggeration is as bad as the first; aside from the explicit attestations of the Bible (2 Kings 25:9; Jer. 39:8; 52:13), this view takes no account of the usual punishments inflicted by the Assyrians on a vanquished

Assyrian conquest of a city. At right, the conquest; at left, deported women and children taken as booty (the women cover their eyes with their hands to blot out the scene).

country — especially if it was obstinate in rebellion. Later, the Chaldeans acted in the same way. This systematic punishment is described by word and pictures on contemporary monuments (Vol. I, § 456). And as for the Temple, what could escape the roaring furnace created by the burning of its wooden parts (Vol. I, §§ 391–395)? Undoubtedly therefore, while some villages were almost totally destroyed, others like Jerusalem remained, though seriously damaged.

Agriculture and stock raising amid such disturbances and depredations must also have suffered long-lasting setbacks. The violence of fanatically patriotic bands who roamed through the desolate country (Vol. I, § 544), and the inevitable reprisals on the part of the new rulers, rendered the situation all the more uncertain, and disheartened the few who were willing and able to think of rehabilitation. On the other hand, the Chaldeans, according to their wont, treated the country as a conquered territory from which everything good, whether product of the soil (Lam. 5:2 ff.), or work of the inhabitants (Lam. 5:13 [Hebrew text]; Zach. 8:10), was to be appropriated. All these factors, especially in the first years, fostered disunity and a quasi-anarchical individualism among those who remained. These feared the Chaldeans and had no confidence in the Jews, and many took refuge in out-of-the-way places (Lam. 5:9), so as to enjoy some calm and safety for themselves and their families.

This state of affairs must have seriously lowered the morale of the minority left behind in Judea. The ancient social organization was demolished by the catastrophe; not only that, but the minority which remained among the ruins was definitely inferior in quality. The flower of the nation, those who more particularly aroused the distrust of the Chaldeans, wound up in Babylonia; the less desirable part of the nation was left at home, the ἰδιῶται, the "lesser folk," among whom foreign elements had infiltrated, as we have seen. These scattered sheep might search for a shepherd to guide them, but they would find only tyrannizing strangers, or at best fanatical fellow countrymen. Where was there a support on which the terrified remnants of Israel could lean, and so rise again? The dynasty of David had ended in chains, the capital was devastated, the beacon of the nation, the Temple, was extinguished; the spiritual dictators of the nation, the prophets (Vol. I, § 430), rose up no more, or at least "they had no visions from Yahweh" (Lam. 2:9). The lot of the abhorred Samaritans seemed more fortunate, for they at least had their sanctuary of Beth-el which functioned regularly (Vol. I, § 457).

This condition of affairs may have been mitigated somewhat after the first years of the catastrophe with the leveling of the ruins and a spontaneous resurgence of social life, and especially with the death of Nabuchodonosor. That the death of this ironhanded conqueror actually brought some respite to the oppressed Jews can be argued from the fact that his successor Evil-Merodach (Amel-Marduk: Vol. I, § 16) liberated the unfortunate Joachin from his thirty-seven years' imprisonment (Vol. I, § 53) and treated him with special honor (2 Kings 25:27–30). It is also certain that, under the fleeting successors of Evil-Merodach (Vol. I, § 16) and especially under the eccentric Nabonidus (§ 4), the instability and weakness of the central government rendered conditions in Judea less harsh. But they did remain harsh, and the inhabitants of Judea could nowhere perceive any ray of hope.

58. No precise details are given as to the spiritual conditions of the people, though one may argue that along with its many evils, the hurricane produced some good. As it roared through the vineyard of Yahweh it devastated the vine branches and struck down the grape clusters. The rotten grapes fell under its lash, but the few healthy ones did not yield and benefited by the air and light. They were the grapes of the "blessing" (Isa. 65:8). Syncretistic cults might take a more profound hold on certain perverse groups (cf. Jer. 44:17, 25; Ezech. 33:25); open distrust of the God of the nation might overpower minds stunned by the tremendous blow (cf. Ezech. 8:12; Jer. 44:18), but there were other superior souls who saw the event as a disposition of Yahweh's providence. These realized that the catastrophe would lead to a moral regeneration; that although the Temple was destroyed, Yahweh always remained in the heavens; though the altar of sacrifices was destroyed, they had at least the palms of their hands upon which they could offer their hearts to God. All human trust had vanished, but Yahweh could reach even into the caverns of hell. These superior souls gave expression to their sentiments in the following words:

> "The crown is fallen from our head;
>   Woe to us because we have sinned!
> Therefore is our heart sorrowful,
>   Therefore are our eyes become dim:
> Because Mount Sion is desolate,
>   The foxes run about upon it.
> But Thou, O Yahweh, dost remain forever,
>   Thy throne from generation to generation."
>
> (Lam. 5:16–19)

In other words, however sorely Jerusalem was afflicted here below, Yahweh still reigned eternally above. From that very contrast a plan of action emerged:

> "Let us search our ways and seek,
>   And let us return to Yahweh!
> Let us lift up our hearts with our hands
>   to God in the heavens! . . .
> I have invoked Thy name, O Yahweh,
>   from the pit of Hell.
> Thou hast heard my voice 'Turn not away
>   thine ear from my relief [. . .]!'
> Thou drewest near in the day when I called Thee,
>   Thou saidst: 'Fear not!'"
>
> (Lam. 3:40 f., 55–57)

Their confidence had only one foundation:

> "My portion is Yahweh — saith my soul —
>   therefore I trust in Him!
> Yahweh is good to him who confides in Him,
>   to the soul that seeks Him.
> It is good to wait with silence
>   for the salvation of Yahweh!"
>
> (Lam. 3:24–26)

Everything converges to one idea, the "return" to Yahweh:

> "Bring us back to Thee, O Yahweh, and we will return;
>   renew our days as in ancient times!"
>
> (Lam. 5:21)

All this is simply pure Yahwism. The prophet is saying that it is necessary to return to the Yahwism born on Sinai and affirmed in the desert, when the temple of Solomon was not yet, even as now it no longer exists.

Prisoners with bound arms being led into slavery. Guard in the rear
about to strike.

59. The Deportees. The deportation of the Jews was carried out
according to the usual system of the Chaldeans, and they had
learned it from the Assyrians, whose monuments often contain pictures of it. Those to be deported were assembled in concentration
camps (in the deportation of 586, Rama, present-day *er-Ram*, about
five miles north of Jerusalem, was such a center; cf. Jer. 40:1; 31:15).
Many, if not all, were bound with chains or ropes so that their elbows
were joined behind their backs, or the left arm of one was bound
to the right arm of another. They were then arranged in columns and,
amid the shouts of the guards and the blows of their clubs, marched
to the regions destined to receive them. As the prisoners marched
farther and farther away from their homeland and their desire to
escape diminished, it is possible that their painful bonds were loosed,
but it is certain that the first half of that very long journey was made
in bonds. Ordinarily the women were not bound, as they had to see to
the food and household goods. Those who could not endure the tortures
and burdens of the march — which must have lasted for some months
(cf. Esdras 7:9) during the summer and autumn heat of the desert of
Syria — dropped by the wayside to become the victims of hunger;
later, the jackals would come to do their work. The whole route
from Jerusalem to Babylonia was dotted with the remains of these
pitiable prisoners.

As pointed out before, the prisoners were the finest flower of the
nation, the "ancients" who by their very appearance inspired reverence,
and the "virgins" who had been the pride of Israel. At the halts of
the difficult journey in their miserable state

> "The ancients of the daughter of Sion
> sat upon the ground and were silent:
> They sprinkled their heads with dust,
> they girded themselves with sackcloth;
> The maidens of Jerusalem
> bowed their heads to the ground."

(Lam. 2:10)

When they were about to depart the Chaldeans

> "Outraged the women in Sion,
> The virgins in the cities of Juda;
> The princes were hung up by their hands,
> The ancients were not respected."

(Lam. 5:11–12)

60. Arrived in Babylonia, the Jews were sent off to various localities. Some of them were employed on the great construction projects which Nabuchodonosor had begun, notably in the district around Babel (Vol. I, § 542). Some worked on canal projects, so necessary in Babylonia; some were farmers on large estates belonging to the king himself, and some were assigned to important Babylonian sanctuaries or large estates. Those who worked on the construction projects probably lived in the suburbs of the large cities, and the others in the agricultural colonies scattered about the countryside. They were under constant surveillance, and their work was subject to the direct supervision and control of their masters, but they did enjoy a sort of restricted liberty similar to that which an American slaveholder in the early days granted to the negroes who did the menial work and caused no trouble.

With the passage of time conditions improved, especially after the death of Nabuchodonosor (§ 57). The more capable and active made progress in various ways and established themselves as opportunity offered. In general, they all bettered themselves to some extent. When they proved that they were somewhat resigned to their lot, the Chaldeans permitted them to build little homes and plant gardens (Jer. 29:5), to establish new families and increase in number. They were permitted, therefore, to build new villages in the districts where they worked. The names of some of these villages have been preserved by history: Tell-Abib, "hill of the ear of corn" (Ezech. 3:15), near the Kebar canal (Vol. I, § 530). The name may be an indication of the fertility of the region, and this was perhaps the most important Jewish center. Some think the name may be a corruption of the Babylonian Till-Abub, "hill of the flood," which would refer to a devastated district under reclamation. Other names which have come down to us are: Tell-Harsha, "hill of the plow" (Esdras 2:59; Neh. 7:61), clearly a symbolic name; Tell-Melah, "hill of the salt" (found there); Kerub Addan; Immer (Esdras 2:59); Kasiphia (Esdras 8:17).

61. These colonies continually developed as centers of social life. The reluctance of the inhabitants was transformed, as times and circumstances changed, into a tranquil acquiescence. It was then that private enterprise and the development of commerce got under way. Conveniences increased, and the captives began to enjoy a bit of leisure; some of them even became rich. Proof of this can be seen in the fact that only a few decades after they were settled in the country by force of arms, the colonists had thousands of slaves (Esdras 2:65) and some of them — a minority — were in a position to donate 61,000 darics of gold and 5,000 minas of silver (Esdras 2:69; cf., however, Neh. 7:70–72). Later on, in the time of Esdras, 100 talents of gold, 650 of silver, and many other precious objects were offered as gifts — sums including the Persian contribution it is true — by only a part of the Jews who remained in Babylonia (Esdras 8:26–27).

In only fifty years, therefore, the original situation was reversed. The rapid decline of the Chaldean government explains it in part, but the chief factor was the tenacious industry of the Jews. In a land which was more fertile and fruitful than Palestine (cf. 2 Kings 20:18) and in the commercial centers of Babylonia which had a large international trade, they seized every opportunity to become producers and merchants — a trait which seems to be inherent in the race. Of course, some few, and some groups did not keep pace with this progress or even regressed, but on the other hand there must have been individuals who, by their industry, gained eminent positions in the commercial field, in government administration, or even at court in the capacity of pages, eunuchs (2 Kings 20:18), etc., and used their influence in a patriotic way to help their fellow countrymen. This can be legitimately inferred because of what happened during the Persian period (§ 63).

62. The Jews eventually did very well in their involuntary exile, where they were in better circumstances even than in their homeland. In fact, many had the opportunity to return to Palestine but chose rather to remain in Babylonia (§ 85 ff.). It may seem strange that they refused to return, when one considers that only two generations before it had taken the chains and clubs of their guards to drag them from the land of their fathers. Many reasons may be offered for this change. In some cases the nationalistic spirit had died out, but for the majority there was no question of apostasy but rather of a compromise between their patriotism and their present manner of life. They had achieved success in Babylonia, had acquired power. Moreover, the repatriation of the Jews had to be sustained, materially and morally. Many, therefore, decided to remain in Babylonia where they could themselves go on living well and, at the same time, assist in the work of repatriation. This was as deserving a work, nationally speaking, as that of those who actually returned.

A similar attitude is encountered in the Zionism of our own day. Many Zionist bankers, both English and American, never seriously consider migrating to Palestine, a country they have perhaps never seen; yet their activity, which induced England to adopt a Zionist policy in the first place, and, later on, their liberal support of the Zionists transplanted to Palestine, were certainly not less valuable to Zionism than the labor of the poor Polish or German Jews who now form colonies in the valley of Esdraelon, in the Zionist city of Tel-Aviv, or in the suburbs of Jerusalem. In like manner the Jews of means in Babylonia aided their fellow countrymen.

63. Material well-being, so profound a concern to the deported, increased little by little as their commercial organization was better established. Recent documentary discoveries provide us with many details of this. In the second half of the fifth century B.C., during the reigns of Artaxerxes I and Darius II (§§ 17, 18), there was at Nippur (Vol. I, § 530) a prosperous Jewish commercial house which, from the name of the proprietor, could be called "*Murashu and Sons Bank.*" A part of the archives of this firm, consisting of some hundreds of tablets containing contracts, has been recovered in the ruins of Nippur by the American expedition from the University of Pennsylvania during the closing years of the past century. The documents are strictly commercial in character with lists of sums, goods, formalities of transactions, etc., and give especially long and meticulous lists of witnesses for every contract.

The Murashu Bank did not limit its operations to the Jews of Babylonia, but dealt with Persians, Medes, Chaldeans, Arameans, and anyone else who traded in that international mart. Business was transacted in movable or immovable goods, rentals of plots, watering of animals up for sale, and trading. The names preserved in these contracts are oftentimes of Babylonian, Persian, Aramean, and other flavors, but more often they are purely Hebrew names, the most interesting of which are the theophoric names formed with "Yahweh." Along with such Hebraic names as Natunu, Shabbata, Haggai, Hanani, etc., there are theophoric names like Gadalyama, Yadihyama, Ahiyama, Yahulunu (for Yahulanu, "Yahweh [is] with us"), Dadiya (cf. Vol. I, § 355), etc.

The house of Murashu is the only one which has come down to us, but it was only one of many others about which all information has been lost. It is also evident that if the Murashu firm and other similar ones flourished in the middle of the Persian period, the first beginnings were much older and must go back to the decline of the Chaldean period.

64. Concerning the moral status of the deported little definite information can be assembled. When the exiles had completed the work assigned to them under the surveillance of the Chaldean inspectors (§ 60) — it is likely that there was one superintendent for every colony — they were left to their own devices, within circumscribed limits. The ancient ethnarchico-political order had officially ceased for them with the fall of the kingdom, but in practice much of it remained in force because of their traditions. Occasional mention is made, for example, of the existence and activity of the "ancients" (Ezech. 8:1; 14:1; 20:1), who undoubtedly enjoyed a special directive authority and, perhaps, were in some manner representatives of their people before the Chaldean governor. Other instances of social superiority are recorded elsewhere during the Persian period (Esdras 8:17); there were doubtless celebrations, and hence a continuation of such customs as had been observed in the homeland.

Priests also must have enjoyed a special prestige. Although they no longer performed the sacerdotal duties connected with worship, they must have been consulted on the many social and religious questions which arose in daily life. Prophetism however seems to have become somewhat rare, concentrated, as it were, in a few outstanding personalities. It gained, however, in quality, for the ecstatic exaltation (Vol. I, § 427) which had accompanied an earlier prophetism (Jer. 8:1; cf. Ezech. 13:17 ff.) now occurred less frequently.

New circumstances gave rise to a new class of spiritual directors, midway between the priesthood and prophetism, which later on had a large representation and increased continually in authority: the *mebhinim*, i.e., the deciders or "knowers," and the *sopherim*, i.e., the "writers" or "scribes" (§ 79). The two names derived from two different functions, but meant about the same thing in practice, for the two functions were performed by the same person. The *mebhinim* (Esdras 8:16) were the learned ones who decided isolated cases of the law concerning which there could be some doubt; the *sopherim* were the custodians and the moral and physical transmitters of that law. They were learned in it, and besides served as its scribes. It is evident that the two offices could be, and in practice had to be, combined. This double legal office also could well be discharged by either a priest or a prophet. Esdras is "the priest and scribe, the writer of the words of the commandments of Yahweh" (Esdras 7:11). Even before him, during the Chaldean period, Ezechiel had been both priest and prophet and at the same time the exponent *par excellence* of the law of Judaism.

65. Those who influenced the deportees in a more decisive manner than the ordinary guides were the spiritual dictators. The name,

Women mourners of Tammuz making preparations for the services in honor
of the dead god. (Athens, Museum.)

writings, and biography of one of them have been preserved: Ezechiel.
He was in the first group deported in 597 (Vol. I, § 530), and came
into prominence during that profound crisis in which one historical
period closed and another opened. He seemed to mirror in himself the
transformation of Yahwism, of which he was a mirror, but also one of
the principal causes. In all justice it was said of him to the Jews:
"Ezechiel shall be a sign for you" or emblem (Ezech. 24:24, 27).

He was not only a priest by birth, but his mind was impregnated
with the sacerdotal spirit (cf. Ezech. 4:14 for a typical example). He
manifested characteristics typical of ancient prophetism in the first
period of his activity, which extends from 594 to beyond the destruction
of Jerusalem. When in the second period the deportees had become
accustomed to the idea that their distant homeland was destroyed, and
later on when they began to consider some means of reconstruction,
the strong-willed prophet changed into a very methodical organizer,
a most exacting interpreter of the law, and the foremost of Yahwistic
"scribes." Such was the policy followed under his leadership in that
crisis of Yahwism: because the gift of prophecy was more and more
rarely given, Yahwism concentrated more and more upon the Law.

The first prophetic activity of Ezechiel in Babylonia is contem-
poraneous with the last of Jeremias' work in Palestine (Vol. I, § 599 ff.).
While Jeremias tried to restrain the fanatical patriots in Jerusalem,
Ezechiel was attempting to disillusion the deportees. Both proclaimed the
same message: Juda's prevalent syncretism had provoked this latest
punishment from Yahweh. And both proclaimed the same political
lesson, namely, by rebelling against Babylonia they would meet with
total destruction. No less than the fanatics in Juda, these deported

with Ezechiel had a superstitious faith in the Temple of Jerusalem
as the dwelling of Yahweh and hence a safeguard against any misfortune. Jeremias, however, had called the Temple a "den of thieves"
because of the conditions there (Vol. I, § 523), and Ezechiel saw from
afar that the Temple was reduced to a receptacle for idols and a
hostelry for the women mourners of Tammuz (Ezech. 8). In view of
such a perversion no alternative remained; that sanctuary of stones
had to be destroyed, but Yahweh said to the genuine and faithful
Yahwists: "I will be their sanctuary" (Ezech. 11:16). This principle,
it is clear, is a forerunner of that other according to which "those who
adore [God] must adore in spirit and truth" (Jn. 4:24).

66. This illusion was deeply rooted in the deportees. In order to
eradicate it the prophet performed strangely symbolic actions which in
a visible form foreshadowed the future, assuming bodily poses which
attracted attention by reason of their eccentricity. All in vain. His
fellow deportees were intrigued by such actions, secretly discussed
them in their private gatherings, willingly listened to the prophet
as he sang his stirring songs to the tune of a zither, and they
believed that he was a genuine prophet who really announced the
"word of Yahweh" (Ezech. 33:30–33; cf. Vol. I, § 427 ff.). But as for
heeding him, that was another matter. The far-off Temple could not,
must not, be destroyed! The glory of Israel would never die!

And yet one fatal day a "fugitive" arrived from the far-off homeland
(Ezech. 24:26; 33:21) and brought the news that it was all over. Judea,
Jerusalem, and the Temple were no more. Now that little group of
deportees which had considered itself the weakest and most unsound
part of Israel had become the only part of it which remained intact. The
prophet sometime before had unexpectedly lost his wife, the delight of
his eyes (Ezech. 24:16), but by the command of Yahweh he did not
publicly mourn for her. He was truly at that time a "sign" or symbol
(Ezech. 24:24–27) of the state of numbness into which the deportees
fell when they learned of the catastrophe of Jerusalem.

The bubble had burst, and they plunged, so to speak, from the
heights down to the very depths. In those dark depths where human
hope was impossible they began to lift their gaze on high. Yahweh
still reigned unchanging in the heavens. Their fellow countrymen in
Palestine were perceiving Him in this light also (§ 58). They saw
something else too: they saw Ezechiel, whose predictions had been
so horribly confirmed by the events, leaning over the edge of the
precipice toward them, making signs of encouragement and hope
to them. He invited them to arise from the abyss, and held out before
them heights much greater than those from which they had been
cast down.

A prophet was destined to oppose always the current of public opinion (Vol. I, § 429). When all had hoped, Ezechiel had despaired; now that all had crumbled to dust, he was attempting to rebuild.

67. The private life of the deportees went on under the direction of these ordinary or exceptional guides among their fellow countrymen. For the most part the Chaldeans let them alone, so they used their Hebrew tongue, although they began at that time to use Aramaic freely (Vol. I, § 51). They preserved their old customs and maintained continual contact with one another, for they paid visits to the various colonies in Babylonia (Ezech. 3:15). But what is more remarkable is that they kept in touch with the homeland by sending and receiving letters (Jer. 29). It is, then, almost superfluous to mention that under these circumstances they were able to observe practically all the precepts of their religion, except the fundamental one of the true and legitimate worship, for that was possible only in the land of Yahweh, Palestine, and in His one and only Temple, now destroyed. They must have practiced circumcision with greater faithfulness than before; it distinguished them from the hated overlords (Vol. I, §§ 133, 135). The religious observance of the Sabbath, for the Babylonians an unpropitious day, must also have been observed with greater solemnity, so as to accentuate the difference (Ezech. 20:12–24). The observance of the great Israelite feasts, beginning with the Passover (Vol. I, § 216), was not abandoned, although the ceremonies were necessarily reduced in length, thanks largely to a spirit of conservatism and adjustment.

Finally, there are indications of gatherings of the deportees (Ezech. 8:1; 14:1; 33:30 ff.; etc.), and one may suppose that some of them served for religious purposes. And while there is no proof that there were real "synagogues," as tradition has it, they are the beginnings of a system which was to create during the *diaspora,* or dispersal, a genuine "synagogue." To hold prayer meetings and to gather for instruction was but a preparation for the "synagogue" (§ 192 ff.).

68. This tenacious observance of traditional practices is of the highest importance because it manifested a twofold reaction among the deportees. Not only was there a reaction against the nation which had deported them, but another more subtle and profound, against themselves. It was in substance "repentance," or that state of soul which in Hebrew is called *shubh,* "return," and which had already been augured in the prayer of the faithful Yahwist: "Return us (root: *shubh*) to Thee, O Yahweh, and we will return (*shubh*): renew our days as of old!" (§ 58; Lam. 5:21.)

As usual, religion and nationalism were fused together in this reaction. That time was no more when an Achaz could consider copying an

Assyrian altar and placing it in the Temple of Jerusalem solely because it was a type of altar used by the victors (Vol. I, § 476). The recent disaster of the kingdom of Juda had confirmed once more what Ezechias, the son of Achaz, had already perceived when the kingdom of Israel fell, namely, that the great Mesopotamian empires Assyria and Babylonia were bent on the destruction of nationalities (Vol. I, § 479). As the stupor first caused by the catastrophe wore off, the reaction among the deported took on a new maturity. To the hatred for those who had caused such immense damage, there was now added the realization that prophets of Yahweh had been correct. Even before the catastrophe, they had deplored the alliance with strangers, and had cursed the imitation of foreign cults and the syncretism which admitted alien gods (Vol. I, § 426 ff.). Ezechiel also had spoken in this vein (§ 65). Now amid all that destruction, there remained only the principles of that Yahwism which had been the source of Israel's glory. It was necessary then to "return" to it by hating the Chaldeans, and loving their own nation.

69. The scene is a very familiar one in which the deported are gathered together, perhaps for religious reasons (§ 67), on the banks of a canal in Babylonia; they stand silent; their traditional songs remain unsung upon their lips, and their harps hang idle on the poplars lining the bank.

> "By the rivers of Babel, there we sat
>   and wept at the remembrance of Sion;
> On the poplars, in the midst thereof,
>   we hung up our harps.
> For there they that deported us
>   required of us the words of songs,
> And our task-masters joyfulness, [saying]
>   'Sing us some songs of Sion!'
> How shall we sing the song of Yahweh
>   in a strange land?
> If I forget thee, O Jerusalem,
>   let my right hand be paralyzed.[1]
> Let my tongue cleave to my palate,
>   if I do not remember thee,
> If I do not make Jerusalem
>   the height of my joy!"
>
>   (Ps. 137 [136]:1–6)

A sentimental and nostalgic interpretation is often given to this scene, but there is much more in it than this. Here in epitome is the rising of one people against another, as well as the protest of

---

[1] The Hebrew has: *let it be forgotten*, but it should be corrected slightly as given.

one religion against another. Here two rival nationalisms, each based on its own homeland and religion, clash. The question: "How shall we sing the song of Yahweh in a strange land?" gives vivid expression to the shocked horror of the Jews. The "foreign land," precisely because it is foreign, is unalterably opposed to the "song of Yahweh." To the deported Jew Babylonia was doubly foreign, in race and in religion. Babylonia was alien and impious, because it stood for everything that was anti-Palestine and anti-Yahweh, in a word, anti-Israel.

70. The feeling that welled up from the depths of their hearts under the weight of their oppression was to be the salvation of the "remnant of Israel," as the deportees had often been called by the prophets. The ten tribes deported to Assyria after the destruction of Samaria were of a different temper (Vol. I, § 457), mixing with the peoples among whom they now lived, and gradually being absorbed by them. The hybrid Samaritans on the soil of the homeland were scarcely any better, even though there remained in them some evidence of the Israelite stock. The reason for this is obvious. Genuine Yahwism had few deep roots in the kingdom of Samaria; open syncretism had flourished there for centuries, unopposed by any energetic or permanent reform. As a consequence, the kingdom had become ethnically weak; its nationalism lacked backbone, and as, under the terrible strain of the deportation, it did not engender a vigorous reaction, it was crushed.

Not so, however, the kingdom of Jerusalem. In it genuine Yahwism may have been seriously contaminated by syncretism at times, but vigorous reforms like those of Ezechias and Josias (Vol. I, § 480 ff.; § 507 ff.) had produced profound effects, the solidity and permanence of which were manifested during the exile. And though the effects of the Yahwistic reforms were obscured by succeeding waves of syncretistic

A canal branching off from the Euphrates in Babylonia. (From Koldewey, *Das wiedererstehende Babylon.*)

abominations, at least there were always present the germs of the national spirit, ready to burst into luxuriant bloom at the first opportunity.

The exile was the opportunity in which Israel was saved by its Yahwism. Even this salvation had been foreseen by the prophets, especially by Jeremias (Vol. I, § 537). The final catastrophe would be that a sieve would separate those faithful to Yahweh in Israel from those who fell away. The latter would be either completely cut off from the nation or would make their "return" to Israel when they recognized their fault (§ 68). In former days Amos had considered Yahweh as the sifter of the nation: "Behold, I will command, and I will shake the house of Israel among all nations, as a sieve is shaken; but not one kernel shall fall to the ground" (Amos 9:9). The chaff will be dispersed, the good seed will remain.

71. Apostates there undoubtedly were. Especially when things began to go well, there were bound to be some who would forget or deny their own national heritage amid the cosmopolitan peoples of Babylonia, just as today poor emigrants may try to hide or even deny their nationality in the foreign land where they fare well. How many of the Jews were renegades it is impossible to say, lacking as we do the data or basis for an estimate. Human nature being what it is, it may be supposed that there were more than a few hundred.

There were others, however, who compensated for their weaker brethren, and when these began to make some headway, and especially when they glimpsed some reasons for hope, they began to make plans. There was first the possibility, then the probability, and finally the certainty of the rebirth of the nation; then they carefully collected what still remained of their ancient patrimony and, at the same time, began to prepare this patrimony and themselves for the future.

Their material patrimony had been completely lost, but not the much more precious moral patrimony. The moral patrimony which always accompanies the dweller of the desert and which had already accompanied the father of the Hebrew nation from east to west (Vol. I, § 180 ff.) this time accompanied from east to west that "remnant" of his descendants which was deported to his original country. Of course, the patrimony now had greatly increased. The historical traditions were no longer limited, as then, to episodes which were concerned almost exclusively with Babylonia, for in the course of centuries the events which had befallen the nation in Egypt and Canaan had been added to it, as well as incidents concerning other peoples with whom the nation had come into contact. Thus a genuine historical *corpus* had been formed; to the first nucleus (the traditions and episodes of the patriarchs) there had been added, little by little, the glorious and tragic chapters of the history of their descendants.

The same can be said, due proportion being observed, of their juridical traditions. It was to be expected that Abraham's family would follow substantially the Babylonian law, inasmuch as they were Chaldeans (Vol. I, § 246), but in the course of centuries many other important laws were added to that primitive nucleus. These were either derived from the peoples of Egypt and Canaan, or elaborated and determined in the long legislative process which was proper to the nation itself, extending from the codification of Moses (Vol. I, § 244 ff.) up to the last reform by Josias (Vol. I, § 509 ff.). Thus a juridical corpus had been formed, containing both patriarchal elements and others of the later times of the kingdom of Juda.

72. This moral patrimony — stored away, so to speak, in two strong-boxes, one historical, the other juridical — they carried with them into exile. Even though naked and hungry, they could say, as a Greek philosopher did in similar circumstances: *Omnia mea mecum porto;* and they could rightly boast of their riches, for that patrimony, which was owned by them alone at that time, was to become, in succeeding ages, the possession of all humanity.

This *fact* has been subjected to various kinds of dramatization. Renan graphically pictured the fate of humanity as depending, during the journey to Babylon, on the more or less secure footing of the animal which carried the sacred book of the future into the land of exile. This may be good theater, but actually the very existence of an animal at the disposal of the deportees, in view of the methods of deportation explained above (§ 59), is more than doubtful, as doubtful, in fact, as the existence of such a book itself.

That there were writings containing the historical and juridical traditions at the time of the fall of Jerusalem is most certain, and the "book of the *Torah*" discovered in 621 B.C. is only one of many proofs of this (Vol. I, § 510 ff.). But there were not many copies of these writings in circulation. Some of these were only partial. They were in great part destroyed by the fire which consumed the Temple, or in the general destruction of the city. Fortunately their contents were preserved in another manner. Along with other accounts which were never set down in writing, they had a much wider circulation by "memory." ("Memory" and "writing" among the Semites have been sufficiently discussed previously and need not be taken up here [Vol. I, §§ 189 ff., 242, 514].) This is especially true in the present case, because those deported to Babylonia were of the better classes, intel-lectuals who were better trained in the use of "memory" and more capable of being "bearers" (a Moslem expression, cf. Vol. I, § 189) of tradition.

It is easy to understand how the deportees, about to depart into exile, would include among their most precious possessions some small roll of leather or folio of papyrus containing written fragments of their moral heritage. However, their bundles had to be thrown together in a hurry, and could not be too bulky. The remainder of their precious legacy was carried in the safer treasure chest of "memory." (Another possibility might be mentioned, although it does not concern those deported to Babylonia: other written copies, complete or fragmentary, may have been preserved in some nook of Palestine which escaped serious damage, or in some Jewish community outside of Palestine. The recent discoveries in the caves near the Dead Sea [Ain Fashka] bear this out. The possibilities of similar future discoveries are tremendous.) (Vol. I, §§ 95a, 95b.)

73. During the vigil which preceded the national rebirth, therefore, the loving care of a faithful Yahwist in Babylonia centered on this moral heritage. It was not only to be a link with the past, but was also to provide a program for restoration. Thus while the rebuilders salvaged the past in good part, they were also planning for the future.

Yahwism was a living thing rather than a complexus of crystallized truths. Its fundamental principles were immutable, but their application could vary according to times and circumstances. With the destruction of the kingdom of Juda and the deportation, not only were circumstances radically changed but the immediate future gave glimpses of entirely new times. When the deported should return to their homeland, their social organization clearly could not be what it was before the exile, in view of the new political situation created in the meantime in anterior Asia. On the other hand, it should not be a repetition of the one which, with its numerous failings, was responsible in the eyes of the faithful Yahwists for the general decadence of the latter times, and for the punishment meted out by Yahweh through the catastrophe of 586 B.C. Yahwistic principles should have to be observed, but modified as necessary to meet the times.

The modifications made did not result in a tolerant compromise but, on the contrary, in a more rigorous application of Yahwistic principles. There was no swing to the left, but a full advance to the right.

74. A predominant principle of pre-exilic Yahwism, for example, was that of *collective responsibility:* not only did Yahweh punish the iniquity of the fathers in their children to the third and fourth generation because their bond of relationship made them as it were one person (Exod. 20:5; 34:7; Num. 14:18), but there are traces of the application of such a principle even in the Hebrew (Vol. I, § 471) and Babylonian (Code of Hammurabi, art. 210, 230) civil law. There arose, therefore, the conviction among the survivors of 586 B.C. that this catastrophe was the punishment of Yahweh solely for the ancient crimes of their fathers. The proverb: "The fathers have eaten sour grapes and the teeth of the children are set on edge!" (Ezech. 18:2; Jer. 31:29; cf. Lam. 5:7) was widely quoted among them. But in the future, this norm of judgment would be abandoned and in its place established the principle of strictly personal responsibility. "As I live — saith the Lord Yahweh — you need no longer repeat this proverb in Israel! Behold all lives are mine; both the life of the father and the life of the son are mine: the soul that sinneth, shall die"; "The soul that sinneth, the same shall die. The son shall not bear the iniquity of the father, and the father shall not bear the iniquity of the son; the justice of the just shall be upon him, and the wickedness of the wicked shall be upon him" (Ezech. 18:3, 4, 20). At first sight, it might seem that this modification of vindictive justice was an act of clemency because it preserved the children of the third and fourth generation from the punishment merited by the father, but, in reality, it manifested an even more rigorous justice, because the punishment henceforth always followed the crime. Also, for the most part, it did away with the possibility that the wicked would not be punished personally but only in the group to which they belonged.

75. More or less abstract programs intended for the nation which would be reborn in Palestine were drawn up along these new lines. They henceforth began to envision a broader horizon. The deportees in Babylonia were the only "remnant" of the kingdom of Juda; the other kingdom, schismatic Israel, had been destroyed almost a century and a half before, and its "remnant" was now fusing with the foreign populations among which it had been settled (§ 70). What did it matter to the exiles in Babylonia what happened to the residue of the schismatic kingdom? If a renascence of the nation was to occur, would it not have to come through the "remnant" of Juda, the legitimate kingdom of David, the Yahwistic monarchy? Such were not their thoughts. After the disaster which affected the entire nation, the ancient rivalry between the two kingdoms disappeared among the exiles of Babylonia, and they were concerned only with "Israel," the nation of Yahweh. In what condition was Israel at this time? Israel was a desolate field, nothing but withered and fleshless bones, in which every spark of life had been forever extinguished. Yet . . . if Yahweh were only to breath over them, these dry bones would come together again, take on new flesh and blood, and become a great host of living human beings (Ezech. 37). Were these resurrected souls to be only of the house of Juda? No, "these bones are the *whole house of Israel*" (Ezech. 37:11; cf. v. 15 ff.).

Thus the unhappy schism of the past was ended forever. It was now necessary to take steps so that in the future the one united nation of Yahweh be held together tightly, close to its God.

76. In the programs worked out at that time by the zealous rebuilders, the future nation was planned as a society which would be entirely penetrated by Yahwism. No more compromises or remissness. The dualism of the Temple and Palace in internal matters, and the contamination of the Israelite by the non-Israelite in external affairs (both of which had occasioned such harm in the old order), were not to be even thought of in the new. In the future nation the palace would be only a department of the Temple, a distinct, official post with its own princely head, but wholly dependent on the Temple, and dedicated to serve the Temple and the nation. The real heart and brain of the nation, the Temple, was to be the geographical center of the tribes of Israel. Not only would non-Israelite elements be excluded from the Temple, all the "foreigners uncircumcised in heart and uncircumcised in the flesh" (Ezech. 44:7, 9), but even the ordinary Israelites would have much rarer access to it than before. It was essential that the nation be perennially aware of the "sacredness," the "awe" which would emanate from the Temple. Only the "holy ones" would be able to enter it habitually, and they were to be chosen according to rigorous rules. Of these, only the priests would offer sacrifices; the simple Levites would be merely liturgical servants of the priests.

Even the topography of the future nation had to be a reflection of its social order. The temple, the abode of Yahweh, would be located on the summit of a very high mountain. From it, Yahweh would watch like a shepherd over his sheep gathered about him. All around the base of the mountain would be the dwellings of the priests; farther down, those of the Levites; still farther away would be the tribes of Israel, the common people, those who were not the "holy." Lastly, the territory of the prince would extend around the very periphery. This last was to constitute a kind of spiritual hedge, protecting the nation within and defending it from profane strangers.

This plan aimed at more than a theocratic state. It envisioned a true religious community, strictly cloistered, governed internally by the priests and served externally by the prince. It reminds one of a medieval Benedictine monastery which was closed off physically by a wall, and otherwise by the canonical enclosure, governed internally by the abbot and served externally by the castle authorities (§ 134).

77. Is there nothing more here than a Platonic utopia? Indeed there is. Chapters 40–48 of *Ezechiel*, in which this objective is sketched, contain also a series of minute prescriptions and detailed laws which are very practical and which had to be observed. Most of them concern

the Temple and its personnel, naturally, for they are of prime importance. These prescriptions are in general similar to the sacerdotal laws in the Pentateuch (Vol. I, § 114); oftentimes the prescriptions are in accord but at other times they differ, and not rarely on some essential points.

The problem is difficult and complex. It seems undeniable that Ezechiel used the preceding legislation as a model, especially *Deuteronomy* (Vol. I, § 515), which would account for the parallel prescriptions; but at the same time he did not intend simply to transcribe that legislation, but to modify and adapt it to the needs of the future nation. We have already seen that the legal modifications made by the deportees in Babylonia were as a rule rather on the rigorous side, and, as a matter of fact, where the legislation differs Ezechiel is usually found to be stricter and more exacting than *Deuteronomy*. Doubtless he had before him a visual prototype for many of his details (for example, the high mountain upon which the Temple was to be built) or even a messianic one (the geographical distribution of the tribes), but his appeal to these lofty motives and the fact that he proposed them for the future nation, proves that he aimed high so as not to hit too far below the mark. The grandiose picture he set up as a model could not be realized in its entirety, but he must have hoped that some of its more outstanding features would be adopted.

78. The differences between the legislation of Ezechiel and that of the Pentateuch were accurately brought to light by the Talmudic rabbis, and here a rather interesting scandal comes to light. Because the two lists of prescriptions were not in complete accord, some rabbis were for throwing one of them out completely and at once. The Mosaic *Torah* was ancient, *Ezechiel* recent; hence, some considered abolishing Ezechiel and excluding his book from the Canon (Vol. I, § 109 ff.). This opinion did not prevail. *Ezechiel* was rescued and remained in the Canon, thanks chiefly to Hananiah ben-Hizqiyyahu. After using up three hundred lamps of oil in nightly studies, this rabbi was successful in showing how the legislation of Ezechiel could be harmonized with that of the *Torah*. Even so, the rescued book always remained under the shadow of suspicion (for other reasons which do not concern the present work) and, as a measure of prudence, its reading was forbidden to all who were not thirty years old (Talmud Babli, *Hagiga*, 13a; *Menahoth*, 45a; *Shabbath*, 13b; St. Jerome, *In Ezech.*, *praefatio*; *Epist. ad Paulin.*; incidentally, the *Canticle of Canticles* was also forbidden to be read by those under thirty).

The scandal of the rabbis was understandable but unjustified. Ezechiel did not abjure the *Torah*, but superimposed upon it another very elaborate story. He intended that the future nation be more rigorously safeguarded by the new legislation than the now prostrate na-

tion had been by the old. Besides, since he envisioned the future
nation against a messianic background, he used in his descriptions and
laws only those elements which transcended contemporary conditions.
The ultimate scope of the religious society (§ 76) for which he drew
up the constitution was the expectation of the Messiah of Yahweh.
In fact, the city or the capital of the future nation was to change its
name and be called no longer Jerusalem but "Yahweh-[is]-there."

With this prophetic name the legislation terminates and the book
of Ezechiel closes.

70. It is almost superfluous to observe that these visions which looked
to the future not only did not exclude, but rather were built up on,
memories of the past, like the stories of a building. Future Yahwism
required the past and perfected it, although it actually contained in
itself its own justification. It is easy to understand how there could be
and had to be, parallel to this work of future legislation, a co-ordination
and systematization of the ancient material which had been recovered.

The *historical* and the *juridical corpora* (§ 71) were constructed
from parts gathered on various occasions from various sources, here
a tradition from the kingdom of Israel, there a document edited in
the kingdom of Juda; here a more detailed account of some episode,
there a more summary report. Some special items of information about
a given person were transmitted orally but did not appear in the
written accounts (cf., for example, Vol. I, § 357 ff.). As for juridical
material, there may have been this or that collection of laws which was
more up to date, from which some ancient norm had been dropped,
but which had continued to circulate up to that time either by "memory"
or in "writing" (§ 72). A given "memorized" or "written" norm may have
been exactly transmitted side by side with a flourishing practice to
the contrary. Hundreds of such examples could be cited. However, the
enormous quantity of material which was recovered and which formed
the twofold corpus was not organized or all together. One historical
tradition, for example, would contain an account of the period of the
northern Judges and did not treat of the southern; another would linger
over Davidic times, but would scarcely mention Saul; a third dealing
with events under the monarchy would be limited almost exclusively
to the Davidic kings of Juda, and would leave the schismatic kings of
Israel in semi-obscurity. Now an organic and continuous history of the
past was wanted. Due proportion being observed, much the same can
be said of the juridical material, for too many laws were antiquated, undetermined, or inadequate. Here too, what was needed was an organic,
practical arrangement of the entire material.

To arrange the nation's patrimony within a systematic framework,
therefore, was a most urgent task. The historical material had to be

arranged in chronological order, its parts connected and integrated one with another and clarified; the juridical material had to be brought up to date, harmonized, completed, and interpreted. In brief, there had to be some editorial board to create a real historico-juridical digest from the collected material. So precious a heritage should not remain scattered about, for it was the genuine and the only residue of ancient Israel. In practice, moreover, it could not remain divided, for laws and history are very often mutually dependent on each other; and while its history was a juridical exegesis, its legislation justified certain of the incidents.

The digest was completed. It must have been much more complex than similar works accomplished by the reform commissions of Ezechias and Josias (Vol. I, §§ 484, 509), for this time there was much more, and more varied material. Entire generations of learned Yahwists labored over it, and their juridical skill merited for them an eminent position in the esteem of the nation. From that time on, the doctor of the Law, that is, the "scribe," ascended to the seat of authority on equal footing with priest and prophet (§ 64). Later, when the prophet's chair had disappeared, that of the scribe was placed above that of the priest.

While the scribes in Babylonia were carrying on their work, the unpredictable happened, and at one blow changed the whole state of affairs.

THE REPATRIATION

80. Some thirty-five years after the destruction of Jerusalem and about forty-five (§ 55) after the first of the deportees arrived in Babylonia, the star of Cyrus (§ 2 ff.) began to rise to the east of the land of exile. Its first rays of light were rather flickering. In fact, after his first unsuccessful attempts against Astyages, it seemed as if it were destined to be extinguished forever, like so many other political meteors which had flashed across the sky. In the year 550 B.C., however, Cyrus won a victory over Astyages, and became, suddenly, the second monarch of anterior Asia, second in power only to the monarch of Babylonia. The peoples subjugated by Babylonia — both natives and deportees — who awaited a radical change in their intolerable political situation, naturally turned their gaze to that new star shining with so brilliant and so unexpected a light. What would the new monarch do? Would he be satisfied to remain in the territory bordering Babylonia on the east and north? Would he not inevitably come to grips with Babylonia? Would he not put an end to the decadent Chaldean monarchy, and bring relief to the peoples groaning under its tyranny?

For the first few years after the ascent of Cyrus, no one could answer these questions with any surety, but there were undoubtedly many dreams that he would bring deliverance. At the beginning of 546 B.C., Cyrus destroyed Lydia with astonishing suddenness, and then extended his conquests, first in the west and then in the east. He became the natural foe, the inevitable destroyer of Babylonia. The deportees in Babylonia pinned all their hopes on him; with breathless expectancy they looked only to him — surely he would be their liberator. Tales of his extraordinary clemency toward the Medes and other conquered peoples showed him to be a generous conqueror who operated on principles entirely different from those of the Babylonians (§ 6 ff.).

81. The Jewish deportees naturally shared these anxious hopes with all the other exiles, and for the most part found them in line with ancient Yahwism. After the nation's collapse they had made their spiritual "return" to Yahweh (§ 68), and were now preparing to build up a new social organization as the nation of Yahweh. For some decades there had appeared to be no real possibility of a renascence, and absolutely no chance for a return to Palestine, the land of Yahweh. They had been laboring for an indefinite, unforeseeable future, sustained only by their faith in Yahweh. Then suddenly a Cyrus appeared on the horizon, and they beheld his triumphant march through western Asia. Was he not perhaps the practical opportunity they were looking for, the means of the hoped-for deliverance? Who had raised up this irresistible hero, this shatterer of thrones and liberator of nations, if not Yahweh? Was it not clear that Yahweh desired also that the throne of Babylonia be smashed and His chosen nation liberated? The mysterious old words now became clear:

> "Who hath raised up this man from the east
>   whose every step brings justice?
> [Who] hath subjugated the nations to him
>   and made the kings tremble?[1]

> His sword strikes them[2] until they are like dust,
>   his bow disperses them like chaff:
> He pursues them, he passes beyond victorious,
>   he tramples not the street with his feet!

> Who hath wrought and done [this]?
>   He who calls the generations from the beginning!
> I, Yahweh, the first
>   and [Who] also am with the last!
>   (Isa. 41:2–4)

Cyrus himself made the claim that the Babylonian god Marduk had given him mastery over all the earth (§ 8). The prophet of Yahweh did not know about Marduk, but he did listen to Yahweh who proclaimed:

> "I have raised [him] up from the north to come,
>   from the rising of the sun, [so that] he may invoke my name:
> and he shall trample[3] the princes as clay,
>   and as the potter treading clay."
>   (Isa. 41:25)

82. More than that, it was the mission of Cyrus to be the real *mashiah* ("anointed," "chosen," "messias") of Yahweh and of Him alone to the exclusion of all the other gods.

> "Thus speaketh Yahweh to His *mashiah*, to Cyrus,
>   whose right hand I have grasped,

---

[1] Thus according to the Septuagint.
[2] *Them* is not in the Hebrew.
[3] *Trample* from *yabus* in place of *yahbs* in the Hebrew text.

To strike down the nations before him,
    so that I may dissolve the loins of the kings,
To open the gates before him
    so that the doors will not be barred.
I will stride before thee,
    I will level the hills;
I will break into pieces the gates of bronze
    and will smash the bars of iron.
I will give to thee the treasures [hidden in] darkness
    and the riches of hiding places."

(It has been pointed out that the campaign of Cyrus against Babylonia was an easy triumph, as if it were only a march over a *level* road without *hills*. He had no need to break many *gates of bronze* or *bars of iron* because almost all doors were thrown wide open at his approach, and the *treasures* of the palace of Babylonia ended up in his possession [§ 6]. What was the purpose of all this? The prophet's song immediately explains:)

"That thou mayest know that I am Yahweh,
    He Who calls thee by name, the God of Israel;
for the sake of my servant Jacob,
    and of Israel my elect,
I have called thee by name,
    I have mentioned thy name though thou knew me not.
I am Yahweh, and there is no other,
    there is no God beside Me."

(Isa. 45:1–5)

Shortly before, the same poem had specified even more clearly the mission entrusted to Cyrus by Yahweh in regard to his chosen nation:

"I am Yahweh Who made all things,
    Who alone stretched out the heavens, . . .
Who saith to Cyrus 'My shepherd!'
    and he fulfills all my desires,
Who saith to Jerusalem 'Be rebuilt!'
    and to the Temple 'Be reestablished!' "

(Isa. 44:24, 28)

Cyrus was the instrument the Lord would use in freeing the deported Jews, and in the reconstruction of Jerusalem and the Temple.

83. The prophetic vision was completely verified, and the fervent hopes of the deportees fulfilled. Once Babylon was taken, Cyrus' policy was to treat religion kindly and to allow the various peoples to go back to their homeland (§ 7 ff.); all deportees in Babylonia could, if they wished to do so, return to their native land. Not all the Jewish deportees availed themselves of this permission. Over all their most cherished dreams and the difficulties involved in recovering and reorganizing their national patrimony (§ 71 ff.), as well as over the drawing up of plans for the rebirth of the nation, there sounded the clarion cry of the prophet:

> "Go forth from Babylon! Flee from the Chaldeans!
> Declare it with the voice of joy, proclaim this [message],
>
> Let it reverberate to the ends of the earth,
> Say: 'Yahweh has redeemed His servant Jacob!' "

> (Isa. 48:20)

In going out from Babel directly to Jerusalem what should be first on the program, their first solicitude, except that the risen nation should fully and completely live up to its Yahwism (§ 76) and scrupulously observe the Law, especially its prescriptions regarding legal purity and impurity — the protective hedge for the true Israel and its liturgy:

> "Depart, depart, go thence,
>   Touch no unclean thing!
> Go out of her midst, be clean,
>   You who carry the vessels [of the Temple] of Yahweh! . . .
> For Yahweh goes before you,
>   Your rear guard is the God of Israel."

> (Isa. 52:11–12)

Joy over the pardon granted by Yahweh to the nation, and over its purification through suffering and its liberation, breaks forth in dancing and shouting:

> "Rise up, rise up,
>   Stand up, O Jerusalem!
> Because thou hast drunk from the hand of Yahweh
>   The cup of His wrath:
> The bottom of the cup of drunkenness
>   Thou hast drained to the last drop!"

> (Isa. 51:17)

> "Shake thyself from the dust, arise,
>   Sit up, O Jerusalem!
> Loose the bonds from thy neck,
>   O captive daughter of Sion."

> (Isa. 52:2)

> "Rejoice, dance in rhythm,
>   O ruins of Jerusalem!
> Because Yahweh had mercy on His people,
>   He hath redeemed Jerusalem!"

> (Isa. 52:9)

Combined with these cries of joy was the ever present thought that legal observances were a guarantee of the future:

"Arise, arise, vest thyself
In thy strength, O Sion!
Put on thy splendid garments
O Jerusalem, holy city!
For henceforth the uncircumcised and the impure
Will not enter thee!"

(Isa. 52:1)

❈ ❈ ❈

84. Cyrus no doubt willingly granted the Jews permission to return to their homes. Achaemenid devotee of Ahura-Mazda, the invincible god of heaven, he could have seen some similarity between the object of his adoration and the invisible God "He-is" (Vol. I, § 209) adored by the deportees from Palestine. For theoretical and for very practical reasons he had bowed down to the god Marduk and to a greater number of other Babylonian gods quite different from Ahura-Mazda (§ 8); he would certainly not balk at bowing before Yahweh "He-is," toward whom he may even have felt some attraction. The far-off Temple of Yahweh had been destroyed by the ancestors of the "wicked" Nabonidus, but it was to be rebuilt even as the Babylonian temples of Esagila and Ezida (§ 8). The idols of other repatriates were being restored little by little, but there were no images of Yahweh to be restored to the Jews. In this Yahweh was similar to Ahura-Mazda, who was not ordinarily represented by statues or pictures, but was adored as the invisible one dwelling on the tops of mountains (Herodotus, I, 131). Moreover, the sacred vessels of the Temple which had been carried to Babylonia when the temple was destroyed, were to be restored.

85. Cyrus' decree of repatriation to the Jews has fortunately been preserved. Not the least among the proofs of its authenticity is its agreement with the religious policy of Cyrus, and even with the expressions used elsewhere by him in official documents (§ 8).

"Thus saith Cyrus, king of Persia: Yahweh, the God of the heavens, has given me all the kingdoms of the earth,

Persian fire altars. (Sarre.)

and he himself hath charged me to build him a house in Jerusalem, which is in Juda. Who is there among you of all his people who desires to go? His God be with him, and let him go up to Jerusalem, which is in Juda, and to build the House of Yahweh, the God of Israel, as he is the God who is in Jerusalem. And all the remnant [of this people] must be aided by the people of the respective places where they dwell with silver, gold, and goods and cattle, besides that which they offer freely for the House of the God which is in Jerusalem" (Esdras 1:2–4).

This document may not agree *verbatim* with the last paragraph of the original, as it may have been shortened by the redactor (2 Para. 36:23 contains an even more abbreviated summary). And, since the document was intended to be proclaimed publicly, another official document may have been deposited in the regal archives at the same time, with briefer oratorical sections, but greater detail concerning the administrative arrangements. It was this diplomatic certificate, written in Aramaic (Vol. I, § 51), that was discovered in the archives of Ecbatana in the time of Darius I, and preserved in its original language in *Esdras* 6:2–5 (§ 99).

With this decree, they had only to get started on the return journey. The careful plans of so many years had now to be realized in fact.

Preparations for the departure were not hasty, for the deportees were well scattered, and many private affairs had to be settled before leaving the country. Also, a list of those who were to be actually repatriated had to be drawn up. Many refused to take advantage of the decree and preferred to stay in Babylonia, but the majority of these were inspired not by any lack of zeal for the national cause, or because they were apostates from Yahwism, but by more honorable reasons (§ 62).

86. The preparations were finally completed, and the caravan began its journey in the year 537 B.C., probably in the spring (according to the apocryphal 3 *Esdras* 5:6, it was the first day of the month of Nisan). They took one of the roads which led to Palestine by way of Syria, and must have arrived during the summer of the same year.

According to available figures, the caravan was made up of 42,360 Jews, plus 7,337 slaves, 736 horses, 245 mules, 435 camels, 6,720 asses. They carried with them, also, many precious Temple furnishings restored to them by Cyrus, and other rich private offerings intended for the Temple. The number 42,360 is given by *Esdras* 2:64 and by *Neh.* 7:66 and is substantially confirmed by 3 *Esdras* 5:41 and Josephus, *Antiquities*, XI, 1, 3 (except for minor divergences in the codices). If, however, the figures of the related groups of the caravan are added together (*Esdras* 2; *Neh.* 7), a total of 30,000 is obtained. Who were these other 12,000? They were perhaps Jewish women. In view of the great labors and hardships to be endured in Palestine perhaps only the richer Jews brought their wives with them, while the poorer Jews left theirs behind in Babylonia. Or were they, perhaps, Israelitic remnants of the ancient kingdom of Samaria who during their exile had come into contact with and joined up with the deportees of Juda? No definitive answer can be given, but the first hypothesis seems to be the more acceptable.

At the head of the caravan were twelve leaders (Neh. 7:7; the parallel passage of Esdras 2:2 lacks one name — an oversight). The choice of twelve, which coincides with the number of the tribes of the *entire house of Israel*, was an indication of the plans of the caravan (§ 75). Zorobabel and Joshua head the list of the twelve. About the latter there is no difficulty: he is the high priest Joshua (called *Iesus*, "Jesus," by the Vulgate in the books of Aggeus and Zacharias), son of Josedec, who had been deported to Babylonia (1 Para. 6:41). Josedec was the son of the last high priest of Jerusalem, Seraias, who had been killed by Nabuchodonosor at Ribla (2 Kings 25:18–21; cf. Vol. I, § 542).

87. Zorobabel causes a difficulty. Indeed, during the course of the narrative, other personages of about the same rank appear side by side with him. First of all there is "Sheshbassar, the prince of Juda" (Esdras 1:8; the Vulgate has Sassabasar), who received the furnishings of the Temple of Jerusalem from Cyrus and headed the caravan toward the homeland (Esdras 1:11; 5:14–16); there was also an unnamed royal functionary described as *tirshatha* (Esdras 1:63; Neh. 7:65, 70), who held some authority in religious matters. How are these three personages related? More especially, how shall Zorobabel and Sheshbassar, whose activities seem to be identical, be considered? Are there three, or only two persons? Or are they all one and the same person, treated and named differently by different documents?

The question has been debated at length, and oftentimes complicated by gratuitous or farfetched hypotheses. The following data is certain: (1) Sheshbassar is one of the leaders of the caravan (Esdras 1:8–11); so is Zorobabel (Esdras 2:2; 3:2; 4:2); (2) Sheshbassar laid the foundations of the Temple in Jerusalem (Esdras 5:16); Zorobabel begins the reconstruction of the same Temple a first time (Esdras 3:8 ff.) and then a second time (Esdras 5:2 ff.; Agg. 1:14; Zach. 4:9). (3) Sheshbassar is the "prince of Juda" (Esdras 1:8); Zorobabel, a grandson of Joachin (1 Para. 3:17–19) the captive king in Babylonia (§ 57), has by reason of his descent the right to the princely rank. Sheshbassar received the title of *Pehah* "governor" (Esdras 5:14) from Cyrus; Zorobabel enjoyed the title of "Pehah of Juda" in the second year of the reign of Darius I (Agg. 1:1). These well-established facts point to the conclusion that Sheshbassar and Zorobabel are one and the same person. Taking into consideration that *Tirshatha* was probably an honorary title given to a *pehah* (somewhat like "excellency" bestowed today on a "prefect" of a province), one may conclude that the three in question are one and the same person. Difficulties against this position can be based on a textual criticism of the documents, or on the fact that both names are clearly Babylonian. It is understandable that a Jew would receive a Babylonian name besides his Jewish name in Babylonia (cf. Dan. 1:7), but it does seem strange that both names would be Babylonian. To identify them, therefore, is somewhat debatable. However, the above conclusion, though not absolutely certain, seems to be preferable.

* * *

88. The first concern of the repatriates, when the caravan arrived in Palestine, was to return to their abandoned fields, vineyards, and paternal homes. The assignment of properties was made by the leaders of the caravan on the basis of lists drawn up in Babylonia. These lists were highly prized because they testified to the purity of the race; they are substantially preserved in *Neh.* 7; *Esdras* 2. A study of these lists is very instructive. They show, for example, that priestly and Levitical families were rather in the majority among the repatriates (Neh. 7:39 ff.; Esdras 2:36 ff.), as was to be expected, for these repatriates were animated by the Yahwistic spirit fostered in the circles devoted to the study of the *Torah* in Babylonia. They further show that the various places in which they settled (Neh. 7:26 ff.; Esdras 2:21 ff.) were chiefly around Jerusalem (Bethlehem, Nethophah, Anathoth, etc.), which shows that they belonged to the tribes of Juda and Benjamin. An ingenious modern interpretation claims that the expression "sons of Sena'ah" (Neh. 7:38; Esdras 2:35; cf. Neh. 3:3) means "the sons (that is, citizens) of Jerusalem" since the name appears nowhere else, and the number of persons who belong to it is very great, 3,930 (or 3,630). In fact, because it is the center of the settlement, this locality is named last in the geographic lists.

It was anything but easy for those who returned to take possession. The simplest cases were those in which the paternal house and field had been ruined and deserted; they could then take possession without difficulty, managing as best they could at first, and hoping that time and good will would do the rest. But where the paternal homesteads had been occupied and were in good condition because others, finding them abandoned, had restored them or at least put them to use again, there were many thorny problems to be solved. These new proprietors were either Jews of low estate who had been spared deportation (§ 55), or came from the surrounding peoples and had entered the vacated country (§ 56). To overcome these difficulties there was needed, besides a fervent spirit among the repatriates, financial resources, and on this score they had little to worry about (§ 61 ff.). Still, the task was very arduous, and more than half of the first year was spent in reaching a temporary working arrangement (cf. Neh. 7:72; Esdras 2:70 with Esdras 3:1–8).

Grove of cedar on Libanus.

89. Once this was accomplished, they turned to more noble endeavors. Seven months after their arrival, the repatriates gathered at Jerusalem and, amid the ruins of the Temple, *rebuilt the altar* on the very spot it had occupied before 586 B.C. Thus was inaugurated, at least on a small scale, the religious ceremonial (Esdras 3:1–6). It has been recently maintained that the restoration of the altar was effected by Jews who had remained in Jerusalem, but the reasons given are not very solid. Even if this were true, those who returned all filled with zeal for liturgical and legal purity, would have regarded it with suspicion of syncretism, or at least of some legal irregularity, and would have demanded that it be replaced. The existence of an altar for liturgical functions is presupposed by *Aggeus* (2:14).

To implement further the Yahwistic program elaborated in Babylonia, the rebuilding of the Temple, the spiritual citadel of the new community (§ 76), was begun. Contracts were drawn up with skilled workmen, a certain quantity of materials was accumulated, especially cedar from Lebanon which was transported by way of the sea (Esdras 3:7). Thus, the second month of the second year from their arrival, Zorobabel and Joshua (§ 86) laid the foundations of the new structure. The occasion was celebrated by a solemn feast, for the event was a pledge of the future. For many of the old people attending the festival, the event was also a reminder of the past, for in their youth they had looked upon the splendor of that other Temple upon whose sad ruins they now stood. And so, during the festival, joyful voices which spoke of the future mingled with the heartbroken sobs of those who mourned the past (Esdras 3:8–13; 5:16).

These sobs which accompanied the festivities were an omen of the future. More than a year passed after their return, and only the foundations of the Temple had been laid. Yet even this little would have been satisfactory had it meant that all major difficulties had been overcome, that the top of a steep hill had been climbed, so that one could continue easily on down the other side. The real state of affairs, however, was just the opposite. The little that had been accomplished at the cost of so much effort, was only the beginning of a steeper hill than the one just mounted.

90. In the first place, the economic condition of the repatriates was no longer flourishing. The reserves they had brought with them from Babylonia must have been heavily depleted by the settling of the families in their proper places, and by the preparations for the building of the Temple. Despite these expenditures a secure and favorable environment for their projects had not been won, nor had they been able to provide many things called for by the grandiose plans. Their rigidly Yahwistic projects found some supporters among the fellow countrymen who had remained in Palestine (one indication of this is mentioned in the Greek text of 3 Esdras 5:50), but many more were indifferent if not actually annoyed at what they considered the utopian enthusiasm of the new arrivals. Undoubtedly too they met with open hostility from the foreigners who had settled in Juda during the exile, to whom the exclusive Yahwism of the repatriates appeared to be a declaration of war. In brief, the repatriated, totally isolated and even boycotted, here and there had to struggle against furtive attacks which amounted to a guerrilla warfare of ill will and spitefulness.

Nor is it difficult to imagine the living conditions of the repatriates in their respective districts. Some now lived near relatives who resented their presence and showed their irritation; others sought what shelter they could find in a half-destroyed paternal home; some, settled in their well-preserved old homes, had to buy them back at exorbitant prices from the foreigners who had taken possession of them; and others, finally, lived out in the open, in traditional Bedouin style. The provisional settlement completed in the first half year (§ 88) had not advanced beyond the dreary conditions mentioned above, but were inferior to the prosperous conditions of life in the land of exile (§ 62).

If, therefore, their glorious Yahwistic projects were to be realized, conditions had to be bettered and stabilized. With financial reserves almost spent it was time to put hands to the plow, to wield the hoe in the vineyards, and to take up the shepherd's staff. At times, perhaps, they might do well to brandish their axes to defend themselves from jealous neighbors and hostile foreigners, just to keep them in line. Yahwistic projects were praiseworthy, but self-preservation came first, and these means were necessary to insure their very lives.

The rebuilding of the Temple called for great quantities of material as well as for enormous man power. The Temple of Solomon was finished in seven years, thanks to the system Solomon had inaugurated of requisitioning material and labor from all quarters (Vol. I, §§ 397, 399, 404 ff.). Now, with even a much lower goal, materials and man power were scarce, especially the latter, for as more and more concerned themselves with providing a more stable livelihood and looking after their daily bread, there were fewer who were able to volunteer their work for the building of the Temple.

It dawned on them with consternation that they were in a bad way.

91. To make matters worse, difficulties with the neighboring peoples and fellow inhabitants had arisen almost from the beginning. Yahwistic fervor had induced them to redouble their efforts to advance the work on the Temple. News of the project had traveled north to the Samaritans, who considered themselves Yahwists also. Why not? Was not Yahweh also included in their pantheon? Was he not the *numen loci* of practically all of Palestine (Vol. I, § 457)? They, therefore, believed it their duty to come and help in the reconstruction of the Temple of Yahweh, making a formal proposal to that effect to Zorobabel and Joshua. Perhaps they also thought that a common Temple would in the future lead to a fusion of the two groups, to the greater benefit of the whole country.

Willing hands were indeed needed, but not from that quarter. If the Samaritans helped with the material construction, they would thereby destroy that spiritual edifice which the ardent workers in Jerusalem had built in Babylonia, and which they jealously guarded in their hearts. The prophet had warned Jerusalem: "Henceforth the uncircumcised and the impure will not enter thee" (§ 83); if the Samaritans were welcomed, they would bring with them the basest sort of syncretism. The reply, therefore, was perfectly logical: "[It does] not [concern] you and us [together] to build a house to our God; but we ourselves alone will build to Yahweh, God of Israel, as King Cyrus, the King of Persia, has commanded us" (Esdras 4:3). In a word, they did not recognize the Samaritans as belonging to the nation of Israel, nor their right to collaborate on the Temple of the God of Israel, Yahweh, *their God.*

The consequences of this refusal were also perfectly logical. At first, the Samaritans had demonstrated their interest in, and even their sympathy with, the new arrivals, but now they were offended by such exclusiveness and would pay them back in kind. If there was no room for the Samaritans amid the repatriates, then there would be no room for the repatriates amid the Samaritans, nor amid all the rest of the "people of the land." Hostility grew apace. Fed by the Samaritans, it found an easy entrance into the minds of the foreigners settled in Palestine and even of many Jews who were annoyed at the presence of the repatriates. The phrase "people of the land" in this place comprises both of these groups. It was a kind of united front formed in opposition to the builders, and it enclosed them in an ever more menacing circle of "boycott."

92. What happened next is referred to vaguely in *Esdras* 4:4–5, 24: "The people of the land caused the hands of the people of Juda to be idle, inspiring in them a fear to work and hiring against them [wicked] advisers to bring their project to naught. [And this lasted] all the days of Cyrus, King of Persia, until the reign of Darius, King of Persia." Precisely what did happen? To suppose that the Samaritans and the "people of the land" had recourse — as was done later on — to the central government, and obtained from Cyrus a decree stopping the work, is a possible hypothesis, but not the only one. Rather, the numerical and social predominance of the anti-Yahwist coalition, and even more the connivance of some high functionary of the state won over by its gold, would clarify the obscure words cited above, and would explain how they were able to hold in check even the authority of the *pehah*, although this was not absolute (§ 87). They must have achieved their ends by means of obstacles, scorn, threats, even physical force; the builders and their leaders were thus rendered helpless.

The work itself suffered. Not only were there too few hands for the task (§ 90), but, in the face of that wave of hostility, they were in no position to defend themselves. There was no dearth of Yahwistic ardor, but that alone could not miraculously build the Temple. Ten times the number of workers, ten times as much money, and even ten times as many arms to defend what was being built up so gradually, were needed. As things stood, the enterprise was wholly impossible. It was decided, therefore, to call a halt, thus to eliminate the chief cause of the hostility. They could only await better times, preserving in their hearts both their projects and the Yahwistic faith which had prompted them.

93. The work must have been interrupted almost before it had begun, and very little accomplished. In fact, when the work was resumed in the time of Aggeus and Zacharias (§ 97), so insignificant and unworthy of mention must have been the results of this first attempt that there is no explicit description of what had been done. For all practical purposes the work of restoration began with Aggeus and Zacharias (Esdras 5:1–2; cf. the much-disputed passage, Agg. 2:18).

Doubt has been thrown, recently, upon the historicity of this first attempt. It is claimed that the reconstruction of the Temple was only begun in 520 B.C. under Aggeus and Zacharias, before whose time only a temporary altar was in use (§ 89). Against this hypothesis we can advance the psychological attitude of the repatriates. It is not likely that such ardent Yahwists, repatriated at a cost of such great sacrifices in order to achieve a well-defined purpose, would let almost twenty years pass without at least trying to realize the central point of that program, the reconstruction of the Temple. The apparent discrepancy between the accounts can be explained by the different viewpoints of the documents involved, some written without regard for chronology (Esdras: § 108 ff.) and independent accounts (Aggeus and Zacharias). Some accounts of diverse provenience repeatedly affirm the unsuccessful attempt made by Zorobabel-Sheshbassar (Esdras 4:1–5, 24; 5:16; cf. Zach. 4:9); others make no mention of this first attempt, precisely because it was unsuccessful, and dealt only with the attempt in 520 B.C. under Aggeus and Zacharias, which did achieve its purpose (Esdras 5:1–2; Agg. 2:18).

94. The failure of the first attempt seriously affected the morale of the repatriates. Disillusionment must have dampened the Yahwistic ardor of some of those who had returned from Babylonia, convinced that they would find the hills leveled and rough places filled, and that their road would be smooth and easy (Isa. 40:4), that Yahweh himself, before whom all peoples are as nothing (Isa. 40:17), would escort them, that Yahweh would then make all the enemies of Israel disappear to the last man (Isa. 41:11–14), and that he would make Israel a toothed harrow which would thresh the mountains and pulverize the hills (Isa. 41:15–16). Filled with these and other enthusiastic hopes, they learned that a few despicable idolaters could impede their greatest work. In the face of this mystery, not a few of the repatriates must have asked themselves, as others had after the catastrophe of 586 B.C., whether Yahweh had not again hidden his face from them. Such tormenting questions always sow a kind of desolate skepticism in weaker souls.

When it became clear that they could not work on their spiritual fortress, they busied themselves in improving their material welfare. Up to that time this had been rather precarious (§ 90). But even here inconveniences were encountered. The construction of the Temple, an outgrowth of the Yahwistic spirit, was at the same time a source of nourishment. Enthusiasm for the project had stirred up their hearts, and was contagious. The exhilaration of a large crowd working together to realize a common ideal led them to love the ideal itself. Once the work was stopped and the enthusiasm dampened, the principal concern of every man became his *own* welfare, his *own* house, his *own* vineyard. Few indeed were so thoroughly imbued with the Yahwistic ideal that they did not falter at the stoppage of the work. How many, hemmed in by monotonous domestic cares, could preserve in the solitude of their hearts the original flame of enthusiasm which had blazed up within them as they had carried forward the first beams, or had with their fellows hewed out the first stones for the Temple? Under the circumstances a rebirth of individualism was only to be expected. How many would pass this new test, however enthusiastically they had welcomed the glowing projects of Ezechiel (§ 76 ff.)?

95. The silence of the documents makes it all too plain that the suspension of operations had evil consequences. The work on the Temple was suspended in the second year after the return (§ 92), i.e., at the end of 536 B.C.; not a word was breathed about it for the next fifteen years, i.e., until about 520 B.C. Enthusiasm for private interests, however, did not lag. Aggeus (1:4, 9) informs us that during those fifteen years, private dwellings with elaborate and costly roofs were constructed, and probably represented a considerable amount of building; yet the house of Yahweh was neglected and jackals skulked over its ruins (Lam. 5:18). This neglect may have been due only to circumstances which were still unfavorable to the resumption of the building of the Temple. It seems this reason was habitually alleged (Agg. 1:2), the real reason probably being quite different, a desire to tend to more pressing affairs which involved individual interests (Agg. 1:9). Other abuses traceable to selfishness and greed became widespread among them (cf. Agg. 2:10–19). The suspension of the work on the Temple was like a heavy layer of ashes over the Yahwistic fire which they had brought back with them from Babylonia.

The fire, however, was not extinguished. To stir it up again, an energetic and inspiring leader was needed. He would, naturally, be a prophet, as was usual in Israel (Vol. I, § 430).

96. Cyrus was succeeded by his son Cambyses (§ 10), who passed through Palestine on his expedition into Egypt. Nothing is said in the Bible about his dealings with the community at Jerusalem, but the papyri of Elephantine reveal his attitude toward the Hebrews in general. Although he showed his contempt for the religion of the Egyptians, and committed sacrileges against it, he respected the temple which the Jewish colony had constructed at Elephantine (§ 172). We may conclude from this that the capricious son of Cyrus was unexpectedly well disposed toward the children of Israel. But the Jews of Jerusalem did not benefit by this, or perhaps it was their growing indolence that prevented them from seeking to profit from it. When Darius I (§ 13) ascended the throne, the Persian empire was entering upon a period of disturbances which seemed at first to threaten its solidity, and did awaken, especially in Babylonia, aspirations of independence. Under the circumstances, the cohesion of the various parts of the empire was somewhat loosened (as soon as peace was restored, Darius undertook a drastic reorganization), and in the more distant or less important provinces, officials could act more or less independently of the central government.

The time, therefore, was ripe for a resumption of the work on the Temple. Active Samaritan hostility had not ceased (§ 91), but in such a time of crisis their hostility could not be as efficacious as before. Besides, the monarch had been changed, and perhaps in the meantime other state functionaries who had been corrupted by the gold of the anti-Yahwist coalition fifteen years before (§ 92) had been changed also. The idea was to work quickly and to present these hostile neighbors with a *fait accompli*. If, in the course of their labors, the Persian authorities should try to hinder the progress of the work, sufficient authorization was available to prove the legality of its continuance. The one stumbling block which could prevent them from taking full advantage of the situation was the decline of community spirit, and the resurrection of individualism (§ 94). But prophetism intervened at this point, and once again was the salvation of Israel.

97. The sixth month of the second year of Darius I (the year 520), the first day of that month (August 29), when Zorobabel and Joshua had gathered a group together — probably amid the ruins of the Temple, for some liturgical function at the restored altar (§ 89) — the prophet Aggeus unexpectedly stepped forth and began in strong language to upbraid the two leaders and the assembled crowd for their neglect of the House of Yahweh. Pointing to the surrounding ruins, he contrasted them with the well-built homes they had put up for themselves, and from this and other considerations urged them to shake themselves out of their shameful lethargy and begin at once to rebuild the Temple (Agg. 1:1–11).

The words of a prophet, even when they were not accepted but had led to the stoning of the prophet, always made an impression (Vol. I, § 429)! On this occasion the Yahwism imbedded in the souls of the repatriates would not allow him to be stoned; instead, his words were followed by obedience. The twenty-fourth day of the same month (September 21), work on the reconstruction of the Temple was resumed (Agg. 1:12–15).

The prophet followed this up by fanning the flame smoldering under the ashes. Other encouraging and comforting orations were made by him on the twenty-first day of the seventh month (October 18), and the twenty-fourth day of the ninth month (December 18).

His voice had hardly been raised when another voice began to encourage the workers with visions of a glorious future. The prophet

Zacharias, of sacerdotal lineage, addressed the workers on the first day of the eighth month (October-November) of 520 and, later on, followed this by other allocutions and oracles, until the fourth day of the ninth month (November-December) of the fourth year of Darius I, i.e., 518 B.C. (Zach. 1–8; cf. 1:1; 7:1).

98. Thus far the documents. They leave room, however, for a special hypothesis which is not based on precise data but is nevertheless not improbable. Was the resumption of work due solely to the intervention of the two prophets, or also to the arrival of a new caravan of repatriates from Babylonia? It is a matter of record that, precisely at this time, Babylonia was plagued by disturbances and wars (§ 13) which would certainly have induced those who could, to leave. Cyrus' decree permitting the Jews to depart had never been revoked. Moreover, the Jews still in Babylonia, especially the more zealous of them, had followed with anxious eye the activities of their fellow countrymen in Palestine (§ 62); and had doubtless helped in the renascence of the homeland by gifts of money. They certainly would not be pleased at the little accomplished up to that time. It is possible, then, that in the early days of Darius I a new group of Jews in Babylonia, disquieted by the disorder there and attracted by the projects of the Yahwistic restoration in the homeland, left the land of exile to re-enforce by money, labor, and their Yahwistic spirit, the fellow countrymen who had returned to Israel in the year 537 B.C.

Whatever may be said of this possibility, it is a fact that the work progressed rapidly once it was resumed. However, the builders were dismayed at the realization that their painful lack of resources would result in a building far inferior in richness and splendor to the Temple of Solomon. Some of the older generation still surviving could recall having seen, in their youth, the old Temple. Their depression was dissipated by a second exhortation delivered by Aggeus in the seventh month, declaring in Yahweh's name that the future destiny of the new edifice would infinitely surpass that of the old. In fact, the glory of Yahweh would be manifested in the triumphant messianic future, and the precious gifts which the pagan nations would bring to it as they became a part of the universal kingdom of Yahweh (Agg. 2:1–9) would make up for the inferiority of the new building.

99. The internal difficulty was thus overcome, but there then arose an external one. The hostile intervention of the Persian authorities, always a possibility, now became a reality (§ 96). The satrap Tattenai (called Sisinnes in 3 Esdras 6) of the satrapy Abar-Nahara (§ 13) and hence having jurisdiction over Palestine, was informed of what was going on and sent his officials to conduct an investigation. It does not require extraordinary intelligence to suppose that the satrap had

been informed of this resumption of work by the same people who fifteen years before had succeeded in having it interrupted, namely, the Samaritans. The officials asked who had ordered the construction to proceed, took down the names of the "ancients" of the people (§ 64), and drew up a detailed report with Tattenai's consent, and sent it on to King Darius. This must have been near the end of 519, when Darius I began to enjoy a secure advantage over the revolutionary movements and to grasp more tightly in hand the reins of his empire. This would also explain the zeal of the satrap and his associates; all desired to appear in the sight of the king as watchdogs of the central government, and as vigilant observers of any suspicious movement which might jeopardize the interests of the empire.

The Jewish builders easily justified their legal rights and, in fact, actually embarrassed the inspectors somewhat by citing the decree of Cyrus permitting the repatriation of the Jews and the reconstruction of their Temple in Jerusalem (§ 85). This decree from the founder of the empire impressed upon the inspectors the delicacy of the matter. Like good politicians, therefore, they avoided any embroilment by referring the whole matter to the central government. In their report they called attention to the fact that the Jews vindicated their legal rights by appealing to the decree of Cyrus; they made no judgment on the decree in question but at the same time suggested that the government search its central archives to see if there existed any trace of it.

The report arrived in Ecbatana and received the attention which a matter of that kind warranted from an organizer such as Darius I. The decree was searched for and found in the archives (§ 85), and the reply sent to Tattenai by Darius was in conformity with the letter and spirit of the decree of Cyrus. As long as his subjects remained obedient and peaceable, Darius desired to favor them and keep them satisfied, following the classic example of Cyrus (§ 7 ff.). The Great King therefore commanded that the reconstruction of the Temple be permitted and assistance given from the royal treasury of the satrapy to the "ancients of the Jews," to help them build the Temple and offer up the daily sacrifices "so that they may offer sweet-smelling sacrifices to the God of heaven and may pray for the life of the King and his children" (Esdras 6:10: Aramaic text). The sanction with which the order of the Great King concluded was typically Persian: if anyone refused to comply, he was to be impaled on a beam of his own house, and the house was to be made a dungheap (6:11).

The official documents containing this correspondence are preserved in *Esdras* 5:7–6:12 and today, especially after the discovery of the papyri of Elephantine (which are so similar both in content and phraseology [166 ff.]), their authenticity can hardly be doubted.

Temple of Zorobabel (Reconstruction by Schick).

100. The sanction specified by the decree was just what was needed to check the Samaritans. For the time being, hostilities were suspended. There is some reason to suppose that a *rapprochement* was attempted with the Yahwists of Jerusalem. The indication of this attempt is found in *Zach.* 7:2 ff., although the Hebrew text is highly doubtful. Whether one reads with the Masoretes, *Beth-el*, or prefers to correct it to *Beth-[isra]el* (other corrections do not seem to be well founded), it still deals with an embassy sent to Jerusalem by the northern districts designated collectively as the "house of Israel" (*Beth-israel*), or called that from their principal religious center which was precisely Beth-el (Vol. I, § 457). It is noteworthy that the embassy was sent to consult Jerusalem on a point of religious observance. They desired that the two peoples be uniform in their worship, the northerners apparently believing that their Yahwism was not different from that of the re-patriates at Jerusalem (§ 91). Since this embassy arrived the fourth day of the ninth month of the fourth year of Darius I (§§ 97, 99), one can logically perceive in it the result of this king's decree.

101. All obstacles were thus overcome, and with the help of the government subsidies, the construction this time achieved its goal. The temple was completed in the sixth year of Darius, that is, 515 B.C. in the month of Adar (February-March). According to the greater number of texts, it was on the third day of this month, but more probably it was the twenty-third, as given by other texts. From the time the work was resumed under the urging of Aggeus (§ 97), that is, from September 21, 520, to its completion, about four years and a half had passed. The dedication of the new edifice was solemnly celebrated, and in the next month, Nisan, the first Pasch was also celebrated (*Esdras* 6:13–22).

102. The new Temple must have copied, in its general lines, the Temple of Solomon (Esdras 6:3 ff.), and yet was greatly inferior to it in the quality of its material and ornamentation. The fact that it was completed in four and a half years despite difficulties and shortages, whereas Solomon's took seven years with an abundance of material and workmen (Vol. I, § 397), is a good indication that it was a mediocre structure. The grandiose plan of the future Temple drawn up and illustrated by Ezechiel (§ 76) remained to be realized, therefore, at some future date.

From *1 Machabees* 4:38, 48 it is evident that the new Temple, like Solomon's, was surrounded by the usual interior and exterior court (Vol. I, § 393). Some modern scholars, however, are of the opinion that lay persons could enter beyond the exterior into the interior court where the altar of holocausts stood, and where the priests offered sacrifice. The reason for the wall, they hold, was the humiliation once suffered by Alexander Jannaeus (§ 302) on the feast of Tabernacles. As he stood at the altar ready to offer the sacrifice, he was unmercifully pelted with the citrous fruits which the by-standers held in their hands (Josephus, *Antiquities*, XIII, 13, 5). It was as a result of this incident, it is argued, that the king caused the erection of a wooden partition separating the two courts.

This opinion does not appear to be well founded, however, for in the mind of Ezechiel the distinction between "sacred" and "profane" was too fundamental a one to be so quickly neglected. Moreover, the railing put up by Alexander Jannaeus was only a substitute for the wall of separation demolished in 159 B.C. by Alcimus (§ 270), and had existed between the two courts from the beginning.

The furnishings also of the new Temple must have been fewer than and much inferior to those of the older Temple, especially in its early days, but were certainly increased little by little both in quantity and quality. The most sacred possession, the Ark, was missing. In the other Temple the Ark was the only object present in the *cell* or "holy of holies" (Vol. I, § 395), but since the Ark had been destroyed along with the Temple, in the new one the cell remained empty (cf. Josephus, *Jewish War*, V, 5, 5). (A pious popular legend mentioned in 2 Mach. 2:1 ff. refused to admit the possibility that such a holy object could be destroyed and asserted that the prophet Jeremias had hidden it on Mount Nebo, in a cave unknown to anyone.) According to a rabbinical tradition (Mishna, *Yoma*, V, 2), the empty place in the new Temple was occupied by a stone three fingers high upon which the high priest placed the thurible when he entered into the "holy of holies" each year on the feast of Expiation (Yom Kippur).

In the "holy" place was the altar of gold for the incense, and the table for the loaves of proposition (Vol. I, § 395); there was only one lampstand of gold, not ten, and it had seven branches (1 Mach. 1:21 [Vulgate 23]; 4:49–51; cf. Pseudo-Hecatus of Abdera in Josephus, *Contra Apion.*, I, 22 [198]).

The Temple completed, Zorobabel disappears from history. Despite the good intentions of some modern scholars who claim that he died a tragic death (they have a habit of multiplying gratuitous hypotheses and then retracting them), nothing more is known of this zealous Israelite leader, who was to be a "signet ring in the hand of Yahweh" (cf. Agg. 2:23; Ecclus. 49:11 [13]).

THE PERSIAN PERIOD

103. There are disappointingly few documents which take us up to the sixth year of Darius I (515 B.C.; § 101), and even fewer for the succeeding period. From the completion of the Temple on into the period of Hellenism, the historian has to grope his way, to push forward on a terrain covered by the waters of ignorance. Here and there he will find a tiny landing-place, or a large island, or the summit of a mountain submerged in the sea; despite this, the continuity of history is interrupted by a gap extending over more than three centuries.

Journey through such a documentary Cyclades invites the activity of a critic only too eager to "reconstruct" history, all the more so because this epoch covers the formation of that typically "Jewish" mentality which will lead to the rise of the Machabees, and amid which Christianity will make its appearance. Undoubtedly the reconstructive ability of these critics offers many advantages. Often, a steady concentrated peering into clear deep waters can make out much that is hidden there, on condition, of course, of not mistaking figments of the imagination for reality. Also, one may never forget that one of the chief arts of a "reconstructive" criticism is the *ars nesciendi*.

104. There are no documents concerning the remainder of Darius I's reign (522–485 B.C.; §§ 13–15). A brief reference to the reign of Xerxes (485–465 B.C.; § 16) in the book of *Esther* (1:1 ff.: Hebrew text) will be taken up later.

For the reign of Artaxerxes I (465–424 B.C.; § 17), we have, first of all, a collection of documents interesting both because of its location in the present-day texts and for its content. It has been brought out above that in *Esdras* 4:4–5 it is stated (in Hebrew) that the first attempt to rebuild the Temple failed, and that the suspension of work endured "all the days of Cyrus, King of Persia, until the reign of Darius, King of Persia" (§ 92). One would expect that the report would mention the completion of the Temple under Darius. Instead, this logical and chronological thread is only resumed in 4:24 (in Aramaic), while the intervening section (4:6–23) treats of events of the time of Xerxes and

Artaxerxes; this latter is certainly Artaxerxes I. It is beyond doubt, therefore, that this section, inserted in the middle of the account of the deeds of Darius I, is chronologically out of place. The proper chronological order should be Darius-Xerxes-Artaxerxes, but here the order is Darius (suspension of work on the temple) -Xerxes-Artaxerxes-Darius (completion of the Temple).

The cause of this displacement must be that this group of documents refers to another suspension of the work undertaken by the repatriates of Jerusalem, not the work on the Temple (already completed under Darius), but the work on the walls of the city. The introduction, in fact, says, in the Hebrew: "And in the reign of Ahasuerus [Xerxes], at the beginning of his reign, they wrote an accusation against the inhabitants of Juda and Jerusalem. And in the days of Artaxerxes, along with[1] Mithredath, Tab'el and his other colleagues wrote to Artaxerxes, King of Persia, and the letter was written in Aramaic and edited in Aramaic" (Esdras 4:6–7). The main part gives in Aramaic the text of a letter sent to Artaxerxes by the Persian officials Rehum and Shimshai and the Samaritans, in which the Jews of Jerusalem are denounced to the king for having begun to rebuild the walls of the city. Since in the past this city had been turbulent and seditious, they counsel him to order the work stopped, unless he wants the city to become a fortified center of rebellion (4:8–16). This letter of the officials is followed by the reply sent to them by Artaxerxes, ordering them to stop the work on the walls, and lastly there is a note to the effect that the order had been carried out by the officials by force of arms (4:17–23). The section ends here, and the narrative goes back chronologically to the time of Darius, as stated above.

105. This section creates some problems. Aside from Josephus (Antiquities, XI, 2), who puts this exchange of letters back in the time of Cambyses (§ 10) (thus saving the chronological order), the fact remains that the letter of Tab'el, which seems to be ahead of its proper place, is not afterward mentioned; the alternative is that it was only a simple copy of the missive of Rehum and the response of Artaxerxes, to which the writer added a few remarks, now lost (4:24).

However, the section brings us back to the time of Xerxes and even to the time of Artaxerxes. Who were the writers of that "accusation against the inhabitants of Judea and Jerusalem in the time of Xerxes"? What was the burden of their accusation? Events of the time of Cyrus (§ 92), and the contents of the section in question justify the suspicion that the

---

[1] Though "along with" is regarded by others as the proper name Bishlam, there seems to be better reason for considering it as an Aramaic expression, leaving it as it stands; cf. the Greek. Mithredath was certainly a Persian official; some suppose that Tab'el was a Jew; others that he was a foreigner (Tab'el would be the Aramaic equivalent of the Hebrew Tobhiyyah, Tobias?).

Samaritans were again at work. The exact charges made during Xerxes' reign are not indicated, but the mere fact that the editor puts this information in his introduction to the pericope treating of the reconstruction of the walls of Jerusalem, indicates that in his mind the accusation was the same in both cases.

It would have been perfectly natural if there had been an attempt made to rebuild the walls even in the time of Xerxes. The Temple, of the highest importance for morale, was practically useless for defense. The walls of the city still lay upon the ground, as they had ever since 586 B.C. An open city in those times was really not a city. It might be a warehouse, or a caravan stop, but it was not a city. Desert bandits could have taken and sacked it without great difficulty. The great care with which the ancient Canaanites girded their tight little cities with walls (Vol. I, § 101) was fully justified. Nineve was able to resist the invasion of the Scythians only because of her strong walls, and from the beginning Babel awaited Cyrus' attack with confidence (§ 5). In Jerusalem's case walls were even more necessary, for the aggressors, the Samaritans and the "people of the land" (§ 92), were not hypothetical and far distant enemies, but were all around it, always alert in their hostility, constantly suspended above the Temple and the defenseless suburbs like a sword.

It is quite likely the repatriates tried to remedy their situation toward the end of Xerxes' reign. In 470 B.C. Persia's land and naval defeat at Eurymedon disclosed her inability to check the power of Greece (§ 16). The defeat must have had unfavorable repercussions inside the Empire, especially in the western sectors nearer to Greece. It is, then, probable that during the five years in which Xerxes continued to reign after this event, and especially toward the end of this period, the Jews of Jerusalem took advantage of the changed circumstances and began to rebuild their walls, which course of action provoked the accusation sent by the Samaritans to the royal court (Esdras 4:6).

106. The zeal of the accusers apparently did not achieve the desired effect, for in the succeeding reign of Artaxerxes, the Jews were still working on the walls. Precisely what had transpired is not clear, for our sources are silent. Either the conspiracy in which Xerxes lost his life, or the disorders which plagued the beginning of the reign of Artaxerxes (§ 17) made it impossible for the court to take energetic steps in an unimportant incident on the edge of the Empire, while at the very center the throne itself was endangered; or, supposing that orders had come to suspend operations, they were ignored at Jerusalem. Thus operations continued under Artaxerxes, but at a very slow pace, owing largely to the difficulties of the enterprise itself, and to the opposition of the Samaritans.

Once Artaxerxes was master of the situation and secure upon his throne, he took steps to cope also with minor threats to his power. The Egyptian revolt of Inarus and later that of Megabyzus, in whose satrapy Jerusalem belonged (§§ 17, 13), were warnings he took seriously. From the very beginning he stamped out every suspicion of a desire for independence, for such thinking could become dangerous to him. The walls were well advanced, perhaps nearly complete, thanks to the man power and money brought by the repatriates from Babylonia (Esdras 4:12; § 120), when the Samaritans again began to denounce the builders to the court. This time their plan succeeded as reported (§ 104). They had portrayed Jerusalem as an ancient nest of disorders, and the builders as conspirators, and Artaxerxes immediately sent word to suspend all operations at once.

107. But not everything depends upon this one section. *Another* source gives further particulars, and helps to determine the period in which the event took place. In the twentieth year (Neh. 1:1 ff.) of Artaxerxes I, that is, in 445 B.C. (or at most 446 B.C.; cf. § 124), a number of Jews returned to the Persian court in Susa, and there relayed some new and recent information: the repatriates "were in great misery and reproach, and the walls of Jerusalem are broken down and its gates burned by fire" (Neh. 1:3). That this destruction and fire was not the one caused by Nabuchodonosor a hundred and fifty years before, is clear enough; it must, therefore, have referred to the one which followed the accusation made by the Samaritans to Artaxerxes. Zealous Persian officials carried out the order of the king by force of arms (§ 104), not only preventing the completion of the work but also tearing down and burning what had already been finished, by this time doubtless a considerable amount. If, however, the information reached Susa for the first time in 445 B.C. (or 446 B.C.), the event must have taken place some months before, that is, between 447 B.C. and 446 B.C. This was, therefore, a period of real triumph for the Samaritans, and a serious setback for the Yahwists of Jerusalem. The girdle of walls representing several years of labor was thrown to the ground, and the enemies who surrounded the Yahwistic community caused them much affliction.

At this point in the history of Judaism, our sources present two men endowed with the energy demanded in leaders of the people. They were to restore the community both materially and morally, and their names were Esdras and Nehemias. The question of the chronological order of their activity at Jerusalem is of fundamental importance.

108. The Chronological Question of Esdras and Nehemias. Practically everything known about these two men is found in the two books called *Esdras* and *Nehemias* (*1 Esdras* and *2 Esdras* in the Vulgate). In reality there is only one book, the division into two books being wholly arbitrary and unknown to the ancients (cf. Josephus, *C. Apion.*, I, 8; Melitus of Sardis, in Eusebius, *Hist. eccl.*, IV, 26; Jerome, *Prol. galeat.; Ad Domnion. et Rogat. in Esdr. et Nehem. Praef.*). It was introduced into the Hebrew text only about A.D. 1450, and from then on was commonly employed by printers to correspond to the Greek and Latin texts. Esdras-Nehemias was once the last chapter, as it were, of one complete work: *Paralipomenon-Esdras-Nehemias*, from which it became detached at some unknown date (Vol. I, §§ 110–112); thereafter it was treated as if it were a work in itself. It treats of a rather late period in the history of Israel untouched by the other books; *Paralipomenon* treats of the preceding period already described in *Samuel-Kings*.

The newness of theme had repercussions on the manner in which it was handled. In this last period of his history, the Chronicler, who is its only author, gathered together his documents (genealogies, catalogues, decrees of the Persian kings, correspondence of bureaucratic officials, etc.), often simply transcribing them as they stood, and often neglecting to show their relationship by means of explanatory or introductory notes. Thus it came about that considerable parts of his compilation are preserved in Aramaic (Esdras 4:8–6:18; 7:12–26) while the rest is in Hebrew; and in other even longer sections, Esdras (Esdras 7:27–9:15) and Nehemias (Neh. 1:1–7, 72; 12:31 ff.) speak in the first person. All this goes to show that the Chronicler drew heavily upon very old sources of information, even if he did write in Aramaic (§ 67), and that among these sources there were the personal written "Memoirs" left by Esdras and Nehemias.

It is unnecessary to insist upon the fact that the crude and unadorned character of these documents makes them all the more valuable from an historical point of view.

109. A cursory glance at the contents of the compilation reveals an important though negative fact, namely, that the documents are not here arranged in precise chronological order, i.e., beginning with the more ancient and coming down to more recent events. As a result, the chronology fluctuates backwards and forwards. The reason for this disorder is involved, but is of no particular interest to us; in any case the proof of it is quite obvious.

One proof of it, or so it seems to us, is the position of the *dossier* which, interrupting the account of Darius' deeds, is not in chronological order. Aside from the fact that the entire unit of *Esdras-Nehemias* has been anachronistically placed before *Chronicles* which being older once preceded it (§ 108), other proofs of this same phenomenon occur in Nehemias itself (thus, ch. 3 does not seem to be in the right place; ch. 5 relates events which surely occurred after those reported in ch. 6

[cf. 5:41]; ch. 8–10 allude to events which are later than those of ch. 12:27 ff.; cf. also §§ 134, 136 f.).

This point once established, we can conclude that when one document follows another in *Esdras-Nehemias* without any comparison or chronological reference from the Chronicler, one may not presume that the second of these documents is chronologically later than the first. It may be later, as it sometimes is in other chapters, but the mere fact of its after position is no guarantee of that fact.

110. The story of Esdras is chiefly found in *Esdras,* 7–10, and that of Nehemias exclusively in *Nehemias,* 1–13. *Esdras* 7–10 is not related in any way to *Esdras* 1–6 (*Esdras* 6 in fact terminates with the completion of the temple under Darius: § 101), nor to *Nehemias* 1–13 which follows immediately. Let us see if the chronological data can determine the sequence of one of these two accounts.

Esdras came from Babylonia to Jerusalem in the seventh year of Artaxerxes, king of Persia (Esdras 7:1–7), and Nehemias from the Persian court at Susa in the twentieth year of Artaxerxes (Neh. 1:1; 2:1). These dates would be very clear if there had been only *one* Artaxerxes who sat on the Persian throne, but there were three, Artaxerxes I or Longomanus (§ 17), Artaxerxes II or Memnon (§ 19), and Artaxerxes III or Ochus (§ 21). The dates given are then of little use because the Chronicler does not single out which Artaxerxes it was that had dealings with Esdras and Nehemias.

The question is an open one still, as the coming of Esdras before Nehemias cannot be based on the precedence of the report on Esdras over that on Nehemias.

Artaxerxes III Ochus does not fit in for evident chronological reasons, particularly because of the Elephantine papyri (§ 166 ff.). Esdras, then, came to Jerusalem in the year 458 B.C. (the seventh of Artaxerxes I) and Nehemias in 445 B.C. (the twentieth of Artaxerxes I); or, if two Artaxerxes are referred to, then Nehemias came in the year 445 B.C. (the twentieth of Artaxerxes I) and Esdras in the year 398 (the seventh of Artaxerxes II). In the first case Esdras would have preceded Nehemias by thirteen years; in the second he would have followed him by forty-seven years.

So great a difference will necessarily have to be taken into account by the historian. If the texts are read in the order of the Chronicler, Esdras, an eminent scribe of the *Torah* and a reformer (§ 146 ff.), played his part in Jerusalem before the walls of the city were rebuilt and the community materially sealed off by itself. Nehemias, on the other hand, was pre-eminently the builder of the walls and social reorganizer who came upon the scene thirteen years after the reform of Esdras. If, however, the report of Esdras' actions (Esdras 7-10) is chronologically out of place and should instead follow the report on Nehemias (Neh. 1-13), it would then follow that Nehemias was first, and that in the forty-seven years which ensued, the community morale weakened, thus preparing the ground for the "great scribe" and reformer, Esdras.

In either explanation Esdras and Nehemias must have been together in Jerusalem for some time, and worked together (cf. Neh. 8). After this Nehemias returned to the Persian court of Susa in the thirty-second year of Artaxerxes I (in 433 B.C.), but he was to return to Jerusalem some time later (Neh. 13:6 ff.).

111. This question has been thoroughly debated and the text has been carefully exploited in favor of either side. A recent hypothesis limits Esdras' activity in Jerusalem to scarcely a year (458-457 B.C.) and provides it with a dramatic ending; but all the facts about Esdras cannot be compressed into so short a time, and the theory itself demands a drastic manhandling of the texts (it is denied, for example, that Esdras and Nehemias ever did collaborate as indicated in Neh. 8:9; 12:[33]36, on the ground that the name of Nehemias is a later addition to the text).[2] Another and now discarded hypothesis held that Esdras never existed, but was a fiction of the later priestly class which desired to exalt one of its members to offset the influence of the "layman" Nehemias. The only documentary proof adduced for this is that the author of *Ecclesiasticus*, in his praise of ancient heroes, praises Nehemias but does not even mention Esdras (Ecclus. 44-50). True, this author does not mention Esdras, but the omission may be explained in various ways (after all, other important names, such as Asa and Josaphat, kings of Juda, are also omitted). Above all, however, here is a case where the critical principle of "learned ignorance" should apply (§ 103), though not of course as a club to destroy what other sources have clearly affirmed. Systems built on mere negative evidence have happily had their day.

The principal reasons for the contention that Nehemias preceded Esdras, contrary to the order of the texts, are as follows.

112. When Nehemias obtained permission from Artaxerxes I to return from Susa to Jerusalem (Neh. 2), and when he described the program for the material and moral restoration of Jerusalem which he undertook (Neh. 1-6), and again when he spoke of exiles who were repatriated before he was (Neh. 7:5 ff.), there is not one single mention of Esdras or of any of his activities. Now, if Esdras had arrived only thirteen years ahead of Nehemias (§ 110) his memory would hardly have been so passed over in silence.

---

[2] The name that would arouse suspicion here of being a later addition would be that of Esdras, not Nehemias (cf. A. Van Hoonacker, in *Revue Bibl.*, 1924, pp. 61-62).

113. The activity of both Esdras and Nehemias for the community at Jerusalem was undoubtedly inspired by a most pure and disinterested Yahwistic spirit. Yet Nehemias, in rendering a public account of his operations, openly accused the governors and leaders who had preceded him, and their clerks too, of having oppressed and despoiled the community (Neh. 5:15). If Esdras had exercised the highest authority in Jerusalem only thirteen years before, this tirade of Nehemias would seem to condemn him unjustly.

114. On Nehemias' arrival, the ruins of the city walls still lay upon the ground (Neh. 2:11 ff.) and only a few houses had been restored for such a large city, and few of them were inhabited (7:4). Nehemias at once undertook to reconstruct the city and get people into it (2:18 ff.; 7:4 ff.). Upon Esdras' arrival, the city was walled and inhabited (Esdras 7–10), which seems to show that Nehemias preceded Esdras by many years.

115. In Esdras, however, there is a text which indicates with some probability the completion of the circle of the walls. Speaking of the past, and in the name of all the people, Esdras says: "We are slaves; but our God has not abandoned us in our servitude, but has extended His mercies to us in the sight of the kings of Persia, giving us life: rebuilding the house of our God, restoring its ruins and giving us a *gadher* in Juda and Jerusalem" (Esdras 9:9). *Gadher* usually means (*wall of*) *enclosure*, (*wall of*) *protection*, and, of course, the word could have been understood both in its material sense (for example, as a wall which encircles a vineyard; cf. Isa. 5:5) and, by extension, in a moral sense. In what sense did Esdras use it? Perhaps only in a moral sense, as if the Temple which was mentioned previously and the Yahwistic laws given to the community were its protective *enclosure*. This moral sense is also included, for immediately mention is here made of Juda, that is, the territory outside the capital. But considering that the capital was supposed to be the material and spiritual stronghold of the entire community (§ 76) and that the capital was open and at the mercy of the surrounding enemies (§ 105) as long as the walls were down, it can be appreciated that the material wall which encircled Jerusalem was also a spiritual protection of the whole Yahwistic community and that it was a physical and spiritual *gadher* for *Juda* and *Jerusalem*. Is it not in this twofold sense that Esdras is using the word here, and is saying that the walls of Jerusalem had already been built by Nehemias forty-seven years before? In 458 B.C. (§ 110) he could not possibly have referred to a material, but only to a moral *encirclement*, and then his words seem openly to contradict the facts (§§ 107, 125 ff.), which show that such a protective moral encirclement did not exist and that the community was at the mercy of its surrounding enemies.

116. When Nehemias arrived in Jerusalem, a handful of foreigners,

Sanballat the Horonite, Tobias the Ammonite, and Geshem the Arabian, ruled over the inhabitants of the city, and of the environs (Neh. 2:10, 19, etc.; § 125). On the other hand, there is no trace of these or any other foreign dominance under Esdras, proof perhaps that the walls built by Nehemias forty-seven years before had served as a true *gadher* of material and spiritual protection.

117. Nehemias came from Susa principally to rebuild the walls (Neh. 2:5 ff.), and they were completed shortly after his coming. If this be the case, there would be good reason for a return under Esdras, who would not concern himself with the walls in any way, but would concentrate on the organization of the liturgy and of a pure national Yahwism.

118. *Nehemias* 12:22 lists the high priests in Jerusalem as follows: Eliashib, Joiada, Johanan, Jaddua. From another passage it is clear that at the time of the first mission of Nehemias, i.e., in 445 B.C., Eliashib was the high priest in charge (Neh. 3:1; cf., however, 13:[4, 7] 28). Eliashib probably held office from 453 to 432 B.C., and his son and successor Joiada from 432 to about 410 B.C. (cf. § 145, footnote). There is no doubt that Esdras was contemporary with a Johanan, son of Eliashib (Esdras 10:6), who was not only a high dignitary of the Temple of Jerusalem, but, from other passages in which he is mentioned, seems to have been the same person as the third high priest referred to above (cf. Neh. 12:10–11 [where Jonathan is an evident mistake for Johanan]; 12:22–23). That he is called "son of Eliashib" instead of "son of Joiada" creates no difficulty, as the word "son" here has the sense of "descendant," as it frequently has among Semites, and in the case of Johanan, rather than recall his descent from his father, the writer preferred to mention his grandfather, Eliashib, during whose pontificate Jerusalem once again came to life thanks to the labors of Nehemias. Now, the documents of Elephantine (§ 172) show that around 410 B.C. Jehohanon (Johanan) was high priest in Jerusalem at the same time that Bagoas was governor there. This is also attested by Josephus Flavius (*Antiquities*, XI, 7, 1), who supposes that both continued to function until a little after the period of the [ἄλλου] ʼΑρταξέρξου, i.e., Artaxerxes II.[3] Under these conditions, everything seemingly points to the fact that Johanan, the high dignitary of the Temple and contemporary of Esdras, was the same high priest of the time of Artaxerxes II, and hence that Esdras came to Jerusalem under this monarch.

119. Aside from the strange omission of Esdras in *Ecclesiasticus* (§ 111), we find the following names mentioned in descending order in *Neh*. 12:26: Joiaqim son of Joshua, the high priest who was a contemporary of Zorobabel (§ 86), then Nehemias, and, last, Esdras. Also,

---

[3] The word ἄλλου is lacking in some codices.

in *Neh.* 12:47, the expression, "in the days of Zorobabel, and in the days of Nehemias," is used, no mention being made of Esdras. Do not these memories of the past, connecting Nehemias with the times of Zorobabel and hence placing him explicitly before Esdras, faithfully reflect the chronological order of the facts?

120. Other more elaborate but not less weighty arguments in favor of Nehemias' precedence over Esdras have been advanced, but need not be repeated here.

There is, however, a grave difficulty against the foregoing thesis. In the letter of denunciation sent by Rehum and Shimshai to King Artaxerxes I (§ 104), we read: "Be it known to the king that the Jews, who departed from your midst to come to us, have arrived in Jerusalem and are rebuilding the rebellious and wicked city, etc." (Esdras 4:12). Which caravan of Jews from Babylonia, departing with the permission of the Great King, can this be, if not the caravan of Esdras, authorized by Artaxerxes (Esdras 7:1 ff.)? According to this, Esdras would have arrived under Artaxerxes I, and before Nehemias.

Yet the identification of this caravan with that of Esdras is not absolutely imperative. There is, indeed, an explicit mention of the caravan of Esdras, but there may have been other caravans of repatriates about which no details have come down to us. Such a caravan may have been one from the time of Aggeus and Zacharias (§ 98), or perhaps it was one led by Hanani, the brother of Nehemias, who returned with other Jews from Jerusalem to Susa, and informed his brother there of the sorry condition of the city (Neh. 1:1–13); he may have been the leader of the caravan in question, and may have returned to Susa after the attempt to rebuild the walls failed, and the Samaritans enjoyed their victory (§ 107).

In conclusion, it must be admitted that absolute certainty cannot be attained by either side in the question of the precedence of Nehemias or of Esdras. In view of the above considerations, however, the precedence of Nehemias seems to us to be the better hypothesis, and we now resume the biblical narrative along these lines.

NEHEMIAS

121. From the time of Darius I (§ 97), the Jewish community of Jerusalem continued to be governed by two heads concerning whom we have information from the time of Zorobabel on (§ 87); they were the *pehah* and the high priest. The *pehah,* who may have been a Jew, was the civil ruler and represented in a special manner the authority of the Persian King. The high priest acted as the ethnarch, and it was his duty to provide for the complex organization of the Temple and to safeguard the internal interests of the community with the help of the "ancients" (§§ 64, 99). He was also the most authoritative representative of the community in dealings with the *pehah* and the Great King. Whether there was a genuine separation of the religious and civil powers we cannot say with certainty, and we know less about any subordination of the civil to the religious powers, as provided for by Ezechiel's ideal plan (§ 76). The two powers often overlapped and clashes were frequent, but there was some kind of a theoretical distinction between them. Whenever in practice one power had to be subordinated to another, the civil power prevailed over the religious (cf., for example, the incident cited by Josephus Flavius in *Antiquities*, XI, 7, 1; § 152). The satrap of the satrapy of Abar-Nahara ruled over both heads, as in the case of Tattenai, *circa* 519 B.C. (§ 99). The *pehah* and high priest were immediately subject to his jurisdiction, although they had the right to appeal directly to the Great King.

The high priest Joshua, contemporary of Zorobabel (§ 86), was succeeded in office by his son Joiaqim; Joiaqim by his son Eliashib, the contemporary of Nehemias (§ 118); Eliashib was succeeded by his son Joiada who held office during the second mission of Nehemias (§ 145, footnote); Joiada by his son Johanan, in all likelihood a contemporary of Esdras (§ 118); Johanan by his son Jaddua (Neh. 12:22; [12:10–11]; Josephus Flavius, *Antiquities*, XI, 7, 1). The list of those who held the office of *pehah*, however, is not known.

122. The community of Jerusalem lived under this series of two heads in a manner which is not clearly understood today, until the first half of the fifth century B.C. The rebuilding of the walls, begun probably in the last years of Xerxes and ending in disaster under Artaxerxes I around 446 (§ 107), was undertaken to assure the city and consequently all Yahwistic territory of the protection it lacked and which only a good *gadher* (§ 115) could provide. The enterprise, therefore, testified to the Yahwistic spirit of the repatriates. The labors were long drawn out (§ 106) and in the course of time the primitive fervor must have cooled somewhat. If the encouragement and help which came from their fellow countrymen who remained in Babylonia compensated in part for this (§ 120), other difficulties arose to plague them.

Besides the details in the book of Nehemias, there are many others in the book written by the prophet Malachias, whose activity in Jerusalem must have preceded the arrival of Nehemias by a short interval, i.e., around 450.

Economic conditions were difficult also. The *pehahs* were men whose ambition it was to fill their pockets with legitimate or illegitimate tribute from rich and poor alike (Neh. 5:4, 15; Mal. 1:8). In one way or another the rich continued to make progress despite these heavy burdens, but the poor, especially when the harvests were scarce or failed absolutely, had a hard time of it. Since they had to pay their taxes no matter what the circumstances, they were forced to turn to their rich fellow countrymen for the necessary loans. The loans were arranged, but with incredible conditions; the poor had to mortgage everything they possessed, fields and vineyards, and these practically always fell into the hands of the rich. When these were lacking, the poorer classes put up their sons and daughters as bond, and these usually had to remain on in slavery (Neh. 5:2–5). Naturally enough, even Yahwistic cult and organization felt the effects of this state of affairs, since the whole community bore the expense. No longer were pure and healthy animals used for the sacrifices of the Temple as the law demanded, but inferior and defective ones, the discards from the regular flocks (Mal. 1:8–14). The people practiced fraud in regard to the tithes and other contributions, giving less than was prescribed or offering unwanted objects (Mal. 3:8–9; cf. Neh. 10:32 ff.).

How different all this from the radiant visions of Ezechiel (§ 76)!

123. Moral conditions were not much better, being so largely connected either as cause or as effect with material conditions. Most serious in this regard was the frequency of mixed marriages, in which Jews took to wife the daughters of the surrounding foreigners. One cannot but be surprised that the Yahwists of Jerusalem, heirs to the grand, nationalistic plans of Ezechiel, should have associated with the hostile peoples who surrounded them or have entered into marriages with them. One probable explanation may be the fact that so few Jewish women returned with the repatriates from Babylonia. If we accept the hypothesis that the 12,000 persons in the caravan of Zorobabel who were not included in the partial lists were women (§ 86), the proportion of men to women would have been about three to one, a very serious disproportion for a polygamous people. Whether that hypothesis is correct or not, it concerns only the caravan of Zorobabel; there is no doubt that women were in the minority in Jerusalem. We must also remember that commercial relations were necessary with the surrounding peoples, and these were bound to lead to meetings and acquaintanceship, and of course the romantic element entered in too. Sometimes material advantages prompted them to repudiate, shamefully, the companion of their youth so as to make way for a more beautiful woman, or one whose parents and relatives were influential (Mal. 2:13–16).

The priestly class, which should have held out against these abuses, allowed itself to drift along with the current. The priests calmly allowed circumventions of the liturgical laws, and profaned the altar of Yahweh by sacrificing unworthy victims. Yahweh disdained such a mockery of religious cult and declared himself ready to throw the contents of the entrails of those victims into the faces of the sacrificing priests (Mal. 2:3). As moral guides too the priests had fallen away from the ancient example of the Levites. The *Torah* had been distorted as it passed through the lips of such priests, and, having become a vehicle for personal ideas and favoritism, had become also a stumbling block for many.

So much for the general state of affairs. It was not so general as to indicate that the ancient Yahwism was in imminent danger of extinction. The fact that there were men like Malachias who had the courage to denounce abuses; the continuation of the work on the walls which must have been extremely difficult considering their financial circumstances; the urgings which must constantly have arrived from the Yahwistic circles in Babylonia; the willingness with which only a few years later they responded to the leaders who with wisdom and energy recalled the community to its primitive objectives — all this is so much proof that it was only a layer of ashes that had accumulated on the fire of Yahwism (§ 95). But the layer was very thick and seriously threatened to suffocate the fire.

The man who scattered the ashes and caused the flame to spring forth afresh was this time not a "prophet" (it is significant that the prophet Malachias concludes the series of prophets in the Canon [Vol. I, §§ 109, 430]), nor was it a priest like Esdras, but a *layman*, Nehemias.

124. Nehemias was a Jew who had done well for himself (§ 61) in the land of exile, where he was born; he had become the cupbearer of Artaxerxes I at the court of Susa. The ease with which he could conduct business with the queen (Neh. 2:6) leads to the supposition that he was a eunuch (the Greek text of 2 *Esdras* 11:11 [Neh. 1:11] expressly states that he was).

In the twentieth year of Artaxerxes, in the month of Kisleu (November-December, 445), he was visited at court by his brother Hanani, just back from Jerusalem with news of the sorry conditions prevailing in the city and the whole community (§ 107). He was profoundly affected by this news — a clear indication that these developments were of recent occurrence. As he went about his duties at the royal table King Artaxerxes noticed his preoccupied and mournful air, and asked the reason for it. Nehemias seized the opportunity to plead the cause of his countrymen, and replied that he was much grieved at news he had recently received concerning the city where his ancestors were buried: the city had been destroyed and now stood with no protecting wall around it. If, therefore, it pleased the Great King, let him be sent there for a certain time with authorization to rebuild it. The case struck a sentimental chord in the heart of the queen, who was present at the banquet, and she intervened in his favor. Nehemias was asked how long it would take him to make the trip, do what he proposed doing, and return, and when he had answered, he was granted permission to set out.

Tetrobulus of
Artaxerxes I.

It is evident that this favorite cupbearer held the keys to his master's heart. The kindly intervention of the queen cannot be overlooked, of course, but it must not be forgotten that the same king who now granted permission to rebuild had given the exactly opposite order only a few years previously. Now, besides granting the necessary authorization, he was depriving himself of his trustworthy cupbearer, no small sacrifice in an oriental court, where a cupbearer, if so minded, could easily dispose of his monarch with a few drops of poison. The Persian court was not unaccustomed to such sinister results of favoritism. But this was not all. As the cupbearer was to depart unaccompanied by a caravan of his fellow countrymen, and as the royal officials in the far-off province were still under the orders of the Great King to oppose any reconstruction, Nehemias was given credentials to present to the satrap of Abar-Nahara (§§ 99, 121) to the effect that he be supplied with building materials from the royal properties, and also that he be given a protective escort for the journey (Neh. 2:1–9). To put an official stamp on his mission. Nehemias was given the title of *peḥah* (§ 121) of Juda (5:14). After this stroke of good fortune, the favorite set out on his journey to Jerusalem.

All this supposedly occurred in the month of Nisan, in the twentieth year of Artaxerxes I (March-April, 445). However, this does not fit in with the fact that Nehemias had been visited by his brother Hanani in the month of Kisleu (November-December) of the same year. Since both items come from the same source (Nisan from Neh. 2:1 and Kisleu from 1:1), i.e., from the original "Memoirs" written in the first person by Nehemias, it can hardly be supposed that two different systems of ancient chronology (§ 36) were involved. The cupbearer of the Persian court surely followed the Babylonian system. The difference can be attributed to an error of transcription (for example in Neh. 1:1, the nineteenth year of Artaxerxes could have been given; or in 2:1 the twenty-first), or perhaps to an interchange of words (in which case Kisleu should be read for *Nisan* and vice versa without changing the year).

125. Nehemias set about his preparations with absolute secrecy, for his life at court had taught him to appreciate the intrigues and plottings that went on behind the scenes there. He became a topic of discussion only when he presented his credentials at the offices of the satrapy of Abar-Nahara for validation. To the satrap himself, perhaps, the whole affair was a matter of indifference, but it was more than that to some of the sheikhs around Juda and Jerusalem who, after the humiliation inflicted on the Jewish community, had there ruled unchallenged. The unexpected arrival of the Jewish courtier become *pehah* must have been disquieting to them. Although his plans were not known, it was certain that his coming was aimed at bettering the fortunes of his fellow countrymen, and hence to abolish all trace of foreign intrusion and domination. The names of three of these sheikhs have been preserved; they were Sanballat the Horonite, Tobias the Ammonite, and Geshem the Arab.

Only the name of this last is known (Neh. 2:19; 6:1, 2; in 6:6 the form *Gashmu* is used); that he was called an "Arab" leads to the supposition that he may have belonged to one of the Arabian tribes of Nabateans which had penetrated the territory of Edom (§ 56) and of which mention is made in Abdias, in the beginning of Malachias (1:1–5), and, in later times, in Diodorus Siculus (XIX, 94). Much more is known of the other two from the recently discovered documents. Sanballat is called the "Horonite" (Neh. 2:10, 19; etc.) because he came originally from Horonaim, in the foreign land of Moab (rather than from the Israelite city Beth-Horon). Tobias is simply the "Ammonite" of the hostile people of Ammon, and in addition is called the "slave" (*'ebhedh*), perhaps because of his lineage. It is evident that in telling his story, the favorite intended to highlight the foreign character of his adversaries, and also to affix dishonorable titles to them. Even when they have a perfect right to honorable titles, these are not mentioned. The papyri of Elephantine (§ 172) state that in the time of Darius II, Sin-uballit (the same person as Sanballat) was still *pehah* of Samaria, but he is never given this title by Nehemias; the omission was quite deliberate. Nehemias, however, did let fall an indication of his rank as *pehah* when he described Sanballat as haranguing the "army of Samaria" against the Jews (Neh. 3:34, Hebrew text [4:2 in the other]). The "slave" Tobias is disdainfully called an Ammonite, which suggests that he should be classed with the Tobiads, a dynasty of sheikhs, which long ruled with luster and power in this very region of Ammon, as Josephus and the papyri of Zeno both testify (§ 218 ff.).

These leaders, therefore, were on their guard when the cupbearer arrived, and were determined to oppose his every move by co-ordinated action. Informed of the state of affairs by his brother Hanani, and perhaps also by the royal officials, Nehemias acted with the astuteness of a diplomat and the insight of a psychologist.

126. He had the reserve of a diplomat. When he arrived at Jerusalem, probably in the June following his departure from Susa, no one could penetrate his mask of silence concerning the real purposes of his mission; even his own fellow countrymen could find out nothing. He allowed three days to pass, perhaps to rest up from his journey, but also to get his bearings, to get the over-all picture. Then he began to act, going about to see for himself what work had been done. It was still necessary to work in secret in order

Cedron and the southern extremity of Ophel in winter.

not to arouse opposition in one quarter, or intemperate enthusiasm in another. He himself tells what he did: "[When three days passed], I arose at night, I and a few men with me, but I did not mention to anyone what my God had put in my heart to do for Jerusalem, neither was there any beast with me, only the beast which I rode. I went out, therefore, by the Valley Gate at night and [passed] right in front of the Fountain of the Dragon and towards the Dung Gate, and stood there inspecting the walls of Jerusalem which had been torn down [perusim] and the gates thereof consumed by fire. I then passed the Fountain Gate and the King's Pool, and there was no place for the beast to pass [to pass beyond] from where I was. And I made my way up the Torrent by night and stood inspecting the wall; I then returned and re-entered by the Valley Gate in order to go back. But the superintendents did not know where I had gone nor what I was doing, and to the Jews and priests and elders and superintendents and the rest of the master craftsmen I had told nothing up to that time" (Neh. 2:12–16).

Evidently this was a technical inspection. Yet the reconnoitering did not extend, or at least was not described as extending, to the entire circle of the walls. Nehemias went out at night from the "Valley Gate," whose location is uncertain (§ 133), and skirting the "Fountain of the Dragon"[1] advanced toward the "Dung Gate." There is no doubt that this gate opened into the Valley of Hinnom where the refuse was deposited, from which it derives its name; on the other side of it he passed the "Fountain Gate" and the "King's Pool" which evidently are in the ancient southeastern district of Ophel (Vol. I, §§ 96–98). From there he "ascended" the "Torrent" (*naḥal*), a name which in the Bible always refers to the Cedron, which flanks Ophel to the east and contains the fountain of Gihon. Up to what point he advanced in this direction is not reported, but it is said that he "returned" and re-entered by the Valley Gate. Instead of completing the entire circle of the walls, then, he probably limited his trip to its (western) southern and eastern points, and at a certain point retraced his steps.

The part of the walls therefore which he inspected — or at least the part that is described — was the most ancient sector, and was the object of great solicitude on the part of the Canaanites and later, of David, before the city began to expand toward the north as a result of the building during the era of the kings (Vol. I, §§ 97, 398, 486). His inspection revealed that the walls were breached but not leveled to the ground, so that gravely damaged sections alternated with others that had suffered little or no damage. The most important section strategically, toward the Fountain Gate or the Pool of the King, seems to have been more seriously damaged. In fact, the stones of the wall which had fallen into the valley years before, and the wild vegetation which had grown up in the meantime in the watery area (as is true even today), made it impossible for his beast to advance farther. Since the spot was so very important, a greater destruction had been visited upon it.

127. What the close-lipped diplomat saw during his secret inspection led him to make an important decision. It was imperative that he act with great energy and dispatch if he was to profit by his twofold advantage: the enthusiasm which his unexpected announcement would arouse in his fellow countrymen, and, second, the opportunity of presenting his foes with an accomplished fact, before they could get their own offensive into motion.

The elders were convoked and Nehemias laid before them the results of his inspection trip. He emphasized the necessity of rebuilding the walls in order that "we may no longer be an object of reproach." Up to this point they were not greatly impressed, however, because they already knew their sorry situation, and his words told them nothing new. What was new and so unexpected as to seem impossible, was Nehemias' announcement that the Great King had changed his attitude,

---

[1] This is the only place in the whole Bible where it is mentioned. Some would identify it as the 'Ain Rogel (Vol. I, § 96), but this is not certain.

and had granted them permission and help to rebuild. The presence of the cupbearer as he announced the great news was a guarantee of the present, and a pledge of the future. — "Let us rise up and build!" the crowd shouted. The spark had been enkindled, the fire blazed, everyone "took courage for the good work" (Neh. 2:17–18).

So as to put up the enclosing wall not piecemeal but all at once, thereby to insure protection against hostile raids from without, the work was divided into sections, each one entrusted to a group of builders. One group was made up of inhabitants from a certain locality (for example, from Jericho: 3:2), another of a clan of relatives, another of an association of those in the same class (such as the priests: 3:1) or an association of workers or craftsmen (such as the goldsmiths or perfumers: 3:8, 32). Nehemias 3 mentions forty-two groups. Some associations, for example, the bakers (cf. Jer. 37:21), or localities which were certainly reoccupied by the repatriates, e.g., nearby Bethlehem, are not mentioned, but the omission means nothing, for we do not know what method of assigning the sections was followed. Perhaps, too, the list is incomplete. The fact that the more wealthy among the inhabitants of Teqoa refused to take part in the enterprise (3:5), while the lower classes from this same district participated (3:27), is much more significant. It may be safely supposed that other like cases which showed that the program of Nehemias was not everywhere favorably received, were not mentioned. These were probably those who had fallen away from the Yahwistic spirit (§ 123) or who were so closely bound to the dominant foreign sheikhs in Jerusalem that they had not the courage to do anything displeasing to them (§ 130).

The sectors, of course, differed both in extent and in state of disrepair, but they were apportioned in accordance with what each group could accomplish. The sector containing the Horse Gate, for example, which gave on the Cedron Valley and was in the Temple area, was entrusted to a group of priests who lived opposite that part of the wall (3:28).

How long it took to partition the work and make the preliminary preparations is not known with certainty, but if the work was completed in only fifty-two days, from the first half of August to the end of September, there certainly could not have been much delay. Nehemias must have begun the work in the August following his arrival, not in the August of the following year as some have reckoned. Josephus, it is true (Antiquities, XI, 5, 8), thinks the work took two years and four months, but he is mistaken, for he puts the termination in the twenty-eighth year of the reign of Xerxes, whereas the year in which Nehemias began and completed his undertaking was either 444 or more probably 445 (§ 124). In passing it may be noted that Athens, then in the age of Pericles, had begun the construction of "long walls" some years before, in order to connect the city with Piraeus, and perhaps in that very same year, 445, the architect Callicrates built the third and last "long wall." Nehemias, however, built under the protection of Persia; Pericles, to keep Persia far from his city.

128. The plan and the preparations for work, of course, came to the notice of ever watchful foes (§ 125) who were so sure of themselves and considered the task so difficult that they were at first content to scoff at the project, and at anyone who believed it to be possible. Nor did they fail to intersperse their jests with threats calculated to intimidate the vacillating, and lead them to imitate the example of the wealthy Teqoans (§ 127). They therefore spoke disparagingly, and depicted the whole affair as an insane attempt to rebel against the Great King (Neh. 2:19-20), the age-old strategy used by Megabyzus (§ 17) and perhaps also by Pericles.

The work was soon begun and proceeded with impressive rapidity. The sections were all started at the same time: breaches and gaps were filled up one after another, gates and towers began to appear, entirely new sections of walls were built up from the ground. The visible success attending their efforts was something extraordinary, but was to be expected considering the mental attitude, for the people "was [all] enthusiasm for the work" (3:38 [4:6]). Once more the breath of Yahweh had infused a vigorous life into the bare, dry bones (§ 75).

This energetic beginning was terribly irritating to their enemies. Jokes were cast aside, and more efficacious means to hinder the work were sought. Disdainful superiority did not disappear in the face of the undeniable fact that the wall was being built up, but rather inspired Tobias the Ammonite to utter these typical words: "Of course let them build, poor people! If a fox jumps upon it, he will open a breach in their wall of stones!" (3:35 [4:3].) He was certain, in brief, that even if the wall were completely rebuilt it could all be knocked down, as must have been true in the not too distant past (§§ 107, 122). These words of the oriental sheikh will bring to the mind of the modern historian the fable of Aesop, in which the fox who failed to reach the grapes, leap though he did with might and main, finally consoled himself by concluding that the grapes were probably sour anyway.

The opposition now saw that arrogant words alone would not stop the walls from rising; the times called for action. They furnished arms to bands of the surrounding peoples whom they hoped to introduce into the city, where they would slaughter the workers and destroy everything. This old Bedouin strategy, once employed by the sons of Jacob against the inhabitants of Sichem (Vol. I, § 148), was now to be directed against their descendants. The plan failed, however, because the Jews inhabiting the territories from which the bands were re-

cruited sensed the danger, and with all possible solicitude hastened
to alert Nehemias and the workers of Jerusalem. Hammers and trowels
were laid down, and in their stead the workers took up arms and
waited for the attack. But when the attackers saw that the Jews
were armed and ready for them, they abandoned their plan. The
Jews then returned to their labors, but the threat of future attack did
not allow them to dispense altogether with armed protection. On the
other hand the labors they were engaged in were very heavy, demanding
every able-bodied man.

129. The situation was critical, and the difficulty was overcome only
by the energy and astuteness of Nehemias. He was adamant about the
work being finished as quickly as possible. His own words about the
measures adopted breathe an impassioned urgency: "From that day
[when the attack was frustrated] half of my young men went on
with the work, and the other half was armed with lances, shields, bows
and coats of mail: and the leaders [stood] behind each one of the
houses of Juda who were building the wall. Those who carried burdens
were armed:[2] with one hand they worked and with the other they
carried a sword. And each one of those who did the building had his
sword girded at his side and thus they labored. The trumpeter also
stood at my side; for I had said to the elders and the superintendents
and to the rest of the people: the work is great and extensive and we
are scattered upon the wall far from each other; rally together with
us to the place where the trumpet sounds; our God will fight for us.
Thus we labored on the task, and half of them were armed with a
lance from daybreak until the stars came out. At that same time also
I said to the people: Let every one with his servant pass the night
in Jerusalem, so that [the servants] may serve us as guards during the
night and as workers during the day. Neither I nor my brothers, nor
my servants, nor the guards who followed me, none of us took off
our clothes [at night]; each kept his weapon in his right hand"[3]
(Neh. 4:10–17 [4:16–23]).

The cupbearer who had been accustomed to the delicacies and pomp
of the court of Susa knew also how to bear serious privations. There
can be no doubt that his personal example, even apart from his leadership, inspired the others and helped to raise the wall higher and
higher each day.

The enemy then tried a new method of attack. Since mockery and
later armed attempts had failed, a typically oriental trick, the snare,

---

[2] *Were armed,* following the Septuagint, which reads *ḥamushim*. So also according
to the Septuagint the phrase *who were building the wall* refers to *houses* not to
what comes after.

[3] *In his right hand;* the Hebrew has "the water" which may be mistaken for the
word for "hand."

was attempted. Four times in succession Nehemias was invited to important meetings which were to be held in the valley of Ono, to the northwest of Jerusalem near Jaffa. But he needed no court experience to see through this invitation, and he resolutely refused. In the meantime the wall was almost completed and only the gates remained to be put in place. The adversaries therefore, insisted for a fifth time, and this time Sanballat also sent a letter to Nehemias, informing him in a friendly way of the disquieting talk which was making the rounds about him. It was said among the neighboring peoples that he had rebuilt the walls so that he could rebel against the Great King, and that he had found in Jerusalem some prophets-with-a-price, who preached that he was "king of Juda." This disturbing talk must certainly have reached the ear of the Great King; hence Sanballat, as *peḥah* of Samaria and official of the Great King, desired only to do well by his fellow *peḥah,* Nehemias of Jerusalem, whom he now invited to a meeting, in order to discuss what should be done and how things could be set straight as among good friends.

This persistence of Sanballat and his companions in attempting to draw Nehemias into a meeting outside Jerusalem may seem at first sight to be a very crude move, but in reality, this invitation by those who opposed the energetic restorer was not merely naïve. They knew well that they had sympathizers in the bosom of the community inside the walls of Jerusalem, and hoped that the invitation from the outside would have a corresponding stimulus from within, and would succeed in luring Nehemias from the city. Apart from their kinship with the Jews and other interests which they had in common (§ 123), the repeated accusation that Nehemias was preparing for rebellion and a restoration of the monarchy must have made an impression on some of them, especially in view of recent examples which were adduced as proof (§ 128).

130. The affirmation in Sanballat's letter that there were in Jerusalem prophets who predicted a kingdom of Nehemias may have had a basis in fact. Not that Nehemias actually encouraged them or prompted such predictions; they may have resulted spontaneously from a fanatical nationalistic zeal, which was always found, tinged with religion, in Israel. The vast majority of the community opposed these fanatics and were faithful to the command of Nehemias, but this did not prevent such outbursts from occurring in their midst. Sanballat and his companions naturally made the most of this chance to add to the internal disturbances, bribing other false prophets with cold cash to imitate the regular prophets while taking their cues from those who paid them, so as secretly to undermine the authority of Nehemias. Nehemias himself, in fact (6:10–14), relates

that once when he went into the house of a pseudo prophet, a certain Shema'iah ben-Delaiah, probably in a state of ecstasy (*'asur*, in Neh. 6:10; cf. Vol. I, § 420 ff.), exhorted him to flee with him to the Temple for protection against an attempt on his life, scheduled for the next night. This solicitous oracle was only a trick of the bogus prophet, just as the attempt was a figment of his imagination, and Nehemias, sensing this, refused to take refuge in the Temple. "But I knew [what he was driving at]; and behold, God had not sent him when he had spoken the prophecy in my regard, but Tobias and Sanballat had hired him, that I might be afraid and might do thus [as he had exhorted me] and commit a sin: in this manner I would have acquired among them a bad name, for they planned to discredit me." Nehemias then invoked Yahweh the Israelite to wreak just retaliation on his adversaries, and immediately added as a warning to other pseudo prophets: "Be mindful, my God, of Tobias and Sanballat, and repay them according to these their deeds! And be mindful also of the prophetess No'adiah and of the other prophets who tried to make me afraid!" (Neh. 6:12–14.)

Sanballat and his colleagues, therefore, far from being fools, were well versed in their subversive work; they even tried to utilize in their favor one of the most decisive forces in Israel, prophetism. Of course, what they worked with was a false prophetism, the kind that would sell out Yahweh himself for sicles and minas, a prophetism which had always been the chief obstacle in the path of the genuine prophetical movement (Vol. I, § 424 ff.). It is noteworthy, finally, that a pseudo prophetess, a Deborah in reverse (Vol. I, §§ 308 ff., 420), is also involved.

The above-mentioned letter and scheme were not the only efforts made by the opposition. In a displaced fragment (Neh. 6:17–19, which evidently precedes 6:15–16), Nehemias relates that Tobias conducted a busy correspondence with many of the more eminent men of Juda "because many in Juda were bound by oath to him" (6:18), and that these dared even to speak his praises before Nehemias, while promptly revealing all his plans to Tobias. The "oath" or bond which held these two-faced Jews may be explained in various ways, being traceable in part to financial considerations, but chiefly to family ties. Nehemias, in fact, mentions significantly (6:18) that Tobias was the son-in-law of Shekaniah and that his son had wed the daughter of Meshullam — both certainly Jews — and later on he will add (13:4) that the same Tobias was even related by marriage to the high priest, Eliashib (§ 144).

131. Despite these threats from the outside, despite the co-operation which these threats met with on the inside, despite the economic and social crises which later on were to become intolerable (§ 135) and which no doubt seriously hampered the work, the reconstruction of the walls was completed on the twenty-fifth day of the month of Elul

Southeastern section of Jerusalem, with the Valley of Siloe and the
"Wall of Nehemias."

(end of September), exactly fifty-two days after it had been started
(Neh. 6:15).

The time taken to complete the work may seem little indeed. Yet
with all the energetic resoluteness of Nehemias, the work could not
have been completed in less than two months if they had had to raise
up the walls which had been razed to the ground. This was not the case,
however. It has already been pointed out how Nehemias, in his nocturnal
tour of inspection, found some walls that had been *breached* (§ 126);
it was, therefore, more a question of restoring them. Moreover, the
restoration was facilitated by the fact that the materials needed were
not far from the breaches in the wall; the stones which had been pushed
over were only a few paces distant. While this explains very nicely the
short time needed to complete the work, it also helps to confirm a
conclusion already drawn from other documents (§§ 107, 122), that these
same walls had been destroyed only very recently, just on the point of
being completed, say between 447 and 446, after a long period of
rebuilding. It is out of the question even to think here of the destruction
of Nabuchodonosor over a century and a half before; the materials from
those ruins had been utilized by the repatriates of Zorobabel in the
building of their homes (§ 95) and perhaps also of the Temple.

132. An analysis and comparison of the various texts discloses more details. The perimeter of the walls is described three times: in the inspection trip of Nehemias (§ 126); in the list of the sections into which the work was divided; in the description of the inaugural ceremony, when two groups in procession traveled the entire perimeter, both departing in opposite directions from one point and meeting again at the other extremity of the walls.

It has been noted that in the nocturnal inspection trip, strangely enough, no mention was made of the north sector, whereas the (west) south and east sectors were described more or less in detail. The list of the sectors, however, begins with that very northern part in which the first sector, extending alongside the Temple from the "Sheep Gate" to the "Tower of Hanan'el," was assigned to the high priest Eliashib and his lesser colleagues. The precedence of this northern sector becomes even more interesting from the terminology which the list employs in its regard, and which is different from that employed for the other sectors. Although for the first sectors of the northern part, it is said that the wall was *built* (Neh. 3:1–3), for the other sectors not so far to the north, or in other parts, it is said that it was *restored* (3:4 ff.). The difference in terminology does not seem to be accidental but must have some relation to the omission of a visit to the north during Nehemias' nocturnal inspection trip. Probably the northern part which had always been the most vulnerable of the city (Vol. I, §§ 97, 398) had been leveled to the ground in the destruction wrought by Nabuchodonosor and again in that of 447–446. This total destruction was known to all, and it would have been superfluous to visit it; during his inspection trip, then, Nehemias did not proceed as far as the northern part. When it came time to rebuild he took advantage perhaps of the *tabula rasa* to alter the line of the wall somewhat to meet the demands of the quarter adjacent to it, which was the more recent and therefore called *mishneh*, "second," in Neh. 11:9; Sophon., 1:10; cf. 2 Kings 22:14, and the only direction in which the city could expand (Vol. I, §§ 97, 398, 486). Because of the greater difficulties involved, this section was entrusted to the high priest and his colleagues. The wall of Nehemias here must have followed in general the line of the preceding wall, which was the one Ezechias (Vol. I, § 486) built, but not precisely at every point of the way, for it tended to go wide of the line and enclose more space.

Finally, the entire circumference of the wall is clearly described on the occasion of the ceremonial dedication, but the identification of the various points mentioned leaves the present-day scholar in great perplexity. The two processional groups started from the same point of the wall which was between the "Dung Gate" and the "Tower of the Furnaces" which may have been the "Valley Gate" (§ 133). The first group which walked toward the right made the following itinerary: point of departure, the Dung Gate, Fountain Gate, steps of the "City of David," Water Gate, Temple. The second group which took the opposite direction made the following itinerary: point of departure, Tower of the Furnaces, Large Wall, Ephraim's Gate, Yeshanah's Gate ("Old Gate"?), Fish Gate, Tower of Hanan'el, Tower of Me'ah, Sheep Gate, Gate of the Watch, Temple (Neh. 12:31–40).

The itinerary of the first group is in great part similar to that of Nehemias on his nocturnal tour of inspection (§ 126), passing along the (west) south and east sectors. The itinerary of the second group went through the rest of the area, in the (west) northern sector.

Even though the single places cannot all be identified, this second itinerary is, on the whole, sufficiently clear and beyond dispute. There is more argument over the western sector of the wall from which both groups started; if it was not the Valley Gate it was very close to it. Where was this Valley Gate situated?

133. Since "Valley" (*gai*) alludes without doubt to the Valley of Hinnom, the common opinion is that the gate in question led into this valley, as did the "Dung Gate" (§ 126). Besides, it is evident that the "Valley Gate" was one thousand cubits (about 500 yards) from the "Dung Gate" (Neh. 3:13) and that this last was the gate immediately preceding the "Fountain Gate" (Neh. 2:13–14; 12:31–37). Since the "Fountain" was most likely Gihon (§ 126), the "Dung Gate" must have been to the southwest, toward the confluence of the Tyropoeon with the Valley of Hinnom (Vol. I, § 95); from this point the "Valley Gate" must have been within a radius of not more than 500 yards.

According to the above opinion, the "Valley Gate" should not be located on the higher slope of the western hill near the present Jaffa Gate, which would be farther away than the 1000 cubits so precisely laid down, but rather toward the lower slope of the hill looking out directly upon the Valley of Hinnom.

Against this opinion, however, it has been explained that the words "of the Valley" do not necessarily imply that the gate in question actually overlooked the Valley of Hinnom; it sufficed that the street which ran into the valley came from it. Hence, it was supposed that the said gate was on the flank, not of the Valley of Hinnom, but of the Tyropoeon, which at a certain point had been crossed by the ancient circle of walls extending to the north. The reasons adduced are the ruins of an ancient enclosure which were discovered during recent excavations made to the west of Ophel, and the lack of pre-Machabean material which the same excavations have certified for the western hill. Thus, in the time of Nehemias the circle of walls of Jerusalem had enclosed only Ophel to the south, to the exclusion of the western hill; it then ascended along the Tyropoeon, bearing, higher up, toward the west in the direction of the "Tower of the Furnaces" (present Jaffa Gate), where it met the northern (ancient) wall of the city.

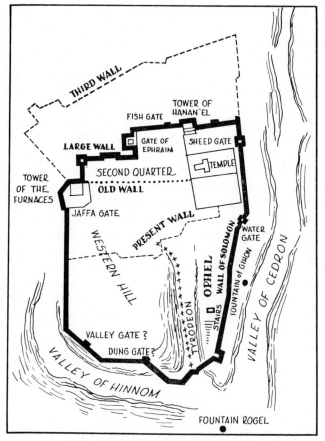

Jerusalem at the time of Nehemias.
(Modern walls also indicated.)

This new opinion, however, does not seem to be justified by archaeological data. The ruins discovered to the west of Ophel most probably belonged to a wall which had formed part of the city from ancient times, when the western hill was added to it. The fact that on this hill no pre-Machabean material was found must be attributed in great apart to the fragmentary and incomplete character of the excavations themselves. An examination of the lower part of the ancient wall girding the western hill leads to the conclusion that it belonged to an earlier period, and there is reason to suppose that in the time of Nehemias this hill formed part of the city.

There is no doubt about the northern line of the walls. On the farther side of the northern (ancient) wall the new or "second" (*mishneh;* § 132) quarter had been added, and this in turn had been enclosed within a new section of wall which, starting from the "Tower of the Furnaces" ascended in zigzag fashion, skirted the northern side of the temple and extended to the Cedron. This was the northern wall which had been almost totally destroyed, and which was "built" with some alteration of line by Nehemias (§ 132).

134. When the structure was finished a dedication festival was celebrated, during which two processional groups walked around half the circumference and met again at the Temple. Even the report of this item (Neh. 12:27–43) is chronologically misplaced in the collection of documents made by the Chronicler (§ 109) and is the subject of additional comment by the redactor.

With the reconstruction of the walls, the desired *gadher* (§ 115) or protective enclosure of the community, was a reality. Still, to insure an efficacious protection it was necessary that at the various gates of the enclosure a regular system of watches be instituted. Nehemias wisely stationed guards at the gates by day, commanding that they be not opened in the morning until the sun was hot, and that they be closed in the evening in the presence of the guards. He appointed as superintendents of the guards and of the whole city Hanani, his brother (§ 124), and Hananiah, head of the *birah* (Neh. 7:2; cf. 2:8), i.e., a military-type section near the Temple on the northern side (7:1–3; cf. § 218).

The ideal of the medieval Benedictine monastery (§ 76), sealed off physically by walls and cloistered from the outside world, was now on the way to realization. Still lacking was a royal prince to serve as a representative to the external world, but Hanani and Hananiah compensated for this by acting as stewards within.

❖ ❖ ❖

135. Thus far, Nehemias had indeed accomplished a great deal by providing a secure or almost secure asylum for the community, but much now remained to be done for its spirit. The ideals of the time of Ezechiel, not only materially but spiritually as well, had still to be achieved.

Two problems demanded an immediate solution. The "holy city" (Neh. 11:1, 18) according to the ideal of Ezechiel was ready, but there was a partial lack of "citizens" on the one hand and a partial lack of "holiness" on the other. After the work was finished, "the city was very wide and large, but the people few in the midst thereof, and the houses were not built" (7:4). In other words there were some houses (§ 95), but too few to fill up the newly enclosed space, and too few certainly to insure the optimum population. The inhabitants were few, as those who had first taken up their dwelling in Jerusalem had, for the most part, moved out again to their properties, or native cities (11:3), probably during the preceding disorders, and because of difficult living conditions (§ 122).

Concerning "holiness," there was a twofold deficiency. Intermarriage with the surrounding foreigners (§ 123) had rendered suspect the Israelite origin of many persons, and a demographic revision of the community was urgent if the nation was to be kept "holy." Furthermore, the economic crisis (§ 131) had reached a critical stage. The drain on the resources of the community for the reconstruction was felt especially by the poorest classes, their patience exhausted by harsh creditors. Thus "there was a great cry of those of the people and of their wives against their fellow Jews." This "great cry" (5:1) may indicate a real insurrection of the poorer classes who had not enough to eat, and saw their own children becoming the slaves of their creditors (§ 122); it may also have been merely a poignant protest designed to attract the attention of the well-intentioned *pehah* to their sad plight. No matter how it was manifested, the "great cry" proved that "holiness" was lacking even in the social relations of the community.

136. Nehemias provided as best he could for the repeopling of the city and for the double deficiency in holiness.

In the first place he examined the lists, which were preserved in the archives of the Temple, for the names of those who had returned with Zorobabel (§ 86), and thus made certain of the Israelite lineage of the members of the community. It is recorded that 642 persons could not prove their lineage, and also that three entire sacerdotal houses did not really belong to the sacerdotal caste (Neh. 7:61–65). With regard to the foreign women who had entered the community by reason of mixed marriages, apparently nothing was done for the time being; it was only later that radical measures were taken against them, after special solemn pledges, necessitated by the particular gravity of the evil, were taken by the people.

The repopulation of the city is reported in Neh. 7:72a+11:1 ff., which form one account into which the data contained in Chapter 7:72b + 8 + 9 + 10 was later anachronistically inserted. The above-mentioned section reads: "The priests, the Levites, the porters, the singers [and part of the people],[4] the *nethinim* and all Israel dwelt in their cities [here is inserted the above-mentioned report], but the leaders of the people dwelt in Jerusalem. Then the rest of the people cast lots: one [lot

---

[4] *And part of the people,* is probably a later addition.

taken] out of ten to dwell in Jerusalem, the holy city, and the other nine [remained] in the [lesser] cities. The people furthermore blessed all those men who willingly offered to dwell in Jerusalem." This immigration, in part obligatory and in part spontaneous, must have considerably augmented the population of the "holy city." Besides the *pehah*, his officials and the "leaders of the people," there now dwelt in the city a greater number of priests, Levites, merchants, workmen, and others who in the past had preferred to live a more pleasant life in the country.

With equal energy and greater tenacity, Nehemias fought to better the economic conditions of the poorer classes. Contrary to the appearances of the report and its position in the arrangement of the documents (Neh. 5 is inserted in the middle of the report on the rebuilding of the walls), the difficulty was not settled simply by an authoritative command nor did it take only a few days. The authoritative command was issued shortly after the work on the walls was completed, rather than during the operations; then Nehemias, moved by the "great cry" of the people, assembled the creditors who were crushing the poor and reproved them bitterly for the way they were treating their fellow countrymen, and made them swear to cancel the debts and the interest due on them (5:1–13). Between promise and fulfillment in a matter touching one's purse, however, there is quite a gap. To make certain that these would not remain empty promises, Nehemias himself set the good example. He himself would be a continual reminder — for twelve years — to those who had pledged themselves. Indeed, Nehemias is careful to report, immediately after mentioning the oath, that for the whole duration of his first mission (twelve years) not only did he not exact from the community the tribute which was his due as *pehah*, but he was very liberal toward it on frequent occasions (5:14 ff.). The economic crisis, therefore, was solved thanks to his persevering generosity which was contagious and produced similar results.

137. Not a little time had passed while these measures were being carried out. The walls had been completed on the twenty-fifth of Elul (§ 131) which was the sixth month (August-September), only three or four days before the seventh month, Tishri (September-October). But the report inserted in the midst of the account of the repopulation of the city (§ 136) contained in chapters 7:72b+8+9+10, treats of events which occurred in the month of Tishri, and precisely of those which occurred on the first and twenty-fourth days of this month. Evidently it cannot be the Tishri of the same year in which the walls were completed, but still another Tishri, as all these innovations could not have been accomplished in less than a week. Hence, the position of this report is anachronistic. If this month is not taken to be the Tishri of a still later year, one may hold that it was the Tishri of the year immediately following, so that an entire year was employed in deciding upon and applying these measures, and on the first day of the following Tishri there was a general convocation. Indeed, the month Tishri began the new year, according to one of the two systems of computation (cf. Lev. 23:24; Num. 29:1–6; Mishna, *Rosh hashshanah*, I, 1; according to the other system it began with the month Nisan).

At the beginning of the year 443, therefore (§ 124; but cf. § 127), or of a later one, there was a general assembly, and on the twenty-fourth of the same month yet another. The two assemblies were related to each other because the first was substantially only a preparation for the second, and between the two fell the seven days of the feast of Tabernacles. The purpose of these two assemblies was the public proclamation of the *Torah* and the renewal of the pact which by means of the *Torah* bound Israel to its God Yahweh.

The first assembly unexpectedly brought to the fore a new personage, *Esdras* (§ 146). Although of sacerdotal lineage, he nevertheless appears here in the character of a "scribe" (§§ 64, 79), and is always so designated in the narrative (Neh. 8:1, 4, 9, 13). His duty was to proclaim the *Torah* (8:1 ff., 18) publicly, and also to be its exegete and catechist (8:13).

The *Torah* read and explained by him on that occasion was the "book of the *Torah*" (8:3), "the book of the *Torah* of Moses" (8:1), the "book of the *Torah* of God" (8:18), the "book of the *Torah* of Yahweh their God" (9:3), all of which leads us conclude that the book in question was of some length. Indeed when it was "opened" solemnly in the presence of all the people (8:5) and the lector began to read, with the help of several others (8:7–8), they read for seven days in succession, and the reading was still continued later on (8:18; 9:3). If this was a new "book," the *Torah* contained in it was not; it was that given by Moses on Sinai (9:13–14). It was the *Torah* which had been despised in the early days of their dwelling in Palestine by the Israelites who "threw it behind their backs" (9:26); it was the *Torah* to which Yahweh later on tried to make them return (9:29); it was the *Torah* which "our kings, our princes, our priests, our fathers did not practise" at any time with fidelity and integrity (9:34). It was, therefore, the *Torah* of Israel's long tradition.

138. A study of the two new elements which made their appearance in the solemn assemblage — the "scribe" and the *Torah* — will help to clarify a few points. It is a matter of record that during a certain period of his life the scribe Esdras was in Babylonia with the exiles there; that he was known as a "scribe learned in the *Torah* of Moses, whom Yahweh the God of Israel had given" (Esdras 7:6); that even the contemporary Great King Artaxerxes recognized him as a "scribe of the *law*[5] of the God of heaven" (Esdras 7:12, 21: Aramaic text); finally, that he came from Babylonia to Jerusalem with that *law* "in his hand," evidently a very definite volume; and he came with the intention of having it faithfully observed (Esdras 7:14, 10). According to this writer's opinion, the arrival from Babylonia here indicated occurred much later than the solemn assemblage held in 398, in the time of Nehemias (§§ 110, 147), but this does not exclude the presence of Esdras forty-five years before at that gathering. The thirty-year-old scribe (Jeremias was perhaps even younger when he began his career as a prophet; Jer. 1:6; Vol. I, §§ 427, 509), who already had a reputation among the doctors of the *Torah* in Babylonia because of his experience in the *law*, could have attracted the attention of Nehemias, who took him along when he departed from Susa — or at least summoned him shortly thereafter to Jerusalem — to help bring about the moral regeneration of the Yahwist community. There is no doubt whatsoever, therefore, that the young scribe and his *Torah* came from Babylonia.

We have already pointed out that in Babylonia many years of loving work had gone into the preparation of a twofold *corpus,* one historical and one juridical, the purpose of which was the collection and preservation of Israel's scattered moral patrimony. It was meant to be a written *digest,* a condensation of the Yahwism of the past, and a guide for the Yahwism of the future. It was also brought out that generations of scribes contributed to this immense work, the authority of which grew as the work progressed and penetrated more and more deeply into the Yahwistic life of the community. More and more it became a substitute for prophetism, now on the wane (§§ 71 ff., 79). If, therefore, a young "scribe" lately come from Babylonia made his appearance at the solemn assembly convoked by Nehemias, bearing a voluminous codex in which was contained the *Torah* of Yahweh and of Moses, and this *Torah* not only summed up the time-honored traditions of Yahwism but was also to be in the future the fundamental law of the Yahwist community, it would seem that the grandiose digest was already completed at that time, and that Esdras had brought a copy of it with him from Babylonia to serve as the Yahwistic foundation of a regenerated Israel.

139. What has been said up to this point will explain the profound wisdom that prompted Nehemias to assemble the people in the month of Tishri. The dynamic cupbearer had left Susa to gird the community of Jerusalem with a *gadher* (§§ 115, 134) of protection, but he was too wise to limit that protection to a material *gadher,* or to think that the

---

[5] The Aramaic text here has *datha,* which is synonymous with the Hebrew *Torah.*

future of the community would be assured merely because it was enclosed by a few feet of stone wall. He was more deeply concerned with the spiritual *gadher,* with the divine breath which alone could recall to life a deserted area full of dry human bones (§ 75). This spiritual element could be nothing else than a "return" to the "old" (§§ 58, 68), and this "old," i.e., the unadulterated tradition of genuine Yahwism, was now ready in Babylonia, condensed in that digest of the *Torah* which the scribes had only just completed. Now that the walls were completed and other more urgent difficulties were being dealt with in a systematic way, Nehemias pressed on to the application of the *Torah.*

First of all, the "Law" was publicly proclaimed (Neh. 8). On the first day of Tishri the Israelites gathered in Jerusalem from their nearby homes, and Esdras read to them the more salient portions of the *Torah.* The reading lasted from morning until noon, but it was not just a simple reading. A dozen other Levites co-operated with Esdras, repeating and perhaps translating it (into Aramaic), explaining, making practical applications and recommendations prompted by the passages which were read slowly, one after the other. The next day another gathering over which Esdras presided was held to consider exegetical and legal questions, and here it was learned that the *Torah* commanded the celebration of the feast of Tabernacles or "Booths." It was agreed that they would observe this prescription, and during the seven days of its duration Esdras continued the public proclamation of the *Torah.*

This method of public proclamation — quite similar to a present-day series of mission sermons — was not new in Israel (cf. Vol. I, §§ 463, 483, etc.), and would continue to be used with modifications. Indeed, this procedure of reading a Hebrew passage of the sacred text, of translating it at once into Aramaic, then explaining and applying it, gave rise, in the ancient synagogues, to the Targum.

The reading of the *Torah* made a profound impression from the very first day. On realizing how lax they had been concerning the venerable prescriptions of ancient Yahwism up to that time, the people cried out in sorrow. This in turn gave way to a desire for the scrupulous observance of the Law and for a more exact knowledge of it. To satisfy such zeal, Esdras spent himself not only on the first two days of the month and during the seven days of the feast of Tabernacles, but also during the intervening days.

During these first twenty-three days of Tishri, Esdras was unquestionably the main figure in the public eye. Although Nehemias was equally responsible for the program he is named only once.[6] It would, however, not be correct, on the basis of the greater prominence given to Esdras

---

[6] Neh. 8:9; for the attempt to suppress his name here, see the footnote to § 111.

here, to conclude that he preceded Nehemias (§ 110 ff.). The young scribe was the center of attraction during this brief period because the occasion required the exercise of his particular function. Nehemias, who had called him, was neither scribe nor priest, and so could not be expected to figure in ceremonies which fell within the competency of the scribe. This is further confirmed by the fact that in the following ceremony, in which the whole Yahwistic community renewed the pact of alliance with Yahweh, Esdras was not mentioned at all (Neh. 9–10: Hebrew text),[7] nor was his name among the signers of the pact. But the name of Nehemias there headed the list of the signers (10:2), for in this act it was not the "scribe" who functioned — it was, instead, the whole nation, with the man who restored it at its head.

After celebrating the feast of Tabernacles from the fifteenth to the twenty-second of Tishri, with an added festive octave day as prescribed (cf. Lev. 23:34, 42; Num. 29:12, 35), another convocation took place on the twenty-fourth of Tishri (Neh. 9–10); it was to be the practical conclusion of all that had transpired from the first of the month onward.

140. After the imposition of a fast and the donning of official insignia of lamentation, the community listened to another reading of the *Torah,* and again publicly confessed its long-standing nonobservance of the prescriptions contained therein. All this was true of the past, but the thoughts of the community and of its dynamic restorer turned chiefly toward the future. Recalling to mind the ancient Yahwistic practices, they proceeded to the renewal of that pact or alliance which bound Israel to Yahweh. This pact had been entered into on Sinai (Vol. I, § 243), had been renewed at intervals (Vol. I, §§ 285, 294, 510), and its written records had from of old been placed within and near the Ark (Vol. I, §§ 253, 274). This time also the document testifying to the pact was set down in writing, as in a regular contract. To make it official, it was signed by the principal priests and Levites and by the more eminent members of the laity, and of these the first signature was that of Nehemias (§ 139).

The signatures preserved from this document do not tell us much. The text itself would have been interesting, but it is missing. Following the signatures is an oath taken by all the people, binding them "to walk in the *Torah* of God, which had been given by Moses, the servant of God" (Neh. 10:30). This information is contained in a tract which owes its origin to the redactor, and which probably resumes at this point the

---

[7] In Neh. 9:6 the Greek text prefixes *And Esdras said.* This is received with great favor by some critics, but it is a begging of the question, being a later addition characteristic of the translator. For that matter, even if this reading were correct, it would prove nothing.

original "Memoirs" of Nehemias (§§ 108, 124). Immediately thereafter the literal text of the "Memoirs" begins again in the first person plural, and some of the specific provisions which come under the terms of the oath are mentioned (10:31 ff.). It is not, therefore, arbitrary to suppose that the text of the written document treated of identical or similar provisions.

An oath was sworn not to contract marriage with foreigners; rigorously to observe the law of the Sabbath and other feasts; not to transact any business on those days with the surrounding peoples; to observe every seventh year as the "sabbatical" year in which all debts would be forgiven; to make an annual contribution of one third of a sicle toward the Temple expenses; to divide by lot the contribution of wood for the holocausts; to bring to the Temple every year the first fruits of the soil and the first-born of animals and men; to give one tenth of the produce of the soil to the Levites who would come to the fields to collect them and who would then in turn give one tenth to the Temple.

141. The first and most important point taken up was that of mixed marriages. As we have seen (§ 123), such marriages were frequent in the community at Jerusalem and must have continued to be so even during the first days of Nehemias. How were they to be judged according to the strict letter of the law? According to the codex discovered during the time of Josias (Vol. I, § 515), marriage with the seven Canaanite nations dwelling in Palestine was strictly forbidden (Deut. 7:1–4; cf. Exod. 34:16; Jos. 23:12); yet in another place, the same codex permitted marriage with foreign women in general although it stipulated that a special ceremonial rite be followed (Deut. 21:10 ff.); by another rule the high priest was excluded from this permission (Lev. 21:14). But were the foreigners living in Palestine in the time of Nehemias included in the first prohibition of *Deuteronomy?* Were they still to be considered as belonging to the seven Canaanite races covered by the prohibition? There were, of course, some zealous Yahwists at that time who maintained that they were (cf. Esdras 9:1), but others less zealous must have answered in the negative and contended that the contrary permission in *Deuteronomy* could be used. The new circumstances and the necessities of daily life, for that matter, had made them easily forget the old code, just as, somewhat later, they were to forget even more easily the solemn oaths sworn in regard to the new (§ 144).

Legally permissible or not, the mixed marriages were certainly harmful to the spiritual compactness of the community, a point which Nehemias had learned only too clearly (§ 130), and the community was easily made to see. In the first fervor of the Yahwistic renewal they solemnly swore to prevent mixed marriages. Their fervor was genuine, but it did not last.

142. Another isolated and late bit of information tells of Nehemias' activity in the field of morals. Toward the middle of the second century B.C. the following statement was made by the Jews of Jerusalem: "The same things[8] are related both in the public Acts [ἀναγραφαῖς] and in the Memoirs [ὑπομνηματισμοῖς] regarding Nehemias: and [it is also related there] that he founded a library and gathered together [ἐπισυνήγαγεν] the books concerning the Kings and Prophets, and those of David and the letters of the Kings concerning the gifts [ἀναθεμάτων]" (2 Mach. 2:13). It may be reasonably doubted that the "Memoirs" cited as the source of this information were the authentic memoirs of the cupbearer of Susa (§§ 108, 124, 140); they are nonetheless deserving of attention, for even if apocryphal, the information they contain is based more or less upon the original memoirs, from which it may have come forth intact. This information is, moreover, recommended by the appeal made to the "public Acts" (very probably the official records [regesti] of the Temple archives [cf. Josephus, *Contr. Apion.*, I, 6–7]) and by the complete agreement between the information given by both.

Here Nehemias appears in the true role of a Yahwistic reformer. Concerned with the literary heritage of the preceding Yahwism, he therefore collected "the books concerning the Kings and Prophets, and those of David" (cf. Vol. I, § 109 ff.), joining them, no doubt, with the fundamental codex which had only recently been brought from Babylonia by Esdras (§ 138), and depositing the whole in some part of the Temple suitably set apart as a "library." Judas Machabeus will take similar action after calamitous times (§ 259). The restorer was also concerned about future Yahwism, and so he deposited in the same library, likewise under zealous custody, "the letters of the Kings concerning the gifts." These "gifts" certainly referred to the Temple of Jerusalem, and the "letters" were the decrees issuing on various occasions from the Great Kings of Persia in favor of the Temple and the community in general (§§ 85, 99, 104, 124). Since such documents were precious guarantees for future Yahwism, the shrewd restorer, accustomed to the bureaucratic procedure of the Persian court, prudently put them in a safe place. There is certainly a most remarkable agreement between the information from the second century B.C. and the actual facts of the fifth century B.C.

✿ ✿ ✿

143. The first mission of Nehemias was coextensive with all those developments (of uncertain chronological order) which attended the hasty reconstruction of the walls, and lasted twelve years, from the twentieth

---

[8] That is, the report concerning the miraculous origin of the fire in the rebuilt temple (2 Mach. 1:20 ff.).

to the thirty-second year of Artaxerxes I, from 445 to 433 B.C. (Neh. 5:14, 13:6; § 110). In 433 Nehemias returned to Susa. It is not at all necessary to suppose that his enemies' underhanded dealings had lessened his esteem in the eyes of the Great King, so that he considered it opportune to present himself again at court to regain his lost favor. From what followed, it appears that his favor had not diminished; in fact, the twelve-year absence of the trusted cupbearer can hardly be explained if the kindly attitude of the Great King had changed.

Even though physically present in Susa, however, the heart of the great patriot remained in Jerusalem. In view of the many contacts and correspondence which the Jews of Babylonia had with the repatriates, there can be little doubt that Nehemias was accurately informed about events in Jerusalem, and that he followed with an affectionate anxiety the fortunes of the institutions which had cost him so many struggles and sacrifices. There came a time when the information was so alarming that it seemed all his work was endangered. He could contain himself no longer, and having again obtained permission from his benevolent Great King, hurried back to Jerusalem. This second mission is to be put sometime after his return to court (433), and not much before the death of Artaxerxes I (424 B.C.).

When he arrived at Jerusalem, Nehemias found that of the two *gadher* rebuilt by him (§ 139), the material one was still intact, but large and dangerous breaches had been opened in the spiritual one. It will be recalled that not many years before, a pact of alliance between the community and Yahweh had been solemnly renewed, and that certain very definite pledges had been sworn to, chief among which were the prohibition of mixed marriages, the observance of the Sabbath, and the support of the liturgical services of the Temple. But the memory of the pledges, together with the solemn oaths, had begun to fade after the departure of Nehemias for Susa.

144. The old adversary Tobias (§ 125) had not given up the idea of keeping a finger in the affairs of this sealed-off community. The Temple of Jerusalem — like other sacred places of antiquity (§§ 40, 44) — served as a place of deposit of large quantities of money and merchandise, and because of this made a fine "market place" for business affairs (cf. Mk. 11:15; Jn. 2:14). On the other hand, banking and commerce will crop up again as an old tradition of the Tobias family (§ 218 ff.); if Tobias so tenaciously opposed Nehemias' reforms against foreigners, he was certainly in part prompted to do so by his realization that these spelled a loss to his commercial interests. With the departure of the intransigent reformer, Tobias returned to the attack, and had succeeded in obtaining a foothold within the Temple itself. His obliging intermediary in this matter was the high priest himself, Eliashib, related

to Tobias by marriage (Neh. 13:4; § 130). This relative had given him
the use of a considerable space in the sacred enclosure which was supposed to be used for Temple goods. The bank of the Tobiads, with central headquarters in Ammon, had established a Jerusalem branch! The
whole affair shows Eliashib, so zealous a worker in the reconstruction
of the walls (§ 132; Neh. 3:1) to have been a double-dealer, serving
two masters. It also unveils the mutual support which the big money
man and his opportunist relative gave to each other. Nehemias' intransigence was fully justified by the existing situation.

This scandal in high places would hardly have been possible had the
bulk of the people remained faithful to their oaths; as it was, it was an
unfortunate public example of the general decadence which had occurred
within a few years. Tobias set himself up in the Temple, but many
Levites and other ministers who should have been there to render their
services retired to their homes in the country. Their unwillingness to
stay near the Temple was not altogether without reason, for it followed
the very significant decision taken by the contributors to the Temple
no longer to pay their tithes. Sabbath observance had fallen to an
equally low level. With his own eyes Nehemias saw, in Jerusalem and its
environs, people working on their farms, selling, buying fish brought in
by the mariners of Tyre, and similar profanations of the holy day. The
thorny problem of mixed marriages had become even worse; the Jews
had taken to wife not only Moabite and Ammonite women — understandable in view of the nationality of Sanballat and Tobias (§ 125) —
but also Philistine women from Asdod. In fact the new style
seemed to favor Asdod, for half of the children born of such
unions "spoke the language of Asdod and could not talk the
Jews' language" (Neh. 13:24). This is all the more strange, as the
differences between the two languages could not have been very great;
they were most likely different dialects. If children born and reared in
a Jewish environment did not use the Jewish language, it was probably
an intentional state of affairs, especially in the Orient where the most
ordinary street urchin can generally get along in five or six different
languages. The offspring of this hybrid Judaism, then, knew the parent
tongue, but under the influence of Philistine mothers, despised it and
refused to use it.

145. Other abuses were abolished by specific commands of Nehemias,
given with his usual resoluteness. It was due to him that the furnishings of Tobias' bank were cleared out and the Temple goods
restored to their rightful place. He summoned the Levites back to
service, reimposed the obligation of tithes, forbade the opening of
the gates of the city during the Sabbath rest, during which time foreign
merchants were not allowed to come near the walls. He dealt with those

who had married foreign women as each case required: some he cursed, some he had beaten, from some he cut off the hair, and he made all swear that neither they nor their children would contract such marriages in the future. Among the guilty was an unnamed son of the high priest Joiada ben-Eliashib,[9] who followed the example of his grandfather in his relations with foreigners, and had married one of Sanballat's daughters. Nehemias merely says: "I drove him away from me" (13:28; § 155).

With this account of the cleansing of the field he had sown, the personal "Memoirs" of Nehemias, such as they are, come to an end. Nothing more is known about this remarkable man. His last words were: "Ah, remember me favorably, O my God!" (13:31), and with this admirable summary of his whole life, he disappears from the pages of history.

ESDRAS

146. Esdras, who had proclaimed and interpreted the *Torah* (§ 138) during the first mission of Nehemias, does not appear at all during his second visit. It may be supposed that he returned to Babylonia with Nehemias at the conclusion of the first mission (§ 143), and that he did not attend him on the second, continuing his activities as "scribe" amid the doctors of the law in Babylonia instead. There he remained, according to the hypothesis preferred by this writer (§ 110), until the time of Artaxerxes II. Thus the youth who in his thirties had been the coadjutor of Nehemias (§ 138) was now an old man of about

---

[9] It may be well to point out here that some modern students are in error in thinking that during the second mission of Nehemias the high priest was still Eliashib. Their reasons are that Neh. 13:4 reports how Eliashib granted to Tobias the aforementioned storeroom in the Temple and that in 13:28 these words occur: *and among the sons of Joiada, son of Eliashib, the high priest, (there was only one) the son-in-law of Sanballat the Horonite.* Even aside from the old age which would have to be assigned to Eliashib, whose married grandson (son of his son) Nehemias chased away, the arguments are inconclusive. The episode alluded to in 13:4 is not said to have occurred during but *before* the second mission, for the verse begins with the words: *before this,* and in verse 6, Nehemias himself repeats: *and during all this I was not in Jerusalem.* Moreover, they err in the interpretation of the reference (13:28). In the phrase, *Joiada son of Eliashib, the high priest,* the words *the high priest* do not refer to Eliashib but to Joiada. This could not be put any differently because in Hebrew *Joiada ben-Eliashib* is all one appellative, corresponding to our name and surname. Both Eliashib and Joiada occupied that office, but here it is attributed to the one actually holding it. One may say, therefore (cf. § 121), that Eliashib had been high priest until shortly after the end of the first mission of Nehemias, that is, around 432, and shortly before he died had granted Tobias his storeroom in the Temple. His son Joiada, succeeding him in office, was the high priest during the second mission of Nehemias.

seventy-five. It is admitted by the followers of the various opinions that the behavior of Esdras during his organization of affairs at Jerusalem "shows signs of senility." His scribal authority had, of course, grown not only among his fellow countrymen but also among the Persians. The prestige which Nehemias had gained in his office of cupbearer to the king was surpassed by that which, at a certain point, was attained by Esdras, the priest and scribe, one of the most illustrious doctors of the *Torah* of Moses, the greatest exponent of Hebrew scholarship in Babylonia. Such a man, advanced in years, must have appeared to the Persians as the natural representative of his fellow countrymen remaining in Babylonia. (Cf. special note on this paragraph, p. 464.)

It is important, therefore, to keep in mind the lively interest with which the ardent Yahwists of Babylonia followed the happenings in Palestine (§§ 62, 98, 120, 124). It will explain the missions both of Nehemias and of Esdras, the old man. If, shortly after the return of Nehemias to Susa, disquieting news began to arrive from Jerusalem, news which decided him to undertake his second mission (§ 143), it may be argued that once he had forever disappeared from the scene, similar news would begin to filter back to Babylonia. The conditions in which the aged Esdras found the community of Jerusalem show that the Jews, a stiff-necked and uncircumcised people at heart, inexorably succumbed to a numbness of soul after a brief blaze of fervor (§ 141).

Such news reached the circles of ardent Yahwists in Babylonia, not a few of whom at that time must have occupied high offices and enjoyed great influence. They decided upon action. Nehemias' work would have to be repeated. The Yahwistic spirit would have to be transfused once again from Babylonia to Jerusalem; another caravan of proven quality led by a person with ample civil powers and unquestioned moral authority — one who would be, in short, another Nehemias — was needed. Only in this manner could the fire beneath the ashes, periodically in danger of dying out, be again revived (§§ 95, 123).

Esdras was the man for the job, especially since he had instructed the same community when he was a youth. His advanced age was not an insurmountable obstacle; they could take special care of him. For that matter, he was not the only old man to have labored for Yahweh, and his gray hairs might help bring about greater results. The Great King probably knew of this representative of Babylonian Judaism, but even if he had not, influential fellow countrymen at court exerted themselves on his behalf, and spoke to the Great King about him,

Drachma of Artaxerxes II.

of the timeliness of his mission to Palestine, of the advantages of allowing him to depart with his fellow countrymen, and of giving him ample powers. What had been obtained from Artaxerxes I by his cupbearer alone was this time obtained with perhaps equal facility from Artaxerxes II by the many powerful Jews of Babylonia, accustomed by now to receive from Yahweh "mercy in the sight of the kings of Persia" (Esdras 9:9). These benevolent *kings of Persia* had been the following: first, Cyrus (§ 85), then Darius I (§ 99), then Artaxerxes I (§ 124); now it was the turn of Artaxerxes II.

147. In the seventh year of the reign of Artaxerxes II, that is, in 398 B.C. (§§ 110, 138), the Great King issued a decree with the following heading: "Artaxerxes, King of Kings, to Esdras the priest, scribe of the law of the God of Heaven: greetings"; the original Aramaic text is preserved in Esdras 7:12-26. The preceding decrees of Cyrus and Darius I (§§ 85, 99) had been favorable; this one was warmly sympathetic. Esdras could depart for Jerusalem with as many fellow countrymen as he wished; the purpose of his mission was to "investigate in Juda and Jerusalem concerning [the observance of] the law which is in your hand" (Esdras 7:14; cf. § 138); let him bring to the Temple of Jerusalem the offerings donated by the Great King and the Jews who were his subjects; let him take whatever else was necessary for him from the stores of the satrapy of Abar-Nahara (§§ 13, 99, 121, 124, 159), up to one hundred talents of gold and one hundred large measures of various goods. Besides, he and all the other servants of the Temple were to be exempt from all tribute; he was to have the power to choose as his coadjutors and subordinates certain jurists who would at the same time teach the law and also judge according to it; whoever did not observe that Law and the law of the King would meet with punishments ranging from fines to death.

Fortified with these broad powers, Esdras gathered around him all who were willing to follow him to the homeland. The journey began on the twelfth of Nisan (March-April) of 398. The caravan consisted of about 1800 men, 250 of whom were servants of the Temple. Counting women and children, the whole group numbered about 8000 or 9000 persons. Of greatest importance was the money which the repatriates brought with them (§ 61), money furnished in part by the Persians, but especially by the rich Jews of Babylonia. The journey lasted about 110 days and the caravan arrived at Jerusalem the first day of the month of Ab (July-August) of the same year. The fourth day after its arrival the precious offerings brought from Babylonia were presented to the Temple.

148. The activity of Esdras was necessarily brief on account of his age, but it must have been both intense and varied. There is no

indication that he occupied himself with rebuilding the walls of the
city, with repopulating it, or with anything of a similar nature, for all
those problems seemed to have been settled previously (§§ 110, 114 ff.).
Esdras' activity is explicitly described only in one case: the old yet
ever new problem of mixed marriages.

Shortly after his arrival in Jerusalem, it was reported to him that
foreign women had entered the community as wives, that "the holy seed
had been mingled with the peoples of the lands" (Esdras 9:2), and that
the primary offenders in this regard were the princes and the more eminent of the people. At this news, Esdras, an old man and of a different
temper from Nehemias, did not rain blows on the guilty, or cut off
their hair; instead, he assumed the desolate demeanor of a Hebrew
smitten by the worst possible misfortune, counting on the effect his
venerable age would produce in this sad state. "I rent asunder my coat
and mantle, I tore the hair from my head and beard, and I sat down
appalled" (9:3). The people gathered about him and he remained in
that attitude until evening. He then arose and, with torn and disheveled
garments, made his way to the Temple, where he knelt down, raised his
hands to heaven and prayed to Yahweh, confessing this public transgres-
sion. He addressed God in a loud voice also directed, of course, at the
curious and pitying crowd which had gathered. In accordance with the
Semitic mentality, the crowd was moved with pity at the sight of this old
man who, although elevated to the highest peak of the entire nation, now
presented such a pitiable sight. The people wept at his words, their
hearts were softened by his reproaches, and they repented, experiencing
a speedy and fervent change of heart.

As they were sitting down, someone in the crowd raised the question
of the foreign wives, and all, beginning with the guilty priests and
Levites, swore to put them away, permitting children to go with their
mothers. To put the oath into practice, for Nehemias' experience had
taught them a lesson (§§ 135, 141, 144), a public meeting was scheduled
in Jerusalem within three days, and it was to be attended by all the
repatriates. Those who did not come would suffer the confiscation of
their property and would be expelled from the community. On the
appointed day the meeting was held.

It was the twentieth day of the month of Kisleu (November-Decem-
ber), which is the rainy season in Jerusalem, when "all the men of
Juda and of Benjamin were gathered together . . . in the street of the
Temple of God, trembling because of the trouble and the rain" (10:9).
The "trouble" was, of course, their sense of guilt over their past sins.
Esdras, who had awakened their conscience, presided over the meeting.
The people acknowledged their fault before him, and the remedy which
inevitably had to be applied. And yet there were practical difficulties

involved in dismissing all at once, and during so inclement a season, large groups of women and children who had long journeys to make. "The people are many, it is the rainy season, and we cannot stand outside, and this is not the task of a day or two, for many of us have sinned in this matter" (10:13). There was nothing else to do but to set up a commission, as is customary in all meetings of this kind. The commission was decided upon, and Esdras was made its president. It functioned for three months, during which time the mixed marriages were examined case by case, and the foreign wives sent to their respective countries. Thus the racial "sanctity" of the community (§ 135) was assured.

149. As with Nehemias (§ 145), so too we lack information regarding the death of Esdras. The figure of the great "scribe," however, provided a basis for later amplifications which developed the theme of his lifework. Thus he became the head of the "Great Synagogue," which was to be the true reorganizer of postexilic Yahwism, and the zealous custodian and restorer of Sacred Scripture. He is said to have miraculously dictated ninety-four (Vulgate: 204) sacred books; twenty-four of which were for common use and formed the three parts of the Canon (Vol. I, § 109 ff.), the other seventy being a treasure house of "apocryphal" or recondite wisdom (4 Esdras 14:18–47). He is looked upon as the principal source of all those oral prescriptions which, in the later law, acquired an authority equal to and greater than the *Torah* of Moses (cf. Mk. 7:8 ff.; Mt. 15:3 ff.). There are other exaggerations of this kind.

That such portraits of the great scribe, widely transmitted as they were from rabbinical to Christian tradition, had no historical foundation, was recognized even in ancient times especially by St. Jerome, who stigmatized the contents of *4 Esdras* as "dreams" (*Ad Domnion. et Rogat. in Esdr. et Nehem. Praef.*). The element of truth underlying all these elaborations is, in all likelihood, the fact that Esdras, like Nehemias before him, spent himself while in Jerusalem in collecting, preserving, and injecting ever greater order into the precious deposit of Yahwistic writings (§ 142). It is impossible to determine, however, just how great a part he personally took in this project (§ 156 ff.).

"IN GURGITE VASTO"

So on the deep and open sea I set
Forth, with a single ship and that small band
Of comrades that had never left me yet.
Inferno, 26, 100–102

PERIOD OF UNCERTAINTY AND MYSTERY

150. Once he has explored the period of Nehemias and Esdras the modern historian must again launch out into the deep. Before him there lies no voyage through well-charted chains of islands (§ 103), but rather a vast expanse of the open sea, offering only rare ports of call. Our knowledge of the period from Artaxerxes II up to the second century B.C., except for a few isolated facts which constitute what Cicero called a *solivaga cognitio*, is a complete blank.

Does so profound and prolonged a silence result only from the ravages which time has wrought upon all documentary evidence? Hardly. That some of the records should disappear, and others be fused, regardless of chronological considerations, with preceding documents, is of course very probable, but it is also likely that simply nothing occurred during this period which merited being handed down, and the life of the community of Jerusalem settled down to a methodical routine, only rarely disturbed by an internal event deserving of note, and even more rarely by any extraordinary development. The ancient ideal of the medieval monastery (§ 134) had been sufficiently realized; the twofold material and spiritual *gadher* (§ 139) with which Nehemias and Esdras had girded the community had worked out rather well, and the Jewish community had become, in fact, a "separated" people. Later on the "separated ones" (*perushim*, "Pharisees") would form a special faction in the very heart of the community, but from the time of Esdras on, it was the entire community which was separated from everything that did not pertain to Judaism.

No political problems arose to disturb them. The Achaemenids had given repeated proofs of their benevolence (§ 146), it being to their own interests to keep peaceful and loyal that singular people located on the edge of the empire. In practice, the Jews had only to be careful not to get into difficulty with the *pehah;* the rest was taken care of by the high priest and the ancients (§§ 64, 99, 121).

151. Some disturbances from without there must have been, however. The uprising of the satraps under Artaxerxes II, together with the revolt of Egypt (§§ 19–20), might very well have had repercussions in the Jewish territory which was directly involved in the matter, but nothing of the sort happened. Slightly more is known about the uprisings of the satraps and of Egypt under Artaxerxes III Ochus (§ 21). In this instance the mere possibility finds some confirmation in a report which though of later date, need not be rejected for that reason. Eusebius (*Chron.,* II, ad annum Abrahae, 1657, in Migne, *P.G.*, 19, col. 486), confirmed and clarified by George Sincellus (ed. Dindorf, Bonn, 1829, I, 486; he also appeals to "many Greek Historians"), and by Orosius (*Histor.*, III, 7), relates that Artaxerxes Ochus, on the occasion of his expedition into Egypt, had deported a goodly number of Jews from Palestine to Hyrcania, on the banks of the Caspian. This deportation was certainly punitive in nature, and one naturally thinks that a number of Jews had tired of the quiet life in Jerusalem, had entertained thoughts of a nationalistico-monarchic restoration, and had joined in the general revolt against Persia which occurred around 351 in lands bordering on their country. Once the Persian monarch had regained the upper hand over the rebels, he took his revenge by deporting them. It is also probable that some traces of this campaign of Ochus are preserved in the book of *Judith*, which mentions both Holofernes, who, according to Diodorus Siculus (XXXI, 19, 2–3), fought with the Persian army against Egypt, and the eunuch Bagoas (Judith 12:11, 13, etc., Greek text), the subordinate leader and Ochus' future poisoner (cf. § 152, footnote).

The information given by Solinus (*Memorabil.*, 35, 4; ed. Mommsen, Berlin, 1864), according to which Jerusalem was replaced as the Jewish capital by Jericho (*successit Hierichus: et haec desivit, Artaxerxis bello subacta*), may possibly be connected with this episode, but no other notice states that Jericho became the capital only to be destroyed in the Persian period, nor is it clear to which of the three Artaxerxes Solinus makes reference. A suspicion arises that the two proper names, Jericho and Artaxerxes, have not been transmitted exactly. At any rate, so isolated and meager a notice can support only hypothetical conclusions.

It is sufficiently probable, however, that the last days of the Persian domination, especially under the cruel Artaxerxes Ochus, were grim ones for the Jews of Palestine. The hope of a liberator who would make the Achaemenids suffer what they inflicted upon the Chaldeans may well have grown, and when Alexander the Great put in his unexpected appearance, and showed such extraordinary strength, many must have thought once again of the benevolent Cyrus (§ 80).

152. So much for external disturbances. Concerning the internal

life of the community, Josephus records a grave incident. In
the time of the [ἄλλου] 'Αρταξέρξου, that is, Artaxerxes II (§ 118), the
high priest in Jerusalem was a certain John, that is, Johanan (§ 118),
and the captain or *strategos* of Artaxerxes was named Bagoas. Johanan's
brother Jesus (Joshua) was very friendly with Bagoas, and perhaps
because of this friendship he intended to supplant his brother in the
office of high priest. Relations between the two brothers must have been
very strained. One day as they were arguing in the Temple itself, the
high priest slew the ambitious Jesus, a ghastly fratricide never before
committed by a high priest in such a place; Bagoas seized this chance
to intervene, and when someone tried to prevent him from entering
the Temple because he was not a Jew, he asked: "Am I not a better man
than one who has committed murder in the Temple?" and went on in.
For each of the two lambs offered daily in holocaust, the year around,
he imposed a tax of fifty drachmas; this went on for seven years, and
probably was not the only punishment inflicted (*Antiquities*, XI, 7, 1).

In the past, this episode was placed in the time of Artaxerxes III
Ochus whose *strategos* was known to be the eunuch Bagoas (§§ 21–22,
151). Josephus was thought to have made a chronological error, as he so
often does, and to have reported for the times of Artaxerxes II an incident
which had happened under Artaxerxes III. The papyri of Elephantine,
however, have removed all doubt on this point and have proved
Josephus right; the fratricide occurred under Artaxerxes II, since it is
established by the papyri (§ 172) that under Darius II, around 410, the
high priest Jehohanan and the governor Bagoas were contemporaries in
Jerusalem. Evidently, the latter was a predecessor, bearing the same
name,[1] of the *strategos* of Artaxerxes III, as the high priest Jehohanan
was the Johanan, the contemporary of Esdras, in 398 (§§ 118, 121). The
fratricide must have occurred well along in the reign of Artaxerxes
II; there is ample time for it, as both the reign of Artaxerxes II
(405 [404]–358) and the pontificate of Johanan were very long, and
Jaddua the son of Johanan (Neh. 12:10–11) was still the high priest
in 332 under Alexander the Great (*Antiquities*, XI, 7, 2; 8, 2 ff.; §§ 24,
215). On the other hand, to suppose that the fratricide occurred shortly
after the reform of Esdras does not seem to fit in with the state of mind
which the reform had brought about among all classes, especially
among the priests. It is usually supposed that Johanan and Jaddua had

---

[1] The name *Bagoas* (*Bagohi*) was apparently frequently borne by high officials
of the court who were, ordinarily, eunuchs; in fact, it is synonymous with "eunuch"
in the following passage of Pliny who says, speaking of various species of psalms,
that "*Clarissimae omnium, quas regias appellavere ob honorem, quoniam regibus
tantum Persidis servarentur, Babylone natae uno in horto Bagou* [*var.*: Bagoo, Baguo,
Bagoi]; *ita vocant spadones, qui apud eos etiam regnavere*" (*Natur. Hist.*, XIII, 41).
There is a similar synonymous use of the word in Ovid, *Amores*, II, 2, 1.

each pontificated about forty years, and that the son succeeded the father around 370; the fratricide then may have taken place about 380 B.C.

153. The extreme gravity of the deed is evident, but this does not justify the drawing of any undue conclusions. Esdras had completed his reform twenty years before, and behold, the spiritual citadel of Yahwism, that very Temple which was the realization of Ezechiel's dreams, was now defiled by the murder of a brother, by the supreme head of Yahwism.

Is this misdeed an accurate index of the spiritual level of the community? There is no evidence to support such an indictment. This merely personal affair between two brothers, brought on by the ambition of the scheming Jesus and by the violence of the irascible Johanan, was one in which the community had no part. One man could be ambitious and another violent without reflecting the spiritual state of the community. The incident does, however, reflect friction existing between the two heads of the community, the *peḥah* and the high priest (§ 121), the predominance of the former and the final subordination of the latter.

154. Josephus reports still another dispute which concerned the family of the high priest. The substance of the account is as follows. Upon Johanan's death, his son Jaddua succeeded him as high priest. Jaddua's brother Manasses was a priest also, and to him a certain Sanaballat, a man of Cuthean origin sent by Darius, "the last king," as satrap to Samaria, gave his own daughter Nicaso as wife. Sanaballat had arranged the marriage in order to win the favor of the Jews of Jerusalem, but his plan miscarried. The more eminent members of the community and Jaddua himself disapproved of the marriage of Manasses with a foreign woman, and demanded that he either send her away or renounce his sacerdotal functions. Manasses, deeply attached both to his wife and to his priesthood, consulted with his father-in-law Sanaballat, who promised him that he would not only help him preserve his priesthood without his having to give up his wife, but he would also make him high priest, and would build a temple for him on Mount Gerizim equal to that of Jerusalem; he also promised to obtain a decree of authorization from Darius himself. Meanwhile, many other priests of Jerusalem, likewise involved in marriages with foreign women, took refuge with Manasses, thus swelling the ranks of schismatic priests from Jerusalem. However, Darius was defeated by Alexander the Great at Issus in Cilicia. Sanaballat thereupon withdrew his obedience from Darius and humbly made his obeisance to Alexander, who received him with favor and granted him permission to build the projected temple on Gerizim. The temple, indeed, was quickly built, Manasses became its high priest, and Sanaballat died soon after (*Antiquities*, XI, 7, 2: 8, 1-4).

155. At first glance, this account contains items which are undoubtedly historical, but also an amazing chronological error. Nehemias had previously reported that he had expelled the son of the high priest Joiada ben-Eliashib for having married a daughter of Sanballat (§ 145), but he did not name him nor say what happened to him afterward. But as he was called the son of Joiada ben-Eliashib, he was surely the brother of Johanan, son and successor of Joiada in the office of high priest (§§ 121, 145, footnote). Furthermore, the incident occurred during the second mission of Nehemias, and therefore under Artaxerxes I, between 433 and 424 B.C. (§ 143).

That the account of Josephus refers to the same incident cannot be reasonably questioned. The identity of the deed in itself, its circumstances, the name of Sanaballat — Sanballat, etc., permit no hesitation on this point. But Josephus places the incident a hundred years later in the reign of the "last king" Darius, that is, Darius III (335–330) and his conqueror Alexander the Great. This being the case, it will not be a surprise to find that the Manasses of Josephus, who should correspond to the unnamed victim of Nehemias, is no longer the brother of the high priest Johanan, but his son, and the brother of Jaddua was the son and successor of Johanan; nor will it be any greater surprise to find that Sanballat who had been the *pehah* of Samaria during the first mission of Nehemias in 445 (§ 125) is still the governor of Samaria more than a hundred years later (to suppose that there were two successive Sanballats is a desperate conjecture which would lead to a repetition of the personage of the priest, his son-in-law, the incident of the latter's expulsion, etc.).

Between the divergent reports of Nehemias and Josephus — or better, between the two chronologies — the one given by Nehemias, a contemporary, is obviously to be preferred.

Josephus' account may, however, contain enough truth to have given rise to the anachronism. The Pharisee historian wanted to explain in his account the origin of the schismatic temple built by the hated Samaritans on Gerizim, and so he repeated the opinion then being circulated in orthodox Jewish circles, and which was perhaps also written down in some polemic work against the Samaritans (§§ 161, 164). This common opinion could not have erred in regard to the period during which the temple was established, namely the time of Alexander the Great (§ 162); it must have also preserved an exact record of actual conditions, for it attributed the initiative of the foundation to the priests who fled from Jerusalem and were protected by the authority of Samaria. The anachronism begins when, in order to harmonize these incidents with the biblical narrative, they are identified with the history of Nehemias, which in fact did offer some points of resemblance.

156. Aside from these isolated incidents we know nothing definite about this period. But there is no doubt that in the depths of the sea of ignorance over which we chart our course there was unfolding a particular kind of activity, some of whose results we see rising sporadically to the surface.

The community of Jerusalem had always kept close contact with fellow countrymen in Babylonia, from whom it received moral and material aid. As time went on, the circles devoted to the *Torah*, which formed the seedbed of Yahwism, must have in part been transferred to Palestine. A particularly clear proof of this was the mission of Esdras, which was planned and organized by these circles, and his caravan was largely made up of their numbers (§ 146).

The activity of these circles in gathering and saving the ancient national patrimony was not exhausted by the completion of the twofold *corpus*, the *historical* and *juridical*, now harmonized with and incorporated into the official *digest* (§ 79). This grandiose digest had been, indeed, the most urgent task at hand, for, derived from ancient Yahwism, it was the indispensable foundation for the Yahwism of the future. Besides this, tradition had also transmitted other material. The material securely stored in the digest was principally historical and juridical, but ancient "prophetic," "lyrical," and "sapiential" material was also in circulation. Was all this material, bound up with the history of Yahwism in the past and so full of salutary admonitions for the Yahwism of the future, to be passed by or possibly be allowed to be lost? Not so. The *Torah* or *digest* would remain first in importance, exerting the highest authority, but the "prophetic," "lyric," or "sapiential" writings of ancient Yahwism, of subordinate and subsidiary authority, might very well have enjoyed a secondary importance.

157. Thus editorial attention was extended to these writings both in Babylonia and in Palestine-Egypt. Wherever a fragment of the ancient patrimony of Israel came to light, there also a saving scribe might come to gather it up and put it in a safe place. When he did not appear the fragment usually was lost, for of that patrimony there has come down to us only what passed through the hands of the scribe, and what was incorporated into the Canon was put there only because it was recognized as inspired by God.

This eminently preservative and conservative labor extended over entire generations, beyond the Persian and well into the Greek era. Work on the *Torah* had been slow too.

To the writings of more ancient prophetism there were now added those of the last representatives of the Yahwistic charism. It mattered little whether these appeared in Babylonia during the exile, as Ezechiel (§ 65 ff.), or in Palestine after the repatriation, as Aggeus, Zacharias

(§ 97), and Malachias (§§ 122, 123). The charism was in decline, and had at one time entirely disappeared. The scribe had more and more taken the place of the prophet (§§ 64, 79), and it was he who saved the literary heritage of known or unknown authors, regrouping it according to criteria partly chronological and in part dictated by other exigencies. It was thus he formed the prophetical *corpus*. When it was admitted to the Canon, the new *corpus* was assigned to its second part (Nebhi'im), and of this it formed the second section called the "Later Prophets" (Vol. I, § 109 ff.).

158. Besides the prophet, ancient Israel had also its poets and sages, but, unlike the prophets, these two classes had not disappeared in the period now under consideration, but still flourished. Ancient collections of national "lyrics" (Vol. I, §§ 287, 309), liturgical songs for use in the Temple, more authoritative and widely used individual compositions, various repertoires of "sapiential" aphorisms which were in use since ancient times (Vol. I, §§ 401, 484), were also sought out. Various elements were selected according to special standards, and from them was formed a core to which other lyrical and sapiential compositions posterior to the exile were gradually added. From this new collection there resulted another *corpus* which, when admitted to the Canon, formed its third part, under the general title of *Kethubhim* or "Writings" (Vol. I, § 109). It was to be expected that this work would take longer to form than the prophetical *corpus*, which had stopped growing with the cessation of prophetism. The men who gathered the "Writings" had to reckon with materials to which the poets and the wise men were continually making new contributions, for they were flourishing (especially the sages) as never before.

The third *corpus*, the "Writings," is characterized by something peculiarly its own. As the material for it was gathered simultaneously in the community of Babylonia-Palestine, and in the community in Egypt which had emigrated from Palestine, there resulted a great difference in the size of the collections emanating from the two regions. The *corpus* handed down to us by the Palestinian scribes is much more limited, and does not include certain lengthy works for which we are indebted to the Egyptian scribes. These other "books" were sometimes written originally in Greek. It is evident that the collectors of the two regions employed a different criterion of judgment in this matter.

For further information we must now leave Jerusalem and go in search of Israel in other lands.

THE SAMARITANS

159. The origin of this special race of Palestine, half Israelite and half foreign, practically idolatrous yet claiming to be Yahwistic, has been already dealt with (Vol. I, § 457). The tenuous bonds still linking the kingdom of Juda to that race, the many attempts made by Juda before the exile to annex it again to itself (Vol. I, §§ 479, 482–483, 505, 517), the attempts made by the Samaritans after the exile to enter the spiritual orbit of the Yahwistic community of Jerusalem and the hatred resulting from their repeated rebuffs, have also been touched upon.

Up to this moment, however, there had existed between the two an hereditary aversion, a political antagonism, a religious alienation, which were all consequences of the ancient relations between the kingdoms of Israel and Juda. These had not yet added up to a full-scale religious schism which would officially separate the two peoples and set them definitely against each other.

For some time after the exile, Samaria and its territory was in a more flourishing political condition than was Jerusalem. Its more fruitful soil, its location athwart the roads of commerce leading from Syria to Egypt, its location close to the satrap of Abar-Nahara (§§ 13, 147) who resided in Damascus, and the absence of grave internal dissensions, meant that the community was well supplied with material and moral resources. In religious matters the Samaritans always considered themselves to be adorers of Yahweh, and gave him a place in their pantheon, perhaps even a pre-eminent place; this was enough to make them look upon the Temple of Jerusalem as their temple also. They blandly allowed the anti-idolatrous invectives of the prophets to pass in one ear and out the other; the exclusive worship of the rigorous Yahwists of Jerusalem impressed them as being puritanical fanaticism, not to be accepted literally. The essential was to adore Yahweh; whether he was adored under the form of a calf (Vol. I, § 414), or without any material representation, in the company of other gods or alone — these were questions of secondary importance in which one might follow his respective traditions. How this outlook of the Samaritans colored their attitude

Samaria (Sebastiyeh): ruins of the city gate.

toward the repatriates of Jerusalem has already been described. Although rebuffed by the official representatives of the community in Jerusalem, they did not give up; on the contrary, their partially successful attempts to penetrate the closed community of Jerusalem prove that some of the Yahwistic repatriates were not entirely opposed to their views (§§ 129–130).

160. Such was their relationship, at least up to the period of the second mission of Nehemias, that is, before 424 B.C. The contemporary biblical documents yield no information as to whether this state of permanent antagonism was resolved by an agreement and reconciliation, or by complete schism and rivalry.

Later on it will become apparent that the antagonism was resolved in a radically hostile manner. At the beginning of the second century B.C., the author of *Ecclesiasticus* affirms his hatred for the Edomites and the Philistines — which was only to be expected, given the ancient enmity existing between Israel and these two foreign peoples — but he immediately adds as the climax that besides these two there is a "third which is not a people," "the foolish *goi* that lives in Sichem" (Ecclus. 50:25–26 [Vulgate: 27–28]; cf. the Hebrew fragments). The zealous scribe of Jerusalem used the strongest language possible to express the aversion he felt toward the Samaritans of Sichem (Vol. I, § 88), hating them more than he did the Edomites and the Philistines; in fact, for him they are not even a "people," but rather, to use an epithet reserved for pagan

Samaria (Sebastiyeh): Roman road.

nations, *goi*. He describes them as *foolish*, which is practically equivalent to calling them "impious" or "atheistic." Such intense hatred is not ordinarily felt toward strangers, but occurs among relatives when one branch wants to deny any kind of relationship with the other.

After this explanation it is unnecessary to dwell on the attitude of the Samaritan woman in her meeting with Jesus Christ; her anti-Jerusalem statements, the remarks of the Evangelist (Jn. 4:5 ff.; cf. also Lk. 9:52–53), and other indications in the Gospel testify to the hatred which existed in the first century A.D., and which had been felt by the author of *Ecclesiasticus* two centuries earlier.

161. What had happened, therefore, after 424 B.C.? How had the ancient antagonism provoked a schism and rivalry?

The silence of the Bible is in part compensated for by Josephus, who informs us that John Hyrcanus, in 128 B.C., destroyed the Samaritans' temple on Mount Gerizim, and that this event occurred 200 years after it had been built (*Antiquities*, XIII, 9, 1; cf. *War of the Jews*, I, 2, 6). From this it would appear that the Samaritans had around 328 B.C. built their own temple on Gerizim, one "resembling the Temple of Jerusalem" and likewise dedicated to Yahweh. This would fall in the period of Alexander the Great; in fact, Josephus expressly refers to his previous account of the exiled priest Manasses (cf. *supra*, § 154).

Was the construction of this rival temple only the beginning of the official religious schism or its final confirmation? In the account of the exiled Manasses two elements must be accurately distinguished: the one, the flight of Manasses to Samaria, which is an evident elaboration of the episode of Nehemias, erroneously transferred to the time of Alexander the Great; the other, the construction of the temple, likewise assigned to the time of Alexander the Great. It has already been brought out that the two elements could have been artificially joined together in an anti-Samaritan polemic (§ 155). But while the item dealing with Manasses is chronologically false, the other, the construction of the temple under Alexander, is most probably exact.

162. The 200 years' duration of the temple is also a proof independent of the first. Where Josephus obtained this figure we do not, of course, know, but it agrees with the other circumstances. Besides, the construction of the temple was an open challenge to the community of Jerusalem, a challenge which in the social mentality of the ancients, had a political significance. It is unlikely that such a brazen schism occurred under the Achaemenids, who had looked with favor upon the Temple and Yahwistic community of Jerusalem, and whose best interests would not be served by arousing deadly rivalries in this far-distant province. The tradition preserved by Josephus, who places construction of the schismatic temple in the period of Alexander, must be correct. At that time, by reason of the sudden destruction of the Persian empire, the favors and privileges conceded by the Achaemenids had been abolished, and the individual peoples could freely indulge in their provincial rivalries.

The construction of the Samaritan temple must have been a long desired local objective, held in check by the Achaemenids but urged by a strong faction in Samaria. It is quite possible that in the faction which planned an open schism there were several priests who had fled from Jerusalem because they would not put up with the rigorous Yahwism which had been restored there. The probabilities are all in favor of Josephus when he relates that a member of the sacerdotal family, who turns out to be the one expelled by Nehemias, took refuge in Samaria, where he was followed by other priests. In fact, Samaria was the ordinary sanctuary of apostates from Jerusalem, the refuge of malcontents from the Yahwistic community especially from the time of Alexander on (Josephus, *Antiquities*, XI, 8, 6–7). There would then result the following succession of events: rebellion of priests against the reform of Nehemias and their gradual emigration to Samaria; the sacerdotal-Samaritan faction in favor of the construction of a temple on Gerizim rivaling the one in Jerusalem, but held in check by the Achaemenids; actual construction of the temple at the fall of the Achaemenids. Thus, the temple of Samaria would be not the beginning, but the final confirmation, of an old schism.

163. The exiled priests from Jerusalem brought with them to Samaria,

besides their sacerdotal descent, something highly important in winning authority
for their ministry, namely, the
book of the *Torah.* The legal
codex which had served as
the basis for the reform of
Nehemias and was a résumé
of ancient Yahwism (§ 137 ff.)
was too venerable to be neglected by these priests, who
therefore brought a copy of
it to Samaria with them, and
made it the moral foundation
of the schismatic Yahwistic
community. That foundation
remained unshakable, and has
been venerated through the
centuries down even to our
own day.

The little community of
about 200 Samaritans living
in the squalid streets of
Nablus (Vol. I, § 88) repre-
sents all that remains of the

The Samaritan Pentateuch at Nablus.
(Vester, Amer. Colony.)

ancient schism.[2] The ancient codex preserved in their synagogue is written in the Samaritan script and dates perhaps to the twelfth century
A.D.; it is the object (of fables and) of the highest veneration, and
is the fundamental law of the community. This sacred book of the
present-day Samaritans is the *Torah,* the Pentateuch of the Hebrew
Canon. Not only does it contain all five parts of the Hebrew
Pentateuch (Vol. I, § 111), but the text itself is substantially the same;
in fact, the six thousand variants in which the Samaritan text differs
from the Hebrew are almost always due to merely scribal differences,
except for a few instances in which a Samaritan hand has clearly made
changes in its own favor (e.g., in Deut. 27:4 the name Mount Gerizim
has been substituted for Mount Ebal), or the Samaritan reading
is better than the Hebrew. The exact correspondence of the two
texts was noted by St. Jerome: *"Samaritani etiam Pentateuchum Moysi
totidem litteris scriptitant, figuris tamen et apicibus discrepantes"*
(*Prolog. galeat.*).

---

[2] In August, 1933, the head of the Samaritan community of Nablus told the author
that the members of the community numbered exactly 206.

Of decisive value is the fact that the Samaritans recognize the entire and exact Pentateuch of Jerusalem, and nothing else, as the sacred book. (A *Book of Josue* of Samaritan origin is a compilation dating only from the twelfth century after Christ, and need not detain us.) Bearing in mind the sharp separation and fierce mutual hatred which existed between Samaria and Jerusalem from the period of the construction of the Samaritan temple on, it is clear that the *Torah* must have entered Samaria before that period, that is, before the reign of Alexander. Precisely when it did enter, it is impossible to say. It is unlikely that the first of the priests exiled from Jerusalem, that is, the one expelled by Nehemias, brought it there; it was more probably brought in by one of the many other priests who followed him later on. As time went on, it was among these men that the project of a clear-cut schism was worked out in detail; they had everything to gain by the possession and exhibition of so authoritative a document. It seems certain also that the sacred codex was carried away from Jerusalem before the later parts of the Canon, that is, the *Prophets* and the *Kethubhim* or *Writings*, were completed (§§ 157–158). If these sections had been completed at the time when the *Torah* was carried northward, the exiled priests would certainly have taken care to bring them along also.

164. The coming of the sacerdotal element and of the *Torah* must have brought to the internal life of the Samaritan community, along with schism, also a kind of Yahwistic reform. The Samaritans were certainly syncretists and idolaters before the exile of Juda (Vol. I, § 457), and perhaps also after the return of the exiles from Babylonia, but it is surprising not to find any indication of their idolatry after the erection of their schismatic temple. Angry and sometimes calumnious accusations were made in Jerusalem against them, but there was no further mention made of calves or other idolatrous representations of Yahweh. The disappearance of these objects which had existed in Samaria

Present-day synagogue of the Samaritans at Nablus. (Vester, Amer. Colony.)

can be attributed to those priests who organized the Yahwistic schism, and who there built the temple which was, as Josephus brings out, "similar to the Temple of Jerusalem" (*Antiquities*, XIII, 9, 1). True, Josephus relates that the Samaritans spontaneously consecrated their temple to Jupiter during the reign of Antiochus Epiphanes, and appeals to an exchange of letters to support his claim (*Antiquities*, XII, 5, 5), but the evidence adduced by the Pharisee of Jerusalem is very suspect, as the letters may have been taken from some anti-Samaritan polemic (§§ 155, 161). Even if such a proposal did come from Samaria, it doubtless represented the wishes of a local Hellenistic faction, one of which existed in Jerusalem also, and not of the entire Samaritan community. From 2 *Mach.* 6:2, it seems that the consecration of the Samaritan temple to Jupiter was the result of brute force, as in the case of the Temple at Jerusalem (§ 239).

Money of *Flavia Neapolis* from the time of Antony. Left: the emperor. Right: a mountain with two summits (Ebal and Gerizim?). One has a temple, the other a tower.

❀   ❀   ❀

165. The fortunes of the Samaritans after their definite schism are not fully known. They spontaneously submitted to Alexander as he marched toward Egypt, and he took a certain number of them with him to Thebais, giving them plots of land and assigning them to guard that country (*Antiquities*, XI, 8, 6). This notice seems to be confirmed by the frequent mention, in Egyptian papyri of the third century after Christ, of a locality in Middle Egypt called

A contemporary Samaritan woman. (Vester, Amer. Colony.)

"Samaria." While Alexander remained in Egypt, Andromachus, set up by him as governor in Syria, was burned alive by the Samaritans. In retaliation for this Alexander, on his return from Egypt, severely punished the city, in all probability razing it to the ground and settling Macedonian colonists upon its site (Curtius Rufus, IV, 8; Eusebius, *Chronicon, II, ad annum Abrahae*, 1684, in Migne, *P.G.*, 19, cols. 489–490).

When Ptolemy I took over Palestine, he transported other Samaritans to Alexandria, together with Jews from Jerusalem (§ 190), and again destroyed the city. Demetrius Poliorcetus did likewise around 296 B.C. when he fought against Ptolemy I (§ 30). After a period of tranquillity the Samaritans reappear in the Machabean period as allies of the enemies of Jerusalem (1 Mach. 3:10 ff.), but they had chosen the losing side, and later on three of their districts fell under the control of Jerusalem (1 Mach. 10:30, 38; 11:28, 34; a fourth district is mentioned in 11:57; for the incorrect reading of 5:66, cf. § 260, footnote). The situation became worse under John Hyrcanus, who, after destroying the temple on Gerizim (§ 297), besieged Samaria, "a very well fortified city," around 108, and after a year's siege succeeded in capturing and destroying it (*Antiquities*, XIII, 10, 2–3; *War*, I, 2, 7). Even discounting the obvious exaggeration in the smug account of Josephus, it is certain that the city was completely destroyed to satisfy an ancient hatred which had grown more virulent under the Machabees.

In 63 B.C. Pompey annexed the territory of Samaria to the Roman province of Syria and rebuilt the city, declaring it a "free city"; later it was restored and fortified somewhat better by Gabinius (*Antiquities*, XIV, 4, 4; 5, 3; *War*, I, 7, 7; 8, 4). When Herod obtained it from Augustus (§ 343) he developed it into a center of the first rank, and built a great temple there and populated the city with veterans and merchants. He changed its name to Σεβαστή ("august") in honor of his imperial protector, and the name has been transmitted to the present as "Sebastiyeh" (Vol. I, § 84).

Finally, the city of *Flavia Neapolis* was built in the Samaritan territory near ancient Sichem in the reign of Vespasian, and was named in his honor. It was peopled almost exclusively by pagans. This name is preserved in the present-day Nablus, in which the descendants of the ancient schism dwell (§ 163). Because of their isolation they have preserved, even today, a typical physiognomy which is quite different from that of the Judaeo-Palestinian.

ELEPHANTINE

166. The unexpected discovery of the letters of Tell el-Amarna (Vol. I, § 43 ff.) has a happy counterpart in the discovery, likewise on Egyptian soil and equally precious for the history of Israel, of the documents of Elephantine.

The island of Elephantine is located less than six miles north of the first cataract of the Nile (Vol. I, §§ 21, 23). Opposite it, on the east bank of the river, rises the city of Assuan, the Syene of the Greeks. The entire district containing the island and the city was called by the ancient Egyptians *Yebu, Yeb,* that is, country of the elephants (cf. Josephus, *War,* IV, 10, 5), probably because these animals were first seen there; hence, the name of the island also. This district had always been of great importance to ancient Egypt for a variety of reasons. A little to the south of the city of Assuan was a quarry of magnificent granite which had supplied the stone for Egyptian buildings since ancient times. Inasmuch as the Nile was navigable from this point northward, the area around the first cataract was a place for unloading and reloading for trade with Ethiopia to the south. Finally, the district was the southern boundary of Egypt, as has been pointed out (Vol. I, § 21). Strategically

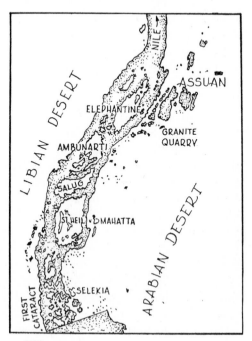

Papyri of Elephantine still rolled up and sealed.

this boundary was of the highest importance, as it was the key point for a foreign invasion. The Nile itself was a most convenient means of penetration, and when an invader coming from Ethiopia to the south gained mastery over the first (the last) cataract and of the Elephantine-Assuan district, the way north to the Delta lay practically open before him.

167. A locality so far away from the land of the Hebrews had never figured in the history of Israel, and one would never suspect that it could, for the Bible mentions it only a few times in passing (Ezech. 29:10; 30:6; cf. Isa. 49:12?) as being the most remote border of Egypt. Unexpectedly, however, it has played a part in the history of Israel — indeed, a part of the first magnitude.

Ever since Napoleon's Egyptian expedition local monuments had attracted the attention of scholars, but toward the end of the century, Greek and Semitic inscriptions from Yeb began to come to light. In 1903 and 1904, papyri made their appearance. One was purchased at Luxor, then nine more at Assuan, all discovered in that territory — so it was said — by Bedouins who were doing some excavating. For the most part, the papyri were intact, still rolled up as they were in the beginning, their knotted cords and lotus seals unbroken. The desert sand had preserved these fragile documents for over twenty-three centuries in a remarkable manner, thanks to the complete lack of moisture. Rain may fall at Thebes every ten or twenty years or so, but at Assuan rain is unknown. The exceptional importance of the find was immediately recognized, and when it was learned where the papyri had been found, German (Rubensohn) and then French (Clermont-Ganneau) expeditions repaired to Elephantine to begin methodical explorations of the area. From 1906 on, other papyri and many "ostraca" were found.

All these documents are of unimpeachable authenticity and fall under the following headings: letters, legal and administrative documents, literary documents, lists of names, fragments, and the like. Aside from the "ostraca" and the fragments, they number about sixty, and all are in Aramaic (Vol. I, §§ 51, 494). From the dates which several of them carry they were all written during the course of the fifth century B.C. from 495 to 400. An examination of their contents proves that they come from a Jewish community which had settled in Elephantine before Cambyses conquered Egypt in 525 (§§ 10, 171).

* * *

168. For what reason and in what period did Palestinian Jews make their surprising decision to settle in a land six hundred miles distant from the Mediterranean? The reason is perfectly clear — to form a guard for that port of entry into Egypt which comprised Elephantine and Assuan. These Jews formed a military garrison and were stationed there by the Egyptian authorities in the interests of the country.

When exactly was this garrison sent there? Certainly before Cambyses, but any date farther back than 525 is only guesswork. Herodotus (II, 30–31) speaks of a mutiny of Egyptian soldiers guarding Elephantine which occurred under Psammetichus I, one which was very likely caused by the discontent of the natives with the foreign troops who had been hired in great numbers by that Pharaoh (Vol. I, § 41). Again, in the time of Manasses, king of Juda, a large number of Jews migrated to Egypt, which number may have increased with the decline of the Assyrian power after Ashurbanipal, and with the consolidation of the independence of Egypt under Dynasty XXVI (Vol. I, §§ 41, 505, 508). Added to these vague general references is a bit of information which, although it comes from a later source, may well be a faithful echo of the facts. The Letter of Aristeas, 13 (§ 192) states that auxiliary Jewish troops aided Psammetichus in his war against the king of Ethiopia; a reference, doubtless, to Psammetichus II and his successful expedition against Nubia (Vol. I, § 42), which therefore antedates the de-

The island of Elephantine seen from Assuan.
(Vester, Amer. Colony.)

struction of Jerusalem in 586. If this information is correct, as it seems to be, because indirectly confirmed by a Greek inscription of Abu-Simbel, it may be supposed that some of these mercenaries were left as a garrison at Elephantine. How Psammetichus II procured the Jewish mercenaries is not explained; perhaps they were freely offered by Sedecias at the urging of the pro-Egyptian faction then influential in Jerusalem, in view of the expedition in Nubia (Vol. I, § 533); or they may have been imported into Egypt by Nechao II during the brief period of his mastery over Palestine (Vol. I, §§ 14–15, 519–520).

Yet it is difficult to see how even a settlement which took place before 586 was the direct predecessor to the garrison mentioned by the documents. An inscription on an Egyptian statue (Louvre A, 90) states that under the Pharaoh Hophra (Vol. I, § 535) and shortly after 586, another mutiny occurred in the garrison of Elephantine, composed at that time of Palestinians, Syrians, and Greeks. But the documents under discussion state that the garrison, at least the island garrison, was chiefly composed of Jews from the time of Cambyses on. It is likely, therefore, that the turbulent and heterogeneous garrison set up by Psammetichus II before 586 was replaced by a nucleus of Jews recruited from among the fugitives who took refuge in Egypt after the catastrophe of 586, taking the prophet Jeremias with them (Vol. I, § 545). The garrison mentioned in the documents was the descendant of this nucleus.

169. A grave difficulty rises here. How was it that these descendants of the declining kingdom of Juda wrote and even spoke Aramaic, if up to the fall of Judea, Hebrew, although no longer the classical tongue, was spoken, and if the exiles from Judea generally spoke Aramaic only in Babylonia (§ 67)? One answer is that at some point of time the Jewish garrison of Elephantine substituted Aramaic for Hebrew, as their fellow countrymen in Babylonia had done. Against this is the fact that the exiles in Babylonia accomplished the change through direct contact with Aramaic-speaking peoples, whereas the Jews of Elephantine lived among people who spoke Egyptian. It is true that Aramaic was the international language, but could this language, because it was international, have had such an influence that it could supplant the Hebrew tongue in a Jewish garrison far from Aramaic peoples? Must it then be held that these Jews came to Egypt when they already spoke Aramaic? It is then difficult to see how they were recruited by Psammetichus II or Nechao II in Palestine, where Hebrew was spoken at that time. Perhaps they came from other settlements, perhaps from Babylonia-Assyria where they were the remnants of deportees not from the kingdom of Juda but from Israel, whence they had penetrated into Egypt in the steps of Ashurbanipal, in his victorious

campaign (Vol. I, § 40)? They may also have been Samaritans who had come under Aramaic influence before 586 (§ 159).

It is plain that the linguistic difficulty is grave. If, in trying to avoid these last conjectures, it be claimed that the garrison was recruited from the kingdom of Juda shortly before 586, there still remains the difficulty of explaining how Aramaic came to be substituted for Hebrew. Up to the present this has not been satisfactorily done.

❋ ❋ ❋

170. The colony was a military one in a very broad sense. In reality, it was a large group of families which had transferred there in hopes of finding a better living. To arouse their personal interest they were allotted plots of land which were to be handed down from father to son, and which because of the fertile soil on the island assured them a decent living, easily supplemented by small commercial ventures not lacking in that locality. The men were obliged under certain circumstances to military service, but this must not have been a burden. It was a Hebrew community, with all its moral baggage of customs, language, and religion. The Egyptian rulers did not interfere in the internal affairs of the community, and the Jews were free to live according to their customs and laws, to marry only among themselves, and to avoid marriages with foreigners, to adore whom they wished. If they fulfilled their military obligations nothing more was asked of them. Yet in practice it will be seen that grave opposition did develop.

Concerning the size of this community, which may have varied considerably over the years, no precise information is available. It is certain that more than a few dozens of families were involved, for their civil and religious organization bears witness to a large number. The data offered by Strabo can serve as a point of reference (XVII, 820); he estimates that in the time of the Romans the garrison of Elephantine comprised three cohorts or about fifteen hundred men.

The Jewish garrison began "in the days of the kings of Egypt," that is, under Dynasty XXVI. With a change of rulers, it came under the Persian, Cambyses (Papyrus 30, line 13; § 171). Not only did this capricious son of Cyrus unexpectedly regard the religious practices of the garrison kindly, but there are many indications that the court of Susa counted in a special way on the fidelity of this foreign colony in the hinterland of Egypt. Of the satrapies of the empire of the Achaemenids, Egypt was the farthest from the center, the most isolated geographically, and the most unified in national traditions, and hence the most difficult to hold in subjection to the empire, as its frequent rebellions testify. The satraps and Persian magistrates, therefore, found a natural support for their power in that foreign Jewish community which, by reason of its religious traditions, kept strictly apart from the surrounding Egyptians who adored an immense pantheon. The spirituality of this cult, moreover, bore some resemblance to the Persian adoration of the god of heaven (§ 84). On the other hand, the Egyptians looked upon the Jews of Elephantine not only as religious enemies, but as supporters of a foreign power, as lackeys and spies of the court of Susa as well, and felt that the garrison which they had invited into the country to defend their southern boundary had turned out to be, once the sovereign had been changed, a serpent in their bosom. This explains their religious and political opposition.

171. The Jewish garrison did not suffer from the anti-Persian uprisings which occurred in Egypt under Darius I and Artaxerxes I (§§ 15, 17), or at least there is no indication of this. Beginning with the rebellions which flared up around 412 under Darius II (§ 18), the hostility of the Egyptians burst forth into violence behind which there lay both religious and patriotic grievances.

What happened at that time is related in the following document (Papyrus 30, Cowley edition) which, in many respects, is the most precious of all those discovered. It is a letter, sent to Palestine by the heads of the garrison. The following translation is from the Aramaic; it must be noted that in some places the rare word employed, or a manifest error of the scribe, or damage done to the papyrus, makes its reading somewhat uncertain. The numbers in brackets indicate the lines of the papyrus; explanatory footnotes follow the same numbers. (Cf. the photograph of this papyrus in Volume I, page 391.)

"[1][1] To our Lord Bagaos, governor of Juda, your Servants Yedoniah

---

[1] Cf. *ANET*, 492. [1] The Aramaic form *Bagohi* is the same as the Greek *Bagoas* (cf. § 152, footnote). — [4] The *King Darius* is Darius II; hence, the date given here is the year 411 B.C. — *Arsames* is the Persian governor of Upper Egypt with jurisdiction over Elephantine; as is evident from what follows (cf. also line 30), Arsames was absent at the time of the events recorded, having gone to the Persian court, possibly to make the usual administrative report. — [5] *Khnub, Khnum* (in Egyptian = "ram") as the god of Elephantine and of the region of the first cataract. He was pictured with the head of a ram. — It is to be noted that *the priests* of this god, being idolaters, are designated in the Aramaic text by a different word (*kumrayya*) from that used (lines 1, 18) for the Yahwistic *priests* (kahanayya). — *Vidaranag* (or *Vaidrang*) was the military *superintendent* (the Aramaic has *phratarak*, a Persian term) of Yeb or Elephantine; from lines 7–8 it is seen that his son *Nefayan* was the military commander of Syene or Assuan. Father and son, therefore, were neighbors. — [6] For *temple* the Aramaic has *'agura'* which very likely is derived from the Babylonian *ekur*, "temple tower," "temple"; the temple is described in lines 9–12. — The temple was dedicated to the God Y H W, pronounced *Yahu* or *Yaho* but there is no doubt it signified Yahweh, that is, Y H W [H]: cf. Vol. I, § 208. — [7] For *Nefayan* see line 5. — [10] The meaning of the last words is doubtful. — [11] The word *which* before *with the rest* is either poor grammar or a mistake in writing.

and his colleagues, priests in the fortress of Yeb [Elephantine]. Of [your] happiness [2] may the God of heaven take the greatest care of our lord at all times, and may you find favor in the sight of King Darius [3] and of the sons of the [royal] palace a thousand times more than at present, and may He grant you a long life; and may you be joyous and strong at all times.

"[4] Now, your servant Yedoniah and his colleagues speak thus: In the month of Tammuz in the fourteenth year of King Darius, when Arsames [5] departed and had gone to the King, the priests of the god Khnub in the fortress of Yeb [made] a pact with Vidaranag who was commander-in-chief here [6] in these terms: 'May the temple of the god Yaho which [is] in the fortress of Yeb be wiped out there!' Later on this accursed Vidaranag [7] sent a letter to his son Nefayan, who was in command over the troops in the fortress of Syene, saying: 'The temple which [is] at Yeb [8] in the fortress, let it be destroyed!' Later on Nefayan led the Egyptians together with other troops; they came to the fortress of Yeb with their arms, [9] they entered that temple and razed it down to the ground. They smashed the columns of stone which were there. It also happened that the gates [10] of stone five [in number], built with squared blocks of stone which were in this temple, they destroyed: their doors were put [to their own uses?] — and the hinges [11] of these doors [were of] bronze; and their roof, all of cedar wood (which) with the rest of the decorations and all the other things which were in that place [12], they burned with fire. The basins of gold and silver and everything else which was in this temple they took and used them [13]² for their own advantage.

"Now back in the days of the kings of Egypt our forefathers built this temple in the fortress of Yeb; and when Cambyses [came] to Egypt [14] he found this temple built. The temples of the gods of Egypt were all destroyed but no one did any damage to this temple.

"[15] But when this occurred, we and our wives and our children wore sackcloth, fasted and prayed to Yaho, lord of heaven, [16] who has let us see [our triumph] over Vidaranag, that dog! The circlets were

---

² [13] The *kings of Egypt* are the native Pharaohs, no doubt those of Dynasty XXVI, after which *Cambyses [came] to Egypt*, conquering it in 525 B.C. — [14] For Cambyses' attitude toward the Egyptian religion, cf. § 11. — [16] The general import of this line is clear enough: Vidaranag has been punished by superior authorities for having permitted the destruction of the Jewish temple, but the phrase *The circlets were taken away from his feet* perhaps alludes to the distinctive marks of the dignity of Vidaranag, of which he was deprived on the occasion of his (capital?) punishment. There are references to the use of rings for the ankles also in *Isa.* 3:16, 19; *Koran*, 24, 31, but it is a feminine fashion. Others translate the passage in this wise: *The dogs have torn off the muscles of his feet*, and have supposed that the culprit was crucified. — [18] *Johanan* is the same name as Jehohanan. [21] For the *year 17 of King Darius* see line 30.

taken away from his feet and all the treasures which he had acquired were lost. All the men [17] who sought to do evil against this temple have been killed and we have seen [our victory] over them.

"Even before now, at the time when this evil [18] was perpetrated against us, we sent a letter [to you, O Bagoas], our lord, and to Johanan the high priest and his colleagues the priests who [are] in Jerusalem, and to Ostanes the brother [19] of 'Anani and the nobles of the Jews. They have not sent a letter [in reply]. And yet, from the month of Tammuz of the fourteenth year of King Darius [20] up to this day, we have been clothed in sackcloth and we have fasted; our women have become as widows; we have not anointed ourselves with oil; [21] we have drunk no wine. Besides, from then until [this] day of year 17 of King Darius, oblation and incense and holocaust [22] have not been offered in this temple.

"Now, your servants Yedoniah and his colleagues, and the Jews, the citizens of Yeb, all speak thus: [23] If it is pleasing to our lord [Bagoas], regarding this temple that it be rebuilt — since it is not permissible for us to rebuild it — behold, to the persons [24] [who are the object] of your goodness and of your affection here in Egypt, let a letter be sent from you to them regarding the temple of the god Yaho [25] so that it may be rebuilt in the fortress of Yeb as it was built before! And oblation and incense and holocaust will be offered [26] on the altar of the god Yaho in your name, and we will pray for you at all times, we and our wives and our children, and all the Jews [27] who are here. If this temple is rebuilt, you will have merit before Yaho god [28] of heaven more than he who would offer holocausts and sacrifices equal in value to a thousand talents. Now as to gold,[3] [29] we have given instructions on this point to our messenger.

"Furthermore, we have sent [news] of the whole affair in our name in a letter to Delaiah and Shelemiah, sons of Sanballat the governor of Samaria.

"[30] Furthermore, of all that has been done against us, Arsames knows nothing.

"On the twentieth of Marheshwan, year 17 of King Darius."

172. This remarkable document agrees in many details with the information contained in the Bible and in Josephus.

First, *the persons*. There must have been more than one *Bagohi*

---

[3] [28] *Now as to gold, etc.* The vagueness of this remark is really very enlightening. *Gold* seems to be just the right kind of lubricant needed to arouse the bureaucratic machine to move more quickly. "Backsheesh," or a "tip" has always been a deciding factor in the Orient. — [29] The name *Sin-uballit* is the more exact form because it is Babylonian, but the Hebrew *Sanballat* is the same name. — [30] See line 4 for Arsames. The date with which the document concludes (cf. lines 4 and 21) falls in the latter part of November of 408 B.C.

or Bagoas (§§ 21, 152), but the present one must be the Bagohi of Artaxerxes II (§ 152), as the chronology attests. *Jehohanan* or Johanan, *high priest . . . in Jerusalem* (line 18), the contemporary of Esdras (§§ 118, 121) and, according to Josephus, the murderer of his own brother (§ 152), is also familiar. *Sin-uballit* or Sanballat, the *peḥah* of Samaria and Nehemias' persistent rival (§ 125 ff.), is even more familiar. From the manner in which he is mentioned here it seems that Sanballat was still alive in 408, but he was then certainly very old. The mention of his sons Delaiah and Shelemiah as the addressees of the other letter from the Jewish garrison suggests that they had been entrusted by their old father with the administration of affairs.

Secondly, *the facts.* What is entirely new and most surprising is that the Jewish garrison of Elephantine had had a temple to Yahweh from the times of the Pharaohs who preceded Cambyses, that is, from the first decades of its Egyptian stay. Were the builders of this Egyptian temple in honor of Yahweh ignorant of the great law regarding centralization of cult, sanctioned by the *Torah* and the objective of insistent attempts on the part of the kings of Juda (Vol. I, §§ 460, 462, 481, 517)? The law stipulated that only in the Temple of Jerusalem was it licit to offer a true cult to Yahweh. Or if they did know about it, did they consider themselves not obliged to observe it? There is no doubt that a genuine temple is involved. Abstracting from the ample proportions indicated by the description given of it (line 9 ff.), from this and other papyri it is known that oblations, incense, and holocausts were offered there and that an altar was regularly used. From these facts one must conclude that the law concerning the one Yahwistic temple might very well have been known at Elephantine, and yet was neglected or considered to be not binding in a foreign land, just as later on the same view will prevail at Leontopolis in Egypt (§ 274 ff.), and according to some, even on the threshold of Palestine at 'Araq el-Emir (§ 219).

173. Whatever the mentality of those builders and their descendants, it is certain that members of the priestly caste in Jerusalem held quite different views on the matter. A very significant detail comes to notice. When the temple of the Egyptians was destroyed, the garrison hoped to receive aid by writing a letter to *Johanan the high priest and his colleagues the priests who [are] in Jerusalem* (line 18). They failed, for no reply came from Jerusalem. Was this silence an accident, or was it not rather a diplomatic silence? The high priest, indeed, must have found himself seriously embarrassed by the arrival of this letter. If he showed favor and encouraged the reconstruction of the illegal temple of Elephantine, he would thereby repudiate a fundamental principle of the *Torah*, and would deny the exclusiveness of his Temple in Jerusa-

lem. On the other hand, this was certainly not the time to repulse harshly those who had turned to Jerusalem from such a distance, and with such religious and national zeal; a rebuff could be interpreted as an approval of the anti-Yahwistic persecutions of the Egyptians, and might lead to a formal apostasy of those who were being persecuted. Psychologically, the best solution was that the high priest diplomatically made no answer at all. Surprised and embittered by this silence, the garrison turned, according to this document, not to the sacerdotal caste of Jerusalem, but to the civil authority of that very city, namely, to Bagoas, and to the authorities of Samaria, Delaiah and Shelemiah, the sons of Sanballat (line 29). This new approach to Samaria is full of meaning. At this time, 408 B.C., the rupture between Samaria and Jerusalem was certainly complete. Whether the Samaritans' temple was built on Mount Gerizim or not, a numerous and powerful sacerdotal faction in Samaria wanted a local temple to rival the one in Jerusalem (§ 162). When therefore the garrison saw that no answer was forthcoming from Jerusalem, it hoped to receive an encouraging word from Samaria. It may be objected that Samaria represented schism and Jerusalem legal orthodoxy; granted, but those who had to live hundreds of miles away, amidst people who were hostile to any kind of Yahwism, undoubtedly took a broader view of the matter and looked upon Yahwists of any type as their brethren, particularly since the temple of Elephantine placed the garrison there in a position, in regard to orthodox Jerusalem, very similar to that of schismatic Samaria.

174. Fortune has been kind enough to preserve the reply of Bagoas and Delaiah, who were apparently good friends. It is not really a letter but rather a memorandum which must have been set down for the personal use of the bearer

The "Memorandum" of Bagoas. Above, Hebrew transliteration; below, the facsimile of the original Aramaic. (From *Encyclopedia Judaica*.)

of the preceding letter after his audience with the two personages mentioned (Papyrus 32, Cowley edition).

"[1] Memorandum of what Bagoas and Delaiah said [2][4] to me. Memorandum, as follows: You must speak in Egypt [3] before Arsames regarding the house of the altar of the God [4] of Heaven, which existed in the fortress of Yeb, [5] since ancient times, before Cambyses, [6] which this accursed Vidaranag destroyed [7] in the year 14 of King Darius; [8] to rebuild it on its site as it was in the past, [9] and oblation and incense may be offered on [10] this altar, as in the past [11] was done."

The one who had to decide the question was, of course, the Egyptian governor Arsames, before whom the messenger was told to present himself. Perhaps also Bagoas and Delaiah, who were on good terms with Arsames, sent another letter of recommendation to him by another messenger. Everything indicates that permission to rebuild was granted but no documents are available to state whether the rebuilding was accomplished or not. There is a highly important difference between the letter and the memorandum: the letter mentions *oblation, incense, holocaust, and sacrifices* which were offered in the destroyed temple (lines 21, 25, 28); the memorandum permits only *oblation* and *incense* to be offered in the rebuilt temple; the *holocaust* and *sacrifice* which required animal victims are not mentioned. The omission cannot have been merely accidental, and almost surely explains the motive of the violent uprising of the Egyptians against the rites performed in the Temple of Yahweh.

The letter (line 5) names as the first instigators of the uprising *the priests of the god Khnub*. The uprising was then chiefly a matter of religious fanaticism, a defense of their god. Khnub was pictured with the head of a ram, in conformity with his name, and sacred rams were guarded reverently as personifications of the god, were embalmed after death, and buried in a place apart. Devotees of the ram-god knew that not far away in the Temple of Yahweh the throats of kids and lambs were cut in sacrifice, and their carcasses burned in holocaust; yet these same animals were in a way personifications of the god Khnub. They knew that those who adored Yahweh slaughtered many lambs on the occasion of their Pasch. This continual sacrilege committed by these foreigners was simply intolerable; long-repressed anger broke out with a destructive fury against the Temple of Yahweh, once a favorable

---

[4] [2] The first draft of the document probably began with this second *Memorandum,* but since it is not known who was speaking in the text, the messenger later on added line 1. — [3] For *Arsames* see the preceding document, line 4. — The *house of the altar* refers to the ruined temple; the explicit mention of the altar deserves notice. — Cf. *ANET,* 492.

The god Khnub with the head of a ram.

opportunity presented itself. Such a moment had occurred during the absence of Arsames. In the reply of Bagoas and Delaiah, then, *oblation* and *incense*, both unbloody rites, were allowed, and the rebuilding of the temple, but *holocaust* and *sacrifice* are not even mentioned. Past experience counseled a prudent removal of so grave a provocation to new outbreaks of fanaticism.

175. One document relative to the Hebrew Pasch antedates the destruction of the temple, going back to the fifth year of Darius II (419 B.C.); unfortunately it is seriously damaged (Papyrus 21, Cowley edition), so that the word *pasch* is missing (although it has been preserved in two of the "ostraca" found there) and only a partial enumeration of its prescriptions has survived. A certain Hananiah who, according to another papyrus, had arrived in Elephantine that same year, 419, and had perhaps, like Nehemias, occupied an office of considerable importance in the Persian court (§ 124), sent word to Jedoniah that King Darius himself had sent a decree to Arsames[5] prescribing the feast of azymes, forbidding them to drink of fermented beverages during the celebration, and ordering them to keep away from the rest of the people. This segregation may perhaps be traceable to the fear that the immolation of the paschal lambs would provoke a reaction on the part of the adorers of the god Khnub. No reference, however, is made to immolation in our document. The care which the court of the Achaemenids exercised over the far-distant and tiny Jewish garrison is worthy of note. Nehemias and Esdras also benefited by a like solicitude.

176. Other bits of information regarding the religious and civil conditions of the garrison can be sifted from other papyri.

While it was so profoundly attached to its temple and had struggled so sincerely on the occasion of its destruction, the Yahwism of these Jews was of a type that would not have gained the approval of Nehemias or Esdras, nor, in general, of the circles devoted to the *Torah* in Jerusalem, for their highly diluted Yahwism was similar to that of the Samaritans (§ 159). It was not so much a question of monotheism as of henotheism. Not only are *the gods* and *all the gods* mentioned in the formularies of salutation, but even the names of these rivals of Yahweh and the offerings made in their honor are preserved. *Ashim-*

---

[5] The same Jedoniah and Arsames are mentioned in the letter to Bagoas; cf. lines 1, 4.

bethel, 'Anath-bethel, and *Herem-bethel* are named,[6] and an oath was sworn invoking *'Anath-iahu,* that is, the goddess 'Anath combined with that of Yahweh. What would Esdras have said if he had heard such blasphemies?

These gods take their seats in hierarchical order at the table prepared for them by their devotees in the Jewish garrison. A papyrus of 419 B.C., a list of money offerings made for religious purposes by the persons of the garrison (Papyrus 22, Cowley edition), begins with the following notation, which leaves no room for doubt: "These are the names of the Jews who have given money for the god YHW: each one two sicles of silver . . ."; the names of the subscribers follow, the first of which is a lady (perhaps the sister or wife of some high magistrate), followed by some dozens of names, chiefly those of men. One cannot help but admire the Yahwistic devotion of these contributors who each gave two sicles, although the Jewish law demanded only half a sicle (Exod. 30:13; Neh. 10:33 requires only a third of a sicle), but the crudity of their Yahwism stands revealed in the closing lines: "Cash on hand with Jedoniah son of Gemariah, in the month of Phamenoth: Money: *keresh* XXXI, sicles VIII. Of this, XII *keresh* VI sicles for YHW; for Ashim-bethel VII *keresh;* for 'Anath-bethel XII *keresh.*"[7] Yahweh (YHW), therefore, was given the place of honor at the banquet table and was served a slightly larger portion (only 6 sicles more) than the goddess 'Anath-bethel. A common table, and Yahweh must share it with the foreign gods whom Jeremias had so feared and disapproved when he pleaded with the refugee Jews who had fled to Egypt (Jer. 44). Finally, it ought not to pass unnoticed that this Jedoniah who acts as cashier and distributor of the collections for all the gods is the one who that very year received the order (§ 175) from Darius II regarding the Pasch and who, some ten years later, would write a mournful letter to Bagoas on the occasion of the destruction of the Temple of Yahweh. Everything points to the conclusion that he was the ethnarchic head of the garrison. What a difference between him and Nehemias and Esdras!

177. The garrison was divided into various *deghel.* The word means ensign or banner (Cant. 2:4), hence, also a "group" of persons united under one flag. During their wanderings in the desert, the Israelites had been grouped into various *deghel* (Num. 2:2 ff.), and each group was named after the official who commanded it; some of these names are Persian and Babylonian. A clear distinction was made between those who belonged to a *deghel,* with its military obligations, and those

---

[6] For *Ashim* (or *Asham*) cf. 2 Kings 17:30. For *'Anath,* Vol. I, § 86. For *Herem,* cf. Vol. I, § 271. For *Bethel,* cf. Vol. I, §§ 104, 126, 143.

[7] *Keresh* is the famous gold "daric"; it was worth ten sicles. Cf. *ANET,* 491.

who belonged only to the *qiryah*, "city"; the latter were not held to military duty and were the civilians or the bourgeois.

Other papyri, especially a small group of the same kind as must have constituted the archives, gives a glimpse into the social life of this semi-military population. For the most part, these are juridical papers concerned with immovable property. Money was loaned out at a very high interest rate, variously estimated to have been 24 or 60 per cent! Nuptial dowries were set down in writing. Women were more emancipated juridically than in Palestine, taking part in commercial enterprises, and receiving property with full rights. They could also institute divorce proceedings.

178. Other historical and literary papyri remain. An Aramaic version of the trilingual inscription carved out by Darius I at Bisutun (§ 12) is, perhaps, an official communication which issued from the court of the Achaemenids, who were ever solicitous of their authority over this distant Jewish community. A few columns remain of an Aramaic version of the story of Ahiqar, very widely known in ancient times, and noted for its similarities to the *Life of Aesop* and to the *Book of Tobias* of the Bible ('Αχιάχαρ[ος], Itala: *Achicarus*, Vulgate: *Achior*). It served as instructive and pleasant reading.

The modern scholar, however, would gladly sacrifice this lengthy fragment of a popular story for even a few lines of any text of the Bible used by the garrison of Elephantine, but of this nothing has been found, not even a line.

179. The ultimate fate of the garrison is not known, but it is probable that the Jewish colony was in the end suppressed or dispersed by new and violent persecutions. A fragment of a letter which seems to be dated sometime after 407 B.C. (Papyrus 34, Cowley edition) alludes to grave disorders and human victims. It is certain that when Egypt shook off the Achaemenid yoke in 404 B.C. (§ 20), the garrison was left defenseless and surrounded by hostile Egyptians. It was to be expected that on such a long-awaited occasion the inveterate hatred of the priests of Khnub should flame out once again, as it had in 411, and in an even more violent manner. Despite everything, however, the garrison continued to exist for some time, and the last document in time (Papyrus 35, Cowley edition) is dated the fifth year of the Pharaoh Amirteus (§ 20), that is, 400 B.C. After this date, there is nothing but silence.

When Artaxerxes Ochus conquered Egypt a half century later (§ 21), only the papyri, providentially hidden beneath the sands, remained to tell of the garrison.

THE DIASPORA

ALEXANDRIA — ROME

180. The term Διασπορά, "dispersion" (Judith 5:19 [Vulgate, 23]; 2 Mach. 1:27; Jn. 7:35; James 1:1; 1 Pet. 1:1), was frequently used by the Jews in Hellenistic times to designate all Israelites who lived outside of Palestine.

An element of national feeling is implied in this term. Israel was the "heritage of Yahweh," to be preserved as a unity in the holy land of Palestine which Yahweh had given to Israel. The isolated Israelite who either by choice or force dwelt outside of that land was one "dispersed" in the midst of the *goim* or pagans; he was a "son of the diaspora." Despite this connotation of official commiseration, and abstracting also from those who were more than once forcibly deported from Palestine, there were many among the "dispersed" who at different times and in different circumstances preferred life in a foreign land, far from the holy land. We have definite knowledge of some of these groups of expatriates, but the knowledge is meager; modern discoveries, which have introduced us to the important, and unsuspected, colony at Elephantine, have greatly widened the possibilities of future knowledge, and have given rise to the wildest kind of guesswork. Many other groups similar to that at Elephantine may have existed, but of these nothing is known, thanks to the withering hand of time.

There were many reasons behind this sporadic emigration. The subjects of Achab who settled in the "free ports" of Damascus when the Syrians were defeated by the king of Israel in 857 (Vol. I, § 435; cf. § 432), were drawn there by the commercial possibilities. Motives of commerce, adventure, or politics had led to emigration toward Egypt (§ 168) ever since the time of Manasses. Then too there were the forced deportations. The deportation of the ten tribes of the kingdom of Israel by the Assyrians served to scatter Israelite stock among the peoples of northern Assyria (Vol. I, § 457); the deportation of the kingdom of Juda by the Chaldeans planted Judaism in Babylonia (Vol. I, §§ 530, 542, 545), and at some undetermined time a Jewish colony was sent to Elephantine. The deportation of Palestinian Jews to Hyrcania under Artaxerxes III Ochus (§ 151) occurred toward the middle of the fourth century.

In their new environment some of the expatriates were absorbed and eventually lost all national characteristics; others retained and even intensified theirs (§ 186). In any case, wherever the Jews went, Judaism was disseminated in varying degrees.

181. Babylonia and Jerusalem were from the beginning the principal centers of Judaism in the ancient world, and these two were closely bound to each other as well as to other minor centers; the ties existing between Elephantine and Jerusalem are attested by the documents cited above. Babylonia and Jerusalem were the principal strands of a network which was to extend gradually throughout the ancient world, until that world was almost completely enveloped in its meshes.

A third center, cosmopolitan Alexandria, was soon to be added to the first two, and to be equally important. If, before the Babylonian exile, there had been any region toward which Israel always looked with nostalgia, it was Egypt, the land of the good life, the cradle of the nation, and indeed, many Palestinian Jews would return thither. But Hellenism, and more particularly the founding of Alexandria (§ 190), made the call of Egypt even more seductive, and in many cases an imperious call. An entirely new situation was in the process of formation: an international wind filtered into the closely shut-up Palestinian community, and foreign allurements, mirrored in a thousand and one facets of social life, all concentrated in Alexandria, stirred up in the minds of the simple dwellers of Judea, first curiosity, then interest, finally approval and desire. The wish to preserve the old traditions and the national and religious heritage persisted, but at the same time some began to realize the overwhelming superiority of the Hellenic world in art, science, politics, the refinements of life, commercial organization; in short, all phases of social life except religion. It was this spontaneous admiration, plus the exigencies of daily life, that drew Palestinian Jews to Egypt in ever increasing numbers. The ancient land of nostalgic memories was now enhanced by a splendor up to that time unknown. Immigration therefore and Hellenism proceeded apace and in a short time made Egypt a second Palestine. Alexandria became a Jewish center superior in many ways to Jerusalem itself.

182. The "dispersion" became still more widespread. Transported from Palestine to Egypt, Judaism was carried elsewhere from Egypt. Under the Ptolemies, Alexandria was the greatest port of the Mediterranean; it was not only the natural outlet for all the land of the Nile, but it was also one of the busiest ports of call for Phoenician and Greek commercial fleets, the masters of the Mediterranean marketplaces.

It was the crossroads of the eastern, of the Hellenistic, and later, of the Roman world. Diverse civilizations radiated out from it in many directions. Here came and went Phoenicians from Syria, Carthage, or the Balearics, Ionians from Asia Minor, Greeks from the Peloponnesus or the Dodecanese, Italians from *Magna Graecia* or Italy itself. A traveler reaching Alexandria on a Phoenician ship from the Pillars of Hercules or from Sardegna could thence set out with a caravan of Egyptians for the heart of Ethiopia, or with Hellenes for the feet of the Himalayas. Alexandria was the port of call for the whole known world, and Strabo (XVII, 1, 13 [p. 798]) rightly called it "the greatest emporium of the inhabited earth." It is unnecessary to insist on the fact that the central position of this Egyptian city greatly favored the "dispersion" of the numerous and enterprising Jewish colonists who had taken up their abode there (§ 191).

183. Antioch also became a very important center of the diaspora shortly after Alexandria (Josephus, *War*, VII, 3, 3). The capital of the Seleucids, it dominated the roads to Asia Minor, upper Syria, and Mesopotamia, and enjoyed direct access to the Mediterranean (§ 37).

The Egyptian and Palestinian coasts were not the only points from which the "dispersion" radiated, of course. In the meantime, another dispersion was taking place at the other extremity of the Hellenistic world, i.e., Babylonia, that other center of the world-wide network of Judaism. The conspicuous commercial and social position which the Hebrews had attained there during the Persian period (§§ 62–63), necessarily led to a certain kind of diffusion, the extent of which, however, cannot be traced. The large number of those who remained behind, even after the various "returns," undoubtedly felt the effects of the ethnological upheavals caused by Hellenistic colonization. The various Hellenistic cities which sprang up everywhere, from the Mediterranean to the threshold of India, and whose advantages attracted colonists from various parts of the empire of Alexander (§ 33), must have also attracted some families of Jewish merchants from Babylonia. Here too the lack of documents prevents our painting a very precise picture, but the discovery at Elephantine in the heart of Egypt leads one to hope that a similar fortunate discovery may one day be made in, say Bactria, on the frontiers of India (§ 34).

We are not, however, wholly bereft of information. From the pseudo-Hecataeus of Abdera (in Josephus, *Contra Apionem*, I, 22 [192]), one gathers that Jewish soldiers served in the army of Alexander the Great, at least when it arrived in Babylonia, and their number was apparently not small (cf. *Antiquities*, XI, 8, 5). When the campaign was finished, a good part of these assuredly became colonials in the new Hellenistic cities. The same pseudo-Hecataeus (*C. Apion.*, I, 22 [194]) explicitly testifies to Jewish settlements in Egypt and Phoenicia in the time of the Diadochi (§ 27). Josephus reports that Seleucus I Nicator (§ 35) had granted the Jews who had gone to the Hellenistic cities founded by him the same rights of citizenship as those conceded to the Macedonians and the Greeks. These cities were located both in Asia, to which the Jews of Babylonia could migrate, and upper Syria, including Antioch, to which the Jews of Palestine, especially, could go (*Antiquities*, XII, 3, 1). The same Josephus also tells of a decree of Antiochus III the Great (§ 39), in which it is ordered that two thousand families of Babylonian Jews are to be transported to Lydia and Phrygia where disturbances had broken out, so that by their industry and loyalty they may guarantee the peace in those regions. These families were granted special favors (*Antiquities*, XII, 3, 4). If this decree is authentic and was carried out — and the doubts raised against it do not seem justified — a strong nucleus of the Jewish diaspora existed in the very center of Asia Minor.

184. Since the diaspora had grown to such a great extent by the third century B.C., it is not surprising that the following centuries were to witness very definite results from it. The words which the Sibyl (*Oracula Sibyll.*, III, 271) directed to the Jewish people around 140 B.C.: "Every land shall be full of thee, and every sea," are evidently exaggerated, but, due allowance being made for hyperbole, they do reflect the true state of affairs at that time. A decree of the Roman Senate which was issued during the tenure of Simon Machabeus in 139–138 B.C. expressed favor toward the Jews of the diaspora (§§ 289–290). The decree was in the form of a circular, and the copy which has come down to us is the one that was addressed to Ptolemy king of Egypt (1 Mach. 15:16–21), and the appendix to this copy supplies also a list of the other states to which the circular was sent (1 Mach. 15:22–23). The appendix creates several difficulties (the copy, which is probably not a literal one, does so also. Apart from a few unfamiliar names, we find recorded there in order the kings of Syria, Pergamum, Cappadocia, the king of the Parthians (?), and finally, many of the Greek islands and cities of Asia Minor. In all these places there dwelt Jews who attracted the attention of Rome.

Finally, Rome itself became part of the diaspora. Its Jewish community, which was the last in point of time of the larger centers of the world-wide network, became, from the first century B.C. on, the principal center of dispersion in the West (§ 195).

185. More recent documents from various sources confirm the great extent of the diaspora. Cicero (*Pro Flacco*, 28) reports that during the governorship of Flaccus in Asia in 61 B.C. there were Jews at Apamea, Laodicea, Adramytium, and Pergamum, and he must have been referring to a large and powerful community in the following passage: *quum aurum Iudaeorum nomine quotannis ex Italia et ex omnibus nostris provinciis Hierosolymam exportari soleret, Flaccus sanxit edicto ne ex Asia exportari liceret.* From them Flaccus confiscated considerable sums, especially in the first two localities. Although referring to a somewhat earlier time, Strabo the Cappadocian expressed himself in still stronger words, cited approvingly by Josephus. At the time of the campaign of Scylla against Mithridates (84 B.C.), the nation of the Jews "has already made its appearance in every city, and it would not be easy to find a place on the inhabited earth which has not given refuge to this people, and which has not been occupied by it" (*Antiquities*, XIV, 7, 2). — Agrippa's letter, written in A.D. 40 to the emperor Caligula, thus describes the extent of the diaspora: "[Jerusalem] is the metropolis not only of the region of Judea but of very many others because of the colonies she has sent out on different occasions to neighboring lands: to Egypt, Phoenicia, to Syria, and the so-called Coelesyria, to the most remote territories, Pamphylia, Cilicia, to many parts of Asia up to Bithynia and to the most remote corners of Pontus; likewise to Europe, Thessaly, Boeotia, Macedonia, Aetiolia, Attica, Argus, Corinth, to the more populous and better parts of Peloponnesus. Not only are the continents full of Jewish colonies but also the most important islands, Euboea, Cyprus, Crete. I do not speak, however, of the lands on the other side of the Euphrates; except for a small area, all the satrapies, Babylonia and the others which have a surrounding fertile territory, contain Jewish inhabitants" (*Legat. ad Caium*, 36). — Josephus (*War*, II, 16, 4 [398]; VII, 3, 3 [43]; etc.) and Philo (*In Flaccum*, 7; etc.) make almost the same claim on their own authority, and, occasionally, are borne out by a study of ancient inscriptions which in the Christian era reveals that the Jews were almost everywhere present in the ancient world.

It is common knowledge that from the beginning Christianity made use of roads already opened up by the Jewish diaspora. It is sufficient to recall here that at the Christian Pentecost in Jerusalem there were present pious Jews "from every nation under heaven," and specifically "Parthians, Medes, Elamites, inhabitants of Mesopotamia, Judea, Cappadocia, Pontus, Asia, Phrygia, Pamphylia, Egypt, the parts of Libya near Cyrene, inhabitants of Rome — both Jews and proselytes — Cretes and Arabians" (Acts 2:5, 9–11). In his voyages to Asia Minor and to the Mediterranean regions, including Latium, St. Paul found Jews everywhere. So, too, there were various ancient churches which were predominantly Asiatic, as for example, the church at Lyons, in Gaul, which kept in contact with the church of Ephesus, which supplied it with rulers. There were other similar cases.

186. The Jewish diaspora was notable for the unity existing between the various communities. Even the smaller centers of the network which covered practically the whole civilized world (§ 181) were intimately linked to one another. The exchange of letters between communities, which made up a good portion of the most ancient Christian literature, was normal among the communities of the Jewish diaspora, even though they were widely separated (cf., for example, Acts 28:21). These letters were, of course, only one expression of the mutual interest of the communities, an interest which extended to individuals as well as to whole groups, and concerned economic and spiritual aid.

Abstracting from the inevitable apostasies, indifferentism, the more or less degenerate spiritual environment — which did not affect the masses too seriously — the resistance which the groups of the diaspora manifested was surprising. To borrow an example from chemistry, here was an "emulsion" on the ethnico-religious plane. A drop of oil, shaken in a tube of water, is dispersed, subdivided into a thousand globules, none of which mixes with the water itself. This is a fairly exact picture of the Jewish diaspora as a whole. These small communities isolated though they were in these far-distant lands, often developed spiritual force which gave them an inner unity and made them react against their environment. These small ethnic globules remained Judaism in the midst of, and in opposition to, non-Judaism. To change the metaphor somewhat, they were dispersed cells, each isolated in a reactionary environment, but strengthened by its communion with other distant cells; and it was a communion which incorporated the scattered cells into a single organism. The different degrees of reaction to the various non-Jewish environments, of course, led to different types. There was the Judaism of Babylonia, closed off and concentrated upon itself, and different from the Judaism of Egypt, which was profoundly permeated by Hellenism. Despite these differences of various degrees and importance, there remained a common basis, guarded with such tenacity that it kept alive the internal unity of the diaspora and prevented the Judaism of the diaspora from degenerating into "non-Judaism." For the most part the net result was an "emulsion," but not a fusion.

187. A phenomenon on so large a scale in regard to place, time, and numbers has no parallel in history. Why has not little Israel met the fate of so many other ancient peoples? Although more numerous and more progressive, these latter were liquidated under oppression by tyrannical regimes and disappeared from history. The paradoxical tenacity of the diaspora must be attributed to Jewish *nationalism,* provided that this term be given its strict historical meaning of a "religious nation" or "national religiousness" — in short, Yahwism. Israel

itself offers the clearest proof of this. The kingdom of Samaria, which formed with its ten tribes the more numerous part of Israel, had been deported to Assyria, but its deportation ended with a "fusion," not the "emulsion" of the Jewish diaspora. To this day, no certain traces of the ten tribes can be found in any of the sources. Most of Israel, uprooted from its own country, had no spiritual resistance and, being absorbed by its new environment, disappeared. Not so the deportation from the kingdom of Juda, with which the paradoxical diaspora begins. Why this difference between two parts of the same nation? This: the kingdom of Samaria lacked the singular "nationalism" of the kingdom of Juda; it did not have that Yahwism which, purified and refined by the catastrophe of 586, completely refashioned the nation of Yahweh during the Babylonian exile. The vision of the prophet of the exile, contemplating an expanse of dry bones which the breath of Yahweh would reanimate (§ 75), was a strictly historical synthesis.

188. The internal organization of the different communities of the diaspora varied according to time, place, and the juridical position of the community in relation to the rest of the local population.

Except for the more ancient though sketchy bits of information about the community of Babylonia (§ 60 ff.), our only other source of information is the Talmud of a well-advanced Christian era. This source, however, may go back to a somewhat earlier period.

In the Hellenistic world the communities were given various names. Some of these have been preserved, e.g., πολίτευμα (civic corporation), κατοικία (immigrant colony), λαός (people), ἔθνος (race), πλῆθος (universitas), σύνοδος (assembly), and others more or less synonymous. Later on another term, συναγωγή (civic congregation), became more prevalent than the others commonly used in Hellenistic jurisprudence. This term was in common use, but later came to be restricted to designate the corporate body of the Jews.

189. Although the internal organization of the various communities differed, there were two offices which were regularly found among them, and these were discharged by the "archon" and the "archisynagogus."

The archon (ἄρχων — ruler, a name which derives from that of the celebrated Athenian magistracy) was also called the ἡγούμενος or director. The office was not a personal but a collegiate one, varying in different places as to the number of individuals, length of term, and extent of powers. The college of the archons took care of administrative and judicial affairs which affected the community, but had nothing to do with matters pertaining to cult. These last were the charge of the archisynagogus (ἀρχισυνάγωγος, head of the congregation), who provided for and presided over the place and the people in the ritual gathering or "synagogue" (§ 192). The archisynagogus could be at the same time also an *archon,* and there could be more than one archisynagogus at the same time, in name, if not in actual fact (cf. Acts 13:15).

Along with these magistracies, and regularly found in various times and places, there were the occasionally mentioned πρεσβύτεροι (elders, "ancients"). The γερουσία (senate) was composed of these elders, with a γερουσιάρχης (head of the senate) at their head. The last two offices and terms are attested by various documents; there is also evidence of an ἐθνάρχης (head of the people or race) for Alexandria.The "ancients" and their senate, however, were subordinate to the *archons* and did not exercise any official duties or magistracy, although because of ancient tradition their authority was great. Other secondary magistracies, or better, duties, which were discharged almost exclusively in the synagogal gatherings, but which carried with them no directive power, do not concern us here. For the type of polity attained by the communities of the diaspora, the positions of Alexandria on the one hand, and of Rome on the other, are characteristic.

*   *   *

190. Alexandria. From its earliest beginnings, Palestinian Jews were attracted to Alexandria, where Alexander the Great had granted them the same rights as the Greeks (Josephus, *War,* II, 18, 7; *C. Apion.,* II, 4; cf. *Antiquities,* XIX, 5, 2). Other Jews, partly because it suited them and partly because of circumstances, emigrated there during the reign of Ptolemy I, who assured them the same equality of rights (*Antiquities,* XII, 1, 1). The reasons for such inducements are readily explained by the length of time required for the building of this grandiose city, and the urgent need of populating the new sections as they were added on.

The city was far from being completed at the death of Alexander, and even during the long reign of Ptolemy I the work continued vigorously and without interruption, but it was not completed until the reign of Ptolemy II. The city was built according to the plan of the architect Dinocrates and became the new capital in place of Memphis. Visitors from distant regions came to admire the magnificence of the metropolis conceived by the genius of Alexander.

The city was built on a strip of land which lay between the Mediterranean to the north and Lake Mareotis to the south. The island of Pharos, lying to the north of this strip in the Mediterranean, had been joined to the city by a dike some 1300 yards long which was called the "Eptastadium." Thus, on both sides of the dike two harbors were formed, the "Great Port" on the east and "Eunostus" to the west, and these were protected by other constructions. A canal was also dug to connect Eunostus with Lake Mareotis, thereby facilitating access from the hinterland to the strip upon which the city lay. Within the enclosure of the walls, which were about nine miles long, the buildings were laid out according to a plan which according to modern critics called for straight streets which intersected at right angles. The city was divided into five sections called after the first letters of the alphabet (Alpha, Beta, etc.). The southeastern district retained the name *Rhakotis*, the name of the village which was there before the new development, and the larger and more aristocratic northeastern area was commonly called "New City" (Neapolis). The royal palace and the other principal buildings were built in this latter section and extended to the west into the Bruchium quarter. Directly south of the royal palaces in the fourth area or "Delta" (*War*, II, 18, 8), were to be found the Israelite immigrants, spread out along the eastern walls near the area of the temple of Nemesis (Nemesion) where Pompey would later be buried. Soon even this district became crowded, and the Jews spread out over various other parts of the city, although their more compact settlement in the "Delta" section was maintained (Philo, *Legat. ad Caium*, 20; *In Flaccum*, 8).

191. Immigration from Palestine continued even after the Diadochi and the first Ptolemies, and as Judaism spread from Alexandria beyond Egypt (§ 182), so too it spread to the hinterland. Philo claimed that during his lifetime the Jews living in Alexandria and in all Egypt, "from Katabatmos near Libya to the borders of Ethiopia," numbered a million (*In Flaccum* 6). The geographical extent of their diffusion is fully confirmed by modern discoveries which have brought to light traces of

Air view of present-day Alexandria.

Capharnaum: general view of the ruins of the synagogue. (Lake Tiberias in the upper portion.)

the Jews in the valley of the Nile from the shore of the Mediterranean to "the borders of Ethiopia," that is, to Elephantine (§ 166). That they numbered a million is quite likely. Diodorus Siculus (XVII, 52) states that by the middle of the first century B.C., three hundred thousand freedmen dwelt in Alexandria alone. Add to this the number of slaves, guests, etc., and the capital alone must have reached almost a million. A tenth part of these, that is, one hundred thousand, could easily have been Jews. The other great cities of the Pharaohs and the rest of Egypt all the way up to Ethiopia, could without any difficulty have provided room for nine times as many Jews as Alexandria itself. Confirmation of this is found in Strabo (in Josephus, *Antiquities*, XIV, 7, 2; cf. XVI, 6, 1) according to whom Cyrene, the Libyan city closely related to Alexandria, had a population which was divided into four classes, and of these the fourth was made up of Jews. Their emigration from Alexandria to Cyrene may have been in the direction of Memphis, Thebes, and other Egyptian centers, also. It is to be noted also that the Jews of Alexandria and of Cyrene had their own "synagogues" at Jerusalem (Acts 6:9; § 195).

192. An outline of the internal organization of the community of Alexandria (about 200?, 150? B.C.) is given in the Letter of Aristeas (310). It mentions along with the πολίτευμα and the πλῆθος, also the "priests," the "πρεσβύτεροι of the translators," and ἡγούμενοι (§ 189); the terms συναγωγή, ἄρχων, ἐθνάρχης, and γερουσία do not appear. Toward

Apse of the synagogue of Capharnaum.

the Christian era when the first two of these last four terms had become common, Strabo said that the Jews of Alexandria and Egypt had their "ἐθνάρχης, who ruled the ἔθνος and passed judgment and had charge of the duties and legal prescriptions similar to the *archon* of an autonomous citizenry" (in Josephus, *Antiquities*, XIV, 7, 2; cf. XIX, 5, 2). According to Philo (*In Flaccum*, 10), the emperor Augustus in A.D. 11 instituted the γερουσία for the Jews of Alexandria whose ethnarch had died, and he did not prevent a successor of this latter from being elected (cf. *Antiquities*, XIX, 5, 2). Finally, from Philo himself (*In Flaccum*, 10; 14) one gathers that the *archons* were different from those who made up the γερουσία, and presided over it (cf. Josephus, *War*, VII, 10, 1). In conclusion, the Jewish community, at least toward the Christian era, appeared to be ruled by a monarchical government, at the head of which was an *ethnarch* assisted by *archons*. The democratic element was represented by the γερουσία, which had more direct contact with the everyday needs of the community. According to a rabbinical tradition (Tosephta, *Sukka*, IV; cf. Philo, *In Flaccum*, 10), it was made up of seventy-one members like the Sanhedrin of Jerusalem. This juridically sealed-off community lived its own life in Alexandria, although it enjoyed all civil rights; its autonomy was limited in external affairs only by its subordination to the monarchy of the Lagidae.

In this city there arose the principal edifice devoted to prayer, the προσευχή (*oratory* or "synagogue" in the present-day meaning; cf. § 188), basilical in form with two rows of columns. There were many other lesser "synagogues" in Alexandria and in other centers; an inscription tells of the "synagogue" of Schedia, about thirteen miles from Alexandria and already built by the time of Ptolemy III.

193. It was in these "synagogues" of Egypt, and to benefit their religious services, that the most audacious event of official Yahwism was undertaken, one of the most decisive steps in the history of the human spirit: the translation of the sacred Hebrew Scriptures into Greek. The audacity of this act, decided upon out of sheer necessity in the interests of Yahwism itself, was understood only later when the far-reaching consequences of the step were seen; opinion concerning it then changed radically. In the first century of our era the Jews of Alexandria still celebrated a special feast to commemorate that translation, "thanking God for the ancient benefit which constantly renews itself" (Philo, *De Vita Mosis*, II, 7). Later rabbis were, on the contrary, filled with bitterness toward it, affirming that the day on which that translation was made was a sad one for Israel, comparable to the day of the golden calf, and that the eighth day of the month of Tebeth was to be a day of fast, being the mournful anniversary of that translation, and because on that occasion darkness covered the earth for three days (*Sopherim*, I, 7; *Meg. Taanith*, 50).

The laments of the rabbis, from their point of view, were fully justified. By renouncing the sacred tongue of the sacred nation and placing translations of the *Torah* and other Hebrew scriptures into a pagan language on a par with the originals, an irreparable breach was opened in the spiritual *gadher* which up to that time had encircled and jealously guarded the nation of Yahweh (§ 139). The national-religious exclusiveness of Israel crumbled somewhat, making Judaism much more accessible to non-Jews. This approachableness, however greatly it facilitated the conversion of proselytes from among the pagans (§ 208), was yet bought too dearly for nationalistic Yahwism, for it was through that same breach that Christianity, with its universal appeal, would pass. From this first Greek translation is derived the greater part of the other ancient versions of the Bible — the *latina vetus* (Itala), the Syriac-Hexapla, the Coptic, the Ethiopian, the Armenian, the Gothic, and the Arabic versions. Japhet was indeed entering the tents of Sem (Gen. 9:27).

The translation of the Bible into Greek was a grandiose enterprise also for the history of the literature of mankind, both because of the enormous difference which existed between the fading original language and the language in the process of transformation into which it was translated, and because the entire "official" literature of a people — if the Bible can be considered such — had never before been translated into a language so diverse. Under this aspect it was Sem who entered the tents of Japhet.

194. The Bible was translated into Greek to meet the religious needs of Alexandrian and of Egyptian Jews, among whom knowledge of Hebrew must have been rare from the very first, and toward the beginning of the Christian era, a most singular exception. Philo himself, the typical exponent of Alexandrian Judaism, shows his ignorance of Hebrew. The prevailing Hellenism forced the Jews to choose one of two alternatives: it being impossible to carry out their worship without sacred scriptures they had either to renounce their cult, or "Hellenize" their scriptures. The Egyptian Jews naturally chose the second alternative and translated the Scriptures into Greek, and used this translation thereafter both in private and in their synagogues (Justin, *Apolog.*, I, 31; Ps.-Justin, *Cohort. ad Graec.*, 13; Tertullian, *Apolog.*, 18).

The translation which has come down to the present is conventionally called the "Septuagint," because the Letter of Aristeas mentions its seventy-two translators. From the same letter, however (Pseudo-Aristeas, 30, 314–316), and other indications, it seems certain that this translation had been preceded by other Greek translations, at least partial ones which were later absorbed or set aside by the Septuagint. When the Letter of Aristeas was written (around 200?, 150? B.C.), the Septuagint enjoyed an official and exclusive recognition, which it preserved and increased until the time of Philo, when its popularity began to diminish (cf. Josephus). Under the influence of anti-Christian *animus*, the Septuagint was repudiated in the second century A.D. and other translations were substituted for it (Aquila, Symmachus, Theodotion and perhaps the anonymous *Quinta, Sexta,* and *Septima*); but these also were in Greek. The Greek Bible was indispensable for Alexandrian Judaism and for practically all the rest of the diaspora as well.

The Septuagint was not the work of one translator, nor was it completed all at one time, nor did it follow the same norms. It grew little by little according to the need and the opportunity. It is apparent from philological data that it is the work of more than one translator even in the case of a single book (for example, *Jeremias*). For accuracy and exactness of translation, the *Torah* holds first place; next the historical books or "early Prophets" and with them *Paralipomena;* the "later Prophets" (Vol. I, § 109) are less well done, especially *Daniel,* and the translation of the *Kethubhim* or "Writings" is uneven. As a general rule, the accuracy of the translation is in direct proportion to the liturgical use to which the various books were put, and also to the antiquity of the respective collections as such. It is certain that the translation began with the *Torah,* which was fundamental for liturgical uses, and as occasion permitted proceeded to the other parts of the Canon.

All three parts of the Canon, "the Law and the Prophets and the other Writings" are mentioned by the grandson of the author of *Ecclesiasticus* as having already been translated into Greek when he published (c. 130 B.C.) his Greek translation of a work written in Hebrew by his grandfather, Jesus (Ecclus., prologue). It is not known which

Palimpsest fragment of the version of Aquila (2 Kings, 23: 19–24). Writing underneath in Greek uncials; upper writing in square Hebraic. (From Burkitt, *Fragments of the Book of Kings.*)

or how many books were included in this translation, at least in the third part (i.e., in the "Writings" or *Kethubhim*). It is generally admitted today that the *Torah* had already begun to circulate in its Greek translation at the beginning of the third century B.C.; the translation of the other two parts of the Canon followed in the same and the following century.

195. Rome. The diaspora led to permanent settlements in Rome at
a much later date than in Alexandria. Aside from the brief embassies sent by the Machabees in the second century B.C. (§§ 264, 289),
and from a vague remark of Valerius Maximus (I, 3, 2), we have no
certain knowledge of a Jewish settlement in Rome until soon after

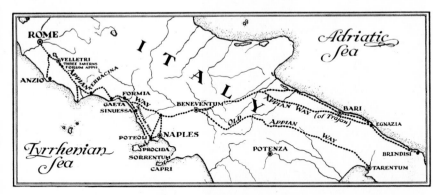

Italy and the roads to Rome.

63 B.C., when Pompey, fresh from the conquest of Jerusalem, transported many prisoners to Rome and there sold them as slaves (Philo,
Legat. ad Caium, 23; cf. Josephus, *War,* I, 7, 6–7). Many of these
slaves won their freedom in various ways, and remained on permanently
in the city as freedmen. Were these the first Jews in Rome? It does not
seem so. If we remember that in 59 B.C. when Cicero delivered his
oration in defense of Flaccus, he discerned many Jews among his
audience, and dwelt upon their large number, their moral unity and
spirit of enterprise (*illa turba quaesita est; scis quanta sit manus, quanta
concordia, quantum valeat in contionibus;* in *Pro Flacco,* 28). If his
words concerning the *aurum Iudaeorum nomine quotannis ex Italia*
which was exported to Jerusalem (§ 185) are also brought to mind,
remembering that *Italia* means chiefly Rome, there is good reason
to hold that the Jewish colony at Rome in 59 B.C. must have been
a good bit older than the one made up of the slaves Pompey had
brought in scarcely three years before. This colony must have greatly
increased in numbers, but even before this many Jews must have been
attracted to Rome by commercial interests from various ports of the
Mediterranean, especially from Alexandria, Cyrene, and proconsular
Africa, all of which constituted the granary of Rome. The magnificent
networks of roads which connected Rome with the ports of southern
Italy, those to the east connecting with Greece and the Orient, and
those to the south and west connecting with Africa, attracted peoples

Tiberius.

of all conditions to Rome, and among them some certainly were Jews of the diaspora.

With dynamic ingenuity the freed Jews of Rome and their other countrymen there insinuated themselves everywhere, chiefly through their many little businesses which prospered amid the Roman people. Among the lower classes, they succeeded in winning a degree of influence. Like the Jews of Alexandria (§ 191), they and their descendants maintained their own "synagogue" in Jerusalem; it was therefore called the synagogue of the freedmen, or of the "Libertines" (Acts 6:9). Those who bore this expense must have been quite well off. The fact also bears witness to the attachment these sons of the diaspora had preserved for the holy city so far away, and this despite their bonds of slavery.

196. Julius Caesar had a special liking for the Jews of Rome, and granted them many privileges (§ 320). In recognition of this the Jews at his death (44 B.C.) lamented at his pyre for several nights (Suetonius, *Divus Iulius,* 84). Augustus also was benevolent toward them, and during his lifetime (in 4 B.C.), there were more than eight thousand Jews in Rome (§ 366); nor did these comprise the whole community (Josephus, *Antiquities,* XVII, 11, 1; *War,* II, 6, 1). Under Tiberius, however, a sad event occurred to disturb the well-being of the community. In A.D. 19 a number of Jews had succeeded in extracting large sums of money from a woman named Fulvia, who was a "proselyte" to Judaism. These sums were supposed to be sent to the Temple at Jerusalem, but instead were slipped into their own pockets. The affair touched off the tongues of a cynical populace, and the sarcasm of conservative patricians, especially as Fulvia's husband Saturninus was a friend of the emperor. The emperor, already in a bad mood because of another scandal which had occurred in the city in the temple of Isis, ordered the expulsion of all Jews from Rome. Not only did he deprive them of their privileges, but he deported four thousand persons,

a number probably made up of Jews and worshipers of Isis, to Sardinia (*Antiquities,* XVIII, 3, 5; Tacitus, *Annal.,* II, 85; Suetonius, *Tiber.,* 36). However, the persecution did not long endure; that step had probably been taken on the advice of Sejanus, Tiberius' omnipotent minister, and a man hostile to the Jews (cf. Philo as quoted by Eusebius, *Chronicon, II, ad annum Christi,* 35 [*Abrahae,* 2050], in Migne, *P.G.,* 19, cols. 537–538). When Sejanus fell in 31, Tiberius restored to the Jews the privileges they had obtained from Caesar and Augustus, and they were free to return to Rome (Philo, *Legat. ad Caium,* 24). There is no record of any disturbance involving the Jews of Rome under Caligula.

Poppaea.

The first years under Claudius were also favorable, for he had confirmed the Jews of Alexandria and of the rest of the Empire in their ancient privileges (Josephus, *Antiquities,* XIX, 5, 2–3). Later, between the years 49 and 50, Claudius expelled them from Rome (Acts 18:2), and the reason is given by Suetonius (*Claud.,* 25) in his famous passage: *Iudaeos impulsore Chresto assidue tumultuantes Roma expulit.* Today it is commonly admitted and cannot be seriously doubted that the *Chrestus* who, according to the Roman historian, served as *impulsor* of the Jewish tumults, was the *Christ* or Messias of the Hebrews. Around 49–50, therefore, there existed in the Jewish colony at Rome at least two factions in violent opposition to each other. One followed an unnamed Messias, and the other refused to recognize him as such. Evidently the first faction were the Christians whose name in ancient times was sometimes changed to *chrestiani* (from χρηστός for χριστός: cf. Tertullian, *Apologet.,* 3; Justin, *Apolog.,* I, 55). The edict of expulsion, however, was executed very remissly or was little more than a ban on religious gatherings (Dio Cassius, LX, 6; cf. XXXVI, 17). It is certain that under Nero, Claudius' successor, the Jews were again in Rome in great numbers (Acts 28:17 ff.) and perhaps more powerful than before. Poppaea, the favorite and the later wife of Nero, acted as their protector before the emperor; it was commonly believed that she was inclined toward the Jewish religion (Josephus, *Antiquities*, XX, 8, 11; *Vita*, 3).

197. The Jewish rebellion and the catastrophe which followed it in 70 seem not to have provoked any special measures of restraint against the Jews of Rome, and certainly none were leveled against them in Antioch (*War*, VII, 5, 2). Only one demand was made, viz., that all the Jews of the empire divert to the temple of Jupiter Capitolinus the two drachmas which they had been paying to the Temple of Jerusalem, now destroyed (*War*, VII, 6, 6; Dio Cassius, LXVI, 7), but even this tax apparently was not rigidly enforced except by Domitian, when *iudaicus fiscus acerbissime actus est* (Suetonius, *Domitian.*, 12).

On the whole, the conditions of the Jews in Rome were ordinarily good, though not perfect as in Alexandria. They did not constitute a city within a city as in the Egyptian metropolis, but they did enjoy privileges not granted to other national groups and other religions, and still less to Christianity. Up to Hadrian the Jewish religion was a *religio licita* in Roman law, and the brief expulsions under Tiberius and Claudius did not abrogate this legal recognition. Thanks to the privileges granted by Caesar and Augustus, the Jews of Rome not only enjoyed freedom of worship, but also the autonomous administration of their social patrimony, and the power of imposing obligatory contributions. They also exercised civil and penal jurisdiction within their *collegia*, subordinate, however, to Roman authority in the more serious cases. Finally, in view of the prescriptions of the Jewish Law regarding the Sabbath, they were also exempt from military service (Josephus, *Antiquities*, XIV, 10, 6 ff.; XVI, 6, 2 ff.; *War*, VI, 6, 2; Philo, *Legat. ad Caium*, 23).

198. The Jewish colony of Rome was divided into many συναγωγαί (§ 188) or *collegia*. Some of them were named after benefactors of the Jews, even though pagans; thus, there was the συναγωγὴ τῶν Αὐγουστησίων, named after Augustus; the one of the ᾿Αγριππησίων, named after M. Vipsanius Agrippa, the friend of the Jews (§§ 344, 350) and builder of the Pantheon of Rome (Josephus, *Antiquities*, XVI, 2, 1–5). The *synagoga Bolumni*, or Βολουμνησίων, was named after the Roman legate in Syria, Volumnius, who was also viewed with favor by the Jews (Josephus, *Antiquities*, XVI, 9, 1; 10, 8). A fragmentary inscription seems to bear certain witness also to a synagogue of [H]POΔIΩN, *Herodiani*, doubtless named after Herod the Great, a friend of the three preceding personages. Other groups were named after the quarter of the city in which the members lived. Thus, there were the *Suburenses* or Σιβουρήσιοι, inhabitants of the Suburra; the συναγωγὴ Καμπεσίων or of the *Campenses*, inhabitants of the Campus Martius, the συναγωγὴ

Καλκαρησίων or of the *Calcarenses*, which name is derived either from the *Calcaria* region near the Circus Flaminius where the lime kilns of the *calcariarii* may have been numerous, or from the corporation of these workers. Others had various names: thus the συναγωγή βερνακλησίων, or βερνακλώρων, was composed of the *vernaculi*, meaning the *urbani*, or those born in the city; in that sense, perhaps, it was used in contra-distinction to the συναγωγή 'Εβρέων, composed probably of those who spoke only Hebrew (Aramaic) because newly arrived in Rome from Judea and using that language in their synagogal worship (§ 200). Some were members of the συναγωγή Τριπολειτῶν. Some have interpreted the name as signifying the merchants of African Tripolitania, especially of Leptis Magna and Sabrata, who were drawn by their commerce to Rome, but more probably they must have been some of those who emigrated from Tripoli of Phoenicia. There are other names some of which are rarer and others of doubtful meaning: 'Ελαίας ("olive tree"? "Elias"? "Elea"?); Σεκηνῶν (African port of Scina?; named after *Sicinius*?); thus, also, the later συναγωγή "Αρκης Λιβάνου, mentioned only once; its members seemed to have come from the citadel of Arca on the slopes of Libanus, which was the native land of Alexander Severus, a good friend of the Jews.

The συναγωγαί of Rome which are attested by documents up to the present time are thirteen in number, but there were undoubtedly others and in all must have numbered more than twenty. Dating from the first century B.C. and afterward, as the incessant immigration from various ports of the Mediterranean gradually created new groups or greatly increased the size of those already in existence, they were erected in various quarters of the city as their names at times indicate. The oldest and most numerous settlement was in the section called Trastevere, extending along the curve of the river from the Porta Portuense to the Porta Settimiana. Outside of this section, Jews were to be found near the Porta Capena and along the Appian Way, on the Celian Hill, near the *Agger* to the north of the Esquiline Gate, in the neighborhood of the Porta Nomentana and the Porta Salaria, as well as in the quarters already mentioned, Suburra, Campus Martius, and Circus Flaminius.

Catacombs served as cemeteries for the various groups and in general corresponded to the location of the groups. The three Jewish catacombs of the Appian Way (Randanini vineyard, Cimarra vineyard, Via Appia Pignatelli), which go back to the second and third centuries A.D., were used by the groups around the Capena Gate, the Appian Way, and in general of the southern and southeastern section of the city. To the east, more toward the north, the catacombs of the Via Labicana (Ap-polloni vineyard) were used for the most part by the groups of the

Grave markers from the tombs of Donatus (top) and Eulogia. Note the 7 and 5-branched lampstands, and a chest containing the "rolls" of the Scriptures. (Müller-Bees, *Jüd. Katak. u. Inschriften, Monteverde*).

Seven-branched lampstand with lamps. Tomb of *Sa[lutia]*. (Müller-Bees.)

Suburra; on the opposite side, to the west, the vast catacombs of Monteverde were used by the groups of the Trastevere; the northern groups used the catacombs on the Via Nomentana (Villa Torlonia-Mussolini) and perhaps also on the Via Salaria. There were also other places on the periphery of Rome which were used for Jewish burials.

199. The various συναγωγαί of Rome were each ruled by a separate and distinct government. While preserving cordial religious and civil relations with one another they were juridically entirely independent. There is not the slightest trace of a γερουσία or other central power which — as in the Judaism of Alexandria and of all Egypt (§ 192) — included in its jurisdiction all the συναγωγαί of Rome, by subjecting them all to one central authority; the arguments adduced in favor of such a condition are not conclusive. Each συναγωγή had its own proper building set aside for prayer, and always called προσευχή[1] (Philo, *Legat. ad Caium*, 23; cf. Juvenal: *"In qua te quaero proseucha?" Sat.*, III, 296; § 192); it corresponded to the present-day "synagogue." Each συναγωγή of Rome was governed by a head approved by the magistrates peculiar to the diaspora (§ 189) and to Alexandria (§ 192). Inscriptions often mention the "archon," the "archisynagogus," and the γερουσιάρχης but never the γερουσία (not even of a particular community), although

---

[1] In the Acts 16:13, the term seems to mean a place in the open for prayer.

the preceding term necessarily demands its existence. The πρεσβύτερος is clearly mentioned only once in a fragment. The προστάτης, who seems to have been, in Rome at least, the "representative" of the συναγωγή before the civil authorities, is only mentioned twice. On the contrary the ἐθνάρχης, the magistrate peculiar to Alexandrian and Egyptian Judaism, nowhere appears. Other secondary magistrates and honorary titles are also frequently mentioned but need not be considered here.

Reconstruction of the Synagogue of Capharnaum.

The respective powers which were attached to these offices were those which were ordinary in the diaspora: the "archisynagogus" had the direction of the προσευχή or the "synagogue" as in present-day usage, and the other duties were apportioned among different magistrates.

200. As an indication of the social environment of the Jewish colony in Rome, it is important to point out that of the five hundred or more Jewish inscriptions known today, 75 per cent are in Greek, 23 per cent in Latin, a dozen or so contain the Hebrew greeting *shalom* or *shalom 'al Yisra'el* ("peace," "peace to Israel"), one is half in Greek and half in Aramaic, and only one is wholly in Aramaic. In a word, the sacred language of Israel, to judge from the inscriptions, had practically disappeared, and its place was taken by the language into which the Septuagint had been translated (§ 194), the language also of the merchants of Alexandria and, for that matter, of the sellers of "roasted peas and nuts" at the Porta Capena. As a matter of fact, the Jews in the two ports of Rome, Ostia and then at Porto, were numerous, and

carried on an extensive trade with the Hellenistic world across the sea. Among the little people around the Porta Capena it was not at all unusual to see the Jew who plied his little business, *plebeio sermone,* selling sticks of sulphur or pieces of glass (Juvenal, *Sat.,* III, 11 ff.; Martial, I, 41, 3 ff.; XII, 57, 13 ff.), or a tattered Jewess who for a few obols would, in barbarous Latin, predict the future, or for a *scrupulum* interpret dreams for gladiators and slaves (cf. Juvenal, *Sat.,* VI, 541 ff.).

Worship in the synagogue was probably conducted in Greek as in Alexandria (§ 194), except possibly in the συναγωγή Ἑβρέων for the reasons already given (§ 198). The same was true also of the liturgy of contemporary Christianity, which in the first two centuries adopted Greek as its language in Rome. It is not altogether impossible that in some cases, for example, in the συναγωγή βερνακλ·σίων, the Latin language was at least partially used.

JEWISH PROSELYTISM

201. The historian of religions finds himself confronted with the fascinating task of analyzing the slender documentary evidence which has come down to him, and of reconstructing from it the attitude assumed by the classical Greek and Roman world when faced with the diaspora.

In the beginning, when the diaspora was still an inconsequential thing, this strange Jewish race must have aroused only a neutral curiosity, especially in Alexandria, where the mixture of the most diverse peoples and the most unusual customs had accustomed the people to any surprise. Later on, however, this neutrality was to be abandoned. When this strange race spread over the whole world without fusing with its environments; when Jewish communities everywhere formed impenetrable spiritual citadels, and especially when the members of these citadels had the temerity to consider themselves spiritually superior to the surrounding worshipers of Jupiter and Artemis, and shunned all moral contact with their neighbors — although they were themselves oftentimes rude and uncultured — then the reaction set in. Retaliation for being repulsed took the form of revulsion directed at these miserable wretches who lived as parasites on the body of Hellenism without ever adapting themselves to it, and who, although aware of the social superiority of the pagan world, doggedly held themselves apart from it. The "emulsion" which resulted from the Jewish diaspora (§ 186) seemed like a mysterious act of pride.

Fundamentally, the difficulty was a religious one. There was no dearth of foreign religions in the Hellenistic and Roman world, from those of the Numidians and of Egypt to those of Asia Minor, of the Parthians, and of India. All were free to follow their own particular forms of worship and feasts; naturally they had their national gods, but all of them had certain elements in common. All had temples in which their respective gods dwelt; here they burned incense, sacrificed animals, banqueted and danced, and enjoyed other activities. Their gods were visible, and could be touched and kissed. But the Jews of the diaspora had nothing like this; they had no temple, sacrificed no animals, had no visible, tangible god at all. No other foreign religion like it had ever appeared.

Indeed, one could seriously doubt whether it was a religion. The abhorrence the Jews manifested for the various divinities including those of the cities in which they dwelt (*C. Apion.*, II, 6 [65]), and their unswerving *contemnere deos* (Tacitus, *Hist.*, V, 5), was sufficient to stamp them as an impious race, *contumelia numinis insignis* (Pliny, *Nat. hist.*, XIII, 4, 46). Besides, they had none of those things which make up a religion and could therefore be called "atheists," as Apollonius Molo actually and logically did (ἀθέους; in *C. Apion.*, II, 14 [148]). It was said, it is true, that this race had its one and only temple in Jerusalem, and that they kept in constant contact with it. It was also told how their god dwelt in the *cella* of that temple (Vol. I, § 391), a mysterious and extraordinarily powerful god. That these reports had no foundation in fact, and that the Jewish temple was in reality an "atheistic" temple was definitely confirmed in 63 B.C. by Pompey the Great, who entered the temple and pushed boldly into the *cella*, where he found *nulla intus deum effigie vacuam sedem et inania arcana* (Tacitus, *Hist.*, V, 9).

202. Such were the basic notions entertained by the Hellenistic and Roman world concerning Judaism. In view of such bias one can understand how the most fantastic tales, the one contradicting the other, were believed, and one can also understand the sarcastic jests of the Hellenes and the hostile conclusions drawn by the Romans.

Sophisticated Alexandria was the great source of anti-Jewish calumnies. Here not only pure fictions were composed, but also cleverly woven combinations of fantasy and fact, derived from the Bible which was now known in its Greek dress. As far back as the middle of the third century B.C., the Egyptian priest Manetho had spread it about that the Jews had descended from the lepers and other offscourings of the Egyptian people, and had incorporated the figure of Moses and other biblical tracts in his tale, as was shown in the preceding volume (Vol. I, § 233). Others of whom names and fragments of writings have been preserved followed Manetho in the same vein: Mnaseas (or Mnapheas) around 200 B.C.; the rhetorician of Rhodes, Apollonius Molo, and the Alexandrian Lysimachus, around 100 B.C.; the Egyptian priest and Stoic philosopher Chaeremon who was the teacher of Nero. The Alexandrian grammarian Apion was the most rabid of them all. He had taught at Rome with great success and had enjoyed the esteem of the court, and had returned to Rome during the reign of Caligula so as to be able to defend the anti-Jewish faction there when conflicts arose in Alexandria (§ 391). The calumnies invented by him and by others were sympathetically listened to, embellished in the retelling, and multiplied apace. And they were accepted as genuine even by serious Roman historians, all the more readily because the common opinion seemed to be verified by the Judaism with which they came into contact.

Manetho's story about the lepers crops up in Tacitus, who remarks that the name Iudae was in ancient times Idaei and was derived from the name of Mount Ida on the island of Crete, their cradle (Hist., V, 2–3). There were different opinions concerning the type of divinity adored by the Jews: Lucanus limits himself to the mention of an incertus deus (Pharsal., II, 593); Juvenal states that nil praeter nubes et caeli numen adorant (Sat., XIV, 97), but others held that the god Bacchus was involved (Plutarch, Sympos., IV, 5). This last opinion was promptly rejected by Tacitus for the decisive reason that: Liber festos laetosque ritus posuit, Iudaeorum mos absurdus sordidusque (Hist., V, 5). The charge that they adored animals is even older. Apion had asserted that the head of an ass was adored in the Temple at Jerusalem, and appeals to the time of Antiochus Epiphanes as proof (C. Apion., II, 7 [80–81]). Such stimulating gossip fared well, and traces of it appear in Diodorus Siculus (XXXIV, 1), in Plutarch (Sympos., IV, 5), and in Tacitus (Hist., V, 3–4), who also explains its historical origin (he forgets what he had himself written about Pompey the Great's inspection in the temple: § 201). Identical charges will be leveled against the Christians (cf. Tertullian, Apolog., 16; Minucius Felix, Octavius, 9). Others thought they saw a relationship between the divinity of the Jews and Jewish abhorrence for pork. Why did not the Jews eat pork? Evidently because they adored it (Plutarch, Sympos., IV, 5; Petronius, Fragment 97 [ed. Bucheler, fr. 37], in Anthologia Latina, ed. Baehrens, IV, Leipzig, 1882, p. 98). The abhorrence for pork was otherwise differently explained: Tacitus gives an historical reason, that the Jews remembered their ancient leprosy and abstained from the flesh of that animal which is subject to it (Hist., V, 4); Juvenal gives an anthropological reason: the flesh of a pig was equivalent in their eyes to human flesh (Sat., XIV, 98), hence, the Roman satirist envies the longevity of the pigs owned by the Jews (VI, 160), as if they really raised them.

203. Other observances were interpreted in a similar manner. The Jews used unleavened bread in their Pasch because in the beginning it was made with stolen grain; they fasted often because they became accustomed to long fasts in the desert; they rested on the Sabbath because on this day their desert trials ended with the arrival in Palestine (all of this is in Tacitus, Hist., V, 4); anyhow, the Sabbath rest was due to laziness (Juvenal, Sat., XIV, 105–106). The Sabbath was also confused with fasting, and even the emperor Augustus, a friend of the Jews, shared the widespread belief that a Jew diligenter sabbatis

ieiunium servat (Seutonius, *Divus August.*, 76; cf. Petronius, Fragment 97; Martial, IV, 4).

Circumcision, of course, was the target for special jests. Josephus replied to the accusation of Apion by citing the example of the Egyptian priests who practiced it (Vol. I, § 133), and in an argument *ad*

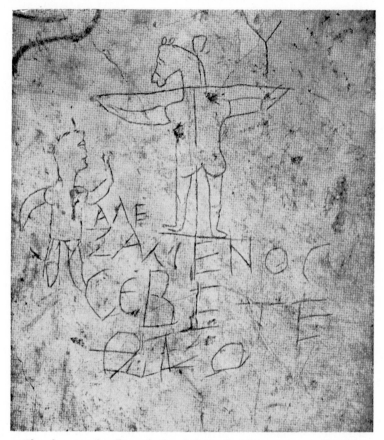

The famous "graffito of the Palatine." (The man to the left venerates a divinity with the head of an ass; behind it is a cross; the Greek inscription reads: *Alexamenos venerate his God.*)

personam, in part insisted on the hygienic benefits resulting from it (*C. Apion.*, II, 13 [137–144]). But he had no answer for the obscene jokes which others made about it. A "circumcised" man meant "a Jew." Other painfully clear and disparaging terms were also used: ψωλός or *verpus* (masculine modification of the obscene *verpa*), or *recutitus*, "lacerated skin." Petronius, Martial, Persius, all reveled in these epithets, but it is easy to imagine how much more the frequenters of the baths or the "gymnasia" enjoyed their broad humor on those rare occasions when they surprised a Jew there with his characteristic mark.

204. The social behavior of the Jews was apparent to all; a thousand and one incidents declared their tenacious clannishness and their separation from the non-Jew. The two went together: *apud ipsos fides obstinata, misericordia in promptu; sed adversus omnes alios, hostile odium* (Tacitus, *Hist.*, V, 5). If someone asked the direction from a Jew, he would only oblige a coreligionist; if someone was thirsty and asked the way to a fountain, the Jew would only show the circumcised the way (Juvenal, *Sat.*, XIV, 103–104). Why such sectarianism? Obviously they had secret agreements and dark pledges. In Alexandria at least it was whispered that the Jews took an oath "not to befriend any stranger, especially a Greek" (*C. Apion.*, II, 10 [121]). It was whispered about that every year the Jews seized a Greek stranger, fattened him up for a year, and then immolated him according to their rites. One part of the ritual was to sample his viscera, and to swear eternal hatred for the Greeks (*C. Apion.*, II, 7 [91 ff.]). Besides being "atheists," therefore, they were also μισάνθρωποι (Apollonius Molo, in *C. Apion.*, II, 14 [148]), or exemplars of that *odium humani generis* of which the Christians also were later accused (Tacitus, *Annal.*, XV, 44). If one needed to be convinced of their true character, one had only to examine the fanatically sectarian precepts which they imparted to their "proselytes," which required of them that they *contemnere deos, exuere patriam, parentes liberos fratres vilia habere* (Tacitus, *Hist.*, V, 5).

Hatred for such an abject and at the same time presumptuous, atheistic, sectarian, parasitical and puritanical race was too good for them; much better to show one's spite and contempt. That here and there some Jews were outstanding for their special talents did not alter the general opinion. Jewish excommunication of foreigners was repaid by ostracism; puritanical segregation, by social isolation. The *barbara superstitio* of Cicero (*Pro Flacco*, 28) finds a response in the *teterrima gens* of Tacitus, just as the *despictissima pars servientium* of this latter (*Hist.*, V, 8) is similar to the *perniciosa ceteris gens* of Quintilian (*Institut. orat.*, III, 7, 21). The words of Marcus Aurelius contain a fitting summary of the attitude of the ancients. He had rubbed elbows with the most uncultured barbarians during many long campaigns, but when he passed through Palestine and was surrounded by the crowds of Jews, *faetentium Iudaeorum et tumultuantium*, it is said that he exclaimed nostalgically: *O Marcomanni, O Quadi, O Sarmatae, tandem alios vobis inertiores* [or *ineptiores*] *inveni!* (Ammianus Marcellinus, XXII, 5.)

* * *

205. Prudent care should be exercised in evaluating the witnesses adduced here. They illustrate the attitude of one mentality against the other, or in other words of one spiritual world against another. But such a world does not comprise all the individuals in it, and the mentality which will pass into history as being characteristic of it may well have been the common and the prevailing one, but not the only one. In these spiritual worlds there are always those better-informed persons who do not share in the views of their contemporaries. Many in fact had seen through them, and thus sounded a warning to future readers.

The Hellenistic and Roman worlds, perhaps more than the others, provided fertile ground for such disagreements. The profound upheavals of whole peoples initiated by Alexander had broken down secular barriers, had jumbled together widely different ideas, and particularly had imported into the Mediterranean countries from Asia Minor, in the form of new religious concepts, human problems which had hitherto never been considered. Naturally the majority remained insensible to these new ideas and continued to live and think along the lines of their traditional culture; others were profoundly affected by them and, being dissatisfied with the prevailing mentality, were in search of something new. It was amid this vast but tranquil world of paganism, and amid that smaller group of troubled human minds that the Jewish diaspora appeared; scornfully rejected by the complacent pagan, it aroused in troubled human spirits now interest, now kindness, and at times even love and acceptance.

It is not surprising that Horace, the Hellenistic *parcus deorum cultor,* looked upon the miserable Roman Jews, all religion and rite, with calm indifference. It is even more understandable that Petronius, that most amoral of the Roman writers, should devote his cutting Latin from Suburra to heaping ridicule upon the generally despised Jews. That austere Tacitus should lose his calm when treating of them and should give credit to the wild tales told about them, may reflect his intuition of the fact that in this *teterrima gens* which held itself aloof, as it were, from the majesty of the Empire, there was something that eluded his sense of history. There were many others like him. In contrast to these, however, there was the old patrician, embittered by the degeneration of ancient customs; the disgusted *cliens,* fed up with his humiliating position; the thinker, who sought in vain for a solid foothold amid the tempest of ideas; the slave, who thought back with longing to Spartacus; the matron, profoundly affected by the mystic oriental cults; the critic, who asked himself whether the pagan religion did not explicitly invite men to be thieves like Mercury, drunkards like Bacchus, adulterers, practicers of incest and pederasty, like Jupiter himself among the gods.

Many of these unexpectedly came into contact with Judaism, and finding it so different from the prevailing ideas, so original in its abstract concepts, and especially so solid in its moral principles, they may have wondered whether — despite some of its difficult prescriptions and the low social status of its representatives — it did not have in it that beneficent new element which they were seeking, the principle of "salvation." For some time, in fact, the Hellenistic world had spoken of a religious *soteria,* and as far back as the third century B.C. the cult of Serapis the "savior" had migrated from Alexandria and captivated the Roman Empire.

206. Judaism found a favorable hearing and made proselytes among these thoughtful souls. Judaism made every effort to approach them and draw them nearer to itself, and, if complete spiritual adherence was not possible, partial union or even a benevolent disposition was welcomed; it was better than nothing. Major obstacles to acceptance were dissimulated or put aside until they would be proposed gradually later on. There was no open talk of racial superiority, exclusive nationalism, or similar topics, for this would have closed the door to those who were outside seeking to be admitted. The fundamental principles of Yahwism, applicable to all humanity and not to the Jews alone, were singled out and stressed, as for example, the belief in only one God, who was spiritual, omnipotent, creator of all things, and lord of all men; general moral principles were expounded too (§ 213). Those who took the first step were no longer hated foreigners and suspected idolaters, but were considered as followers and as the hope of Israel, and while they did not become members of the household, they did become good friends of the family (§ 214).

Was this a renunciation of Israel's proud boast that it was the privileged nation of Yahweh? It was rather a modification of attitude, for while still retaining its privileged position, it was no longer so exclusive; the privileges of the nation could now be communicated to others always safeguarding, of course, the pre-eminence of Israel. To use an example in the material order, Israel was like a ship which, urged along by the breath of Yahweh, at first sailed alone, but later pulled in its wake a string of barges.

One naturally compares this Judaism of the diaspora to the one prepared in Babylonia by Ezechiel and put into effect in Palestine by Nehemias and Esdras. The comparison is instructive. The ancient ideal of a medieval monastery ringed off by a wall and the enclosure (§§ 76, 134) had vanished with the diaspora, at which time Judaism had thrown its doors open to all and the order of the day was *compelle intrare* (Lk. 14:23). Although in Palestine the willing Samaritans, half relatives and half Yahwists (§ 159), had been uncompromisingly rejected, in the diaspora the Jews sought out the uncircumcised devotee of Venus or those who adored the Roman Emperor. In the previous era they had carefully gathered together liturgical prescriptions concerning the number of the lamps of the Temple, or the viscera of the sacrificial victims; now they insisted upon a unique and spiritual deity. The difference was profound; it was not an abandonment of previous positions, but rather a transformation. It was the result of the changing times, and also was an announcement and preparation of a new era.

207. The Jews of the diaspora did their best to propagate Judaism in whole or in part, and to create an atmosphere of sympathy toward it. The ancient nationalistico-Yahwistic superiority was no longer so exclusive; it even assumed missionary guise. Israel desired to be numbered among the various peoples who contributed to Hellenistic civilization. Although hopelessly outclassed in the sciences, the arts, and every branch of culture by other peoples, Israel was conscious of the fact that in one way it surpassed all the others, could make the greatest contribution, and stand as the foremost people of all. A paradox! Israel the spiritual head and guide of the pagan nations! Israel dared claim this spiritual leadership, was firmly convinced of it, and labored to see it realized at the very moment that the pagan peoples, future subjects and obsequious disciples of Israel, officially treated it with loathing and scorn (§ 204).

Israel's consciousness of this new missionary role among the pagans prompted the Jews to search the Yahwistic scriptures to justify it. The ancient prophet had spoken of a "servant of Yahweh" who was to be chosen by God to be a light to the pagan nations and a savior who would bring salvation to the ends of the earth (Isa. 49:6; cf. Acts 13:47). Indeed, in carrying out his mission of salvation, the "servant of Yahweh" would be persecuted, despised, rendered an object of horror, a lamb led to slaughter; yet he would take upon himself the iniquities of many and would obtain justice for the many wicked (Isa. 50:6; 52:13–53:12). Who was this "servant of Yahweh," martyr to his mission of salvation? Looking about them they concluded that he could be none other than the Israel of the diaspora, contemptible in the eyes of the pagans, yet their greatest benefactor. So absolutely convinced were they of this that zealous readers of this part of the scriptures added the name *Israel* in the passages where the prophet mentioned the "servant of Yahweh." It was an exegetical gloss for the benefit of future readers.[1]

Another well-known part of the Yahwistic scriptures (Isa. 2:2–5; Mich. 4:1–5) had foretold that in the long-awaited fullness of time, the

---

[1] The gloss is evident in the text of the Septuagint, Isa. 42:1, but not certain in the Hebrew, 49:3. At any rate, Israel (Jacob) is also called the *servant of Yahweh* in other passages of wider context: 41:8; 42:19–22; 43:10; 44:1, 2, 21; 45:4; 48:20.

house of Yahweh would be elevated above the whole earth and that all the pagan peoples would willingly gather there, exclaiming:

"Come, let us ascend to the mount of Yahweh,
to the house of the God of Jacob,
so that He may teach us concerning His ways,
and we may walk along His paths;
for from Sion proceeds the *Torah*,
and the word of Yahweh from Jerusalem!"

With the abolition of the Palestinian cloister and the spread of Judaism throughout the whole world, was not the fullness of time here foretold drawing near? The time had come for Israel to be the teacher of the whole world, propounding the *Torah* of Jerusalem, and instructing the pagans to walk in the paths of Yahweh.

These are the historical presuppositions which permit Paul to apostrophize the Jew of the diaspora in general, and of Rome in particular, with these words: "You are called 'Jew' and rely upon the Law, and glory in God, and know his will and approve the better things, being informed by the Law; you are confident that you are a guide to the blind, a light to those who are in darkness, an instructor of the unwise, a teacher of children, having in the Law the pattern of knowledge and of truth" (Rom. 2:17–20).

208. Writing was an efficacious way to spread Judaism especially among the cultured classes. Although the Septuagint translation was made for the use of Jews primarily, it also served for those outside the fold and brought the Hebrew scriptures to the direct notice of the pagans; the results of this were sometimes hostile (§ 193). Works dealing with Hebrew history were also written by Hellenistic Jews from the latter part of the third century B.C. and after, and the following names have been preserved: Demetrius, Eupolemus, Artapanus, the genuine Aristeas, Cleodemus; fragments of their writings have been preserved by Alexander Polyhistor (in Eusebius, *Praepar. evang.*, IX, 17–39; Clement Alex., *Stromata*, I, 21, 141; 23, 153–156). These fragments make it clear that such histories had as their purpose the exaltation and defense of the Hebrews, who are portrayed as the pioneers of human civilization, Abraham being a teacher of astrology, Moses the inventor of the alphabet, and so on, and such claims were even taken up by Christian writers of a later era.

While these writers were concerned with the ancient history of their nation, a contemporary history was written by Jason of Cyrene. The second *Book of the Machabees* (2 Mach. 2:23–28 [Vulgate, 24–29]) is simply a "résumé" of his five books. Next, Flavius Josephus (§ 26) treated the whole of Hebrew history in his *Jewish Antiquities*, completing it between A.D. 93 and 94. This was followed by his *Contra Apionem* (or as it is entitled: *On the Antiquity of the Jews*) which was completed around 96. Elsewhere he had already written his eye-witness account of the *Jewish War*, a Greek edition of which, made upon an Aramaic edition, appeared shortly before 79. He was personally cold to religious values, but constantly endeavored to exalt his nation on the international plane, as had his predecessors. Justus of Tiberias, his contemporary, also wrote a general Hebrew history, and another which dealt with the war against Rome, but both have been lost.

We know too of a Philo the Elder, of Theodotus, perhaps a Samaritan, and of an Ezechiel, a tragedian, all of them versifiers on ancient themes of history.

209. These writings were somewhat useful in spreading Jewish propaganda in cultured pagan circles, but they betrayed the partisan hand which composed them. One had only to glance over them to exclaim with Horace: *credit Iudaeus Apella, non ego*. They thought to introduce themselves into these circles wearing pagan dress, by having recourse to ancient and once popular systems, either interpolating authoritative writings of others into their own, or making them up out of whole cloth, using false names. Thus on the one hand we have the false writings of Pseudo-Hecateus of Abdera, the letter of the Pseudo-Aristeas (§§ 192, 194), who went so far as to pose as a pagan, and most of the oracles of the Sibyl (§ 184); on the other hand, there are the occasional spurious citations from Homer, Hesiod, Phocylides, Aeschylus, Sophocles, Euripides, Aratus, and others, all of which are directed more or less openly to the greater glory of Judaism. An outstanding representative of these measures during the middle of the second century B.C. was Aristobulus, perhaps an Alexandrian, who in his work (fragments in Eusebius, *Praepar. evang.*, VIII, 10; XIII, 12) usually tries to prove that Greek philosophy depends on ancient Jewish ideas, and that Pythagoras, Socrates, and Plato, indeed, even Homer and Hesiod, drew copiously on a very old Greek translation of the Bible. Of course, this most ancient translation is pure imagination on his part, just as many verses of the Greek classics which he cites are falsifications of his own or of other Jews.

Toward the beginning of the first century B.C., other Hellenistic Jews published works of a philosophico-religious or polemic character. The *Book of Wisdom* (Vol. 1, § 400), included in the Canon by the Catholic Church, falls in this category, as, in the following century, do the writings of Philo of Alexandria (§§ 390, 391).

210. The most successful propaganda, however, was that which resulted from the thousand and one daily contacts between individuals and small groups. The persistence, energy, and inexhaustible patience of the Jews for their cause are summed up in the famous phrase of Horace:

veluti te Iudaei cogemus in hanc concedere turbam (Sat., I, 4, 142–143). Once they fixed their eye on a possible proselyte, they surrounded him with attentions, invitations, prayers, enticements of every kind, until he succumbed to the gentle pressure (*cogemus*) behind them. The testimony of Matthew (23:15), according to which the Jew was ready to cross the sea or land to "make one proselyte" was aimed at one section of Palestinian Judaism (§ 212), but it applied to the whole diaspora as well.

Any stray lamb was accepted into the sheepfold. The majority of these were persons of low estate: slaves, freedmen, plebeians. Many were women, some of whom were of high station, and, not rarely, persons of importance. Many were drawn to Judaism because of the internal motives already indicated (§ 205); others were drawn by the external means of Jewish propaganda, and still others came for less noble motives. In the diaspora it was practically impossible to make proselytes by threats and violence as in Palestine (Josephus, *Life*, 23). Some took the step so as to enjoy exemption from military duty, or for commercial advantage, or to be able to marry a Jewess (cf. among others the story of Syllaeus, in *Antiquities*, XVI, 7, 6; § 353), or for love of something strange, or in some cases simply because it was the fashion. This latter applied especially to women. It is stated in *War*, II, 20, 2, that all the women of Damascus with few exceptions professed Judaism, which fact must be attributed in great part to a local fashion. It is readily understandable that oftentimes these conversions were superficial and temporary, and were later repudiated. "Many of the [Greeks] agreed to enter into our laws; and some have remained: but there are those who, not being willing to bear the hardship (καρτερίαν), again have withdrawn" (*C. Apion.*, II, 10 [123]).

211. These sheep departed before they had become accustomed to the sheepfold, but others remained, though they oftentimes halted on the threshold. The success of the propaganda was undoubtedly great; wherever Jews settled in any numbers, they won, after a time, either sympathizers or "proselytes." These latter, therefore, were to be found practically all over the world, like the diaspora itself (§ 184). Josephus writes of his time: "Even among the masses [of pagans] there has been for a long time a lively desire for our religion; there does not exist a city whether of the Greeks or barbarians, or a single people among which the practice of the seventh day on which we rest, has not penetrated, and among which the fasts and the burning of lights, and many of our usages regarding food, are not observed" (*C. Apion.*, II, 39 [282]). It would be safe to assume that these words contain some rhetorical exaggeration, but they are substantially true: the public observance of the Sabbath, of lights, and fasting is sarcastically recorded also by Persius (*Sat.*, V, 180 ff.), and

Sarcophagus of the Queen Helen of Adiabene.

is attested by Tertullian, who noted that these practices were wide-spread even in his times (*Ad Nationes*, I, 13; cf. Dio Cassius, XXXVII, 17, although more vague). However, no one would presume to attribute the great diffusion of these Jewish observances solely to a genuine and conscientiously religious proselytism; in most cases it was the result of a formalistic, superstitious mimicry, or, especially where the women were concerned, it was the fashion. Seneca attests to this mimicry: *Illi* [the Jews] *tamen causas ritus sui moverunt; maior pars populi* [non-Jewish] *facit, quod cur faciat ignorat* (in St. Augustine, *City of God*, VI, 11).

Even an approximate estimate of the number of sympathizers or "proselytes" of the Jews is impossible. It is not surprising that at Antioch, the capital of the Seleucids, they should be very numerous and form a sort of addition to the local Jewish community (*War*, VII, 3, 3), as that city was one of the most populous centers of the diaspora (§ 183). Paul, in his voyages throughout the territory of the diaspora, could say that he everywhere found both genuine "proselytes" and σεβόμενοι or φοβούμενοι (§ 213). There are occasional references to them at Antioch of Pisidia (Acts 13:16, 26, 43, 50), at Iconium (Acts 14:1), at Philippi (Acts 16:14), at Thessalonica (Acts 17:4), at Athens (Acts 17:17), at Corinth (Acts 18:7). That the Jewish cause was successful even at Rome, the allusions of the Roman writers (Horace, *Sat.*, I, 9, 68–72; Ovid, *De arte amat.*, I, 75, 415; *Remedium amor.*, 217–218; *Tibullus*, I, 3, 17–18; Juvenal, *Sat.*, III, 10 ff., 296; VI, 156 ff., 542 ff.; XIV, 96–106, etc.) amply prove, and so too the inscriptions on the Jewish catacombs. Several tombs of "proselytes" have been found mixed in with those of the Jews, but no tombs of σεβόμενοι have been found yet in any of the Jewish catacombs. Three Roman inscriptions pertaining to these latter have been discovered, all of them outside of the Jewish catacombs, for since they had not yet accepted the Jewish Law in its entirety, they were not allowed the honor of resting with the children of the Law. Among these sympathizers in Rome there must have been persons of very high station, especially among the women. Poppaea was perhaps one of these; Fulvia certainly was (§ 196).

212. In Palestine itself, Judaism must have made much slower progress among the Hellenists. The words of Matthew (23:15) (§ 210) are, perhaps, directed to those Scribes and Pharisees who sought to procure their own personal glory, and to make themselves heads of their groups; later on it seems that in Palestine proselytes were viewed with an unfavorable eye. At any rate, even here the following special cases are reported: the eunuch of Queen Candace (Acts 8:26 ff.), Azizus, king of Emesa, and Polemon, king of Cilicia related by marriage to Agrippa II (*Antiquities*, XX, 7, 1–3), and especially the royal house of Adiabene. During the reign of Claudius a certain Izates ruled over this region, located beyond the upper Tigris, with Arbela as its capital. At first only a sympathizer, he later allowed himself to be circumcised. His mother Helen, who came to Jerusalem together with Izates' five children, also embraced Judaism when he did. She was very generous in her charitable deeds there and also made provisions there for her tomb, which was adorned with three pyramids (§ 283). She returned to Adiabene after Izates' death and herself died soon after. The bodies of both were carried to Jerusalem and buried in the tomb which she had prepared (*Antiquities*, XX, 2–4; cf. *War*, V, 2, 2; 3, 3; etc.). This tomb has been found in the region usually called "Tombs of the Kings," in the northern suburbs of Jerusalem. A sarcophagus found there in 1863 bore an inscription consisting of two lines; the upper line in Syrio-Oriental characters read *Saddan regina*, the lower line in Aramaic-Palestinian characters read *Saddah regina*. The skeleton inside was five feet five inches in length. A ceramic fragment bearing the ancient Hebrew characters HLN' (Helen) was also found there. It seems that *Sadda(n)* was the Adiabenic name of the queen, and Helen her Greek name.

✿   ✿   ✿

213. Those who were won over by the Jewish propaganda fell into two classes: "devout" or "God-fearing" people (σεβόμενοι or φοβούμενοι τὸν θεόν) and true "proselytes" (προσήλυτοι), a word which corresponds to the ancient Hebrew word *gerim*. The two terms, however, were not always used with the same meaning; sometimes the first (σεβόμενοι) was employed more in the etymological than in the technical sense, so as

Synagogue of Capharnaum: capital with seven-branched lampstand.

to include also the second. The "devout" or "God-fearing," in fact, formed the lowest and least perfect grade: they were sympathizers not yet united to the chosen people, and so their tombs were not to be mixed in with theirs (§ 211). The genuine proselytes formed the higher grade. After they had been circumcised, they became a real part of the chosen people, and enjoyed, theoretically, all the rights of one born a Jew; in practice some few limitations were placed on them.

In much later times these genuine "proselytes," that is, ex-pagans who had been Judaized and circumcised, were also called "proselytes *of justice*" insofar as they observed the justice of the Jewish Law. This differentiated them from the so-called "proselytes *of the gate*" who were neither true "proselytes" nor even of the "devout," but were called thus solely because they lived within the gates, or rather, the territory of Israel. They were also called "proselytes *of the dwelling*." In both these cases the original meaning of the Hebrew term *gerim*, which in its strict sense meant "foreign guest," is unmistakable (cf. the Greek μέτοικοι). The true "proselytes," however, even though foreigners by racial descent, were now put on an equal footing nationally and religiously with the Jew by birth. Little was required of the "devout." Besides giving assent to the doctrines (§ 206) implicit in monotheism, they were usually obliged to the observance of the Sabbath, fasts, contributions to the Temple, and a few prescriptions regarding food. The "proselytes," inasmuch as they were circumcised and Israelites in religion, were held to the observance of the whole Law (cf. Gal. 5:3) just as those who had been born Jews.

214. Circumcision represented a major obstacle to those desirous of passing from the class of the "devout" to that of "proselytes"; the first class was numerically larger than the second. It is almost always to this first class that the allusions of the classical writers cited above refer. From the viewpoint of Judaism adequate compensation awaited those who took the step. The "proselyte" entered in, became one of the household, whereas the "devout," no matter how great a friend he was to the family, remained always an outsider (§ 206). Insofar as he was outside the citizenship of Israel and was not included in the pacts of the promise (Eph. 2:12), a Jew could not visit him in his house nor sit down to table with him without contracting legal impurity. Cornelius, the centurion of the Italian cohort at Caesarea in Palestine, was a φοβούμενος τὸν θεόν and very highly esteemed by the local Jews (Acts 10:2, 22), yet Simon Peter realized that it was unlawful for a Jew to become familiar with him and visit him in his house, precisely because he was a "foreigner" (10:28).

The official reception of a "proselyte" consisted of circumcision, washing by immersion or baptism, and an offering of a sacrifice in the Temple; for a woman there was no circumcision but the last two rites were observed. Sacrificial rites came to an end with the destruction of the Temple by the Romans, but even before A.D. 70 there must have been some laxity in their observance in the remote parts of the diaspora. The rite of immersion does not seem to have been inspired by the legislation regarding purification (Lev. 12 ff.; Num. 19), as if it washed away the previous idolatrous condition, but seems rather to have signified an initiation — or better, a spiritual change, a μετάνοια — as if it gave rise to a new condition of life. During the baptism two men skilled in the Law stood beside the one who was being immersed, reciting some of the principal precepts of the Law. For a woman, two godmothers assisted and the men skilled in the Law recited the verses outside. The rite seems to go back beyond the destruction of Jerusalem (see the difference of opinion between the schools of Shammai and Hillel, in the Mishna, *Pesahim*, 8, 8), although some hold that the baptism was added only later, and that in ancient times the only rite necessary to become a "proselyte" was circumcision. There is some evidence to show that when a man became a "proselyte" he assumed a Hebrew name also.

THE GREEK PERIOD

THE TOBIADS — ANTIOCHUS IV EPIPHANES
THE SADOQITE DOCUMENT — LEONTOPOLIS

215. Turning again to Palestine, we find that we are at once plunged into a sea of nescience, as far as the history of that land is concerned (§ 150). We know nothing certain of the fate that befell the people of Jerusalem immediately after the fall of the Achaemenids and the conquest of Alexander. It has already been pointed out that the account of the idyllic relationship between the community and Alexander which flourished, according to Josephus, during the high priesthood of Jaddua, is accorded scant credence by modern historians (§ 24). Aside from the fact that this account is interwoven with the partisan report of the exiled Manasses and with the construction of the Samaritan temple on Gerizim (§§ 154, 161 ff.), it does not fit in well with Alexander's pressing need to get to Egypt. It harmonizes much less with the fact that after the fall of Tyre and Gaza, Jerusalem and its territory were automatically conquered and could consider no resistance at all against Alexander, such as the account presupposes. What may be historically true in this idyll is, at most, Alexander's benevolent tolerance toward the community of Jerusalem, which suffered no damage of any kind from the new sovereign; but even this was his usual policy. If the last days of the Achaemenids had been really difficult for the Jews of Palestine (§ 151), Alexander's tolerance or indifference brought them some relief, because they now continued to live as a community without disturbance from without.

216. The head of the community was always the high priest. During Alexander's conquest, Jaddua, the son of Johanan (already noted §§ 152, 172), occupied this office, and according to Josephus (*Antiquities*, XI, 8, 7) died about the same time as Alexander (323). Jaddua was succeeded by his son Onias I (cf. 1 Mach. 12:7 ff.), and Onias I by his son Simon I the Just, who died leaving a son still in infancy; hence, instead of the child, Simon's brother Eleazar, a contemporary of Ptolemy II Philadelphus (§ 37), became high priest. Eleazar was succeeded by his uncle Manasses, both pontificating for only a short time. Manasses was succeeded by the son of Simon I the Just, Onias II, a contemporary of Ptolemy III Euergetes (§§ 39, 220). Onias II was followed by his son Simon II, a contemporary of the author of *Ecclesiasticus* (Ecclus. 50:1 ff.), that is, circa 220 B.C. Simon II was followed by his son Onias III, who, during the time of Antiochus IV Epiphanes, was the last in the regular series of high priests (§ 228; for these details cf. Josephus, *Antiquities*, XII, 2, 4; 4, 1, 2, 10).

217. The supreme sovereigns of the community, from the death of Alexander to the battle of Panium (§ 39), were the Ptolemies of Egypt, except for the brief interruptions already noted (§ 37 ff.). In general, the Jews of Palestine fared well under them. Provided the local tributes were paid, the Ptolemies ordinarily did not bother them, nor did they ever outrage the Yahwistic sensibilities of the community by an explicit program of Hellenization. Then too, the continued emigration of Palestinians to Egypt, and especially to the capital Alexandria (§ 181), and the way the Ptolemies fostered this emigration, created between them a sympathetic bond which persisted even after the Seleucids had gained control over Palestine.

Although it was not explicitly imposed, Hellenism began slowly but inexorably to penetrate the territory of the Yahwistic community even during the time of Alexander and the Diadochi, and more so in the time of the Ptolemies. Jews who had enrolled with Alexander (§ 183) or who had colonized Egypt (§ 191) returned from time to time to revisit the homeland; Hellenistic merchants plied their trade on the Palestinian coasts, or Greek veterans came to enjoy well-earned retirement in that country. There were, besides, their contacts with their fellow countrymen in the ever growing diaspora (§ 186), or the thousand social exigencies which brought them in contact with the surrounding Hellenism. All of these factors were as so many breaches made slowly in that jealous *gadher* which encircled the Yahwistic community (§ 139).

There were not wanting also powerful personages on the threshold of the community and even within its territory who made it their business to widen these breaches.

218. The Tobiads. Until recently what little information we had about this family came from Josephus (*Antiquities*, XII, 4, 1 ff.). Recent discoveries of monuments and papyri have augmented that information and help clarify the historical connections between some of its members, and it is now possible better to evaluate the importance of this family and the part it played in the internal and external affairs of Judaism.

At the time of Nehemias' restoration Tobias (§ 125) was able, with the connivance of the high priest Eliashib (§ 144), to install a business office within the confines of the Temple itself. Tobias was an Ammonite and

Ammon must have been the center of his enterprises, but he had good
reason for maintaining an office in an important "trade center" like
Jerusalem. This was in the fifth century.

In the middle of the third century B.C. there is an exact repetition
of names, places, relationships. It was the same situation all over again.
This information is contained in the recently discovered Hellenistico-
Egyptian papyri, all coming from a certain Zeno, who was the commercial agent of Apollonius, the minister of Ptolemy II Philadelphus
(§ 216). One papyrus dated in the year 259–258 is a contract for the
sale of a seven-year-old slave girl to Zeno. The document was drawn
up *in Birta of the Ammonites* and *the horsemen of Tobias* are named
as witnesses; Tobias is mentioned several times. Who this Tobias was
is revealed by two other papyri bearing the date 257. One is a letter
(in two fragments) from Tobias to Apollonius, in which he tells him
that he is sending a eunuch and four slaves; the other is also a letter
from Tobias to Apollonius, but it contains a second letter from Tobias
which Apollonius is to send to King Ptolemy II. The letter to the king
is quite brief: "Tobias to King Ptolemy, salutations. – I am sending you
two horses . . . [a list of the animals sent as gifts follows]. It is well."

Josephus tells us (*Antiquities*, XII, 4, 2) that Tobias had married
a sister of Onias II, the high priest of Jerusalem, and adds a description of the *Birta* (XII, 4, 11: he attributes its building to Hyrcanus, the
nephew of Tobias). The Aramaic term *birta'*, "fortress," is equivalent to
the Hebrew *birah* (§§ 134, 345), but Josephus renders it in Greek as
βᾶρις. It was the stronghold of Tobias.

In the middle of the third century, therefore, there lived in a
"fortified place" in Ammon a man named Tobias who although he
was dependent upon the king of Egypt, at that time sovereign over
Palestine, commanded the border patrol and was on good terms with
his sovereign and that sovereign's ministers. He also engaged in commerce, as had Solomon before him (Vol. I, § 385), and had acquired
great influence in Jerusalem itself, thanks to his ties with the high
priest. He was, therefore, a personage of local consequence, a powerful
ras, not entirely autonomous, but sufficiently influential to approach
Ptolemy himself with a measure of confidence. He had a genuinely
Israelite name, *Tobhiyyah*, "Yahweh [is] good" (§ 104, footnote).
Related though he was to the high priest of Yahweh, his outlook on
things was entirely Hellenistic and in his letters he dared to invoke
the gods. It was natural to suppose that he was a descendant of Tobias,
the ancient adversary of Nehemias, as the name, place, relationship,
habits, mentality, and everything else point in that direction. The
preservation of traditions was no less strong among the Tobiads than
among other Semitic families.

219. The description which Josephus gives of the βᾶρις-Birta tells of white stone, huge sculptured animals, sumptuous halls and courts, and especially of subterranean excavations extending for many stadia in the rock. In the event of a hostile incursion, these were protected by apertures so narrow that only one person at a time could pass through. The ruins of these works have been discovered in Transjordan, east of Jericho. There are subterranean excavations in the rock at 'Araq el-Emir and at the mouth of these the name *TWBYH*, "Tobias," is twice carved in Aramaic letters of a Hebrew type. It has not been possible as yet to establish with certainty to what precise period this type of letter belongs, for it can be ascribed to a period which extends from the fourth to the second century B.C. A short distance away are the ruins of a great building which is called today *Qasr el-'Abd,* "Castle of the Servant." This is undoubtedly the *Birta.*

'Araq el-Emir. (Vester, Amer. Colony.)

Given the tenacity of Semitic place names, it is possible that the phrase "of the Servant" was a reference to the honorary title conferred on the ancient Tobiads as servants or ministers of the Ptolemies. It is not probable

The "Tobias" inscription at 'Araq el-Emir.

that the title is one of disparagement similar to "Ammonite servant," that is, "slave," given by Nehemias to his enemy Tobias (§ 125). Another question is, however, whether it was a genuine "castle." From the plan of the building, from the ornamentation and other details some scholars have held it to be a temple. Abstractly considered, this is not impossible. Elephantine (§ 172) and Leontopolis (§ 247 ff.) go to prove that a man with power and influence could, without difficulty, construct a temple more or less Yahwistic in inspiration, according to his own ideas, on the threshold of Palestine. As a matter of fact, however, although the archaeological identification is far from certain, the name *Birta* used in the papyri points primarily and directly to a "fortress," and only secondarily to a temple. Even Josephus, in his description of the building, in no way indicates, directly or indirectly, that it was supposed to be used for religious purposes. He affirms that it was built by Hyrcanus, the grandson of Tobias, but this can mean at most that the grandson restored or amplified the preceding construction; the papyri make it clear beyond a doubt that the *Birta* already existed in the time of Tobias, the grandfather of Hyrcanus.

220. This Tobias of the time of Ptolemy II had a son Joseph whose star shone brightly during the reign of Ptolemy III Euergetes (§ 216). He figured prominently in an account which was amply embellished by Josephus (*Antiquities*, XII, 4, 2 ff.).[1] Reducing this to solid fact, one

[1] The chronology of this account is certainly false, for it is apparent that the activity of Joseph Tobias is placed after the marriage of Ptolemy V Epiphanes to Cleopatra Syra (§ 40; cf. *Antiquities*, XII, 4, 1). The two mentions of Euergetes

Reconstruction of the presumed temple of 'Araq el-Emir. (From Butler, *Princeton Univ. Expedition Syria.*)

gathers that this Joseph was for several years the taxgatherer of the
levies owed by Palestine to the Ptolemies; that, perhaps for that reason,
he took away from his uncle, the high priest Onias II, practically all
active participation in political and administrative affairs; that he greatly
increased the economic and civil power of the Tobiads; and that he had
a son by the name of Hyrcanus. None of this presents any difficulty;
these were merely the ancient family traditions whereby this Tobias
gathered into his hand the important reins of the government of the
Jewish community, and left to the high priest, the true head of the nation,
only such tasks as concerned the victims for the altar or the incense
for the censers in the Temple of Jerusalem. Had not his ancestor Tobias
aspired to do as much during the time of Nehemias?

One cannot conclude with certainty from Josephus when this Joseph
Tobias died. Indeed, he so intertwines the disappearance of Joseph
and the rise of his son Hyrcanus that the history of Hyrcanus begins
as pure fiction (*Antiquities*, XII, 4, 6 ff.). Hyrcanus had seven older
half-brothers, and in his struggle against them he was supported by
the Ptolemies: this is the kernel of truth in Josephus' story, and it
leads us to suppose that the family of the Tobiads was divided on
matters political. If Hyrcanus was supported by the Ptolemies, the
half-brothers, his opponents, must have sided in with a powerful rival
of the Ptolemies. Who was he? The battle of Panium, which marked
the passing of Palestine from the scepter of the Ptolemies to that of the
Seleucids (§ 217), is the most natural explanation of the division which
separated the Tobiads. Hyrcanus remained true to Ptolemy, probably
Ptolemy V Epiphanes, but his half-brothers went over to the side of
the new sovereign, Antiochus III the Great, and then to Seleucus IV.

221. The political division must have meant also a division of the
possessions and powers which had, up to that time, made up the family
estate of the Tobiads. The passing of Palestine over to the Seleucids
did not mean that their effective authority was at once accepted in all
parts of the new dominion; there remained, as always, the "baronies",
especially if these were strong and situated away from the central
government. The "barony" of the Tobiads remained, being in the
out-of-the-way region of Ammon; Hyrcanus, faithful to the old order,
became its head, maintaining normal relations with the Ptolemies across
the desert to the east of the Dead Sea. On this occasion Hyrcanus,
according to Josephus, built the βάρις-*Birta,* but, as was pointed out, the
building was much older (§ 219) and was at most restored or enlarged.

The half-brothers of Hyrcanus retired to Jerusalem (cf. *Antiquities,*

(XII, 4, 1; and XII, 4, 2), which are chronologically correct, are not found in the
good codices and bear all the earmarks of being later interpolations.

XII, 4, 9; 4, 11), where they could enjoy the direct protection of the Seleucids whom they had supported. Naturally, the direction of the administrative affairs of the nation, which had been previously usurped by their father Joseph Tobias (§ 220) from the high priest Onias II, remained in their hands, and so they retained their own power in Jerusalem and in the territory west of the Jordan. In Jerusalem they found support in the new high priest Simon II, son of Onias II (*Antiquities*, XII, 4, 11), but Hyrcanus, from his fortress in Ammon, had not given up trying to interfere, mostly by political means, in Jerusalem.

During the period which followed the battle of Magnesia, which had been a real catastrophe for the Seleucids (§ 40), Hyrcanus' secret activities must have been stepped up. Quite naturally many in Jerusalem who had endured the Seleucid domination unwillingly while lamenting the passing of the Ptolemaic power, now took advantage of the occasion. Indirectly Hyrcanus fanned the flames, seeking to win to himself those who were discontented with the new government. He exercised a special influence over the high priest, to whom he declared that the administrative power in the hands of his half-brothers was an open usurpation of his power, and he promised that he would restore it to him as it had been before the coming of Joseph Tobias. To convince the high priest, Hyrcanus, who was rich, must have lodged considerable sums with him, to be kept in the Temple according to an ancient practice (§ 144). His determined efforts were crowned with success. Under the high priest Onias III, son and successor of Simeon II, two highly significant facts emerge: the wealth "of Hyrcanus the [descendant] of Tobias" (2 Mach. 3:11) was deposited in the Temple of Jerusalem, and was not entrusted to the official administrator at that time, the Benjamite Simon (§ 225), but to the high priest in person; also, under Antiochus IV Epiphanes, circa 173 B.C., the same Onias III "drove the sons of Tobias out of the city," and these took refuge with Antiochus (Josephus, *War*, I, 1, 1). For Hyrcanus it was a complete victory. The new high priest had been won over to the Ptolemaic faction and his half-brothers were driven out of Jerusalem.

222. The triumph, however, was short-lived. The dominion which Antiochus IV Epiphanes exercised over Palestine was steadily more direct and effective, and could not long tolerate the existence of baronies like the Ammonite barony of Hyrcanus which were loyal to the enemy, the Ptolemies. In all likelihood, then, Hyrcanus was conquered by Epiphanes, as Josephus testifies (*Antiquities*, XII, 4, 11, due abstraction being made from his chronology), but sometime after the year 168–167, in which period the high priest Jason twice fled from Jerusalem to Ammon, and there gathered armed followers against the faction of

Epiphanes (2 Mach. 4:26; 5:5–7). Who else in Ammon could provide such means, and was hostile to the Seleucids, but Hyrcanus Tobias?

It has recently been proposed that Hyrcanus, the son of Joseph Tobias, was the Ephraimite Messias, the son of Joseph; he, like the Jewish Messias and son of David, was to liberate Israel (cf. the story in the Talmud Babli, *Sukkah, 52a*). Tobias, the son of Joseph, has been made into an actual eschatologico-messianic figure. History provides no objective basis for such interpretations. The appellation "son of Joseph" was common to both Hyrcanus and to the Ephraimite Messias, and it was assuredly the family name of thousands of Israelites. It does not seem to be the family name of the Ephraimite Messias, but designates his tribal descent; he came from the tribe of Joseph (Ephraim and Manasses).

223. To recapitulate, it has been seen that the Tobiads followed the policy which was traditional in their family from the time of Nehemias to Antiochus IV Epiphanes. They meddled in the internal affairs of Jerusalem and of the Jewish community in order to hold their influence in administrative and civil rather than in religious affairs. As the family was not equal to the task by itself, it had constantly to be looking for a patron. Under Nehemias it had been Sanballat, *peḥah* of Samaria, and later it was the dynasty of the Ptolemies. Consistently, a foreign patron was called upon to oppose Juda. When the Seleucids took the place of the Ptolemies in Palestine, the family still pursued its traditional policy, varying it to fit the choice of new patrons. The Ptolemies and Seleucids were both equally foreigners; Hyrcanus chose the Ptolemies; his half-brothers chose the Seleucids. It led to division in the family and the antagonism between the two factions.

After his ephemeral victory, Hyrcanus fell back before the Seleucids, but his pro-Seleucid half-brothers won only a Pyrrhic victory. While the Ptolemies had remained outsiders, never attempting to foist Hellenism upon Judaism, the Seleucids had no wish to remain outsiders, and made an attempt to absorb Judaism by hellenizing it. Between the Ptolemies and Jerusalem there could exist a bridge to span the gap, and the pro-Egyptian Tobiads offered themselves to fulfill this function, for their own purposes. There was however no reason for this bridge between the Seleucids and Jerusalem, for the new policy demanded that the Seleucids become Jerusalemites, and that Jerusalem become a Seleucid town. Hyrcanus' brothers were favorable to the Seleucids and blended into the general picture of the Palestinian subjects, with the result that their services along these lines became unnecessary.

Antiochus Epiphanes, the Hellenizer of Judaism, was the ideological successor of the Tobiads, and, being more powerful than they, supplanted them. The resistance raised against him by Hyrcanus was doomed to failure because it depended on a foreign power which was weaker than Epiphanes; the reaction of the Machabees, however, because it was a national force and issued from the people, was successful.

224. Antiochus IV Epiphanes. The passing of Judea under the scepter of the Seleucids did not at first produce revolutionary consequences within the community. But this new acquisition of Antiochus III the Great was a very unstable one, especially so because of the warm friendship which bound most Palestinian Jews to the Egypt of the Ptolemies (§ 217). This friendship could be broken up by fair means or foul, by creating a greater friendship with the new masters, or by destroying the old one by force, and methodically changing the actual state of affairs. As a matter of fact, in either case the Seleucid ruler would find supporters in Palestine among those Jews who, for a variety of reasons, looked favorably upon the new regime. Among these there would be the half-brothers of Hyrcanus, the high priest Simon II (§ 221) who was under their influence, and those who wished to throw the doors of Jerusalem open wide to Hellenism, and they hoped to be helped along in this by the new government.

Such helps as these were not enough to overcome the difficulties involved in such an enterprise. After the disaster which had struck him at Magnesia (§ 40 ff.), and the permanent consequences which this entailed in his relations with Rome, Antiochus III was bereft of the means to win them over by friendship, or of imposing conditions upon them which would lead to the moral conquest of Judea. On the other hand, the undertaking called for extreme delicacy, for such a moral conquest would necessarily have to face a religious problem posed by these new subjects. How was he to resolve it? The Ptolemies had habitually sidestepped it with benign tolerance, and had scrupulously steered clear of anything that concerned a local religion. A Seleucid, however, adversary and supplanter of the Ptolemies, could not imitate such a policy; he had explicitly to declare himself either for or against it. To be a supporter of a narrow Yahwism would mean sacrificing Hellenism, long the program of the Seleucids and basic to unity in the empire, to an insignificant religion of a very secondary province. To oppose it, given the well-known character of its adherents, would be to plunge headlong into a situation fraught with unpredictable political consequences, the net result of which would benefit only the Ptolemies.

For such reasons Antiochus III was persuaded not to take radical measures, and instead adopted as his policy a tacit *modus vivendi*. The territory of Judea belonged to him, but the majority of the inhabitants favored the Ptolemies; he could count upon powerful local supporters who looked forward to reaping a personal profit by their attachment to him, and upon the strictly enforced payment of the tribute.

225. The *modus vivendi* of Antiochus III was continued under his son Seleucus IV Philopator, but at the same time conditions were becoming so critical that they would soon lead to its abandonment.

In his brief reign Seleucus tried by good deeds to win over the influential Ptolemaic faction in Jerusalem. Mention is made of his contributions to help defray the expenses of Temple worship (2 Mach. 3:3), but after Magnesia this faction was greatly strengthened, since Hyrcanus Tobias had rallied the supporters of Ptolemy, and won over the high priest Onias III to whom personally he had entrusted great riches, depositing them in the Temple (§ 221). Yet the faction which supported the Seleucids still held strong positions, led as it was by the half-brothers of Hyrcanus. The direction of administrative affairs which had been usurped by the Tobiads (§ 220) was now carried out by Simon, of the tribe of Benjamin, but a pawn of the Tobiads and possibly related to them also by marriage. In this state of affairs, the pro-Seleucid faction of the Tobiads prepared to strike a blow which would result in grave material and moral damage to the pro-Ptolemaic faction of Onias III and Hyrcanus Tobias. It was known that Seleucus IV was in sore straits because of the annual revenues he had to send to Rome according to the terms of the peace treaty (§ 41); it was well known, on the other hand, that large sums had been deposited in the Temple of Jerusalem (§§ 40, 44) and that they belonged not only to Hyrcanus Tobias but certainly also to many other supporters of the Ptolemies. It would be a simple matter, then, for the king to send some functionary who would quietly and without violence confiscate these riches. The act would be at the same time a concrete declaration of his sovereignty over the country, a financial blow to the opposing faction, and of course it would be of great help to him in his payments to Rome.

226. This attractive course of action was advanced by the well-informed Simon (2 Mach. 3:4 ff.) and Seleucus agreed to it, entrusting the mission to his minister Heliodorus, the same person who would shortly afterward be his assassin. Heliodorus came to Jerusalem with all the outward appearances of friendliness, but when he disclosed the reason for his mission and the news spread around, the assembled people were horrified both at the profanation of the sanctuary, and also at the loss of the sums deposited there. This explains the popular reaction against Heliodorus, but it is altogether likely that the leaders of the Ptolemaic faction further incited the people for political reasons. Heliodorus and his servants prepared to empty the coffers containing the monies, and while Onias the high priest and all the people prayed and pleaded with Yahweh, there appeared first a horse with an awesome rider, then two other personages, who proceeded to flog Heliodorus,

Ruins of Ascalon.

reduced him to a state of abject misery and drove him from the sanctuary. His life was spared through the intercession of Onias, but he thereupon abandoned his project and returned to King Seleucus.

In our account the incident is set forth as being definitely miraculous, but
the rationalistic interpretation of the fact could not be older than it actually is, beginning as it does with Simon himself. Seeing that his plans had
gone awry, he went about saying that Onias the high priest had arranged
the whole affair as a show of his power. No doubt a detailed explanation
of the affair was next in order, and the gist of it was that the awesome
horseman could be none other than one of the knights of Hyrcanus Tobias
(§ 218) and that the other two were his muscle men, previously hidden
in the Temple, ready to play the part of rescuing angels. These accusations were accompanied by fights between the two factions, and blood
flowed (2 Mach. 4:3). Onias then went to pay a visit to King Seleucus,
the one "who sends the tax-gatherer" (Dan. 11:20; Hebrew text), hoping
to prove that it was not his fault that the taxgatherer collected blows
instead of money, and promising him that Jerusalem would be peaceful
again. But there would be no peace.

227. When Seleucus IV died and was succeeded by Antiochus IV
Epiphanes, the rivalry between Hyrcanus Tobias and his half-brothers,
that is, between the Ptolemaic and Seleucid factions, continued, and was
soon further complicated by new faces, new schemes. It is a matter of
record that about the year 173 Onias, the friend of Hyrcanus, "chased
the sons of Tobias out of the city" (§ 221), nor is anything more said
about Simon who had instigated the mission of Heliodorus. But in their
stead other antagonists of Onias had arisen. About the same time —

precise dates are not available — one of Onias' brothers began to come forward and to compete with him for the office of high priest. His name was Jesus, but he was ashamed of his Hebrew name and had changed it to the Greek name *Jason,* which was quite similar. *Nomen, omen:* Jason had a program and urged his candidacy for the office of high priest as a step in its execution. His program was to hellenize Jerusalem completely. Such a program by its very nature made Jason an enemy of his brother Onias III and of Hyrcanus Tobias, but in return it gained him the support of the half-brothers of Hyrcanus, of all the Hellenized Jews of Palestine, and lastly, of Antiochus IV.

Jason calculated shrewdly in posing as the champion of Hellenism, for the Hellenistic element was entering a prosperous phase due to Antiochus' new policy. Unable now to do anything against Rome, Epiphanes had only to pay his tribute; but Egypt, which faced him across Palestine, was not Rome. He therefore thought it time to begin that moral conquest of the country which Antiochus III the Great (§ 224) had not been able to carry out. That conquest or moral assimilation could not be achieved except by a process of Hellenization. During the first phase the program of Hellenization was to be pursued by favoring already existing Hellenistic centers such as the cities of Gaza, Ascalon, Samaria, Scythopolis, Gadara, and others, and by cultivating those men who were favorably disposed and in the public eye. The second phase was to subdue all resistance, and this could always be managed by force. It was this program that Epiphanes had proposed to launch throughout his whole kingdom, which was widespread but not homogeneous and which needed some moral bond to hold it together (§ 42).

228. Jason, of course, was favorably received when he presented himself and his program before Epiphanes, especially in view of the fact that his proposal was accompanied by promises of large sums for the royal strongboxes, at that time in dire need of replenishment (2 Mach. 4:8–9). The illicit bargain was agreed upon and Jason was recognized by Epiphanes as high priest in place of his brother Onias III. The decisive interference of Epiphanes in the internal affairs of the community of Jerusalem must have occurred immediately after Onias had driven the Tobiads out of Jerusalem, probably in the same year 173, and represented the immediate reaction of the Tobiads, who had taken refuge with Epiphanes (§ 221). As a result, the ideological contrast between the two factions was more sharply drawn; no longer was it a matter of personalities, and individuals counted only insofar as they represented sides either for or against Hellenism. The Tobiad half-brothers of Hyrcanus followed the ancient family traditions and championed Hellenism under their new patrons, the Seleucids.

They also made use of ambitious innovators in Jerusalem like Jason. Hyrcanus Tobias and his conservative Ptolemaic friends like Onias III, fought against it. All of these men, even those who belonged to the victorious faction, were destined to failure, and the only one of them to emerge as victor was Antiochus Epiphanes, the true representative of the Hellenic ideal (§ 223). This ideology triumphed briefly, that is, until it came up against personal interests and political situations, and in its turn it was vanquished when confronted by the Yahwistic ideal as represented by the insurrection of the Machabees.

✿   ✿   ✿

229. The official Hellenization of Jerusalem began with the high priest Jason. It comes as no surprise to see at his side in the execution of this program a certain Menelaus, the brother of that Benjamite Simon who had been administrator under Onias III, and a creature of the Tobiads (§ 225; cf. 2 Mach. 4:23 ff.). As was usual in Hellenic cities (§ 33), Jason built a "gymnasium" in Jerusalem, and there young men performed their athletic exercises in the nude, and were divided into groups of "youths" (epheboi) distinguished by their Grecian hats (the *petasus*) (2 Mach. 4:12: Greek text). Young men from the sacerdotal caste also joined in the games, which little by little drew them away from the liturgical services of the Temple, to which they soon preferred their gymnastic exercises and the throwing of the discus (2 Mach. 4:14).

Hellenization extended even to so fundamental a rite of Yahwism as circumcision. Because this left a distinguishing mark which was very noticeable in their nakedness during the games, and exposed them to the intolerable gibes of non-Jews (§ 203), they had recourse to a surgical operation (ἐπισπασμός) which more or less supplied the missing part; those who made use of this expedient "[re]made the prepuce[s]" (1 Mach. 1:15 [Vulgate, 16]; cf. 1 Cor. 7:18), and thus was their Hellenistic honor saved.

They also felt it necessary to show that they were up to date in their intercity relations. Jason had previously proposed to Antiochus that the citizens of Jerusalem be inscribed in the municipal registers of the capital Antioch (2 Mach. 4:9), and on the occasion of the quinquennial games at Tyre sent three hundred drachmas of gold for the offering of sacrifices to Heracles (Melqart). The messengers who carried the money, however, considered this destination so unworthy that they asked the recipients to use the money for their famous arsenal, which was then under construction (2 Mach. 4:18 ff.).

230. This secret rebellion of the messengers of the high priest is very significant, as is also that act of explicit idolatry which he ordered to be performed in pagan Tyre. However, nothing indicates that anything similar had been done by his orders at Jerusalem and, above all, in the Temple, and this seems to show that Hellenism had made progress on the surface only. The Jews liked the more showy and theatrical aspects of the new civilization, but they had not yet understood nor assimilated its spirit. The rustic bumpkin who moves to the city and who, in order to appear citified, dons top hat and tails and attends elaborate concerts, will give some idea of the kind of figure Jason's faction in Jerusalem represented in the eyes of a true Hellenist.

This does not, certainly, diminish the importance of all these manifestations of that provincial and incipient Hellenism which were at least a direct road to the true spirit of the new civilization, but at the same time it must be remembered that in Jerusalem and Judea the Yahwistic outlook was too firmly entrenched to be changed in a few years time. Jason's faction was certainly a minority faction with roots in the city, an active and enterprising minority, as minorities usually are, but outnumbered by the people of the land; the same is true of those lesser centers where Hellenism had little or no foothold, and the ancient national traditions thrived. In Jerusalem, the stronghold of Yahwism, the Temple was so greatly venerated that no one had as yet dared to attack it. Liturgical services may have been to some extent neglected, and the solemnities more or less curtailed, but this was only a result of coolness or estrangement; there was not yet any aggressive hatred shown toward it and the Temple was at least tolerated. A true Hellenist would go much further and state positively that the Yahwistic Temple was incompatible with the spirit of the new city. That was a step which Antiochus IV, an authentic Hellenist in contrast to Jason and his followers, was soon to take.

231. The superficiality of the Hellenism of Jerusalem did not escape the watchful eye of Epiphanes, and he was not satisfied with it. Descending with his army toward Jaffa to meet a possible attack from Egypt (§ 43), he used the occasion to visit nearby Jerusalem, where he was received with great ceremony and blazing torches by a very humble Jason (2 Mach. 4:21-22). His over-all impression must not have been favorable. The project he had in mind for Judea was a very definite one; it consisted in "destroying their superstition and replacing it by Greek *mores,* so as to change that most horrid people for the better,"[2] and yet he now found that little or nothing had been accomplished. Jason was trifling away his time, and lacked the courage to put the ax to the roots, i.e., to the Temple and all Yahwistic practices. Moreover, the fact that Jason descended from the ancient sacerdotal lineage and

---

[2] "Demere superstitionem et mores Graecorum dare. . . . teterrimam gentem in melius mutaret" (Tacitus, *Hist.*, V, 8).

was the brother of the deposed Onias III was enough to make him suspect. He would be replaced at the first opportunity.

The opportunity came rather suddenly, toward the end of 170. Jason had pontificated for about three years (2 Mach. 4:23), and at this time sent his coadjutor Menelaus (§ 229) to court to take care of administrative matters. Aware of Antiochus' discontent, perhaps, Menelaus intrigued to get the office of high priest for himself, and so was very generous in his promises of money. That did it. The fact that he was of the tribe of Benjamin and not of sacerdotal lineage must have recommended him in the eyes of the king, who hoped that he, Menelaus, would prove to be a more energetic hellenizer than Jason had been. When Menelaus returned to Jerusalem with the royal nomination, there was nothing for Jason to do but flee. He took refuge in Ammon for the reason given above (§ 222).

232. What Menelaus did at first to promote the Hellenization of Jerusalem is not reported, but he soon found it very difficult to pay the sums which he had promised to Antiochus. Not only did they seem impossibly out of proportion, but even the revenues from taxes were unexpectedly diminished, for now, for the first time, there is mention of a royal official, a certain Sostratus, who had been installed in the "acropolis" of Jerusalem to "gather" the taxes (2 Mach. 4:27–29). The new official represented another sign of Antiochus' possession of Jerusalem, already a fact when he granted to Menelaus a high priesthood that was nothing but a shadow, and was burdened with crushing debts.

The insolvent Menelaus was summoned to court, and Sostratus as well. It seems that on this occasion he left his brother Lysimachus as his successor (διάδοχον: perhaps in the sense only of "vicar") in the office of high priest, but in the meantime he himself had appropriated many golden objects from the Temple of Jerusalem, which he sold at Tyre and elsewhere so as not to have to appear empty-

Waterfall of Daphne, near Antioch.
(Vester, Amer. Colony.)

handed before his master. This was in the beginning of 169 and Epiphanes, who had repaired to Cilicia in the region of Tarsus and Mallos to put down a revolt, had left Andronicus behind as governor of Antioch. Menelaus approached him while at court and tried to win him over to his side with the gold he had stolen from the Temple. But suddenly he found himself face to face with a new adversary who was present on the scene and seemed to have been almost forgotten, Onias III.

233. After he had been supplanted by his brother Jason (§ 228), the high priest Onias III had taken up residence at Antioch. He was perhaps constrained to live there by Antiochus, who wanted the legitimate representative of the office of high priest under his control in case anything developed, and who seemed moreover to have regarded him highly. It would have been dangerous for him to live in the royal city, for among the many Jews residing there (§ 183), not a few must have been favorable to Jason, and inclined to do violence to the person of the ex-high priest, so Onias had taken refuge in a suburb of Antioch, close to the sanctuary of Apollo and Daphne, where his life was assured him by the right of sanctuary.

From Daphne, of course, Onias kept in touch with the fortunes of his Temple, and having received word of Menelaus' depredation, bitterly reproved him for it when he arrived in Antioch. This reproof from so important an exile, and perhaps also the vague fear that King Antiochus might one day restore Onias to his post, convinced Menelaus that Onias had to be done away with. He arranged the matter with Andronicus, who lured Onias from the sacred enclosure of Daphne with false promises of security, and, once he was outside, killed him (2 Mach. 4:33 ff.).

234. From another source comes information of another homicide perpetrated by the same Andronicus. When Antiochus IV Epiphanes ascended to the throne, he had trampled on the rights not only of his nephew Demetrius, then a hostage at Rome, but also of another son of the preceding king, Seleucus IV, who was still of a very tender age, and seems to have been called Antiochus (§ 41). Epiphanes was unconcerned about the far-off Demetrius, but he was concerned about little Antiochus, for the child was apparently much loved by the people. For the first years, Epiphanes acted as if he was co-ruler with the child, and its tutor. Along about this time, toward the beginning of 169, when Epiphanes was still in Cilicia, Andronicus suddenly slew the young Antiochus (Diodorus Siculus, XXX, 7, 2; cf. John Antiochenus, Fragment 58, in Müller, *Fragmenta hist. Graec.*, IV). What had moved Andronicus to perpetrate so politically dangerous a regicide? The very least one can say of it is that he was convinced that it would please Epiphanes. But over and above this there remains the suspicion that Epiphanes had secretly ordered the deed, and had disposed things in such a way that it might be accomplished on another's initiative when he himself was far away from the capital. Thus he himself would appear innocent in the eyes of the people. The fury of the populace exploded into such violence that Epiphanes put Andronicus to death.

The murders of Onias and of little Antiochus were almost simultaneous. Many of the non-Jews were especially aroused by the second deed, and demanded justice, while many of the Jews in Antioch reacted in like manner toward the first. On the king's arrival the popular protest was unanimous, and the head of the murderer was demanded. This explains why a Jewish source of information attributes the punishment of Andronicus to the murder of Onias, while the non-Jewish source attributes it to the regicide, each side being concerned with its own interests and ignoring the other.

235. Meanwhile, the pecuniary pledges of Menelaus became still further complicated. While Antiochus was waging his first campaign of 169 in Egypt (§ 43), Lysimachus in Jerusalem was methodically despoiling the Temple, acting on the orders of his brother Menelaus and thereby aiding him in his difficult situation. Eventually, however, the people were aroused and killed the sacrilegious thief. From a juridical standpoint, once the sacrilege was proved, the killing was justified as a legitimate penalty. Menelaus was therefore accused as being responsible for the sacrilege which had provoked the killing of Lysimachus, and three messengers were sent from Jerusalem to Tyre, where Antiochus had arrived (probably on his return from Egypt) to support the accusation. But with the help of a powerful courtier Menelaus had the three messengers put to death, and shortly after, confident of the royal protection, re-entered Jerusalem (2 Mach. 4:39–50).

Things remained thus unsettled until the following year, 168, when Epiphanes waged his second campaign in Egypt (§ 43; cf. 2 Mach. 5:1 ff.). The intervention of Rome was seriously embarrassing for him, but it gave him opportunity to march against his adversaries in Palestine, where the rumor had been spread that he had died. Jason quickly moved from his refuge in Ammon and broke into Jerusalem with an armed band. Once sure of the possession of the city, he began to put to death the supporters of Menelaus, and forced them to take refuge in the acropolis, under the protection of the royal troops (§ 232). Jason's short-lived success was of the greatest importance for the consequent fate of Jerusalem, for it convinced Antiochus that he would have to force Hellenism upon Judea (§ 227), and forego all compromise or bargaining. To Antiochus, locked in combat with the Ptolemies, Jason's coup must have spoken of base treason aimed at him by the Ptolemaic, anti-Seleucid and anti-Hellenistic party. There was no alternative but to destroy these three branches of the same trunk; the ax had to be put to the roots.

236. When Antiochus stepped out of the "circle" of Popilius Laenas (§ 43) and therefore from Egypt, he returned to Palestine, furiously determined to settle accounts with his betrayers. He quickly took Jerusalem, all of which had been taken by Jason, save the acropolis. Jason again fled to Ammon, but soon was obliged to flee thence to Sparta, where he died (§ 279). The suspicion arises that Antiochus' troops pursued the rebel even into the loyal "barony" of Hyrcanus Tobias, and that on this occasion this latter was decisively vanquished.

Jerusalem was a scene of carnage. Naturally the supporters of Jason were the first to be killed, but others also certainly who were suspected of being hostile to the Seleucids, friendly to the Ptolemies, or simply adverse to new ideas. Many others were deported and sold as slaves. Then Antiochus, to recoup some of his war expenses, and at the same time to humiliate the stronghold of Yahwism, entered and despoiled the Temple, going all the way into the "holy place," and carrying away the golden lampstand and altar (§ 102) and a large quantity of other objects and precious furnishings. He also took possession of the treasures deposited in the sacred enclosure, the high priest Menelaus acting as guide in the discovery of the gold of Yahweh (2 Mach. 5:15; cf. 1 Mach. 1:21 [Vulgate, 23] ff.). He then returned with his booty to Antioch, not because he believed that his mission in Jerusalem was ended, but because he had been away since the beginning of the campaign, and there was urgent need for him there. He left his general Philip Phrygius (§ 44) and Menelaus in Jerusalem; Menelaus could pursue his own revenge at his leisure.

After more than a year had passed,[3] that is, at the end of 167, he decided to finish the program which had scarcely been inaugurated by his despoiling of the Temple. He could not now direct his thoughts in the direction of Egypt because of Rome's veto, but he could very well make his province of Judea a solid moral bulwark against that enemy kingdom by completely hellenizing it. He would himself personally direct the process.

Despite the serious blow it had endured in that theft and bloodshed, the Yahwism of Jerusalem was still a moral and material force to be reckoned with. Epiphanes was aware of the fact, and therefore sent Apollonius at the head of a sizable force to execute his plans. This Apollonius is not mentioned by name in 1 Mach. 1:29 [Vulgate, 30], being there described as "collector of the tribute," but he is named in 2 Mach. 5:24, and is described as μυσάρχης, that is, probably, "commander

---

[3] The date given in 1 Mach. 1:29 [Vulgate, 30] "after two years" is a round number, unless some other system of computation is meant (cf. § 36).

of the Mysians" who constituted a picked body of troops. It was clearly a matter of the iron fist.

237. To force, Apollonius added craftiness. Foreseeing opposition, and desirous both of sparing losses to his men and avoiding a tedious siege, he approached the city feigning a friendly attitude. One day, however, while the loyal Yahwists were immobilized by the Sabbath rest, he broke into the city, slaughtered the inhabitants, sold men and women into slavery, and laid about him with a heavy hand. After this preliminary step, he aimed at securing a lasting and undisputed control of Jerusalem. The encircling walls were therefore dismantled so that they could no longer serve for defense, and, perhaps with stones taken from the walls, a fortress, *Akra,* was built within the city. These walls, which had cost Nehemias so much trouble, and which had arisen as a symbol of his ideal of Yahwistic reconstruction, now were fallen and transformed into a permanent reminder of pagan tyranny.

The Akra was a veritable dagger thrust into the heart of Jerusalem. Close to the Temple, like a hawk guarding its prey, it was girded by a large wall re-enforced with towers. There for a quarter of a century it stood opposite Yahweh's Temple, an impregnable sign of pagan power (§ 285). Its precise location has been the subject of various hypotheses. The most common opinion, based on the data supplied by Josephus, is that it was situated on the crest of Ophel near the elevation overlooking the spring of Gihon (Vol. I, § 96 ff.). If such were the case, it would be to the south of the Temple. Recently, however, Père Vincent and Père Abel have questioned this data of Josephus, and have adduced serious archaeological and topographical reasons to support their contention that the Akra was situated on the slope of the western hill of the city which faced the Temple. If this is true, it was to the west of the Temple and dominated both the "City of David" on Ophel and the more recent expansion of the city toward the northwest.

238. While the Akra was being built the hurricane again struck the city. "Not long after" (2 Mach. 6:1), Antiochus sent an "old Athenian" to Jerusalem to direct the methodical transformation of the ruins of Yahwism into Hellenistic institutions. That an old Athenian was chosen for this mission shows a desire to draw upon the purest source of the new civilization, Athens, the mother of Hellenism. The king wished to give his Hellenistic program the note of genuineness. However, there is a Latin variant which has: "an old Antiochian" instead, which suggests that he was a member of the γερουσία or "senate" (§ 189) of Antioch, and in view of this position was charged with the task of transplanting the Hellenistic institutions of the capital to the city chosen for Hellenization.

Under the technical direction of a specialist who was backed up by

Syrian arms, the transformation of the city was rapid.
No time was to be lost in
dawdling, as Jason (§ 230)
and the other ordinary Hellenistic Jews had done; the
instructions of the king to the
messenger were precise, *demere superstitionem* (§ 231),
put the ax to the roots. With
perfect logic the most un-

Tetradrachma of Antiochus IV. The King to
the left; Jupiter to the right.

shakable foundations of the Yahwistic religion: the Temple and its mono-
theistic cult, the practice of circumcision and the observance of the Sabbath, and the books of the *Torah;* all these were systematically attacked.

239. On the fifteenth of December, 167 B.C., the "Abomination of desolation" was erected in the Temple of Yahweh (1 Mach. 1:54: Greek
text).[4] It was probably a statue of Jupiter Olympus, and it perhaps
had the features of the same Antiochus to whom the cult was directed.
On some of his coins the king is portrayed as Jupiter.

The perennial sacrifices and oblations of the cult of Yahweh had
now ceased and a Greek altar had been erected over the altar of
holocausts. Pagan sacrifices were offered ten days later, on the twenty-
fifth day of December, on the festival of the sun-god who was reborn at
the winter solstice. Thus was the Temple of Yahweh in Jerusalem dedicated to Jupiter Olympus.

But a temple had also been built for Yahweh by the Samaritans on
Gerizim. Even this Yahwistic temple was incompatible with Hellenism.
It was forced to change its name, and was dedicated to Jupiter Xenios,
or the Hospitable One (§ 164).

With the Temple of Jerusalem paganized, it was necessary that the
pagan cult be spread outside its walls also. Everywhere there appeared
idolatrous statues; in the streets and squares of Jerusalem, before the
doors of the principal buildings, in the smaller villages throughout the
country, braziers and altars were set up, incense was offered and animals
were sacrificed. The animal of preference was the pig, for two reasons:
it was most hateful to the Hebrews as being a most impure animal
and, besides being sacred to Demeter, it played an important part
in the purification rites of the Eleusinian mysteries. It was a fitting
humiliation to hold up as a purifying element, or at least as something

---

[4] This is the famous phrase of Daniel, Hebrew (9:27) 11:31; 12:11 (cf. Mk.
13:14). It was, perhaps, a partially cryptographic substitution to designate with
disdain the god *Ba'al-shamin* (Vol. I, § 107) or "Lord of heaven"; cf. *RB*, 1930,
pp. 188–189.

pure, that which until then the Jews had considered as impurity itself.

Peremptory orders from Antioch imposed the pagan cult under penalty of death to anyone who refused; rich rewards were promised to the prominent persons who obeyed. Every month an inspection was carried out in the various places to see that the orders were obeyed (1 Mach. 1:58 [Vulgate, 61]). The Temple, which in the past had been used for sacred prostitution (Vol. I, § 501), was now filled with harlots and was the scene of Hellenistic orgies (2 Mach. 6:4), but the pagan cult was also required in places prepared for it elsewhere. On the monthly celebration of the king's birthday participation in the sacrifices was obligatory, and during the festival of Dionysius all were obliged to go around in procession wearing crowns of ivy (2 Mach. 6:7). Participation in the rites might consist simply in putting incense in the brazier, but on occasion it involved the eating of some of the immolated flesh, especially if it was pork.

To these positive prescriptions were now added others, negative but equally severe, and aimed at the eradication of all traces of Yahwism. It was forbidden to circumcise infants, to observe the Sabbath or other feasts, to have in one's possession the books of the Law — these were to be turned over to the authorities, torn up, and burned. Violation of these prohibitions was punishable by death.

240. Was all this simply an application to Jerusalem of the juridical norm governing the Hellenistic πόλις (§ 33)? Although there is the purely juridical question, there is the "human" problem. Hellenism did not recognize the human problem of "liberty of conscience," for up to this moment all the religions it had met in its path had bowed down before it in compliant acceptance; Yahwism alone did not bow down, and the human problem was raised. With this we come into contact with a typical religious persecution, the first known to history.

❊   ❊   ❊

241. The hurricane which broke upon the vineyard of Yahweh shook loose many of the loose or rotten grapes (§ 58). In the wake of persecution there were many apostasies, long prepared for by the growing enthusiasm for Greek customs and spirit, and by the simultaneous coolness toward Yahwistic ideals and national customs. Mass defections were common, especially in cities along the Mediterranean which were directly exposed to the influence of Hellenism, and in Jerusalem where the behavior of Jason the high priest was a continuous scandal which invited apostasy. Considerable impetus in that direction was also given in Jerusalem by the Syrian garrison stationed in the Akra (§ 237). But in the less populous centers, those out of range or in country areas where

Sarcophagus of the seven brothers, called "Machabees" (discovered in
1876). (Rome, S. Pietro in Vinculi.)

Hellenism was more superficial and ancient national traditions were
more deeply rooted, the new program won few supporters.

However, even in the above-mentioned cities there were rebels and
consequently martyrs, and these were not few. Special mention is made
of mothers who circumcised their sons even after the anti-Yahwistic
edicts, and who on that account were killed together with their little
ones. In some cases the rulers sought to terrorize the populace. Two
anonymous mothers, accused of having circumcised their sons, were
carried about the city with their babes tied to their bosoms, and then
thrown from the walls. Anyone who was discovered observing the
Sabbath in caves was liable to be burned by fires built at the entrance
of the cave by the Syrian officials. Others paid with their lives for
their veneration for the sacred scriptures of Yahwism, if apprehended
with the books of the *Torah* in their possession.

242. The famous example of Eleazar (2 Mach. 6:18 ff.), who preferred to die rather than even pretend to eat pork, does honor to the
scribal class to which he belonged. The other celebrated example of the
anonymous mother (2 Mach. 7) who was present at the martyrdom of
her seven sons, encouraging them to stand fast, and who then followed
them to death out of loyalty to the laws of her people, is described as
if it happened under the very eyes of Antiochus himself. Both incidents — which reappear in the apocryphal 4 Mach. 5 ff.; 8 ff. — form
as it were separate parts in the account of the persecution, but the presence of Antiochus at the martyrdom of the mother and her seven sons
makes their chronological position doubtful. It has been held that at
least the second incident occurred during this persecution, but in Antioch, where the king happened to be at that time, not in Jerusalem.
It seems more probable that both martyrdoms, that of Eleazar and
of the mother, took place during the brief persecution of 168 and
therefore in Jerusalem under the eyes of Antiochus, then present in the

city, but that they were placed out of their chronological order and narrated on the occasion of this second persecution to suit the didactic purposes of the writer.

243. Although many others were not martyrs, they avoided apostasy by quitting inhabited centers, which were effectively controlled by the Syrian authorities. It is important to note that there was a considerable exodus from Jerusalem itself (1 Mach. 1:38 [Vulgate 40]), which shows that much of the Yahwistic heritage still remained in the capital. At first, this unexpected disappearance of the citizens seemed a blessing to the new masters, for Hellenistic-minded inhabitants were called to take their place, settled comfortably in the vacated houses, and thus strengthened their position. Later on, however, the Hellenizers perceived that they had won only a Pyrrhic victory, for the citizens who had left the city only prepared their counterattack elsewhere.

Many of these émigrés from the city took up their abode in the country. Those who did not relish the prospect of martyrdom could no longer remain in the cities where the pagans were absolute masters, and nothing could be hoped for from the fallen priests and elders. The only thing left to do was to scatter over the steppes, where the vexations of the new masters could not easily overtake them, and there lead the nomadic life of the Bedouin, living today in a cave, tomorrow with a trusted friend, one day losing oneself in the solitude of the desert, and reappearing later on some solitary height. This meant bidding farewell to family possessions, but what mattered that if their moral patrimony was saved. The wandering life in the open desert, for that matter, was an ideal which lay dormant in the hearts of many Israelites. Indeed, in every period there were ardent Yahwists who looked upon the first sojourn in the desert as the golden age of the nation, and who felt that it was a departure from ancient purity for Yahwism to settle in the cities (§ 246). Whence it happened that "many who sought justice and judgment [the practice of the moral precepts of Yahwistic religion] went down into the desert to dwell there, they and their sons and their wives and their cattle" (1 Mach. 2:29–30).

It is obvious that these scattered Jews did not form a real political faction nor a genuine religious confraternity; they were simply saviors of the national traditions, faithful to the *Torah*, the devout or "pious"; in fact, that is what they were called, Hasidhim ('Ασιδαῖοι, Vulgate, *Assidaei*). Confronted with persecution, these Assideans were up to this time only passively resistant.

Perhaps there were also, under these circumstances, secessions within Yahwism which were strictly corporate in character.

244. The Sadoqite Document. A fragmentary Hebrew codex, published in 1910, was discovered in that veritable mine of treasure, the *genizah* of Old Cairo, and is commonly known today as the *Sadoqite Document* or *Fragment*. Unfortunately, the nine folios which compose it are in a deteriorated condition and what is worse, its contents so persistently defy any certain assignation in history that it is difficult to draw any solid conclusions from them. Written in good Hebrew, with some Aramaisms and rabbinisms, it tells of a Jewish community established at Damascus and bearing the name of the "Sons of Sadoq" or of the "New Alliance." This bit of information is as isolated as the type of community therein described is new.

In it there appears a "Master of justice," "Unique Master," "Legislator," who was raised up by God to save Israel 390 years after the destruction of Jerusalem by Nabuchodonosor. But his teachings were not accepted by the Israelites, seduced as they were by the "Man of lies." Hence, after twenty years the "Master of justice" emigrated with some of his disciples, the "Penitents of Israel," to Damascus, where he founded the "New Alliance," the "Alliance of penance." The "Master of justice" was the offspring "of Israel and Aaron," the "Star" come forth from Jacob (cf. Num. 24:17). Yet he seems to be different from another "Master of justice" who will appear at the end of time. The "Master of justice" died at an undetermined time, and about forty years after his death "all the men of war who went with the man of lies have disappeared." These have often been identified with those who "build the wall and plaster it" (cf. Ezech. 13:10 ff.); these, given over to luxury and avarice, profane the sanctuary, for which reason the Most High had already punished them in the past, and "the head of the kings of Javan (Greece) came to wreak upon them the divine vengeance." The members of the "New Alliance" will hold themselves apart from these "Sons of perdition." They will observe the Sabbath, the Jewish festivals with their fasts, and a large quantity of other rigid prescriptions including monogamy, with exactitude. A complex body of legislation almost militaristic in character was, in fact, imposed on the "Sons of Sadoq," by which they were guided even in the minutest details of daily life. At the head of the community were, not the priests, but simple laymen. They thus awaited the Messias of Aaron and of Israel who would come to save those faithful to him, and to exterminate all others.

245. How should such a document, so lacking in precision and so similar to other Jewish writings which are only superficially historical, be interpreted? It is unquestionably the product of a reform movement which opposed a majority it judged to be wicked and corrupt, but which, nevertheless, prevailed. Aside from this enlightening point we are reduced to conjecture only. Suffice it to state that the numerous hypotheses concerning it have assigned the document to periods ranging from 170 B.C. up to the seventh century A.D., abstracting from Margoliouth, who wrongly attributes it to a Sadducean-Christian sect which flourished at Damascus in the ninth century A.D.

According to the chronological data of this document, the "Master of justice" should have appeared 390 years after the destruction of Jerusalem (586 B.C.), that is, in 196 B.C., and his emigration to Damascus would occur twenty years later in 176 B.C., and thus would clearly fall in the period of the Seleucids. But have the figures a real or only a symbolic value? Are they an exact chronicle of events, or an apocalyptic elaboration of a program of dates? No one can answer with certainty, considering the widespread use of symbolic artifices encountered in Jewish literature from the second century B.C. on down. The "Sons of perdition" who "build the wall and plaster it" are possibly the Hellenized priests of Jerusalem of the time of Antiochus IV; some scholars have perceived in them the Pharisees, building the "wall" of tradition which complemented the *Torah*. In this second case, the "Sons of Sadoq" would necessarily be the Sadducees; but they would not be the Sadducees known elsewhere in history, for they were surely in no position to level many recriminations against the Hellenized priests. They must then have been a special kind of Sadducees, strict and reformed (a reform which would be related to the meaning of *sedeq*, "justice," applied to the *Torah*?). Who could the "man of lies" be? Herod the Great, Ben-Kosebha, etc., have been thought of here, but with equal right it may have been some unknown of whom we have no other information. Uncertainty likewise prevails as to the "head of the kings of Javan," Greece perhaps but also a possible symbol of Syria, Rome, or another pagan country. The "men of war who went with the man of lies" and the eventual war waged by them are also obscure. Scholars more commonly claim that the document was written when the Temple of Jerusalem was still standing and functioning, that is, before A.D. 70, but not a few others consider as literary fictions the mention of the sanctuary, of the moral corruption which raged there, etc.

246. It would be imprudent to reconstruct the past on so shaky a foundation, but, on the other hand, no one has the right to exclude any reasonable hypothesis without a hearing, not even if it places the origin of the "New Alliance" in the times of the Seleucids and perhaps before the Machabees. In that case, the new community would be a practical protest on the part of souls embittered by the state of contemporary Yahwism. Since they could have no hope in the sacerdotal caste which ruled in Jerusalem, these Yahwists moved to the region of Damascus, far from the plots of a civic Hellenism (§ 243) to begin there a simple, austere life inspired by the ancient Yahwism of the sojourn in the desert (Vol. I, § 406). Mistrusting the priesthood, but

unable to abolish it out of reverence for the *Torah,* they retained
it in their social organization, but
relegated it to a lower status, while
the direction of the community was
entrusted to laymen.

If these hypotheses could be
proved, it would mean that as early
as the time of Antiochus IV there
was a movement opposing the de-
nationalization of Israel, hinging
upon a life apart or "separated"
(*perushim;* § 150) from victorious
anti-Yahwism, and mistrust of the
contemporary priesthood, and a return to the old in preparation for
the future.

**247. The Jewish Temple at
Leontopolis.** In Lower Egypt,
about nineteen miles from Cairo
and some thirteen miles from ancient Heliopolis (Vol. I, § 24),
there is toward the northeast a

Obelisk at Heliopolis.

locality called *Tell el-Yehudiyeh,* "hillock of the Jews," the name of which
makes one suspect an ancient Jewish settlement. The researches made
there at the end of the past century by Naville and later by Flinders Petrie
yielded archaeological proof that the settlement was really a Jewish one
and went back to pre-Christian times. Josephus knew of its existence and
called the place Leontopolis, locating it in the nome or province of
Heliopolis.[5]

It is certain that before the middle of the second century B.C. there
was a Jewish community at Leontopolis and, what is more important,
a Jewish temple, but its origin is described in a different and contra-
dictory manner by Josephus.

In his earlier work, *Jewish War* (§ 208), he states that the high
priest Onias son of Simon — hence Onias III (§ 216) — fled from Jerusalem when the city was taken by Antiochus IV, and took refuge in Egypt
with King Ptolemy. The latter granted him the above-mentioned place,

---

[5] Another *Tell el-Yehudiyeh,* farther north in the center of the Delta, at Tell
Mokdam near Mit Ghamr, is ruled out chiefly for archaeological reasons. It is also
too far north. The data of Josephus which places Leontopolis only 180 stadia from
Memphis (*War,* VII, 10, 3) is inexact (as he so often is) and the *Tell el-Yehudiyeh*
near Heliopolis exceeds this distance; Tell Mokdam exceeds it even more.

and here the deposed high priest built a temple somewhat different externally from the one in Jerusalem, being in the form of a tower sixty cubits high; inside it was the same except that instead of a lampstand (§ 102) it had a lamp of gold (*War*, I, 1, 1; VII, 10, 2–3). In his later work, *Antiquities,* he takes a different view. The one who fled to Egypt and built the temple is no longer Onias III, but a son of his who was also named Onias but had never assumed in Jerusalem the office of high priest which belonged to his family. He was still a boy when his father Onias III died, but when he saw that Antiochus IV chose as high priests first Jason, then Onias "who was also called Menelaus" (*Antiquities*, XII, 9, 7; the unexpected identity of names is noteworthy for it seems definitely to attest a confusion of persons: cf. §§ 227, 229, 231), and finally Alcimus, who was not of the line of the high priests (although he was a priest, § 263), Onias fled to Egypt, where he entered into relations with Ptolemy VI Philometer and Cleopatra. Sometime after this, while on a military campaign conducted by the Jews in Ptolemy's service, he espied the ruins of a temple dedicated to the goddess Bast[6] and in a letter to the royal couple asked permission to build a temple there similar to the one in Jerusalem, giving as his reason a passage in Isaias (Isa. 19:19), which foretold that Yahweh would have an altar in Egypt. Ptolemy and Cleopatra replied by letter, expressing their surprise that so unclean a place be even considered as a site for a temple to God, but leaving the matter up to Onias' judgment. The temple was built "like indeed to that in Jerusalem, but smaller and poorer" (*Antiquities*, XIII, 3, 1–3).

248. In these two works, then, Josephus is evidently giving two different accounts, and he is so little mindful of their diversity that he blithely refers the reader of his later work to the earlier one, as if he there told the same story. It is quite possible that the tradition thus enshrined in Josephus, attributing the temple at Leontopolis to Onias IV, depends upon some partisan source which, in order to belittle the importance of this Egyptian sanctuary, festooned it with legends, making up the letters, stressing the detail of the uncleanness of its site, etc. The chronological question however is something else. Theoretically it would seem that the later work, *Antiquities,* is more likely to be the correct one; in it Onias IV is said to have built this temple, whereas in the older *Jewish War* it is attributed to Onias III. Where Josephus is involved, such a presumption is of little value. Of much more value is the fact that in 2 Mach. 4:33 ff., Onias III was reported slain at Daphne (§ 233), and so could not have been the

---

[6] The goddess Bast had the face of a cat, but in those times she was likened to Sekmet and Tephnut, who had the face of a lioness; hence, the name *Leontopolis.*

founder of the temple of Leontopolis. On the other hand, the account
which makes him the founder and which is reproduced in the earlier
work is quite unattested, meeting with no confirmation in other manuscripts; the only echo of it to be found is in the Talmud (Babli, *Menahoth*,
109*b*, ed. Goldschmidt, Leipzig, 1909, VIII, p. 797; cf. Jer., *Yoma*, VI,
3, ed. Schwab, Paris 1882, V, p. 234 f.), but besides being embroidered
with childish nonsense and self-contradictory, it is so inexact as to relate
that Onias (III), son of Simon, "went to Alexandria in Egypt and there
built an altar," thus making the temple of Leontopolis an altar in
Alexandria.

249. In conclusion it would seem that the founder of the temple was
Onias IV, and that he took this initiative when he came of age, some
years after the death of his father Onias III. The historical circumstances offer an adequate explanation of his step. After the assassination
of his father, he realized that the policy of the Seleucid monarchs
rendered his own succession to the office of high priest — at least a
secure and stable succession (cf. § 263) — increasingly improbable. He
thereupon took refuge in hospitable Egypt, where the rival monarch,
Ptolemy VI, welcomed him into his territory, hoping thereby to widen
the division brought about in Palestine by the decrees of Hellenization.
The presence in Egypt of the legitimate heir to the high priesthood
might serve as a spiritual magnet, drawing to Egypt the Palestinian
Jews who were opposed to Hellenism, just as the new temple proposed
by Onias might one day perhaps rival that of Jerusalem. Onias, to
make his request more acceptable, offered his services to Ptolemy
not only as the high priest, but also in another capacity more useful to
that king, namely, as a captain of his soldiers.

It seems certain that the colony at Leontopolis, after its organization
by Onias at least, was military in character, although this was not so
pronounced here as at Elephantine (§ 177). Onias himself picked the
site for Leontopolis during one of the military campaigns which he
conducted for Ptolemy, as recorded in *C. Apion.*, II, 5 [49 ff.]. His
two sons Helcias and Ananias later were also captains in the army of
Cleopatra (§ 301) according to Strabo (in *Antiquities*, XIII, 10, 4; 13,
1–2). The excavations conducted at Tell el-Yehudiyeh have brought
to light what may be interpreted as an entrenched camp. There is,
finally, proof of its military tradition at the time of Caesar. At first
the Jewish colony at Leontopolis opposed Antipater by force of arms
because he had given help to Caesar, but when Antipater produced
letters of recommendation from the high priest of Jerusalem, a supporter
of Caesar (§ 319), it yielded.

250. That the temple of Leontopolis was viewed with a jaundiced eye by the sacerdotal circles of Jerusalem was to be expected, for, like Elephantine, it was a flagrant violation of the law of centralization of worship, more serious however in that its head was the natural heir of the high priesthood of Yahweh. According to later tradition, the sacrifices offered in the temple of Onias were not considered valid, although the fulfillment of a vow made expressly through that temple was (Mishna, *Menahoth*, XIII, 10), a surprising difference in criteria which proves that even in Jerusalem the sacerdotal lineage of the founder of the temple carried some weight. Also, out of regard for him there were no violent attacks or clamorous disavowals of his enterprise; no certain trace of anything of the kind has survived. Here too the Mishna laid down a special norm which forbade the Jewish priests from Leontopolis from offering sacrifices in the Temple at Jerusalem (*ibid.*): and yet priests who wished to marry would write from Egypt (and therefore from Leontopolis also) to Jerusalem to assure themselves of the descent of the woman, thus preserving the priestly line unsullied (*C. Apion*, I, 7).

251. How great an influence did the temple of Leontopolis exert? In the supposition (it is well-founded) that the Jewish temple and colony there was of a Palestinian type, in contrast to many other Jewish centers of Egypt which by now had long since adopted the Greek language and customs (§ 191 ff.); that these other Egyptian Jews remained in touch with Jerusalem and its Temple even after the building of the temple at Leontopolis; and allowing due weight to the customary silence of Jewish writers (except Josephus)[7] toward the temple of Onias, one must conclude that its influence must have been very slight and limited. The vast majority of Egyptian Jews must have considered the local temple as something which arose at the initiative of Onias, a man in a difficult situation; it had therefore to be judged in the light of many extenuating circumstances, and in practice it was tolerated, although the true center of Egyptian Yahwism remained, as always, the Temple of Jerusalem. And so it is that we find Philo, who never even mentions Leontopolis, betaking himself "to the paternal temple," that is, to Jerusalem, to offer his sacrifices (*De providentia*, ed. Mangey, II, 646).

The final fate of the temple of Leontopolis, however, is known. After the fall of Jerusalem, the Romans took special pains to wipe out the chief hotbeds of the Jewish revolt, and Vespasian gave orders to Lupus, governor of Alexandria, to destroy the temple of Leontopolis. Lupus began

---

[7] The passage of the *Oracula Sibyll.*, V, 492–511, seems to be not an allusion to the temple of Leontopolis but a kind of abstract vision. However, the local community and names of its members are known from inscriptions and papyri.

by closing it, perhaps in A.D. 72, but died shortly afterward. Paulinus succeeded him in office and first despoiled, and then destroyed it entirely, probably in 73 (*War*, VII, 10, 4).

We read in Josephus that the temple of Leontopolis lasted for 343 years, but this is almost certainly a scribal mistake for 243, which would mean that the temple was founded in 170 B.C., a round number which agrees with other data.

THE MACHABEES

JUDAS — JONATHAN — SIMON

252. Triumphant Hellenism made the mistake, not uncommon to victors, of underestimating its foe. Victorious in the cities, its chief objectives, Hellenism failed to pay sufficient attention to the desert, partly because of the greater difficulty involved, and partly because its importance was not properly understood.

That was a fatal mistake, because the Assideans (§ 243) were there and their Yahwism also. The Assideans, it is true, were only isolated individuals who had fled from Hellenism, and were at that time putting up only a passive resistance; but the danger was clear that that resistance might become active, with the banding together of the individuals under one head and the formation of a Yahwistic organization. This is what actually happened, and in very short order.

There lived at that time in Modin, the present-day *el-Medieh*, a small village about nineteen miles northwest of Jerusalem in the direction of

The Machabee Family

d. = died   *m. = married*

Mathathias, d. 166 B.C.

John, d. 160 B.C.	Simon, 143–134 B.C.	Judas, 166–160 B.C.	Eleazar, d. 162 B.C.	Jonathan, 160–143 B.C.
Judas, d. 134 B.C.	John Hyrcanus, 134–104 B.C.	Mathathias, d. 134 B.C.	Daughter, m. to Ptolemy (1 Mach. 16:11 ff.)	
Aristobulus I, first husband of Alexandra, d. 103 B.C.	Antigonus, 104 B.C.	Alex. Jannaeus, 103–76 B.C. m. Alexandra, 76–67 B.C.	Son Son	

Hyrcanus II, 63–40 B.C.   Aristobulus II, 67–63 B.C.

Alexandra m. Alexander, d.49 B.C.   Antigonus, 40–37 B.C.

Mariamne (d. 29 B.C.), wife of   Aristobulus III, d. 35 B.C.
Herod, the Great, 37–4 B.C.

Alexander and Aristobulus
both executed in 7 B.C.

236

Lydda, a family of sacerdotal lineage whose head was
Mathathias "son of John, of
Simon, of Hasmoneus" (*Antiquities*, XII, 6, 1; cf. 1
Mach. 2:1). From this last
ancestor the family was thereafter called the Hasmoneans.
Mathathias had five sons who
rank in seniority as follows:
John called Gaddis, Simon
called Thassi, Judas called
Machabeus, Eleazar called
Avaran, Jonathan called Apphus. The family was also
called the Machabees after the
surname of the third son.[1]

The hillock of Modin. (Vester,
Amer. Colony.)

Surrounded by the stalwart sons of whom he was very proud, the
priest Mathathias was a man cut to the pattern of ancient times. He
felt only disdain for the civil usages of Hellenism, and the pagan profanation of Yahwism made him boil with indignation. Nor was he one
to keep silent and dissimulate. At the first signs of persecution he
openly manifested his disapproval, and in the manner of the ancient
prophets went about, together with his sons, dressed in mourning. He
could no longer participate as a priest in the liturgical service of the
Temple which had been profaned, but he could at least protest vigorously in this way. What could the persecutors do to him? He was
old, true enough, but he had always at his disposal five strong sons
and the vast, uncharted desert. They would stake everything there:
"Why should we live any longer?" (1 Mach. 2:13.)

Such was his mental state when one day the enforcement commission
(§239) arrived, unfortunately for it, at Modin, there to put into effect
the edicts of the king in regard to pagan worship. Many Jews yielded
and sacrificed to the idols, but Mathathias, who was approached with

---

[1] Both names of the family, *Hasmoneans* and *Machabees*, are obscure, especially
the first. In the passage cited from *Jewish Antiquities*, it is not stated whether
Hasmoneus is a different person from the preceding *Simon* or just another name of
the latter, "of Simon the Hasmonean." As to its meaning, nothing certain is known
(to derive it from the problematic word *hashmannim* of Psalm 68:32, in the
meaning of "opulent," "eminent," lacks foundation; rather should one consider it a
geographic appellation from *Heshmon*, a locality of the tribe of Juda: cf. Josue
15:27). The name Machabeus is commonly traced to *maqqabhah*, "hammer," in the
sense that Judas was the "hammer" which smashed the oppressors of Israel (cf.
"hammer of the heretics," etc.), but even this derivation is not free from doubts,
and the others are still more uncertain.

particular solicitude and was promised special rewards as befitted the principal personage of the place, disdainfully refused. They were still discussing the point when another Jew presented himself to offer sacrifice. At this sight the old man could contain himself no longer. He killed the renegade Jew and the royal commissioner, and then destroyed the pagan altar. After this, he and his sons fled into the desert, inviting all who were faithful to the laws of their fathers to follow them.

253. There was much talk about the incident, for the news spread with the surprising rapidity of the desert grapevine. Many of the Assideans who were disunited in their passive rebellion gathered around the rebel priest who had seized the offensive. From that day on the individual Yahwists of the desert began to take on the form of a Yahwistic organization.

But they first had to be disabused of some naïve notions. The news of the rebellion of Modin and the rallying of the people around the rebel had reached Jerusalem also, and immediately soldiers were sent from the Akra to disperse the gathering. They found a group of about a thousand Assideans and astutely chose the Sabbath day on which to negotiate with them (§ 237). The Jews refused to apostatize, and as they would not violate the Sabbath by defending themselves, they were killed on the spot without a fight. On the point of expiring they invoked heaven and earth to bear witness that they were unjustly slain, but the tragic gesture must have brought meager consolation to Mathathias and the other groups of Assideans, who realized that by so acting they were playing into the hands of their oppressors. They therefore decided that in the future they would defend themselves even on the Sabbath.

The courageous old man and his sons set to work at once, especially as the number of their followers was increasing daily. When they had gathered arms and formed a small nucleus of an army, they proceeded to go about the villages and towns, and sought to counteract the work of the oppressors. Hellenists and renegade Jews were either put to death or forced to flee; pagan altars were destroyed, and infants who were not yet circumcised were subjected to the rite.

Soon afterward old Mathathias died, but on his deathbed he encouraged his followers to continue the work they had begun, and recommended that his second son, Simon, be placed at the head of administrative and political affairs, and his third son, Judas, be given command of the military. He was buried at Modin in the tomb of his fathers (166–165 B.C.).

254. Judas Machabeus. When the proud old man had passed from the scene, Simon the prudent one and Judas the warrior were left in command of the insurrection in accordance with his wishes. They were aided by the other brothers. The circumstances, however, called for

an intense military effort, and as Judas had been designated especially for this purpose, he rose to the fore and outshone his other brothers.

The first of the family to be honored with the name Machabeus, Judas was a genuine hero: one of those youths produced according to the ancient Israelite mold, who from early childhood toughened their bodies and tempered their spirits while guarding the paternal flocks in the desert. There they had battled wolves, dealt with the nocturnal thief, sang the ancient national songs during periods of repose, in a word, became masters of the sword and harp, and much at home in the desert. Bodies and souls of such character were of the type of young David (Vol. I, § 356), and produced heroes when dedicated with enthusiasm to a great ideal. The figure of Judas, therefore, became an epic one in later tradition, and it was sung of him that:

> "He was like a lion in his deeds,
> and like a lion's whelp roaring for its prey."
>
> (1 Mach. 3:4)

The first days of his command Judas gave over entirely to organizing his available forces. These had first to be armed and then trained, for without this they would have availed him nothing. The wandering life they were forced to live in the desert meant that they could outfit themselves only in secondary centers, poorly stocked at best; this made the outfitting of the army both very difficult and inadequate to their needs. Something enduring had first to be created; enthusiasm and personal valor would supply for the rest until better times should come.

The Syrian authorities of Jerusalem were informed of all this activity and prepared to meet it. They estimated as best they could how many armed men Judas could have, and as the Syrian garrison of Akra was not sufficient to guarantee a crushing victory, sought re-enforcements in Samaria. With tactical superiority assured there was no cause to doubt that the rebels would be dispersed and annihilated. But their calculations erred, and erred precisely in that they counted only the number of armed men, without taking account of the spirit which animated them.

The one who had made the estimate and had gone to Samaria for re-enforcements was Apollonius, who two years before had treacherously perpetrated the first slaughter in Jerusalem (§ 237). His name alone was sufficient to fill Judas and his men with fury. They ran forth to meet him, and the anger and valor of the rebels gained the victory despite the equipment and superior numbers of the mercenary troops. Apollonius' army was destroyed, and he himself killed on the field; Judas took possession of his sword, and it was to serve him to the end of his life. Among other fruits of the victory, not the least was a plentiful supply of arms abandoned by the defeated troops.

Beth-Horon. (Vester, Amer. Colony.)

255. The defeat was certainly not a disaster for the Syrian authorities, but at the same time it was not to be taken lightly. Seron, general of the Syrian army, assumed the task of repairing the damage, hoping that by his victorious intervention he would win renown and that his merits would attract the favorable attention of King Antiochus. But he too committed the error of underestimating the enemy, thinking that the forces he had at hand (they were certainly numerous) were sufficient to subdue them. For good measure he joined to these the renegade Jews who had been forced to flee by the insurgents, and promised that they could re-enter their homeland under the protection of Syrian arms.

Seron came down from the north and passed through Modin, the nest of the Machabees, but encountered no resistance. Pushing forward to Beth-Horon, about fifteen miles from Jerusalem, he came upon Judas who, from an elevated post, surveyed the road which led to the capital. The sight of the powerful forces on the march outnumbering themselves frightened some of Judas' men. They were, in fact, outnumbered and, what was worse, were weakened by the starvation diet which the wretched life in the desert had forced upon them. The flaming words of the champion of Israel reminded them of their wives, their children, their venerated traditions, and effectively changed their hunger into fury. When Judas finished speaking they spilled down the hill of Beth-Horon like hungry wolves, fell upon the troops of Seron, pushed them back into the road where it was flanked by valleys, broke through the center so that the wings were scattered in the valleys, and, after putting to rout the best troops massed in a square, proceeded to give chase to the scattered remnants. Eight hundred of the enemy were slain on the field of battle; the others found refuge in the Hellenistic cities of the Philistine coast.

256. This defeat was not a very serious matter for Antiochus, but its effect on the morale was very great, and clearly indicated that up to then the real state of affairs had not been understood. The king was all the more annoyed at this because it occurred (in 165 B.C.) at the very

Emmaus. (Abel.)

moment he was departing on his expedition to the Orient against the
Parthians (§ 44). Since it was not possible to delay the expedition which,
because of its importance, demanded the presence of the king, he gave
to Lysias, who had been left in Antioch as regent, the express responsibility and the means of subduing the vexatious rebellion of Judea.

Lysias immediately put Ptolemy, the son of Dorymenes, the governor
of Coelesyria and Phoenicia, in charge of operations, and he made
ready an army, entrusting its command to Nicanor, son of Patroclus,
who was aided by the general Gorgias. The army, according to one
source, numbered 40,000 men and 7000 horses (1 Mach. 3:39), but
according to another "not less than" 20,000 men (2 Mach. 8:9) and this
latter figure seems to be closer to the truth. Besides being better
equipped, it was also very much larger than the army of Judas which
numbered only a few thousand; here also there are two figures, 6000
according to 2 Mach. 8:16 (Vulgate, 7000), and 3000 according to
1 Mach. 4:6.

The Syrian commander pitched camp at Emmaus, or modern
'Amwas, slightly southwest of Beth-Horon (§ 255) and southeast of
Gezer (Vol. I, § 76). He was so sure of subduing the insurgents in short
order that slave merchants from the coast were gathered there with
large amounts of money, ready to purchase the Jewish slaves who
would soon be available. Judas gathered his men together at Mispah,
site of ancient national memories (Vol. I, §§ 89, 344 ff.), and after
encouraging them proceeded to attack Emmaus from the southern
side, where it was least protected. In the meantime, Gorgias had
also departed with a detachment of 5000 troops and 1000 cavalry
to surprise the camp of Judas, which, of course, he found empty. The
Syrian encampment, however, thinking that it was protected in the

front by Gorgias who was pushing forward against the enemy, had neglected to take measures of safety, and its soldiers were scattered outside the camp. Thus, bursting forth unexpectedly from the south, Judas won an easy victory; 3000 of the enemy were killed and the rest put to flight. On his return from his fruitless march, Gorgias saw from the top of the mountains what had happened to the encampment of his soldiers at Emmaus, and overestimating the strength of the enemy forces, he avoided battle and retired toward the coast.

257. The following year, 164, brought forward Lysias, who came to Judea in person at the head of a strong army. Rather than a real campaign, about whose maneuvers we have no specific information, this must have been more in the nature of a show of force whose aim was to affirm Syrian authority in Idumaea to the south of Judea. At Beth-sur (1 Mach. 4:29: the Vulgate again has Beth-Horon), about nineteen miles south of Jerusalem, an engagement took place, probably between a single detachment of Lysias' troops and the forces of Judas; Judas preferred guerrilla warfare. The Syrian detachment was worsted and Lysias almost immediately broke off the campaign and retreated to Antioch. This retreat was attributed by Jewish tradition to the reversal suffered by Lysias, but in reality he had other and graver reasons for it, and he had probably accomplished his purpose in Idumaea. His presence in Antioch as regent was now a necessity, for vague rumors had begun to filter back to Antioch about Epiphanes' expedition to the Orient, and simultaneously, the first reports of his death (§ 44).

Under such conditions, it was to the interest of both parties to come to at least a provisional agreement. The Jewish nationalists could obtain from Lysias the recognition of the liberties for which they had rebelled; by granting them, Lysias would have the advantage of being able to dedicate himself with more freedom to the most delicate situation of the regency. The diplomatic exchanges reported in 2 *Machabees*, 11:13 ff.,[2] very probably took place at this time.

---

[2] These documents which are not cited in 1 *Machabees* are reported in 2 *Machabees* as the termination of the first expedition of Lysias, and with perfect logical and chronological reason. But the various episodes of this book are not arranged in chronological order. Indeed, the author of 2 *Machabees*, who merely synopsized the work of Jason of Cyrene (§ 208), bearing in mind his particular purpose had already previously narrated the death of Epiphanes (2 Mach. 9:1 ff.), and immediately had subjoined to it by way of contrast the purification of the Temple (10:1 ff.). He placed the account of the first expedition of Lysias, which had already occurred, after the purification of the Temple, at which time, as a matter of fact, the second expedition of Lysias occurred. As is clear from 1 *Machabees*, the chronological order of the three happenings is as follows: the first expedition of Lysias (concluded with the diplomatic exchanges); the purification of the Temple; the second expedition of Lysias: cf. 1 Mach. 4:26–35; 4:36 ff.; 6:17 ff. — The sole difficulty is the reference which Antiochus V Eupator makes in his letter

258. Judas had sent John and Absalom to Lysias to represent him in the diplomatic negotiations. They returned with a letter from Lysias to the Jews, and also with two letters from Antiochus V Eupator. One of these was addressed to Lysias, and in it the king commanded him to make peace with the Jews, and to grant them the liberties they asked. The other was addressed "to the γερουσία of the Jews, and to the other Jews" (2 Mach. 11:27; cf. § 189), and granted the desired liberty and amnesty to the insurgents. From this second letter we learn that Menelaus, the Hellenized high priest (§ 231), was at Eupator's court, and had intervened to obtain an agreement. Evidently the victories of the Machabees had shaken his blind faith in the Seleucids and the Hellenistic faction, and he felt that he would be more secure in his office if all open breaks were eliminated once and for all, even if it meant tempering somewhat his Hellenistic ardor.

Besides these three letters, a fourth has been preserved in our texts. It was from legates of Rome, which power now begins to enter directly into Jewish affairs. With this letter, "Quintus Memmius [and] Titus Manius [*variants:* Manlius, Manilius], legates of Rome," confirmed the liberties granted by Lysias, and invited the Jews to communicate to them their own desires as soon as possible; these they would support before the king in Antioch, as they were about to set out for his court. The two Romans are not with certainty met with elsewhere in history; nor can it be perceived at first glance by what right they took part in the dealings between Judas and Lysias, or confirmed the concessions he had granted, but their presence and their proposals tally exactly with the system then pursued by Rome. The two legates were one of the many embassies which Rome had, on one pretext or another, sent throughout the Orient always with the ultimate aim of extending Roman influence by infiltration of new spheres, and by keeping a finger in foreign affairs. In fact it frequently happened that local questions were referred to the Roman legates if they happened to be present, either because of the authority of Rome's name, or because the patronage of Rome was being courted

---

to Lysias (2 Mach. 11:22 ff.) to the death of his father Antiochus IV Epiphanes, who was at that time still alive. The report of the death of Epiphanes was false, yet, coming from such a great distance and under obscure circumstances, it was accepted as true even at court in Antioch (an entirely similar case occurred to Herod the Great: § 337). It was precisely this report which led Antiochus V and Lysias, in the gravity of that moment, to solicit a peaceful settlement with the Machabees. Other scholars, however, suppose that the diplomatic dealings reflected in our text occurred after the purification of the Temple, and after the real death of Epiphanes. Others, with little critical sense, assign three expeditions to Lysias in Judea; others, with too much, assign only one.

(cf. Polybius, XXV, 53, 4 [ed. Büttner-Wobst, XXIII, 17, 4]). Whatever the excuse for being with Lysias, their true purpose was to survey the Syrian scene; probably also the representatives of Judas Machabeus had asked their aid. They were all the more willing to take part in the proceedings, for the false rumor of the death of Antiochus Epiphanes offered a new pretext for interfering in the affairs of the Seleucid kingdom.

259. The peace settlement reached between Judas and the Seleucid sovereign was only a compromise based on the abstract principle of mutual toleration: liberty of worship for Yahwism, and thenceforward the Assideans and Hellenists would live together in Jerusalem, side by side, without disturbing each other. Was this possible? Evidently it was a dream in which no one had any faith. The Temple might become Yahwistic again, but the official high priest remained Menelaus, the instigator of the persecution now opportunely become "moderate." The Assideans might be able to re-enter Jerusalem undisturbed, but the Akra and its Syrian garrison remained still. However, Judas began to utilize the advantages granted him by the compromise; as for the rest, he reserved for himself liberty of action.

He entered Jerusalem with his armed forces, and his first care was for the Temple. It was in a neglected and squalid condition, for after the first fervor of Hellenism had worn off, there followed a lack of interest in the building. Yet when the Jews began to remove the pagan accretions there was no lack of resistance and hostility, especially on the part of the inhabitants of the Akra (1 Mach. 4:41); these however were held at bay by the soldiers of Judas. The pagan altar was thrown down and all other pagan emblems were thrown out; a new Yahwistic altar was built according to the prescriptions of the *Torah*, and the furnishings which had disappeared in the various depredations were replaced.

The dedication of the purified Temple was celebrated on the twenty-fifth of December, 164 B.C., precisely three years after its profanation (§ 239). Judas arranged that this feast should be renewed every year, and thus, from that time onward, the event was recalled by the feast of *H a n u kk a h*, which became practically synonymous with the Greek 'Εγκαίνια, and the Latin *Encaenia* (Jn. 10:22). It is interesting to note that as the profanation of the Temple had taken place on the occasion of the solar festival (§ 239), so also *Hanukkah* was characterized by a grand display of lights, and was named the feast of *Lights* by the Jews who spoke Greek (*Antiquities*, XII, 7, 7; cf. § 211).

Thereafter, the Yahwistic cult was carried out regularly in the Temple by priests chosen from among those who had not apostatized. It was probably during this period that Judas collected the sacred

Jamnia (*Yebna*).

books which had been dispersed during the persecution and war. In the same source (2 Mach. 2:13), the collection of the sacred books made by Nehemias (§ 142) is mentioned in passing.

260. Judas and the Assideans had unquestionably achieved a splendid triumph, but more than anything else it was an affirmation of principle, for if they wanted to be more secure than the actual unstable state of affairs allowed, they could not rest on the untrustworthy laurels of their compromise with Lysias and Antiochus Eupator. Judas and his men were too intelligent not to share the judgment expressed by Epiphanes, that Hellenism and Yahwism were incompatible and mutually exclusive (§ 231); they realized the necessity of continuing to expel by force the Hellenism which Epiphanes had imposed by force.

For his armed companies, which were obliged to move quickly, Judas then created two strategic bases. One of these was in Jerusalem, "the hillock of Sion," that is, the hillock of the Temple itself. This he girded with high walls protected by towers after the dedication, thus making of it almost a fortress. He left a permanent garrison of his soldiers there, so that the Temple became, even in a military sense, the counterpart of the Syrian Akra (§ 237). The other fortified base was Beth-sur, which commanded the approach to Idumaea, about which Judas had his well-founded suspicions (§ 257); Beth-sur was at the same time a protection for Jerusalem from the south.

During this same time, Judas extended his anti-Hellenistic program outside of Judea in order also to revivify the Yahwistic nuclei which had been more severely tried by the persecution. He pushed on with his soldiers first to Idumaea — according to the better reading of *1 Mach.*

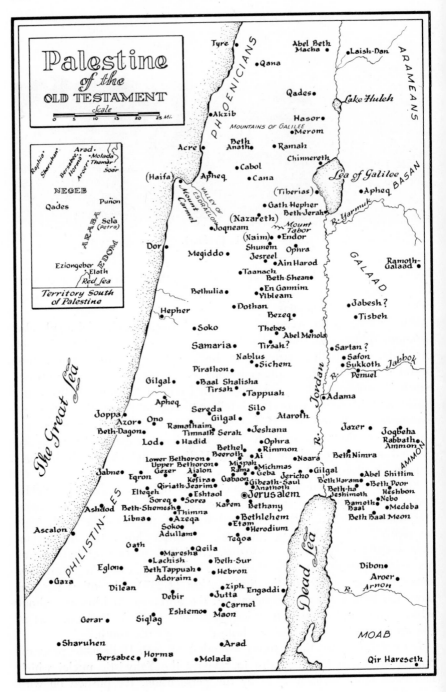

Palestine of the OLD TESTAMENT

Maresa.

5:3 — and thence to Transjordan. Following this, he divided his forces into two expeditions. One of them, composed of three thousand men commanded by his brother Simon, he sent to Galilee, while the other with eight thousand men, commanded by him and his other brother Jonathan, went off to Galaad. This second group was chosen because aid had been urgently requested by the Jews exposed to the most severe persecutions "in the [district] of Tobias" (1 Mach. 5:13). This name, if we suppose it to be correctly transmitted, leads one naturally to think of 'Araq el-Emir and of the "barony" of Hyrcanus Tobias, which, having fallen shortly before into the hands of Antiochus Epiphanes (§ 236), had become a haven for this latter's faithful followers. These took revenge regularly on the local Jews because of the successes of the Machabees. Yet the campaign of Judas, which is minutely described, seems to have been waged farther to the north, in Galaad, properly so called, and it may be that his intervention in the region of the ancient Tobiads has been omitted in the report (1 Mach. 5:24–54).

During his absence, Judas had left a small force in Judea under the command of Joseph and Azarias, with the responsibility of guarding over the region without making any forays to the outside. To emulate the glory which Judas was winning in Galaad, however, they decided on an incursion into Jamnia, the present-day *Yebna,* a city in the Philistine plain along the Mediterranean at about the same latitude as Jerusalem; it was a Hellenistic center fortified by Gorgias. The latter welcomed the opportunity to revenge his previous defeat at Emmaus (§ 256), and easily bested the two inexperienced Jewish captains, who lost two thousand of their soldiers on the field of battle. By way of compensation, however, Judas, on returning from Galaad, resumed operations in Idumaea. Among other cities he occupied Hebron (Vol. I, §§ 91, 127 ff.), then Maresa,[3] more to the northwest, which corresponds to the present *Tell Sandahannah* (Vol. I, § 75), and the Philistine city of Azotus (Asdod; Vol. I, § 328).

261. There is no doubt that all this activity of the Assideans did not please the court of Antioch, and that the victories of Judas were as so many blows struck at the shaky compromise which had been concluded. When the news of the real death of Epiphanes (§§ 44, 257, footnote) arrived, Lysias ignored the wishes of the dying man, who had designated Philip, and seized the government of the kingdom for himself, in the name of the nine-year-old Antiochus V Eupator. In the beginning, he would certainly have preferred to avoid a new open conflict with the nationalistic Jews, either through fear that the supplanted Philip might arrive at any moment from the Orient, or because the new governor of Coelesyria, Ptolemy Macron, was well-disposed toward the Jews and was recommending a conciliatory policy toward them (2 Mach. 10:12). But the news of the death of Epiphanes increased the aggressive activity of the insurgents to such a degree that Judas immediately set out to get rid of the Syrian Akra, the menace and disgrace of the Yahwistic capital (§ 237). He first prepared his engines of war and other equipment, and began a regular siege. Some of the besieged, however, succeeded in passing through the blockade, and, joining with "some wicked men of Israel" (1 Mach. 6:21), hurried to Antioch and informed the government there of the critical condition of the Seleucid fortress in Jerusalem. They urged that immediate aid be sent to the Hellenistic faction in order to avert its capitulating to the nationalists, and thus leaving them a clear field. Who were these "wicked men of Israel"? If this time it was not also the high priest Menelaus (§ 258), it was certainly his partisans, who like him saw that Judas and the Assideans could not be held in bounds, and perceived with sorrow that the dream in which Hellenism and Yahwism lived together in Jerusalem, was dissolving into thin air.

262. Upon receiving this news, Lysias was forced into action. Putting himself at the head of a large army and thirty-two war elephants, and bringing along for his own good the young king Eupator, he took up again the old plan of attacking Jerusalem from the south (§ 257), using Idumaea as his base of operations. Beth-sur, the strategic base of Judas (§ 260), was besieged, and leaving a detachment of troops there to blockade it, Lysias pushed on toward Jerusalem. In the meantime, Judas,

---

[3] Thus should *1 Mach.* 5:66 read instead of *Samaria* (Μάρισαν instead of Σαμαρίαν).

after lifting the siege of Akra, had descended from Jerusalem to assist his beleaguered men. When he arrived at Beth Zekaryah, some six miles north of Beth-sur, the two armies met. Lysias had placed his elephants, protected by heavily armored soldiers, in the center, and the cavalry to the sides, and thus deployed they approached Beth Zekaryah. Judas' soldiers furiously attacked the center, and succeeded on the first attempt in pushing back the vanguard and killing six hundred of the enemy. They then attacked the elephants, and at this point occurred the celebrated deed of Eleazar Machabeus, the younger brother of Judas. Seeing a larger elephant which was better armed than the others, and thinking that the king himself rode it, he opened up a path through the enemy with his sword, hurled himself under the beast, and drove his sword into its belly, being immediately crushed to death beneath the beast thus wounded. Ironically, the king was not on the elephant at all, being far too young to be exposed to such danger. From that day forward the dead Eleazar was called Ḥawaran (§ 252; "sword thruster": from the root ḤWR, "to perforate"), a name that recalled to all the cause of his death, and of his glory.

The center of the Syrian army withstood the attack, however, and nothing remained for the soldiers of Judas but to fall back as best they could to Jerusalem. There they shut themselves up in the "hillock of Sion," or the fortress of the Temple (§ 260), and were besieged by Lysias, who began to prepare his engines for the assault. Shortly afterward Beth-sur fell and the besiegers were freed from any danger to the rear, and were re-enforced by the detachment which had blockaded the fallen stronghold. The besieged soldiers on Sion defended themselves bravely and constructed war engines to match those of the enemy. Their situation however soon became critical because of the lack of provisions in the city; that year had been a "sabbatical year," and hence there had been no harvest. Many of the defenders fled away secretly, and very few remained to fight.

Their fate would have been sealed if there had not then occurred, luckily for them and unluckily for Lysias, what Lysias had been fearing. News suddenly arrived that Philip, the regent designated by Epiphanes on his deathbed (§ 44), was approaching Antioch with an army. For Lysias any delay might prove fatal, so he hastened to offer peace according to the conditions of the previous compromise (§ 257), and the besieged likewise hastened to accept them. Yet once the capitulation was made, the fortress of Sion, contrary to the terms of the pact, was dismantled; the Akra, of course, remained untouched, and the commandant Hegemonides (2 Mach. 13:24; Greek text) was placed at the head of the whole region. It also seems that the obligation of offering holocausts for the Seleucid monarch (1 Mach. 7:33) in

Demetrius I.

Temple was again included in the pact. The insurgents, however, received another consolation: the high priest Menelaus was deported to Berea in Syria, and was killed there as the instigator of the disorders of Judea (2 Mach. 13:4 ff.; *Antiquities,* XII, 9, 7). In the meantime, Lysias directed his efforts against Philip (§ 45).

263. The peril which had threatened the Machabean faction had been extremely grave. Many of the Assideans must have asked themselves what would have happened to them had the providential appearance of Philip in Antioch been delayed even a short time. The Hellenized Jews must likewise have asked themselves the same question from the opposite viewpoint, for that circumstance had ruined their imminent triumph. But what had happened served only to confirm both sides in their own convictions with the classical stubbornness of Israelite factions (Vol. I, §§ 454, 458, 531). Judas did not disarm nor did the Hellenized Jews abandon the thought of winning out in the end.

They immediately prepared a clever plan. It was necessary to replace the dead Menelaus in the office of high priest, an office which remained — at least nominally — the highest in the nation. The Assideans had been able to object to the authority of Menelaus with full legal justification, for he was not of sacerdotal lineage (§231). It was imperative, therefore, to take this valid charge away from them and see to it that a descendant of the seed of Aaron became high priest in conformity with the Law, and that he also be well-disposed to Hellenism. Once a Hellenistic high priest was legally elected, Judas and his faction would become religious as well as political rebels. The Hellenists of Jerusalem moved to carry out their schemes.

It is not known with certainty what happened to their plan during the turbulent months which witnessed first the struggle between Lysias and Philip, and then the ruin of Lysias and Antiochus V Eupator when Demetrius I arrived on the scene (§ 46). But when Demetrius I was sufficiently secure on his throne, the Hellenized Jews sent a delegation to him to discuss the question of the high priest. Their leader was the candidate for that office, Eliaqim by name, and he was duly descended from Aaron. But like most Hellenists he had denied Yahwism during the persecution of Epiphanes, and like Jason (§ 227) had changed his name to the Greek one of Alcimus. The delegation and its leader insisted on the political implications of the question. They offered to King Demetrius a symbolic crown of gold and a palm, and accused Judas and the Assideans of persecuting the king's faithful subjects, and of keeping Judea in turmoil. Furthermore, the leader represented himself as having been unjustly deprived of the high priesthood. They had spoken only in the interest of the king and for the tranquillity of Jerusalem. If, therefore, the king wished to re-establish order there, he should send someone he could trust to ascertain the facts, to set things in order by force, and to establish Alcimus again in office.

Had Alcimus previously been high priest? Josephus answers affirmatively (*Antiquities*, XII, 9, 7; XX, 10; cf. 2 Mach. 14:3, 7) and attributes his election to Lysias and Antiochus V. Indeed, it is possible that upon Menelaus' death, Lysias had granted the request of the Hellenists of Jerusalem by making Alcimus his successor. But, as a matter of fact, even if he was appointed, Alcimus could not have exercised his office except for a very brief period (cf. 1 Mach. 7:5) because of the opposition of Judas and the Assideans. One may then conjecture that Onias IV was called to function in Jerusalem in order to replace the Hellenized Alcimus. When Onias was later driven out by the forcible imposition of Alcimus, he repaired to Egypt where he founded Leontopolis (§ 249).

Demetrius immediately understood that the delegation gave a true picture of affairs, and that his own interest demanded that he lean on the faction which sent it. He therefore recognized Alcimus as the high priest, and sent his general Bacchides to Jerusalem with an army to carry out there what the delegation had proposed. This was toward the middle of 161 B.C.

264. In the same year, however, Judas had taken a step similar to that of the Hellenized Jews. The danger which threatened his faction in the last expedition of Lysias had taught him clearly that the nationalist forces, however great their good will and courage, were all too inadequate to struggle against the Seleucids. Guerrilla warfare could go only so far, but if the monarch of Antioch decided to finish them off with a powerful expedition, disaster was inevitable; only the providential appearance of Philip in Antioch had saved them before. They would therefore have to look for powerful support elsewhere. But where? Judas bethought himself of distant Rome.

The remembrance of the friendly attitude of Quintus Memmius and Titus Manius (§ 258) certainly influenced this decision, but even more decisive must have been the distrustful attitude which Rome still evinced toward Demetrius I (§ 46), and its inclination to embroil itself in the affairs of the Orient (§ 258). It seemed that for Rome the two went together: to be present wherever Demetrius was in the Orient, and to create obstacles for him. At this very moment there occurred the typical case of Timarchus (§ 46). Timarchus proclaimed himself independent in Babylonia, and was recognized and supported diplomatically by Rome. It was the old principle, *divide and rule,* which guided Roman policy. In order to weaken the power of the other states, the Conscript Fathers were willing to grant scraps of that power to future competitors, thereby creating friends easily at the expense of others. Justin (XXXVI, 3, 9) had already remarked this practice in speaking of Antiochus VII and the independence of the Jews which the Romans had recognized at that time; he added this subtle consideration: *"Amicitia Romanorum petita primi omnium* [the Jews] *ex orientalibus libertatem acceperunt, facile tunc Romanis de alieno largientibus."* Such maneuvers however were of worth only in the field of diplomacy, for Rome did not send so much as a company of soldiery to the effective support of these clients to whom she dispensed what belonged to others. If they wished to secure real possession of this, they had to conquer by their own arms. Timarchus was regaled with fine words but received no material help; in fact, he was vanquished and put to death by Demetrius, but the Conscript Fathers were not moved, nor did they lift a finger to help their client.

Judas Machabeus thought that he would derive profit from the attitude of Rome from the moment that his case became a reproduction in miniature of Timarchus'. By turning to Rome, he offered her the twofold advantage of gaining yet another political foothold in the Orient, and of raising another barrier to Demetrius. He therefore chose Eupolemus and Jason (these Hellenistic names are noteworthy, since they are borne by the trusted emissaries of the head of Jewish nationalism) and sent them to Rome, "a very long journey," to "establish friendly relations and an alliance with them and to take away the yoke . . . of the Greeks . . ." (1 Mach. 8:17–19).

265. The two unknown Jews who presented themselves at the Curia of Rome and proposed to the Conscript Fathers that they enter into "friendship and alliance" with an obscure chieftain of Judea, might perhaps have caused some to think of the famous story of the fly which alighted upon the shaft of the plow and said that it would help the oxen to pull it. But the Conscript Fathers at the time of the two Scipios and Aemilius Paulus were not of that sort, and they took good care not to spurn *any* alliance that was offered to them; and if any fable came to the mind of the old men of the Curia, it was rather the one about the lion who entered into an alliance with a mouse whose tiny teeth one day freed him from the cords of a snare into which he had fallen. The desired alliance was therefore concluded. By its terms the Romans and Jews pledged themselves to support each other in the event of a war with a third power, and to give no assistance to the enemy's allies. The treaty was written down on tablets of bronze, and a copy of it was sent to Jerusalem; at the same time a letter of the Conscript Fathers was dispatched to Demetrius which deplored the yoke imposed by him "on our friends and allies, the Jews" and admonished him threateningly to change his tactics (1 Mach. 8:31–32).

It is not established whether this letter arrived at its destination before Demetrius' last campaign against Judea, but even if it had, Demetrius, who had spent much time in Rome and had learned to read between the lines of the documents of the Curia, must have quickly understood that there was here no real commitment, and that Rome had

The Curia of the Senate (Roman Forum).

merely tightened another diplomatic knot without the least intention of engaging her legions. In fact, as subsequent events proved, Rome did not depart from her policy of nonintervention: even when her "friend and ally" Judas again was struggling against Demetrius, she disclaimed any interest in him, sent him no help, and did not even move when she learned that her ally had fallen in the struggle. It was the story of Timarchus all over again.

In substance, the text of the treaty which was made public in Jerusalem may have lifted up the spirits of the Jewish nationalists who read with eagerness that they were the "friends" and "allies" of Rome. For the rest, there remained, not indeed a piece of paper, but a plaque of bronze, worth only a few sicles.

❀   ❀   ❀

266. Upon the arrival of Bacchides in Jerusalem the struggle began anew, this time fought with legal weapons. The shrewdness of the Hellenized Jews, who stood righteously behind Alcimus, a high priest who fulfilled the requisites of the law, had its effect upon their adversaries. Bacchides and Alcimus, indeed, presented a friendly exterior and sought to come to some agreement with Judas. But Judas did not trust them; to his mind the army which Bacchides had brought with him boded no good. Others, however, did trust them; now that religious liberty had again been obtained and had been guaranteed by the promises of Bacchides who spoke in the name of the king, and had been confirmed by the election of a high priest descended from Aaron, they believed that there was no longer any reason for continuing the struggle. To fight on in these circumstances would mean that their cause had degenerated into a purely political movement, whereas they had rebelled only to defend their Yahwism, which was now assured. Those who reasoned in this wise were the Assideans in general; they acted accordingly, and thus a schism ensued between the followers of Judas. The Assideans made up the bulk of Judas' forces, but among them there were not a few who for various reasons were more closely bound to Judas and the family of the Machabees. The former trusted Alcimus, negotiated with him, and turned their backs on the latter who remained faithful to Judas and were distrustful of the whole affair.

The trusting Assideans, however, paid dearly for their experience and hastened to rejoin Judas and his party. Brought before Alcimus and Bacchides under the strictest guarantees, sixty of them from around the environs of Jerusalem were put to death on one day alone. This was the beginning of a methodical purge which was extended to the whole region, to get rid of suspected persons. Information concerning one slaughter perpetrated at Bezeth — the place is not identified with certainty — has been preserved; the victims had been thrown into a large cistern. When the purge was over, Bacchides left the reins of government in the hands of Alcimus, assigned him a sufficient escort of troops, and returned to Antioch.

As was to be expected, the victory of the Hellenists and the government of Alcimus touched off a regime of persecution, but the reaction of Judas was immediate; he again took to the desert, where he reorganized his bands of faithful followers and the disillusioned Assideans who returned to him. In a short time the nationalists regained the advantage and put such pressure on Alcimus that he was again forced to ask for help from the king.

267. This time the king sent a new army and the "master of the elephants," Nicanor, probably the same person who had taken part in the expedition which had terminated in the encounter at Emmaus (§ 256). At first he tried to capture Judas by trickery, inviting him to a friendly meeting, but the trap was discovered, and open hostility followed (1 Mach. 7:27–30). Another tradition refers to the close friend-

The height of Adasa (Khirbet 'Adasch). (Abel.)

ship which sprang up between Nicanor and Judas but was broken up sometime later by Alcimus, at whose instigation an order was issued by King Demetrius that Nicanor send Judas to him as a prisoner (2 Mach. 14:18 ff.).

A first encounter occurred at Caphar-salama, which cannot be identified with certainty but is perhaps not far from Jerusalem. Nicanor suffered a reversal and withdrew to Jerusalem. There he assumed a contemptuous and threatening attitude even toward the Hellenized priests and the other adherents of the Seleucid faction, probably because he suspected that he had been secretly betrayed. Not long afterward, with the approach of re-enforcements from Syria, he advanced as far as Beth-Horon (§ 255) to meet them. Judas awaited in ambush on the heights of Adasa with only three thousand armed men, and fell upon him as he was returning to Jerusalem. It must have been the usual surprise attack, and it seems that Nicanor was among the first to fall, two circumstances which led to a general disorganization and consequent slaughter. It was the thirteenth of the month Adar (March) of 160 B.C., from that time on declared a festive day and called "The Day of Nicanor." Nicanor's head and right arm were cut off and displayed in Jerusalem. But it was the last victory of Judas Machabeus.

268. Demetrius at once sent an army of twenty thousand men and two thousand horses under the command of Bacchides, accompanied by Alcimus, to avenge the death of Nicanor. They made contact with Judas at Elasa, probably near *el-Bireh,* some ten miles to the north of Jerusalem. Judas had his usual three thousand men, but this time they became frightened on seeing even from a distance the strength of the enemy, and many secretly fled away. Judas was left with eight hundred soldiers, "and he was troubled in mind because he did not have time to rally them together" (1 Mach. 9:7). The cunning desert chieftain then made a bad decision, and disdainfully rejecting the prudent exhortations of his men to retreat, decided on a frontal attack. With their usual valor augmented by the heat of battle, they succeeded in breaking the right wing of the enemy and pursued it for a great distance. But the left wing wheeled into position behind them, and Judas was slain with many others on the field of battle; the survivors fled. It was April, 160 B.C.

Jonathan and Simon recovered their brother's body and buried it in the paternal tomb at Modin (§ 253). His loyal followers mourned him for a long time and chanted the elegiac refrain:

> "How is the mighty one fallen,
> who saved his people Israel?"
>
> (1 Mach. 9:21)

269. Jonathan Machabeus. The death of Judas was an extremely grave blow to the nationalist faction, especially since the victors immediately proceeded to press their advantage, being determined to blot out every trace of the previous insurrection and to stifle any similar desires which might rise in the future. Bacchides ruled from the Akra and Alcimus from the Temple. Both made good use of a serious famine which unexpectedly struck the land to re-enforce their political position. To receive help one had either to be or to pose as a Hellenist. As a result, the few who were faithful to nationalism disappeared from view, the

El-Bireh: remains of fortifications. (Abel.)

Cistern in the desert of Teqoa. (Abel.)

old Hellenists triumphed, and those who had held aloof or had been wavering now abandoned themselves to the current and passed over to the Hellenistic faction. The most lucrative posts and the more responsible offices were given to the old Hellenists, but even without previous merit one could get ahead by turning informer. To be a spy against the nationalists, to point out to Bacchides the hiding place of some family faithful to the Machabees or a secret meeting place of the Assideans, brought a reward in provisions, money, or other ways. Those who conducted this systematic man-hunt had ample resources at their disposal, and the results can easily be imagined. They are summed up in these words of the narrator who went back in thought to the ancient dictators of the spirit of Israel, now seen no more (Vol. I, § 430): "And there came about a great tribulation in Israel, such as was not since the day when a prophet was no longer seen among them" (1 Mach. 9:27).

The nationalists who disappeared from view took refuge in their trusted desert. The famine which raged through the cities was also felt there, but to them hunger was an old acquaintance (§ 225), and too, the desert has resources of which the city is ignorant. They were pitifully few in numbers; worse still, they were leaderless. Yet this handful of starving, wandering men hoped against hope.

270. They now had to choose a leader. Of the five Machabee brothers, Eleazar and Judas had died in battle; Simon, as the dying Mathathias had arranged, continued to be the counselor and political leader (§ 253); but the great need now was for someone to take over the office of general, left vacant by the death of Judas. The experience of past battles indicated that the youngest of the Machabees, Jonathan, would be a worthy successor to Judas, so he was put at the head of the insurgents. To the eldest of the Machabees, John, was entrusted the care of the baggage and of the camp, and the surname "Gaddis" (§ 252: probably "forager") may have been given him because of this.

The rebels probably concentrated in the vicinity of Modin (§ 252), a fact which did not escape Bacchides, whose zealous spies served him well. To surprise completely the core of nationalist forces, and especially its new head, he then took up so dogged a chase that the pursued could no longer maintain their position, but had to draw back to an unapproachable and inhospitable place, the desert of Teqoa (Vol. I, § 65), which lies south of Jerusalem and along the western shore of the Dead Sea. There they settled "near the water of the cistern of Asphar" (1 Mach. 9:33). David in his stormier days had taken refuge in these same localities (Vol. I, § 362).

To obtain greater freedom of movement and to secure the safety of the families and goods, Jonathan decided to send his brother and the baggage entrusted to him to his friends the Nabateans. The caravan, once in Transjordan, was to proceed down along the eastern shore of the Dead Sea. When it had reached a point near Madaba, to the southeast of Mount Nebo (Vol. I, § 275), John Machabeus lost his life in a surprise raid made by the inhabitants of the place. The caravan was lost. Custom demanded that the injured parties exact blood vengence for this deed, and not long afterward they succeeded in so doing, for during the celebration of the marriage of a young noble woman of Madaba, Jonathan and his warriors crossed the Jordan, fell upon the nuptial procession, and killed them all. Meanwhile, Bacchides had been informed of Jonathan's foray into Transjordan, and was waiting to surprise him when he came to recross the river. After a brief encounter

The Jordan looking toward Madaba. (Abel.)

there, Jonathan and his men swam across the stream and vanished into the desert safely.

To guard against the new guerrilla warfare, Bacchides fortified some of the more important points which would assure his control over the desert, and installed garrisons in them. Then to make certain that the local chiefs did not secretly help the rebels, he took hostages from them and brought them to Jerusalem.

In May of 159 B.C., something new occurred. Alcimus commanded the demolition of the wall of the inner court of the Temple, which separated the (inner) enclosure reserved for the priests from the one into which the Israelites were admitted. It is possible that he intended to rebuild it in a Hellenistic way. One modern opinion quite without foundation would have it that he wished to abolish altogether this sign of separation of Jew from Greek, as being now inopportune. But it is difficult to believe that even when Hellenism held the upper hand, pagans were permitted to penetrate into the Temple, licitly, as far as the inner court and in front of the door of the "holy" place. On the other hand, it is probable that once the wall was demolished, the two courts remained without any separating wall until the time of Alexander Jannaeus (§§ 102, 302). It is a fact that when the work was begun, Alcimus was stricken with apoplexy and died shortly after in great agony. The accident was considered to be a divine punishment for having demolished "the works of the prophets" (1 Mach. 9:54), the reference being to Aggeus, who was responsible for building the Temple (§ 97). With Alcimus dead, Bacchides no longer had anyone who needed his special protection, and since, on the other hand, Jonathan was roaming the broad stretches of the desert, Bacchides found nothing more to occupy him in Judea, and so returned to Antioch.

"And the land of Juda was at peace for two years" (1 Mach. 9:57). According to Josephus (*Antiquities*, XX, 10), Alcimus had no successors, and the office of high priest remained vacant for seven years.

✿　　✿　　✿

271. During the two years of truce, Jonathan and his men grew stronger, living in the desert. Internal dissension within the Hellenistic faction led to the neglect of the struggle against the rebels, and they were not disturbed. One might say that during this period each side pretended to ignore the other, and avoided coming to grips.

But at the end of 157 B.C., some of the zealous Hellenized Jews thought that the truce was a good time for a surprise attack; surely Jonathan had now grown careless. Let Bacchides be summoned again with an army, and he would capture him. Bacchides was in fact asked to come and actually started out, perhaps not very willingly. But first he wrote that a surprise attack should be made quickly on Jonathan and his men. The attack failed, however, because Jonathan and his men had been warned. When Bacchides arrived, irritated by the unsuccessful attempt, he revenged himself on those who had mismanaged the project by killing some fifty of them. This is what we read in 1 Mach. 9:58 ff., but it is probable that the narrator was taken up only with his own argument, and so made no mention of other and more grave reasons which had prompted the new expedition of Bacchides. Had Jonathan at that time not directly annoyed the Hellenistic faction, it is difficult to see why Bacchides would have come from Antioch with an army to seize him, and much less would he have entrusted to the Hellenists at Jerusalem the striking of that blow which was the reason for his own visit. It can be conjectured that Bacchides came, rather, to quiet the possibly violent dissensions in the Hellenistic faction of Jerusalem, which threatened the foundation of the Seleucid authority in Judea, and whose effects could be seen in the interruption of hostilities against Jonathan, and in the lack of a successor to Alcimus. Even the capital punishment ordered by Bacchides at that time and later (§ 272) points to something more serious than the failure of the surprise attack against Jonathan. At any rate, as long as he had come, Bacchides decided to take some action also against Jonathan.

But Jonathan had taken refuge at Beth-bassi, probably to the southeast of Bethlehem (Vol. I, § 356), and had fortified himself there very carefully. He then left his brother Simon in command of the fortress, himself remaining free to roam in the surrounding sectors to procure the necessary supplies from the nearby Bedouin tribes, and especially to be ready to attack Bacchides from the rear whenever he made his attack on the fortress. Bacchides did begin the siege, but in the middle of the desert his position was very inconvenient, and supplies were difficult to obtain. Besides, Simon made sorties from within and damaged the siege-engines, while from without Jonathan posed a continuous threat against the lines of communications. After some time had elapsed, Bacchides had still not gained the upper hand, and the siege threatened to detain him in the desert indefinitely. In the face of such a prospect he raised the siege and dropped the whole affair; he had come to Judea grudgingly, and was anxious to hurry back to Antioch.

272. He tarried in Jerusalem before he departed, however, and put to death several other Hellenists. This measure is depicted in the narrative as Bacchides' revenge for the reversal suffered in the siege of Beth-bassi. That is a partial explanation, but there is more to it than that; by this new purge he hoped to root out the chief trouble-makers in the party, and so to leave a peaceful situation in Judea which would no longer require his presence.

In the meantime, Jonathan had been informed of those dissensions, and also of Bacchides' desire to have no more trouble from Judea. He then cleverly seized the opportunity to send representatives to Bacchides before he departed, to discuss the return of prisoners and a general accord. This suited Bacchides perfectly. The prisoners were returned and Jonathan received solemn guarantees that he would not be molested in the future. When Bacchides returned to Antioch, Jonathan transferred to Michmas (Vol. I, § 350) about nine miles north of Jerusalem, fortifying the place and setting himself up as its master. His political status there was most unusual: in the eyes of the Syrian authorities he was no longer a rebel, for he had come to an understanding with Bacchides; yet he had not explicitly renounced his nationalistic program, and still less had he made peace with the Hellenized Jews of Jerusalem. This point had not been touched, and he had implicitly reserved his right to full liberty of action. He had become, therefore, one of those local chieftains frequently met with in the Orient, who rely upon their own resources and at whom the central authority, because of its own weakness, had to close one eye or even both. Thus, the Yahwistic Michmas became the opposite of Hellenized Jerusalem, and it was there that "Jonathan began to govern the people and made the wicked disappear from Israel" (1 Mach. 9:73). This constituted the reaction of the Assideans against the "wicked" Hellenists who until then had been powerful.

✻   ✻   ✻

273. From 157–156 to 153 B.C. we lack definite information about Judea, but it is easy to imagine that the Yahwistic reaction centered in Michmas grew ever more extensive until it had gained the greater part of Judea. The Hellenized Jews of Jerusalem would, as usual, send to Antioch for aid, but the ever mounting difficulties which King Demetrius had to face (§ 46) did not permit him to send to that disturbed land other troops and other Bacchideses. As long as they paid their tribute they could settle their own religious and provincial wranglings. But the Hellenized provincials fared very badly left to themselves, for when Hellenism and Nationalism struggled for mastery, as the one declined, the other correspondingly increased. Shortly before 153 B.C., Jonathan had practically become the arbiter of the affairs of Judea.

Despite all this, he had not yet revolted directly against the very center of Hellenism, Jerusalem. His plan was well thought out. He profited from past experience and realized that his power rested upon the desert, the countryside, and the smaller centers. When these districts were solidly won over to his side, Jerusalem would be sur-

Alexander Balas.

rounded by such a spiritual blockade that even its physical conquest would cost little. The possession of Jerusalem without solid support from without had in the past resulted in an illusory success. Further, while he was winning over the open areas, time was passing and political conditions were becoming ever more favorable to himself, in view of the progressive decline of Demetrius. Jonathan already glimpsed the day when the ripened fruit would fall into his hand almost without his shaking the tree, and he was astute enough to wait quietly for that full ripening. He well deserved his surname "Apphus" (§ 252: ? "dissimulator" [of his own thoughts], "astute"). In some Greek manuscripts a copyist's mistaken duplication of the final "s" of the preceding word makes his name "Sapphus."

274. In 153 what he had foreseen actually came to pass. Alexander Balas, pretender to the Seleucid throne, disembarked at Ptolemais (§ 46). This port (St. John of Acre; Vol. I, § 52) facing Carmel was very important to Demetrius, for its possession would put the whole of Judea, now dominated by Jonathan, at the disposal of the pretender. Demetrius therefore moved to forestall Balas by securing Jonathan's support. He abandoned the Hellenized Jews who had proved to be incompetent and troublesome, and wrote to Jonathan, choosing him as his ally and imposing upon him as an official duty the gathering of troops and fashioning of arms, besides consigning to him the hostages held in the Akra (§ 270). Jonathan had already been gathering troops and making weapons for quite some time, but what was important now was that he had official sanction to do so. The ripened fruit was falling into the hand of the "Dissimulator."

As Jonathan had not despaired in adversity, so now he remained master of himself, coolly calculating these more prosperous times. He must now avoid the mistake of binding himself to only one wheel of fortune, seeing that prosperity might also be derived from other sources. Demetrius today made him an offer, but it was clear that he acted out of fear of Balas; tomorrow Balas would certainly make his bid and he would surely offer more than Demetrius. The "Dissimulator" was, then, cultivated by both sides; he accepted Demetrius' offer but reserved the right to hear what Balas might have to say.

Upon receipt of the letter from Demetrius, Jonathan immediately went to Jerusalem and, having notified the authorities and those in the Akra of it, began at once to act as the representative of the king.

But he neither disavowed his old principles nor did the local Hellenists think for a moment that he had. So well understood was this that at his first acts, the foreigners and the foremost members of the other party fled away or into hiding, and the troops which had been distributed in the fortified places of the district by Bacchides (§ 270) dispersed. The Akra in Jerusalem and the fortress of Beth-sur to the south (§ 262) were the only places of refuge left to the more ardent Hellenized Jews. Once he had received the hostages and sent them back to their families, Jonathan immediately set about rebuilding in Jerusalem the counterpart of the Akra, that is, the fortress of the "hillock of Sion" which had been dismantled from the time of Lysias (§ 262). He raised up its walls again — a necessary precaution, and one which meant more than the letter of Demetrius.

Meanwhile, however, another letter arrived — the expected counter-offer of Alexander Balas. Considering him as already a king, Balas treated Jonathan as almost an equal. He constituted him the high priest of Judaism, granted him the title of "friend of the king," the most coveted title at court, and at the same time sent him the purple insignia and a crown of gold. Thus, the offers of Demetrius were far surpassed, especially when, with the conferring of the office of high priest upon him, Jonathan officially assumed the highest position in the nation. He readily accepted all these new concessions or recognitions, including the office of high priest. Since he came from a sacerdotal family (§ 252), he donned the pontifical mantle and functioned for the first time on the feast of Tabernacles in October of 152 B.C.

In putting on the mantle for the first time Jonathan may have thought that, while it was offered to him by an uncircumcised and idolatrous king, it was by way of compensation, sprinkled with the blood of thousands of Yahwists, among the first of whom were his brothers Eleazar, Judas, and John, and it was woven with the hardships of other thousands of starving wanderers, beginning with those of his father Mathathias. It was these dead who offered him the mantle, rather than Alexander Balas. It was indeed a heavy mantle.

275. The office of high priest did not interfere with his duty as head of the army; on the contrary, it seems more likely that it helped it. After the mention of the feast of Tabernacles, there is immediately subjoined the information that "he gathered together an army and prepared many arms" (1 Mach. 10:21). It was what the times demanded: it would have been tempting Yahweh to expect that He would send angels from heaven every time a Heliodorus took a notion to profane the Temple (§ 226). Under the circumstances it was necessary that those of good will be ready to serve Yahweh with their arms, as well as venerate Him in their hearts, and that they have

"The praises of God in their mouth
and a double-edged sword in their hand,
to wreak vengeance upon the *goim*,
chastisements among the [pagan] peoples."
(Ps. 149:6)

This union of the sword and censer had undeniable practical advantages, so the faithful Yahwists kept silence, although in theory there was some obscurity as to whether this union was in accord with the Yahwist principles of most ancient times, which had kept these two functions separate. These points were not explored at the time, but became an issue later on when the practical advantages which led to a neglect of the theoretical discussion (§§ 298, 302, 311) had vanished.

When Demetrius heard of the concessions Balas had made, he made in turn even greater offers, which included — among other generous benefits in taxation, administration, and military matters — even the yielding up of the jealously guarded Akra (1 Mach. 10:25–45, which probably gives the trend of the letter). Such great generosity, however, was suspect. A man like Demetrius who acted in this manner only because he was on the edge of an abyss might on the morrow, when he was no longer in danger, break faith with his promises. It would be better to push him down into the abyss and to support Balas, and that is what Jonathan did. Joining Balas, he left Demetrius to meet his fate.

Balas showed his gratitude. He invited Jonathan to the splendid nuptial feasts at Ptolemais (§ 47) and there treated him with special honors. On this occasion a minor attempt to turn Balas against

Lydda.

him was made by some Hellenized Jews, who made a special trip to Ptolemais to accuse Jonathan. The incident is significant in that it demonstrates that even after the Machabean triumph the opposing faction had not lost all hope and was secretly working against him. It is not surprising that Balas was unwilling to be alienated from so valuable a partisan as Jonathan and would not listen to their charges; instead, he made Jonathan "first friend of the king," "general," and

Jaffa (Joppe).

also "meridarch," that is, "head of a part" [of the realm], namely Judea.

276. The ability and fidelity of the high priest "general" was soon put to the test. When the new pretender Demetrius II came upon the scene, and Apollonius the governor of Coelesyria had gone over to his side, Balas prepared to defend Antioch to the north, while Jonathan remained in the south. Apollonius sent a direct challenge to Jonathan to come down and engage him in battle on the coastal plain, and Jonathan, with Simon and ten thousand men, came down from Jerusalem, took the port of Joppe (Jaffa), and defeated Apollonius at Azotus (Asdod: § 260). When the fugitives took refuge in the local temple of Dagon (Vol. I, §§ 332, 343), Jonathan burned both city and temple and thence moved forward to take possession of Ascalon. When Balas heard of these successes of his "general," he promoted him from the rank of "first friend of the king" (§ 275) to that of "relative of the king" — the highest rank at court — and sent him the golden buckle which went with the rank. He also gave him as his personal possession the other Philistine city of Accaron.

When Ptolemy VI advanced with an army from Egypt to execute his sly plans against his son-in-law, Balas (§ 47), Jonathan accompanied him from Joppe up to the River Eleutherus, the modern *Nahr el-Kebir*, a little to the north of Tripoli. Ptolemy then went on alone to prosecute his war, and in the struggle both he and Balas were killed. Jonathan had returned to Jerusalem and seized the opportunity provided by this dynastic war to re-enforce his own position. He first laid siege to the Akra in Jerusalem, occupied as always by the Syrian garrison (§ 274). It was perhaps on this occasion that he busied himself in extending his northern confines and annexing some localities which were dependent on Samaria. The anti-Machabean faction then repeated its old attempt (§ 275) to discredit him, and denounced his activity to Demetrius II when the latter was established upon his throne.

Jonathan had opposed Demetrius when he was still a pretender and had defeated his partisan Apollonius, but now that Demetrius had become king and Balas was dead, he had no reason for preferring anyone else to him, if the terms were right. Demetrius II must have come to a similar conclusion; it was to his interests to win over such a powerful national leader by friendliness, rather than to try to conquer him by force of arms. Invited to present himself to Demetrius in Ptolemais, Jonathan diplomatically accepted, going there in a frame of mind similar to that of the king. The gifts brought by Jonathan neutralized the denunciations of the anti-Machabeans, diplomatic negotiations overcame all difficulties, and an agreement was reached, both sides yielding certain points. Jonathan was to tolerate the Akra and its Syrian garrison in Jerusalem, but he was allowed to annex to Judea three toparchies which belonged to Samaria, namely, Apherema (Ephron: Vol. I, § 459), Lydda, and Ramathaim (1 Mach. 11:34: Greek text). It seems, furthermore, that by the single payment of three hundred talents, Judea would be exempted from the tribute due to the crown. The usual decorations accompanied the completion of the accord, and Jonathan who had already been confirmed in his office of high priest, was also made "first friend of the king" (145 B.C.).

277. The agreement represented a great step forward for the political ambitions of Jonathan. The ample concessions of Balas in 152 (§ 274) had not, properly speaking, increased the territory of Judea, nor loosened the bonds which tied it to the throne of the Seleucids, as for example, the tribute especially levied by the commandant of the Akra. By this accord reached seven years later, Jonathan's territory was extended, and the last remaining vestiges of Seleucid authority were the two fortresses of Akra and Beth-sur. This was not full independence, but it was not far from it, and Jonathan the "Dissimulator" was well able to bide his time, awaiting the opportune moment.

Later on, Demetrius, thinking himself to be now secure on the throne, dismissed the army which had put him there and retained only his Cretan troops (§ 47). This caused widespread discontent which in Antioch broke out into an open revolt that was destined to play its part a little later in the appearance of the

Antiochus VI.

new pretender Antiochus VI, who was under the protection of Trypho (§ 48). Demetrius found himself facing the revolt without troops and sent an urgent appeal to Jonathan for soldiers. The Machabean, having first extracted a promise of the withdrawal of the garrisons of Akra and Beth-sur, sent him three thousand of his picked troops. These served Demetrius well, for in conjunction with the Cretan troops, they quelled the rebellion in Antioch, burning houses, slaughtering a great number of the inhabitants, and looting the city on a large scale. The capital under control, Demetrius allowed the three thousand Jews to depart with their spoils, but would not hear of the withdrawal of the garrisons from Judea. For this, Jonathan soon afterward had his revenge.

278. When Antiochus VI appeared on the scene, the usual offers were made. The new pretender confirmed Jonathan in the office of high priest, confirmed the annexation of the toparchies (which here become four; 1 Mach. 11:57; cf. §§ 276, 165), the usual titles "friend," "cousin of the king," and other privileges, and gave Simon Machabeus the office of "general" of all the region of the "Ladder of Tyre" (the promontory between Ptolemais and Tyre) to the confines of Egypt. The two Machabees, needless to say, went over to the side of Antiochus VI, especially as Simon's new office gave them an opportunity to act legally in their own interests even outside their territory.

Their resentment against Demetrius prompted them to act zealously against him and in favor of Antiochus VI. Brief incursions into Transjordan and then on the Philistine coast made them masters of the situation. Ascalon yielded of its own accord, Gaza after a brief resistance. While Jonathan was conducting an expedition up to Damascus, Simon attacked the fortress of Beth-sur; after a prolonged resistance it capitulated and he took possession of it, thereby finally abolishing this redoubt of Hellenism. It became a Machabee fortress. While Jonathan continued his expedition toward Damascus, an army of Demetrius penetrated Galilee up to Hasor (Vol. I, § 309). The encounter there at first went badly for the Machabean, but he gathered his fleeing soldiers, filled them with renewed spirit, and led them again to the attack, turning the tide in his favor.

Following this defeat, Demetrius' supporters brought up an army for the counterattack. Jonathan had returned to Jerusalem, but went up against them, as far as the region of Emath (Hamath: Vol. I, § 60), but the enemy withdrew without joining in battle. Meanwhile, Simon was fortifying Adida, the strategic center near Lydda, with an eye to his own advantage. Returning from his expedition, Jonathan in turn began to rebuild the walls in Jerusalem, demolished since the time of Antiochus Epiphanes (§ 235), and at the same time undertook other works which were designed to render the "hillock of Sion" impregnable (§ 260). He still further reduced the power of the one remaining redoubt of Hellenism, that towering Akra, by surrounding it with a high wall which isolated it from the rest of the city.

279. These war efforts did not exhaust the energies of the Machabees. To strengthen his position Jonathan had need also of diplomatic recognition, so, while each successive Seleucid monarch was becoming weaker and weaker, he turned his thoughts to Rome, far away, but always present in the Orient. The experience of his brother Judas with Rome did not encourage him to hope for much (§ 265), but Jonathan did not expect a tribune with four legions to be sent to him. The shadow of protection which the name Rome implied was, in certain cases, worth more than legions. He therefore sent Numenius and Antipater to Rome to renew the former friendship. Only the bare mention of this embassy is preserved. It is probable that it was received at Rome with the same courtesy extended to the embassy sent by Judas Machabeus, but produced no more than Jonathan expected, namely a certain diplomatic luster and prestige. Others think that Jonathan did not send an embassy to Rome, and that the mission of Numenius and Antipater should be identified with the embassy of Simon. But it is a question more of names than of facts (§ 290).

Another power which had great influence in Asia Minor was Sparta (§§ 3, 19 ff.). A legend had sprung up there — due no doubt to Jews who had emigrated to Sparta (§ 236) — that the Spartans and Hebrews were related, because they were both descended from Abraham (1 Mach. 12:21). At any rate, the diaspora had brought about much intercourse between Sparta and Palestine, going back to Arius I, the Spartan king of the house of the Agiadae, who reigned from 309 to about 265 B.C. The embassy of Numenius and Antipater passed through Sparta on its return from Rome, doubtless there too to seek support, merely diplomatic support, for the Machabees.

280. All this warlike activity and diplomatic energy of Jonathan alarmed Trypho. True, the Machabee had actively supported Antiochus VI, who was protected by Trypho, but the latter planned to replace Antiochus as king, and did not like to see Jonathan become too powerful and the head of an autonomous state. He therefore schemed to eliminate him in one way or another. Trypho advanced with an army toward Judea, Jonathan went up to meet him with forty thousand soldiers, and they met at Beisan (Vol. I, § 86). What the motive was behind this deployment of forces which did not join in battle, is not known. Perhaps Jonathan feared an attack, and so marched against Trypho; the latter, seeing the strength of his adversary, perhaps despaired of conquering him and so resorted to trickery. Or perhaps Trypho had invited Jonathan to mobilize, proposing to him vaguely some important enterprise, and when they met at Beisan he openly confided his plan to dethrone Antiochus VI, offering him a part in the project. Upon Jonathan's refusal, Trypho had recourse to treachery. Whatever the meaning of these obscure preliminaries, Trypho feigned the warmest friendship for Jonathan, suggested to him that he dismiss his soldiers except for a small personal escort, and that he follow him to Ptolemais where he would hand over to him the city and the forts. The Machabean, for years accustomed to good fortune, saw in this proposal of Trypho the normal conclusion of his preceding successes, and did not suspect a plot in one who had no apparent reason for hatching one.

So Jonathan dismissed his army, keeping only three thousand men, and of these two thousand were sent into Galilee; the other one thousand went with him to Ptolemais. Hardly had he entered the city when Trypho's followers closed the gates of the city, slaughtered the thousand men, and sent Jonathan to Trypho as a prisoner. The two thousand men who were in Galilee managed with difficulty to force open a path through the troops sent against them, and made their way back to Judea.

This was at the close of 143 B.C.

281. Simon Machabeus. Great was the sorrow of the Jewish nationalists at the imprisonment of Jonathan, and great the joy of their Hellenistic enemies who immediately said: "They do not have a man who knows how to command and conquer (ἄνδρα ἄρχοντα καὶ βοηθοῦντα [Semitic phrase]); now, therefore, we will make war on them and destroy their memory from among men" (1 Mach. 12:53). The observation had some truth in it. Simon Machabeus, the only brother remaining of the five, was especially known as a political ruler and administrator (§ 253), while he had given only second-rate proofs of his ability in warfare as a "general," under the command of his brother Jonathan (§ 278).

Nevertheless, the hopes of the Hellenists were naïve. Simon was not the second-rate war leader they imagined, nor was the Machabean faction so disorganized as to have need still of a nomad chieftain who relied on the stratagems of the desert. It need not be said that Simon was chosen by popular acclaim to fill the post of the imprisoned Jonathan, and it is interesting to note that his first care was to prepare for war, a very prudent step in view of Trypho's treachery and its consequences. Simon immediately set about to provide works of fortification for Jerusalem, "and he gathered together all the men of war, and made haste to finish the walls of Jerusalem, and fortified it round about" (1 Mach. 13:10). This rebuilding and fortification of the walls, which had been begun by Jonathan (§ 278), was again intended to insure the city against external attack, but it must have had also the other purpose of isolating in a more rigorous manner the enemy nesting within, that is, the Syrian Akra, which was still blockaded by the troops of the Machabees. It was already surrounded by the wall erected by Jonathan, but perhaps this did not suffice to cut off the garrison from all replenishment of supplies, especially on the side closer to the walls of the city and the countryside. It was therefore opportune to re-enforce the walls for this reason also. Simon also secured the port of Joppe (§ 276) by fortifying the city and putting a strong citadel there.

282. Trypho, as was to be expected, led an army into Judea, and Simon advanced to meet him at Adida (§ 278). Trypho did not intend to attack Simon, but he wanted to get close to the Akra and to force the blockade around it, thus bringing the supplies urgently requested by the besieged. Bringing his prisoner Jonathan with him, he planned to make what use he could of this important pawn. He proceeded down along the coast, and, opening negotiations with Simon, informed him that he was willing to liberate Jonathan if they paid him one hundred talents of silver — on the pretext that this was tribute due to the king — and the two sons of the prisoner as hostages. Coming from Trypho, the proposal was obviously insincere, but to avoid any ill will on the part of the people, Simon ordered that the talents and hostages be sent. Trypho did not liberate Jonathan but pushed on southward by way of Adora, to the south of Hebron, circling around and around Jerusalem, with the Akra, now reduced to extreme need, always his goal. But Simon and his army wheeled to face him and forestalled every approach to the blockaded fortress. Seizing an opportune moment, Trypho prepared a swift raid with his cavalry which was to circle around Simon, make for the Akra, and replenish its supplies in a surprise move. But the night before the plan was to be put into effect, a heavy snowfall, a rare occurrence in Palestine (Vol. I, § 67), made it impossible for him to do so. Trypho abandoned the Akra to its fate, and began his march toward Syria, passing to the east through the region of Galaad. His prisoner Jonathan no longer being useful to him, Trypho had him put to death (and his two sons also, according to the Vulgate of 1 Mach. 13:23) when they reached Bascama, an unidentified locality in Transjordan. It was toward the beginning of 142 B.C.

283. Simon recovered the body of his brother, the fourth one to lose his life in the interests of the nation, and proceeded to build a monument to commemorate what his family had done for the cause. Jonathan was buried in the family tomb at Modin (§§ 253, 268), and a stone mausoleum was erected there in the form of seven pyramids: two for his father and mother, four for his brothers who were killed; the seventh was reserved for himself when his time should come. The

use of pyramids has a parallel in the tomb of Queen Helen (§ 212), but it is more interesting to note that the mausoleum also contained columns decorated with war trophies such as panoplies and spurs. These certainly were intended to commemorate the deeds of the dead but they betrayed all too clearly their Hellenistic inspiration. Such was the temper of the times that traces of Hellenism left their mark even on the tombs of those who had died in fighting it.

The monument, so grandiose that it could be seen even from the Mediterranean, was an exact, perhaps even an international symbol of the political situation. In the twenty-five years that had elapsed from the persecution of Antiochus Epiphanes up to the coming of Simon Machabeus, Yahwistic Judea had carried out a grandiose program under Machabean leadership, and the splendid monument which arose there in the native place of the Machabees to commemorate, to be sure, the past, also gave a warning for the future that Yahwism, nationalism, and Machabees must be indissolubly linked together.

284. Shortly after he had had Jonathan slain, Trypho disclosed his political game by also killing Antiochus VI (§ 48), and proclaimed himself in his stead "king *autokrator*," as he is called on his coins. But he went too far both in his title and in his methods, for Demetrius II, whom Jonathan and Simon had supported before they went over to Antiochus VI (§ 276), was still alive and willing to fight. Jonathan's murder was more than a crime for Trypho; it was a mistake, for it caused Simon, the survivor, to return to Demetrius II, who had lost all power in the southern part of the divided realm. It seemed too good to be true that he should find a powerful ally in the head of the Jews, and this time he responded to the proposals of the Machabean by granting most liberal concessions of all kinds; anything he would get from Simon was to his gain. The Seleucid monarch recognized all of Simon's ancient titles, abolished all past and future tribute which Judea owed to the crown, gave permission to the Jews to fortify their territory — which Simon was already doing on a large scale — and, finally, as a sign of honor, invited the Jews to enroll in his army.

After these concessions what remained of the sovereignty of the Seleucids over Judea? According to the ancient political mentality there still remained a *jus*, a right, although an abstract and nominal one; in practice, nothing of it remained. The concessions were so interpreted by the Jews, who fixed the year

Demetrius II.

170 of the Seleucids (§ 36), that is, 142–141 B.C. as the first year of a new national era, and began to date events from it. In the year 170 the yoke of the [pagan] nations was lifted from Israel and the people of Israel began to write, in their contracts and agreements: "The first year of Simon, high priest and general and prince of the Jews" (1 Mach. 13:41–42). They now had achieved complete independence.

285. Yet the Akra remained to remind them of their former dependence. The long siege had been hard on the garrison and many in it were dying of hunger. There being no hope of help from Trypho, and much less from Demetrius II, the besieged came to terms with Simon and obtained a safe-conduct for their withdrawal. Simon entered the Akra on the twenty-third of the month Iyyar (May) of 141, and not only was that day celebrated with special joy, but it was made into a yearly feast. Finally, after twenty-five years, the pagan dagger thrust into the heart of Jerusalem (§ 237) had been withdrawn.

Shortly before the taking of the Akra, Simon had gained control of Gezer (Vol. I, § 76 ff.) which had become an important Hellenistic and military center.[4] In the hands of the Machabean it would protect his communications from Jerusalem to Joppe (§ 281) and would prevent a new possible thrust on the part of Trypho. Simon cleared the city of its inhabitants and resettled it with zealous Yahwists; he fortified it and also built there for himself a residence which was later to become the residence of his son John Hyrcanus, who was put in charge to watch over the important sector (1 Mach. 16:1, 19, 21). Archaeological exploration of Gezer has brought to light the plan of the palace of Simon. In the material examined by Macalister there was a stone with the following fragment scratched on it in cursive letters: Πάμπρας: Σίμωνος κατοπάζη πῦρ βασίλειον — "Pampras [prays thus]: May fire reach the palace of Simon!" A genuine imprecation, therefore, confirmed by certain magical signs engraved upon the same stone. It has been rightly conjectured that its author was some Hellenistic enemy of Simon's who had been forced to work on this palace, probably because he was his prisoner. Unable to express his bitterness aloud, he put it in writing, and left this fine magical "charm" in the very palace of his enemy.

286. Simon's political position was now very strong, and no immediate threat weighed upon him. Yet there *was* a shadow which, in the judgment of many among the more scrupulous Yahwists, had clouded the very origins of his high priesthood. The Machabee family had obtained this office through concessions made to Jonathan by Balas (§ 274), and this had been subsequently confirmed, though always by

---

[4] In 1 Mach. 13:43 it should be Γάζαρα, that is, "Gezer," as *Antiquities*, XIII, 6, 7, has it, instead of Γάζαν, that is, the Philistine city of "Gaza" (Vol. I, § 328).

Seleucid kings. Strictly speaking, therefore, the investiture had been made by foreigners; it had been an intervention of non-Jews, pagans even, in the designation of the highest office in Jewish Yahwism. This unpleasant shadow was dispelled by a kind of official declaration, democratic in character, on the eighteenth day of the month of Elul (September) of the year 140 B.C. The people,[5] gathered together for the occasion, recalled to mind how deserving of national praise was the Machabee family, and it was then decreed that the survivor of the five brothers, and his descendants, be confirmed in office. Hence, "Jews and priests consented that Simon be their prince and high priest forever, until there should arise a faithful prophet" (1 Mach. 14:41). A copy of the decree was made on tablets of bronze which were put on a column and exhibited on Mount Sion.

The title "high priest forever" was one of grandiose solemnity (cf. Ps. 110 [Vulgate, 109]:4), and according to the desire of these electors, meant that after so many adversities Yahwism had found its lasting equilibrium. Simon's authority was to be perpetuated in his children by reason of the immutable divine decision, for "Yahweh swears and does not repent."

287. Simon was not proclaimed as "king of Israel" in so many words, out of regard, perhaps, for the Seleucid monarch, but more certainly because of the Yahwistic persuasion that the "king of Israel" had to be of the line of David, which Yahweh had chosen in the beginning to be the depository, and that forever, of the scepter of Israel (2 Sam. 7:16; Ps. 89 [88]:37–38; 132 [131]:12). Some of David's descendants were still alive, but lived in obscurity and privacy. On the occasion of the national renaissance they had not been particularly conspicuous and had shown little or no initiative or interest in the movement; the Machabees did. In view of these facts, the popular decree followed a middle course; it did not assign the scepter of Israel to the Machabees, but granted them a kind of official lieutenancy which would last "until there should arise a faithful prophet." Who could scrutinize the future designs of Yahweh? The prophet, the official herald of Yahweh, had not been seen for centuries (Vol. I, § 30), but Yahweh could easily raise up another man when He wished, perhaps He even might select him from the obscure descendants of David. For that matter, was it not the ancient and universal conviction in Israel that its greatest prophet of future times, the Messias, would issue forth from the line of David? The phrase in the decree regarding the future prophet was

---

[5] The Jewish people, of course, which means, practically speaking, the Machabee's faction. The Latin of 1 Mach. 14:24 has "populus Romanus," which is a result of the influence of the preceding phrase. The Greek (14:25) does not have the adjective.

intended to cover this possibility of divine intervention – a theocratic phrase in a democratic decree.

There was no difficulty about excluding the ancient line of high priests, now represented by Onias IV, who had deserted his post and had tried to substitute his schismatic temple of Leontopolis (§ 249) for the Temple of Jerusalem. There was abundant reason for considering that line as ruined, and its place taken by the Machabees, who were also of sacerdotal lineage, and who deserved so well of Yahwism.

The popular election of Simon legalized his position according to the principles of Yahwism. He was at the same time "high priest," "general," and "ethnarch." The corresponding Hebrew word for this last Greek term (§ 189) was rich in meaning and more definite, that is, "prince of the people of God." There is also a Greek transcription of this Hebrew phrase: Σαραμέλ (or 'Ασαραμέλ) which has been misinterpreted as a place name (1 Mach. 14:28 [27]); it can only be plausibly explained as the title of an office (Hebrew: sar 'am 'el, "prince of the people of God"). Thus was the quasi-regal dynasty designated and confirmed amid popular enthusiasm. Public sentiment once again glossed over ancient scruples as to the propriety of uniting the sword with the censer (§ 275), especially since this union had given the finest proof of its efficacy in the case of Jonathan and more particularly in that of Simon. The union endured, at any rate, and later on it was found that the enthusiasm had gone too far in sanctioning it (§§ 298, 302).

The dynasty so constituted is conventionally termed the dynasty of the Hasmoneans (§ 252).

288. Having taken over the Akra, Simon established a Jewish garrison in it. Subsequently, perhaps especially under John Hyrcanus, the famous citadel was gradually demolished and disappeared entirely. It is possible that its stones were gradually absorbed into other works already begun by Simon. We know that he quickly set about improving the strength of "the hillock of the Temple on the side facing the Akra, and he dwelt there and those who were with him" (1 Mach. 13:52 [53]), and it is likewise certain that he endeavored to rebuild and fortify the walls of the city (2 Mach. 14:37). If the Akra actually stood on the western hill opposite the Temple (§ 237), one may see in Simon's building of dwelling-place for himself the beginning of the palace of the Hasmoneans, which was built on the side of the hill which was opposite the Temple.

At the same time Simon was engaged in diplomatic activity.

289. The question of Simon's embassy to Rome is connected with that of Jonathan's (§ 279). Numenius and Antipater were sent to Rome by Jonathan, and set out toward the end of 144 B.C. or at the beginning of 143. At the end of this year Jonathan was made prisoner by Trypho,

and in the beginning of 142 was killed while the embassy certainly was still en route. When the senate of Rome learned of the death of Jonathan, it sent a diplomatic message of condolence to Simon, seizing the occasion also to renew with him the alliance contracted with his brothers before him (1 Mach. 14:16–19); at the same time, Simon likewise received a friendly letter from Sparta which described the honorable reception given to Numenius and Antipater there (14:20–23). Hence, one must conclude that the two ambassadors sent by Jonathan to Rome and Sparta returned to Jerusalem, perhaps in the first months of 140 B.C., and that in the meantime news of the death of Jonathan reached Rome and Sparta by other channels. We learn that Simon dispatched the same Numenius to Rome again with a golden shield weighing a thousand minas to renew the alliance (14:24), and that Numenius returned later with commendatory letters from Rome given by "Lucius, the consul of the Romans, and addressed to many other governors of the Orient besides Ptolemy, king of Egypt" (§ 184).

Another source provides us with other information. Josephus (*Antiquities*, XIV, 8, 5) describes a *Senatus consultum* which is in every respect similar to the aforementioned recommendation of Numenius. This "act" took place under the praetor *Lucius* Valerius, at the instance of three Jewish ambassadors: Numenius and two Alexanders (one of whom is surely an *Antipater*[6]); they too had brought a golden shield to Rome. But Josephus dates the decree much later, assigning it to the time of Julius Caesar and Hyrcanus II (§ 320, note).

290. What is to be said of these reports? How many and of what character were the embassies which they presuppose? It is certain, first of all, that the decree mentioned by Josephus cannot be dated to the time of Hyrcanus II, for many evident reasons. The period of John Hyrcanus I (§ 296) can be considered as a possibility at most, but even here there are grave difficulties, taking into account the embassies of Simon and Jonathan. It would mean that the same *Numenius* had been sent three times to Rome within the interval of a few years; two of these times he would have been accompanied by "*Antipater* son of Jason" and would have brought a shield of gold there and negotiated with *Lucius*. So many similarities in different embassies is much more difficult to admit than some confusion in or tampering with the respective accounts.

The problem has been much debated. It is very probable that the decree of Josephus should be referred to the time of Simon, and that it had been obtained precisely by his embassy. This embassy must have departed from Jerusalem around September of 140 B.C. (§ 289), either as a response to the senatorial condolences, or to confirm the

---

[6] Compare *1 Mach.* 12:16; 14:22 with *Antiquities*, XIV, 8, 5; the reading there: "*Alexander* son of Jason" is merely an alteration of "*Antipater* son of Jason."

alliance with the help of the glittering golden shield. The embassy arrived in Rome during the year 139 B.C. at which time, in fact, *Lucius* Calpurnius Piso was consul; thus, it returned to Jerusalem during the course of the year 138 B.C. (1 Mach. 15:10, 15). One has to be somewhat on the alert in this matter of the names of the ambassadors. The same Numenius might understandably go twice to Rome in the space of five or six years, chosen perhaps for his ability first by Jonathan, and then by Simon. He had Antipater as his companion during the first embassy and, according to Josephus, also during the second. But it is probably here that the confusion arises in the accounts, perpetuating the companions of Numenius from one embassy to the other. Moreover, Josephus' alteration of the names does not in general arouse confidence in their correct transmission.

The embassy was a great diplomatic success for Simon. The circular decree of the senate (§§ 184, 289) publicized the pact and warned the various states of the Orient against hostile acts against the "ally," Simon. It also recognized his jurisdiction over the Jews of the diaspora and requested the said states to send to Simon those persons who had rebelled against him and had fled to their territories. But beyond the realm of diplomacy it meant nothing. Rome did not send forth anything but the circular decree, which ended up, as usual, in the chancelleries of the various states, after having reminded the various sovereigns and ministers for a time that there existed in Jerusalem a man named Simon who was the high priest and ethnarch of the Jews.

291. In these first years of Simon, internal affairs went along well in his dominions, and are described by the narrator in idyllic terms, taken in part from the description of the Solomonic golden age (Vol. I, § 400). Simon's subjects "cultivated their land in peace, and the land yielded its products and the trees of the plains their fruit; the ancients sat in the public squares and treated together concerning profitable affairs, and the youths dressed themselves in splendid robes of war. . . . Israel rejoiced with great joy, and each one sat under his vine and under his fig tree, and there was none to make them afraid" (1 Mach. 14:8–12). The lyricism of the description is clear, yet it cannot be denied that it was actually true in part, and largely justified by the remembrance of the persecution of Epiphanes or of Bacchides. After the long fast even good plain bread seemed delicious. But an objective observer would easily have foreseen new clouds obscuring the idyll: the well-being of Simon's dominions was in inverse proportion to the power of the Seleucids, and the more the latter decreased the more the former increased. However, with Antiochus VII (§ 49) the throne of the Seleucids regained the brilliance of authority, and the Hasmonean princedom entered into a corresponding period of shadow.

292. Antiochus VII, who had landed in Syria to conquer the throne of his brother Demetrius II against Trypho, was at first too weak to engage Simon in a struggle. Indeed, even before he began to act, he took care to win Simon over to his side by confirm-

Antiochus VII.

ing the terms made by Demetrius, adding to them the right to coin money, and greater promises for the future. But the very words in which these concessions were couched (1 Mach. 15:1–9) show that Antiochus still looked upon Judea as being under the sovereignty, or at least the suzerainty of Syria.

When the struggle began Trypho soon found himself with few followers and took refuge at Dor, south of Carmel on the coast halfway to Caesarea. There he was besieged by Antiochus, but succeeded in escaping by sea and reaching Apamea, where he died (§ 48). During the siege Simon sent two thousand soldiers to Antiochus with war materiel and money, but Antiochus unexpectedly refused the re-enforcements and other proffered assistance. The truth was that he held a definite advantage over Trypho, and was unwilling to jeopardize his plans for Judea by accepting help. Even during the siege of Dor, he sent a courtier, Athenobius, to demand that Simon surrender Joppe, Gezer, the citadel, and other occupied places outside of Judea, on the grounds that they belonged to the Seleucid crown. If he refused to do so, Antiochus demanded the payment of five hundred talents of silver as tribute for these places, and another five hundred as compensation for damages. Athenobius arrived in Jerusalem and received a negative reply, which was perhaps expected. What had not been foreseen, but made a deep impression on the courtier, was the sumptuousness which surrounded Simon.

On his return to Antiochus, Athenobius reported Simon's answer, and described what he had seen. At that moment Trypho was fleeing from Dor and Antiochus pursued him northward, first charging Cendebaeus, who commanded the coast, to proceed against Simon, and to crush him by force of arms. Cendebaeus, following out his orders, fortified Kedron, probably present-day Qatra, southeast of Jamnia (§ 260), and from there began to make sorties into Simon's territory. No longer able to bear the hardships of the field, Simon placed the responsibility of repulsing the enemy on his two eldest sons, John Hyrcanus and Judas, and they fully upheld the family traditions.

Mount "of the Forty" overlooking Jericho.

They advanced toward the enemy's territory, passing through Modin where their uncles lay buried (§ 283). Judas was wounded in the attack, but John inspired his soldiers by his example and routed Cendebaeus' forces. After this reversal Antiochus VII, busy elsewhere, did not again disturb Judea for a number of years.

293. There was one however who, relying on Antiochus, gave thought as to how he might disturb Judea, and bring Simon's career to an inglorious end. The Machabean in his old age had given over the command of the army and the ordinary administration to his sons, and also to one of his sons-in-law, Ptolemy, son of Abubos (Ḥabub), who had been made governor over the district of Jericho. Simon had reserved to himself the duty of making inspections which contributed to the improvement of conditions in the land, and which gave him the consolation of witnessing the rebirth of the nation. Ptolemy, on the other hand, coveted the position of the Machabees and plotted to become the sole head of the nation. He counted on the hostility which existed between Antiochus and Simon, but concealed his plans from the Seleucid king, intending to deal with him later, when he could present him with a *fait accompli*. Everything hinged upon his doing away with Simon and his sons at one blow, and upon his occupying Jerusalem. When he would report these two deeds to Antiochus as already accomplished and by one who professed to be his subordinate, that king would surely help him consolidate his position.

The traitorous son-in-law therefore chose an occasion when Simon was inspecting his district of Jericho, and received him with great pomp in the fortress of Doq, on the mountain of the Forty near Jericho (Vol. I, § 80 ff.). The old man was accompanied by his sons Mathathias and Judas; John Hyrcanus had remained at Gezer (§ 285). The inevitable banquet was prepared, and when the no less inevitable drunkenness prevailed among those at table, Ptolemy had Simon and his two sons and some of their servants murdered. It was February of the year 134 B.C.

After this bloody deed, Ptolemy at once sent messengers to Antiochus to ask him for help and for soldiers. At the same time he sent his men to Gezer to dispatch John Hyrcanus. There Ptolemy's plan failed: warned in time, no doubt, by some faithful servant of the family, John was waiting for them, captured them and put them to death. He then immediately betook himself to Jerusalem to forestall his rival, and there took possession of the heritage of the last murdered Machabean.

THE HASMONEANS

294. *The First Book of Machabees* ends with the death of Simon, last of the Machabees, and only briefly mentions the coming of his son, John Hyrcanus. With Simon the period of buoyant rebellion led by the sons of Mathathias, the priest, came to an end, and there began the usual vicissitudes of a dynasty, that of the Hasmoneans. The Hasmoneans were also Machabees (§§ 252, 287), but no longer the Machabees of the heroic and errant life of the desert. They too fought, but their wars were much more dynastic than Yahwistic affairs. Worse still, they themselves were no longer representatives of the larger and better part of a rebellious people, for they had by degrees become the heads of parties who based their support on one portion of their ancient followers, and made enemies of the other, and in the end they dealt with and made compromises with that spiritual world against which the ancient Machabees had battled until they won the supremacy.

Unfortunately for the new period which is to be treated, our only informant is Josephus. A chronicle of the pontificate of John Hyrcanus which was available to the author of *2 Machabees* (16:23–24) has been entirely lost, perhaps even by Josephus' time. An occasional reference in rabbinical or Hellenistic sources is insufficient to help check the accuracy of our only informant, who is at times prejudiced, and at others, careless and obtuse.

295. John Hyrcanus. He was the third son of Simon, younger than the two who were slain with their father at Jericho. Because of his special aptitude for war he had been placed at the head of the district of Gezer, which had special strategic importance (§ 285), and it was there the news of the murder perpetrated by Ptolemy and his henchmen reached him. These latter done away with, he immediately took steps to assure himself the succession to his father's dignity, and hastened to Jerusalem. He arrived there before Ptolemy, and the people immedi-

280

ately rallied to his side, recognizing him as the legitimate heir of Simon. When the traitor Ptolemy arrived a little later, he was not even able to enter the city.

But the game was not over yet. Ptolemy took refuge at Doq, where the assassination had taken place, and where he also held as hostage Simon's wife and perhaps others of his family. He was soon besieged by John Hyrcanus, but the siege was a long one and complicated by the difficulties of the sabbatical year which was upon them. Ptolemy eventually escaped, after first killing his hostages, and took refuge with Zenos Kotylas, a prince of Philadelphia (Rabbath Ammon: Vol. I, § 374). Ptolemy's resistance was certainly in part due to his hope of seeing King Antiochus VII, whom he had expressly invited, arrive on the scene (§ 293). Come he actually did, and probably in that same first year of John Hyrcanus (134 B.C.), but too late for Ptolemy.

Antiochus, in fact, with an eye to his own advantage, wished to settle the question left hanging by the defeat of Cendebaeus, and to revindicate his rights of sovereignty over Judea. His greater strength quickly made him master of the situation. Gezer (§ 285) and Joppe (§ 281) with the region to the north were reoccupied. A great part of the population returned toward Jerusalem which was besieged. The siege was long, and was aggravated by famine conditions caused by the sabbatical year, and by the fugitives who had fled to the city. Hyrcanus tried to send these away, as they were useless for the defense, but Antiochus would not let them pass, and they remained for some time between the walls of the city and the trenches of the besiegers, rejected by both sides; many died of hunger. However, on the feast of Tabernacles they were readmitted into the city; Antiochus granted a truce of seven days in honor of the feast, and in addition sent an offering of bullocks for the sacrifices in the Temple.

This regal gesture was intended as a hint that, if they wanted peace, he was well-disposed toward the Yahwistic religion, provided that his rights of sovereignty be recognized. The gesture was a good argument for peace, but Antiochus had undoubtedly other reasons for urging it. He had in mind a campaign against the Parthians, and had launched this campaign against Judea precisely so as to secure his rear; the sooner it was concluded, the better for him. Too, Antiochus no doubt felt a twinge of fear at the thought of complications with Rome.

296. It is certain that Hyrcanus at some time in his reign turned to Rome, as had his father and his uncles the Machabees, and that he had obtained a decree confirming Rome's friendship and alliance with the Jews, and ordering the restitution of Joppe, Gezer, and other places occupied by Antiochus (*Antiquities*, XIII, 9, 2). It is not clear whether this embassy took place during or after this war. Mention is

Feast of Tabernacles at Jerusalem. (Vester, Amer. Colony.)

also made in a decree of the city of Pergamum, of a *Senatus-consultus* which imposed a similar restitution to the Jews of what was taken from them by "King Antiochus, son of Antiochus," and granted to them terms favorable to their commerce (*Antiquities*, XIV, 10, 22). This decree, which apparently refers to the time of Antiochus IX Cyzicenus (§ 51), has been said to apply to the times of Antiochus VII. (See also the Roman decree in *Antiquities*, XIV, 8, 5, mentioned in § 289.) It is highly probable that Hyrcanus, hard-pressed as he was by Antiochus VII, sent an earnest message to Rome, inviting her to intervene at least diplomatically in his behalf, and that, whether the sources referred to above refer to this period or not, Antiochus probably knew of this step, or may even have received an explicit warning from Rome. At any rate, under the circumstances Antiochus saw that his own best interests would be served not by clashing with Rome but by making some kind of peace with Simon, at the same time imposing upon him the obligation to help him in his campaign against the Parthians.

The kindly disposition of Antiochus toward the Yahwism of the besieged Jews procured for him the title of "pious" (§ 49), and led to the making of a peace. However, a group of the king's counselors, perhaps suborned by the Hellenized Jews, counselled him to destroy that turbulent nation. But Antiochus VII was intelligent enough to profit by the experience of Antiochus Epiphanes, and keeping his eyes fixed upon reality for his own good, rejected the proffered advice. The terms of the agreement were moderate: Antiochus left the disputed cities, Gezer, Joppe, etc., in the possession of the Jews, perhaps because of the warning from Rome; but he exacted tribute. He also demanded that they yield up their arms, pay him an indemnity of five hundred talents of gold, deliver up hostages, and, to preclude further opposition, dismantle the city walls. In substance, all of his old powers were left to Hyrcanus, but he had to recognize the sovereignty of the king of Antioch over him.

In his campaign against the Parthians, Antiochus was assisted by a Jewish contingent of soldiers led by Hyrcanus himself, in fulfillment, probably of the terms of the truce. In the disaster which was visited upon this ill-starred campaign in which Antiochus lost his life (§ 49), Hyrcanus seems not to have suffered, and soon was once more in Jerusalem. At this same time Demetrius II again took possession of the kingdom of Syria, where a period of profound decadence now set in (§ 50). For this very reason there began for Hyrcanus a period of prosperity which was to increase steadily during his long reign. On this point the judgment of Josephus is accurate: "[Hyrcanus] after the death of Antiochus revolted from the Macedonians and submitted no more to them either as a subject or as friend. His affairs prospered and flourished more and more during the times of Alexander Zabina and especially under these brothers [the Antiochuses of § 51]; the war which they waged with one another gave Hyrcanus an opportunity to enjoy in peace the revenues of Judea, and to gather an immense quantity of money" (*Antiquities*, XIII, 10, 1).

297. Under these favorable circumstances he conceived and carried out a plan of territorial expansion. Nationalistic hopes were not excluded from this plan, and in it clearly Yahwistic preoccupations were evident; so too were the interests of this dynastic head, namely the strengthening of his family and the increasing of its political influence. After a bitter siege which lasted six months, he conquered Madaba in Transjordan (§ 270). Then he turned to the north of Judea to settle an old score with the hated Samaritans. He took Sichem from them and destroyed the temple of Gerizim. Much later, about 108 B.C., he entrusted his sons Antigonus and Aristobulus with the command of an all-out expedition against the city of Samaria, which fell despite the attempt of Antiochus IX Cyzicenus to aid it (§ 165).

Even previous to this expedition, Hyrcanus had extended his dominion to the south, where he imposed Yahwism by force. Having entered Idumaea and taken possession of Adora (§ 282) and Maresa (§ 260), he did not expel the foreigners as the Machabees ordinarily had, but obliged them to embrace Yahwism by accepting circumcision. By such proselytism, the Idumaeans were incorporated into the Jewish nation (§ 213). Their full revenge came a century later when Herod, the Idumaean with an iron hand, sat upon the throne of Hyrcanus, the missionary with sword in hand. To all these conquests must be added that of Scythopolis (Beisan: Vol. I, § 86) during the siege of Samaria; it gave Hyrcanus control over the valley of Esdraelon and access to Galilee, to the north.

298. Internally the long reign of Hyrcanus was very prosperous, as was to be expected after such conquests, and as Josephus expressly affirms. Regarding the moral unity of the nation, one item of great importance occurs: Hyrcanus, who "had been a disciple" of the Pharisees and "much beloved by them," suddenly went over to the Sadducees, became the enemy of the Pharisees, and began to persecute them. At the time of Hyrcanus the two camps of "Pharisee" and "Sadducee" were already clearly differentiated, and among other characteristics of the Pharisees there was a tendency of separation from anything foreign or modern, while the Sadducees looked with favor upon both. Why did Hyrcanus break with the Pharisees and go over to the Sadducees? Josephus gives as the reason an incident which happened during a banquet.

When Hyrcanus requested those at table with him to advise him in the way of perfection, a Pharisee named Eleazar suggested that he relinquish his office as high priest and limit himself to "governing the people." Asked his reason, Eleazar replied that in the time of Antiochus Epiphanes the mother of Hyrcanus had been a slave, and as her son he was not fit to exercise the pontifical office (a rabbinic norm states the presumption that a slave woman had been violated, hence her children were legally unclean). At this Hyrcanus became exceedingly angry; the Pharisees present also showed signs of anger, but suspecting that they feigned their display, Hyrcanus, on the advice of a Sadducee friend, put them to the test by allowing them to determine what penalty Eleazar deserved. The Pharisees fixed the penalty of "stripes and bonds." Hyrcanus, who believed that the death penalty should have been imposed upon him, now looked upon all Pharisees as Eleazar's accomplices, and from that day he broke with them, forbidding the people to follow their prescriptions and observances (*Antiquities,* XIII, 10, 5–6).

How much truth there is in this anecdote it is difficult to say. It is given in substance in the Talmud also (Babli, *Qiddushin,* 66a), but put in the times of "King Jannaeus," who is surely Alexander Jannaeus. On the other hand, the Talmud (*Berakhoth,* 29a) confirms the fact that Hyrcanus was hostile to the Pharisees. But even if the break did occur under Hyrcanus (the figure of Hyrcanus may have been confused with that of Jannaeus: § 300), no doubt there was a very much more grave reason for the rupture. For that matter, the very demeanor of Hyrcanus in the anecdote indicates that he vaguely sensed the hostility not only of Eleazar but of the whole Pharisaic faction toward him. Why this unmistakable hostility?

The reason that comes immediately to mind is the union of the sword with the censer, concerning which nothing had been said in the past for pragmatic reasons (§§ 275, 287); to such scrupulous traditionalists as the Pharisees this must now have seemed intolerable. It is noteworthy that the Pharisee proposed that Hyrcanus retain his office as prince, but relinquish the office of high priest. Another very likely reason may have been the state of affairs which was developing under Hyrcanus. He was the first one in his family to hire foreign troops the better to carry out his plans for territorial expansion. The consequent increase in the internal organization and external relations demanded an open-minded and modern administrative personnel which Hyrcanus could ordinarily find only among the followers of the aristocratic faction of the Sadducees. The Pharisees, on the contrary, who were all for tradition and who disdained anything new, were incapable of rendering any valuable service in the administrative exigencies of the Hasmonean government, and could only have viewed with horror this hiring of foreign troops. Hence, the preponderance of the aristocratic Sadducees in the direction of public affairs, and the slighting of the democratic Pharisees whose influence was among the lower classes. Hence, also the jealousy of the latter, expressly attested by Josephus. That Hyrcanus, a disciple of the Pharisees, suddenly cast them aside — whether the banquet incident was true or not — was only natural, once it was seen that they could contribute little or nothing to his government, and looked askance at his high priesthood.

299. It has been recently pointed out, in connection with the story in point, that the death penalty demanded by Hyrcanus was the punishment for those who insulted the "king," while stripes and prison, proposed by the Pharisees, were for those who insulted the "priest." From this and from other learned reflections on the text of Josephus, it has been concluded that Hyrcanus had already assumed the title of "king," but was not recognized as such by the Pharisees. The conclusion is not very convincing. In the first place, too much stress is laid either on the anecdote itself or on the words in which Josephus relates it; nor is it clear why the Pharisees should protest against the high priesthood of Hyrcanus, since they allowed him to continue to "command the people"; in the hypothesis it is the contrary which would be expected.

On the other hand, while it has been expressly stated that the title of "king" was adopted after Hyrcanus (§§ 300, 301), it is found that he used the two following types of inscription on his money: JOHN HIGH PRIEST AND THE COMMUNITY (ḥebher) OF THE JEWS; or JOHN HIGH PRIEST AND HEAD OF THE COMMUNITY OF THE JEWS. It is probable that the second inscription is the more recent, for it more accurately brings out his personal power; that is, the dynastic ideal was becoming stronger. However, the title "king" does not appear on his money.

Another move which made Hyrcanus appear more like an ordinary Hellenistic prince was his hiring of foreign troops. In giving this bit of information Josephus brings out the fact that he was "the first of the Jews" to have done this (Antiquities, XIII, 8, 4); but surely the historian means that he was the first since the exile, for long before the exile David had employed foreign mercenaries (Vol. I, § 375). He thereby departed farther and farther from the methods of his father and uncles, who attacked foreign pagans with a few hundred hungry and badly armed men; but they were authentic Jews, warmed by a Yahwistic flame. Now the honor of the nation was at least in part entrusted to the descendants of those who had only yesterday been enemies, men who might help demolish a few Idumaean villages, or undermine the walls of Samaria, but who would certainly not fail to perform a similar work of destruction and sapping within the Yahwistic nation itself. There is a taste of bitter irony in Josephus here, when he states that these foreign mercenaries were paid with three thousand talents of silver which Hyrcanus took out of the tomb of David in Jerusalem, now violated for the first time (Antiquities, XIII, 8, 4; cf. XVI, 7, 1; according to VII, 15, 3, this amount also helped him pay Antiochus VII the tributes owing to him by the treaty: § 296). Would Mathathias or Judas Machabeus have so acted? The contrast illustrates the evolution which had taken place in a half century, and also the effects of stability in the dynasty.

The reign of John Hyrcanus lasted for thirty-one years, and was a period of genuine rebirth for the Jewish nation, if not precisely for Yahwism. At John's death in 104 B.C. Judea was independent and strong; its dominions were almost as extensive as in the times of David, and everything was going well. But upon him a judgment must be passed similar to the one passed on Solomon in comparison to David his father (Vol. I, §§ 375, 382). The strength and prosperity of Hyrcanus' government were to a lesser degree the result of a personal activity which a propitious political situation made possible for him, and to a much greater degree they were the result of what his Machabee uncles and father had built up by some thirty years of extraordinary labors.

300. Aristobulus I. John Hyrcanus was succeeded by the eldest of his five sons, Aristobulus I, who ruled for only one year (104–103 B.C.).

His real name was Judas, and his other name, Aristobulus, was a con-cession to Hellenistic fashion, to which he made many other concessions as well, for Josephus records that he was called "a lover of the Greeks" (*Antiquities*, XIII, 11, 3).

Josephus relates that Hyrcanus had wished his wife to be the "mistress of all" after his death, but Aristobulus and his brother Antigonus threw his mother and three brothers into prison, where the mother died of hunger. Aristobulus was therefore crowned king, the first king since the time of the Exile. Out of jealousy he had his brother Antigonus slain; shortly afterward, however, his remorse for this crime induced an illness in him from which he died.

It is difficult to say how much of this account is fact, and how much is traceable to tales spread by the Pharisees, toward whom Aristobulus maintained the hostility begun by his father Hyrcanus. It is strange that a fratricide caused him to die of remorse, when the murder of his mother bothered him not at all, nor is it easy to explain why Hyrcanus should have left a woman as "mistress of all" at a time when the high priesthood was the key to every door. The statement that Aristobulus I had been the first to crown himself king is contra-dicted by Strabo (XVI, 2, 40), who says that the first to bear the title of king was his successor Alexander Jannaeus. Lastly, the same Josephus, who a few lines above has narrated the matricide, fratricide, and the imprisonment of his brothers, ends by calling Aristobulus an honest and honorable man, citing Strabo, who on the testimony of Timagenes, likewise called him a good man (*Antiquities*, XIII, 11, 3). There are, then, reasons for suspecting that Josephus gathers here the most disparate opinions and reports them all together, calumnious and true, paying no attention to the fact that they are mutually contra-dictory. Nor is this the only such case in his works.

It is also possible that the two figures John Hyrcanus and Alexander Jannaeus were confused, so that the figure of Aristobulus midway between them was decked with their deeds. We have already seen that the Talmud attributes the anecdote of the Pharisees (§ 298) to Jannaeus; later, just as Hyrcanus was supposed to have done previously, Alexander Jannaeus left his throne to his wife Alexandra Salome, which he had every right to do, as he had assumed the title of "king." Hyrcanus, on the contrary, had only the title of high priest, and so could not have designated the heir to the hereditary title, as Jannaeus did. But a later tradition has him doing this, and transferred more than one aspect of the later and more ferocious enemy of the Pharisees, Jannaeus, to the earlier and less ferocious figure of Hyrcanus.

On the extant coins of Aristobulus inscriptions similar to those of his father appear: JUDAS HIGH PRIEST AND THE COMMUNITY (*hebher*) OF

THE JEWS; the fact that there is no mention of a "king" shows that Strabo, not Josephus, was correct.

In his brief reign, Aristobulus also waged a campaign to the north of his dominions, to extend his territory beyond the confines attained by Hyrcanus. He is said to have subjugated one part of the Itureans and obliged them to circumcision. Aristobulus then, despite his predilection for Hellenism, continued, in the interests of his dynasty, the coercive methods of his father, who forced Yahwism on the Idumaeans (§ 297). It is more true to say that he conquered upper Galilee into which, perhaps, the tribes of the Itureans had returned, rather than a genuine zone belonging to the Itureans who inhabited Antilibanus (Vol. I, § 59), which was too far from Judea.

301. Alexander Jannaeus. Aristobulus left no children when he died, but only his three brothers, held prisoners, and his wife Salome, called in Hellenistic fashion Alexandra. She set the brothers at liberty, and conferred the high priesthood and all authority on the eldest. Although there is no explicit testimony of the fact, it is quite certain that she also then became his wife. The newly elect was named Jonathan, abbreviated to Jannaeus, and he had the usual secondary Hellenistic name, Alexander. He ruled for twenty-seven years, from 103 to 76 B.C.

Strabo (§ 300) attests that he was the first to call himself "king," and this is confirmed by his coins, some of which bear the usual inscription JONATHAN HIGH PRIEST AND THE COMMUNITY (hebher) OF THE JEWS, whereas others have bilingual inscriptions: the one in Hebrew reads JONATHAN THE KING, and in Greek, OF THE KING ALEXANDER. The scruples of the legitimists who worried over the lineage of David (§ 287) had now been set aside.

Of an impetuous character, enterprising, inflexible before obstacles, Alexander Jannaeus brought these qualities into the government of his kingdom. Ever advancing in the direction begun by John Hyrcanus, he became engulfed in political intrigues and warlike undertakings because of his mania for power. He continued the practice of imposing Judaism by force, more for his own advantage than for religious motives. His hostility toward the Pharisees, whom he considered the internal enemies of his dynasty, knew no bounds, and the many excesses he committed against them were such as only a man of his character could contrive.

He began by laying siege to Ptolemais, whose port would be useful to him. Seeing that they could count on no help from Antiochus VIII and Antiochus IX, who were struggling between themselves (§ 51), the besieged turned to Ptolemy VIII Lathyros who, having been driven out of Egypt by his mother Cleopatra III, was then reigning over Cyprus. On the approach of Ptolemy Lathyros at the head of a strong army, Alexander raised the siege and feigned friendliness toward him, at the same time secretly inviting the wrathful Cleopatra to take action against her own son. When Ptolemy learned of this sly move, he attacked the territories of Alexander, taking and sacking Asochis near Sepphoris in Galilee. Alexander went to meet him with a powerful army at Asophon on the banks of the Jordan. At first the tide of battle was favorable to the Jews, but the tactical ability of the enemy general, Philostephanus, wrested the advantage from them and they were completely routed. It was in fact a real slaughter, for it was said that thirty, and even fifty, thousand men were slain. After the victory Ptolemy systematically devastated the surrounding territory in a deliberate attempt to terrorize the Jews.

Cleopatra was alarmed at her son's victories, and sent an army against him into Palestine commanded by the Jews Helcias and Ananias, sons of the high priest Onias IV, founder of Leontopolis (§ 249). It was not long until Cleopatra had taken Ptolemais, forced Ptolemy to flee to Gaza, and had become master of Palestine. Yet, upon the generous advice of the Jew Ananias, she did not annex it to Egypt, but restored it to Alexander Jannaeus, who had sought refuge with her. Thus, with Cleopatra and Ptolemy both far away, the Hasmonean was again master of his dominions.

302. Nothing daunted by past dangers, Alexander undertook new compaigns to enlarge his borders. After ten months of siege he conquered Gadara to the south of the Lake of Tiberias on the eastern side of the Jordan, and to the south the fortress of Amathus. Descending thence into the Philistine zone, he captured Raphia, Anthedon, and, after a year of siege, Gaza, once the refuge of Ptolemy Lathyros; this he destroyed. It was the year 96 B.C. in which Antiochus VIII Gryphus died, and Alexander Jannaeus returned to Jerusalem where the internal situation demanded his presence.

The hostility of his dynasty toward the Pharisees was naturally repaid in kind, and the mutual aversion was even increased under him for a variety of reasons. The ancient incompatibility of the censer and sword (§§ 275, 287, 298) had become in the minds of the Pharisees even more evident in the case of Alexander Jannaeus, a "king" who had usurped the rights of the descendants of David (§ 287). He was, for them, a common soldier who spent the whole year making war and mingling with uncircumcised foreigners; an Israelite whose hands were always wet with human blood and whose conscience was further burdened by thousands of Jews whose deaths were traceable to his craze for conquest; a politician who, because he was always on the move, fighting his battles, necessarily neglected the offices of high priest; a man who had espoused a widow, in violation of the ancient Yahwistic law which

forbade a priest to do so (Lev. 21:13–14; but cf. Ezech. 44:22).
Alexander Jannaeus, in short, could not be and should not be the high
priest. These considerations and certainly others also were driven home
by the Pharisees to the lower classes who were their stanch adherents,
and the animosity toward the king became general.

The story of altercations at court between Alexander and Simon
ben-Shetah, a renowned Pharisee and his supposed brother-in-law (cf.
Bereshith rabba, c. XCI), is commonly believed to be a later rabbinic
legend, but there is no reason to doubt that grave tumults occurred
in the Temple itself, according to the report of Josephus (*Antiquities*,
XIII, 13, 5; *War*, I, 4, 3). During a feast of Tabernacles, as the war-
loving high priest offered sacrifice at the altar of the Temple, he was
disrespectfully pelted by the bystanders with citrons which they had
brought to the feast (§§ 102, 270). It was by no means a friendly gesture, for the citrons were many and much larger than pine cones, and only
slightly less solid. It was later related (Talmud Babli, *Sukkah*, 48*b*) that
the incident had involved an anonymous "Sadducee" because during the
sacrifice he had poured out the libation of water on the ground and not
on the altar, as prescribed. If this Sadducee was Alexander, which is
quite probable, and if the motive for the violence was the one alleged,
then that trifling liturgical irregularity had served as a spark to set off
an explosion that had been long preparing, and whose ingredients were
the grievances which the Pharisees had successfully disseminated among
the lower classes against the Hasmonean.

303. Alexander reacted violently to this "citric" provocation, and his
soldiers slaughtered six thousand men. This bloodshed naturally caused
the popular hatred against him to boil up even more, and in the end
he no longer trusted his Jewish troops but enlisted others from
Cilicia and Pisidia.

To summarize the situation: the ancient Machabees had been principally sustained in their national struggles by the Assideans (§§ 253,
266); the direct descendants of the Assideans are now the mortal enemies of the descendant of the Machabees. The man sitting on the
throne fashioned for him by the struggles of his ancestors against aliens,
has recourse to these same foreigners in his fight against those who had
supported his ancestors. Lacking only to complete the full reversal of
roles was the fact that the descendants of the Assideans should in their
turn have recourse to foreigners to combat this descendant of the
Machabees. This also came to pass.

Carried away by his mania for conquest, Alexander soon undertook
campaigns in Transjordan against the inhabitants of Moab and Galaad.
At first successful, he fell into an ambush set by the Arab king

Obedas. Extricating himself only with difficulty he fled to Jerusalem. At this defeat his enemies at home broke out into open revolt.

The Pharisee revolt against the Hasmonean dynasty was undoubtedly a very serious one. Unfortunately, there remains only the brief statement that it endured for six whole years and cost the lives of not less than fifty thousand Jews (*Antiquities*, XIII, 13, 5). These losses were, for the most part, suffered by the rebels, for Alexander was chiefly served by his hired foreign troops. Evidently impressed by the tenacity of the rebels, Alexander finally offered them peace, but so furious were they against him that they declared peace to be impossible as long as he lived. They then turned for help to King Demetrius III Eucaerus (§ 52), the last Seleucid monarch to have a hand in the internal affairs of Judea. Thus was the official apostasy consummated.

At that moment a miracle would have been most opportune: if only the old Mathathias and his five sons lying in their mausoleum in Modin (§ 283) could rise up in those bodies which bore the wounds of Syrian swords, and look around! Would they recognize the sons of their ancient followers in those Pharisees who now called upon the same Syrian swords to invade the sacred land of Israel? But the miracle did not come to pass and those heroes of Israel were certainly spared this posthumous and most cruel wound of all.

304. The apostasy was repaired in part, fortunately. In the year 88 B.C. all Asia Minor rose against Rome under Mithridates, king of Pontus, and in Rome itself a struggle broke out between Marius and Scylla. Accepting the invitation of the Pharisaic faction, Demetrius III came down with an army and, joining with the troops of the rebels, defeated King Alexander at Sichem. Alexander was forced to flee as an exile to the mountains like his forebears, the Machabees. But then the unexpected happened. Many of the rebels suddenly perceived the abyss toward which they were heading and reversed their dirction. They saw that the victory of the Seleucid monarch would mean a return at one bound to the times of Antiochus Epiphanes; and when it came to a choice between an Epiphanes and a Jannaeus, was it not perhaps better to reach some reasonable agreement with the latter? Faced with this decision, many Jews retained enough nationalism and Yahwism in their hearts to prevent the Seleucid monarch from reaping the fruits of his victory. Six thousand of them deserted Demetrius and passed over to Alexander. Demetrius quickly sensed which way the fickle wind was blowing, and judged it prudent to withdraw to Syria.

The revolt was not thereby quelled, for many of the insurgents persisted in their opposition to Alexander. But he was now strong enough to deal with them, and they were pursued and repeatedly defeated by him. Seeking refuge at Bethome, perhaps the present *el-Betuni*, slightly over four miles northwest of Jerusalem, they fell into his hands. Even then Alexander ran true to form and displayed the depths of his bestial character. The prisoners of Bethome were transported to Jerusalem and eight hundred of them were crucified. Before the eyes of these agonized sufferers, he had the throats of their wives and children cut "as he sat feasting in a place apart with his concubines" (*Antiquities*, XIII, 14, 2; *War*, I, 4, 6). This earned him the appellation "Thracida" from his fellow countrymen; even the contemporary Scylla, for all his famous proscriptions at Rome, could come to Jerusalem for a lesson in refined vengeance from the high priest of the God Yahweh.

The horrible spectacle of the crucified made the other rebels who had already returned to Alexander quake with fear, expecting at any moment to meet the same fate as their former comrades. About eight thousand of them slunk away by night to the desert, and remained as wanderers during the remainder of Alexander's life. No record of other struggles between him and the Pharisees has come down to us. Not that there was peace — rather, seeing that it was too difficult to triumph over the foreign companies which Alexander was continually hiring, and not wishing to imitate him in that degradation of the nation, his opponents preferred temporarily to withdraw from politics. They also refused to recognize the Hasmonean as high priest and took to the desert, like their predecessors the Assideans.

305. Alexander gave himself up to wine, not so as to forget the fifty thousand Jews who had died in the civil war, but rather in imitation of the usual customs of the lowest type of Hellenistic soldier. He felt so great a need for both wine and arms that, although sickened from too much drink, he continued to maintain his camp, and to fight. In the struggle between Antiochus XII and the Nabatean Arabs south of Judea, he tried to oppose the passage of Antiochus with fortifications at Capharsaba, northeast of Joppe; but in this he was frustrated, for the fortifications were burned and the enemy continued on his way. Antiochus XII was defeated and killed, however, and the Nabatean king Aretas III (about 85–60 B.C.) extended his dominions all around those of Alexander, from the south along Transjordan and up to Damascus to the north. A struggle between them was inevitable. Aretas attacked and penetrated Judea up to Adida (§ 278) but then retired, after reaching some kind of an agreement with Alexander (§ 309). What it was we do not know.

Other campaigns followed from 83 B.C., prompted by the mania for conquest. In Transjordan he was able to annex the Hellenistic centers of Pella, Dium, Gerasa, the fortress of Gamala, and other localities to the south and east of Lake Tiberias. In annexing these territories, he

Gerasa.

generally forced the inhabitants to accept Judaism (§§ 297, 300); refusal to do so meant destruction.

After an illness of three years, Alexander died in 76 B.C. while conducting a siege of the fortress Ragaba, near Gerasa in Transjordan. Thanks to a tenacity undaunted by repeated defeats, he left the territory of his dynasty greatly enlarged over what it had been at the death of Hyrcanus. Starting from Idumaea on the south, it embraced a large strip of Transjordan to the east up to above Lake Tiberias, and to the north and west, Galilee, while on the Mediterranean it included the coast of the Egyptian frontier up to Carmel, with the exception of the free city of Ascalon.

Internally his kingdom had always been divided into two factions: the Neo-Sadducean and the Pharisees. On his deathbed Alexander made a radical decision. He left his throne to his wife Alexandra Salome, but recommended to her that she make friends with the Pharisees, that she promise them not to make any decision concerning the government without them, and finally that she entrust them with his dead body, a pledge to be abused or honored with worthy funeral rites, at their good pleasure (*Antiquities*, XIII, 15, 5). This return to discretion, advised by the most ferocious enemy of the Pharisees, must have been in his mind for a long time. He knew from experience the strength of that faction which had its foundation in the people, and if he had succeeded for good or ill in defying it with the help of foreign troops, there was every reason to fear that his successor on the throne would not know how to handle the situation successfully, especially if she were a woman. Better, then, to remove the grave danger to the dynasty by promoting a reconciliation.

The widow comported herself in all things according to his advice. On her return to Jerusalem she negotiated with the Pharisees, made known her new plans for governing, and consigned to them the body of her husband. Faced with this unexpected proposal, the Pharisees were forthwith won over and gave the dead king a most solemn funeral, "enumerating the deeds of Alexander" and lamenting "that a just king had been taken from them" (*Antiquities*, XIII, 16, 1).

The place where the Pharisees mourned the "just king" must have been near that other place where twelve years before eight hundred of their companions had died on the cross, forced to gaze in their agony upon their wives and children being butchered before them (§ 304). The slaughter had not been forgotten and vengeance was being plotted (§ 306), but it would indeed be curious to know if this deed was one of those included by the Pharisees, now lamenting "the just king," in their enumeration of his deeds.

306. Alexandra Salome. The reign of Alexandra (76–67 B.C.) was the golden age of the Pharisees. Her husband had left two sons: the elder, Hyrcanus, was a mild man and loved the quiet life; the younger, Aristobulus, was all activity and daring. Alexandra kept the reins of government in her own hands, chose Hyrcanus as high priest, and left Aristobulus aside. It was here that she made a mistake, for the restless younger son would not be satisfied with his role as a simple spectator. From the moment his mother and brother sided in entirely with the Pharisees, he reached an understanding with the Sadducees.

The relations between Alexandra and the Pharisees are reflected in the words of Josephus: "She allowed the Pharisees to do everything, and ordered the people to obey them. She also restored again those practices which the Pharisees had introduced according to the traditions of their fathers, and which her father-in-law Hyrcanus had abrogated (§ 298). So she had the name of queen, but the Pharisees had the authority" (*Antiquities*, XIII, 16, 2).

The new rulers began by showing favor to their own party and at the same time took revenge on the Sadducees. Exiles were recalled, prisoners liberated, and some of the more notorious counselors of the late king were put to death. They had feigned forgetfulness, at the funeral of the king, of the eight hundred men he had had crucified, but they had not for a moment forgotten that slaughter and were now determined upon revenge on those who had advised it. Very soon the aggressiveness of the Pharisees led the queen to build up her corps of mercenaries so as to be ready for any eventuality. The acts of revenge next aroused the fears of former officials in the government, especially in those who had been the companions of Alexander Jannaeus. One day, led by Aristobulus, they presented themselves to the queen and asked her to guarantee their safety. Alexandra astutely combined her own interests and the present circumstances, and entrusted to their custody various fortresses of the realm where they would be both useful to the crown and safe from the Pharisees. The queen however retained under her direct control the fortresses of Hyrcania, Alexandrium, and Machaerus, in which she kept her treasures. She kept the restless Aristobulus at a distance by sending him with troops to Damascus to conduct an unimportant little campaign in which he had no occasion to distinguish himself.

307. The dominance of the Pharisees in civil and religious matters had grave and lasting consequences. The γερουσία (§ 258) or Sanhedrin, which was the continuation of the old assembly of the "ancients," and represented the consultative college of the high priest in the government of the nation, had up to that time been essentially an aristocratic-sacerdotal college, that is, made up of followers of the Sadducean party. Under the supremacy of the democratic Pharisees, the Sanhedrin changed its character; its aristocratic-sacerdotal members were reduced to a minority, and at their side arose the majority group composed of doctors of the *Torah* or scribes, who from that time on were the arbiters of the college. Their detailed legislation, elaborated "according to the traditions of the fathers," had the force of genuine decree in accordance with the expressed will of Queen Alexandra, as mentioned by Josephus (§ 306). In addition the Pharisees had the enthusiastic support of the people, and their precepts and programs were willingly accepted by the ordinary people, who saw in all this juridical elaboration the salvation and approval of the ancient laws of the nation. This current, approved by the crown and acceptable to the people, began to cut the opposing Sadducean current off from the life of the nation, and Pharisaic views became increasingly influential in civil and religious matters.

That the new masters pursued their objectives with a fiery zeal, giving no quarter to their enemies, can be taken for granted on general principles. It is also attested to by Josephus, who states that under Alexandra "all the country was at peace, except for the Pharisees" (*Antiquities*, XIII, 16, 2). Their insatiable zeal was such that it stamped upon the countenance of the nation those features so typical of it at the beginning of the Christian era. Beginning with the reign of Alexandra, Judaism became essentially Pharisaical, and despite partial reactions and adverse circumstances, remained so.

Tombs of Absolom, Zacharias, and James
(note the "whitened sepulchers").

308. The advance of Tigranes, king of Armenia, across Syria, and his capture of Ptolemais menaced the peace of Alexandra's realm, but the prudent queen dispatched ambassadors to him bearing gifts, and begged him not to despoil her territories. More effective than the gifts was the news which reached Tigranes that the Romans under Licinius Lucullus were invading his Armenia, and he was forced to depart in haste (§ 52).

Later still an internal threat, resulting naturally from the situation, manifested itself. Alexandra fell ill, and seemingly seriously so. At that moment Aristobulus, who had become increasingly alienated from his mother because of her docility toward the Pharisees, began to fear a Pharisee *coup*, and to prevent it seized the fortresses in which his friends and supporters were stationed (§ 306). Within fifteen days he had twenty-two of these in his power, and at the same time recruited soldiers from the nearby countries. The Pharisees were frightened and hurried to the queen, but she replied that she was too exhausted to be any longer concerned with the government. Shortly afterward she died (67 B.C.), at the age of seventy-three. Her coins contain the inscription in Greek: QUEEN ALEXANDRA, both words being abbreviated. It is not certain to what Hebrew form her other name *Salome* corresponds and it also appears in other variations, *Salma, Salina, etc.*

It is natural that the Pharisees should cherish the most pleasant memories of the reign of Alexandra; later tradition would describe it as an enchanted reign in which rain fell regularly on the eve of the Sabbath, grains of wheat were as large as marbles, those of barley were like the pits of olives, and lentils were like golden denarii (in *Megillath Taanith*, 23 *a*). It must have been a prosperous period, as only one faction had absolute control in it, but it was also the last prosperous period enjoyed by the Hasmoneans. The dispirited words of the dying queen can be applied to the entire dynasty, which now enters a period of decline, inaugurated by civil war between Alexandra's sons. It is not easy to assess with fairness the extent of Alexandra's responsibility for what happened after her death. It is to be remarked however that Josephus himself charges the decline of the Hasmoneans to her, accuses her of preferring only the present and not the future, and of having followed the judgment of an evilly disposed group, thus depriving the throne of the support of great men (*Antiquities*, XIII, 16, 6). Strong language for a Pharisee!

309. Aristobulus II. At the death of Alexandra, the enterprising Aristobulus was virtually master of the situation, thanks to his foresight. Hyrcanus, who had been high priest, now became also the legitimate king, but he remained on the throne only three months (*Antiquities*, XV, 6, 4). Aristobulus marched against him and defeated him near Jericho, thanks to the defection of many of Hyrcanus' soldiers who deserted to his side, and then proceeded to besiege him in the Temple at Jerusalem. Here the two brothers reached an agreement. Hyrcanus, as his temperament inclined, retired to private life to enjoy his revenues, but had to yield all his offices; Aristobulus became both high priest and king. To ratify the agreement, Aristobulus transferred his dwelling to the royal palace, and Hyrcanus settled down in the palace of Aristobulus.

In truth, the agreement settled matters very nicely, and would have endured a long time and with profit, if a third person had not entered upon the scene who was not inferior to Aristobulus in either energy or intrigue. He was the Idumaean Antipater (Antipas) whose father, likewise named Antipater, had been made governor of Idumaea by Alexander Jannaeus. It seems that Antipater the son succeeded his father in this office. At any rate he was very powerful by reason of his wealth and his friendship with the surrounding rulers, chief of whom was Aretas III, king of the Nabateans (§ 305); Antipater had married Cypros, daughter of a noble Nabatean family. Antipater was very friendly to Hyrcanus, whose indolence indicated to the Idumaean that he might become an obedient instrument in his hands. By the same token Antipater was also hostile to Aristobulus, whose character represented a serious obstacle to his ambitious ideas. Aristobulus' *coup*, making himself king and high priest, upset Antipater's plans, but did not cause him to lose hope.

He began by stirring up Hyrcanus and by winning over to himself some of the most influential Jews: Hyrcanus was not to take his brother's tyranny lying down, but should demand his rights, for otherwise his very life was in danger, and one fine day Aristobulus would finish him off. Hyrcanus, ever indolent, did nothing. Antipater then increased his calumnies against Aristobulus, pointing out to Hyrcanus his imminent peril, and urgently invited him to seek refuge with King Aretas. Antipater's tenacity convinced the indolent one. The diplomatic ground was prepared, and one night the Idumaean fled with Hyrcanus from Jerusalem to Petra, where King Aretas held his court.

The diplomatic preparation had been this: Aretas was to restore Hyrcanus to the throne of the Hasmoneans by force of arms, and would receive in exchange the return of the territory conquered by Alexander Jannaeus (§ 305). Aretas kept his word. He advanced with a powerful army and, accompanied by Hyrcanus, first defeated Aristobulus in battle, and then besieged him in Jerusalem. As a consequence, many of the Jews went over from Aristobulus to Hyrcanus; the ordinary people, that is, those favoring the Pharisees, sided with the besieger Hyrcanus, while the priests, that is, the Sadducees, remained faithful to Aristobulus (*Antiquities*, XIV, 2, 1).

310. The party spirit blazed up anew so violently that while some of the more prominent Jews who desired peace had sought refuge, as was the ancient custom, in Egypt, Onias, a pious man venerated as a wonder-worker, was stoned because he had refused to comply with the Pharisees' demand that he curse the besieged. There is no reason to suppose that this Onias was a Sadducee. On the contrary, he was a man with a profoundly religious and Yahwistic conscience, and the fault which brought on his stoning was his failure to approve hatred toward one part of his nation. How much the hatred which the Pharisees preached in the name of Yahwism was really based upon Yahwism was brought out shortly afterward on the occasion of the Passover. The besieged priests, lacking animals for the Paschal sacrifices, requested their fellow countrymen, the besiegers, to furnish them with the required animals at any price. The price demanded was enormous, but the terms were accepted. When however the besieged lowered the money over the walls, the besiegers took it but then would not deliver the animals to them. Thus did the Pharisees act on the feast of the Passover, the greatest festival of Yahwism. Antiochus VII himself had offered the besieged a truce and animals for the feast of Tabernacles (§ 295), though he was neither Jew nor Yahwist. But then he was not a Pharisee either.

Soon afterward a famine visited the land; Josephus looks upon it as a divine punishment for the impiety committed.

Against the fortified walls of Jerusalem, desert fighters like the Nabateans had little success, and the siege dragged on. The issue was soon resolved from without. Once Syria had been annexed to the Roman Empire, in 65 B.C. (§ 52), Pompey had sent his legate Scaurus before him to Damascus, where he heard of the war between the brothers. Sensing a golden opportunity, Scaurus moved southwards into Judea, following the usual policy of Rome of meddling in the affairs of the Orient (§ 258). As soon as the brothers learned of his arrival, they turned to the representative of Rome to seek his support, and both promised him four hundred talents. The astute Roman saw clearly that Aristobulus, already king and high priest, was in a better position to fulfill his promise than was Hyrcanus, who was dependent on the mediocre soldiery of Aretas. Other money also flowed from Aristobulus, for later on Gabinius, another legate of Pompey, was accused of having received three hundred talents from him (*Antiquities*, XIV, 3, 2). In conclusion, Scaurus decided the contest in favor of Aristobulus and ordered Aretas to withdraw. When this was done and he had received the talents, he returned to Damascus. Freed from the siege, Aristobulus pursued Hyrcanus and Aretas, and inflicted a crushing defeat on their troops.

311. But Antipater, the director of this diplomatic game, did not admit defeat, and, when Pompey arrived at Damascus in the spring of 63 B.C., presented himself before him to plead the cause of Hyrcanus. At the same time, not only did a precious gift and an ambassador from Aristobulus reach the conquerer, but also Jewish representatives, who came to express the dissatisfaction of their nation over the Hasmonean government in general, their desire to do without a royal dynasty, and their preference for the ancient ethnarchico-sacerdotal regime.

This Jewish legation is very significant, for it proves that amid the struggling Sadducees and Pharisees, amid the hatred for and servility to the Hasmoneans, there was still a strong group in the nation which had remained faithful to the ancient ideals. The head of Yahweh's nation — according to this group — should be the first of Yahweh's priests, who would govern from the Temple and with the authority which came from the Temple: no crown on his head but only the pontifical miter; no sword in his hand but only the liturgical censer. Thus, the ancient union of sword and censer (§§ 298, 302) which had shown itself to be a source of so much trouble, would be dissolved, and this would have the immediate political advantage of allaying the suspicions of the Romans, who would much prefer that the head of a peculiar nation such as the Jews should wear a miter instead of a crown.

In view of these many embassies, Pompey ordered

Road from Jericho to Jerusalem.

The fortress Alexandrium.

the two brothers to appear before him and present their views. But these were complicated by so many other personal grievances, brought forward against Aristobulus by Antipater, acting in the capacity of Hyrcanus' advocate, that Pompey put off making a decision until later, wishing first to settle his account with the kingdom of the Nabateans. The delay was obviously a pretext to give him a free hand in his expedition against the Nabateans. On the other hand Aristobulus suspected, from Pompey's behavior, that his future decision would not be as favorable to him as had been Scaurus', and thus imperiled, the choleric Hasmonean began to act in a way the Roman must have considered as illogical, flighty, and contradictory, for it inclined him alternately to rebellion and to peace.

Aristobulus at first accompanied Pompey on the expedition against the Nabateans, but when they reached Dium (§ 305) he separated from him and shut himself up in the fortress of Alexandrium (§ 306). At this hardy move Pompey broke off the campaign and marched against him. Three times Aristobulus came forth from the Alexandrium to negotiate with the Roman, hoping to hear the longed-for decision, but returned each time into the fortress, so as to have it in case of a conflict. Pompey finally demanded that he surrender this and other fortresses to him. Aristobulus obeyed, but fled to Jerusalem to prepare to resist him there. Pompey arrived at Jericho and from there marched upon Jerusalem. Terrified, Aristobulus came out to meet him, promising him money and free ingress to the city if he did not attack. To this Pompey consented; Gabinius was sent to receive the money and take possession of the city, but the troops of Aristobulus were ready for the defense

and would not comply with either of
the terms. Pompey then put Aristobulus in prison and invested the city.

312. Within the walls, as usual,
there was a difference of opinion. A
minority composed of followers of
Aristobulus, blindly fanatical, were
all for resisting the Romans, but
seeing that they were alone in their
view, shut themselves up in the fortified Temple and let the rest of the
city fend for itself. The majority of
those left in the city were supporters
of Hyrcanus and yielded the city to
Piso, the legate sent by Pompey. A
garrison was placed in the palace,
and when negotiations with those
barricaded in the Temple resulted in
failure, a regular siege began. Hyrcanus naturally furnished all possible
help to the besiegers.

Pompey.

The plan was to attack the northern part which was the weakest
because of the nature of the terrain (Vol. I, §§ 95 ff., 390). On this side,
the Temple was protected by walls fortified with towers, and by a
moat in front of the walls, but there was no natural valley to impede
an approach here, as on the other sides. The Romans began to fill in the
moat, a long and difficult task both because of its depth and the
attacks made by the defenders in the towers. But the Romans made
progress, especially on the Sabbath days, for the besieged believed
that they were allowed to repel an armed attack on that day (§ 253),
but not to interfere with warlike actions in general. Once the moat
was filled in, the engines of war brought from Tyre were moved into
position and began to batter the walls.

In the meantime, inside the Temple which was bombarded by arrows
and other projectiles, the liturgical services went calmly on, and the
daily sacrifice was offered with a magnificent punctuality which was
admired by Pompey himself.

After a siege of three months, the Temple was entered. First to
penetrate the breach was Faustus Cornelius, son of the dictator Scylla,
followed by the centurions Furius and Fabius. This was at the beginning

of the autumn of 63 B.C., probably on a Sabbath;[1] Marcus Tullius Cicero was consul at Rome.

313. After the conquest there followed a slaughter. As the Romans broke in, the priests engaged in offering sacrifice continued with the ceremony and were cut down near the altar. A few of the defenders tried to resist, but many threw themselves down from the rocky precipices which surrounded the Temple on two sides. It was estimated that twelve thousand Jews died, but probably the greater part of these did not fall under the Roman sword, for "many were killed by their own countrymen, of the adverse faction" (*War*, I, 7, 5), that is, by the Pharisees, supporters of Hyrcanus, who went in after the Romans to carry out with ease their inexorable vengeance.

On this occasion, perhaps on that same day, Pompey made his famous inspection of the interior of the sanctuary, going all the way into the "holy of holies." Of all the objects of gold and the two thousand talents found there in various places, he touched not a one, yet the momentary presence of that pagan in a place where only once a year the high priest alone could enter made all the Jews of whatever faction shudder with the greatest horror: "nothing in all those misfortunes afflicted the people so much as that their sanctuary, which up to that time had been seen by no one, was laid open to foreigners" (*War*, I, 7, 6). Besides military considerations, there must have been a great deal of curiosity in Pompey's action. So many tales had been told about the mysterious Temple that on this occasion, when he had the chance, he wanted to see with his own eyes what it actually

Roman road near Maresa.

---

[1] The "day of fast" attested by Josephus (*Antiquities*, XIV, 4, 3) is probably equivalent to a Sabbath because of the confusion between the Sabbath and a fast day, common to non-Jews (§ 203). Here, Josephus seems to depend on a non-Jewish source (cf. Schürer, I, pp. 298–299). Others interpret it as the "day of fast" *par excellence*, that is, the day of Expiation or Yom Kippur, and hence it would be in October, the tenth day of Tishri, but this seems a bit too late considering all that Pompey did soon after in that same year.

did contain. It is not difficult to picture him, sword in hand, suspicious and alert, as he crossed the "holy place" (Vol. I, §§ 391–392). Filled with emotion, he lifted the curtain which was in front of the pentagonal door, prepared to gaze upon the head of an ass (§ 202) or some monstrous image; instead, when he peered about the darkness of the "holy of holies" he saw only a *vacuam sedem et inania arcana* (§ 201).

Was it Cnaeus Pompey who performed the act, or was it all humanity?

314. His conquest accomplished, Pompey was impatient to be off to Asia Minor, and settled his affairs quickly. The next day he ordered the Temple to be purified and the regular liturgical service resumed. Then, when the leaders of the resistance were put to death, he established Hyrcanus as high priest and ethnarch, but without the title of king. He imposed a tribute upon Jerusalem and the land, and detached from it the various districts which had been Judaized by force, among which were Scythopolis, Pella, Samaria (§ 165), Maresa, Jamnia, etc., and all the cities of the coast such as Gaza and Joppe up to Caesarea to the north. All these places were annexed to the recently created Roman province of Syria. Freed from Jewish dominance, the Hellenistic cities of Transjordan initiated a new era out of gratitude, dating all future events from the period of Pompey. The ethnarchy of Hyrcanus — which took in Judea, Galilee, a small part of Transjordan then called Perea, and some sections of Idumaea — enjoyed internal autonomy, but was placed under the surveillance of the governor of Syria. Pompey left Scaurus with two legions to govern this province, and then departed to Cilicia, taking with him Aristobulus with his two daughters and his two sons, Alexander and Antigonus, destined to embellish the triumph which the conqueror was to enjoy in Rome in 61. The elder of the two, Alexander, managed to escape during the voyage. Many prisoners of war were also brought to Rome and enormously increased the Jewish colony of the city (§ 195).

Thus, the contest between the two Hasmoneans ended with the defeat of both. Aristobulus was forced to march in front of Pompey's triumphal chariot, but the unwarlike Hyrcanus, who remained at Jerusalem, ended up even more ignobly; he became a mask for the grinning face of the real winner, the Idumaean Antipater.

THE ROMAN DOMINATION

315. Hyrcanus II. The preceding relations between Jerusalem and Rome now began to bear fruit, though not the fruit promised the Machabean brothers, the "friends" and "allies" of Rome; it was, rather that which the Conscript Fathers had vaguely awaited since the days of Judas and Simon. Whether or not Judea was incorporated officially in the Roman province of Syria by 63 B.C. (that is doubtful), it is certain that it was a tributary under the direct control of Rome. This was only a step, but others would surely follow.

The subjection of Judea, to view the matter fairly, was advantageous to the people. Independence had been an occasion for internal divisions and struggles so rabid that leaders of the factions had enlisted the help of foreign soldiers and had invited the intervention of the Seleucids (§§ 299, 303). They had also so disturbed those who desired peace as to bring about a spontaneous request for the abolition of the monarchy and a return to a sacerdotal rule (§ 311). Under the severe rule of Rome disturbances of this kind could occur only with difficulty and would be less grave, and on the other hand, there would also be provided the greatest religious liberty, internal autonomy, and assurance against molestations from surrounding people, for the standards of the Roman legions were enough to command respect for the places in which they were raised. There was, of course, tribute to be paid, and it seems to have been heavy (Josephus speaks of ten thousand talents being taken by the Romans "in a short time"; *Antiquities*, XIV, 4, 5), but remembering the fifty thousand Jews who were slain in the civil wars under Alexander Jannaeus alone, and the semi-anarchy of those times, it was worth the price (§ 303).

In fact, under the new Roman regime, Judea remained tranquil for some years. It was during this time that Scaurus led the expedition against Aretas, king of the Nabateans, which Pompey had to interrupt because of the complications with Aristobulus. That expedition did

Petra (at the base of the mountain). (Vester, Amer. Colony.)

not fare well, since the capital Petra did not lend itself to a regular siege, and the surrounding region was an inhospitable desert. The situation was saved by Antipater, a friend of Aretas as well as of the Romans, who first supplied the troops of Scaurus with provisions and then induced him to come to an agreement with Aretas. Scaurus retired on being promised three hundred talents, and these were guaranteed him by Antipater.

In 61 B.C. Scaurus was replaced as governor of Syria by Marcius Philippus, and the latter in 59 by Lentulus Marcellinus, both of whom governed the province as *propraetores*. Because of the ever greater importance now assumed by Syria, and because of the complicated difficulties connected with it, it was resolved to send a *proconsul* there. The first of these was A. Gabinius, in 57 B.C. Although there is no hint of his two predecessors having intervened in the affairs of Judea, Gabinius must have busied himself with them from the very beginning of his proconsulate.

316. After the catastrophe of 63 the followers of Aristobulus had been left defeated and dispersed, but had not abandoned all hope. An occasion for an attempt at recovery presented itself to them around 58, when the eldest son of Aristobulus, the Alexander who had succeeded in escaping

during the journey toward Rome (§314), appeared in Judea. Immediately setting about the reorganization of the remnants of his faction, he collected ten thousand infantry and fifteen hundred cavalry under his banner, and with them proceeded to reconquer step by step those centers more favorable to him, including the fortresses of Hyrcania, Alexandrium, and Machaerus, the traditional holdings of the Hasmoneans (§ 306). Meanwhile, Hyrcanus "was unable to oppose his power" (*Antiquities*, XIV, 5, 2). Gabinius intervened on his behalf, sending against Alexander a division commanded by Mark Antony, the future triumvir, and soon afterward he himself came down with the rest of the army, to which the troops of Hyrcanus and Antipater were added. Defeated near Jerusalem, Alexander shut himself up in the Alexandrium, where he was besieged for a long time. Through the intercession of Alexander's mother who was favorably known to the Romans, an accord was reached in virtue of which the three afore-mentioned fortresses were ceded to the Romans and razed to the ground. With unexpected clemency Alexander was allowed to go free.

During the siege of Alexandrium, however, Gabinius had taken new political measures. Besides ordering the reconstruction of Samaria (§ 165), Scythopolis, and other localities which had been destroyed by the Hasmoneans, he divided the territory of Hyrcanus into five districts (σύνοδοι or συνέδρια), each one governed by a college of prominent Jews which was responsible for the district to the proconsul. The centers of the districts were Jerusalem for upper Judea, Gazara (Gezer) for lower Judea, Amathus (§ 302) for northern Transjordan, Jericho for southern Transjordan, and Sepphoris (§ 301) for Galilee (*Antiquities*, XIV, 5, 4; *War*, I, 8, 5). This partition was doubtless intended to facilitate the collection of the taxes, but this was not the only and perhaps not even the principal purpose behind it. Gabinius thus planned to bring about a real break-up of the nation, for although the division might further various local and often conflicting interests, it would deprive the remnants of the Hasmonean faction of any basis for unity. There was, of course, Hyrcanus left, but Gabinius took care of him also; as "high priest" he left him absolute mastery of the censers of the Temple and the lambs for the altar; as "ethnarch" he left him only the title, since each college in the five districts was autonomous, and within its own territory had juridical and administrative authority equal to that of the others. It was, therefore, a genuine and clear separation of Church and State, and naturally Hyrcanus, who had always agreed with Aristobulus, Antipater, and everyone else, did not dream of opposing Gabinius, who thus left him stripped of all civil power.

317. The one who once again became defiant was Aristobulus, the brother of Hyrcanus. In the year 56 he succeeded in escaping from Rome with his other son Antigonus and in re-entering Judea with him. He quickly found followers and repeated the attempt of his son Alexander, but being first defeated and then besieged at Machaerus, he was sent back to Rome by Gabinius, and there held in prison. His sons, nevertheless, were given their liberty by the Roman senate, and they returned to Judea.

With a tenacity worthy of his father and one which clearly reflected the sentiments of the people, Alexander attempted a new uprising in 55. Taking advantage of the absence of Gabinius, who on his own initiative had gone off on an expedition into Egypt to restore Ptolemy XI Auletes (§ 54) to the throne, Alexander gathered an army, killed many Romans, and laid siege to others who had taken refuge on Mount Gerizim. On his return from Egypt, Gabinius found Judea in full revolt. Antipater, who had been very useful to him during the Egyptian expedition — he had supplied him with provisions in the desert and had gotten him a favorable reception by the Jews settled in the Delta — again came to his assistance, and by his arguments persuaded many of Alexander's adherents to leave him. Alexander with thirty thousand men attacked Gabinius near Mount Tabor (Vol. I, § 310) and was badly defeated.

This last revolt clearly brought out this fact, that the various attempts at revolt were becoming steadily more anti-Roman in character, and were losing little by little any semblance of a struggle between the Hasmoneans. Shortly after this defeat, Alexander became the son-in-law of the high priest Hyrcanus by marrying his daughter Alexandra (Antiquities, XV, 2, 5).

Pompey and Crassus, who with Caesar had already formed the first triumvirate, had been consuls at Rome during this same year, 55 B.C., and at the year's end Crassus, who had obtained the proconsulate of Syria, came to replace Gabinius. Wishing to match the renown of his two colleagues in warlike deeds, as he already did in wealth, the new proconsul undertook a campaign against the Parthians in which, in 53, he lost his life. Shortly before the campaign, he came to Jerusalem and, if only not to belie the one title to fame he enjoyed, despoiled the Temple of two thousand talents in money and eight thousand in objects of gold, including a very large bar of gold, all of which were gifts continually being made to the Temple from the diaspora. He could not have chosen a better way to intensify the hatred of the Jews for foreigners. Hence, while the victorious Parthians threatened the province from the east, a revolt broke out anew in Judea, led this time by an obscure Pitholaus who had once been a partisan of Aristobulus. Although Cassius Longinus (§ 323), who succeeded Crassus, had few troops, he easily prevailed over the revolters; at the end of the war he was able to sell thirty thousand Jews as slaves, and also, on the advice of Antipater, had Pitholaus put to death. Favored by Cassius Longinus as he had been by Gabinius, Antipater functioned as the real governor of Judea. In gratitude for the help he had received, Gabinius settled the affairs of Jerusalem "as was agreeable to Antipater's inclinations" (*Antiquities,* XIV, 6, 4). But there soon arose, even for Antipater with his policy of surrender to Rome, a highly embarrassing question: Which Roman to choose?

318. The fire that was smoldering in Rome in 51–50 suddenly flared up. The old rivalry between the two surviving triumvirs, Caesar and Pompey, developed into open warfare when the senate lined up on the side of the latter. On the twenty-third of November, 50 B.C. (January 12, 49), Julius Caesar started the civil war by crossing the Rubicon with only the Thirteenth Legion. Striking swiftly, a characteristic of his tactics, he took over the various centers supporting Pompey, surprising them beginning their preparations, and forced the senate and Pompey to fly to Greece (January of 49 B.C.). The outcome of the personal rivalry between the two leaders was decided on June 6 (August 9) of 48 B.C. at Pharsalia, where Pompey was completely defeated. Shortly thereafter the defeated hero fled to Egypt and there was killed by Ptolemy XII (§ 54). A few days later Caesar arrived at Alexandria with a very few soldiers. Upon learning that his rival was dead, he began to act as arbiter in matters concerning the Ptolemies (§ 54), and thus irritated the partisans of Ptolemy XII, who, noting the smallness of the forces at his command, attacked him. Caesar was obliged to burn his ships, and for six months was besieged in Alexandria in the quarter where the Palace (§ 190) was located. When re-enforcements came, he defeated Ptolemy, settled the affairs of Egypt, and moved to battle Pharnaces, king of Pontus. To reach the new battlefield Caesar hurriedly traversed Judea in the summer of 47 B.C.

Three years later, on the Ides of March of the year 44 B.C., twenty-three wounds inflicted by the daggers of Cassius and the other conspirators left him lying dead in the Curia, at the feet of the statue of Pompey.

319. When Caesar wrested Rome from Pompey, Aristobulus was in prison. Caesar thought of a way to make use of him. He freed him, appointed him to the command of two legions, and charged him to march to Syria to win those regions over to his (Caesar's) side. But supporters of Pompey learned of this, and Aristobulus was poisoned. About the same time, Pompey sent an order to Metellus Scipio, proconsul of Syria, to kill Alexander, Aristobulus' son, and the order was carried out in Antioch. Evidently the faction favorable to Pompey feared that the sons of Aristobulus would support Caesar, not only because of the trust Caesar placed in their father, but also by way of opposition to

Hyrcanus and Antipater, who from the beginning openly supported Pompey, their chief benefactor (§ 314).

Pharsalia and the death of Pompey, however, upset the plans of both, or rather, of Antipater, who was the real power. After Pharsalia the supporters of Pompey were still very strong, but the astute Antipater was an expert political pilot, and had no difficulty in changing his course to sail with the wind. Sensing that Caesar would emerge the victor, he deserted his allies, and threw in his lot with him. With a man like Caesar, actions spoke louder than words, so Antipater acted. While Caesar was besieged in Alexandria,

"Caesar . . . with fierce eyes." (Dante.)

Antipater collected three thousand Jews to support the troops led by Mithridates, king of Pergamum, to help Caesar. He directed and aided their passage across the desert, fought valiantly in the capture of Pelusium, won over to Caesar's cause the Jewish colony of Leontopolis, which was at first hostile to him (§ 249), and finally, contributed to Caesar's final victory in a battle below Alexandria. Caesar was famous for his generosity toward his enemies, and much more so toward his friends. The important aid given to him by Antipater in the most critical moment of his career was enough to make him his sincere friend, and made him feel kindly toward the Jews; they in turn lamented his death (§ 196).

He went to such lengths that he neglected other obligations of gratitude. When he passed through Judea in 47, Antigonus, Aristobulus' surviving son, appeared before him to claim his dynastic rights, mentioning also that his father and brother had died for Caesar's cause. But Caesar desired to hear also his favorite, Antipater, and he, with diplomatic eloquence, had little trouble in showing that Aristobulus' whole family was nothing but a band of agitators who were disliked by their own country and were the enemies of Rome. Naturally this last accusation sufficed to leave Antigonus with empty hands, at least for the time. Instead, Caesar recognized Hyrcanus as high priest of the Jewish nation; at the same time, he declared Antipater a citizen of Rome and immune from taxes, and officially confirmed him in the office of procurator (ἐπίτροπος) of Judea, which he had in fact occupied up to that time.

320. But these were only the first drops of a rain of acknowledgments and concessions[1] which made Hyrcanus more of a puppet than ever, for it was Antipater who manipulated the strings, who grew more and more powerful. Soon afterward, Hyrcanus was recognized as ethnarch or also civil head of the entire nation, with absolute control in questions affecting the internal affairs of Judaism. This appointment, therefore, abolished the politico-administrative divisions introduced by Gabinius (§ 316), and restored organic unity to Palestinian Judaism. In regard to the internal order to be established in the country, broad powers were granted to Antipater, who was empowered to make decisions at his own discretion (Antiquities, XIV, 8, 5). Besides, permission had been granted to rebuild the walls of Jerusalem, thrown down since the time of Pompey. The territory of the nation was widened too, for the cities of Galilee which had previously fallen to Syria and Phoenicia, and also of the port of Joppe, which was most useful to Jerusalem, were now restored to Hyrcanus. The whole territory was held to the ordinary tribute, but dispensed from it in the sabbatical year, when the Law proscribed any produce. Roman troops were not to enter the territory at all, or requisition goods there for military purposes, or there fill up their levies of recruits for the legions.

Special consideration was shown to the family of Hyrcanus, and his office was declared hereditary. Diplomatic etiquette was also taken care of, so that whenever he or his sons or ambassadors came to Rome, they could, if they so wished, amuse themselves by gazing, from seats reserved for them among the senators, at the spectacles provided by gladiatorial combats, or battles to the death between wild animals.

The benefits were extended to the diaspora (§ 197). Henceforward the Jewish ἔθνος was a corporate body at whose head stood an ἐθνάρχης. It was recognized and protected by Rome. Other vassal states and allies of Rome were informed of the privileges Rome had conceded to it and expected them to respect. In keeping with diplomatic custom, there were

---

[1] At this point Josephus gives a long series of decrees (Antiquities, XIV, 8, 5; 10, 2–25) which are represented as emanating from the year 47 and later, either from Caesar and the other Roman authorities, or from various cities in Asia, all of which redound to the greater glory of Hyrcanus or the Jews in general. The very quantity of the material involves other delicate questions. Some decrees seem to be anachronistic (the Roman decree given in XIV, 8, 5, should be referred neither to Hyrcanus II nor Hyrcanus I, but to Simon Machabeus; cf. §§ 289, 296); many others are fragmentary, badly preserved, or have been altered, and would require separate discussions. In general, however, they must contain much that is authentic and one may discern from them the outlines of the juridical position achieved by the Jews in the Empire at the time of Caesar and immediately afterwards.

placed (so we are told) in the Capitol, and in the sanctuaries of cities hostile to Judaism, as for example Sidon, Tyre, Ascalon, bronze tablets attesting Rome's privileges toward and protection of the Jews.

321. Who could complain amid such abundance? Certainly not Antipater, who, after he had accompanied Caesar to Syria, returned to Judea and busied himself with propaganda tours in favor of the Romans and of Hyrcanus, and in trying to quiet the malcontents (*Antiquities*, XIV, 9, 1). Shortly afterward, he took thought for his own personal interests, and here the narration of Josephus must be quoted verbatim: "Seeing that Hyrcanus was of a slow and slothful temper, Antipater made his eldest son, Phasael, governor of Jerusalem and the places round about: to his next [son] Herod, he committed the governorship of Galilee, though he was very young, being only fifteen years old" (*Antiquities*, XIV, 9, 2). Whether Herod was fifteen or twenty-five years of age,[2] he was indeed very young, but also very perspicacious and energetic. His father put him in charge of the northern part of the country, and over Jerusalem he put his other son, intending that the two would work in harmony, with himself as supervisor over all. Both sons took to their offices with enthusiasm. Herod succeeded in overcoming a certain Ezechias, described as a brigand and a bandit chieftain who infested the roads of Galilee, but who may very well have been something else (§ 322). After capturing him, Herod had him put to death and dispersed his followers. This won for him the recognition of the local populace and of Sextus Caesar, a relative of Julius Caesar and now the new governor of Syria. Phasael, not to be outdone by the good name his brother was making for himself in the north, brought to the government of Jerusalem an energy and an integrity which were quite novel. As a result, in Josephus' words, "This conduct procured from the nation a respect for Antipater such as is due to kings and such honors as are usually accorded to one who is a monarch" (*Antiquities*, XIV, 9, 2).

For all the titles conceded to him by Caesar, what remained to Hyrcanus but the censers and the lambs of the Temple?

But all the Jews were not like Hyrcanus, and there were many reasons for hating Antipater and his two haughty sons. Apart from the fact that they were Idumaeans, that is, bastard Jews (§ 297), descendants of the ancient enemies of Israel (Vol. I, § 140, etc.); apart from the fact that they exacted huge sums of money from them; apart even from the fact that Antipater sent the tribute to Rome in his own name and not in the

---

[2] The codices uniformly have *fifteen,* but scholars commonly presuppose this to be an error and correct it to *twenty-five.* One can only conjecture about the text, but the reckoning is based on the fact that Josephus gives Herod's age as seventy years when he died in the year 4 B.C. (*Antiquities*, XVII, 6, 1).

name of Hyrcanus, though with the full consent of the latter, their most serious grievance was that Antipater stood for foreign domination over Israel. It was a dominion imposed, as it were, by surprise, hypocritical, apparently conformable to the Law, but for all of that, not less harsh nor less real. It was perhaps the more galling because all external appearances were kept up. The offices of "high priest" and "ethnarch" remained, and were filled by a genuine Jew; but he was a perfect imbecile, this Hyrcanus, chosen deliberately so that the bastard Jew, Antipater, could do as he liked. This was insult added to injury.

322. Some, therefore, undertook to arouse Hyrcanus from his slumber, and to awaken him somewhat to the realities of the situation. They did not have recourse to violence, which in any case was entirely impossible, but rather concentrated on a legal question. Their accusation was directed against young Herod, but the shot was really aimed at his powerful father. The case of Ezechias (§ 321) was reopened, and exception taken to the fact that Herod had put him to death in violation of the law, according to which only the Sanhedrin of the nation in Jerusalem could pass the death sentence.

But why was it that the case of Ezechias was the one to be reopened? Because it provided a sound legal ground to stand on? This may have entered into it, but it is difficult to believe that such was the main reason. The subtle casuists of the Sanhedrin were certainly not lacking other and more worthy cases in which they could entangle Herod than that of a "brigand." The real reason must have been that the executed Ezechias was *not* the bandit leader he was said to have been, but rather a Jewish nationalist and patriotic leader who had harassed the pagan and foreign centers of Galilee. Making himself the spokesman of the widespread anti-Roman sentiment, Ezechias had acted in substantially the same way the Machabees had a century earlier. Thus an adequate explanation is given for the thankfulness which was manifested toward his executioner, Herod, by both the local populace and even by Sextus Caesar. The new Machabean of Galilee had met his Antiochus Epiphanes in the son of the Idumaean Antipater. The Sanhedrists, then, made an issue out of this case, not because of the "brigand" it involved, but because he had been a "nationalist."

Phlegmatic Hyrcanus, who probably failed to grasp the political aspects of this case, agreed with those who brought their complaints to him, and made a resolute gesture: he summoned Herod to appear in court. But the resolute gesture was to end in embarrassment.

Herod presented himself before the Sanhedrin of Jerusalem in an insolent manner, well-groomed, clothed in purple, and surrounded by soldiers, whereas custom demanded that the accused present himself disheveled, clothed in mourning, and humbly. At the same time there arrived a letter from Sextus Caesar, directing that Herod be acquitted. At the appearance of such an accused one, the members of the Sanhedrin were struck dumb, even those who had made the charges. Only one Pharisee, Sameas (probably the famous Shammai), arose to speak, but instead of accusing Herod, he denounced the general state of affairs which made it possible for him to adopt such an attitude. The courage of Sameas revived the courage of the Sanhedrin, and it probably would have condemned Herod had not Hyrcanus, who was mindful of the letter from Sextus Caesar, secretly induced him to leave Jerusalem. Herod sought refuge in Damascus and was made governor of Coelesyria by Sextus Caesar. He then gathered troops around him and marched on Jerusalem to revenge himself on Hyrcanus and the accusers. It was only with great difficulty that his father succeeded in calming him and caused him to turn back. But for a man of Herod's stamp, this meant only that his revenge was postponed (§ 339).

323. All this had occurred between 47–46 B.C. In 44 the assassination of Caesar rendered Antipater's position somewhat insecure and brought him face to face again with the question of which Roman party to choose (§ 317). This time the uncertainty was of brief duration. One of Caesar's murderers, the same Cassius Longinus who had previously been governor of Syria and had had dealings with Antipater (§ 317), came to Syria as proconsul. Antipater, until then a supporter of Caesar, had to bear in mind the republican ideas of the new proconsul. Cassius was in need of money for military action against Caesar's party, and laid upon Judea a tribute of seven hundred talents. Antipater divided the burden among his sons. Herod was the first to collect the amount assigned to him, having become Cassius' friend, and in recognition for his service was named to his old post of governor of Coelesyria. In Judea, however, the collection went much more slowly, and when the inhabitants of Gophna, Emmaus, Lydda, and Thamma did not deliver their allotment they were sold as slaves.

Among the collectors of tribute there had been a certain Malichus (or Malchos) who was ill-disposed toward Antipater and plotted to supplant him. He seized upon this tribute as an occasion to fan the popular discontent against the Idumaean extortioner who so served foreigners. Antipater was suspicious of Malichus' schemings and began to gather together an army for his own protection, whereupon Malichus roundly denied any insidious design against him and again entered into friendly relations with him. This was the subtler plan, for as Antipater was too strong to be attacked openly, Malichus turned to guile. He corrupted Hyrcanus' cupbearer with his bribes, and as a result, Antipater was poisoned as the two of them sat at table (43 B.C.).

Herod reacted at once, and although Malichus denied having had anything to do with the crime and was on his guard against him, he was able to have him slain not far from Tyre, thus frustrating Malichus' plan to seize the reins of power. Thenceforward, Herod would carry on the work of his father, Antipater, with equal cunning and even greater resoluteness, and, with an absolute disregard for men or anything else, he would bring it to realization.

324. When Cassius departed from Syria (42 B.C.), that territory was almost reduced to a state of anarchy, thanks to the depredations and turmoil induced by the contending rivals. Aristobulus' surviving son, Antigonus (§§ 314, 319), took advantage of this situation to attempt once more to recoup his fortunes. He was supported by a few petty rulers who were faithful to Cassius, especially by Ptolemy of Chalcis and Marion of Tyre. The latter annexed some localities of Galilee, and Antigonus began his advance toward Judea. Herod intervened promptly, defeated him and threw his troops into a rout.

Herod obviously acted as the custodian of the highest office of the nation out of self-interest. He had repulsed Antigonus more for his own interest than for Hyrcanus'. But now he realized that it would be to his advantage to cultivate Hyrcanus again, so as to be able to watch him and circumvent him the more easily. Consequently, although Herod was already married to Doris, the mother of his firstborn Antipater, he was again reconciled with Hyrcanus and married Mariamne, the daughter of Alexander the Hasmonean and of Alexandra, Hyrcanus' daughter (§ 317). His purpose and foresight in so acting was clear, for by entering into a family relationship he thereby established rights which could be urged when the succession to Hyrcanus II would be open, especially in view of the fact that Cassius had already explicitly promised him the kingdom of Judea once he had put down the pro-Caesar party (*Antiquities*, XIV, 11, 4).

325. In the two battles at Philippi (October, 42 B.C.) where Cassius lost his life, the political situation changed once more. The republican and anti-Caesar faction had been broken for good, and its adherents gravely compromised. Because of their friendship for Cassius, Herod and Phasael were included among these, along with Hyrcanus, who had put himself into their hands. The many Jews who lamented the overlordship of the Idumaean family, the inertia of Hyrcanus, and the foreign domination, decided that they should seize this opportunity to break the most important link in this chain, and to get rid once and for all of the Idumaean family now also compromised in the eyes of the Romans. After Philippi, Mark Antony had become the master of Asia. Among the many other ambassadors who appeared before him while he was still in Bithynia, there arrived a delegation of Jews to denounce what amounted to usurpation on the part of Herod and Phasael, and the complete indifference of Hyrcanus.

But Herod also came in person to save the situation, throwing himself on the side of Antony. Both by money and by reminding Antony of the friendly relations which had existed between Antony and his father Antipater (§ 316), he so completely won him over to his cause that the delegation of Jews was not even given a hearing. A second embassy sent by Hyrcanus to Ephesus, where Mark Antony had gone, came with a clever plan: feigning ignorance of any change of policy on the part of Hyrcanus (or of him who acted for him), it represented the Jews as having been persecuted by Cassius, whereas in reality they had always been for Caesar's party. It therefore requested the liberation of the Jews sold as slaves, and restitution of the territories lost (§ 324) during that ill-starred government. Antony believed them, or pretended to because it suited him, and issued the decrees requested. Herod's cause was now won, and to accelerate his victory two other delegations sent by the Jewish complainants, one to Antioch, the other to Tyre, helped. Despite the two delegations, Antony, suborned as usual by Herod, named the brothers Herod and Phasael as "tetrarchs" of Judea and had several members of the second delegation put to death. The term "tetrarch" at that time had lost its ancient signification of "the head of a fourth part" of a territory, and was the usual title of petty sovereigns. The preceding state of affairs was thus officially sanctioned, and the cherished dream of Antipater realized. Hyrcanus no longer had any official duties outside the Temple; sovereignty in civil affairs now belonged, even in title, to the two Idumaeans. It was the autumn of the year 41 B.C.

326. But the dream had a tragic awakening. A storm (the Parthians) had been brewing in the Orient as far back as the days of Julius Caesar, and now it drew closer. It was up to Mark Antony to meet it, but instead he began at this time his amorous dalliance with Cleopatra (§ 54), whom he followed to Egypt. For both enterprises — preparations for war with the Parthians and his extravagant expenditures for Cleopatra — he needed immense sums of money, and these he tried to extract from the whole of Asia by means of crushing tributes. While he was playing the fool at the Egyptian court and had left the legions of Syria to their fate, the Parthians, called in by the remnants of the republican faction defeated at Philippi, began their invasion early in the year 40 B.C.

Many Roman garrisons deserted, and while one horde of Parthians led by the Roman Quintus Labienus marched on Asia Minor, another led by Pacorus, the Parthian king, the son of Orosus, and by the satrap Barzapharnes, descended upon Syria and Palestine.

So great was the exasperation caused by the Roman tributes and the hatred against the two Idumaean brothers, that to many Jews the deluge of barbarians seemed like a liberation. Antigonus, who had persisted in seeking revenge after his last failure (§ 324), quickly grasped the situation and saw in it his golden opportunity, and at once set about making terms with the Parthians, all the time gathering rebels about him. To the Parthians he promised, if they gave him the kingdom and killed Herod, one thousand talents and five hundred women (a new kind of money, this, coined by the great-grandchild of the Machabees). The Parthians came and joined with Antigonus, as it was to their own interest to do so. He forced his way toward Jerusalem, his soldiers increasing in number along the way. Once he had broken through the defense ring and had taken possession of the Temple, where he was probably received with favor by the Sadducean priests, Antigonus was attacked by Herod and Phasael, who were holding out in the palace. The people were divided between the Hasmonean and the Idumaeans, and civil war ensued. Antigonus then sent a Parthian captain, also named Pachorus, into the city, as if to act as peacemaker. Phasael, in whose home he had put up, was invited to present himself before Barzapharnes to state his case. Herod suspected the trap, but Phasael did not. Accompanied by Hyrcanus he set out toward the Parthian headquarters in Galilee. There, after a number of delays engineered in the hope of laying hold on Herod also, the two were imprisoned. Herod was warned in time and, with a few soldiers and members of his family, succeeded in fleeing from Jerusalem. On reaching Masada, a powerful fortress on the west bank of the Dead Sea, he left his wives there for safety, and himself turned toward the Nabateans of Petra.

So Antigonus remained the master and, through the Parthians, held Hyrcanus and Phasael in his power. With his own teeth he bit off the ears of the first so that he might never be able to be the high priest again, "the high priests were to be complete, without blemish" (War, I, 13, 9); the second killed himself by dashing his head against a stone.

✿   ✿   ✿

327. Antigonus. In the year 40 B.C., the last of the Hasmoneans was both "high priest" and "king," thanks to the Parthians and the desire of many of the Jews. His coins bear the inscription: OF THE KING ANTIGONUS in Greek, and in Hebrew: MATTATHIAS HIGH PRIEST, Mattathias being his Jewish name.

In compensation for the services they had rendered, the Parthians proceeded to plunder the country. Antony eventually sent a strong army against them and Ventidius, its commander, opened the campaign in 39 B.C. His uninterrupted string of victories meant the liberation of Asia Minor, the defeat and death of Labienus, and the reconquest of Syria.

When the Parthians launched a new invasion in 38, Ventidius inflicted a complete defeat upon them which cost them the life of their king Pachorus. With the barbarians out of the way, Ventidius proceeded next to subdue the local chieftains who had supported them, and laid siege to Samosata. In the course of these operations Antony replaced Ventidius by Sosius who continued them, and thus found himself in an engagement with Antigonus, the king of the Jews.

On their retreat from Palestine the Parthians led away the ex-high priest, Hyrcanus, as prisoner. He was treated with great consideration by their king, Phraates, and shown much respect by the Jews of Babylonia. Later, through the repeated invitations of Herod, he was able to return to Jerusalem (§ 333).

Antigonus moved quickly, for he saw that he was deprived of Parthian support. He laid siege to the fortress of Masada, defended by Herod's brother, Joseph, but did not take it. Leaning more and more on the aristocratic Sadducees and the sacerdotal faction, he also won over, by his money, the commanders of the first Roman detachments which penetrated into Judea as the Parthians retreated. As a result he was not directly disturbed either by Ventidius or his lieutenant Silo.

328. Very soon, however, a much graver threat was to cast its shadow over his throne; it was Herod again. A man of steel, Herod was not one to wallow, discouraged, in the disaster that had struck him, not even when, upon approaching Petra (§ 315), he learned that he would not be received by the king of the Nabateans for whom he had done favors in the past. To add further to his woes, he learned during the journey that his brother Phasael had killed himself, and thus Herod found himself entirely alone for the present and also for the future, in the desert of Idumaea. With his clear and realistic intuition, Herod saw that amid such great ruin his only hope was Rome, whereupon he immediately set out for Egypt and, after a brief stop in Alexandria, embarked for Rome despite the inclement season, arriving there after a fortunate voyage by way of Rhodes and Brindisi. Antony had made peace again with Octavian, and both were at Rome at that moment.

With his usual skill perhaps made more persuasive by money and further promises, Herod aroused in Antony a cordial interest for his cause. Antony, for that matter, had every reason to support this man who had been ruined by the Parthians, for this would be a blow struck at Antigonus, who had profited by it. Antony's interest was shared by Octavian, who, in turn, undertook to befriend Herod because he was the son of that Antipater who in Alexandria had come to the aid of Julius Caesar, his father by adoption. The favor of the two masters of Rome and of the world was ratified by the senate, which issued a decree declaring Herod "king."

Ptolemais (Akka).

Herod was as much surprised as anyone at this outcome. On his way to Rome he had never dared dream of so much. His plan had only been to obtain the throne for Mariamne's brother, Aristobulus, who was also the grandson of Hyrcanus II, on his mother's side, and of Aristobulus II on his father's side (§ 324; cf. *Antiquities*, XIV, 14, 5). With Aristobulus established upon the throne, Herod had hoped to become his all-powerful minister, as his father Antipater had been under Hyrcanus. In fact, Herod had reasoned that the Romans would follow their usual policy, and would not bestow the crown of Judea on anyone but a genuine Jew, and if possible, on a member of the ruling family. Herod was an Idumaean, and not of the Hasmonean dynasty, but this time the senate, or, rather, Antony and Octavian, departed from the ancient rule. Herod was something of a Jew, and on the point of marrying into the Hasmonean family; he was a trusted friend of Rome and already recognized as a "tetrarch" (§ 325); he was a rival of Antigonus, that enemy of the Romans and friend of the Parthians to whom he owed his kingship. Herod therefore was also made "king," as his rival had been.

Faced with such good fortune, Herod took pains to act the part of the legitimist and the modest soul. Feted by Antony and Octavian, he accepted the celebrations. Led to the Capitoline to assist at the ritual sacrifice to Jupiter, he went along as he would go up in the Temple at Jerusalem to sacrifice to Yahweh. In only seven days everything was concluded, and he was ready to depart from Rome and to win for himself the kingdom that had been decreed to him. It was the autumn of 40 B.C., in the consulate of Domitius Calvinus and Asinius Pollio.

329. To wrest the kingdom from Antigonus was not easy. Herod disembarked at Ptolemais in 39, conquered it, and recruited some soldiers there. With the help of Roman troops he seized the port of Joppe, and hurried thence to liberate his besieged relatives in the fortress of Masada (§ 326). Antigonus shut himself up in Jerusalem and awaited help from the Parthians, meanwhile bribing with money the auxiliary Roman troops who were supporting Herod. Herod, however, went on winning over soldiers from his rival. In 38 a new invasion of the Parthians (§ 327) complicated the situation, and while the Romans were dealing with this, Herod repaired to Galilee to fight against powerful local brigands. These were probably supporters of Antigonus, or at least anti-Roman nationalists like Ezechias (§ 322). Meanwhile, Antigonus, farther to the south, defended himself as best he could; he succeeded also in defeating and killing Joseph, the brother of Herod (§ 327) who had been aided by troops in the service of the Romans. Other uprisings occurred against Herod in Galilee also. To bring the long war to a successful conclusion, Herod went to Antony who was busy with the siege of Samosata (§ 327), and obtained from him two Roman legions; after various encounters with the rebel nationalists and the troops of Antigonus, he besieged the latter in Jerusalem.

It was the spring of the year 37 B.C. During the siege Herod took care also to settle his legal position with regard to the question of the dynasty, and during a brief interval betook himself to Samaria to celebrate there his nuptials with Mariamne (§ 324). Shortly afterward Sosius (§ 327) arrived with a large army to help in the siege of Jerusalem. Yet, even after both forces were united, the besiegers certainly could not have had eleven legions and six thousand cavalry, plus the reserves as stated in *Antiquities*, XIV, 16, 1. The city, attacked from the north as usual, held out for almost three months before it fell, probably in June of the same year 37. The customary slaughter followed, intensified by the desire of the victorious Jewish party for revenge, and of the Roman soldiers for booty. Herod tried with partial success to put a stop to the disorders, and got rid of the destructive Roman legions as quickly as he could, sending them away with rich gifts.

Herod showed no mercy to King Antigonus. At the fall of the city Antigonus threw himself at the feet of Sosius and pleaded for mercy, for which act Sosius insulted him beyond measure, called him a woman, and had him brought as a prisoner to Antioch, to Antony. Herod however could not rest easy as long as this rival of his remained alive, for one day or another, given a change in circumstances, Antigonus might persuade the Roman senate of the justice of his claims. Money, therefore, and urgent pleas were poured out from Jerusalem toward Antioch, and finally, to restore Herod's peace of mind, Antony gave order to have Antigonus beheaded.

Such was the end of the last descendant of the Machabees who had governed Israel. He was the first king conquered by the Romans to suffer that fate at their hands (Strabo, in *Antiquities*, XV, 1, 2).

HEROD THE GREAT

330. If the title "Great" should be awarded a prince who, with little at his disposal, carried on an obstinate struggle in the face of extraordinary difficulties and attained to enormous power, Herod fully merits the title. If, however, there enters into the judgment a consideration of the means whereby that power was attained and exercised, then Herod can still be called "the Great," but only in irony.

He was a very complex type of person. Endowed with exceptional qualities of mind and body, he was insensible to fatigue, adept in the handling of arms, a good leader of soldiers, and capable of prodigious activity. In political questions he had a clear grasp on reality which, aside from any abstract ideology, pointed out to him where his practical advantage lay, and in the attaining of this, his steely temperament did not know the meaning of fear or distraction, nor was he ever hampered by any sort of moral considerations.

Herod's dominant characteristic was an obsession for power. Everything in him was subordinated to the power of his scepter and the glory of his throne. He had a family, he was a father, he had his human affections, but when his mind, driven by that fixed idea, was crossed by a fleeting suspicion of opposition between his affections and his scepter, he did not hesitate to kill relative after relative, son after son, in order to allay that suspicion. *Regnare necesse, vivere non necesse.* But his ambition was also lucid and calculating. If his scepter was threatened by someone higher than himself, Herod adapted himself to the circumstance of the moment, became subservient, prodigal, flattering before the higher potentate; let the threat come from an underling who could supplant him only by intrigue and conspiracy, and Herod showed himself without the mask, a maniacal and tyrannical inquisitor with sword in hand. The fixed rule of his policy was friendship with Rome, the evident *conditio sine qua non* of his rule; Herod never quarreled with Rome. But who represented Rome for Herod? First it was Julius Caesar, then Caesar's assassin Cassius, then his enemy Antony, then his rival Octavian. At first Herod was all for Julius

Caesar, then he transferred to Cassius, then reversed himself so as to be for Antony, and finally wound up siding with Octavian. Fickleness? Fickleness would hardly be the proper word for the times and the circumstances in which Herod found himself. It was rather due to political intuition which enabled him infallibly to pick the strong party; it was also the result of his mania for power, which led him to fill in promptly with the stronger man, even at the price of great sacrifices of money and personal prestige.

331. Yet such a man, cold-bloodedly Machiavellian in politics, was also violent and tormented in his private life. During his long reign the vicissitudes brought on by his burning jealousy had almost as decisive an importance as the political events with which they were in part connected. That he married ten wives is hardly surprising in a Semite and an Oriental despot; in any case the affection he bore for nine of them did not equal the love he bore Mariamne.

His marriage with Mariamne was undoubtedly dictated by politics (§§ 324, 329), but this was not the only reason, and perhaps was not even the principal reason for it. Herod's love for this beautiful and virtuous woman, in whose veins there flowed the blood of the heroic Machabees, was without bounds. In her presence this crude Idumaean must have experienced a sense of inferiority and embarrassment. He had desired her as his wife in order to establish family connections with the Hasmoneans, but along with her superiority in lineage Mariamne brought with her a physical and spiritual nobility, and her threefold excellence had made Herod her subject, for with his usual perspicacity he had appraised such a magnificent woman at her true value. Moreover, on repeated occasions Herod's deep-seated sense of inferiority was accentuated by Mariamne's behavior. With that dignity which seems born in a superior person, she on more than one occasion made all too apparent the enormous moral distance which separated her from her husband. Herod had understood, and was silent; his silence was that of profound humiliation. It was the disappointment of one who, though a despot in a political domain, suddenly finds himself, on a human plane, a humble slave. In men of Herod's temper, such a state of mind regularly results in tragedy, for eventually a certain point is reached when the man prevails over the monarch, and Othello takes the place of Machiavelli.

Was Herod a sensual man? Probably not, if we judge him according to the standards of ancient times. His ten wives are no more an indication of it than were the concubines of the high priest Alexander Jannaeus (§ 304). One episode showed his mastery over himself, although it might be that this too was dictated by his astute political sense. The famous Cleopatra, who had seen a Julius Caesar and a Mark Antony at her feet, had designs also on Herod during her sojourn in Judea (§ 337). Whether it was a genuine sentiment or simply a snare to compromise Herod before Antony — where a woman like Cleopatra is involved, both hypotheses are likely — it is certain, at any rate, that she made explicit and insistent advances to him. But Herod did not weaken; in fact, he played with the thought of doing away with Cleopatra once and for all, thus freeing himself, Antony, and the whole human race of such a woman. In the end he decided against so perilous a project. His resistance was undoubtedly strengthened by political considerations, but when his behavior is compared with that of Antony

Cleopatra.

(who also had sound political reasons [§§ 54, 326] for breaking with Cleopatra), Herod's superiority to the triumvir stands out. Cleopatra was not accustomed to such defeats, and both as a diplomat and as a woman thereafter despised him.

332. As king, Herod was an intelligent Hellenistic ruler, a seeker after magnificence and display, fond of sumptuous buildings and of the material modernization of his domain. The realm existed, naturally, to serve the throne, and not vice versa; when this service was guaranteed and absolute, little else mattered. Herod knew that he was not loved by his Jewish subjects, and being intelligent, would have preferred to be loved, but this being impossible, there remained for him the principle: *oderint, dum metuant*, let them hate, provided they also fear me. Politically prudent, he hardly ever offended the religious sensibilities of his subjects. He wished to gain their favor by completely rebuilding their Temple, but this was done only for reasons of internal politics, and was not a manifestation of his Yahwistic leanings; it simply fitted in well with his passion for sumptuous buildings. A Hellenist and a skeptic, while he was rebuilding Yahweh's Temple he was also putting up temples in Palestine in honor (*horribile dictu*) of the living Roman emperor.

Since ancient times, conflicting judgments have been passed upon this very complex figure, Herod, and traces of them crop up in our various sources. Today Josephus is practically our only source of information concerning him, but he was at times slavishly dependent upon his predecessors who wrote about Herod. The first of these was Herod himself; following a common practice he composed his "Memoirs" (*Antiquities*, XV, 6, 3). It is doubtful, however, that Josephus actually read these (although he refers to them); he seems to have known them only at second hand. There is no doubt that Herod's "Memoirs" were intended to be an *apologia pro vita sua*. In a similar vein there is Nicholas of Damascus' work, but however well informed this member of Herod's court may have been, he is quite too benevolent to be objective; Josephus drew freely upon his writings. Unfavorable to Herod were the works of Ptolemy (of Ascalon?) and of Strabo (since lost), both of which utilized authors who had preceded them. There seems too to have been some anonymous source extant which was also unfavorable to Herod, and it was used by Josephus. The rare rabbinical references to Herod are understandably unfavorable to him and often fantastic.

❋   ❋   ❋

333. When Herod saw that he was master of Jerusalem, rid of the Roman legions and without threat from Antigonus, he set about making his throne secure. Forty-five of the wealthiest followers of Antigonus were slain, and all their wealth transferred to Herod, who needed it badly to pay his debts to Antony. Fearing that along with these corpses, which were carried out of the city, gold and silver objects might also be secretly carried away, he ordered the corpses to be inspected for such objects. He then turned his attention to the Sanhedrin, and although he did not kill all of those who wished to condemn him in former days (§ 322; cf. *Antiquities*, XIV, 9, 4), he did decimate their ranks. In contrast, he was very kind to those who had been his supporters or had changed over to his side. He showered honors upon the two Pharisee leaders, Pollio and Sameas (§ 322), because during the siege they had counseled yielding the city to him. The people were in the power of the Pharisees, and so were hostile toward Herod, but it is probable that the counsel of the two men had done much to lessen these hard feelings, and, as a consequence, to limit Herod's revenge. The Sadducees of the sacerdotal faction who were loyal to the Hasmoneans were slaughtered in larger numbers, and the forty-five wealthy victims may have been of this group.

Herod kept a watchful eye upon the survivors of the supplanted dynasty of the Hasmoneans. Of the men, there remained the old man Hyrcanus II, now living in Babylonia, and the brother-in-law of Herod himself, Aristobulus (§ 328), who was sixteen years of age. There was, therefore, no immediate threat to the throne from this quarter, but Herod was not entirely at ease about Hyrcanus, who had once held the highest power and was now outside his jurisdiction. He resolved to have him brought back home, where he could watch him more closely and prevent the Jews of Babylonia, who held him in great esteem (§ 327), from attempting to do anything in his behalf. And in fact, by letters and gifts to the Parthians, Herod succeeded in having Hyrcanus sent back to Jerusalem, where he received him with great marks of respect, at least in the beginning. Hyrcanus could no longer hold the office of high priest because of his mutilated condition (§ 326), and Herod, who was of Idumaean descent and wished to avoid irritating the people by himself assuming this position, summoned an obscure member of a priestly family from Babylonia and made him the high priest. His name was Ananel.

334. This choice meant that Herod had set aside the Hasmonean Aristobulus, his brother-in-law, for the obvious reason that he did not want him to be too much in the limelight; Herod, of course, could always justify himself by arguing that a boy of sixteen was entirely too immature for so great a responsibility. But at this point feminine jealousies and dynastic quarrels began to break out, and from that time on were to cause Herod more anxiety and trouble than had the triumvirate of Rome. Herod's mother-in-law, Alexandra, mother of Mariamne and Aristobulus, protested against this exclusion of her son; in fact, she really wanted to exercise official control in court over the actions of Herod, as a queen mother usually did in an oriental court (Vol. I, §§ 460, 467), especially since in her judgment Herod's power derived from the dynastic rights of the Hasmoneans. She was, furthermore, extremely proud of the exceptional beauty of her two children, Mariamne and Aristobulus. It seems that like his sister, Herod's wife (§ 331), Aristobulus was very comely.

Herod, of course, was deaf to Alexandra's protests. Then the woman — for in this she does not deserve the name of mother — conceived an infamous plan. She thought to win Antony over by playing on his notorious proclivities, and through Dellius, a friend of Antony, had her beautiful children brought to his attention; she also saw to it that a picture of them reached Antony. (The Hellenistic custom regarding personal portraits is noteworthy here; traditionally, the Jews prohibited them.) Antony was very circumspect, however, and would not consent to have the wife of Herod come to him, proposing only that Aristobulus be sent. Herod, under pretext of domestic policy, forbade the youth to depart, and shortly thereafter put an end to the pressure which was exerted on him from all sides, by appointing Aristobulus as high priest. A very bad sign, indeed, when Herod yielded.

The Jericho of Herod: to the right beyond the ruins, the place where
Aristobulus was drowned.

Suspected of intrigue to gain the throne for her son, Alexandra was
subjected to a surveillance so strict that it soon became intolerable;
she decided to seek refuge in Egypt with Cleopatra, with whom she
was already in touch. Mother and son were hidden in two coffins,
but Herod was apprised of this in time and caught them in the act. This
time also he was clement and did not punish. Another bad sign, that,
when Herod did not punish.

335. The quarrel was concentrated on the son, for Herod thought of
the mother only as an annoying and troublesome woman. Then, unfortunately for the young man who was already so compromised, it
happened that, the first time he pontificated, i.e., on the feast of
Tabernacles in 35 B.C., he was welcomed with great acclaim by the
people, who saluted in him the heir of the Machabees. Perhaps there
came to their minds that same feast day in 152 B.C., when Jonathan
Machabeus had pontificated for the first time (§ 274). At any rate the
political implications of the acclamation hastened the carrying out of
the sentence which Herod had already decided upon for the ill-starred
youth: this idolatrous Hasmonean should no longer live. But everything
was done in such a way as not to implicate Herod. A few days
after the feast, Herod and his court took part in a little feast prepared
by Alexandra near Jericho, and the young priest was feted with especial
cordiality by his brother-in-law, the ruler. It was hot, however, and
many sought refreshment in the spacious pools which surrounded the
palace. Their swimming skill was admired and various contests were
organized. The young priest was also invited to enter the water, and
because he was not very sure of himself he would be watched over

by expert swimmers. The "expert swimmers" approached him, accompanied him, watched over him, and then — unfortunately — held him under water so long that he drowned.[1]

How great was Herod's sorrow when the sad news reached him! He lamented and wept over his brother-in-law almost as much as the boy's mother Alexandra and his sister Mariamne, and then gave him a most solemn funeral. And then, as there was nothing else that could be done, he reappointed Ananel (§ 333) as high priest.

Not even Herod believed that others were taken in by his actions or absolved him from blame for the crime; however, that was the official version of it, and he played his part. But he quickly set a watch on Alexandra, who from that moment on thought only of revenge and turned again to Cleopatra. Cleopatra signified her willingness to injure Herod, for she had more than a vague desire for his territories, and worked upon Antony to such an extent that when he returned from Armenia he called Herod to Laodicea to stand trial for his action.

336. It was the spring of 34 B.C. Herod dared not disobey the command of Antony, and realizing perfectly well the gravity of the situation, and that his journey to Laodicea might be without return, he made arrangements in Jerusalem to cover even the eventuality of his own death. What worried him most was not the death of Aristobulus, for that would have meant absolutely nothing to Antony, but rather Cleopatra's desire to annex Palestine and, further, a well-founded fear that his wife Mariamne had begun to occupy Antony's mind. Before departing, therefore, he set up as regent his uncle Joseph, who was governor of Idumaea and also his brother-in-law, for he had married Herod's sister, Salome. To him he also entrusted the custody of Mariamne, at the same time giving him a secret order to the effect that, when it became known that he had been put to death by Antony, he was to kill her, to prevent her from falling into the hands of the Roman.

Despite his dire forebodings, Herod was fortunate at Laodicea, where his ability and his money settled the matter in his favor. He suffered only one setback; he had to yield to Cleopatra almost all of the Palestinian coast and in addition the district of Jericho, whose palm trees and balsam groves the romantic Egyptian loved so much. But Herod liked these things also and continued to enjoy them, although he had to pay Cleopatra for the privilege. Moreover he assumed the burden of collecting tribute for her from some districts of the Nabatean Arabs, which Cleopatra had obtained at that time also.

337. Conversely, affairs went badly at Jerusalem. While Herod was at

---

[1] Thus the report in *Antiquities*, XV, 3, 3; the other, in *War*, I, 22, 2, which is somewhat different, is less probable.

Laodicea Joseph had confided to Mariamne and to her mother Alexandra the secret order he had received, intending thereby to furnish decisive proof of Herod's special love for his wife. One day, however, a rumor circulated in Jerusalem that Herod had been killed by Antony; Alexandra then pleaded with Joseph to let them seek refuge with a Roman legion encamped near the city, hoping in this way to be saved from the disturbances which would surely break out in the city; perhaps too she hoped later on to work on Antony through Mariamne, and thus obtain the throne. But almost at once letters arrived from Herod, stating that his affairs had gone well and that everything had been settled satisfactorily. Alexandra's project was then abandoned. Unfortunately for her, however, others had learned of it.

After his return, Herod was told of this plan by Salome, his sister and the wife of Joseph. She suspected that her husband was involved in an affair with Mariamne, and in addition, she was at odds with Mariamne and her mother. Mariamne defended herself before Herod, but imprudently let slip the fact that she knew of the secret order given to Joseph. This was enough to convince Herod of the "affair." Not daring at that time to take action against Mariamne, he had Joseph killed and Alexandra thrown into prison.

Cleopatra's passage across Judea, her meetings with and designs on Herod (§ 331), took place at this time. Bearing in mind the facts known up to this point, it is easy to understand her secret political purpose behind these attempts to compromise Herod before Antony, for the move struck at his weakest side. Nor should Cleopatra's fickleness be excluded from consideration. Herod's self-control is even more strikingly manifested here, after his recent painful experience with Mariamne. Political considerations undoubtedly stiffened his resistance, but who can say how much he was also helped by the thought of Mariamne, who in his mind appeared to be so noble, and at the same time so base a creature, for whom he felt at one and the same time a reverent affection and so violent a jealousy. He played with the idea of doing away with Cleopatra during her stay in Judea; was this suggested to him by political motives only or by a natural feeling of deep revulsion?

338. In 32 B.C. the rivalry between the two colossi of Rome, Octavian and Mark Antony, broke out into the open. Herod stood ready with his troops to support Antony, but was providentially saved from participating in this struggle against Octavian (for which he would have had to pay dearly afterward) by the jealousy of Cleopatra, who did not want him to gain new merit in Antony's eyes. She therefore had him sent to fight against the Nabatean Arabs, who had suspended payment of the tribute owing to her.

The war against the Nabateans which began in 31 B.C. at first went well for Herod, and he won battles at Diospolis and at Canatha; yet it was at Canatha that Herod was defeated when Athenion, Cleopatra's general, came to the help of the enemy. At that time a violent earthquake shook Judea, and thirty thousand persons were buried in the ruins. Herod fought for time, reorganized his troops, and in the end completely defeated the Nabateans, thereby acquiring dominion over them.

In the meantime, the battle of Actium (September 2, 31 B.C.) had decided the fate of Antony and of the world (§ 54). Herod quickly perceived that Octavian had become the stronger, and true to his political policy, passed over to his side. He proceeded to help in his final triumph, and joined with Q. Didius, governor of Syria, who had also become a supporter of Octavian, to block the passage of Antony's gladiators from Cyzicus to Egypt (Dio Cassius, LI, 7). In the spring of 30 B.C., following his usual policy of facing dangerous situations boldly, he presented himself before Octavian on the isle of Rhodes.

339. This time also, as on his earlier journey to Laodicea (§ 336), Herod was going to face the unknown, and again he decided to order his affairs for any eventuality. Hyrcanus was now old, but despite his colorless character remained a source of concern for Herod, because he might become an instrument in the hands of the intriguing Alexandra. Herod had him put to death, and to explain the killing, adduced the correspondence in which Hyrcanus had appealed to the king of the Nabateans for help and shelter. These letters had been composed at the instigation of Alexandra, but intercepted by Herod. Josephus reports the fact as found in the autobiographical "Memoirs" of Herod, but shows that he does not believe it, and sketches out another version of the charge against Hyrcanus. It is very probable that there was some such correspondence, but it was perhaps a forgery on Herod's part, seeking as he was a legal basis for the assassination of the old man. Hyrcanus' crime was that he was a Hasmonean, and also that he had long ago cited Herod before the Sanhedrin (§ 322), a "crime" which Herod had never forgotten.

Next he set his brother Pheroras up as regent, and sent his own mother and his sister Salome to the fortress of Masada for safety; because of the incompatible temperaments among the women, he sent Mariamne and her mother Alexandra to the Alexandrium, entrusting their custody to a loyal minister, the Iturean Soemus. In the event his cause should not succeed at Rhodes, Pheroras was to save the household of Antipater sheltered at Masada, and Soemus was to kill the two Hasmoneans at the Alexandrium. These were substantially the same dispositions he had made on the occasion of his voyage to Laodicea. Then he set out for Rhodes.

Site of Hippos.

At Rhodes Herod won Octavian over by his frankness. Not trying to dissemble his past loyalty to Antony, Herod gave his new master to understand that that same loyalty was his from that moment on, as he had been wiser than Antony. Antony's lack of wisdom was highlighted by a long tirade against Cleopatra, in which a spade was certainly called a spade. Octavian had already shown clemency to Antony's veterans, and had no reason for creating new enemies, so he accepted the services of Herod, and for the time being reconfirmed him on the throne.

340. Shortly afterward Herod prepared a splendid reception for Octavian at Ptolemais when the latter passed by on his way to Egypt. In addition, he undertook to provide provisions for his army for the march across the desert, and personally offered him eight hundred talents. This calculated prodigality had the desired effect. On the first of August, 30 B.C., Alexandria was taken by Octavian; shortly afterward Antony and Cleopatra killed themselves, and Octavian became master of the world. In Rome Horace composed on this occasion his famous and joyful *"Nunc est bibendum, nunc pede libero — pulsanda tellus,"* but in Jerusalem Herod must have danced with an even livelier joy, if for nothing else than the death of that viper, Cleopatra, who had schemed more against his kingdom than against his virtue. He hastened to Egypt to present his congratulations to Octavian, and also to strike the iron while it was hot.

So deftly did he strike it that he obtained from Octavian what he was looking for, the restitution of the lands ceded to Cleopatra: the district of Jericho and the coastal towns of Gaza, Anthedon, Joppe, and

Straton's Tower (Caesarea). In addition, he also received the cities of Gadara, Hippos, and Samaria, and a corps of Gallic soldiers who had formed Cleopatra's guard of honor. With these grants, and the good dispositions of the conqueror toward him, Herod's position for both the present and the future was at last secure.

At the end of 30 B.C., he accompanied Octavian from Egypt to Antioch, and then returned to Jerusalem.

341. But just as he attained the heights of his political career, tragedy began to stalk through his family affairs. During his absence at Rhodes, Mariamne and Alexandra, entrusted to the care of Soemus in the Alexandrium, had extracted from him the confidential order he had received to kill them in the event that misfortune befell Herod. There is little doubt that, since the situation on the occasion of the voyage to Laodicea was here duplicated, the women had rightly suspected the same secret instructions. Since things might go badly for Herod, Soemus sought to gain the good will of the two queens by divulging to them more than he should have. This time when Herod returned from Rhodes Mariamne did not tell him what she knew, but was very cool and distant to him. He had expected a different reception after the danger he had escaped. Added to the tension were Salome, Herod's sister, and Herod's mother, who could not bear the air of disdain with which they had been treated by the two Hasmoneans.

The rancor between the women grew during Herod's stay in Egypt, and so too did Mariamne's hostility toward the returning monarch. The lion-tamer so antagonized her love-struck lion that he began to work his claws. One day when Herod was more tender than usual and Mariamne all the more haughty, she dared remind him that he had killed her brother Aristobulus and her grandfather Hyrcanus. Herod flew into a rage, and his roars could be heard throughout the palace. His sister Salome saw her long-awaited opportunity, and while tempers were still at white heat, sent to the king a cupbearer who had been bribed to play his role. This man told Herod that Mariamne had charged him to mix a philter for the king, but not being acquainted with the drug which was to go into it (for Mariamne kept that herself), he had come as a conscientious servant to inform the king. Herod then had Mariamne's most trusted eunuch put to the torture to learn about the drug. The tortured slave spoke the truth, saying that he had no knowledge of any drug, but let slip the fact that Mariamne's estrangement from Herod went back to the day Soemus had revealed to her his secret orders to kill her in case anything happened to the king (§ 339). Herod now considered himself doubly betrayed, for he was convinced that the confidence told to Mariamne could only have come about from an adulterous intimacy. Soemus was soon killed; Mariamne was violently accused by the king himself in the privy council of the throne, and was condemned to death.[2]

342. Mariamne was speedily executed, chiefly because the implacable Salome convinced her brother that there would be tumults among the people if he procrastinated. Mariamne's mother, Alexandra, fearing that she would be included in the sentence, was so base as to reproach her daughter publicly for her harshness and ingratitude toward Herod, and abused her by pulling her hair. Mariamne, however, comported herself in a manner worthy of her Machabean forebears, and remained serene and dignified, facing death without flinching. She left behind her five children, three boys (§ 350) and two girls. The words of Josephus can be heartily endorsed: "Thus she died, a most excellent lady both for her chastity and her magnanimity; but she lacked moderation and had too much contention in her nature" (*Antiquities*, XV, 7, 6).

It was the end of 29 B.C.

Once the crime was committed, a most violent desire for his victim reawakened in Herod, and the executioner now became an Othello. He wandered through the palace shouting at the top of his voice for Mariamne, and in his madness ordered the servants to call for her by name as if she were yet alive. He then gave himself over to drink in an effort to forget her, but in vain. Next a plague broke out in the land, and to escape it and to distract himself he went off to Samaria to hunt, but there, weakened by the preceding strain, he contracted the plague and was at the point of death with serious mental disturbances.

When Alexandra heard of this she moved to take possession of the fortress of the Temple of Jerusalem, having in mind a probable succession. But shortly afterward Herod recovered, and it was not long before Alexandra followed her daughter in death.

A little later, in 27 or 25 B.C., it was the turn of Costobar, an Idumaean nobleman who had married Salome after the death of Joseph (§ 337). He was suspected of wishing to withdraw Idumaea from Herod, and then was accused of having for twelve years hidden the sons of

---

[2] The parallelism of the two episodes is evident, the one on the occasion of the voyage to Laodicea, the other on the occasion of the voyage to Rhodes. Hence it is possible that the two reports may overlap on some points (for example, Josephus states that Mariamne was guarded in the Alexandrium not only by Soemus but also by a certain Joseph, who seems in all likelihood to be the Joseph of the first episode); but there is not sufficient reason for holding that the two episodes are a double elaboration of the one fact. The repetition of the circumstances of the voyage and Herod's unchanging mentality, account for the similarity of details in the two stories. The account in *War* (I, 22, 3–5) differs from that in *Antiquities;* according to it, Herod killed not only Joseph, but also Mariamne, on his return from Antony. This account is certainly synthetic, as well as anachronistic (cf. Schürer, I, pp. 385–386).

The forum of Augustus at Samaria (Sebastiyeh).

Babas (or Sabba), distant relatives of the Hasmoneans. Costobar was put to death, and the boys along with him.

❋   ❋   ❋

343. In the wake of these killings there began a period of silence within the house of Herod, the silence of a cemetery. All the adult Hasmoneans had been put to death. That peace was to be disturbed anew when other Hasmoneans who were now infants grew up and, remembering their ancestors, took action.

During this long family truce, Herod acted more the part of a Hellenistic administrator and restorer of his reign, than of a politician concerned with foreign relations.

He had little to do with outside affairs now. Being a king, "friend and ally" of the Roman people, his territory was exempt from tribute and not subject to the burden of playing host to Roman garrisons. He had full power of administering both finances and justice in his state, and he had his own army, made up largely of mercenaries (Gauls, Germans, Thracians) and a handful of Jews. It was an army which the Roman emperor could use when it suited him. In his foreign policy Herod was obliged to conform to the views of Rome, and without the emperor's permission he could declare war against no one. His power in regard to the dynastic succession was strictly personal, and he could make no arrangements for an eventual succession without imperial approbation.

Shortly after 27 B.C., Herod lavishly rebuilt Samaria, and gave it the name of his imperial patron, upon whom the Roman senate had, on the sixteenth of January, 27 B.C., conferred the title of "Augustus" (§ 165). The splendid temple Herod built in Samaria was dedicated to Augustus, which reveals Herod's religious mentality, as well as the respect he had for the Judaism of Jerusalem, for he built this pagan temple outside of what was strictly Jewish territory. This concern diminished little by little. Around 22 B.C., he began the total renovation of the maritime city which had been called Straton's Tower, and which from that time on was called Caesarea, in honor of Augustus, as usual. The project took twelve years and was very costly, but the result was a splendid but decidedly Hellenistic city, equipped with a good port. There too was a temple in honor of the goddess Roma and of the divine Augustus.

344. At various times and according as opportunities presented themselves, Herod undertook many other works designed both for beauty and for strategic security. He renovated Anthedon (§ 302), and called it Agrippeion in honor of Agrippa (§§ 198, 350); he built Antipatris between Caesarea and Lydda in honor of his father; in honor of his brother Phasael (§ 326), he built Phasaelis in the valley of the Jordan, to the north of Jericho; and the fortress of Cypros near Jericho in honor of his mother. He re-enforced and adorned in an extraordinary manner the Herodium, the fortress wherein he was later buried (§ 364), this being the same as the so-called "Mount of the Franks" to the southeast of Bethlehem. He built another fortress of the same name in Perea, and he renovated and fortified the fortresses of Alexandrium, Hyrcania, Machaerus, Masada (§§ 306, 311, 316, 326, 371), and other localities.

Nor was his building activity confined to his own territories. It

Site of Antipatris.

extended also to other lands, both to compete with other Hellenists who had a passion for building, and to honor Augustus still further. Besides the two temples at Samaria and Caesarea, he erected another to Augustus at Panium (§ 39). It seems that these were not the only temples which resulted from his idolatrous adulation, for "after he had filled his own country with temples, he also poured out memorials honoring him [Augustus] in the province, and in many cities he raised up Καισάρεια" (*War*, I, 21, 4). The Greek term leads one to think more of a real though small temple than of a simple statue in honor of Caesar Augustus. However one might wish to see in these words a reflection of a source adverse to Herod, there must be some basis of truth in them; they show that although Herod was at first respectful toward Judaism, he later on grew less and less concerned about offending it. He also contributed to the construction of Nicopolis near Actium, designed to perpetuate the victory of Octavian Augustus, and to works in Ascalon, Tyre, Sidon, Tripoli, Damascus, Antioch, and Rhodes, and also Sparta and Athens.

Naturally, the enormous sums which thus ended up in foreign lands, and above all, this co-operation with idolatry could not be pleasing to the Jews, but Herod devised a very effective way of stopping wagging tongues. With an air of compunction and sadness he would reply that he did not do all this of his own volition, and hinted of "higher orders," the ready excuse of all bureaucrats (*Antiquities*, XV, 9, 5).

345. Jerusalem was certainly not to escape his feverish desire to build, and underwent a more profound transformation under Herod than any of the other cities.

Within the city, Herod built a theater, and in the environs an amphitheater and a hippodrome. In the first two, perhaps from 27 B.C., he fostered the celebration of the "quinquennial" games, in honor of Augustus. In these there were competitions of various kinds in which athletes, gladiators, and wild

Site of the fortress Antonia.

beasts all took part. Worst of all, ornamental trophies were hung up for display. Many pagans from the surrounding districts frequented the games, but the Jews were very critical of them, especially since they believed that the trophies hid idolatrous statues. This time Herod chose to use persuasion, and when authoritative witnesses were gathered on the spot, he had the trophies taken down, and the witnesses saw that the trophies were empty and were supported only by a stake. Many, however, continued to grumble, and a plot was hatched by about ten men, one of them blind, to stab Herod as he attended the theater. But the conspirators were betrayed by one of Herod's spies and were put to death; the spy in turn was killed by the people, and his body thrown to dogs as food, an act which led Herod to respond with other cruel reprisals.

Somewhat later, around 24 B.C., he built his royal palace, using in it a great deal of marble. It was located on the western side of the western hillock of the city (Vol. I, § 95) at the upper portion of the ancient circle of walls, and was defended by a semicircle of three great towers which Herod named in honor of the dead who were dear to him, that is, Hippicus, Phasael, and Mariamne. The pilings of the so-called "Tower of David," which today rise exactly on the northern limits of the palace of Herod, manifest the characteristics of the Herodian era.

The palace also served as a fortress dominating the whole western sector or "upper city." To dominate the eastern sector or "lower city" and especially the Temple, Herod had previously transformed the ancient *birah* (§§ 134, 218) in the time of Antony, and in his honor called the fortress the "Antonia." It was unusually strong, as is seen from the following description of Josephus: "The Antonia was situated at the juncture of the two porticoes of the first Temple [external court], the one toward the west and the one toward the north; it was built on a rock which was fifty cubits high and precipitous on all sides. It was the work of King Herod, and in it he again manifested the magnificence of his genius. To begin with, the rock was covered, from its base upward, with slabs of smooth stones both to ornament it and to deprive of a foothold anyone who attempted to ascend or descend it. Next, in front of the actual edifice, there was a wall three cubits high, and behind this there arose to the height of forty cubits the superstructure of the Antonia. The interior had the spaciousness and appointments of a palace, being divided into apartments of every description and for every purpose, including cloisters, baths, and broad courtyards for the accommodation of troops; so that from its possession of all conveniences it seemed a town, from its magnificence a palace. Although the whole was in the form of a tower, yet at the four corners there were four other towers; three of these were fifty cubits

The Fortress Antonia (after Vincent).

high, while that at the southeast angle rose to seventy cubits, and so commanded a view of the whole area of the Temple. Where the fortress made contact with the porticoes of the Temple there were stairs leading down to both of them, by which the guards descended, for a Roman cohort was permanently quartered there, and at the festivals took up positions in arms around the porticoes to watch the people and repress any insurrectionary movement.[3] Thus, the Temple towered over the city like a citadel, and the Antonia [towered] over the Temple; but in the Antonia there were the garrisons of the three [places: the city, the Temple, and the Antonia]" (Wars, V, 5, 8).

346. The most famous project of Herod, however, was the complete rebuilding of the Temple of Jerusalem. By this time, the venerable old building, rebuilt at the cost of many sacrifices by the repatriates of Babylonia, damaged by the Syrian and Roman wars as well as by the usual ravages of time, was an architectural anachronism in the midst of the sumptuous constructions which had lately arisen in Judea and in the capital. In renewing it from the ground up, Herod could give free vent to his building proclivities, and would file claim to a special title of glory not only in the eyes of outsiders, but also in the eyes of his Jewish subjects.

But viewing the project precisely in its relation to the Jews brought up some very thorny questions. Herod was not a priest, indeed he was not even a genuine Jew, and, on the other hand, his Hellenistic

---

[3] The presence of Roman troops in the Antonia refers to the times immediately preceding the siege of Titus, of which Josephus here treats. As for the term *troops,* the Greek text has τάγμα, which ordinarily means legion for Josephus, but a Roman legion is perhaps too much for the Antonia, and it may be that here the term (as in other cases) has the meaning of *cohort,* which was the tenth part of a legion and consisted of from four to six hundred men.

leanings, more or less idolatrous in this very matter of architectural projects, were widely known. No proof was forthcoming that the respect for the Temple shown by him up to that time was anything more than a simple dictate of politics. Everything led the Jews to distrust him on this point. He might very well demolish the old Temple and then not rebuild a new one; or he might rebuild it, but according to Hellenistic ideals, employing scandalous representations of men and animals so execrated by Jewish tradition. He might perhaps alter its site, its disposition, its measurements, things which had been settled by Yahweh himself. Lastly, who but the priests, the only ones authorized to enter into the "sanctuary," could carry out all the work of demolition and reconstruction? Would Herod, no priest himself, consent to let others do all the work, and never enter the interior to inspect their labors, limiting himself to paying the immense expenses?

It may truthfully be said that these difficulties, although only preliminary, were much more serious than the actual execution of the work. That Herod overcame them is certainly the best of tributes to his subtle understanding and his practical ability. The devil became a sacristan. He knew full well that the people believed he was some kind of a devil, and yet he so convincingly succeeded in urging his services as a Yahwistic sacristan that he was accepted in this role.

347. As was his wont, Herod faced the greatest difficulty without hedging. He, the absolute despot, acted this once in a democratic manner; he gathered the people together to explain his grandiose project. Nothing, he assured them, would be done without adequate preparation, and in nothing would he offend against the traditions of their fathers. On the contrary, the new Temple would not be of modest size and mediocre appearance, as was the one built in the days of Cyrus and Darius; as a matter of fact, it would be an exact reproduction of the Temple of Solomon in size but would exceed it in magnificence.

The unexpected project left his hearers perplexed, for the reasons already mentioned, and Herod realized that he had to dispel their many misgivings by deeds, not by words. He assured them that he would not remove a single stone of the old Temple until he had everything ready for the building of the new one, and then he set to work gathering enormous quantities of material. Ten thousand workmen were engaged in the work; one thousand priests learned how to build walls, and the other skills necessary for construction, for they were the ones who would have to work on the interior parts of the Temple, where no layman could enter. Everything was at the king's expense.

In the eighteenth year of his reign (20–19 B.C.), the work was started; it consisted in demolishing one part of the edifice and immediately rebuilding it. Liturgical services were never interrupted. Work on the "holy place" properly so called (Vol. I, §§ 391–392) lasted a year and a half; that on the atriums (Vol. I, § 393), by reason of the spacious dimensions planned, took eight. The whole work, therefore, was carried out in nine and a half years. However, as is usual in all large con-

Greek inscription from the Temple of Herod prohibiting pagans from advancing further under penalty of death.

structions, it was many more years before it was finished (cf. Jn. 2:20), and was fully completed only in the time of Albinus (A.D. 62–64), that is, just a few years before its destruction (§ 401). At any rate, nine and a half years after the work was begun Herod dedicated it on the anniversary of his ascent to the throne, and for the occasion offered three hundred oxen in sacrifice. But this celebration did not mean as much to the people as had the dedication of the Temple in the time of Judas Machabeus (§ 259).

348. The "holy place" strictly so called was similar in all ways to that of the Temple of Solomon, except that it was a bit higher. The external constructions were enormously increased in size. By means of substructures built along the slopes of the hillside, to the north, west, and south, a large artificially made area was obtained about double that occupied by the Temple of Solomon. In this area there were three courts, each one higher than the other, leading up to the "holy place." The first one, nearest the perimeter, was permitted to all, for which reason it was called the "court of the gentiles"; even the pagan

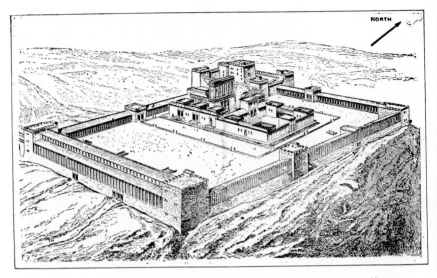

The Temple of Jerusalem at the time of Christ (after De Vogué).

could enter there. But as one proceeded toward the interior, a stone parapet indicated the limit of advance for pagans. Greek and Latin inscriptions placed there reminded them that they were forbidden to pass beyond under penalty of death; one of these Greek warnings was found in 1871. Passing beyond, and ascending several steps farther on, one entered an inner court which was surrounded by very thick walls and was divided into two parts, an exterior one called the "women's court," for the Israelite women could enter it, and an interior "court

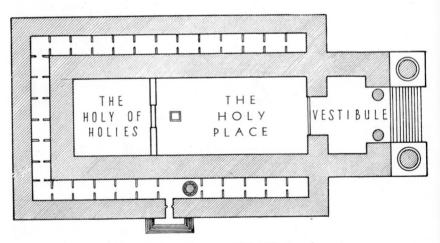

Plan of the sanctuary of Herod's Temple.

of the Israelites," so called because it was reserved for the men. A few steps farther and upward led to the "court of the priests," where stood the altar. A few steps beyond was the "sanctuary."

The "court of the gentiles" was flanked on two sides by two porticoes. The eastern one overlooked the torrent of Cedron (Vol. I, § 95 ff.) and was called the "portico of Solomon" (cf. Jn. 10:23; Acts 3:11; 5:12). The two ends of the southern or "royal portico," touched the valley of Cedron (to the east) and the Tyropoeon (to the west). It was made of one hundred and sixty-two columns, capped by Corinthian capitals of fine workmanship. The columns were so large in circumference that three men together could not reach around them. They were arranged in four rows, so as to form three aisles. This "royal porch" was most sumptuous, "a work deserving to be mentioned more than any other under the sun" (*Antiquities*, XV, 11, 5). Aside from the mention of the sun — which was probably an imitation of the famous example of Horace (*Carmen saecul.*, 9–12) — there is no doubt that it was a remarkable architectural achievement. However, it was clearly Hellenistic, of a type which could be found by the hundreds in the various cities of Italy, Greece, and Asia Minor, and which served as a meeting place for the public. It contained nothing, therefore, that was typically Jewish in character, and still less anything that pertained to the Yahwistic religion; it was simply tacked on to the Temple of Yahweh and had no conceptual connection with it. It was, in a word, the architectural counterpart of all that Herod stood for in the moral order.

349. There was no violation of Jewish traditions in the building of the Temple. Among the ornamental motifs, a vine of gold with enormous pendant clusters of grapes was very conspicuously displayed over the gates of the sanctuary; but nowhere were there any representations of living beings such as were forbidden by common tradition. Later on, an incidental remark reveals that a large golden eagle (*Antiquities*, XVII, 6, 2) had been put up over the main gate of the Temple, which of course provoked the most vehement protests from the Pharisees and from the people (§ 359). When and why Herod committed such an imprudence as this is not known; it was done, probably, only after the work was finished, and the solemn dedication over. That Herod intended to allude to his own apotheosis by this emblem, according to a widespread custom of pagan courts, has been advanced recently, but perhaps without sufficient reason.

❋   ❋   ❋

350. Herod's energy was not exhausted by his building activities. In 25 B.C., eager as always to win the good esteem of Rome, he dispatched

five hundred men to help in an expedition which Aelius Gallus conducted unsuccessfully in Arabia. In the same year, Palestine was visited by a serious famine, accompanied by the usual pestilence; this lasted until the following year. On this perhaps unique occasion Herod was humanly great for although he was deprived by circumstances of the regular tribute, he broke into pieces and sold the golden objects he had in his palace in order to get food from Petronius, governor of Egypt, and did as much as he could to supply the necessities of his subjects. Not however without political purpose.

M. Vipsanius Agrippa.

In 23 B.C. he sent the sons of the deceased Mariamne, Alexander and Aristobulus (§ 342), to be educated in Rome; thirteen and twelve years of age respectively, they were accompanied by a third young boy who died at Rome (*War*, I, 22, 2). There they were welcomed by Asinius Pollio and treated with special kindness by Augustus. On that occasion, Herod obtained from the Emperor also an increase in territory with the annexation of Batanea, Trachonitis, and Auranitis (Vol. I, § 66). Later on, when Augustus came to Syria in 20 B.C., he granted Herod the territory of the recently deceased Zenodorus also; it included the region of Panium (§ 39) and other districts near Lake el-Hule (Vol. I, § 61). At this same time, Augustus appointed Pheroras as tetrarch of Perea. Pleased with these and other proofs of friendship given him by Augustus, Herod condoned a third part of the tribute due him from his subjects, in this way hoping to quiet their ever growing dissatisfaction.

About 18 B.C. Herod visited Italy either to consult with Augustus or to bring his sons home after their education in Rome. In 15 B.C. he was visited in Jerusalem by M. Vipsanius Agrippa (§ 344), son-in-law and first collaborator of Augustus, who had been for some time a close friend of Herod. The guest, of course, was received with the highest honors, and well-disposed as he was in regard to the

Hebrew religion, offered a hecatomb in the Temple. Other proofs of Agrippa's benevolence were given in the following year, when he received Herod after he (Herod) completed various missions at Sinope in Pontus. On that occasion, Agrippa, at Herod's request, confirmed and guaranteed to the Jewish diaspora of Jonias the tranquil enjoyment of its privileges. Herod was content with the successes he obtained during his voyage, and upon his return home, remitted a fourth part of the tribute due him from his subjects.

351. At this time, however, there began again those family difficulties which were to reopen the door on tragedy and slaughter. The opening wedge was driven, of course, by the Hasmoneans. Herod had given wives to the two sons whom he had shepherded home from Rome. To Alexander was given Glaphyra, daughter of Archelaus, king of Cappadocia; to Aristobulus, Bernice, the daughter of Salome, Herod's influential sister. But these two sons of the Hasmonean Mariamne had inherited from their mother not only her fine physical appearance — which made them especially dear to Herod — but also her haughtiness and disdain. The liberal education they had received in Rome had given them a freedom of manner which little suited an oriental court, and especially the suspicious court of Herod. From the outset they let it be known at court that they often thought with great bitterness about the manner in which their mother had died; they thought too about those who had been the perpetrators of that death, and about the dynastic advantage which had resulted from it — for interested parties. From the imprudent words of the young men it was apparent that they contained not only a remembrance of the past, but also some kind of a threat for the future, as if they would one day demand an accounting of all those involved. All this must have taken place during the absence of Herod, who was on a journey with Agrippa.

At court, however, there was Herod's *alter ego*, Salome, obsessed no less violently than her brother by the authority of her own family, and the instigator of the assassinations of her husbands Joseph and Costobar (§ 342), and of Mariamne, for the sake of the dynasty. Her natural suspiciousness was now transformed into real alarm, for she fully realized that responsibility for the death of Mariamne lay on her shoulders, and felt that she was being directly threatened by the remarks of the young men. She openly broke with them. By way of compensation she leaned directly on her brother Pheroras for support, and with two Idumaeans on the one side, and two Hasmoneans on the other, there arose a succession of jealousies, rivalries, and grudges which, in a court like Herod's, fell upon well-prepared ground.

352. On returning from his trip, Herod was informed of everything by Salome and Pheroras, who represented the affair to him as a full-blown conspiracy against the throne. This struck at the despot's weak spot, and his obsession for the scepter prevailed over his paternal predilection for Mariamne's sons. First, however, he took a clever precaution. His first wife Doris had borne him a son, Antipater (§ 324), whom he had sent away from court. After the accusation of the Hasmoneans he had Antipater return, and set him up as a rival alongside the two suspected pretenders, intimating vaguely to him that he might succeed to the throne. An enterprising young man, Antipater immediately became a spy on the two youths who were being watched in their father's house. They, in turn, reacted energetically, and so it was that the family split grew continually wider and gave imminent promise of new tragedies.

There was, however, one difficulty. At Rome Augustus had received the two young Hasmoneans into his court, and remembered them with affection. It would have meant Herod's own head to do violence to two youths who were under Augustus' protection. No other course was open to him except an appeal to Augustus himself, to warn him against the two youths, and to undermine his good will toward them. Herod made his first move, then, in 13 B.C., by sending both the new favorite, Antipater, and Agrippa to Rome, there to be introduced to the emperor, and turn the emperor's mind in his favor as against the Hasmoneans. Antipater not only acted in this wise, but from Rome itself sent letters of such a tenor as to keep the rivalry between the two factions of the Herodean court very much alive. In the following year, 12 B.C., Herod felt no further need of restraint and personally took the two suspects to Rome to accuse them before the emperor and ask him to judge them. Augustus was not at Rome, so he followed him to Aquileia.

A trial before Augustus ensued, in which Herod accused his two sons of conspiring against his life, more out of revenge for their mother than to gain possession of the throne. The king spoke from the depths of anger and certainly overdrew the picture, and the experienced Augustus, knowing the two youths, saw through the exaggerations. The two young men wept; Alexander spoke in his own defense and also for his brother, and the more he spoke the more convinced Augustus became of their innocence. Even Herod was deeply moved by this discourse, and much more by the thought that he was making a spectacle of himself in the eyes of all those present. He must have seemed to them a suspicious and vindictive kind of father, for these people were not endowed with the mentality of his courtiers at Jerusalem. Under these conditions, it was easy for the diplomatic Augustus to smooth over the difficulties and to reconcile father and sons. From now on, he counseled, there should be no suspicions on the part of the father, nor

occasions for suspicion given on the part of the sons, but only an affectionate bond of union between both sides. When he had finished, the
tears began to flow, embraces and kisses were exchanged, and everything was settled. Antipater, who was present at the scene, had to
feign an attitude of joy and to show it before Augustus. How could he
have done otherwise?

353. In the same year Herod was in Rome, something happened which
was to affect his foreign policy deeply. Trachonitis, recently granted
to Herod by Augustus (§ 350), suffered from a series of Bedouin raids
in 12 B.C., but Herod's troops gave chase and drove them out of the
country. Forty of the most powerful of the raiders took refuge in the
territory of Obodas, king of the Nabateans, where they were received
with favor by Syllaeus, Obodas' omnipotent minister. This man had
been Herod's friend and once was on the point of marrying Herod's
sister Salome; but the wedding
had to be called off when
Syllaeus refused to submit to
circumcision (§ 210). On his return, Herod demanded that the
raiders be handed over to him,
and also the repayment of an
old loan he had made to
Obodas. Neither demand was
met. Instead, the incursions into
Herod's territory were steadily
intensified. With the permission
of Sentius Saturninus, governor
of Syria, an energetic campaign
was waged against the Nabateans, who were repulsed with
the loss of twenty-five hundred
men. Other steps to insure the
tranquillity of Trachonitis
(§ 368) were taken. In the
meantime Syllaeus had gone to
Rome, and when the news of
Herod's incursion and victory
came to his ears, he presented
it to Augustus in such a way as
to make Herod appear as a dis-
turber of the *pax Romana* and
of the common security. Augustus was indignant, for he

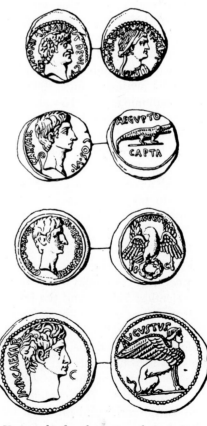

Various kinds of money of Augustus.
(From *Enciclopedia Italiana.*)

had not been informed of this war, nor given Herod the necessary permission to wage it (§ 343). He wrote him a violent letter, warning him that although up to the present he had treated him as a friend, he would from now on treat him as a subject. Augustus' anger was no mere flash of temper, and the ambassadors sent by Herod to plead his defense were rejected, despite their remonstrances.

Herod was terrified and — perhaps for the first time in his political life — convinced that he was ruined. Syllaeus continued to fan the flames at Rome, and as a result Herod did not dare to defend his own interests against the Nabateans, lest Augustus be irritated still further, but was reduced to accepting any abuse of his power without lifting a finger. Fortunately for him, Obodas died, and was succeeded by Aretas IV (9 B.C.–A.D. 40). Augustus was at first ill-disposed toward Aretas also, especially because of Syllaeus, who was plotting to obtain the throne himself. Aretas soon succeeded in winning the good will of the emperor and in obtaining recognition by unmasking the intrigues of Syllaeus. Herod seized this opportunity to re-establish himself in the good graces of Augustus, and sent a new embassy to Rome, with Nicholas of Damascus (§ 332) at its head. Having obtained an audience, Nicholas sided with the ambassadors sent by Aretas, to accuse Syllaeus, and succeeded without much difficulty in depicting him as an intriguer and a calumniator of Herod. He explained that Herod's alleged war amounted to a simple military march in which scarcely twenty-five men were killed, instead of the two thousand five hundred as reported by the lying Syllaeus. Moreover, Herod had acted as he did because of an unpaid loan. By his eloquent refutation of Syllaeus, Nicholas removed all cause for resentment from Augustus, who then restored Herod to his good graces and gave him a *carte blanche* to proceed against his sons Alexander and Aristobulus.

354. During this period the rivalries which had been smoothed over at Aquileia (§ 352) broke out anew, and because of them again Herod had turned to Augustus. Scarcely had the two young Hasmoneans returned from Aquileia when they were again enmeshed in the coils of the relentless Salome and the intrigues of Antipas and Pheroras, and on their part they acted without foresight and manifested little prudence in speaking. Naturally their words, maliciously altered, were reported by zealous spies to Salome, and through her reached Herod's ears. Among the spies is to be numbered, perhaps unwittingly, Salome's daughter, the wife of Aristobulus, Bernice (§ 351). At the prompting of her mother she divulged the secret confidences of her husband. Glaphyra, too, the wife of Alexander and proud of her royal descent, was the occasion of other dissensions. In order to fan the mutual hatred between Herod and Alexander, Pheroras one day revealed to Alexander that Herod was secretly in love with Glaphyra, a sordid affair all too common in an oriental court.

For once, however, Herod put all to silence, sharply reproving Pheroras and Salome. Then came the turn of the three trusted eunuchs of Herod. Falling under suspicion they were put to the torture, and confessed that they were in league with Alexander. This discovery generated in Herod a veritable frenzy of suspicions. Distrusting now even his most faithful friends, he put many to the torture and to death.

After extorting other denunciations from those tortured on the rack at the suggestion of Antipater, Herod threw Alexander into prison. He promptly defended himself by accusing others, and calumnies, denunciations, and countercharges were hurled about with abandon. In the dark mood caused by his obsession Herod did not neglect one of them, but believed them all because he suspected everyone. Josephus is perfectly right when he depicts the old despot as a man tormented day and night by his obsession of treachery, and living in a state of paranoiac anxiety (*Antiquities*, XVI, 8, 5). After Mariamne was killed he exploded in passionate outbursts, in the manner of Othello (§ 342); now his frenzy for the scepter threw him into a savage paroxysm in the manner of a Macbeth, yet with this difference, that the Scottish king was drawn against a background of majestic fatalism, while this Idumaean king did not rise above the bestiality of a Caesar Borgia.

Meanwhile — and this is particularly noteworthy for a psychoanalysis of this old tyrant — he dyed his hair, and made out that he was an energetic young man. A wretched farce, to be sure, and not intended to further any romantic purposes, for in his position as a despotic king cosmetic remedies were entirely superfluous; it was just that his usual drive for power impelled him to masquerade in such a manner, so that even his physical presence would be that of a strong sovereign inspiring fear.

355. Amid so much depravity there appeared for a brief moment a man with a head and a heart, King Archelaus of Cappadocia, the father of Glaphyra and father-in-law of the imprisoned Alexander. When informed of the state of affairs, he came to visit Herod and with much tact and intelligence persuaded Herod to make peace with Alexander and Pheroras. But this ray of sunshine was of short duration, and was obscured by the contrary activity of a Spartan named Eurycles. Coming to the hospitable court of Antipater and won over by his money, Eurycles repeated to him a few phrases of Alexander which could, if viewed in a biased manner, be interpreted as signifying a conspiracy. A short while later two of Herod's guards were discharged by him, and entered into Alexander's service. This simple acceptance for service sufficed to arouse Herod's suspicions; he had the two guards put to the torture, and in the depths of their agony they affirmed that Alexander had charged them to kill the king while they were out hunting, and to pretend that it was an unfortunate accident. The commandant of the fortress of Alexandrium was next tortured and accused of having promised the two Hasmoneans the surrender of his fortress. The torture did not break him, however, and he said nothing of any consequence, but a letter written in the handwriting of Alexander for the occasion was adduced, which showed that the commandant was guilty. All these moves had been planned by Antipater, who in his determination to provoke Herod to decisive action against the two Hasmoneans, had had the letter forged by Diophantes, an expert calligraphist. Although the forgery was discovered, Herod had Alexander and Aristobulus thrown into prison at Jericho.

For fear of Augustus, however, Herod did not immediately proceed against them. But when the old despot felt, hopefully, that he had regained the good graces of the emperor, he again denounced the presumed treachery of the two sons, charging his ambassador at Rome, Nicholas of Damascus, to obtain authorization to proceed against them. After pacifying the emperor, Nicholas obtained this authorization also (§ 353). The emperor, however, with his noble sense of fairness and that intuition of the *ius* which was deep-seated in a Roman, admonished Herod to gather together a regular tribunal at Beyrouth, to allow non-Jews to serve on it, and to pay strict attention to proven facts.

356. Augustus' admonition was observed externally, but its spirit was entirely frustrated, for the mixed tribunal assembled at Beyrouth was completely loyal to Herod. The father accused his sons with disgusting vehemence, and they were not even permitted to defend themselves. In the face of such fury on the part of the old man, all the judges with the exception of Saturninus, governor of Syria and a few others, realized that the death sentence was necessary. Yet Herod faltered, for Nicholas of Damascus, freshly arrived from Rome at that very moment, pointed out to him how bad an impression this execution would make in the city where the two had been educated. But soon afterward new accomplices came under suspicion, whereupon Herod ordered three hundred officials from among the populace of Jericho who had fallen under suspicion to be hanged, and, after that, Alexander and Aristobulus throttled at Sebastiyeh (Samaria). It was the year 7 B.C.

It was at Samaria, thirty years before, that Herod had espoused Mariamne (§ 329); now the monster on the throne, who had shed such scalding tears over his favorite wife, continued to lament over her while strangling her beloved sons.

Augustus, who had done what he could for the sons of Mariamne because of his affection for them, did not conceal his displeasure at the double murder. Macrobius (Section V) reports the following terse remark of Augustus: "It is better to be Herod's pig than his son." Pigs, which were raised in the Hellenistic districts under the jurisdiction of Herod, had never been killed by him, because he did not eat pork; but his sons were, as the present case and, later, that of Antipater testify. The nimble wit of Augustus was also manifested by the pun he used, for his jest was certainly spoken in Greek, in which language the word for pig (*hus*) is very similar to the word for son (*huios*).[4]

* * *

357. Herod had other sons by his other nine wives (§ 331) who survived the two sons of the Hasmonean Mariamne. In addition to Antipater, the son of Doris, another Mariamne of sacerdotal lineage bore him a son who was also called Herod; a Samaritan Malthace bore him Archelaus and Antipas; Cleopatra of Jerusalem bore him Philip; and there were still others. Archelaus, Philip, and probably Antipas were educated at Rome (*Antiquities*, XVII, 1, 3).

In these last years of Herod, tragic events followed closely upon each other. Antipater was now master of the field, and since he was already designated as the successor to the throne, he grew impatient and began to fret. To hasten the day of his succession, he became friendly with Pheroras who, because of his marriage with a woman of low caste, was now in disfavor with his brother Herod. The two won over other persons of the court, among whom was Bagoas, Herod's eunuch, and made preparations to murder the king. But the ever suspicious Salome suspected that something was afoot and so informed Herod. But meanwhile a complication arose.

It seems that Herod had previously demanded an oath of fealty from his subjects, but that the greater part of the Pharisees, following the example of Pollio and Sameas (§ 333), had refused to swear (*Antiquities*, XV, 10, 4). Now — between 7 and 6 B.C. — he demanded also an oath of fealty toward the Roman emperor, of whom he was actually only a local representative. This demand was certainly the result of orders from Rome, for about the same period — that is, about 4–3 B.C. — the citizens of Paphlagonia swore a similar oath to Augustus.

---

[4] This play upon words by Augustus is probably authentic, for he had a sharp wit and ready tongue. However, Macrobius who has taken it from someplace or other, has falsely linked it up with the slaughter of the innocents (Mt. 2:16), in which he reports that a son also of Herod only two years old was killed. This is rather too much to swallow. Here is the passage in Macrobius: "[Augustus] *cum audisset inter pueros quos in Syria Herodes, rex Judaeorum, intra bimatum iussit interfici filium quoque eius occisum, ait: Melius est Herodis porcum esse quam filium*" (*Saturnal*, II, 4). It is not necessary to insist that the slaughter of the innocents was perfectly in keeping with Herod's habitual mode of operation.

Six thousand Pharisees refused to swear this new oath to a pagan (*Antiquities*, XVII, 2, 4). Since the wife of Pheroras was a fervent disciple of the Pharisees, their refusal to swear the oath seemed tied up with the secret schemes plotted by Antipater, Pheroras, and their followers. As a matter of fact, under the influence of Pharisaic ideas, there was drawn up a prophetico-messianic project which centered upon the members of the clique: the kingdom would be taken away from the tyrant Herod by a Messias, who was soon to appear and who would cede it to Pheroras, his wife and their descendants, reserving the final authority for himself. The all-powerful minister and arbiter of all affairs in the new messianic kingdom would be Bagoas. Although the latter was a eunuch (§ 152, footnote), he would receive from the future Messias-King the power to beget children so as to have a regular line of descendants (cf. the messianic passage of Isa. 56:3–5).

But this rosy vision was dissipated by Herod's sword, once he was informed of the situation by Salome. Bagoas and the Pharisees who were most compromised were put to death; Pheroras was banished from the court to his tetrarchy of Perea. The Pharisees who had refused to swear the oath were obliged by Herod to pay fines; these were willingly paid by Pheroras' wife. Antipater saw that he was compromised, and arranged to have himself sent to Rome, to obtain from Augustus the necessary confirmation of the will of Herod appointing him heir to the throne. Even after his departure he kept in touch with Pheroras; and Herod, for his part, kept on the watch to see what he would attempt next.

358. Shortly after his return to Perea, Pheroras unexpectedly died. It was thought that he was poisoned, and servants under suspicion were put to the torture without proof of a crime being obtained. But something more serious came to light, namely, the full extent of the conspiracy woven by the absent Antipater against Herod, which the latter had only vaguely suspected; even the poisons to be administered to the king were found. The inquest was still in progress when there arrived from Rome a freedman sent by Antipater himself; he was carrying new poisons which were to be delivered to Pheroras, thought to be still alive, and destined likewise for Herod.

After these discoveries, Herod thought only of getting Antipater into his power again, of making him come back to Judea from Rome. Dissembling his horrible discovery, he then wrote him affectionate letters, inviting him to return as soon as possible for various political and family reasons. Antipater returned and was promptly handed over for trial to the new governor of Syria, Quintilius Varus (the same Varus whose death so delighted the Germans). He was easily convicted thanks to Nicholas of Damascus, accuser for Herod and with Herod,

Callirrhoe: sulphur springs.

and was put in chains. But inasmuch as he was the heir to the throne confirmed by Augustus, Herod took no immediate action against him. Keeping him meanwhile in prison, Herod wrote to the emperor. It was the year 5 B.C.

359. It was during this period that the old man fell sick and grew rapidly worse. He then made a new will in which he designated Antipas, the son of the Samaritan Malthace, as his successor to the throne (§369 ff.), Archelaus and Philip being discarded because of the suspicions insinuated by Antipater. Augustus was to receive one thousand talents, and his family another five hundred.

When they learned that Herod's illness was incurable, two prominent Pharisees, Judas the son of Sariphäus and Matthias the son of Margaloth, incited their numerous disciples to correct the numerous violations of their national laws by Herod, and to begin by wiping out the scandal caused by the golden eagle in the Temple (§ 349). When the news of the king's death was bruited about, some of the bolder ones pulled down and smashed the eagle in full daylight. Unfortunately for them, Herod was still alive, and when he learned of the incident, although bed-ridden in Jericho, he ordered the two leaders to be burned alive, put to death some forty of the perpetrators of the deed, and deposed the high priest Matthias because he had not prevented the outrage.

360. His condition, meanwhile, grew rapidly worse. From the symptoms described by Josephus it seems that he was suffering from a complication of diseases: a general burning feverishness; insatiable hunger; violent visceral colic with suppuration and emission of worms; swelling of the extremities; difficult and stertorous breathing. The whole picture leads one to suspect that he had an intestinal cancer complicated by diabetes, and perhaps other ailments. Herod had himself moved to Callirrhoe, or modern *Ḥammam ez-Zarah* on the eastern shore of the Dead Sea. From its hot, sulphurous waters he hoped to derive some benefit; at the first bath, however, he was overcome by a fainting spell, and had to abandon that treatment, which was too severe for his condition. He gave orders that he be carried back to Jericho.

361. The disgusting degeneration of his character became manifest as the corruption of his body advanced. Realizing that his death would be welcomed with jubilation by his subjects, he determined that on the contrary it should be the cause of intense sorrow. To that end he summoned many of the most prominent Jews of his whole realm to come to Jericho under penalty of death. When they arrived, he had them locked in the hippodrome. Then, with tears in his eyes, and calling on God, he begged his sister Salome to send his soldiers, as soon as he was dead, to butcher the men held in the hippodrome. Thus he made certain that his funeral would have the tears which it otherwise would lack and which he ardently desired.

In his minute description of this incredible fact, Josephus makes mention of a "black bile" which took possession of the sick man (*Antiquities*, XVII, 6, 5). The physiological description is accurate enough, but the historian, in passing judgment on this dying human hyena, must remember the thousands of corpses he had strewn along the path of his lifetime, and then will not find much difference between his life and his death. This psychological correspondence alone is sufficient to guarantee the authenticity of the fact (questioned by some, because in the glosses of the *Megillath Taanith* it is attributed to Alexander Jannaeus, the usual scapegoat of the Pharisees: §§ 300, 304). The bestial fury of this provision which is entirely in keeping with the character of Herod, dispenses one from seeking in it some political motive (as if Herod wished to take out of circulation all future enemies of his successor, as some have supposed).

362. The provision was not carried out by Salome, but by way of compensation another son was killed. Letters arrived from Rome giving Herod power to act as he saw fit against the accused Antipater. The dying man quivered with joy and seemed to take a sharp turn for the better. But the attacks of his malady were becoming more and more critical; and in one of them Herod tried to kill himself with a knife with which he was peeling an apple. He was prevented from doing so, and the women began to cry from fear. From his prison, Antipater heard the commotion. Hoping that it meant the death of his father, he urged his jailer to release him. When Herod was informed of this by the jailer, he found strength in his rage to prop himself up on his elbow in bed, to order his guards to kill Antipater. The order was immediately carried out.

In the tortured restlessness of his spirit, the agonized Herod changed his will still another time, this time designating Archelaus, the son of Malthace (§ 357), as heir to the throne; Archelaus' own brother Antipas as tetrarch of Galilee and Perea; Philip, the son of Cleopatra, as tetrarch of Gaulanitis, Trachonitis, Batanea, and Panias. Everything, of course, was contingent upon the necessary approval of Augustus.

363. It was his last act. Only five days after Antipater was killed, Herod himself died at the age of seventy years, thirty-seven years after he had been declared king by Rome. It was the year 750 *ab Urbe condita,* B.C. 4, between the end of March and the beginning of April. Some days before there had occurred an eclipse of the moon, which is calculated by present-day astronomers to have taken place on the night of March 13. A few days later it was time for the Hebrew Pasch, on the fifteenth Nisan, which in that year was April 11.

About two years earlier, in Herod's territory, Jesus Christ was born.[5]

---

[5] It is a very well-known fact that by placing the date of the birth of Jesus Christ in the year 754 *ab Urbe condita,* a mistake of at least four years was made. Jesus Christ was born before 750 A.U.C., that is, at least four years before the present era A.D.

THE SONS OF HEROD

364. The last will and testament of Herod was executed. Immediately after Herod's death, Archelaus was recognized as king by the family and was acclaimed by the army. As king, he took charge of the funeral arrangements for his father and they proved to be most sumptuous. Herod's corpse was placed on a bier of gold inlaid with gems; surrounded by relatives, followed by the army of mercenaries and five hundred slaves bearing spices, it was carried to the fortress Herodium, which Herod himself had chosen to be his sepulcher (§ 344).

Once Herod was buried, it seemed that the unity of his realm which he had so desired to preserve was buried in the tomb with him. His last will, with its disposition of the realm and assignation of tetrarchies (§ 362), did not aim at a partition, but only at a subordination of powers. The brothers tetrarchs were to be subordinates, co-operating with King Archelaus in the same way that Pheroras had been subordinate to Herod himself (§ 350). But things did not turn out as planned. It should have been foreseen that, given the great rivalries in the family of the court and the hostility of the people, there was no chance for them to succeed.

At any rate, the one factor essential to the carrying out of Herod's wishes was the approval of Augustus, for without this the will had no value. Archelaus at once began thinking about going to Rome to obtain it. Then about eighteen years of age, he had influential friends in the city where he had been educated, and seemed to have the unanimous backing of the members of his family. Everything augured well. Yet for the sake of prudence he would not accept the title of king, nor take the diadem offered to him by the soldiers, as he wished to appear to defer to Augustus. On the other hand, he desired to establish contact with the people and to dispose them favorably before he departed.

But here his troubles began. When he had gone to Jerusalem for the Pasch, which drew enormous crowds from all quarters of the kingdom,

THE HERODS

(Capitalized names are those mentioned in New Testament;
d. = died or daughter; ex. = executed; k. = king; m. = married.)

Antipater,
Governor of Idumaea (§ 309)
Antipater,
Procurator of Judea, d. 43 B.C.

Phasael, d. 40 B.C.	HEROD THE GREAT 74–4 B.C. married	Joseph, d. 38 B.C.	Pheroras, d. 5 B.C.	Salome, d. A.D. 10

Doris	Mariamne, grand-d. of Hyrcanus II, ex. 29 B.C.	Mariamne, d. of Simon the high priest	Malthace, a Samaritan	Cleopatra of Jerusalem

Antipater, ex. 4 B.C. | | PHILIP m. Herodias | ARCHELAUS   HEROD ANTIPAS m. Herodias, wife of Philip | Olympias

PHILIP, Tetrarch, m. Salome

Aristobulus m. Bernice, d. Salome; ex. 7 B.C.	Alexander m. Glaphyra, ex. 7 B.C.	Salampsio m. Phasael	Cypros	

Alexander   Tigranes   SALOME
m. Philip,
Tetrarch

AGRIPPA I, d. A.D. 44	HERODIAS m. Philip, m. H. Antipas	Aristobulus m. Jotape	Herod, k. of Chalcis, m. Bernice; d. A.D. 48	

AGRIPPA II, d. A.D. 100	Mariamne	BERNICE m. Herod, k. Chalcis; m. Polemon, k. Cilicia	DRUSILLA m. Azizus, k. Emesa; m. Felix, Procurator of Judea	Drusus	Tigranes V, k. of Armenia

Agrippa,   Alexander,
d. A.D. 79   k. of Cilicia

the popular hatred of Herod so long repressed began to manifest itself. Archelaus was asked to cancel some of the taxes and other tributes, and this he granted, promising many more benefits after he returned from Rome. There came to him then the Pharisees, the most tenacious partisans in the feud, to demand the deaths of the counselors of Herod at whose instigation the destroyers of the golden eagle and the two leaders who were behind them were executed (§ 359). The request seemed unreasonable to Archelaus, and he refused. The Pharisees were persistent and proceeded to barricade themselves in the court of the Temple. A small detachment of troops was sent to recall them to their senses, but the soldiers were ill-treated and driven off. At this, all available troops were called in and overcame all resistance.

Three thousand Jews were killed in the Temple and nearby areas. A very bad start for the new king, from the viewpoint of the Pharisees.

365. After this, Archelaus named his brother Philip regent, and departed for Rome with Salome,[1] but shortly afterward Antipas also departed to oppose the projects of Archelaus. Meanwhile, Palestine had not calmed down although Archelaus had quelled the resistance at the cost of three thousand Jewish lives. In fact, Varus, governor of Syria (§ 358), had to intervene to guarantee order, and, to make certain there would be no further disturbance, he prudently left a legion at Jerusalem. At the same time Sabinus arrived in the capacity of financial procurator of Augustus and protector of his rights. Because of his officiousness and personal greed, he did not keep the promises made to Varus to await the new instructions from Rome, and having entered Jerusalem, took up quarters in the royal palace of Herod where he began his exercise of fiscal control over the goods of the crown and of the Temple. He met with resistance, however, on the part of the administrators, who considered themselves dependent on Archelaus and Augustus, and appealed to their decisions. When new crowds poured into the city on the occasion of Pentecost, new encounters in the Temple ensued. Sabinus' soldiers were violently attacked and in serious danger, but freed themselves by setting fire to the porticoes of the Temple. This precipitated a slaughter of the Jews, after which the Temple was despoiled of its treasure; Sabinus appropriated four hundred talents as his share. This massacre and depredation enkindled anew the fury of the rebels, and when they were joined by the king's mercenaries, Sabinus was besieged in the royal palace.

Revolt broke out immediately throughout the whole country, long prepared for such an eventuality. Hatred for Herod was doubtless thus finding an outlet, but certainly, too, messianic hopes made them thrill with anticipation of an imminent liberation from the foreign Idumaean-Roman domination and the installation of a theocratico-nationalistic regime. In Judea two thousand soldiers of Herod's disbanded army attacked the royal troops; in Perea one of Herod's old slaves, Simon, set fire to the royal palace of Jericho and proclaimed himself king. A certain Athronges, a shepherd of Herculean strength, did the same in Judea, and setting up a regular government, ruled for a time by means of guerrilla warfare. In Galilee, Judas, the son of that Ezechias who had been overcome by Herod at the beginning of his reign (§ 321), came to the fore, took possession of the arsenal at Sepphoris and also aimed at obtaining the royal authority. Josephus

---

[1] The parable of Lk. 19:12 ff. should be borne in mind: *"Homo quidam nobilis abiit in regionem longinquam accipere sibi regnum et reverti."*

describes these rebels under the blanket term of "brigands," but for the Romanophile writer this term very often refers in reality to nationalistic insurgents (§§ 322, 329) who used substantially the same means of combating Roman and Herodian authorities as the Machabees had employed against the Syrians. It seems, however, that the insurgents aimed principally at the Herodians, and in general avoided encounters with the Romans.

366. Called on for help by Sabinus, Q. Varus came up with two legions and auxiliary troops. The repression of the revolt was ruthless. Sepphoris and Emmaus were burned and the rebels of Jerusalem disbanded of their own accord, but Sabinus, the cause of the explosion, dared not even present himself before Varus, who had two thousand of the rebels crucified.

Others among the Jews desired only to live in peace, and harbored no messianico-nationalistic fancies. A delegation of fifty men, seconded by the eight thousand Jews living in Rome (§ 196), petitioned Augustus for the abolition of the monarchy[2] and the incorporation of Judea into the province of Syria, so that under the administration of a Roman procurator they could live peacefully according to their traditions.

At Rome, in the meantime, open rivalry had broken out between the Herodian princes. Antipas and Salome had taken position against Archelaus, and each side accused the other of responsibility for the disorders in Judea, while the delegation which had just arrived asked to be allowed to do without either of them. Strange to relate, Augustus decided against the democratic solution and apparently against Roman interests by rejecting the request of the delegation; on the other hand, he did not confirm the provisions of the last will of Herod as they stood but, contrary to Herod's wishes, divided the kingdom into three parts. The better part of it comprising Judea, Samaria, and Idumaea, was given to Archelaus; the title of king was not given to him, but only that of ethnarch, with the understanding, however, that he might later become king if he gave a good account of himself. Antipas and Philip were made tetrarchs of the other two parts of the kingdom, as had been assigned to them in Herod's will. Gaza, Hippos, and Gadara were declared free cities, and Salome received, among other possessions, the city of Jamnia. The territory which was thus divided remained under the direct surveillance of the Roman governor of Syria.

With a noble gesture, Augustus refused to accept for himself the fifteen hundred talents left to him, along with other precious things, by Herod, and kept for himself only a few small souvenirs.

---

[2] See what follows in the parable cited above: "*Cives autem eius oderant eum: et miserunt legationem post illum, dicentes: Nolumus hunc regnare super nos*" (Lk. 19:14).

367. Archelaus (4 B.C.–A.D. 6). Very little is known of the brief reign of Archelaus. Josephus, our only source of information, did not have Nicholas of Damascus (§ 353), his principal source, to draw upon, as he had gone to Rome with the Herodian princes and died there about this time. The reign of Archelaus was cruel and tyrannical, despite the promises he had made to the people of Jerusalem immediately after the death of Herod, and to Augustus in Rome, when he was given the tetrarchy along with a warning that he act with moderation. He deposed in succession two high priests, Joasar and Eleazar, and named to that office Jesus the son of Sië. He repudiated his wife and married his sister-in-law Glaphyra, the widow of the Hasmonean Alexander (§ 351), who in the meantime had also married King Juba of Libya. This marriage between two people related by affinity might appear perfectly normal in Rome where Archelaus was educated, but made a very bad impression in Judea where Jewish law prohibited it. He rebuilt the royal palace in Jericho on a lavish scale, and farther to the north founded the city of Archelais.

During his tenth year of rule (A.D. 6) a deputation of Jews and Samaritans accused him to Augustus of tyranny. Augustus had thought his counsels of moderation had been faithfully obeyed, and was highly incensed to learn differently. Archelaus was ordered to come to Rome, where the emperor heard both his accusers and Archelaus' defense. His defense was so feeble that he was without further ado sent into exile to Vienna in Gaul, and was deprived of his revenues. According to Strabo (XVI, 2, 45), he died there, but St. Jerome (*Onomasticon,* ed. Lagarde, page 101) speaks of a sepulcher of Archelaus in the vicinity of Beth-lehem.

The territory of Archelaus became a Roman province (§ 374).

368. Philip (4 B.C.–A.D. 34). The tetrarchy under Philip comprised Gaulanitis, Trachonitis, Batanea, Panias, Auranitis, and, according to *Luke* 3:1, Iturea. Thus, his territory lay east of the Jordan River and extended from

Caesarea Philippi (Banias).

near its sources to the north, down to the Yarmuk (Vol. I, § 66).
These territories had been only recently annexed to Jerusalem, and
were the least Jewish of any part of Herod's kingdom. Pagans, Hellenists, and Syrians predominated there, but were everywhere mixed
with Jews and even Idumaeans. When waging war on the Trachonitian
brigands (§ 353), Herod had, in order to strengthen the Jewish element
of Batanea, settled there a strong nucleus of Babylonian Jews. These had
led a life of adventure and of razzias under the leadership of a certain
Zamaris, who built a citadel at Bathyra, became a powerful local sheikh,
and guaranteed safe passage to Jewish pilgrims coming from Babylonia
to the Temple at Jerusalem (*Antiquities*, XVII, 2, 1–3).

Like Archelaus, Philip was also educated at Rome, and always remained faithful to her. He had also the juridical mentality of a Roman,
and scrupulously followed it in administering his territory. He built a
city at Panion (§ 39), which he called *Caesarea* in honor of the emperor; it was commonly called *Caesarea Philippi* to distinguish it from
the other Caesarea on the sea (§ 343). On the northern bank of Lake
Tiberias, near the Jordan (Vol. I, § 61), he entirely rebuilt the village
of Bethsaida and called it *Julia* in honor of Augustus' daughter.
Philip was different from the other Herodian princes; mild and pacific
in character, he passed his life in the tranquil administration of his
territories without becoming embroiled in dynastic plots and without
suffering any such disturbances. His wife Salome was the daughter of
Herodias, the famous dancer who was rewarded with the head of
John the Baptist (§ 371). There were no children from this union.

After thirty-seven years of rule in his tetrarchy, Philip died, in the
twentieth year of Tiberius (A.D. 33–34). His territory was then incorporated into the Roman province of Syria. In A.D. 37 it was assigned
by Caligula to Agrippa I (§ 395).

369. Antipas (4 B.C.–A.D. 40). This is the Herod Antipas, referred
to on his coins simply as Herod, who figures in the Gospel accounts
of the ministry and Passion of Jesus Christ. His tetrarchy took in the
two parts of Galilee and Perea, but was broken up into two parts by the
confederation of the cities of the Decapolis (Mk. 5:20; 7:31; Mt. 4:25)
which was placed under the direct supervision of the governor of Syria.
To bring the two parts closer together, and at the same time to satisfy
his inherited desire to build, he restored and fortified Sepphoris (§ 365),
to the north of Nazareth. Directly to the east of Sepphoris but on the
western shore of the lake, he built Tiberias in honor of his great protector, making it the capital of Galilee and his own residence. A beautiful
city, Hellenistic in character, resulted, and it was populated by a population of a very mixed description. Jews who were observant about
the Law avoided settling there, as the city was in part built over a

Site of Bethsaida-Julias.

cemetery. In southern Perea, opposite Jericho, he fortified ancient Beth-Haram, calling it *Livia*, and later on Julia, in honor of the wife of Augustus;[3] this fortress was intended for the protection of the sector from the incursions of the Nabateans. At any rate, to guarantee even better protection against them, Antipas espoused the daughter of their king Aretas IV (§ 353).

"Go tell that fox . . ." Christ once said, referring to Antipas (Lk. 13:22), whose slyness must have been a by-word. This epithet has been interpreted (with little reason) as an allusion to his greed. He took possession of his tetrarchy when seventeen years old; like Archelaus and Philip, he seems to have been educated in Rome (§ 357). In character he somewhat resembled his father, for he was proud and loved pomp, but he lacked his father's industry, and it is in this sense that the phrase of Josephus which describes him as a "lover of tranquillity" must be interpreted (*Antiquities*, XVIII, 7, 2). His passion for Herodias recalls his father's love for Mariamne, but with this difference: his father was master of himself even when tempted by Cleopatra, whereas his son allowed himself to be led to political ruin by his passion. Despite his education at Rome, he certainly was not a skeptic in matters of religion. So far as his passions allowed, he conformed to the Jewish law and went

---

[3] Concerning the double name of the empress (and hence of the city), cf. Tacitus, *Annal.*, I, 8.

Tiberias and its lake.

to Jerusalem for the feasts (Lk. 23:7), but in his so acting there seems to have been a great deal of superstition and fancy.

370. Perhaps Antipas might have lived out his career as a mediocre oriental potentate and have ended up as peaceably as did the tetrarch Philip, had he not met his evil genius, Herodias. Although his relations with Augustus were always those of a simple vassal to his sovereign, Antipas worked himself into the good graces of Tiberias by acting as a spy for this suspicious new emperor, whom he kept informed concerning the Roman magistrates in the Orient (the enmity between Antipas and Pontius Pilate referred to in Lk. 23:12 was probably caused by the reports Antipas had sent concerning the procurator); it was perhaps because of his new political authority that, in A.D. 28, he went to Rome. There he met Herodias, the daughter of the Hasmonean Aristobulus murdered by Herod (§ 356). She had married the son of Herod and Mariamne of the sacerdotal lineage (§ 357), and Salome was born of this union (§ 368). Herodias' husband (Josephus calls him Herod, although in Mk. 6:17 he is called Philip) led a quiet private life, but Herodias was mindful of her descent and was very ambitious, and could not resign herself to so obscure a life. She met the powerful Antipas, and the combination of ambition on the one hand and passion on the other led to an understanding. It was agreed between them that Herodias would leave her husband and Antipas was to send away his wife, the daughter of King Aretas. But Herod's wife learned of this plan, and rather than suffer the humiliation of being repudiated, she managed to have her husband send her to Machaerus, whence she fled to her father. Antipas then married Herodias without further ado,

371. This deed caused a serious scandal throughout the land. It was spoken of with indignation, but secretly, for the sword of Antipas and the claws of Herodias made it advisable not to speak of it openly. But John the Baptist, who had great authority among the people (*Antiquities,* XVIII, 5, 2) and was highly esteemed also by Antipas (Mk. 6:17–20 and parallel passages), had the audacity not only to speak of it openly, but also to reprove Antipas himself for it. John was cast into prison at Machaerus and remained there about a year. His imprisonment was occasioned as much by his open denunciation of the royal adultery, as by the political suspicions aroused by his power over the people. Probably too it was to some extent due to the jealousy of the Pharisees (cf. Jn. 4:1–3). The prisoner was not put to death immediately for fear of the people's reaction, and also in part because of Antipas' sincere though superstitious veneration of John. Herodias, on the contrary, wanted as brief an imprisonment as possible, but, short or long, the victim could not escape her clutches. The evil banquet, during which the adulteress succeeded in obtaining the head of the austere censor thanks to the nimble toes of her daughter Salome, was probably held at Machaerus itself. The fumes of the wine, the sensual excitement, the point of honor involved in his given word to grant whatever the dancer might request, led the tetrarch to capitulate before Herodias. At her mother's suggestion the daughter asked for the head of the prisoner; bloodless but still warm, it was brought in on a platter and handed to the dancer, who in turn offered it to her mother. Holding that bloodstained platter in her hand, the adulteress felt secure.

Machaerus.

But she was mistaken, for there remained the Nabatean Aretas to be reckoned with. Outraged at the treatment accorded his daughter, the wife of Antipas, Aretas was looking for revenge. A border dispute in Transjordan provided him with his opportunity, and in the war which broke out in 36, he utterly defeated Antipas. The arrogant tetrarch then appealed to Tiberius, and the emperor, moved by the laments of his Galilean spy, ordered the governor of Syria to march against Aretas and to capture him dead or alive. Vitellius set out for Aretas' territory with two legions and auxiliary troops, but on arriving at Jerusalem with Antipas, news reached him of the death of Tiberius (March 16, 37). Vitellius, who hated Antipas because of a report which had revealed his dealings with the Parthians (on this point there are chronological uncertainties) had undertaken the expedition unwillingly, and now called off the expedition, returning to Antioch on the pretext that the government had changed. Antipas and Herodias therefore, already gloating over their revenge on Aretas, were left disappointed.

372. A more serious disappointment was yet in store for them, and again it was traceable to Herodias. The new emperor Caius Caligula was a fast friend of Herodias' brother Agrippa, who was then in Rome. At the beginning of his reign Caligula had made Agrippa king, granting him the territories which had belonged to the tetrarch Philip (§ 395). After some tarrying in Rome, Agrippa came to Palestine the following year, in 38, proud of his title of king, his friendship with Caligula, and of all his recent good fortune. At the sight of him in such glory, his sister Herodias burned with jealousy at the thought that her Antipas was a simple tetrarch and that in addition he could be defeated by a Nabatean king without the Romans lifting a finger to avenge him. In her boundless ambition she finally persuaded her reluctant husband to go to Rome to seek the title of emperor for himself, and to better his position generally. Herodias accompanied him. Agrippa, who naturally did not favor their proj-

Machaerus: ruins of the village.

ect, sent his freedman Fortunatus after them to present Antipas in a bad light before Caligula.

Fortunatus carried a letter from Agrippa in which Antipas was accused of negotiating not only with the omnipotent Sejanus against Tiberius, but also with the Parthians against the dominion of Rome, and of having amassed for that purpose arms for seventy thousand men. The three travelers met Caligula, then still in his first period of moderation, at Baiae, and the letter of the favorite, Agrippa, had its effect. Interrogated on the question of the arms, Antipas could not deny the fact (though the arms were probably intended for the war against Aretas or someone else). At this admission the emperor was convinced of Antipas' guilt, and in punishment he was exiled to Lyons in Gaul. Because Herodias was a sister of his friend Agrippa, Caligula was willing to allow her to enjoy her possessions, but for once she made a noble gesture and refused the concession, remarking that, as she had once shared in her husband's good fortune, she was now willing to share disgrace with him. Accordingly she too was sent to Lyons, and their goods, together with the territories of the tetrarchy of Antipas, were given to Agrippa. Although the meeting with Caligula took place in 39, it seems more probable that the deposition and exile of Antipas occurred some months later, that is, in 40.

373. The sight of the tray with the bloodless head of John the Baptist on it must have haunted Antipas continually. The people, according to Josephus, interpreted Aretas' victory as a divine punishment for that crime, but even before that defeat, Antipas had not forgotten his victim at Machaerus. He heard men talk of the works and the miracles of Jesus of Nazareth within his dominions and, with his superstitious and fanciful mind, he thought the new prophet was none other than John the Baptist come back to life (Mt. 14:1 ff. and parallel passages). Antipas greatly desired to see Him both because of what He was and because of His wonder-working powers, but the new prophet avoided meeting him. One day the Pharisees came to tell Jesus that Antipas wanted to put Him to death and that He should go away (Lk. 13:31). It is very difficult to see how this announcement corresponds to Antipas' real intention. His experience with John the Baptist had been politically too dangerous, and psychologically too serious for him to be disposed to repeat it. Some scholars maintain that the threat communicated to Jesus by the Pharisees was of their own making, to induce the unwelcome prophet to depart from those places; but it is more probable that it was, on the contrary, a scheme of Antipas himself, who wanted Christ to leave his dominions, as he was unwilling to take action against Him. If this be so, the epithet "fox" given by Jesus to Herod (§ 369) is well explained.

Antipas' wish to see Jesus was eventually fulfilled (Lk. 23:7 ff.). During the trial of Jesus the tetrarch was in Jerusalem because of the Pasch, and Pilate, hearing that Jesus was a Galilean and a subject of Antipas, sent Him to him. For Pilate this was a deliberate act of courtesy toward Antipas, for while he in truth despised him (perhaps because Antipas had reported to Tiberius on the way he discharged his office [§ 370]), it is probable that he now wished to come to an agreement with the annoying informer. Antipas was overjoyed at the meeting, and interrogated Jesus at length, perhaps expecting to see Him perform some of those miraculous works about which he had heard so much; but Jesus uttered not a word in reply. Although sorely disappointed, the tetrarch was unwilling to assume any responsibility for the accused, however manifestly Pilate's courteous gesture invited him to do so. He therefore left to Pilate whatever decision was to be made about his subject. It may be that this "resurrected John" aroused his fear. At any rate, the disdain of the oriental despot had to be made clear. He sent Christ, His silence still unbroken, back to Pilate, but clothed in a white garment, as fools were accustomed to be clothed.

One may wonder whether in later years, during the tedious exile in Lyons, that same bloody tray which was so indelibly impressed on his memory did not sometimes appear to him against the background of that white mantle.

THE ROMAN PROCURATORS

374. When Archelaus was deposed (§ 367), the territories of his tetrarchy comprising Judea, Samaria, and Idumaea came under the direct administration of Rome. In taking this step Augustus must have had in mind the wishes expressed by the delegation of Jews who came from Palestine after the death of Herod the Great (§ 366). He said to the Jewish people, in substance, what Porcius Festus would say to Paul: *Caesarem appellasti? Ad Caesarem ibis* (Acts 25:12).

When a region came under the direct administration of the Empire, it was annexed to one of the larger provinces. In 27 B.C. the emperor Augustus had divided the provinces between himself and the senate. He reserved to himself the frontier and less secure provinces where strong garrisons were stationed; but provinces in the interior which were tranquil and weakly guarded he had left to the senate. Hence, the division into *imperial* and *senatorial* provinces. The *senatorial* provinces were governed as of old by proconsuls (*legati pro consule*) chosen annually. The *imperial* provinces had Augustus himself as their common proconsul, and were governed by *legati Augusti pro praetore*, appointed by himself. These *legati* of provinces (ἡγεμών) usually belonged to the senatorial order. To some imperial provinces requiring especially delicate handling (Egypt for example), Augustus sent not a *legatus* but a *praefectus*. The procedure followed in other regions annexed after the establishment of the Empire, especially if they offered any particular difficulty, was to send a *procurator*, who belonged, however, to the equestrian order. The office of *procurator* (ἐπίτροπος) was originally a financial one, and existed also in the senatorial provinces, but especially after Augustus, the title *procurator* replaced that of *praefectus* in regions recently annexed (except in Egypt).

375. The territories of Archelaus which we shall henceforth call "Judea" for the sake of brevity, were annexed to the province of Syria, one of the most important *imperial* provinces, thanks to its geographical position. The annexation was neither complete nor total, but was rather a subordination of powers. A *procurator* of the equestrian order was sent to Judea as an ordinary governor with direct power, but in the discharge of his office he came under the jurisdiction of the *legatus* of the province of Syria; this latter had authority to intervene directly in Judea in more serious cases. The proverbial difficulty of ruling the Jews had shown the prudent Augustus the wisdom of such a subordination of powers whereby the ordinary *imperium* of the procurator might be aided or, depending on the circumstances, rectified by the superior *imperium* of the nearby legate.

The Roman procurator of Judea ordinarily was in residence at Caesarea (§ 343). On the great feast days, however, he often went to Jerusalem, which was a better center from which to exercise viligance and control. In both cities the royal palace of Herod served as the *praetorium*, as the residence of the procurator was called. In Jerusalem the procurator often carried out his duties from the fortress Antonia (§ 345), the military barracks.

As military commandant of the country, he had no Roman legions composed of *cives romani* under him, for these were stationed in the province of Syria, but auxiliary troops usually recruited from Samaritans, Syrians, and Greeks. The Jews enjoyed their ancient exemption from military duty (§§ 197, 320). The troops were usually subdivided into "cohorts" (infantry) and "wings" (cavalry). The over-all strength of troops in Judea was in the neighborhood of five "cohorts" and one "wing," making a total of about three thousand men. One "cohort" was the normal complement of the citadel in Jerusalem (§ 345, note).

As administrative head the procurator had charge of collection of taxes and various other duties. Property, personal, and income taxes were exacted from the country inasmuch as it was a tributary to Augustus, and eventually found their way into the *fiscus* or imperial treasury (the taxes from the senatorial provinces were ultimately deposited in the *aerarium* or treasury of the senate). To collect these taxes the procurator made use of state officials, who in turn were assisted by local officials. The other taxes were of various kinds, such as customs duty, import and export taxes, rental taxes for public buildings, market toll, etc. Here as in the rest of the Empire, the collection of these taxes was leased out by contract to financial agents (the *publicans* or τελῶναι) who paid the procurator a fixed amount, and retained as their profit whatever they collected over and above this amount. The employees of these financiers were the *exactores* or *portitores*. It is needless to say how much both the *publicani* and the *exactores* were hated by the people, and how many acts of tyranny and extortion occurred, especially if the contracts were sublet to others, as frequently occurred. The whole weight of the complex money-making system fell upon the taxpayer.

376. As administrator of justice, the procurator had his tribunal, in which he exercised the *ius gladii*, or the power to impose capital punishment. Anyone who enjoyed Roman citizenship could appeal from his tribunal to that of the Emperor; for others there was no appeal. For ordinary cases, the local tribunals continued to exist and function with full liberty. The chief of these was the Sanhedrin in Jerusalem, which had also preserved its legislative authority over the members of the nation. It was, however, deprived of the power to sentence anyone to death; more exactly, the supreme tribunal of the nation could actually sentence a person under its jurisdiction to death, but it could not carry out its own sentence until it was ratified by the Roman procurator.

On the whole the ancient ethnarchic order had been preserved. The real head of the people was the high priest, though his nomination and removal lay in the hands of the procurator, who took pains to decide according to the wishes of the most eminent sacerdotal families (toward the end the procurators ceded these rights to the Herodian princes: § 400). At the side of the high priest the procurator stood as a political superintendent and representative of the imperial treasury. If the sword of justice in the hand of the pontiff now cut off no heads, this was some compensation for the all too many it had caused to fall in the past. The right to inflict punishment by rods, and full legislative power, however, were still his. *Caesarem appellasti? Ad Caesarem ibis* (§ 374). He would not think of going to Caesar with empty hands, or of treating with him as an equal. Many another country would have desired annexation to the Empire under such conditions, in order to enjoy the benefits of the *pax Romana*.

377. It must be said that the Roman authorities consistently followed the rule of absolute respect for the local religion, and often even many local prejudices. On some occasions, to be sure, this rule was violated to a greater or lesser extent, but these political imprudences were quite foreign to the Roman character and were quickly disavowed and atoned for. The Romans even sought to take part in some of the traditional practices, to prove that they not only respected them but also were in sympathy with them. Thus, for example, offerings for the Temple of Jerusalem were more than once made by the imperial family, and Augustus desired that every day an ox and two lambs be sacrificed at his expense "for Caesar and for the Roman people" (Philo, *Legat. ad Caium*, 23:40; cf., however, Josephus, *War*, II, 10, 4; 17, 2–4; *C. Apion.*, II, 6). Special allowances were made for local traditions, and because representations of living things were forbidden by Jewish law (§ 349), the Roman soldiers who mounted guard in Jerusalem were ordered not to carry with them the standards bearing the effigy of the emperor. Roman coins (of bronze only) minted in Judea, did not bear the image of the emperor, but only his

name and those symbols inoffensive to Judaism (coins of gold and silver minted outside of Judea were also in circulation, even
though they bore the forbidden image; cf.
the *numisma census* of Mt. 22:19 ff.). The
cult of the emperor was not imposed upon
Judea, though in other provinces this was
a fundamental act of ordinary government.

Denarius of Tiberius (the
numisma census).

The one contrary attempt made by Caligula (§ 389 ff.) only confirms his
reputation as a paranoiac; at any rate the attempt was frustrated by the
prudence of Petronius.

All things considered, and without trying to gloss over the practical
difficulties especially under the last of the procurators, Judea under
the government of Rome had no reason to look back with longing to
the times of the Idumaean Herod the Great, and still less to those of
the Hasmonean Alexander Jannaeus.

☼   ☼   ☼

378. The Procurators From A.D. 6 to 41. The first Roman procurator of Judea was the equestrian Coponius (A.D. 6–9). Sent with him as
legate of Syria was the senator P. Sulpicius Quirinius, who, though he
did not belong to the patrician family of the Sulpicii and was born of
low estate at Lanuvius near Tusculum, made himself so valuable that
Augustus prized him as *"impiger militiae et acribus ministeriis"* (Tacitus,
Annal., III, 48). This legation of Quirinius in Syria began therefore in
A.D. 6; how long it lasted is uncertain, but certainly not beyond 11–12.
It is very probable that this same Quirinius had previously been legate
in Syria circa 3–2 B.C. The famous fragmentary inscription found at
Tivoli in 1764 (now in the Lateran museum), when compared with
that of Emilius Secundus found at Venice in 1880 (previously known
but in an incomplete copy which was viewed with suspicion), provides
sufficiently solid evidence for this preceding legation of Quirinius. After
Mommsen (*Res gestae divi Augusti,* 2a ed., Berlin, 1883, p. 125 ff.)
pronounced in favor of his preceding legation, it has become the most
common opinion, although the matter still awaits a definitive solution.

Coponius and Quirinius came to Judea to annex it to the political
organism of Rome. According to Roman administrative principles, the
basis of this annexation was a census which would reveal to the emperor, who took personal possession of the new territory, the goods left
by the deposed tetrarch Archelaus, and the demographic and financial
potential of the territory itself. This census, which under Augustus was
occasionally also taken in other places (in proof may be mentioned those
taken in Gaul in 28 B.C. and later, others very probably in Spain, the

periodic censuses of Egypt recorded in the papyri, the inscription of Emilius Secundus for Apamea in Syria; cf. in general Tacitus, *Annal.*, I, 11), was similar to the general census of the "Roman citizens" which Augustus in his *monumentum Ancyranum* declares that he had completed three times, in 28 and 8 B.C. and in A.D. 14. Thus, the two Roman magistrates began the census of Judea which was completed about A.D. 6 or 7;[1] of course they limited themselves to the territories of the suppressed tetrarchy of Archelaus, leaving the other territories, which were not then being annexed to Rome, alone. Galilee, for example, remained under Antipas.

379. The census aroused great discontent among the people, doubtless because of the economic burdens which it presaged, but chiefly because it was official proof of the slavery they were about to begin. It is not certain whether this census of A.D. 6–7 was made according to the Hebrew method, which was based on the place of origin of the families and the groups of relatives, or on the Roman method which — following the *tributum capitis* and the *tributum soli* — was based on the actual domicile of the individual and the place where he held his possessions. If the Roman system was the one employed at this time, the people must have been much disturbed, for they would view the new system as a violation of their national laws. If moreover their new masters acted so rudely at the very beginning, what might they not expect after a few years had passed?

One may well wonder whether the fifty prominent Jews who went to Rome to appeal to Caesar (§§ 366, 374) had not known of and foreseen this inevitable census. They perhaps knew that it would come, but they may have hoped that exception would be made for Judea. At any rate, the mass of the people must have been ignorant of it, or so vaguely informed that when faced with the harsh reality they were filled with dismay.

To carry out the census Quirinius asked the help of the high priest Joasar, son of Boethus, who had been deposed by Archelaus (§ 367). It is not stated in what manner or with what difficulty it was done, but the fact is that the high priest succeeded in making the people swallow this bitter draught, and the census was taken.

380. Amid the general capitulation there was no lack of men who

---

[1] However the famous passage of *Luke*, 2:1–2 is interpreted, the evangelist actually refers there to a census made by Cyrinus (Quirinius). Whether he here means this census of A.D. 6–7 (interpreting πρώτη as a comparative), or gives indication of another previous one made by the same Quirinius, is an old question which cannot be entered into here. At any rate, the evangelist knows about the census of Quirinius of A.D. 6–7 (cf. Acts 5:37). It is also certain that the census of 6–7 was not the one at the time of the birth of Jesus Christ, since in A.D. 6–7 Jesus was at least twelve years old.

refused to yield, and one of these was named Judas. A native of Gamala in Gaulanitis, he passed for a Galilean, and hence was exempt from the census. He became the leader. This Judas is not, it would seem, the son of that Ezechias who had rebelled under Archelaus (§ 365). Judas the Galilean came into Judea and joined a renowned Pharisee named Sadduc in advocating resistance to the census and to the dominion of Rome in general. Appealing to national patriotism they advocated a return to their ancient liberty and to religion, cursing those of their fellow countrymen who "would, after God, submit to mortal men as their lords" (*War*, II, 8, 1). Disorders and encounters led to much bloodshed, but in the end Judas was killed and his followers dispersed. No details about the affair remain, but as the nationalist rebellion was powerful and widespread, the suppression by the Romans must have been violent and ruthless. A quarter of a century later, Gamaliel would speak of it as of an object lesson (Acts 5:37).

381. The immediately important consequences of the movement captained by Judas of Galilee were far surpassed by the later and more permanent results. Judas' followers were Pharisees, and among them was a special group which was quickly differentiated from all the others. To these men the ordinary Pharisaism appeared to be diluted — too weak and inactive. Had not the Pharisees yielded to the exhortations of the high priest Joasar, and bowed their heads to the census? At best they had concentrated their hatred on the publicans, those representatives of the foreign dominion, and these had therefore become the object of great disdain. To the followers of Judas, all this seemed too little. Their aim was to be one hundred per cent Pharisees, both in their theoretical principles and in practice. The foreign domination was a disgrace for Israel, and it had to be shaken from the nation by aggressive action, instead of being borne passively while awaiting, as the ordinary Pharisee did, liberation by the Messias. No more compromise, no more laxity, but action! The whole nationalistic program should be undertaken not with prayers in the Temple, or by diplomatic intrigue, but with daggers in hand. The Roman oppressors called these daggers *sicae* and those who wielded them were known as the *Sicarii* (*War*, VII, 8, 1).

This name, which was of course assumed with pride, became common only in the last period, when it became all too clear that any uprising against the Romans was doomed to failure. They therefore decided upon individual action, on the sporadic activity of the conspirator. Hiding the *sicae* beneath their tunics, they struck their isolated blows against Roman officials and prominent Jews who were friendly to the Romans; their own disdain for death was supreme. Before this last despairing period of intransigence was reached, however, these absolute Pharisees were called by the general term of the "zealous" ones, or "Zealots."[2] In Yahwism the term was a classical one, for the aged father of the Machabees, Mathathias, had addressed this last exhortation to his sons on his deathbed: "And now, my sons, be *zealous* for the Torah, and give your lives for the alliance of our fathers" (1 Mach. 2:50). The followers of Judas of Galilee took these words of Yahweh's dying hero literally.

382. After the failure of the attempt made by Judas of Galilee, the Zealots remained, but dispersed and hidden. They may have become more ardent than before. In his inordinate desire to make the Jewish world resemble the Greco-Roman, Josephus treats the Zealots as if they professed a "fourth philosophy" (*Antiquities,* XVIII, 1, 1), the other three being those of the Essenes, the Pharisees, and the Sadducees; but this is farfetched. Actually, the Zealots were strict Pharisees. Josephus himself, shortly after, affirms with perfect accuracy that the followers of this fourth school "in all the rest agree with the opinion of the Pharisees, except that they have a most ardent love of liberty, and admit only God as their sole leader and lord; they do not mind suffering the most extraordinary deaths, or care what punishments are meted out to their relatives and friends, as long as no man is recognized as lord" (*Antiquities,* XVIII, 1, 6). One has only to picture these bearers of spiritual ferment as everywhere dispersed throughout Judea, bound together by secret ties, raging at each act of oppression by the Romans, and ever poised awaiting the right moment to revolt, to perceive in all this a most fitting preparation for the final insurrection against Rome. It is also the exact historical explanation.

Of course, this group of Zealots was not always and everywhere inspired by unalloyed nationalism and pure Yahwism. In the last days especially many diverse elements were incorporated into them. Along with genuine patriots and sincere traditionalists there were unstable fanatics, adventurers, and charlatans. Common criminals and out and out brigands also joined them, welcoming the opportunity to settle their private feuds and fill their purses by a daily wielding of the *sica* — all in the name of Judaism! This time Josephus can well be believed when he speaks of brigands and assassins (§ 322). After all, he had been an eyewitness to the reality.

❊   ❊   ❊

383. After the census Coponius alone remained, but nothing more is known of his three years in the office of procurator (A.D. 6–9) except

---

[2] In Aramaic it is written *qan'ana* (Hebrew, *qanna'*); it was Graecized to καναναῖος. Hence, the Apostle Simon, called καναναῖος (Mt. 10:4; Mk. 3:18), was not a "Canaanite," but rather a Zealot (cf. Lk. 6:15; Acts 1:13) in the primitive sense of the word.

that certain Samaritans scattered some bones
of the dead in the Temple on the occasion of
the Pasch and thus profaned the Temple.
Nothing also is known of the two succeeding procurators, Marcus Ambivius (or
Ambibulus) (A.D. 9–12) or Annius Rufus
(A.D. 12–15), who was the last procurator
appointed by Augustus.

Money of Pontius Pilate.

The first procurator to be chosen by Tiberius was Valerius Gratus
(A.D. 15–26). He had difficulty from the beginning in finding a high
priest with whom he could get along. He soon deposed Ananus (Annas)
who in four years had three successors, the last of whom was Joseph,
called Caipha (Caiphas). These last two, it need hardly be mentioned,
figured in the Passion of Christ.

384. Gratus was succeeded by a man who never dreamed that his new
office would make him forever famous in the eyes of mankind. His name
was Pontius Pilate (A.D. 26–36). His procuratorship in Judea was a
failure so far as Roman interests were concerned, and the reasons for his
failure were his temperament and his behavior while in office. Here,
fortunately, the data given by Josephus are clarified and augmented
by the Gospels and by Philo (*Legat. ad Caium*, 38).

The least that can be said of Pilate is that he was a cantankerous and
obstinate man. Agrippa I, who knew whereof he spoke, depicted him
also as being venal, violent, rapacious, an oppressor, and a tyrant (in
Philo, *ibid.*). It follows that a man of such character would have a
supreme and hearty disdain for his subjects, and would do absolutely
nothing to win them over, nothing to try to understand them or appreciate their point of view. He was quick to seize any opportunity to
irritate, contradict, and offend them. In short, not only did he hate
his subjects, but he had an overpowering urge to manifest his hatred,
and if it had depended on him, he would gladly have sent them all
to work in the prisons (*ergastula*) and (iron) mines (*ad metalla*).
In this he was prevented, for the Emperor of Rome, to whom the
legate to Syria reported his doings, stood in his way. Hence the equestrian Pontius Pilate had to check himself, and hold back expression of
his spite. But even this servile fear was counterbalanced to some extent.
As a matter of fact, from A.D. 19, when the Jews were expelled from
Rome (§ 196), Tiberius appeared to be hostile toward the Jews, and
Pilate had been sent as procurator precisely during this period so unfavorable to Judaism. Particularly in his first years of office, then, he
could argue that his hostile behavior toward the Jews aped, with courtly
opportuneness, the example which came from Rome.

385. It was probably at the beginning of his procuratorship that Pilate, combining courtly servility toward the emperor and disdain for the Jews, commanded the soldiers going up from Caesarea to Jerusalem to enter the city carrying with them, for the first time, standards bearing the effigy of the emperor (§ 377). Yet he was clever enough to have the standards brought in at night, so as not to provoke resistance; the city would thus be faced with an accomplished fact. The next day the Jews were struck with consternation at such a profanation, and many of them hurried to Caesarea, where for five days and nights they begged the procurator to remove the standards from the holy city. Pilate would not yield. On the sixth day, vexed by their insistence, he had them surrounded by his troops at a public audience and threatened to kill them if they did not immediately return to their homes. It was then that those admirable traditionalists overcame the cynical Roman. Seeing that they were surrounded by soldiers, they threw themselves upon the ground, bared their necks, and declared themselves ready to die rather than renounce their principles. Pilate had not expected such a move, and yielded the point; the standards were removed. With the Zealots still at large he had to be careful.

After this there was the affair of the aqueduct. To bring badly needed water to Jerusalem and to the Temple, Pilate decided to build an aqueduct, bringing the water from the ample reserves to the southwest of Bethlehem (the so-called "Pools of Solomon"). To accomplish this work he dipped into the funds of the Temple treasury. Demonstrations and rioting followed this use of sacred money, whereupon Pilate had many of his soldiers, dressed as Jews, filter among the demonstrators; at a predetermined signal, they brought out their cudgels and began to belabor the crowd. Several dead and wounded were left on the ground.

386. Still later the belligerent procurator attempted something similar to the episode of the military standards. Gilded shields, bearing the name of the emperor, were hung in the palace of Herod at Jerusalem. It has been argued that this episode, which is found only in Philo, may be nothing more than another version of the preceding incident of the standards. This is hardly likely, considering Pilate's character and the fact that this new episode must have occurred much later than the other, probably after the death of Sejanus in 31 (§ 196). This time the delegation sent to Pilate included also four of Herod's sons, but they were unsuccessful in having the shields removed. The Jews then had recourse to Tiberius himself, and he commanded that the disputed shields be transferred to the temple of Augustus at Caesarea. The fact that Tiberius yielded on this point seems to be connected with the disappearance of Sejanus, the enemy of the Jews. Incidentally, it is also said that Pilate had a number of Galileans slain while they were offering sacrifices in the Temple (Lk. 13:1), but concerning

this details are lacking. On the other hand, it can be suspected that the hostility existing between Pilate and Antipas (§ 370) was to some extent at least due to this slaughter of Antipas' subjects, and because Antipas probably acted as a spy for Tiberius and reported to him Pilate's doings.

387. Pilate's habitual hostility toward the Jews becomes very evident in the trial of Jesus.

The accused, who had been arrested by the national tribunal and declared by it guilty of death, was presented to the procurator, for the sentence could not be executed unless it was ratified by the representative of Rome (§ 377). Experienced as he was, Pilate quickly perceived that the accused was the object of a popular hatred incited by the Pharisees, the leaders of the people. He also saw that the accused was innocent. He had therefore two reasons for absolving Jesus from blame and dismissing the case: he could show his spite for the Jews, and could perform an act of justice. From the beginning he declared roundly that Jesus was innocent, but the accusers insisted. Pilate then attempted to saddle the responsibility for the whole affair on Antipas, a courteous gesture which might also serve to temper the zeal of that spy (§ 370). But Antipas wanted no part of it, and, once he had satisfied his curiosity, sent the accused man back to the procurator, who then tried another tactic of evasion, proposing that Barabbas take the place of Jesus. This also failed when the accusers insisted that Jesus himself must face the penalty. Then Pilate made his first concession, and had Jesus scourged. The accusers, however, interpreted the concession as only the first earnest, and wanted Him to be crucified. Pilate still wavered and was unwilling to yield. The accusers then brought forth the political issue, and demanded that the accused be put to death as a proof of Pilate's loyalty to the emperor. And Pilate capitulated. Why?

Actually, Pilate was also threatened with denunciation to the emperor in the matter of the golden shields (but this, probably, after the trial of Jesus), but it was not for this reason that he yielded and thus satisfied the Jews. The two cases are quite different. In the affair of the golden shields, he seemed to be a zealous official solicitous for the honor of the emperor, but if in the case of Jesus an appeal were to be made to the legate of Syria or to Rome, Pilate might very well appear to have been remiss or negligent. This would have been very annoying to him, for at this time his bureaucratic position must have been a trifle shaky, thanks to the reports of Antipas and also because of the rather numerous complaints made against his administration. He had no intention of hurting himself further, and so he gave up the attempt, in this case, to show his scorn for the Jews. Jesus was condemned. There was, it is true, the question of justice, and he himself had declared the accused innocent; but Pilate must have asked himself if one could really speak of justice where some provincial, not a *civis romanus*, was concerned. The skepticism of his famous *Quid est veritas?* well deserves the cynical retort *Quid est justitia?*

388. In the end Pilate himself fell victim to his own methods of governing. In 35 a pseudo-prophet had appeared in Samaria, and many people believed in him. The Samaritans claimed that the sacred utensils of the time of Moses were hidden on Mount Gerizim, and the prophet promised to produce them. On the appointed day many people gathered there in the belief that the showing of these sacred objects would herald the beginning of the new messianic era. They were assembled at Tirathana, at the foot of Gerizim, ready to climb upward when the time came. But Pilate had already stationed his troops on the summit, so as to put an end to the project. In the ensuing encounter several people were killed, many taken prisoner, and of these the most important were later put to death by Pilate.

The zeal of the procurator in preventing the affair was based on more profound reasons than merely the simple "exhibition" promised by the prophet, for he really suspected some kind of open revolt; as the Samaritans said later, the people had grown tired of Pilate's persecutions. Because of this massacre the Samaritan community presented a formal accusation against Pilate to Vitellius, who was the legate to Syria and possessed of full powers to act in the Orient. Since the Samaritans were noted for their loyalty to Rome, the accusation carried much weight. Vitellius promptly suspended Pilate from office, and sent him to Rome to account for his actions before the emperor.

When Pilate arrived at Rome, about a year later, he learned that Tiberius had died (March 16, of the year 37). History knows nothing more of Pilate. Eusebius (*Hist. eccl.*, II, 7) states that he killed himself, while in a later Christian legend the man who condemned Jesus is pictured as the hero of wondrous adventures, some of them worthy of the imagination of a Dante.

389. Marcellus (A.D. 36–37) succeeded Pontius Pilate as procurator, and in turn was succeeded by Marullus (A.D. 37–41). Nothing is known of either one of them. At this time, the Roman magistrates of Syria and Egypt, and the new emperor Caligula himself, demand attention.

Vitellius came to Jerusalem for the Pasch of 36, and on that occasion remitted the tax on the sale of fruits, and restored to the charge of the Temple the solemn vesture of the high priest which had been kept in the fortress Antonia. The following year he began his campaign against Aretas, which, however, he suspended, to the bitter disappointment of Antipas (§ 371).

Serious troubles began for the Jews of Palestine and Egypt under Caligula, when that emperor decided that he was to be venerated as a god. That Caligula had probably become deranged, although this has been recently questioned, was common knowledge of the time. He prized his divinity above everything else, and as he could not wait to be declared a god by the senate after his death, as was the usual custom for the other emperors, he could not endure the fact that in his whole empire only the Jews denied him divine honors.

390. The first disorders broke out at Alexandria in the summer of 38, on the occasion of a visit of Caligula's friend, Agrippa I, then returning to Palestine from Rome with the title of king (§ 395). The privileged position of the Jews in Alexandria (§ 190 ff.) had in times past stirred up the jealousy of the other citizens, and relations became very strained. The presence of Agrippa gave rise to popular demonstrations which ridiculed the new king and his extraordinary good fortune. In fact, a certain Karabas was dressed up in a ragged parody of Agrippa and carried through the Jewish quarters amid the gibes of the people.

Avilius Flaccus, then prefect of Egypt, did nothing to stop these manifestations, perhaps because of his long-standing rancor toward Agrippa. Later, because of Caligula's friendship for the king thus ridiculed, Flaccus began to fear the emperor's resentment, and to forestall it began to flatter him on a subject dearest to his heart: the fact of his own divinity. The Alexandrian populace was willing to go along with him in this, for thus they were striking a blow directly at the hated Jews. A full-fledged persecution was soon legally under way. Statues of Caligula were erected within the synagogues of Alexandria; the Jews were declared foreigners to the city and intruders, and were deprived of all their ancient privileges. Ejected from their homes, they sought refuge in a run-down zone of the Fifth Quarter (§ 190), and there had to live practically in the open. Their goods were seized, four hundred of their homes and their business places, and even the ships which they had chartered and which still remained in port, were sacked. Many of them were also manhandled and killed. Thirty-eight members of the local γερουσία were publicly scourged by order of Flaccus in punishment for not worshiping the emperor, and Jewish women were forced to eat pork in public. In brief, what had happened in Jerusalem under Antiochus Epiphanes, or *epìmane* ("maniac") (§ 42), was now repeated more or less in Alexandria, under that other *epìmane*, Caius Caligula.

But with all this, Flaccus came to a bad end, because in that same year Caligula, acting perhaps on accusations supplied by Agrippa, summoned him to Rome as a prisoner, and then sent him into exile to the island of Andros in the Aegean Sea; there he was killed shortly

Caligula. (Rome, Capitoline Museum.)

afterward. This was the Flaccus against whom Philo wrote his *In Flaccum*.

391. None of this helped matters for the Jews of Alexandria. King Agrippa had previously sent a document to Caligula recommending the cause of the Jews, but then the two contending factions one after another sent deputations to plead their case before the emperor. They departed from Alexandria probably at the end of 38, one on the heels of the other. Heading the anti-Jewish deputation was Apion (§ 202), against whom Josephus wrote his *Contra Apionem* (§ 208). The Jewish deputation was led by Philo, who gives an account of it in his *Legatio ad Caium*. At Rome, however, the deputation of Apion succeeded in winning over the protection of Helicon, the favorite of Caligula, while Philo's suffered grievous disappointments. Although they followed the emperor to Rome and to Puteoli seeking an audience, they did not obtain it until around the autumn of 40, and it was an audience worthy of the character of Caligula. He was at the time visiting the gardens of Maecenas and Lamia, and moved rapidly about the various buildings in the park giving orders for various alterations. The Jewish ambassadors hurried on, always behind him, and tried to set forth their arguments whenever he stopped moving, being meanwhile subjected to the sarcastic remarks of Apion's delegation, which had been admitted to the audience. The flowery declamation they had prepared in advance had to be abandoned. From the start Caligula reproached them for refusing to believe in his divinity. While giving orders to put in doors of crystal, and to rearrange one part of the archives, he asked them curiously why they did not eat pork, and then when they were told to state their petitions and began to do so, he walked away from them and ran into one of the buildings. And so it went. But on that day the unbalanced emperor was not in bad humor, for at last he dismissed them declaring that they were not really wicked, but were to be regarded as imbeciles and deserving of compassion because they would not admit his divinity.

Philo's delegation got no more than this. However, under the new prefect of Egypt, Vitrasius Pollio, the plight of the Jews of Alexandria was somewhat bettered. Conditions would return to normal later on under the emperor Claudius, after the assassination of Caligula on January 24 in the year 41.

392. The events which developed under Claudius appear as the natural consequences of Caligula's reign. We are now fortunately able to add to Josephus' account (*Antiquities,* XIX, 5, 2–3) other such precious documents

Claudius. (Florence, Uffizi gallery.)

as the famous letter of Claudius to the Alexandrians (papyrus 1912 of the British Museum), and the so-called Acts of the pagan martyrs Isidore and Lampon (fragments at Berlin and at Gizeh).

At the death of Caligula the Jews of Alexandria, naturally, sought to shake off the yoke that weighed down upon them, and this led to new and serious conflicts. Claudius, desirous of good order and amenable to the wishes of Agrippa I and of Herod of Chalcis (§ 400), hastened to remove the principal cause of the disorders by issuing a special decree which restored their ancient privileges to the Jews in Alexandria. He guaranteed the free practice of their religion and traditions, and abolished the law by which Caligula, in his "great stupidity and madness," tried to make them worship him as a god (*Antiquities,* XIX, 5, 2). A similar decree in favor of the Jews was directed to the rest of the empire. The letter to the Alexandrians was promulgated in Alexandria by the prefect L. Aemilius Rectus on November 10, 41; it had been issued by Claudius in the preceding October. In it the emperor, among other things, refused divine worship, reconfirmed the ancient Jewish privileges and religious liberty, and commanded them and the pagans to be tolerant of one another. He then especially admonished the Jews not to scheme about increasing their power still more, and in particular "not to bring in or cause to be brought in Jewish navigators from Syria or Egypt, lest he should become seriously suspicious of them. If they did not comply he would punish [them] with great severity as instigators of a pestilence threatening the whole world." This last expression has led some to think that the internal disorders in the Jewish community of Alexandria were caused by Christianity, then being spread there, but the text does not seem to justify this view, nor do the facts. What stands out clearly is the unity of spirit which bound together the various communities of the diaspora (§ 186). Fellow countrymen from Syria and Egypt hastened to help the persecuted Jews of Alexandria. One result of this was that the Alexandrian community became very large and also powerful, and Claudius, an able administrator of the Roman provinces, remarked this with some concern.

From fragments of the Acts of Isidore and of Lampon we learn that Claudius instituted a formal trial for the principal instigators of violence against the Jews, namely, Isidore, the gymnasiarch of Alexandria, and Lampon. These two are mentioned by Philo (*In Flaccum*, 5, 15–17). Summoned before the emperor's tribunal, they were put to death early in the reign of Claudius.

393. To return now to Caligula and his mad belief in his own divinity. Things were going equally bad in Palestine, where the disorders were provoked by Herennius Capito, the financial procurator of Jamnia (this city, after the death of Salome, had become imperial property). A greedy profiteer, Capito was therefore fearful that the Jews, the greater part of his victimized subjects, would do him harm by denouncing him. He shrewdly forestalled them in this by exposing them to the hatred of Caligula. In order to vent their spite on the Jews, the pagans of Jamnia had erected an altar to the emperor at the end of

Final column of the Letter of Claudius to the Alexandrians. (From H. I. Bell, *Juden und Griechen im röm. Alexandr.*)

39, and this the Jews had conscientiously hastened to destroy. Taking advantage of his opportunity, Capito zealously reported the misdeed to the emperor. Wounded in his most sensitive spot, Caligula at the beginning of 40 ordered the destroyed altar to be built more sumptuously than before, and in addition, a statue of himself to be erected in the Temple of Jerusalem.

It was difficult for the mad lord of the Palatine to realize the gravity of this second command. At any rate, his deranged mind was hardly aware of it, and he expected to be obeyed. But Petronius, who had succeeded Vitellius in the governorship of Syria (39–42) and was charged with the execution of the command, grasped the situation at once. Caught between the blind determination of emperor and the inevitable refusal of those who were ordered to obey, he temporized, as a wise man like himself would in such circumstances. To pacify the emperor, Petronius moved from Antioch to Ptolemais with two Roman legions and other auxiliary troops (nothing less than these large forces were required to take care of the revolt which would inevitably follow). There he passed the winter at the beginning of 40, while the statue was being made by artists of Sidon. In the meantime, the news had spread about, and thousands of Jews poured first into Ptolemais and then Tiberias, whither Petronius had gone at the end of the autumn of 40. They besought him to abandon this project. Moving scenes took place, and did not fail to impress Petronius. They were a clear demonstration that the religious roots of Yahwism still lay deep in the people, even two centuries after the Machabees, and much infiltration of Greco-Roman paganism. Thousands of men and women of every age presented themselves in successive groups to Petronius at Ptolemais, beseeching him with loud cries and tears to prevent the profanation of their Temple, and declaring that they would rather die than yield the point. At Tiberias large crowds of suppliants importuned Petronius for forty days, neglecting their work in the fields, although the planting time was drawing near.

394. Amid these trying circumstances Petronius comported himself with great prudence and kindness. After Ptolemais, he wrote to Caligula apprising him of the delay in the erection of the statue owing to the slowness of the workmen (he had ordered the artisans to proceed slowly). He suggested that because the harvest time was drawing near, it would be prudent to go cautiously, lest the irritated Jews might destroy the harvests and provoke a general revolt. Caligula, hiding his anger, approved the course Petronius had followed, but at the same time insisted in his letter that the statue be set up when the harvest was over (Philo, *Leg. ad Caium*, 33–34). At Tiberias, Petronius was profoundly impressed by the suppliants and wrote to Caligula again, at the risk of exposing himself to the vengeance of the emperor, to present the reasons advanced by the Jews against the project, and even defended them (*Antiquities,* XVIII, 8, 5).

Meanwhile, in the spring of A.D. 40, King Agrippa had gone to Rome hoping to influence his friend the emperor in favor of the Jews. How he succeeded in partially fulfilling his purpose is not clear. Josephus states that it was done on the occasion of a banquet. Philo says that Agrippa fainted when he saw how angry the emperor became upon reading the letters from Petronius, and mentions a later suppliant letter sent by Agrippa. It is certain that after his meeting with Agrippa, the emperor instructed Petronius that no innovations should be introduced into the Temple at Jerusalem for the moment; outside the city, however, anyone might erect temples and altars to the emperor. As far as Caligula was concerned, these dispositions were only provisional. He had not really renounced his project, and during this time had another large statue prepared at Rome, which he himself intended to set up in Jerusalem when he made his projected voyage to Egypt. The last letter of Petronius had angered him greatly. Before granting Agrippa's request he ordered Petronius to kill himself as a penalty for his disobedience and remissness toward the rebels.

Cherea's dagger, which brought death to the paranoiac emperor (§ 391), finally settled the question. There was no more talk of the statue, and the courageous Petronius remained alive because the letter commanding him to commit suicide arrived, fortunately, a month after he had learned of the death of Caligula.

The disappearance of the tyrant was a relief for the rest of the empire. The joy of the Jews can be imagined. According to the *Megillath Taanith,* the day on which Caligula's death was announced was to be a festive day on which all fasting was forbidden.

❋   ❋   ❋

395. Agrippa I (A.D. 41–44) was the son of the Hasmonean Aristobulus, who was murdered by his father Herod the Great in 7 B.C. (§ 356), and of Bernice, daughter of Salome (§ 351). Born in 10 B.C., he had had an adventurous youth. While still a child, he had been taken to Rome with his mother, and there had been educated with Drusus, the son of Tiberius, and others of the imperial family, and thus formed many powerful friendships. Steeped in the atmosphere of imperial Rome, he gave himself over to the carefree life of the patrician youths and squandered all his possessions. After the death of Drusus in A.D. 23, he found himself in such financial straits that, to escape his creditors, he left Rome and returned to Judea. He betook himself to Malatha, a fortress in Idumaea, and in his desperate plight considered suicide. His wife Cypros obtained a small employment for him in the government administration of Antipas. Next he joined his friend Pomponius Flaccus, governor of Syria, and after various other adventures, finally wound up in Italy again in A.D. 36. He was received quite favorably by Tiberius at Capri, but was quickly besieged by his old creditors. With the help of Antonia, grandmother of Caius Caligula, he was able to pay his debts, and out of gratitude, but also with an eye to his own interests, he became a close friend of Caligula, and one day expressed to him the hope that he would soon succeed to the throne of the empire. To utter such words even in private conversation, such as this was, was dangerously imprudent during the reign of a man so suspicious as Tiberius. Agrippa's remarks were reported to Tiberius, and Agrippa was put in chains. He remained a prisoner for six months, until the death of Tiberius.

Caligula's advancement was the prisoner's good fortune, for he was immediately released, his iron chain replaced by one of gold of equal weight. Caligula also created him king, and gave him the territories which belonged to the tetrarch Philip (§ 368), and those of the tetrarchy of Lysania, which extended to the northwest of Damascus near Abila of Lysania (the present-day *Suq Wadi Barada*). After this he remained for over a year at court, and then departed for his territories, passing first through Alexandria (§ 390). He arrived in Palestine surrounded by such splendor that Herodias' jealousy, which eventually led to the ruin of Antipas (§ 372), was aroused. The territories belonging to Antipas were given over to Agrippa in A.D. 40, the same year that he returned to Rome to treat of the question of the imperial statue (§ 394). He was still there when Caligula was killed, and in that critical time Agrippa did much to help his friend Claudius, the choice of the praetorians, to obtain the election, for he persuaded him to conquer his indecision and to accept the crown, and he persuaded the senate to recognize him.

Claudius rewarded Agrippa handsomely for the good services he had rendered him. Not only were decrees promulgated at the request of Agrippa in favor of the Jews of Alexandria and of the whole empire (§ 392), but Claudius also confirmed his hold on the territories he had already received, and in addition gave him those of the Roman province (Judea together with Samaria and Idumaea) which was therefore suppressed. The senate also conferred upon him the dignity of consul. Thus the reign of Herod the Great was revived in the person of his grandson, Herod Agrippa I.

396. In his brief but able reign, Agrippa followed closely the traditions of the last Hasmoneans, whose blood flowed in his veins. From the very outset, he sought to be popular, and therefore took the only road which led to that end — he sought to win the favor of the Pharisees. "When he arrived in Jerusalem, he fulfilled all the sacrifices of thanksgiving, not omitting any of those things prescribed by the Law" (*Antiquities*, XIX, 6, 1), and, among other things, he donated to the Temple the chain of gold which Caligula had given him. Even afterward he was not only respectful toward Jewish prescriptions, but was actually zealous for their observance. Josephus writes that he preferred to stay in Jerusalem, and let no day go by without offering sacrifice in the Temple, gladly defraying the costs of worship, and being very liberal to those who sought his help. He consented to the betrothal of his daughter Drusilla to Epiphanes, the son of the king of Commagene, but only after her future spouse promised that he would embrace Judaism. (Actually, he did not keep his promise because of the usual repugnance to circumcision, and thus the marriage did not take place; § 210). He had a number of young men of the coastal Phoenician city of Dora called to account before the tribunal of Petronius for having introduced a statue of Caligula in the Jewish synagogue.

His persecution of the rising Christian community of Jerusalem was prompted by a desire to win the love of both the people and the Pharisees. Indeed, he "set hands on certain members of the Church to persecute them. He killed James the brother of John with the sword, and seeing that it pleased the Jews, he proceeded to arrest Peter also" (Acts 12:1–3). Despite his zeal and the precautions adopted, he did not succeed in having this prisoner suffer the same fate as James.

397. That he assumed the pose of a zealous Jew chiefly for political reasons is evident from the very broad-minded manner of life which characterized him when he was outside strictly Jewish territory. He had statues erected in his palace at Caesarea in honor of his daughters, although the common tradition forbade him to do so. He frequented the Greek theater, for which a fervent Pharisee reproved him. At Beyrouth he built a theater and an amphitheater; under his orders, fourteen hundred gladiators took part in those bloody exhibitions which he had admired when they were presented on a much larger scale at Rome. But neither were these in keeping with the traditions of the Pharisees. His double game is reflected also in his coins: those minted at Jerusalem had no image on them; those minted outside bore the image of the emperor or of Agrippa himself, with various inscriptions.

In one of these he is called φιλορώμαιος, "friend of the Romans." All flattery laid aside, this was true, if for no other reason than that it served his own advantage. Yet even with the Romans his relations were not entirely without friction, because he was extremely desirous of popularity, a trait which the Romans always considered suspicious in a vassal. Once during the last days of his reign, he played host to a meeting of five other princes, vassals of Rome: Antiochus of Commagene, Sampsigeram of Emesa, Cotys of Lesser Armenia, Polemon of Pontus, and his own

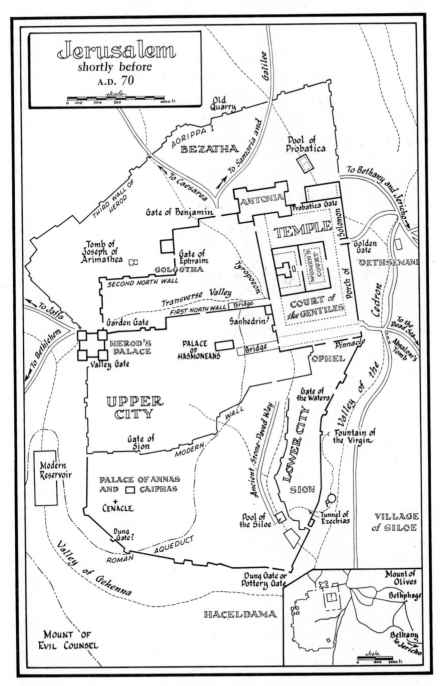

Jerusalem
shortly before
A.D. 70
scale
0 100   300   500   1000 ft.

Remains of the so-called Fourth Wall.
(Vester, Amer. Colony.)

brother Herod of Chalcis (§ 400). The purpose of this meeting is not known, but it was probably nothing more than a kind of spectacular exhibition promoted by Agrippa. But Vibius Marsus, the new governor of Syria, who also came to Tiberias, did not consider it as such. Suspecting ulterior political purposes in the meeting, he ordered the princes to return to their homes at once. Agrippa was offended at the brusque order, and it soured his relations with Marsus, but neither he nor the others dared hesitate for one moment to obey the order.

398. Of greater importance is what happened with regard to the walls of Jerusalem. From the time of Herod the Great on, the city had continued to grow toward the north, the only direction in which further expansion was possible. An entirely new quarter had arisen in the area outside the wall of the city (Second Wall or Wall of Nehemias: §§ 132–133), on the hill called Bezetha, which was a prolongation of the hillock of the Temple, and contained the pool of the same name (Jn. 5:2). Agrippa wanted to incorporate this new quarter into the city, and to gird it with another wall joined to the ancient circle of walls on the east and west. In view of the fact also that the northern front which was to be girded was the city's most vulnerable point in case of an attack, as past experience had shown (§ 312), this wall would have to be unusually solid and strong. Agrippa applied himself to the task, probably after a few months in office, and undertook the construction of this new northern wall.

What happened then is not clear, as Josephus gives three separate accounts, each one quite different from the others. One account has it that when this work had progressed to a certain stage, Marsus, the governor, became alarmed and informed Claudius, who issued an order to halt the work (*Antiquities*, XIX, 7, 2). A second account completely ignores the prohibition of Claudius, and states only that Agrippa was prevented by death from completing the wall, which would have been impregnable had it been finished according to the plan (*War*, II, 11, 6). A third reports that Agrippa himself chose to interrupt the work after it was started, lest Claudius suspect him of hatching some scheme of rebellion (*War*, V, 4, 2). What seems to be certain amid these divergent accounts is that Agrippa began his new wall, and had made considerable progress in its construction, when, for some unknown reason, a halt was called to the work.

Which was the Wall of Agrippa? Until recently the common opinion was that it was the wall which Josephus specifically called the "Third Wall" (*War*, V, 4, 2). It followed substantially the same line as the present northern circle of walls, joining the ancient line on the two sides, one at the tower of Hippicus (our Jaffa Gate) on the western side, the other at the northeastern corner of the Temple, on the eastern side. Excavations made by the Jewish Society of Palestinian Archaeology (Sukenik and Mayer, 1925 ff.) have brought to light various traces of a wall which lies some hundreds of yards north of the Third Wall and could therefore be called the Fourth Wall. Some scholars have concluded from the line which it traces and from the characteristics of these remains that it is Agrippa's Wall. Père Vincent, however, has raised serious archaeological and topographical objections against this theory, and maintains the older opinion.

Whether the work on the grandiose wall was interrupted by imperial decree or spontaneously, it was another case in which the surveillance of Rome weighed upon Agrippa, or upon the one who was supposed to continue the project.

399. The good fortune which had raised Agrippa to the throne after so many adventures did not keep him there. Scarcely three years later, in the spring of 44, he attended a special celebration at Caesarea in honor of Claudius (probably because of his safe return from Britain), and there he accorded an audience to the inhabitants of Tyre and Sidon (*Antiquities*, XIX, 8, 2, and Acts 12:19–23). During this audience, while the common people flattered him and likened him to a god in his sumptuous raiment, he was unexpectedly stricken with violent intestinal pains. He was carried to his house, and died five days later. From the sudden and violent character of the illness, it has been conjectured that he may have died from a ruptured appendix.

During his brief illness the populace showed some signs of grief; yet, as soon as word reached them of his death, a good proportion of the inhabitants of Caesarea and Samaria and the many soldiers present broke out into wild demonstrations of joy, holding public banquets, insulting the dead man, and obscenely dishonoring the statues of his daughters. The probable reason should be sought in the ancient enmities which the pagans of Caesarea and the Samaritans of Samaria felt against the Pharisees of Jerusalem, toward whom the dead man had been so obsequious.

At his death, Agrippa left three daughters, Bernice (§ 402), Mariamne, and Drusilla (§ 410), besides a son of seventeen who was being educated at Rome, and was likewise named Agrippa. Claudius was at first disposed to confer the throne upon this youth at once, but his royal advisers pointed out the boy's youth and lack of experience, so he kept him at Rome instead, and re-established the former regime in Judea; the procurator Cuspius Fadus (§ 406) was sent to rule over all of Agrippa's territories.

✸   ✸   ✸

400. Agrippa II (50–100?). When awarded dominion over all of Palestine by Claudius, Agrippa I saw that the moment was propitious and persuaded the grateful emperor to bestow the territory of Chalcis upon his brother, Herod, with the title of king. This was Herod of Chalcis, and his small kingdom extended through the valley between

Bernice (?). (Museum of Naples.)

Libanus and Antilibanus (el-Beqa'a; cf. Vol. I, § 60), with its capital at Chalcis (modern 'Angiar). This Herod was his son-in-law as well as his brother, for he was married to Agrippa's daughter Bernice. He took possession of the kingdom in 41, and in 44 obtained control over the Temple of Jerusalem, with the right to name the high priest. He died in 48, and for the time being his tiny territory again passed under the jurisdiction of the governor of Syria.

In the meantime, Marcus Julius Agrippa, the son of Agrippa I, had reached his majority. The vacant throne of Chalcis seemed to offer a fair test of his ability to govern, so Claudius in 50 chose him as successor to his uncle Herod, and even gave him the right of superintending the Temple and of naming the high priest.

Agrippa II had been given a completely Roman education, and had been assiduous in his studies. A member of the court of Messalina, he had nevertheless kept alive a strong attachment for his nation, and more than once had spoken in its interests to Claudius. When he returned to Palestine, he continued in this disposition, remaining always benevolent to Judaism, but above all loyal to Rome, and in the final insurrection he cast in his lot with the Romans.

In the year 53 Agrippa made an advantageous exchange of territory. In place of Chalcis, which returned to the governor of Syria, he obtained the much larger tetrarchies of Philip, of Lysania (§ 395), and a small eparchy in the possession of Varus. To these territories, Nero in 54 or 55 added other parts of Galilee and Perea, that is, the cities of Tiberias and Tarichea with their districts, and Bethsaida-Julias and fourteen minor centers (§ 368). To show his gratitude to Nero, Agrippa II changed the name of Caesarea-Philippi to *Neronias* (§ 39).

401. Various items of information concerning his long reign, especially at the time of the insurrection, are extant. He built a theater at Beyrouth, and had copies made of famous and ancient statues and paintings. At Jerusalem, he ordered pavements to be made of white stone, to give employment to eighteen thousand workmen who were left without work when the Temple was finished (§ 347). Being superintendent of the Temple, he had, about A.D. 60, built a gallery on top of the palace of the Hasmoneans opposite the Temple, and from it could very easily see while at table what was happening in the sacred place. This struck the citizens as being an irreverence, so they raised a high wall in the western enclosure of the Temple, blocking out his view. Disputes arose and the affair was referred to Nero, who ordered the wall to remain (§ 414).

The encounter between Agrippa II and St. Paul at Caesarea is well known (Acts 25:13 ff.). The new procurator Porcius Festus found Paul in prison and spoke of him to Agrippa when the latter came to pay his respects. Agrippa expressed a desire to see Paul. In the presence of the king and procurator, Paul gave such a forceful defense of his life and doctrine that the procurator told him in a friendly way that too much doctrine had gone to his head. But Paul turned and appealed directly to the king: "Dost thou believe, O King Agrippa, the prophets? I know that thou dost! — Then Agrippa said to Paul: In a little thou persuadest me to become a Christian!" (Acts 26:27–28.)

402. But Agrippa could not have become a Christian, as things stood. His words reflect a certain broadness of spirit due to his Roman education, but there was also present at this conversation the one who prevented him from living an absolutely honest life, his sister Bernice (§ 399), the

Gamala: location of the fortress.

evil genius in his life. Widowed by the death of Herod of Chalcis (§ 400) in A.D. 48, she went to live with her brother Agrippa, and soon ugly rumors of an incestuous relationship between the two were being circulated. To silence these, Bernice married Polemon, king of Cilicia, who accepted circumcision for that purpose (§ 212). The marriage did not last very long through Bernice's fault, and abandoning Polemon she returned to Agrippa and resumed her former relationship. This was known even at Rome, and provoked the sarcasm of Juvenal (*Sat.*, VI, 156 ff.). The affair continued, and was destined to become more complicated, for Bernice became even more notorious for her relations with Titus. These began about the year 68 (Tacitus, *Hist.*, II, 2), and were renewed in Rome in 75 when Bernice accompanied Agrippa there. Her power over Titus became proverbial: "she did all things, as if she were also his wife" (Dio Cassius, LXVI, 15), and it was also said that Titus had formally promised to marry her (Suetonius, *Titus*, 7). The relationship, however, made a very bad impression at Rome, so Titus unwillingly sent her away (cf. Aurelius Victor, *Epit.*, 10). At the death of Vespasian, Titus became emperor and Bernice returned to Rome, but Titus refused to be dominated by her any longer and *"Berenicem statim ab urbe dimisit, invitus invitam"* (Suet., *ibid.*). After this she disappears from history.

Such was the character of the woman who sat at Agrippa's side as he listened to the burning words of Paul. Despite Agrippa's exclamation, then, the words of the prisoner could have no effect upon the incestuous king.

403. Agrippa worked zealously to prevent the coming war, maintaining a prudent equilibrium between the Roman authorities and the national insurgents. In a long discourse to the people of Jerusalem in 66, he recommended that they be calm and submissive to Rome, and persuaded them to repair the losses inflicted on the fortress Antonia and to pay the overdue tribute. Later he exhorted them to put up with the procurator Florus, but at this the people drove Agrippa from the city, and some even cast stones at him (*War*, II, 16, 4 ff.). He then retired to his own kingdom, where he still worked for peace, and sent three thousand cavalry to help the faction in Jerusalem which opposed war with Rome. But the extremists took possession of the city by main force, and set fire to the palaces of the pacifists, including those of Agrippa and Bernice.

When the war broke out, Agrippa continued to give aid to the Romans with the direct result that the cities of Tiberias, Tarichea, and Gamala rebelled. Vespasian, however, who had previously enjoyed his hospitality at Neronias, reconquered all these places with his own troops. When the war was over Agrippa was rewarded for his fidelity with new grants of territory, and in 75 the emperor Vespasian raised him to the dignity of praetor.

In regard to the history of the war in which he had taken such a great part, he was in close contact with both Josephus and Justus of Tiberias (§ 208). According to a fragment of Justus preserved by Fozius (*Bibl.*, 33), Agrippa died in the year 100, or perhaps even a few years earlier.

❧　❧　❧

404. The Procurators From 44 to 66. The new line of Roman procurators which began at the death of Agrippa I (§ 399), and extended to the outbreak of the insurrection, was, on the whole, much worse than the one which had preceded Agrippa I. To be sure, it was becoming increasingly difficult to govern Judea, where the Zealots (§ 381) were always working in secret. The people felt and resented more and more the yoke of foreign domination, and the masses had reached a stage of permanent irritation. But this multiplication of difficulties was not counterbalanced by a proportionate increase in the diligence and rectitude of the new procurators. Quite the contrary.

As the people became more critical and touchy, the procurators became more blunt and exacting. The prescribed levies were collected only with difficulty and threats. Several of the new procurators came to Judea with the intention of lining their pockets. Hatred and vengeance on one side, disdain and avarice on the other! Partly involved in this vicious circle, and partly added as a new and aggravating element, were the widespread ideas of a messianico-nationalistic nature, the vague hope of a theocratic rebirth leading to liberation from the yoke of foreign servitude, and to the restoration of the ancient glory of the kingdom of Israel (cf. Acts 1:6). The people protested angrily against the terrible conditions then existing, and awaited the coming of an era of radiant felicity in the immediate future. The present struggles served only to whet still more their desire for the future, and their expectation of it was little short of feverish.

405. From the vantage point of twenty centuries, a modern historian can without difficulty discern in this state of affairs an explosive situation which needed but a spark to set it off. Two of the most powerful and widely divergent forces of antiquity stand out in vivid contrast.

First of all there was Rome, the mistress of the whole ancient world, the reservoir of streams of classical culture, and her thirty legions. Opposed to her was Judaism, representing a bit of very ordinary land, a *barbara superstitio* (§ 204), and four makeshift armies. Politically speaking, it was everything against nothing, but in the moral and ethnical spheres positions were reversed. Rome had assimilated cosmopolitan Hellenism (§ 34), but in the process had greatly diluted her own heritage. Under more than one aspect, the matron of the seven hills had become a "great harlot . . . with whom the kings of the earth committed fornication," and the seven hills "upon which the woman sat," had become the heads of a monstrous beast (Apoc. 17). Judaism under the Machabees, on the contrary, had overcome and repelled Hellenism, and at the same time had, by means of her paradoxical diaspora (§ 180 ff.), disseminated her tenacious nationalism throughout the whole of the ancient world.

Face to face with Rome, the Zealots could not assume an attitude different from that with which they had confronted Hellenism. Indeed, they had to display an even greater intransigence. There was now added to the thousand-year-old tradition of the past, to which the Machabees had appealed, the throbbing expectation of the coming renascence which had to be accelerated by forcing the Roman eagles now nesting near the Temple to take flight. The political pygmy which dared to attack the giant was, then, driven to do so by two idealistic motives about which the giant was entirely ignorant. The emperor and the states-men on the seven hills, in contrast to the Pharisees and the Zealots on the hills of Sion, had no religious *Torah* hedged around by an ac-cumulation of "traditions," and never had they dreamed of a radiant messianic era.

It was under the new series of procurators that the two opposing forces came to grips. The war actually broke out in 66, but the conflict was being prepared during the preceding years.

Amman (Philadelphia). Roman Theater.

406. On the death of Agrippa I, Claudius sent Cuspius Fadus as procurator (§ 399). He held office from 44 to 46, and discharged his duties in a worthy manner. On his arrival, he found that the Jews of Perea had risen against the inhabitants of Philadelphia (Amman) over a boundary dispute. He intervened energetically, punished one of the principal culprits with death, and exiled two others, even though all three were Jews. He also put a stop to brigandage which had become widespread especially in Idumaea, and put Ptolemy, the ringleader, to death. An order from Claudius had stipulated that the solemn vesture of the high priest, formerly entrusted to the Temple by Vitellius (§ 389), was again to be kept in the fortress Antonia, but Fadus permitted a deputation of Jews to ask the emperor to revoke the decree. Arrived in Rome, the deputation succeeded in having the decree withdrawn, thanks to the mediation of young Agrippa II. Finally, Fadus dispersed a messianic uprising led by a certain Theudas, who had promised his followers that he would lead them across the Jordan, after miraculously causing its waters to divide. The cavalry sent to the spot by the procurator, however, prevented a repetition of the passage of Josue. Some of the miracle seekers were killed and others were imprisoned. Theudas was beheaded.

407. Fadus was succeeded by Tiberius Alexander, an Alexandrian Jew and the nephew of Philo; he held office from 46 to 48. Claudius had perhaps decided upon him because he was of Jewish origin, but the people seem to have held this detail against the new governor, who came to them not only as the representative of foreigners, but also as a known apostate from the Israelite religion. We know of his term only that a great famine occurred during it (cf. Acts 11:27–30), and that he crucified James and Simon, the sons of Judas the Galilean, the leader of the insurrection provoked by the census of Quirinius (§ 380). This brief bit of information shows that Judas' sons had followed the example of their father, and in a more general way affords one a glimpse of the fires that smouldered beneath the ashes.

408. The fire began to flare up under the next procurator, Ventidus Cumanus, who held office from 48 to 52. A serious incident occurred at the Pasch, when one of the Roman soldiers who had been posted on the walls to keep order in the Temple made a vulgar gesture to show his dislike for the Jews (*Antiquities*, XX, 5). The crowd was furious and blamed Cumanus. Cumanus intervened and asked them to be calm, but, as the crowd became more threatening by the minute, he ordered his soldiers, fully armed, to occupy the fortress Antonia. At this, fearing a charge, the Jews began to flee, and so great was the panic that many in the great crowd were crushed to death. Josephus' figure of twenty thousand dead is surely too high, however.

When this incident died down, another arose which was perhaps the result of the first. An imperial servant was robbed near Jerusalem, and out of patriotic zeal the culprits were hidden by their fellows. In reprisal Cumanus ordered the centers near the place where the misdeed occurred to be sacked, and cast some of the prominent men into prison. While the sack was in progress, one soldier came upon a scroll of the *Torah* and publicly tore it to pieces, to the accompaniment of much blasphemy and scurrilous language. The Jews at once hastened to Caesarea to the procurator, demanding punishment for this sacrilege. To avoid complications, Cumanus had the soldier beheaded.

Another and graver incident marked the final disgrace of Cumanus. Pilgrims going from Galilee to Jerusalem were attacked and massacred at Ginea (Jenin), near the border of Samaria. Cumanus did not punish the culprits because he was, it seems, bought off. The Jews then took the law into their own hands, sacking and burning a number of Samaritan villages. In this they were aided by Eleazar and Alexander, two men who harried these regions and are described in the usual manner as "brigands," but who undoubtedly were genuine patriots or Zealots (§§ 322, 381). Cumanus then took action and his troops clashed with the Jews, killing and imprisoning many of them. Appeal was made to Ummidius Quadratus, governor of Syria, and he, coming to Samaria, crucified the Jews imprisoned by Cumanus, and sent the remainder to Rome to answer for their action before the emperor's tribunal. Cumanus and his tribune Celer and a number of prominent

Samaritans and Jews, among which latter were Ananias, the high priest holding office, and Jonathan, who had been high priest before, made up this group. At Rome the situation was saved for the Jews by the vigilance of Agrippa II, who got to Claudius through Agrippina. Claudius condemned the Samaritans to death, deposed Cumanus, and sent him into exile, and ordered Celer to return to Jerusalem to be put to death as an example to the others. At the suggestion of the ex-high priest Jonathan, Felix was made procurator.

409. Obviously Rome was pursuing a yielding and conciliatory policy, hoping that by these concessions peace would be brought to this turbulent land. Instead, the opposite effect was achieved; the deposition of Cumanus and the extraordinary punishment of the tribune Celer, who was returned and put to death under the very eyes of the Jews, awakened in the nationalists the idea that they could obtain anything they wished if they clamored for it loudly enough, and that even Rome was afraid of them. The sacerdotal-Sadducean faction continued to lose authority over the people because it seemed to be subservient to the Romans and favorable to the foreign oppressors. Nor did its highhanded and arrogant methods — as illustrated later on in the attitude taken against St. Paul by that "whited wall" (Acts 23:2–3), the high priest Ananias — endear this aristocratic minority to the people. It was the Pharisees who were heeded most faithfully by the people. The Zealots, however, steadily parted company with them, until by their direct action they came to be known as the Sicarii. The Pharisees, who had once represented the extreme right wing of Judaism, were now "overcome" by the new current and appeared to be the "conservatives" in search of compromise. They were no longer able to sway the masses as they wished, nor could they impede the practical successes of the fiery Zealot-Sicarii who promised grandiose and miraculous triumphs to excited crowds, and swelled their ranks with persons of every sort, all of them men spoiling for action.

410. Such were the conditions in Judea when the new procurator Antonius Felix took office.[3] A freedman of Claudius' mother, Antonia, he was the brother of Pallans, all-powerful favorite of Agrippina, fourth wife of Claudius and mother of Nero. No one knows why Jonathan asked for him (§ 408), but there is no doubt that the choice could hardly have been worse. The conditions of the time called for an entirely different man. Felix's procuratorship lasted from 52 to 60, and was the real prelude to the tragedy. His conduct did not belie

---

[3] Josephus (*Antiquities*, XX, 6, 1–3; *War*, II, 12, 3–7) differs from Tacitus (*Annal.*, XII, 54) on this point. The latter states that Felix was governor of Samaria and Judea at the time when Cumanus governed Galilee. Today the opinion of Josephus has come to be generally accepted, and rightly so, for he was a contemporary of the facts and was present on the scene.

his origin; it was *free* in the widest sense of the word. Tacitus describes it exactly: *"per omnem saevitiam ac libidinem ius regium* SERVILI *ingenio exercuit"* (*Hist.*, V, 9). Confident of the highest protection at court, beginning with that of his brother Pallans, he acted as if he had arrived in a country which existed only to be exploited for his own advantage; *"cuncta malefacta sibi impune ratus, tanta potentia subnixo"* (Tacitus, *Annal.*, XII, 54). In his private life, he had the overweening desire of the *parvenu* to marry into the highest families, and he is portrayed as *"trium reginarum maritus"* (Suetonius, *Claud.*, 28). One of these princely wives was Drusilla, sister of Agrippa II and of Bernice (§ 399). Felix had in 54 induced her to leave Azizus, the king of Emesa (to whom she had been married less than two years, and who had become a Jew so as to be able to wed her [§ 212]), and to marry him, a pagan.

411. Under the government of this venal and ambitious *parvenu*, the Zealot-Sicarii made tremendous progress, especially after the death of Claudius and the election of Nero (October 13, 54). The usual refuge for these nationalists was the desert, as it had been for the Machabees, for there they were quite secure, and ordinarily out of the reach of the Roman authorities. There too they terrorized the towns and roads by their continual patrols and raids. Nothing escaped them. Emboldened by the support of their secret fellow members and sympathizers, they insinuated themselves under various pretexts into private homes, into public places, and into the Temple itself, especially during feasts, treacherously striking down their intended victims, and quickly vanishing without leaving a trace. Oftentimes those who ran solicitously to aid the stricken man, or raised the loudest cry over the dead victim, were the very persons who had a *sica* hidden in their tunic (*Wars*, II, 13, 3).

At other times they operated on a larger scale and attacked entire villages, burning and plundering and then disappearing into the security of the desert. When opportunity offered, they also propagandized small groups and harangued gatherings, inciting them to revolt, and hypnotizing them with wild messianic promises. Their aggressiveness and infectious fanaticism was helped along by the inefficiency of the authorities. No truce was allowed anyone who loved peace and was averse to public movements. Whosoever was not with the Sicarii was against them, which meant that such a one was likely to come face to face with one of them at any time, whether traveling through the countryside, or praying in the Temple, or even in his own home. "No one felt secure, even when friends came to visit them, for notwithstanding all their suspicions and safeguards, they were slain in the end anyway" (*Wars*, II, 13, 3).

One may not say that Felix did nothing about these fanatics, for he did pursue them and crucified many of them, just as he crucified or meted out other punishments to "an immense multitude" of the followers of Eleazar, the bandit leader for twenty years whom he had captured by treachery. These measures, however, were not only sporadic, and in the judgment of Tacitus *intempestivi* also (*Annal.*, XII, 54), but they were nullified by Felix himself, who secretly used the Sicarii to strike down his enemies. He had them cut down the ex-high priest Jonathan, the very one who had asked of Claudius that he be named procurator (§ 408), but who had wearied him with his constant advice as to how he should govern. The Sicarii were willing to lend their services to eliminate so high a personage of the sacerdotal-Sadducean faction, and, needless to say, went unpunished. But what they did to accommodate Felix on that one occasion, they continued to do all the more willingly for their own purposes.

412. Amid all this turbulence messengers from God, i.e., "those sent by God," sprang up and flourished like weeds. In the hearts of the people there had always remained a vague nostalgia for a prophetism which had long since disappeared (Vol. I, § 430), and the tendency to discover the ancient spiritual dictator in anyone who presented himself as the savior in the present extremity was widespread. If God did not send his prophets in times like these, when would he send them? Would he not surely send the greatest of the prophets, the Messias, inasmuch as they were undergoing such tribulation and humiliation as never before? They therefore looked anxiously around in every direction and exclaimed: "Behold, here is the Messias!" or "There he is," and many declared "I am the Messias" (Mt. 24:23). In reality these messiases were either victims of delusion or charlatans, but many of the people believed in them.

Several of these messengers "sent by God" drew the people to the desert to perform miracles in proof of their mission, and Felix apprehended and punished many of their followers. Our accounts tell of an Egyptian of this same sort who invited a crowd to the Mount of Olives. By a simple command, he promised to make the walls of Jerusalem (Vol. I, §§ 96–97) fall to the ground, and thus all would triumphantly enter into the city. Felix attacked this gathering and killed four hundred of them; two hundred more were imprisoned. The Egyptian saved himself by flight, and a few days later St. Paul suffered the humiliation of being mistaken for him by a Roman tribune (Acts 21:38).

413. Other disputes broke out within the sacerdotal-Sadducean faction over the division of the tithes, and among the people of Caesarea over the right of citizenship as it affected the Jews and Greco-Romans. In Caesarea, there was street fighting, houses were sacked, many Jews were

imprisoned, and in the end the dispute was referred to Rome by deputations from both parties.

The Jews of Caesarea who were thrown into prison found St. Paul already there. He spent the last two years of the procuratorship of Felix there, from 58 to 60 (Acts 24:24). We know that Felix saw him, and liked to talk with him, although it was not a noble motive that prompted him to grant these interviews. Paul expounded his doctrine from the very beginning before Felix and "Drusilla, his wife, who was a Jewess" (Acts 24:24). As a matter of fact, by prolonging the imprisonment of St. Paul and arguing with him, Felix hoped only to be bribed into releasing him (Acts 24:26). Not long after this he went out of office, leaving Paul to languish in prison.

In the year 60, with the affair of Caesarea not yet settled, Felix was recalled by Nero.

414. Porcius Festus, the new procurator, did not fill out even two full years in office, and the period from 61 to 62 was all too short a time for his rectitude and ability to achieve permanent results. Upon his arrival he found Judea in a state of semianarchy and practically in the hands of the Sicarii, who were everywhere bent upon stabbings, burning, and plunder. Festus tried his best to combat this elusive enemy, and sent a strong expedition against an *exalté* who was drawing crowds into the desert with the usual false promises of a messianic inauguration; the prophet and his followers were killed. As for the dispute over the wall raised by the priests of the Temple to spite Agrippa II, Festus was conciliatory to both sides, and succeeded in having the affair referred to Rome (§ 401). St. Paul, whom he found in prison, he treated justly, and presented him to Agrippa II (§ 401). When the prisoner appealed to the emperor, as he could in virtue of his Roman citizenship, Festus sent him to Rome, being himself convinced that Paul was innocent and worthy of freedom (Acts 26:31–32).

This great magistrate, who might well have been the man to straighten out the situation in Judea, died in 62, while still in office.

415. In the interval between the death of Festus and the arrival of his successor Albinus, the high priest in charge was Ananus (Annas), son of the high priest of the same name who had been deposed by Valerius Gratus (§ 383), and who had figured in the Passion of Jesus. A rabid Sadducee and lacking the procurator's moderation, he took advantage of his position to rid himself summarily of those he most hated. A passage in Josephus (*Antiquities,* XX, 9, 1, quoted by Eusebius, *Hist. eccl.,* II, 23, 21–24) states that Ananus "assembled the Sanhedrin of the judges, and brought before them the brother of Jesus who was called Christ, whose name was James, and some others; and when he had formed an accusation against them as breakers of the law, he delivered them to be stoned." The Christians of Jerusalem, therefore, were being persecuted. James, "brother of Jesus," is James "the younger" (Mk. 15:40; cf. Gal. 1:19), and "some others" must be the coreligionists of James, i.e., the more notable Christians.[4] But the principal victim, James, was held in highest esteem even by the Jews because of his austere life, and was called "the Just." For that reason, the proceedings of Ananus aroused general indignation, and he was accused both before the new procurator Albinus, who was then on his way, and before Agrippa II. The king, who had conferred the high priesthood on Ananus only three months before, deposed him, and Jesus, the son of Damneus, was given that high office.

416. The brief rule of Albinus, who held office from 62 to 64, completely undid the little good Festus had been able to accomplish, and resulted in genuine disaster. Albinus was concerned only with money, and with it anything could be obtained from him. At first he applied himself to deal with the now extremely powerful Sicarii, but then he speculated even with them. "There was no sort of wickedness that he did not have a hand in. Not only did he, in his political capacity, steal and plunder every one's substance, nor did he only burden the whole nation with taxes, but he permitted the relatives of such as were in prison for robbery . . . to redeem them for money. Nobody remained in prison as a malefactor, but he who gave him nothing" (*War*, II, 14, 1).

Under such a regime the Sicarii flourished, going so far as to abduct from the Temple the very secretary of Eleazar, the Temple superintendent. They then demanded that ten of their companions who were in prison be released in exchange for him, and so it was done. Albinus was persuaded to grant the release by the ex-high priest, Ananias (§ 409), the father of Eleazar. By the color of his money — to be sure — Ananias had come to exercise great influence over the procurator, to such an extent that he had his own band about him to despoil his colleagues in the priesthood. The Sicarii promptly retaliated by seizing the followers of Ananias so as to insure the release of their companions from prison. In such an anarchical state of affairs the only two things

---

[4] The view that this passage may be a Christian interpolation is steadily losing ground, as the passage appears in all manuscripts; Josephus might very well have referred to Jesus as the "Christ," following the common usage. However, the *other* passage to which Eusebius (*Hist. eccl.*, II, 23, 20) and Origen (*Contra Celsum*, I, 47, and elsewhere) appeal, cannot be found. According to it, the destruction of Jerusalem was the divine punishment for the death of James. The account of the martyrdom of James given by Hegesippus (in Eusebius, *Hist. eccl.*, II, 23, 10–18) concludes with the remark that after this crime Vespasian came "directly" (εὐθύς), and began the siege. Nevertheless, writing of the event more than a hundred years later, as Hegesippus did, "directly" might also have a broader meaning, something like "rather quickly" and may signify a period of five years, from 62 in which year James died, to 67, in which year Vespasian came upon the scene.

that counted were money and the *sica*. The man with the most money and the most skillful in the use of arms attracted followers and became a law unto himself. Two relatives of Agrippa also became leaders of groups of adventurers, thieves, and assassins.

When Albinus heard that his successor was on the way to replace him, he conceived the brilliant idea of emptying the prisons. Prisoners guilty of the graver crimes were put to death; the others he made pay very handsomely for their release, and then let them go free. "Thus," Josephus reflects at this point, not without a touch of irony, "the prisons were indeed emptied, but the country was filled with robbers" (*Antiquities*, XX, 9, 5). The prisons of Caesarea must have been quite large and well filled.

417. Albinus was succeeded by Gessius Florus, who held office from 64 to the outbreak of hostilities, and was the last procurator both in time and dignity. After Albinus it was really difficult to see how there could be a worse governor; yet, when the Jews had some experience with Florus, they praised Albinus as a benefactor, so excessive were the evils Florus brought upon them (*Antiquities*, XX, 11, 1). This judgment of one who had been an eyewitness is verified by Tacitus, who noted that "Jewish patience lasted until the coming of Gessius Florus" (*Hist.*, V, 10).

Florus had obtained the procuratorship through the intrigue of his wife Cleopatra, a friend of Nero's wife, Poppaea. The women, it seems, were two of a kind. Florus came to Judea disposed like "an executioner sent to punish condemned malefactors" (*War*, II, 14, 2). Not only did he commit acts of flagrant injustice, oppression, rapine of every kind, but he openly boasted of these crimes. He gave free rein to thieves, also, on condition that they divide their booty with him. This criminal official acted in this manner out of passion for gain, at first, but later he had another motive: to drive the people to desperation, and force them into rebellion and war "by which means alone he hoped to conceal his enormities" (*War*, II, 14, 3). He therefore despoiled entire cities, and reduced whole communities to misery, with the result that many Jews emigrated to foreign countries rather than endure this rapine. In conclusion, no one did more than Florus to further the program of the Sicarii, to push things to extremes.

The measure was now full to the brim, and the least disturbance would suffice to make the jar spill over in the last misfortune.

418. Josephus gives the following report (*War*, VI, 5, 3): "A certain Jesus, son of Ananus, an ignorant and rustic fellow, four years before the war began (i.e., in 62) and at a time when the city was in very great peace and prosperity, came to that feast whereon it is our custom for every one to erect tabernacles to God in the Temple, and began suddenly to cry aloud near the Temple: 'A voice from the east! A voice from the west! A voice from the four winds! A voice against Jerusalem and the Temple! A voice against bridegrooms and brides! A voice against the whole people!' This was his cry as he went about all the lanes of the city by day and by night. Some of the more prominent citizens were annoyed at this evil omen, and seized the man and manhandled him, not sparing the blows. He did not cry out either in his own defense or against his assailants, but continued to cry out the same words as before. The magistrates then concluded, as it was in fact, that his impulse to cry out came from a more hidden source, and led him to the Roman procurator. Although his flesh was torn through to the bone by scourges, he did not plead nor weep, but with all the strength he had, he uttered at each lash in a most mournful chant: 'Woe to Jerusalem!' Albinus, who was the procurator, asked him who he was, and where he came from, and why he cried out in that manner, but the man did not offer any reply, and did not cease to proclaim the lamentation over the city until Albinus let him go, judging him to be insane. Up to the time of the war, this man did not approach any of the citizens, nor was he seen to speak, but the whole day long, like one who practices a prayer, he repeated the lament: 'Woe to Jerusalem!' He neither called down evil on those who struck him every day, nor thanked those who shared their food [with him]; his one and only reply to everyone was that calamitous prediction. During the festivals he cried out more than ever. And repeating this for seven years and five months, he did not become hoarse or tired, but when he saw that his predictions [were verified] in the operations of the siege, he died. Walking about on the walls, he cried without cease: 'Woe! Woe to the city! and to the people! and to the Temple!' When he added: 'Woe also to me!' a stone hurled by a ballista struck him, killing him instantly. Thus, still crying out those predictions, he breathed forth his spirit."

Is this merely a popular little tale, as so many others we find in Josephus? Considering the duration and notoriety of the phenomenon, and the circumstance that the narrator himself was in a very good position to know personally the man involved, there is good reason to believe that the fact — or whatever one may judge it to be — is really historically true.

THE WAR OF VESPASIAN AND TITUS

419. Gessius Florus continued in his ways. When Cestius Gallus, the governor of Syria, came to Jerusalem on the occasion of the Pasch, an enormous multitude of Jews (Josephus states that there were "three million," an evident exaggeration) came before him to protest against Florus. Nothing came of it. Cestius Gallus made vague promises to call the procurator to order, but the latter continued worse than before.

In the month of Artemisios (May) of 66, the crisis was reached. The imperial decision concerning the dispute over civil rights between the Jews and the Greco-Romans of Caesarea (§ 413) arrived from Rome. By virtue of underhanded dealings at court, the anti-Jewish delegation was successful in obtaining a verdict unfavorable to the Jews, and one which cost them their control over the city. The news was joyfully received by the Greco-Romans of Caesarea, with great manifestations of disdain for the Jews. With an eye to making the synagogue almost inaccessible, these pagans put up shops in front of the synagogue. Florus took the eight talents which the Jews offered him so that he would put a halt to the building, but proceeded to do nothing. On the following Sabbath one of the Caesareans derisively immolated a bird in front of the synagogue, in imitation of the Hebrew rite of the cleansing of lepers, thus implying that the Jews were lepers, as the ancient fable stated (§ 202). The Jews reacted to this, but were worsted. Foreseeing other and more serious incidents, those who could departed from the city and withdrew to Narbata, about sixty stadia from Caesarea. A delegation of protest which they sent to Florus was punished.

420. The Jews in Jerusalem were furious at this news, but soon afterward it was the turn of the holy city. Florus sent to the Temple treasury for seventeen talents, pretending that they were for the emperor, when in reality they were for himself. The amount was not extraordinarily large, especially for Florus, but it nevertheless aroused the people to violent protest. Instead of protesting, however, some of the sarcastic wits among the Zealots went about the city with baskets to gather alms for the needy and mendicant Florus. The procurator took offense at this, came to Jerusalem with his soldiers, and, despite the intercession of the more eminent Jews and of Bernice (§ 402), razed many houses of the presumed culprits. Besides this he scourged and crucified a large number of citizens, some of whom held the rank of Roman knights. These repressive measures extended to some 3600 victims, including women and children. Florus then gave orders that on the following day, the seventeenth of Artemisios, the people were to welcome the two cohorts of soldiers who were arriving from Caesarea. The pretext given was that in this manner the people would show that they had disavowed their preceding attitude, but the real aim was to set off the ultimate conflagration at which the procurator was aiming (§ 417). This is confirmed by the fact that, among other things, he ordered the cohorts not to acknowledge the greetings and to assume a harsh attitude toward the Jews.

Florus' purpose was easily attained. Entering Jerusalem, the cohorts refused to return the proffered greetings. Voices of protest arose from amid the people. At this the soldiers charged the crowd, which fled in disorder, and many were slain or trampled to death by the horses. In the narrow streets of the city, the soldiers encountered sporadic resistance, but finally the vast majority of the rebels took refuge in the Temple. The first thing they did was to isolate the Temple from the fortress Antonia (§ 345) by battering to earth the portico which connected the two. Thus, Florus could no longer penetrate the Temple by way of the fortress, nor, on the other hand, did he have sufficient troops to flush out by other means the rebels in the extremely well-fortified Temple. He then considered that he might extricate himself from the difficulty by making some provisional agreements with the people, and so withdrew from the city leaving only one cohort on guard.

421. This moment in the course of events was like that of a tower which is on the point of collapsing. Having sustained a great blow, it trembles from top to bottom, but before crashing to the earth it hangs momentarily in the air, as if undecided whether to resume its upright position or to fall headlong. Before suffering its ultimate fate, the thousand-year-old tower of Israel also knew this moment.

At Jerusalem the Zealot-Sicarii wished to push things to extremes, but there were moderates among the Pharisees and the remnants of the Sadducean-Hasmonean faction who wished to avoid a rupture with Rome. These, together with Bernice, turned to Cestius Gallus; so too did Florus, but on his own account. Gallus sent his tribune Neopolitanus to conduct an inquest on the spot; the tribune met Agrippa II near Jamnia, and both came on to Jerusalem. When he had collected his information, the tribune returned to Gallus to make his report, and Agrippa, a Romanophile himself, did what he could to restore calm. He harangued the people, painting in vivid colors the disaster awaiting them in the event of a war against Rome, and so extracted from them a promise of obedience to the emperor. For some weeks the situation did not get any worse. Later, when Agrippa refused his consent to the sending of a deputation to accuse Florus before the emperor, and tried rather to induce the people to have patience until Florus was replaced, he was driven out of Jerusalem with stones (§ 403). The Sicarii, of course, were the ones who threw the stones.

The extremists were also busy, and with better success. They took possession of the fortress Masada (§ 326), killing its Roman garrison. Grave as this was, graver still was the decision taken at the instigation of Eleazar, son of Ananias (§ 416), to stop offering a daily sacrifice for the emperor (§ 377) in the Temple. This was equivalent to an open declaration of war.

422. The Jews of Jerusalem who did not share the fervor of the Sicarii were terrified at this action, but their exhortations and protests were of no avail, the sacrifice for the emperor was not resumed. The moderates then began to gather arms so as to overpower the extremists by force, and had recourse to Florus. But this very war was what he wanted, so he did not even deign to reply. Three thousand cavalry sent by Agrippa, however, did arrive (§ 403), and occupied the upper city. The Sicarii, in control of the lower city and the Temple, willingly accepted the challenge, and Jerusalem became a battleground. In the month of Loos (July-August), the moderates lost ground almost completely and in the end were besieged in the palace of Herod. Shortly before this, the palaces of the high priest Ananias, Agrippa, and Bernice had been burned (§ 403), and the fortress of Antonia had fallen into the power of the insurgents. The siege of the palace lasted some time. The troops of Agrippa and natives of the land were allowed free passage if they withdrew from the struggle, but the Roman soldiers, denied this passage, were driven to take refuge in the three towers of the palace (§ 345).

On the sixth of the month Gorpiaios (August-September), the edifice was burned, and the following day the high priest Ananias, discovered hiding in the subterranean passages of the building, was killed by the Sicarii. The Romans commanded by Metilius held out for a time, but finally again asked for free passage, proposing to lay down their arms. The offer was accepted by the Sicarii, who pledged their good faith with an oath. The Romans did in fact file out without being molested, but once they had laid down their shields and swords, they were cut down to a man, with the exception of Metilius. While all the others allowed themselves to be killed without any resistance beyond appealing in a loud voice to the oath that had been sworn, the craven Metilius promised to be circumcised and to become a Jew. Meanwhile, he could learn something of the observance of the Jewish law from the Sicarii who accepted his promise, for that slaughter took place on the Sabbath day (§§ 237, 253, 312).

423. During this same period, grave disorders broke out elsewhere. While the Roman garrison was being massacred in Jerusalem, the Gentile populace slaughtered twenty thousand Jews at Caesarea, with the result that the Jews rose up against the Gentiles in Philadelphia, Pella, Scythopolis, Samaria, Ptolemais, Ascalon, and other places. The pagans, in turn, struck back again at the Jews, so that in all Judea, and in the Hellenistic cities of the coast, pillage, burning, and slaughter were the order of the day. "It was then common to see cities filled with unburied corpses, dead bodies of old men and infants exposed side by side, poor women stripped of the last covering of modesty, the whole province full of indescribable horrors" (*War*, II, 18, 2).

Nor was Alexandria to escape the wave of hatred against the Jews, only there the disorders occurred on a vaster scale. The pile of fifty thousand bodies mentioned by Josephus may be an exaggeration, but it is no exaggeration to say that there was a terrible slaughter.

Amid such great desolation some few were quite satisfied: Florus on the one side, and the Zealot-Sicarii on the other. Their common purpose had been achieved.

424. At this stage, Cestius Gallus felt he should intervene in virtue of his authority as governor of Syria. Mobilizing the Twelfth Roman Legion, he gathered together many other auxiliary troops from the kings tributary to Rome. Among these were strong contingents sent by King Agrippa, who followed him in person. It was with a total of about thirty thousand men that Gallus marched from Antioch along the coast. Along the way he burned Zabulon in Galilee, and farther down, about parallel with Jerusalem, the port city of Joppe (Jaffa) and Lydda.

The feast of Tabernacles occurred during this period. The people who flocked to Jerusalem on that occasion had come armed, and in a surprise attack had inflicted heavy losses on the Roman troops. Despite this, Gallus advanced toward the capital, and set up camp on Mount Scopus so as to attack it from the north, as was customary (§ 312). The quarter of Bezetha was quickly conquered and put to the torch, but when Gallus attacked the Temple, he was driven back. He then unexpectedly ordered a retreat, a move for which Josephus is unable to give an adequate explanation. The reason probably was connected with the results of these first attempts and with Gallus' realization that he lacked both troops and engines of siege for this undertaking. Events quickly proved how difficult an undertaking it was.

Half-sicle of the year I of the insurrection (A.D. 66).

The retreat of the Romans filled the rebels with confidence, and they set to work to harass the rear of the retreating army. Their guerrilla tactics cost the Romans much, and the second half of the retreat was transformed into a veritable rout. At historic Beth-Horon (§ 255) the Roman army fled in disorder, leaving behind them almost all of their military equipment; the bulk of the army, however, succeeded in reaching Antioch. The pursuit ended, the insurgents returned triumphantly laden with booty to Jerusalem, which they entered on the eighth of the month of Dios (the first of November).

425. It is hardly necessary to mention that this success intensified to an inordinate degree the already exalted spirits of the insurgents. They perceived in their victory evident proof of Yahweh's assistance, saw a return of the heroic era of the Machabees, and perhaps also they already contemplated the hillock of Sion, as the prophet had predicted (Isa. 2:2; Mich. 4:1), "established on the summit of the mountains, elevated above the hills," above even the hill of the Capitoline. For these reasons, many friends of the Romans very prudently left Jerusalem; others, wavering and doubtful, were dragged along by the popular enthusiasm and joined the insurgents. As a sign of the new era of liberty which was beginning, Jewish money was coined.

This enthusiasm was all very fine, exhilarating even, but as it cooled, the necessity of serious organization to meet the inevitable attack of the Romans, who would certainly return in greater strength, became obvious. By now even the more eminent of the sacerdotal faction had been carried along by the current, with more or less conviction; and it devolved upon them to direct the necessary reorganization. The measures they took clearly reflect their true state of mind. Still somewhat diffident, and desirous always of leaving the door open for an understanding with Rome, they either eliminated the most extreme Zealots from their organization entirely, or relegated them to secondary offices. At the head of the government, and in charge of the defense of Jerusalem was Joseph, the son of Gorion, and the ex-high priest Ananus (Annas: § 415). The extremist Eleazar, son of Ananias (§ 421), and Jesus, son of Sapphia, were sent south to Idumaea, a region less exposed to the attack of the Romans. The eleven districts into which Judea was divided were put under new administrators. To the north, that is, the region which would first feel the fury of the Roman attack, they sent

Joseph, son of Mathias; he was to govern lower and upper Galilee, and also the fortress of Gamala (§§ 305, 403).

426. This Joseph, son of Mathias and of sacerdotal lineage, is the historian Josephus (§ 208). At that time he had not yet assumed the name of Flavius. He was born in A.D. 37–38, and was twenty-nine years old at this time. In 64 he had been sent to Rome by the Sanhedrin to obtain the release of the priests who had been arrested by Felix, and it was shortly after his return to Judea in 66 that he was given this post. The real reason why he was assigned to the region which would be the first to feel the Roman attack from the north, can perhaps be discovered by sifting the two different explanations which he himself gives. In *War*, II, 20, 3–4, he describes himself as an organizer of the armed resistance; in his *Life*, 7 (written some twenty years after *War*: § 208), he portrays himself rather as one who restrained the extremists of Galilee, seeking only to have them conform to the milder counsels which prevailed among the heads of the government at Jerusalem. There is little doubt that the portrait which Josephus paints of himself in his *Life* tends to emphasize the fact that his actions were conciliatory toward Rome, and it is very probable that this was also the real, though hidden, purpose behind his being sent to Galilee. In that case, the sacerdotal faction of Jerusalem certainly hoped that Josephus would organize that territory for war, but they also expected him to be an influence for moderation amid the extremists who had infested Galilee ever since the time of Herod the Great (§ 322). Since Josephus had lately returned from Rome, he would have a special interest in the latter task. Could anyone who had seen the power of the Empire of Rome at close range harbor any delusions as to the outcome of a war between Israel and Rome?

Josephus did not abjure his nationalism (of the moderate Pharisee variety) when he took over his charge, nor was he insensible to the perfervid patriotism which had by this time pervaded the masses. Still, cold logic would not let him forget the inevitable outcome of the war, nor could he entirely suppress his admiration for the Empire of Rome with which he had recently come into personal contact. He therefore went about his duties like a good patriot, and his prudent moderation was sustained by a firm will impervious to emotional thinking. When later he found himself in an indefensible position, he did a resolute about-face (§ 434).

427. Meanwhile, he labored for the national cause. Assisted by Joazar and Juda, the priests who had come with him from Jerusalem, he wished to establish personal contact with the people of Galilee, and set up there a supreme council of seventy ancients upon whom other

Cana of Galilee.

judges, assigned to the various centers, depended. He fortified many strategic points in Galilee, among which were Jotapata (present-day *Kh. Jefat,* near Cana of Galilee, slightly north of Sepphoris [§ 301]), Sepphoris itself, Mount Tabor (Vol. I, § 310), and, to the northwest of Lake Tiberias, the advance post Gischala (modern *el-Jish*); he also re-enforced Tarichea, Tiberias, and Gamala, which had rebelled against Agrippa II and joined the insurgents (§ 403). At Tiberias, Josephus desired to placate the extremists on one point which happened to be in accord with his own Pharisaical principles; he allowed the angry populace to destroy the palace of Herod there, for it contained traditionally forbidden representations of living creatures. At the same time he provided for the levying and training of troops, and taught them the Roman manner of fighting from a square formation. He soon had sixty thousand men trained and ready.

Yet, despite his zeal, Josephus did not succeed in dissipating some of the rather somber shadows in which suspicions were nurtured of him, if not of his friendship for the Romans, at least of coolness toward the nationalist cause. In view of his state of mind, his conduct must have given some reason for such suspicions. The representative of the anti-Josephus trend was John, son of Levi, better known by the name of John of Gischala, from the place of his origin. Astute and bold, ready for any kind of violence, he was an ideal political chieftain. His violent hatred of Roman tyranny, however, did not prevent him from aspiring to replace it with his own, which would be no less harsh, but much less intelligent, judging from the way he exercised it now in Galilee with his armed bands. Hence his aversion for Josephus, the official representative of nationalistic power and too lukewarm an enemy of Rome. Among other accusations and plots, John on one occasion tried to have him assassinated at Tiberias, and Josephus was barely able to save his life by leaping into the sea. John also tried to have him deprived of the authority which he held from Jerusalem, but Josephus parried this blow neatly by winning over to his side the four persons sent for that purpose.

428. Meanwhile, Jerusalem was being fortified and prepared for war. Walls were repaired, great quantities of arms and engines of war were gotten ready, young men called to arms were being trained. Directing the organization for war was the ex-high priest Ananus (§ 425), but neither was his heart in his work, as Josephus justly observes: "Ananus proposed shortly to withdraw from the preparations for war and to persuade the rebels and those rash ones who were called Zealots to more useful endeavors, but he had to give way before their violence" (*War*, II, 22, 1).

In Jerusalem internal division was as rife as it was in Galilee. Here, the leader of the extremists was Simon Bar-Giora (Aramaic: *bar*, "son [of the]"; *ghiyyora*, "proselyte"), who had previously fought against Cestius Gallus, and was now ravaging in true brigand fashion the territory of the Acrabata, north of Samaria. The high priest was forced to send some troops from Jerusalem against him. Simon then retired and made his way to Masada (§§ 326, 421), whence he made incursions into all parts of Idumaea, whose principal centers had to be guarded to save them from his depredations and burnings.

✿   ✿   ✿

429. The news of the defeat of Cestius Gallus and of the total insurrection of Judea found Nero in Achaia, amid the Homeric surround-

Nero.   Vespasian.

Sepphoris.

ings of feasting, heroic theatricals, and no less heroic buffoonery. Upon receipt of the information, a brief, prosaic halt was called to the Hellenic festival, and immediate provisions were made to avenge the defeat and suppress the revolt. Find only the right man, give him full power to act, and he would see to everything, from gathering the necessary troops to carrying out a full-scale expedition.

Nero's choice fell upon a general who at that moment formed part of his retinue. This man, Titus Flavius Vespasian, was not particularly esteemed by Nero because he was notoriously unappreciative of poetry and heroic verse; indeed, so boorish was he that he had once had the scandalous impertinence to fall asleep while the emperor was declaiming his verses. Nero tolerated him only because he was a useful instrument of war. Despite his countenance, which was that of a stolid Sabine peasant (the Flavii came from Rieti), Vespasian had given proof of his ability in the campaigns in Germany and Britain, and could be very useful in military affairs because of his experience and shrewdness.

To remove him from his sight, and at the same time to put the troublesome business in good hands, Nero sent him to Judea.

430. Vespasian set about preparing his army, and with this in mind betook himself to Antioch. A regular army man and a strict disciplinarian, he realized that one of the reasons for Cestius Gallus' defeat had been the lack of discipline among his troops, which included the Twelfth Legion, *Fulminata* (§ 424). For the time being, then, he set aside this legion and mobilized the Fifth Legion, *Macedonica*, the Tenth, *Fretensis*, and sent his son Titus to Alexandria to mobilize there the Fifteenth,

Apollinaris.[1] He further gathered twenty-three auxiliary cohorts and six "wings" of cavalry (§ 375), and other troops furnished by allied kings, such as Agrippa II, Antiochus of Commagene, Soemus of Emesa, and Malchus, king of the Nabateans. His total force was in the neighborhood of sixty thousand men. Titus led the Fifteenth Legion from Alexandria and joined his father at Ptolemais in the spring of 67.

Even before this arrival, Sepphoris, one of Josephus' key cities, defected from him. It had always been favorable to the Romans, and no sooner had Vespasian arrived with the bulk of his army in nearby Ptolemais, than it swore fealty to him and asked for a Roman garrison to defend it. Vespasian complied with six thousand infantry and one thousand cavalry, commanded by the tribune Placidus. Josephus attempted to recapture the city, but, as he himself states, he was repulsed. To make matters worse, Placidus now began to lay waste large sections of Galilee.

When Titus arrived, Vespasian moved from Ptolemais, encamping with all his army on the borders of Galilee. This alone was enough to cause the armed recruits instructed by Josephus, who at that time was encamped at Garis near Sepphoris, to flee in all directions and to seek refuge in various fortresses. Josephus retreated to Tiberias and asked Jerusalem to send re-enforcements adequate to meet the critical situation, but of course none of these arrived. The majority of the disbanded soldiers had gathered at Jotapata (§ 427); Josephus also repaired thither, arriving on the twenty-first of the month Artemisios (first part of May) to direct operations. And just in time, for the next day Vespasian arrived to attack Jotapata. He had already become master of almost all of Palestine without meeting any opposition. Shortly before he had taken and burned Gadara; once Jotapata fell, there remained the fortresses of Gischala and Mount Tabor, and they would not hold out for long.

431. The unexpected opposition Vespasian encountered at Jotapata lasted for forty-seven days and did much honor to Josephus. The fortified city was on a steep hill and was accessible with difficulty only on its northern side; it was protected by solid walls and towers, and was well-stocked with food. The first violent assaults of the Romans were repulsed. Vespasian then began a regular siege, and at the same time raised an earthen bank to match the height of the walls, and from this he proposed to batter down the defenders' wall. To offset the destruction of the first wall, Josephus had his men put up an inner wall. The ballistae were then concentrated against the citadel, while lower on the wall the battering-rams set to work. The besieged fought

---

[1] In regard to this data, the text of *War*, III, 1, 3, as it is commonly given, must be corrected according to III, 4, 2.

Enemy fortress assailed by Romans. Left to right: ballista, bastion, interlocked shields, battering ram under cover, wooden tower.

back as best they could, hurling every sort of object at the attackers.
They even made a number of successful sorties, and set fire to part of
the wooden towers built by the Romans. Vespasian himself was slightly
wounded by an arrow from the walls.

The Romans rebuilt their towers, and resumed their bombardment
and demolition with a greater intensity than ever. A veritable shower
of large stones fell upon the besieged and paralyzed their defense.
A stone struck off the head of a soldier standing on the walls near
Josephus, and caused it to land about three stadia away.[2] The next
day a pregnant woman was hit and torn asunder as she came out of
her house by a projectile which carried her child half a stadium away.
Yet, even when the walls were breached, the first assault made by the
Romans was unsuccessful, because the Jews with boiling oil and
fenugreek caused the assailants to slip off their scaling ladders and
bridges. By now, however, the defenders were weakened not only by
their losses but also, and especially, by the lack of water. The Romans
pushed inexorably ahead with their operations, and soon completely
dominated the walls of the fortress.

432. While the siege was under way, the neighboring city of Japha took
courage at the resistance of Jotapata, and itself rebelled. Vespasian sent
Trajan, the father of the future emperor of the same name and the com-

---

[2] A stadium is equivalent to 606.75 feet.

Roman battering ram, not
protected, in use.

Roman soldiers assault a wall, protected
by interlocked shields.

mander of the Tenth Legion, against Japha. The inhabitants came out to
assail him, but were driven back and beleaguered in their city. Shortly
thereafter Titus arrived with re-enforcements, and the city was taken
on the twenty-fifth of the month Daisios (first days of June). Fifteen
thousand Jews were killed in the fighting and more than two thousand
were enslaved.

A few groups of Samaritans felt the urge to rebel also, and began
to gather together on Gerizim in a threatening manner. Vespasian
dispatched Cerealis, commander of the Fifth Legion, against them.
Surrounding the assembled multitude on the twenty-seventh of Daisios,
he demanded their surrender. When they refused, he destroyed them,
leaving 11,600 dead on the field.

433. In the end, Jotapata fell. A Jewish deserter had told Vespasian
of the sorry plight of the besieged, and that out of fatigue the sentinels
could no longer keep themselves awake until morning, but fell asleep.
The best moment for an attack, then, would be toward dawn.

One morning, under cover of a mist, the Romans scaled the walls. First
to go up was Titus, with the tribune Domitius Sabinus and a few soldiers
from the Fifteenth Legion. They were not discovered, and after killing
the sleeping sentinels they pushed on into the city. Sextus Calvarius
and Placidus followed with their troops, and in a short time the fortress
was full of Romans, while the besieged still slept. It was the first
day of the month Panemos (first part of July). There was practically
no resistance. The vengeance exacted by the Romans because of the
prolonged siege was terrible; to add to their anger, the centurion
Antony was treacherously killed in the taking of the city by a Jew to
whom he had reached out his right hand as a guarantee that he would
spare his life, and also to help him get out of a cave.

Between the siege and the final assault, forty thousand persons were killed. Many of these had leaped to their death from the precipices upon which the city was built. Only twelve hundred people, mostly women and children, were marched off as slaves. The city itself was razed to the ground.

434. After the fall of the city, the Romans went looking for Josephus, but he could not be found, as he had taken refuge in a cistern which was connected by a secret passageway to a cavern well-concealed in

Romans storming a fortified place. (Rome, Trajan's Column.)

the rock. In this place he found forty other persons and abundant provisions. He lay hidden for two days, waiting for an opportune moment to flee, but so close was the watch kept by the Romans that it was impossible for him to do so. On the third day a slave woman accidentally discovered the men in the cave and spread the news. Vespasian immediately sent two tribunes to the cave to guarantee Josephus his life, but he did not believe them. Vespasian then sent a tribune who had been one of Josephus' friends, urging him to surrender. He was on the point of doing so, but his companions in the cave threatened to kill him if he yielded himself up. Then, according to his account (*War*, III, 8, 1 ff.), they decided to kill each other one by one, in chain fashion, drawing lots to see who should be the first victim, and who should follow in turn. Josephus and another drew the last straws. When all but they were dead, they peacefully surrendered to the Romans. This account has the distinct flavor of a story invented to cover his confusion; thus to throw the responsibility of his safety on providential lots makes one suspect that the reality was quite different, something which did not harmonize well with his valorous conduct up to that time. After Jotapata's fall, however, Josephus' political vacillations were at an end. From that time on he was an open adherent of Rome.

When brought to Vespasian, he was received kindly by him, and even more so by the young Titus. Hearing that within a short time he was to be sent as a renowned prisoner to Nero, the wily Pharisee assumed the role of a prophet, and predicted that Vespasian and Titus would enjoy the imperial dignity. The two corpulent Sabines were, like everyone else at the time, somewhat superstitious, and this prediction uttered by a son of the mysterious Orient was not at all displeasing to them. However, their positive Roman mentality led them to await the fulfillment of the prophecy, and in the meantime they retained this prophet near them, for he could be useful to them in their future campaigns. So it was that the future historian of the war remained with the Flavii, and was treated well, although he was kept in chains (§ 445).

435. Three days after the conquest of Jotapata, Vespasian resumed operations. Passing through Ptolemais, he repaired with his army to maritime Caesarea, and thence to Caesarea Philippi, where he was received with great festivity by Agrippa II and Bernice. At this time he sent a detachment to destroy and occupy Joppe, which had been rebuilt after its destruction by Cestius Gallus (§ 424). He then reconquered the lands which had rebelled against Agrippa, and which had been fortified by Josephus (§ 427). Tiberias surrendered without resistance. In Tarichea, the citizens wanted to surrender, but the Zealots resisted Titus. When the city fell at the beginning of the month Garpiaios (September), the Zealots took refuge in boats on Lake Tiberias, but the Romans followed them on rafts, and there ensued a slaughter which made the lake one mass of floating cadavers. Six thousand five hundred were killed in battle, and, in combing through the population soon afterward, one thousand two hundred who were not fit for work were also killed. Six thousand of them were sent to work on Nero's project, the cutting of the isthmus at Corinth, and more than thirty thousand were sold as slaves. This large number glutted the market, and the price of slaves fell off sharply; a Jew as merchandise lost a good third of his former value.

436. There remained the fortresses of Gischala and Tabor in Galilee, and Gamala (§§ 403, 427). Agrippa had unsuccessfully besieged

Tarichea and the Lake of Tiberias.

Gamala for seven months, and was wounded there while calling upon the besieged to surrender. After very stubborn resistance, which inflicted heavy losses on the assailants, the fortress fell before the methodical battering of the Roman engines of war. This time, out of revenge, total slaughter followed; women and even children were thrown down the steep slopes of the fortress. Only two women did not perish because they succeeded in hiding themselves. Before this assault, which occurred on the twenty-third of the month Hyperberetaios (October), a detachment commanded by Placidus had taken possession of the fortress on Mount Tabor. So only Gischala was left, where John and his men had withdrawn (§ 427). Vespasian sent Titus with a detachment of cavalry to demand the surrender of the city. As that day was a Sabbath, John asked that consideration of the offer be postponed until the following day, and the request was granted without any difficulty. During the night John fled toward Jerusalem, where he and a group of his most fanatical followers were able to find shelter. Gischala itself welcomed Titus, and was left undamaged.

Having thus conquered all of Galilee and Samaria by the end of 67, Vespasian wintered at Caesarea with the Fifth and Fifteenth Legions. The Tenth he sent to Scythopolis (Beisan).

        ✿   ✿   ✿

437. Vespasian was in no hurry. He had organization and discipline, and was proceeding step by step according to a methodical plan. He

knew that he would have to tighten the circle around the rebellion until it was reduced to one center of resistance, and that this would doubtless be Jerusalem. According to this plan, he had everything to gain with the passage of time; for the rebels it was just the reverse.

Among the Jews there was neither organization nor discipline. The .opposition between the reluctant sacerdotal-Sadducean faction and that of the extremist Zealots, who were dragging them in their wake (§ 425), had become ever more acute. The events of the first period of the war which ended in 67, pointed to only one possible conclusion, the ascendancy of the Zealot-Sicarii, the one dynamic force of the nation. The defeats inflicted by the Romans and the loss of the northern part of the country were attributed to the weakness of the aristocrats in charge (and this indeed no one could deny); let these inept leaders be divested of all authority, then, and the Zealots take charge. The arrival of the furious John of Gischala with his followers in Jerusalem reenforced the extremist circles, and they quickly set about their business.

438. The most prominent persons in Jerusalem were cast into prison and then killed, among whom was an Antipas of the Herod family. All traditional laws were disregarded in the choosing of a new high priest by lot. The lot fell to a certain Phannias (Pinehas), a villanous rogue who had not the faintest idea of the dignity which he was receiving. But for this very reason he was all the more acceptable to the democratic Zealots, who thus struck another blow at the aristocratic, sacerdotal-Sadducean caste. The ousted faction then moved to recover its position.

Fortress besieged by Romans. (Rome, Trajan's Column.)

The most influential among them, such as the ex-high priest Ananus (§ 425), Gorion, son of Joseph, the famous Pharisee Simon, son of Gamaliel, and others, thought to crush the arrogance of the extremists by force. Civil war was again enkindled, and the two parties fought over the possession of the Temple itself.

Then the Zealots, judging that they were too few in relation to the aristocratic faction, turned for help to the savage inhabitants of Idumaea, where the extremist Eleazar (§ 425) had been a commander. An army of about twenty thousand Idumaeans responded to the call, but was halted outside the walls by the Sadducean faction; that night, however, the Zealots were able to get them into Jerusalem during a terrible hurricane.

439. Once they had entered, the Zealots and Idumaeans began a reign of terror typical of the politico-religious fanaticism of the Orient. Three brief passages in Josephus are like three rays of light focused on the events which occurred after that first dark night. "Outside of the Temple was a lake of blood, and there, [when] the day broke, eight thousand five hundred men lay dead" (*War*, IV, 5, 1). "I do not believe I am in error in saying that the ruin of the city began with the death of Ananus" (IV, 5, 2); he was murdered as were the more eminent among the priests. Soon "after this, the Zealots and the multitude of Idumaeans fell upon the people and butchered them as if they were a flock of unclean animals" (IV, 5, 3). The slaughter went on for some time, methodically, and counted twelve thousand victims among the aristocrats. After the mass slaughter, regular tribunals were set up to pass judgment on persons who were considered unacceptable, but even when absolved by these tribunals, they were likely to be slain. Thus it happened that the eminent man Zacharias, son of Baruch, after being absolved by the tribunal, was assassinated in the Temple, and his corpse thrown into the valley.

Even the Idumaeans were finally nauseated by this macabre orgy, and retired to their own district. The Zealots, however, now absolute masters of the city, persisted in the mad slaughters, and wallowed in blood. Those citizens who by money or other means succeeded in leaving the capital took refuge wherever they could, even with Vespasian, and spread about the news of what was happening in Jerusalem.

440. The astute Roman realized how well these events helped his cause, and he waited at Caesarea more tranquilly than before. No doubt he even began to smile.

But he did not remain idle. During the winter, Vespasian had secured certain localities by means of garrisons. At the beginning of spring, instead of marching against Jerusalem — as his war council suggested —

he had his troops occupy
Gadara and all the rest of
Perea, which, except for Machaerus, was thus lost to the
Zealots. Later still he went
down from Caesarea with his
army along the coast, oc-
cupied Lydda and Jamnia
among other places (§§ 393,
473), and set a guard over all
the region as far as Idumaea
to the south of Jerusalem.
Next, he went back to Sa-
maria, and then turning eastward, proceeded along the
Jordan until he reached
Jericho on the third of the
month Daisios (end of May).
Here and there along his circular march, he had left detachments of troops, so that
the capital, torn to pieces
interiorly by civil war, was

Outlines of a Roman camp at Masada
in Palestine. (Vester, Amer. Colony.)

externally girded by a chain of enemy garrisons.

441. Only a short time after the general had returned to Caesarea
to prepare his plan of attack on Jerusalem, the news of the death of
Nero, on June 9, 68, reached him. The political situation immediately
became most delicate. Up to the time of Nero, the supreme power had
remained in the family of the founder of the empire by means of
adoptions and marriage, but after Nero it seemed that at Rome the
family of Julius-Claudia was not to be considered. The legions at Lyons
in Gaul had already rebelled under Vindex, and this move quickly
clashed with that of Galba, legate to Tarraco in Spain. At Rome, the
praetors had gone over to the side of Galba, and he became emperor at
the death of Nero. Now that the hypnotic charm of the family of Julius
Caesar was broken, the legions had begun to play the role of political
arbiters, and gained increasing influence. The legions of Germany wanted
their voice heard, and elected as emperor Aulus Vitellius, son of Vitellius,
governor of Syria (§ 371). At Rome itself, the praetors quickly discovered the severity of Galba. Offered money by Otho, they rebelled.
On January 15, A.D. 69, Galba was assassinated in the Forum, and
Otho succeeded him. But Vitellius descended from the north with the
legions from Gaul and Germany, and Otho, defeated at Cremona on

the fourteenth of April, killed himself three days later. Within ten months three emperors on the throne of Caesar had died violent deaths.

442. Things had indeed come to a serious pass. It is remarkable that the legions of the Orient, both those of Egypt and those of Syria-Palestine, took no part in these turbulent affairs. The example of the other legions was infectious, and it is hard to see why these legions also, like those of Gaul and Germany, and the praetors of Rome, should not have had something to say. The most prominent general of the legions in the Orient was now Vespasian and his soldiers could expect much from him. But once again the shrewd calculator waited calmly. He had learned from the fruitful Sabine fields that the best fruits are those which fall when they are ripe. His fruit was not yet ripe. Perhaps also the prophecy pronounced in his favor by his Jewish prisoner (§ 434) echoed in his mind. At any rate, he wished to co-operate positively but prudently in proving him to have been a true prophet and, while biding his time, kept him in chains at his side.

When he learned of the election of Galba, Vespasian sent Titus to Rome to pay homage to the new emperor and to receive orders in regard to the prosecution of the campaign. When Titus arrived at Corinth, he learned that Galba was already dead, and as there was now no longer any reason for his voyage, he returned to his father at Caesarea. The father and his son followed attentively the struggle between Otho and Vitellius; but they made no move themselves. Nor did their legions move, either politically or strategically. Actually, in such political conditions as these, it was not prudent to carry on a war; so the war was suspended for the space of a year, from June, 68, to June, 69.

443. In the meantime, the internal situation at Jerusalem and that of the insurgents was critical. Simon Bar-Giora had become very powerful at Masada (§ 428) and had more than forty thousand armed men at his command. With these he harried Idumaea and the south up to the very gates of Jerusalem with his brigandage. Within the city, the faction of John of Gischala prevailed, and tyranny went hand in hand with the most unbridled license. The Zealots, who had risen up in the name of Yahweh to enforce strict observance of the Law, now were occupied not only with robberies and killings, but also with the violation of women. Some of them, dressed up as women, perfumed their hair and painted their eyelids, and did other things better left unmentioned. "They went about the city as in a brothel" (*War*, IV, 9, 10). The stages of their historical evolution is clear: Pharisaism had degenerated into fanaticism, the fanaticism had been organized into gangsterism, and the gangsterism ended up in a brothel.

To free themselves from such a shameful situation, those opposed to John of Gischala had recourse to a desperate measure: they invited Simon Bar-Giora with his brigands into the city. Unfortunately however this did not prove to be either Scylla or Charybdis, but rather a piling of Scylla upon Charybdis. Simon entered Jerusalem in the month Xanthicus (April) of A.D. 69, and was enthusiastically welcomed by the citizens. The Zealots of John, however, disapproved and shut themselves up on the hill of the Temple. Simon attacked the Temple, but encountered resistance; thus, civil war continued, and the city itself was divided between the two leaders.

444. On the fifth of the month Daisios (end of May), Vespasian, without seriously engaging in action, again moved his army, drawing the circle ever more tightly around Jerusalem. In the north he took Acrabata (§ 428), set up a garrison at Beth-el (Vol. I, §§ 126, 127), and then pushed forward to reconnoiter the territory around Jerusalem. To the south, the tribune Cerealis subdued upper Idumaea and conquered Hebron (Vol. I, § 91). There thus remained to the insurgents only the fortresses of Herodium, Masada, and Machaerus, and a small strip of land around Jerusalem. Roman standards were planted on the rest of Judea.

This second step in his strategy being taken care of, Vespasian was again drawn from it by the political situation. Events at Rome were pressing, but Vitellius thought only of stuffing his stomach with food, either with the very ordinary kind which he selected as he assisted at the sacrifices to the gods, or with the most rare and costly foods imported by him from distant lands. In the few months of his rule, he squandered nine hundred million sesterces with his banquets. This was too much even for imperial Rome, and the city was soon seething with discontent. As the first intimations of this reached him, Vespasian drew back to Caesarea, for the fruit was now ripe. The legions of the Orient, both

Vitellius. (Rome, Capitoline Museum.)

those under his command and those in Egypt, had maintained a disciplined silence while awaiting the opportune moment. Now they made themselves heard.

445. On July 1, 69, the legions of Egypt, where an ex-Jew and ex-procurator of Judea, Tiberius Alexander (§ 407), was prefect, proclaimed Vespasian emperor. A few days later,[3] the legions mobilized in Judea did likewise, and the governor of Syria, Licinius Mucianus, had the new emperor recognized throughout the Orient. Many cities sent embassies to Beyrouth to render homage to the new emperor. Vespasian soon afterward went up to Antioch, whence he sent Mucianus with an army into Italy. Along the way the army was re-enforced by the legions of Mysia and Pannonia which had both declared for Vespasian. Accompanied by Titus, Vespasian then went to Alexandria, where he learned that Vitellius had been defeated and killed (December 20, 69). Vespasian was thus left as undisputed emperor.

It was while he was at Beyrouth that the new emperor one day found before him the prophet whom he had kept in chains, and remembered that his surprising prophecy had been verified to the letter. The uncircumcised Roman, unlike the Jews who stoned their own prophets (Vol. I, § 349), gratefully struck off the chains that bound Josephus, and he, now become Flavius Josephus and a free man, followed the emperor Vespasian to Alexandria.

❄   ❄   ❄

446. Vespasian remained at Alexandria until the beginning of the summer of 70, when he set out for Rome by sea. At the end of the winter he had empowered his son Titus Vespasian, "the delight of mankind," to reopen and carry to a conclusion the campaign in Judea.

Conditions in Jerusalem had in the meantime become much involved. To the two factions who were battling between themselves, that of John of Gischala and Simon Bar-Giora (§ 443), a third was added, headed by a son of Simon, the priest Eleazar, and recruited from the dissident followers of John. This new band of Zealots took forcible possession of a sector of Jerusalem which included the inner and more elevated part of the Temple, and contained the "holy place" and the "holy of holies." Thus the city was divided into three camps, each occupied by armed men. Eleazar occupied the sector just mentioned; John occupied the remaining and lower end of the Temple and many adjacent places; Simon had the largest sector, namely, the whole upper city (western) and a part of the lower. Clashes between

---

[3] Thus according to Tacitus, *Hist.*, II, 79–81, and Suetonius, *Vespas.*, 6. On the contrary, Josephus, *War*, IV, 10:2–6, claims that the first legions to proclaim Vespasian emperor were those of Judea; Mucianus was with these at the time.

the different factions were frequent, especially between John and Eleazar, who battled with holy zeal within the sacred enclosure of the Temple. Eleazar from his higher position easily defended himself, but John was better equipped with arms and machines of war, and attacked with such furious insistence that he inflicted losses of men and of a material order upon Eleazar.

447. Liturgical observances were continued, and John allowed the Jews who came to offer their sacrifices to pass through his sector into that of Eleazar after first searching them. The examination was less thorough if they were pilgrims from the diaspora, but more rigorous if they were Palestinian Jews.

Despite this safe passage, however, the lives of those Yahwists allowed to pass were not safe. Many times, while they were engaged in the ceremonies of the sacrifice, projectiles hurled by John's ballistae, catapults, and other machines landed among them, killing pilgrims, priests,

Sicle of the year V of the insurrection (A.D. 70).

and Levites near the altar of Yahweh. "The dead bodies of aliens were mingled with those of natives, those of priests with laymen; and the blood of all who were slain formed a pool within the courts of God." (*War*, V, 1, 3). Was this the legal purity which the Zealots, the most rigorous of Pharisees, had proposed to inaugurate?

Enormous reserves of foodstuffs accumulated for the war against the Romans were also destroyed. In a war of attrition John and Simon raided each other's territory, and when they withdrew, entire stores of grain and other provisions were burned or scattered around. "Almost all the grain, which might have sufficed them for many years of siege, was burned" (V, 1, 4). Yahweh's holy city had become like a cage wherein savage beasts snarled and tore at one another. Their master, however, was approaching, bringing iron and fire with him.

448. From Alexandria Titus had marched overland to Caesarea. To the three legions and troops gathered by Vespasian (§ 430), he joined the Twelfth Legion, *Fulminata*, which in the meantime had been reorganized and imbued with a spirit of discipline. He filled up the depleted ranks of the other legions, and incorporated into them the auxiliaries placed at his disposal by the confederate kings. The total number of forces under his command must have been well above sixty thousand men. The council of war called by Titus was presided over by Tiberius Alexander (§ 445), who, besides his other qualifications, had under Nero given excellent proof of his ability

North wall of Jerusalem (Third Wall).

as a director of strategic operations in the campaign of Corbulo against the Parthians. Taking part in these deliberations were four generals: Sextus Cerealis, commander of the Fifth Legion; Larcius Lepidus, of the Tenth; M. Tittius Frugi, of the Fifteenth, and the commander of the Twelfth, whose name is not known.

Having determined on the concentration of the legions around Jerusalem, they set forth in the beginning of the month Nisan (March-April) of 70. The roads were already choked with pilgrims from Palestine and from the diaspora making their way toward the holy city to celebrate the Hebrew Pasch (14 Nisan), but the Romans did not molest the pilgrims, and the city became ever more crowded. When he arrived at Gibe'ath Saul (Vol. I, §§ 85, 347 ff.), Titus encamped and, with a detachment of six hundred cavalry, reconnoitered the northern front of Jerusalem. Furiously assailed by the Jews in their outposts, Titus saved himself with great difficulty, personally taking part in the fray although unprovided with helmet and armor. He was obliged to retreat in all haste. The victory won in this skirmish, like their previous success against Cestius Gallus (§ 425), emboldened the Jews to imagine, perhaps, that the supreme commander of the Roman army would come within reach of their lances every day, and under those same conditions.

449. The attack on the city had to be made from the north (§§ 312, 424), and Titus concentrated the bulk of his army at this point. The Twelfth and Fifteenth Legions encamped on Mount Scopus, which dominates Jerusalem to the north, and somewhat to the rear of these was also the Fifth. While they were pitching camp, the Tenth Legion arrived along the Jericho road, and Titus stationed it on the northwestern slope of the Mount of Olives. While it was taking up its position, the Tenth was violently assailed by the Jews and seriously endangered. Titus hastened to the spot and drove the attackers down

into the valley of the Cedron. This time also he personally engaged in the front line fighting (see the plan of Jerusalem on p. 432).

On the very day of the Pasch, a new development occurred within the city. Because of the enormous crowds of pilgrims, the partisans of the three bands (§ 446) had difficulty in recognizing each other. Taking advantage of the situation, John of Gischala had a sizable group of his soldiers disguise themselves as pilgrims, and thus they were able to penetrate undisturbed into the inner sector held by Eleazar. Once inside they bared their weapons, and soon had gained possession of the whole Temple. There remained in the city, therefore, only the two factions of John and Simon.

450. Meanwhile Titus moved his troops still closer to the walls of the city, and himself encamped before the extreme northwest corner of the Third Wall (§ 298), where there arose the tower of Psephinus. Farther south, in front of the juncture of the Third Wall with the more ancient wall, opposite the tower of Hippicus, he placed a strong division, while the Tenth Legion still faced the eastern part of the city from the top of the Mount of Olives. When the troops were deployed in this fashion, all the trees around about were cut down and the terrain smoothed over so that the siege engines could be brought up for their part in the siege.

Titus' attempts to secure a surrender from the besieged were unsuccessful. The spokesman he sent was Josephus, but that despised apostate and traitor obtained no conclusive answer from the men on the walls. However, the imminence of the peril succeeded in bringing the two leaders of the rival factions, John of Gischala and Simon Bar-Giora, to compose their differences, and from that time on they fought side by side against the besiegers.

451. Immediately the Roman ballistae went into action. Each legion was amply

Northeast corner of the Herodian Walls of Jerusalem.

Herodian foundations of the tower
of Psephinus.

supplied with these weapons, especially the Twelfth, only recently reorganized. The catapults shot huge arrows; the ballistae hurled stones that weighed up to a talent (about a hundred and ten pounds) with a range of two stadia (a "stadium" is equivalent to about two hundred yards). The defenders on the walls were at first cut down *en masse* by these projectiles but soon learned to avoid them, especially when the stone was very large. In the latter case its whiteness and the whistle it made during its trajectory gave ample warning to the sentinels on the walls, who shouted the warning: "Sonny's coming!"[4] and the defenders then ran for shelter before the stone reached them. Perceiving this, the Romans painted the stone shot by the ballista black, so that their trajectory could not be discerned, and the slaughter of the men on the walls began anew.

Meanwhile, down below, the Roman battering-rams were working on three points of the very solid Third Wall. When they had battered it for several days a sortie by the besieged succeeded in burning part of the Roman constructions. But after a brisk battle they were driven off by Titus, who had hastened to the spot. Titus killed twelve of the attackers with his own hand. The Romans then built three other wooden towers (one of which unexpectedly crashed one night) so as to dominate the besieged from a greater height and protect those handling the battering-rams. After fifteen days, a breach was opened in the walls by the most powerful battering-ram the Romans

---

[4] The expression is typically Semitic. As the arrow in Hebrew was called "daughter" of the bow, so in the military slang of the Aramaic sentinels the stone was likely to be designated as the "son" of the ballista. However, many codices of the text of Josephus (*War*, V, 6, 3) have *iós*, "projectile," the Latin *missile*, instead of *viós*, "son."

had, and for this reason it was called *Nikon*, "Victor." The Romans poured into the breach and took possession of the Third Wall and Bezetha, the quarter behind it (§§ 394, 424). It was the seventh day of the month Artemisios (first part of May).

452. In five more days Titus had breached the Second Wall also, and advanced into the ancient city through these openings without enlarging them, for he did not wish to damage the wall. This he did out of regard for the Jews, for he continued to hope they would surrender. He was mistaken. A violent counterattack drove part of the Roman forces outside the newly won wall, and isolated another part of them within the city itself. Titus ran to the aid of the soldiers cut off in the city, and taking part in the fighting as an archer, succeeded in rescuing them. After four days of repeated assaults, he again gained possession of the Second Wall.

At this point Titus suspended operations for four days, as he wished to pay his troops and to give them a chance to rest.

He also used this time to march the entire army in review, doubtless hoping to impress the Jews by this show of force, but although they gathered on the walls in great numbers and admired the grandiose spectacle, the surrender which Titus naïvely expected was not even brought up for consideration.

On the fifth day he resumed operations. His objectives now were the fortress Antonia (§ 345), defended by John of Gischala, and that sector of the "upper city" defended by Simon Bar-Giora. From the

Types of Roman fortification. (Rome, Trajan's Column.)

Roman assault of a fortress using bastions and engines of war. (Rome, Trajan's Column.)

twelfth to the twenty-ninth of Artemisios, Titus raised four earthworks, two opposite the Antonia and two opposite the upper city, one being assigned to each legion. While this work was being pushed forward, Titus, ever hopeful, sent Josephus to circle the walls, appealing to his

View of Bezetha.

fellow countrymen in Aramaic to surrender. For all his efforts, he met
only with derision.

453. So great a number of pilgrims had come for the Pasch and
were now held in the city that a serious famine broke out. Many,
especially of the pilgrims, began to make their escape. They sold
their possessions, swallowed the few gold pieces thus obtained, and
fled to the countryside or to the Romans. Their swallowed coins

Roman council of war. (Rome, Trajan's Column.)

once recovered, they bought food outside the siege lines. Others
ventured outside the walls in search of some kind of food. At night,
or during the intervals of truce, they would slip between the Roman
sentinels, gather up clumps of herbs or the carrion upon which the
dogs fed or which jackals had left, and then would scurry back behind
the walls. Withal, the defenders of the walls kept up their watch, and
seriously harassed the construction of the four earthworks. Titus then
resorted to reprisals in the hope of intimidating the besieged defenders,
and crucified opposite the walls all who ventured forth from them.
Each day more than five hundred were crucified, but to no purpose.

Hardly had the four bastions been completed and begun to function,
when they were destroyed by the besieged. Under those intended to
be used against the Antonia, John of Gischala had dug large tunnels,

Roman signal towers. (Rome, Trajan's Column.)

which he temporarily propped up with wooden scaffolding. Now he set fire to the scaffolding, and when the ground caved in, the bastions crumbled as well. Those which were to be used against the upper city were shortly thereafter burned by Simon's soldiers.

454. This was a serious blow for the Romans. Not only was their labor lost, but it was very difficult to rebuild the bastions because of the scarcity of timber in the vicinity. It was then that the council, both to save the troops, and to spare them from the tricks of the besieged, approved Titus' plan of starving the city into submission. To prevent the wretched foragers from slipping through the lines, and anyone else from leaving the city, it was decided to construct a wall around the city which would be out of range of the besieged and would close them completely within it.

For the veteran Roman soldiers, long used to this type of work, the construction of the proposed wall was not an extraordinary enterprise. Similar circumvallations had been built by their legions in other places, for example, by Caesar around the city of Alesia in the Lyons section of Gaul (*De bello gall.*, VII, 69), and in Palestine itself during the assault on Masada (§ 471). Flavius Silva, at a later date, built another which is still well preserved today, and is the best example of its kind.

To effect this construction, the legions were spread in a chain around the city, each one being assigned the task of building the

section in front of it. Under the personal direction of Titus the wall
was completed in only three days. Starting from the encampment of
Titus opposite the tower of Psephinus, it descended along the western
flank of Jerusalem, ran along the southern side of the Valley of
Hinnom, and ascended to the east in the Valley of Cedron along the
slopes of the Mount of Olives, and when it had been extended
sufficiently northward it turned back toward the west, crossed the
conquered quarter of Bezetha, and completed the circle at its starting
point. It was thirty-nine stadia long, interspersed with thirteen fortified
redoubts in which garrisons were stationed. Titus himself inspected each
of the redoubts at nightfall. Later on in the night, Tiberius Alexander
made the rounds. Toward dawn the commanders of the legions made
their inspection. The garrisons were continually in touch with each
other during the night. From that day on, no one could leave or
enter Jerusalem.[5]

---

[5] One may call to mind the words which Jesus addressed to the city of Jerusalem:
"*Venient dies in te, et circumdabunt te inimici tui vallo, et circumdabunt te: et
coangustabunt te undique*" (Lk. 19:43). Caesar describes the *vallum* with which
he surrounded Alesia — it is entirely similar to that of Titus and of Flavius Silva:
"*Alesiam circumvallare instituit. Ipsum erat oppidum in colle summo admodum
edito loco, ut nisi obsidione expugnari non posse videretur. . . . Castra opportunis
locis erant posita, ibique castella XXIII facta; quibus in castellis interdiu stationes
ponebantur, ne qua subito eruptio fieret: haec eadem noctu excubitoribus ac firmis
praesidiis tenebantur*" (*De bello gall., loc. cit.*).

Roman legionaries building a wall. (Rome, Trajan's Column.)

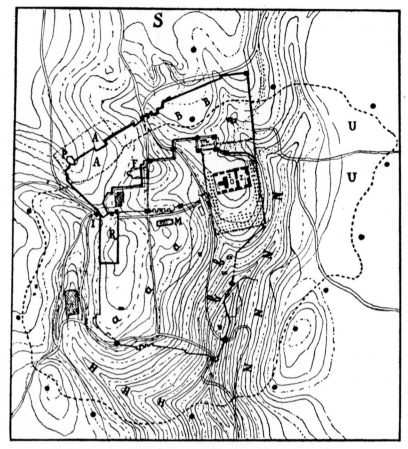

Plan of Jerusalem Under Siege by Titus.
S, Mount Scopus; B-B, Bezetha quarter; A-A, camp of Titus; P, Tower
of Psephinus; m, Fortress Antonia; Z-Z, The Temple; U-U, Mount of
Olives; b-b, Lower City; a-a, Upper City; M, Hasmonean palace; F,
The Holy Sepulcher; I, Tower of Hippicus; R, Court of Herod; H-H,
Valley of Hinnom (Gehenna). Dotted line (-----) shows the encircling
wall with its thirteen fortified watch-towers.

455. The consequences of this encirclement were immediately felt.
Up to now it had been possible to smuggle small supplies of food
into the city, especially from the southeastern part, for the hungriest
had boldly gone out to the very edge of the Roman camps to pick up
whatever leavings they could find. This was now not possible, and they
had to rely on what they had within the city, and that was practically
nothing. The abundant reserves of grain had been destroyed, for the
most part, during the civil war (§ 447), and the influx of Paschal
pilgrims had exhausted the rest. All at once hunger became something
horrible, inhuman, bestial. Everything edible had been eaten; what

little remained was requisitioned by the Sicarii for the defenders of
the walls. These searched everywhere to discover caches of provisions,
torturing anyone suspected of hiding foodstuffs to learn where the food
was hidden. For a handful of grain or rotted barley, when it was still
available, civilians gave their entire patrimony, and when such delicacies
were no longer to be had, they took to eating other things, even the
leather on their shields and their shoes. Bits of old hay became a luxury,
and four Athenian minae were paid for a small quantity of it.

456. Surrounding them was the unyielding wall, and in front of it
a veritable forest of crucified grew daily larger and larger. At length
wood for the crosses became scarce and there was insufficient space
to set them up. But on top of that horrible wall was something much
more impressive than sharp arrows and bloody Roman crosses: abundant
and fresh food, regularly distributed to the soldiers by the commissary,
which the soldiers cruelly displayed before the starving defenders on
the walls.

That sight was so irresistible that many, as if carried away by a super-
human frenzy, left the wall and walked toward the embankment, hoping
against hope to get close to food.

457. The Romans then left off their practice of crucifying those caught
outside the walls, and offered them food, and many died because
they ate so ravenously after their long fast. Then occurred an incident
which aggravated even more the fate of these unfortunate wretches.
Some of the Arabians and Syrians who had been hired as auxiliary
troops by the Romans, one day discovered a deserter in the act of
recovering some gold coins which he had swallowed before leaving

Roman warfare. (Left to right: hauling down trees; impaled
enemy heads; pitching camp.) (Rome, Trajan's Column.)

the lines (§ 453). It was at once noised abroad that the Jewish deserters left the city with their bellies full of gold. No need to say that from that moment on the Arab and Syrian mercenaries slit open the bellies of all Jews who approached the Roman wall. In one night alone, two thousand Jews perished in this manner.

On hearing of this, Titus surrounded the culprits with his cavalry, fully intending to put them to death, but so numerous were they that he could not punish them without weakening the ranks of his army. He then gave most severe orders to the mercenaries not to repeat their misdeeds, and to the legionaries to denounce the miscreants. But the forbidden practice continued, with greater precautions to be sure, and dissuaded many Jews from going over to the Romans.

458. Within the city, the specter of hunger hung implacably over all. Before it all sentiment and affection vanished, but not of course the unshakable fanaticism of John of Gischala, Simon Bar-Giora, and their Sicarii. Josephus describes the interweavings of the two threads of hunger and fanaticism in the following words: "The famine, enlarging its maw, devoured the people by households and families. The roofs were thronged with women and babes completely exhausted, the alleys with the corpses of the aged; children and youths, with swollen figures, roamed like phantoms through the market-places and collapsed wherever their doom overtook them. As for burying their relatives, the sick had not the strength, while those with vigor still left were deterred both by the multitude of the dead and by the uncertainty of their own fate. For many fell dead while burying others, and many went forth to their tombs ere fate was upon them. And amidst these calamities there was neither lamentation nor wailing. Famine stifled the emotions, and with dry eyes and grinning mouths these slowly dying victims looked on those who had gone to their rest before them. The city, wrapped in profound silence and night laden with death, was in the grip of a yet fiercer foe — the brigands" (*War*, V, 12, 3).

"Brigands" is the term Josephus uses for the Zealots; with the city in such a condition they looted the dead, pillaged houses, killed those whom they suspected of desiring to go over to the Romans, and, above all, requisitioned anything that could still serve as food.

459. One day some Zealots who were passing through a narrow lane of the sepulchral city smelled something roasting. The aroma was traced to one of the houses. They rushed inside and found there a woman who was still alive. They threatened to cut her throat if she did not surrender the food to them on the instant. The woman presented her food: her own suckling child. Driven to madness by hunger, she had killed it with her own hand, roasted it, eaten half of it, and now offered the other half to those who called themselves the "Zealous" servants of the

God Yahweh. Such a thing was not new in Israel (Vol. I, §§ 441, 540), but faced with that horrible scene, even the Sicarii trembled. The news of the monstrous event soon was spread throughout the city, and even Titus came to hear of it. Calling on God as a witness, Titus protested that such a misdeed fell upon the heads of those obstinate persons to whom he had unsuccessfully offered terms of surrender, and swore that he would bury such infamy beneath the ruins of the entire city. The name of this woman was Mary. She was of a rich and noble family of Beth-Ezob in Transjordan, and had come to Jerusalem, only to become involved in the siege (*War*, VI, 3, 3–4).

When the combatants within the city reached the point where they had nothing to eat, they consumed the sacred liturgical provisions of the Temple — the oil and wine, which for centuries had been regarded with mysterious respect. Soldiers who had enough strength to stand on their feet were becoming fewer and fewer. All services were then simplified, beginning with those connected with the dead, for these had become the principal task of the city. The bodies were then flung from the ramparts into the ravines, which thereby became pestilential charnel-houses and bogs of rottenness. From a single gate of the city, no less than 115,880 bodies were thrown out in less than three months.

460. To hasten the end of such a horrible situation, Titus then ordered new bastions to be constructed for use against the fortress Antonia, although to obtain the wood necessary he was forced to cut down all trees in the vicinity of Jerusalem for a radius of ninety stadia. There were four bastions this time also, but larger than their predecessors, and all of them intended for the Antonia. They were completed after twenty-one days of hard work. An attempt made by John of Gischala on the first of the month Panemus (July) to set fire to the bastions was nipped in the bud by the increased vigilance of the Roman soldiers. The battering-rams went into action, and when a breach was opened, a Syrian by the name of Sabinus, with a few others, attempted to climb through, on the third of Panemus. But this attempt too was foiled, and Sabinus killed. On the fifth of Panemus, the attempt was repeated at nightfall by some twenty soldiers; these succeeded in surprising and killing the sentinels, and in penetrating the fortress. When the trumpets gave the signal, Titus hastened forward with picked groups of soldiers, and was the first to make the ascent. The struggle continued for many hours, and the Romans suffered some considerable losses — among which was the brave centurion Julianus — but finally they were masters of the Antonia, and chased the Jews from it toward the Temple.

461. The Antonia was conquered on the fifth of Panemus, and on the seventeenth of the same month, Titus had it torn down so as to expose the Temple within which the Jews had concentrated their resist-

Footings of the Antonia; to the right, a projectile from a Roman ballista shown where it landed. (From *Revue Biblique*, 1933.)

ance. For Yahwism, that seventeenth day of Panemus of A.D. 70 was the most tragic day of the whole war, for on it, the sacrifice offered daily for centuries was not offered in the Temple. It was omitted not because of the attacks of the Romans, even as it was not omitted for this same reason at the time of Pompey (§ 312), but "because of a lack of men" (*War*, VI, 2, 1).

From that day to this, the Hebrew religion has not offered up that daily sacrifice to Yahweh (cf. § 488).

462. Once the Antonia had fallen, events moved swiftly. One defense after another collapsed, but not the tenacity of the Zealots. Again and again Titus sent Josephus to try to persuade the besieged to surrender, urging that the Temple, now directly menaced, might thus be saved. But he succeeded only in causing the desertion of isolated individuals, several of whom were priests.

A surprise attack at night against the Temple, even with picked legionaries and directed by Cerealis, commander of the Fifth Legion, was unsuccessful, so Titus again took up the usual siege operations, directly against the Temple. The ruins of the Antonia were leveled out to facilitate an approach from the north, and orders were given to build four new ramparts against the north wall of the Temple. For these wood was brought in from a radius of a hundred stadia. Recognizing the difficulty of defending the portico of the Temple on the northwest corner where it joined the demolished fortress (§ 345), the Jews burned part of it, and the rest of this northern portico was later destroyed by the Romans. The western portico also fell into the hands of the Romans at about the same time, but they suffered many losses through a trap set for them by the Jews.

463. The new bastions were completed on the eighth of the month Lous (August). The battering-rams immediately went into action, and joined the catapults and ballistae which had already started their work. But that Herodian wall had been built with enormous squared blocks of well-joined stones, and resisted both projectiles and other blows. An attempt was made to demolish the northern gate, but with insignificant results. The Romans then tried scaling the walls, and those who succeeded in reaching the top and setting up their standards were furiously assailed by the Jews, thrown to the ground or killed and the standards were lost. Finally, Titus ordered the gates to be set on fire. Because of the large amount of combustible material which the Romans piled up against the gates, the metals fused, the leaves of the gates burned and the fire continued on to the portico behind the gates.

At the sight of the fire penetrating their secure and sacred enclosure, the defenders were struck with consternation, and did nothing toward putting it out or defending themselves. Titus, who now had attained his aim of obtaining free access, ordered his soldiers to extinguish the

Enemy emissaries in the Roman camp. Trajan in the center. (Rome, Trajan's Column.)

fire, and to prepare for an assault by the legions. It was the ninth day of the month Lous. On that day, Titus, in view of the imminent general assault, held a council of war (§ 448) to determine what should be done to the Temple, the objective of the assault. Some of the commanders in attendance were of the opinion that the Temple should be treated simply as a fortress, since that is what the Jews made of it; hence, once taken it should be destroyed. Titus disagreed, and expressed the opinion that the Temple should be preserved even if the Jews had used it as a military fortress. The ex-Jew Tiberius Alexander also shared his view, and in conformity with it, the order of the day was drawn up, and the assault prepared.

464. The next day, the tenth of Lous (August) of A.D. 70 was to be a sad day for Judaism throughout the world and for all the centuries to follow. At the beginning of that day, the positions of the two belligerents were obviously only temporary ones. The Romans held the external court and, by burning the door, had opened the way for an advance against the inner court (§ 348); the Jews, who up to that time had repaired behind the unshakable wall of the inner court, now no longer had any guarantee of safety, seeing that the gate had been burned. The passage from the burned gate, which was now in the hands of the Romans, up to the "holy place," properly so called (Vol. I, § 391), offered no serious obstacle to a Roman assault, since the intermediary subdivisions — the "court of the Israelites" and the "court of the priests" — could be overcome without any great difficulty. Once this was done, the Romans would stand at the "sanctuary," at the very heart of Judaism.

465. During the morning the Roman soldiers were still occupied in extinguishing the remains of the fire which had spread from the gate to the portico. A Jewish sortie from the eastern gate gave serious trouble to the Roman guards at that point; Titus hastened up with re-enforcements, and the Jews were driven back only after repeated counter-attacks and three hours of fighting. Titus then retired to his tent to rest.

A little later the Jews renewed their sortie, this time directing their attack against the soldiers engaged in putting out the flames. Again repulsed, they were pursued by the Romans across the intermediate space up to the "holy place." It is certain that the pursuit was a disordered and haphazard one in which the pursuers threw anything that came to their hands at the fugitives, including the firebrands they were attempting to extinguish. In the heat of the chase and the confusion, one of the soldiers, not awaiting orders and without any dread of such a deed, but rather urged on by some evil spirit (δαιμονίῳ) snatched up a burning piece of wood and, lifted up by another soldier, cast the fiery torch through the Golden Window which opened into the rooms surrounding the sanctuary on the north side (*War*, VI, 4, 5; concerning the rooms here mentioned cf. Vol. I, § 392). These rooms were all of old wood, and probably contained flammable material used for liturgical services; the torrid temperatures of August also helped, and the firebrand thrown by the soldier touched off a blaze which was soon out of control.

Informed at once of the fire, Titus and his generals hastened to the spot, and the legions soon followed. Titus gave orders to extinguish the blaze, but in the confusion his orders were not heard, or at least they were not carried out. At the sight of the flames which usually signified victory and the beginning of pillage, the Roman soldiers were seized with an uncontrollable fury. The newly-arrived legions made common cause with the soldiers already present, and all pushed into the "holy place" with such force that some were crushed at the gates. Instead of controlling the fire, the legionaries helped spread it more and more. At the same time there began a massacre of the Jews who had not succeeded in fleeing. Piles of dead bodies accumulated around the altar of holocausts until it appeared to be an island in the middle of a bloody swamp.

466. Seeing that his intervention was of no avail, Titus tried to save what he could of the furnishings of the Temple. He succeeded in pushing past the legionaries engaged in their bestial orgy, and reached the interior of the "holy place" as yet untouched by the fire. Accompanied by some of his generals, he went on until he stood inside the "holy of holies," re-enacting once more that action of Pompey the Great (§ 313), which, in the centuries to follow, would never be repeated. Here he again tried to make the soldiers respect the holy place and to quench the fire, but neither his authority nor the freely administered blows of his club could deter the excited soldiers. When Titus turned to push some of them back, another tossed a firebrand into the interior, and the Holy of Holies was also destroyed.

Many sacred furnishings were salvaged, and later appeared in the triumph of Titus at Rome (§ 470). The rest became the loot of the soldiers who were so loaded down with booty, which they sold little by little, that the price of gold in the markets of Syria was lowered by 50 per cent.

While the fire was still raging, the legionaries planted the standards of Rome in the outer court of the Temple, opposite the eastern gate, there offering a sacrifice of thanksgiving to the gods of Rome, and proclaiming Titus "emperor," perhaps intending it to be only an honorary title.

*   *   *

467. What happened in Jerusalem and the surrounding territory after the burning of the Temple is summed up in the bare recital of the last calamity which struck the nation.

John of Gischala and many of his followers had made their way to

Enemy embassy with animals for sacrifice in the Roman camp. (Rome, Trajan's Column.)

the city, but about six thousand people sought refuge in the last un-harmed portion of the portico. The Romans then set fire to this remain-ing section and slaughtered all within. They next turned their attention to the upper city which still resisted. John of Gischala and Simon Bar-Giora then began to negotiate with Titus, but no agreement was reached because the rebels asked free passage for themselves and for all their followers, while Titus offered them only their lives. Exceed-ingly angered at their cheek, Titus had the lower city sacked and burned, and also prepared an assault on the upper city.

The Romans made their preparations from the twentieth of Lous to the seventh of Gorpias (September), on which latter date they opened a breach in the walls, after which the rest of the city fell into their hands without resistance. With all hope now gone, the rebels had even aban-doned the strong towers of the palace of Herod (§ 345) and taken refuge in the subterranean passages and the sewers. The legionaries invaded the streets of the city prepared to loot the houses, but found them for the most part filled with corpses or with people dying of hunger. Then began the hunt for those who were hiding under-ground, and those who were discovered that day were all put to death.

468. When he entered the city, Titus decided upon the fate of the city and of the prisoners who were flowing into it. The city was to be entirely razed, the three towers of the palace of Herod (Hippicus, Phasaelus,

and Mariamne) excepted, because of their strength. One
part of the wall of the city
where Titus intended to set
up an encampment for a future Roman garrison was also
spared. The prisoners were
temporarily shut up in the
burned Temple; several thousand of them died from hardships previously suffered and
from the mistreatment they
now received. Of the survivors, only a small number
was destined to add luster to
the triumph of Titus at Rome,
among them John of Gischala
and Simon Bar-Giora; the
others were either sent to
Egypt to work in the mines
or were apportioned to the provinces to fight as gladiators in the circus,
or, if under seventeen, sold as slaves.

The "upper city" of Jerusalem (western hill).
(Vester, Amer. Colony.)

The widespread opinion that the Flavian amphitheater at Rome (the
Colosseum) was built in great part by Jewish slaves is a gratuitous
assertion which has no factual evidence to support it.

469. In the five months during which the siege lasted, 97,000 prisoners
were taken and 1,100,000 died. These are the figures given by Josephus (*War*, VI, 9, 3). The first figure seems likely enough, but the second
seems exaggerated. It is true that a very large number died even
outside Jerusalem, and that when the city was closed up by the siege
it was crowded with Jews from the diaspora (§ 448), but this figure
does not seem to be in proportion to the population density of those
times. Tacitus (*Hist.*, V, 13) gives the number of besieged in Jerusalem
alone as 600,000.

470. Titus left the Tenth *Fretensian* Legion and other smaller units at
Jerusalem, and with the rest of the army moved to Caesarea by the sea.
Thence he made a long swing through Caesarea Philippi, Beyrouth, Antioch, and other places in Syria, everywhere staging great gladiatorial spectacles with his Jewish prisoners. From Antioch he went to Alexandria,
where he left his legions, finally setting sail for Rome with seven hundred
picked prisoners who were to add color to his triumph. He celebrated
his triumph in 71 together with his father Vespasian and his brother
Domitian. John of Gischala and Simon Bar-Giora walked in his tri-

The Tullianum (Mamertine Prison).

umphal procession as notable prisoners. The most precious objects taken as booty were the seven-branched lampstand and the table of gold used for the loaves of proposition. After the triumphal ceremonies, these were deposited in the Temple of Peace.

The ancient Roman custom required that during the ceremonies of the triumphal procession the most important enemy captured in the war be put to death. In this triumph of the Flavii, Simon Bar-Giora was the victim. Dragged along by a noose around his neck as far as the *Carcer*, the present-day Mamertine prison at the foot of the Capitoline, he was slain there in the deepest part of the *Carcer*, known as the "Tullianum." In this grim place men like the Numidian Siphax, Perseus of Macedonia, Jugurtha, and Catiline's fellow conspirators had awaited their fate and were put to death.

Gold coins of Titus struck in memory of the victory of 70. Right: a woman seated under a palm.

As a memorial of the victory coins were struck bearing the figure of a woman seated or lying down under a palm, and the following inscription: *Iudaea capta* or *devicta*. In honor of Titus, but after his death, the senate and the Roman populace erected the famous arch of triumph on the Via Sacra, between the Palatine and the Forum.

The 7-branched lampstand and table of gold. (Rome, Arch of Titus.)

Masada from the east. (Vester, Amer. Colony.)

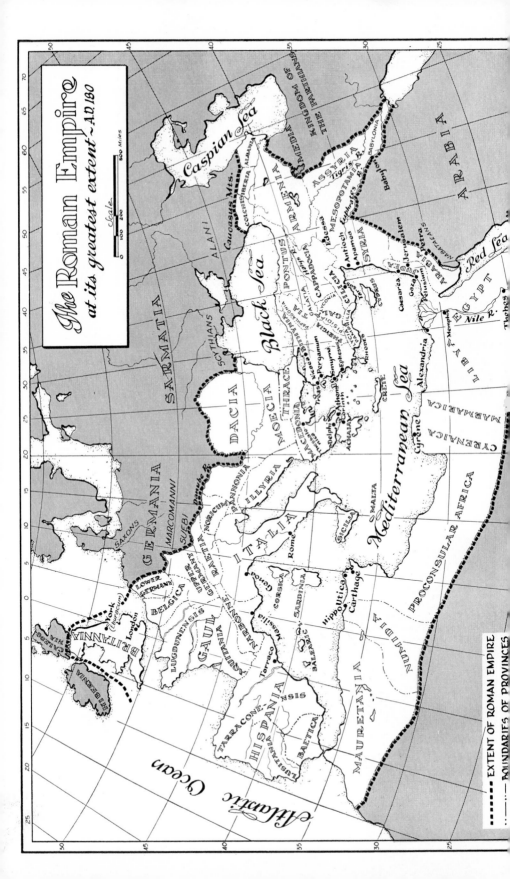

The Roman Empire at its greatest extent ~ A.D. 180

Scale
0 100 200 500 Miles

EXTENT OF ROMAN EMPIRE
BOUNDARIES OF PROVINCES

Carved in relief on it can still be seen the seven-branched lampstand and table of gold.

471. In the conquered land a few fortresses held by the rebels remained to be stormed, namely, Masada, the Herodium, and Machaerus (§ 444). Lucilius Bassus, the new governor of Palestine, took the last two of these cities with comparative ease, but after his death in 73, his successor, Flavius Silva, encountered the most stubborn resistance at Masada, where the last of the Sicarii had taken refuge under the command of Eleazar, the descendant of Judas of Galilee (§ 380). To capture this powerful fortress, Flavius Silva was obliged to conduct a rigorous siege, complete with the construction of a surrounding wall (§ 454), and of an *agger* to reach the summit of the cliff on which the walls were built. When the doom of the fortress became certain and the besieged had lost all hope of deliverance, they by common agreement slew their families and themselves. Thus did 960 of them die, first however setting fire to everything. When the Romans made their final assault on the fifteenth of the month of Xanthicus (April) of 73, they entered the fortress without resistance, and entering, found the dead lying everywhere. Only two old women and five children remained alive, and these came out to the Romans from the cellars where they had been hiding.

472. The tragedy in Palestine had repercussions in Africa. The Sicarii who had fled from Palestine caused riots in Alexandria and Cyrene. On that occasion the Temple of Onias at Leontopolis (§ 251) was first closed and then destroyed by the Romans.

With the fall of Masada, Judea was completely subjugated and became the private property of the emperor. As an imperial province (§ 374), it was governed by a legate who held senatorial rank; the province was completely independent of the province of Syria. The name of the province remained the same, namely, Judea. The legate, who resided at Caesarea, had at his disposal only one legion, the Tenth, *Fretensis*, which was stationed in Jerusalem, and other auxiliary troops.

473. Life was not pleasant in Palestine for the Jewish survivors of the catastrophe. Most humiliating and galling to their religious sensibilities was the knowledge that the two drachmas which they had formerly contributed to the Temple were now being sent to the Temple of Jupiter Capitolinus at Rome (§ 197). Moreover, the holy city of Jerusalem had been reduced to rubble, and its ruins were profaned by the presence of the Roman legion. The Sanhedrin, once the supreme authority of the nation, was dispersed and no longer functioned. The Temple was gutted by fire, the perpetual sacrifice had ceased, the priests, of course, could no longer fulfill their duties. The victorious Messias who was to have appeared to guide the nation to triumph, and to establish

The Dead Sea and a Roman encampment (square in foreground)
seen from Masada. (Vester,
Amer. Colony.)

Masada and the Dead Sea. (Vester,
Amer. Colony.)

his reign of happiness, had not been seen and was nowhere to be found. What did the future hold for Israel?

For one thing, there remained the task of gathering together the precious records of the past with a view to the future. From 68 on, a group of learned scribes, assembled at Jamnia (§ 440) with the permission of the Romans, had been silently laboring to reconstruct amid the ruins the future spiritual fortress of Judaism. Thus was gathered together that immense body of tradition which was later fixed in the Mishna and the Talmud.

THE LAST INSURRECTIONS

TRAJAN — HADRIAN — SHIME'ON BEN-KOSEBHA

474. We are very poorly informed as to what took place in Palestine after the termination of the great war. Our principal source of information up to this point, Josephus, is silent, his task finished. Fragmentary information garnered elsewhere is summary and rather unimportant. Yet during the sixty years which followed the great war, events were occurring which, by and large, can compare with those of the year 70. The items of information relative to these events tersely but eloquently bring out the gravity of the situation.

It is not necessary to dwell on the fact that after the catastrophe of A.D. 70 Judea did not become a desert, even as it had not become a desert after the catastrophe of 586 B.C. A few centers in Galilee, and many in Judea, had suffered the most. Jerusalem and its environs had been cruelly tried, but elsewhere the war had not caused material ruin. Jerusalem itself, it is true, had been destroyed and emptied of its population, but already the presence of the Tenth Legion must have caused the return of many small merchants to serve so large a body of soldiers. Later, the ordinary people worked their way back into the demolished city for one reason or another, and so re-established a tiny, but tolerated, center of local life.

475. The morale of the people has already been alluded to (§ 473). At first the survivors were quite dispirited, almost crushed. But with the passage of time, the resumption of social life and contacts with affluent Jews of the diaspora must have healed over many wounds, reawakened many memories of the past, and even re-enkindled old hopes which seemed extinguished forever. Was it possible that Yahweh would reject his chosen nation forever, or that he would leave his holy city eternally in ruins? Would he abandon the hill of Sion to be abused by pagans? What then of the radiant promises made by Yahweh to the fathers of the nation, of those visions of the prophets who described the future beatitude of Israel, of the "faithfulness" of Yahweh to his covenant with Israel?

447

No, the nation would not fail to rise again. The catastrophe of 70 had been, perhaps, the last and the supreme test which Yahweh desired of his nation, and now that it had passed this test, there had to be a triumph. The extreme severity of the test was itself an indication that the triumph would also be of the highest order: the triumph of the Messias, who would renew the face of the earth, who would place Israel upon the throne which was her due and make the pagan nations her footstool.

These were pleasant dreams, and amid the great external desolation they grew ever more wonderful and necessary. But they had to be guarded jealously in one's heart, and could only be spoken of between intimate and trusted friends. The Roman police were suspicious both in Palestine and outside it, and were on the watch for possible fomenters of nationalistic uprisings (cf. Hegesippus in Eusebius, *Hist. eccl.*, III, 12; also III, 19–20; III, 32, 3–4). The Jews, therefore, while distrusting external reality, inwardly exalted themselves and concentrated upon their dreams. It was the spiritual preparation for a new revolt.

476. Trajan. For the next forty years the situation was to remain as it was, but unfortunately we know practically nothing of what went on in them. But when Trajan, the *optimus princeps,* was conducting his

glorious campaigns (114–116) against the inveterate enemies of Rome, the Parthians, and had advanced beyond the Tigris, revolt unexpectedly broke out behind him. Immediately to his rear in Mesopotamia, the Jewish diaspora was numerous and powerful, and kept in constant touch with coreligionists in Palestine and Africa. Thus an immense strip from the Tigris to Cyrenaica was sprinkled with Jews who fretted and fumed as they thought back over the happenings of the year 70, and longed for the messianic restoration of their nation. The revolt suddenly broke out in that part of the strip which

Trajan.

was farthest removed from Trajan and his army. The Jews of Alexandria and of Egypt in general, and those of Cyrenaica, erupted with savage violence against their non-Jewish fellow countrymen (Eusebius, *Hist. eccl.*, IV, 2). The uprising in northern Africa began in 115, and reached its greatest intensity in 116. What were the reasons behind it? Detailed information is not available, but given the messianic ferment which had pervaded the Judaism of the diaspora and of Palestine, it may reasonably be supposed that one of the provocations to rebellion was the fact that the countries on the lower Mediterranean were, because of the war against the Parthians, practically divested of troops. Given this favorable opportunity, the powerful Jews of Egypt attempted to seize control and to activate their vindictive projects against Rome.

477. The insurrection must have been under way only a short time when something occurred which greatly increased the courage of the insurgents, and confirmed them even more strongly in their messianic convictions. Trajan had victoriously closed the first period of his campaign against the Parthians and had returned to winter at Antioch when, on the thirteenth of December of 115, a severe earthquake, whose tremors lasted for days, literally destroyed that city and ruined large sections of Asia Minor as far as the island of Rhodes. It was reported that Trajan miraculously emerged from it unharmed, and that the survivors numbered only three in all. The messianic hopefuls were quick to see in this tremendous cataclysm clear proof that the solemn hour they were awaiting was at hand (cf. Lk. 21:9 ff.). The prediction that "nation shall rise against nation, and kingdom against kingdom" was being fulfilled in the large scale operations against the Parthians, and "great earthquakes" similar to the one at Antioch had actually occurred; surely the "terrors from heaven" and other events were to be looked for in the near future. It was therefore the opportune mo-

Antioch seen from Mount Silpius. (Vester, Amer. Colony.)

ment to intensify their activity so as to hasten the advent of the Messias.

478. The uprising spread over a large stretch of territory with irresistible speed. When it reached the district of Thebes in Egypt it was seen to be a real threat to the empire with which the prefect of Egypt, Rutilius Lupus, was in no position to cope. Non-Jewish Egyptians were defeated in open battle and took refuge in Alexandria. Here, however, the tables were turned, for the pagans regained the upper hand, sought out the Jews, and slaughtered them. The struggle within the wallls must have been long and ferocious, for the city suffered much damage, and later had to be restored by Hadrian.

In the West, the Jews in Cyrenaica took revenge for the slaughter in Alexandria by slaughtering their non-Jewish fellow countrymen. The account of Dio Cassius (LXVIII, 32) numbers the victims of this massacre in Cyrenaica at 220,000, and states that the Jews comported themselves as cannibals, for they ate the flesh of their victims, bathed in their blood, wrapped their entrails around themselves, and committed other atrocities. It is not difficult to detect in this gruesome picture the work of an unrestrained imagination, but there is no doubt that the Greco-Romans of Cyrenaica were slain in great numbers by their Jewish compatriots.

Recent discoveries furnish a significant detail in this regard. The insurgents of Cyrenaica knew that sooner or later the Roman troops would march against them, and took steps to cut their lines of communications, destroying the roads which were the arteries of the empire. A milestone from the road which connected Cyrenaica with Apollonia, found only recently, attests that it was put up again in 118–119, after having been torn up and destroyed by a Jewish uprising.[1] Even more important is the fact that Eusebius gives the title of "king" to the leader of the Jewish insurrection, Andrew or Lukuas. Naturally, this suggests that the insurrection was of messianic inspiration. Josephus describes a similar case (War, VII, 11, 1) which concerned a notorious Sicarius named Jonathan. This man, immediately after the catastrope of 70 A.D., fled from Palestine to Cyrenaica, where he stirred up disorders which led to the intervention of the Romans.

To put down the revolt of 116, Trajan sent Marcius Turbo with a strong contingent of troops, and after a long time and several encounters, he was successful in his task. Many Jews, not only those in Cyrenaica, but also those from Egypt, who had come to the aid of their coreligionists in Cyrenaica, lost their lives during the suppression.

479. Meanwhile, the Jewish uprising had spread toward the north to the island of Cyprus. Here also exaggerated figures are given:

---

[1] Tumultu iudaico eversa et corrupta erat.

240,000 pagans killed by the Jews, and the city of Salamis totally destroyed. As in the case of Cyrenaica, one may suspect that the Cypriot Jews slaughtered a great number of people and inflicted serious damage on the city. No account is given of the suppression of this uprising, but so great was the hatred thereafter borne by the inhabitants of Cyprus for the Jews that they put to death every Jew who set foot on their island, even if he were cast ashore by a storm at sea.

The Jews of Mesopotamia assumed a threatening attitude while Trajan was at Ctesiphon, the capital of Parthia, and made common cause with many local centers which, even after the Roman conquest, remained faithful to the dominion of the Parthians. The fact that the new hotbed of rebellion was in neighboring territory made it all the more serious a threat for Trajan, whose forces were deeply committed in the east. Lusius Quietus was sent to stamp out the rebellion by severe measures. Edessa was burned, and Nisibi and Seleucia (which Seleucia it was is not clear) were also taken, and in all of these cities there were certainly many Jews. After the terrible massacres which ensued, the Jews living in Mesopotamia were almost wiped out.

Lusius Quietus was then sent to Palestine as governor, but it is not known whether he continued his war of suppression in Palestine which eventually also rose up in rebellion, or whether he merely established a Draconian regime of watchfulness, for the Jewish insurrection was spreading throughout the empire, and threatened to ignite the cradle of the nation also.

According to rabbinic legend, this is the period during which the brothers Julianus and Pappus were killed at Laodicea; the legend is similar in form to those of many Christian martyrs.

* * *

480. Hadrian. The violent suppression of this widespread Jewish revolt terminated shortly after 117, but the resulting calm was only apparent, especially in Palestine, where, perhaps, the insurrection had assumed less serious proportions.

In Palestine, in the first thirty years of the second century after Christ, the traces of the catastrophe of 70 must have practically disappeared. Available information concerning material conditions in Jerusalem is lacking, but it is highly probable that its population, even its native population, had increased from what it was immediately after A.D. 70, and that some parts of the city had been rebuilt after a fashion under the noses of the tolerant and disinterested Romans in charge. In a word, Israel's holy city may have become once more a powerful Jewish center, installed amid the ruins which were still officially maintained. The

Temple still lay in ruins, but even in its desolate condition it was the goal of many pious Israelite pilgrims, one of whom was the famous rabbi Aqiba.

481. Trajan died on August 8, 117, and was succeeded by Hadrian. From the very beginning the new emperor pursued a foreign policy different from that of his predecessor. He not only gave up the idea of a war against the Parthians, but also abandoned the provinces conquered by Trajan, and pulled back the limits of the empire to the Euphrates. This policy aroused open and vehement dissatisfaction among the generals, many of whom had gained their fame under Trajan. But Hadrian brooked no opposition, and since Lusius Quietus and Marcius Turbo (§§ 478, 479) opposed him, he removed the first from Palestine and sent him to Rome, and transferred the second from Egypt to Mauritania (Libya). Later on, Lusius Quietus and three other famous consular personages were put to death by order of the senate, the charge being that they had conspired against the life of the emperor. Hadrian subsequently avowed his ignorance of this condemnation.

482. Indefatigable traveler that he was, Hadrian visited the whole empire, from Britain to Thebes in Egypt, from Mauritania to the Danube. In the spring of 129 he was at Ephesus, and from there he went to the Euphrates, crossing Asia Minor, and then came to Antioch. In the first months of 130, he was at Palmyra, whence he descended to Arabia across Judea, and from there he proceeded to Egypt in the autumn of the same year. After visiting Thebes, he made his way to Alexandria, and then to Cyrenaica to repair the devastation caused by the Jewish insurrection (§ 478). In 131 he was again in Syria.

Hadrian's purpose in these journeys was to see with his own eyes what was necessary to make the frontiers of the empire secure, and would contribute to the well-being of the peoples. He had in mind a complete restoration of the Roman world. He traveled with a small retinue of slaves and soldiers, but with a large number of engineers, surveyors, and other experts who were to study the situation and set up the necessary works. Wherever he had passed there soon began to rise various kinds of public projects ranging from aqueducts to theatres, from streets to ramparts. He fully merited the title of *Restitutor* found on the various types of coins issued under him.

483. His passage through Palestine was only one point in this vast program, and he proposed to be the "restorer" of these regions also. After his beneficent visit, Petra, the capital of Nabatean Arabia (§§ 315, 328) was called *Hadriana Petra,* and we find constructions of his at Gaza, Caesarea, and Tiberias. In Judea, the great ruin to be restored was the capital city, Jerusalem. During his trip through Judea, Hadrian gave orders to rebuild it completely, and gave it the name

Colonia Aelia Capitolina. The new city was to be essentially Hellenistic in type, in keeping with the cultural mentality of its creator; in keeping with his religious mentality (for Hadrian *"sacra Romana diligentissime curavit, peregrina contempsit"* [Sparzianus, *Vita Hadriani,* 22]) a temple of Jupiter was to occupy the place of the Temple of Yahweh.

It is easy to imagine the impression this sacrilegious project made on the Jews. As long as Jerusalem was officially neglected by the Roman authorities, the slow work of rebuilding without seeming to do so could go on; thus too the vague hope might be kept alive of one day being allowed to rebuild the Temple also. It seems certain that this rosy hope had already been expressed by Jews who had Hadrian in mind. The Alexandrian Jew who made the Sibyl speak (*Oracula Sibyll.,* V, 46 ff., 492 ff.) considers Hadrian as a new Cyrus who bears the name of a sea (the Adriatic), and who in his wisdom and power shall restore all things. The priests of Yahweh must present themselves to him so that the Temple of Jerusalem may be rebuilt. Evidently the hopes of the Sibylline poet were founded on Hadrian's fame as the "restorer," which was then in the making. Would that new sovereign, so conciliatory and so anxious for the well-being of his subjects, and who was restoring so many public edifices, allow the greatest treasure of Israel, its Temple, to lie in ruins? No, indeed; it would certainly be restored.

As a matter of fact, it was, but the Sibyl was correct only as regards the fact, and blundered terribly as regards the manner of the restoration. Unfortunately Hadrian was, without intending to be so, a new Antiochus Epiphanes instead of a new Cyrus. His command to construct an Aelia Capitolina with its temple of Jupiter was the official desecration, not the auspicious reconsecration, of the city.[2]

484. Nor was this heavy blow the only one. About the same time (precise details are lacking), Hadrian issued a decree forbidding circumcision. The reasons which impelled the jurists of Rome to seek Hadrian's signature for this decree and which compelled Hadrian to sign it were only the consequence and further application of the principles already established in Roman law. In the past, Domitian had prohibited

---

[2] Some modern scholars advance the hypothesis that at the beginning of his reign Hadrian had really given the Jews permission to rebuild the Temple of Jerusalem, and that afterward, under the persuasion of the jealous Samaritans, he imposed impossible conditions on the enterprise. The principal foundation for this supposition is the episode narrated in *Bereshith rabba,* 64, which is a Midrash legend of no historical value for the point at issue (at most, in dealing with a text of the sixth century, one is reminded of the similar permission granted by Julian the Apostate). Other lesser proofs adduced are even more fragile. See the article "Hadrian" in *Encyclopaedia Judaica,* VII, Berlin, 1931, for the arguments in favor of this thesis; for the opposite view, Schürer, I, pp. 671–673.

castration (Dio Cassius, LXVII, 2; Suetonius, *Domit.*, 7); Hadrian re-enforced this prohibition by making it a crime subject to the death penalty under the *lex Cornelia de sicariis et veneficis* (cf. *Digest.*, XLVIII, 8, 4, 2). This prohibition was doubtless intended to put a stop to the corybantic mutilations so frequent in oriental cults (Vol. I, § 108), and to preserve healthy moral customs threatened by other widespread practices. After this prohibition, Hadrian issued the new decree putting circumcision on the same level as castration, and therefore punishable by the same *lex Cornelia* (cf. *Digest*, XLVIII, 8, 11).

This decree does not seem to have been especially aimed at the Jews, for Hadrian was not particularly interested in prohibiting only the Jews from practicing their thousand-year-old custom, nor was he so politically shortsighted as deliberately to provoke their indignation. The Jews were not the only subjects of the empire who practiced circumcision (Vol. I, §§ 133–134), and the new decree also struck at the Samaritans, who were still subject to it a hundred years later (cf. Origen, *Contra Celsum*, II, 13), and other peoples outside of Palestine (for the Nabatean Arabs, cf. Bardesane, *Libro delle leggi dei paesi*, 43; ed. Nau, in *Patrologia syriaca*, II, col. 603). Hadrian proposed to abolish in the whole empire a usage which to his refined Hellenistic sensibilities seemed barbarous and inhuman. The Jews however quite naturally believed that the decree was aimed at them.

485. Hadrian's plan to build the Aelia Capitolina and his prohibition of circumcision are adduced, separately, as the incentive for the subsequent Jewish insurrection. Dio Cassius (LXIX, 12) prefers the first reason, and affirms that the Jews rebelled so as to prevent the alienation and profanation of Jerusalem. Sparzianus (*Vita Hadriani*, 14) favors the second reason: "*moverunt ea tempestate et Judaei bellum, quod vetebantur mutilare genitalia.*" Both historians are correct, but incomplete, for the two imperial directives may easily be linked together and be considered as simultaneous causes of the rebellion.

Even if taken together, however, the imperial mandates are not an adequate explanation for the desperate rebellion; the mental processes of the rebels must be taken into account. After the catastrophe of 70, and more so after the failure of the insurrection under Trajan, the Jews in Palestine had worked themselves up into a state of feverish excitement. The chalice of Yahweh's indignation had been drunk to the dregs (Isa. 51:17), and further one could not go. Now that the chalice was empty their consolation was necessarily at hand. The humiliation inflicted upon the nation of Yahweh had been most severe, it is true, but no doubt it was also the last. The Messias was at the gates. The most obvious proof of this was that flood of misfortune which for more than a hundred years now had been visited upon the nation. Men therefore went on living in the hope of the final triumph, and their expectation was prolonged month after month, day after day, hour after hour. The lamps they held in their hands were always lit, their loins girded. They watched for every sign that would announce the great "coming," their spirits wasting away in an atmosphere of painful tension.

And finally the signs did appear: a pagan Aelia Capitolina was to be built, and the sacred rite of circumcision was forbidden by law.

It was then that the conflagration began; it was the rebellion of desperate men.

❋   ❋   ❋

486. Shime'on ben-Kosebha [Bar-Cochba]. As long as Hadrian tarried in Syria after his visit to Egypt (§ 482), things remained quiet in Palestine, but once he had departed for Greece in 132, the revolt began. The exasperation of the Jews of Palestine, the influx of Jews of the diaspora, the taste of uprisings which all still remembered, helped make this last struggle of Judaism against Rome as lengthy and perhaps even more bloody a revolt than the one which occurred in A.D. 70. Josephus, an eye-witness of that struggle, gave us a detailed account of it, but the details of this last revolt are incomplete and distressingly brief.

Until very recent times (cf. Vol. I, § 94 b), the figure of the Jewish leader of the revolt had never clearly emerged from history, and there was much uncertainty as to his very name. Coins struck by this man were inscribed: SHIME'ON PRINCE (*nasi*) OF ISRAEL, but rabbinical and Christian sources differ in the title given to him. In rabbinical literature he is called *Ben-* or *Bar-Kosebha;* in the Christian, *Bar-Cochba,* i.e., "son of the star." The second title has definitely messianic overtones (cf. Num. 24:17), and was given to Simeon by Rabbi Aqiba, who looked upon him as the Messias. The other name, *Ben-Kosebha,* is obscure. It may have been nothing more than the customary patronymic, "son of Kosebha," in which case Kosebha was the name of Simeon's father, or again, it may have been a place-name, signifying that he was a "son (native) of" a town named Kosebha, situated in the territory of Juda (cf. 1 Para. 4:22), and indeed this seems quite likely. A further explanation which would derive the name from the root K Z B, "to deceive," making him a "deceiver, liar, false one," has little to recommend it, but in line with this derivation later rabbis, prompted by the failure of the insurrection led by him, by a slight but important alteration of a letter changed his glorious name Bar-Kokhebhah, "son of the star," to Bar-Kosebha', "son of the deceiver." But although this explanation appears in the *Midrash Ekhah rabbathi* (seventh century) and was accepted by the famous Azarias de Rossi, it has against it the fact that Simeon was given that second name even by rabbis who were most loyal to him, e.g., by R. Aqiba, the greatest doctor of his time; this would hardly have been the case if the name had been a disparaging one. It is more probable, then, that enthusiastic followers soon replaced Simeon's original name of Ben-Kosebha' (whether patronym or toponym) to *Bar-Cochba,* which was similar phonetically and indicated a messianic dignity ("son of the star"). As a matter of fact, Christian writers know him only as "son of the star," and certainly they do not recognize him as the Messias.[3]

487. Later and not very authoritative sources state that Simeon was an only son belonging to a family of scribes, and they also mention his uncle Eleazar of Modin. What the rabbis say of his prodigious strength, and of his violent methods of testing his soldiers, is pure fabrication. It is, rather, probable that he issued from the circle of the doctors of the Law, with whom his relations were always most cordial. Undoubtedly his greatest moral victory was the fact that he was recognized as the "Messias-King" by the great rabbi, Aqiba, even if the latter's authority was not enough to induce the other rabbis who followed Simeon to concede him this recognition.

Ben-Kosebha must have asserted his leadership from the beginning of the revolt, judging from his activity in encouraging and directing it. Here at long last was the warrior and victorious Messias King awaited with such intense desire by the masses. Who could doubt this fact when a doctor like Aqiba felt as he did about him? Rabbinical tradition does not, however, point to any miracles which Ben-Kosebha may have performed in support of his mission, but there is a Christian tradition which describes him as trying to appear as a wonder-worker by putting lighted tow in his mouth and then spewing forth flames (Jerome, *Contra Rufin.,* III, 31). Christian sources also state that he persecuted and killed the Christians of Palestine because they would not join him against the Romans, and would neither deny that Jesus Christ was the Messias, nor admit that Simeon was (Justin, *Apol.,* I, 31; Eusebius, *Chron.,* ed. Schoene, II, 168 ff.). Eusebius gives him short shrift: "The leader of the Jews at that time was a man by the name of Barcochba, which means star; actually he was nothing but an assassin and a robber" (*Hist. eccl.,* IV, 6, 2).

488. From the very first the insurgents relied heavily upon the desert, as had the Machabees long before them. There they first went to dwell, and there they skillfully fortified rocks, cliffs, and especially caves; they dug out tunnels which connected the caverns with one another, and also with the redoubts set up in front for defense. In brief,

---

[3] The discoveries at Wadi Murabba'at (*RB,* 1953, 245 ff.; 540 ff., and since) help clarify this question of the name of the Jewish leader (cf. Vol. I, § 94 *a* and *b*).

they resorted to a form of
trench warfare against which
the Roman square was much
less effective than in the open
field.

These guerrilla tactics spread
over the whole region, and were
received with enthusiasm by the
people everywhere. Judea took
on the appearance of a well
dug-in camp. The Jewish diaspora, which kept its eyes ever
focused upon Palestine, was
swept with high hopes for the
success of the vigorous rebellion, and doubtless contributed
both encouragement and aid.
"The whole world was excited
over this event" (Dio Cassius,

Money of Shime'on ben-Kosebha.

Money (Roman coins reminted) of
Shime'on ben-Kosebha. To the left:
stylized figure of the Temple(?).

LXIX, 13). The legate of Judea, Tineius (Tirannus) Rufus, defended
himself with the troops at his disposal and others he received as re-
enforcements, and slaughtered a great many of the combatants and
noncombatants (Eusebius, *Hist. eccl.*, IV, 6, 1), but as the tide of the
insurrection rose ever higher, he was constrained to withdraw gradually
from the whole region of the rebellion without having fought a single
battle in the open, and suffered grave losses while passing by the
fortified areas in the desert. Jerusalem fell into the hands of the insurgents shortly after operations began, and on that occasion Ben-Kosebha
had coins struck to mark the beginning of a new era, starting with the
year in which the holy city was reconquered. The new coins (practi-
tically all of them were Roman coins reminted with the die of the
insurgents) were for the most part marked with the year I or II,
followed by the inscription: OF THE REDEMPTION OF ISRAEL or OF THE
EMANCIPATION OF JERUSALEM (or OF ISRAEL). Other coins of this
period bear the inscription of ELIEZER THE PRIEST, which suggests
that Ben-Kosebha gave the high priest of his time the power to coin
money, recognizing the authority which had been vested in this office
ever since the time of the Roman conquest. But now that the "fullness
of time" had arrived, naturally the ordinary power of the high priest
was subordinate to the extraordinary power of the "messias," Simeon
Ben-Kosebha (cf. § 287).

It is quite likely that during his brief reign Kosebha attempted to
restore the Temple, and while there is no certain and clear evidence

Bethar (Bittir).

for it, that he also restored, partially at least, the liturgical observances there.

489. The success of Ben-Kosebha was like a flash flood, violent but of short duration. The feverish enthusiasm of the masses after the first flush of victory did not bear up long when confronted with the iron organization of Rome. The legate of Syria, Publicius Marcellus, came to the aid of his colleague in Judea, but apparently with only meager success. Forces were then assembled from various places, until they numbered about four legions which were supported by auxiliary forces and, at sea, by the Syrian fleet. Hadrian next summoned from Britain the ablest general of the whole empire, Julius Severus, and entrusted to him the prosecution of the new operations. It seems quite certain that the emperor himself visited the theater of operations, and had the architect Appollodorus draw up plans for attacking and taking by storm the caverns and other fortified localities of the rebels in the desert. On May 5, 135, Hadrian was again in Rome; he had apparently left Judea because everything was going along splendidly there under the direction of Julius Severus.

490. To put down the revolt was a laborious affair, for the defense was very stubborn. No great battles took place, but rather a series of skirmishes, sieges, and assaults, a step-by-step demolition of the forces of Ben-Kosebha. Julius Severus gained control over the main roads, and so was able to isolate the various groups from each other. Ben-Kosebha was soon in difficulty as regards his food supply, and it seems that many of the defenders in the fortified caverns died from snake bites. Rabbinic sources state that fifty-two (or fifty-four) engagements took place during the entire campaign. In its ruined condition, Jerusalem could not have put up the same stout resistance to the Roman attack as in the time of Titus. And even if one assigns the Fourth Wall (Vincent: § 398) to the time of Ben-Kosebha, this hasty construction obviously could not long withstand the Roman engines of war. The capital yielded almost automatically when the Romans took over the surrounding territory.

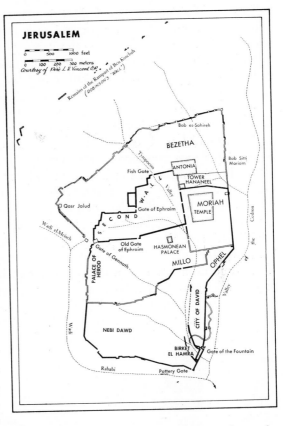

Ben-Kosebha finally shut himself up in his last remaining fortress, Bethar (modern *Bittir*), some seven and a half miles southwest of Jerusalem. He was besieged there, and after some resistance was defeated and killed, probably in the first half of 135. The insurrection had lasted a little more than three years.

491. From the summary given by Dio Cassius (LXIX, 13–14) and from other indications, it appears that the Romans suffered heavy losses while putting down this revolt, but for the Jews the Roman victory presaged a slaughter more ruthless than the one under Titus. That the losses of the Romans were very heavy can also be argued from the fact that when Hadrian sent a written report of the campaign to the senate, he omitted the usual introductory formula which stated that the emperor and the army were well. The emperor may have been in good condition, but certainly the army was not, after that trying campaign. Such great importance was attributed to the victory in Rome that in the second half of 135 Hadrian took anew the title of emperor (*imperator iterum*).

In Judea alone fifty fortresses and nine hundred and eighty-five inhabited centers were taken by storm and destroyed. The number of those killed in battle amounted to 580,000, and others died as a result of the hardships of war. The number of Jewish slaves sold in the markets of Hebron, Gaza, and Egypt could not be counted; the supply of this type of merchandise caused the prices to fall so low that a horse or a slave could be bought for the same price. The more eminent supporters of Ben-Kosebha were of course put to death, and Aqiba was one of these. All things considered, Dio Cassius' statement that Judea had almost became a desert was almost literally true.

492. After having caused this desert, Hadrian took up the business of being here also the *restitutor,* and proceeded without further hindrance to the building of Aelia Capitolina (§ 483). The city was established and was from every point of view the negation of the Yahwistic Jerusalem. Materially speaking, it was a Hellenistic city, constructed according to a plan entirely different from that of the old city; there were baths, and a theater, and the usual public buildings. Over the southern gate of the city which looked toward Bethlehem, a sculptured pig was erected as a trophy. The wild boar was, in fact, the

So-called *Arch of Hadrian* in Jerusalem (arch of the gate of the Forum of Aelia Capitolina).

emblem of the Tenth Legion, *Fretensis,* which had remained to guard Jerusalem after the catastrophe of 70 (§§ 472, 474), and was symbolic of the domination of Roman arms over Jerusalem. What a dreadful mockery to raise *such* an emblem over that city!

Aelia Capitolina was pagan and anti-Jewish by deliberate design. On the site of Yahweh's Temple there arose the temple to Jupiter Capitolinus containing a statue of Jupiter and an equestrian statue of Hadrian. On the western and opposite side of the city there

Tile of the Tenth Legion, *Fretensis,* with its emblem of a boar. (From *Revue Biblique,* 1900.)

was erected, over the spot where a hundred years before Jesus Christ had been crucified and buried, a temple to Aphrodite. The inhabitants of the new city were all non-Jewish in origin, and the Jews who had survived were forbidden under penalty of death to set foot in what had been ancient Jerusalem; they were permitted only "to gaze upon it from afar" (Tertullian, *Adv. Judaeos,* 13).

493. Conditions, therefore, were now reversed. Before A.D. 70 all pagans coming to Jerusalem had been excluded under penalty of death from setting foot in the Temple (§ 348), and they were permitted to contemplate "only from afar" that most holy place wherein Yahweh the God of the Jews had dwelt. Now it was the Jews who were forbidden under penalty of death to enter into their own holy city, and they were not even allowed to gaze upon that very material Jupiter who had been substituted for their immaterial Yahweh.

From that day to this, the entire world has been a city for the Jews; for a Temple, they have only their own hearts.

ADDITIONAL NOTES

Paragraph

2 ff. Cf. *ANET*, 305 ff., the Nabonidus Chronicle.

5 ff. *Op. cit.*, 306, and the Cyrus Cylinder, *ibid.*, 315 f.

36. For the document dated 304 B.C., cf. A. T. Clay, *Babylonian Records in the Library of J. Pierpont Morgan*, New York, 1913, II, 83, n. 1 (cf. pp. 11, 13).

41. Cf. *Cambridge Ancient History*, VIII (1930), 497 ff., 713, concerning the young son of Seleucus IV, who was perhaps called Antiochus (cf. § 234), and whose rights Antiochus IV passed over.

55 ff. Basic to the study of this new period of Israel's history is Kittel's *Geschichte des Volkes Israel* (Stuttgart, 1927–1929). An excellent work, with ample bibliography. More restricted and at times even fantastic is Sellin's *Geschichte des israelitisch-jüdischen Volkes* (Leipzig, 1932). Of minor value and marred by mistakes in the Hebrew is W. O. E. Oesterley's *History of Israel*, 2 vols. (Oxford, 1932). Other works will be noted below.

57. Oesterley believes the Temple of Jerusalem remained standing after the fire. Cf. *op. cit.*, 92.

59 ff. Concerning the deportees, cf. E. Klamroth, *Die jüdischen Exulanten in Babylonien* (Leipzig, 1912); and A. Causse's more general *Les dispersés d'Israel* (Paris, 1929).

63. The documents of Murashu are treated in H. Hilprecht and Albert Clay, *Business Documents of Murashu Sons of Nippur* (Philadelphia, 1898, 1904); cf. also Clay, *University of Pennsylvania Museum, Babylonian Section*, II, 1, 1912. The texts are given in Gressmann's *Altorientalische Texte zum Alten Testament* (Berlin and Leipzig, 1926), 434–439; cf. *ANET*, 221.

80 ff. For the "Return," and the entire Persian period, cf. Touzard, "Les Juifs au temps de la période Persane" in *RB*, 1915, 59–133, and the excellent but very lengthy "L'âme juive au temps des Perses," *ibid.*, 1916, 299 ff., and later. Cf. also R. De Vaux, "Israel . . . La restauration . . . La période grecque" in *DBS*, IV (1947), 769–774.

88. "The sons of Sena'ah" are discussed in E. Meyer, *Die Entstehung des Judentums* (Halle, 1896), 154; Kittel, *op. cit.*, III², 363 f.

108 ff. For Esdras and Nehemias and the question of chronology, cf. A. Van Hoonacker, "Néhémie et Esdras, une nouvelle hypothèse sur la chronologie de l'époque de la restauration juive" in *Le Muséon* (1890), IX, 92 ff.; "Zorobabel et le second temple," *ibid.*, X, 1891, 72 ff.; and his other articles as cited in "La succession chronologique Néhémie-Esdras" in *RB*, 1923, 481 (note) ff. Others who hold for the succession Nehemias-Esdras are J. Vandervorst, *Israël et l'ancient Orient* (Bruxelles, 1929), 204–216; S. A. Cook in *Cambridge Ancient History*, VI (1927), 173 ff.; Oesterley, *op. cit.*, 114–118 and Coucke in *DBS*, I (1928), 1269 ff. For the more customary order, cf. Kittel and Sellin in their *Geschichte*; cf. F. X. Kugler, *Von Moses bis Paulus* (Münster, 1922); A. Médébielle, *Esdras-Néhémie*, in the *Pirot Bible*, 1947, 266–271; R. De Vaux, "Israel" in *DBS*, IV (1947), 765–769.

133. Cf. H. Vincent, "Les murs de Jérusalem d'après Néhémie," in *RB*, 1904, 56–74 (textual criticism, topographical remarks); *ibid.*, 1927, 516–548; Crowfoot, "Excavations in the Tyropoeon Valley" in the *Quarterly Statement* (*PEF*), 1928, 9 ff.,

and at greater length in the *Annual* for 1929, Chap. II; A. Alt, "Das Taltor von Jerusalem" in *Palästinajahrbuch,* 1928, 74–98, is favorable to the new opinion.

146. That Esdras' manner and behavior in regulating matters in Jerusalem "shows signs of senility" is commonly admitted by both sides; cf. *RB*, 1924, 47 and n. 2. Not to be overlooked, however, is the fact that a noble visage can be made to appear ludicrous by a single slip of the brush. Cf. in this regard Médébielle, *op. cit.,* 270.

159 ff. Cf. J. A. Montgomery, *The Samaritans, the Earliest Jewish Sect* (Philadelphia, 1907); M. Gaster, *The Samaritans* (Schweich Lectures, 1923: Oxford, 1926); J. Jeremias, *Die Passahfeier der Samaritaner* (Giessen, 1932).

166 ff. E. Sachau, *Aramaische Papyrus und Ostraka aus einer jüdischen Militär-Kolonie zu Elephantine* (Leipzig, 1911); A. Cowley, *Aramaic Papyri of the 5th Century B.C.* (Oxford, 1923); cf. English text in *ANET*, 491 f. Cf. also L. Hennequin, "Eléphantine" in *DBS*, II (1934), 962–1032; E. G. Kraeling, "New Light on the Elephantine Colony," in *BA*, XV (1952), 50–67.

168. For the inscription of Abu-Simbel, cf. *CAH*, III, 301; E. Schürer, *Geschichte*, III, 32.

180 ff. From this point on the classical work of E. Schürer, *Geschichte des judischen volkes im Zeitalter Jesu Christi* (Leipzig, 1901–1909), is a veritable mine of information and covers the field up to this date. (English translation: *A History of the Jewish People in the Time of Jesus Christ* [tr. by J. Macpherson], 6 vols., 1890. References are however to the German.) More concerned with the doctrines and customs of Israel are G. Moore, *Judaism in the First Centuries of the Christian Era — The Age of the Tannaim* (Cambridge, 1927–1930); M. J. Lagrange, *Le Judaisme avant Jésus-Christ* (Paris, 1931). Also good, with reservations, is J. Juster, *Les Juifs dans l'Empire Romain* (Paris, 1914).

192. For the Synagogue of Schedia, cf. Schürer, *op. cit.,* III, 41, 93.

195 ff. For Roman Judaism, cf. J.-B. Frey, "Les communautés juives à Rome aux premiers temps de l'Eglise" in *Recherches de science religieuse*, 1930, 269 ff.; in *Biblica*, 1931, 129–156. This author has published many unedited Jewish inscriptions in the *Rivista di archeologia cristiana*, 1928–1931; in *Inscriptions juives de Rome et d'Italie* (Paris, 1932); and *Corpus Inscriptionum Judaicarum:* "Recueil des inscriptions juives qui vont du III° siècle de notre ère" (Vatican City, 1936). The Jewish catacombs at Rome have not been fully explored; cf. N. Müller, *Die jüdische Katakombe am Monteverde zu Rom* (Leipzig, 1912); and in collaboration with N. A. Bees, *Die Inschriften der jüd. Katakombe am Monteverde zu Rom* (Leipzig, 1919). Those of the Villa Torlonia are described by R. Paribeni, *Notizie degli scavi* (Accad. Lincei), 1920, 143 ff.; and H. W. Beyer and H. Lietzmann in *Die jüd. Katakombe der Villa Torlonia in Rom* (Berlin, 1930).

199. For the juridical independence of the various "synagogues" of Rome, and for details concerning the lack of a central power, cf. the first article of Frey cited in § 195, and Schürer, *op. cit.,* III, 81. Opposed are Juster, *op. cit.,* I, 420 f., and La Piana, in *The Harvard Theological Review*, 1925–1927.

200. The Jewish inscriptions cited can be found in Frey, in *Biblica*, 1931, 136.

201 ff. All the texts of Greco-Roman authors pertinent to Judaism are gathered together in Th. Reinach's *Textes d'auteurs grecs et romains relatifs au judaïsme* (Paris, 1895).

208. Schürer, *op. cit.,* and Felten, *Storia dei tempi del N.T.* (tr. from the German) (Turin, 1932). For Josephus Flavius, cf. V. Ussani, "Questioni flaviane" and "Su la più antica storia del testo di Fl. Gius.," in *Rivista di filologia*, 1910–1914 (textual criticism); R. Laqueur, *Der jüdische Historiker Fl. Josephus* (Giessen, 1920); W. Weber, *Josephus und Vespasian — Untersuchungen zu dem Jüdischen Krieg des Fl. Josephus* (Stuttgart, 1921); B. Motzo, *Saggi di storia e letteratura giudeo-ellenistica* (Florence, 1924); H. St. John Thackeray, *Josephus, The Man and the Historian* (New York, 1929).

211. Jewish tombs were segregated in the Roman catacombs. Cf. Frey, *Biblica*, 1931, 144.

214. Moore, *op. cit.*, I, 331 ff., and III, 109 ff., gives the Jewish initiation rites.
215 ff. For the Papyri of Zenon, cf. *Papiri greci e latini* in *Pubblicazioni della Soc. Ital. per la ricerca dei papiri gr. e lat. in Egitto* (Florence, 1917), IV, 54 ff. For our position, cf. especially C. C. Edgar, *Selected Papyri from the Archives of Zenon* in the *Annales du service des Antiquités de l'Egypte*, XVIII (1918), XXIII (1923), nn. 3, 13, 84; also, *Zenon Papyri* (Cairo Museum Catalogue), I, 1925, nn. 59003, 59075, 59076 (the last number squares with n. 84 above, and contains Tobias' invocation to the Gods: χάρις τοῖς θεοῖς).
The best and most recent studies on the Tobiads are E. Meyer, *Ursprung und Anfänge des Christentums* (Stuttgart and Berlin, 1921), 128 ff.; H. Gressmann, "Die ammonitischen Tobiaden" in *Sitzungsberichte der preussischen Akademie der Wissenschaft*, 1921, 663–671; A Momigliano, "I Tobiadi nella preistoria del moto maccabaico," in *Atti della R. Accad. delle Scienze di Torino*, 1932, 165–200; cf. also the geographical remarks of H. Vincent in *RB*, 1920, 161 ff.; and of F.-M. Abel, *ibid.*, 1923, 409 ff.; 1924, 566 ff.
219. The archaeological finds at 'Araq el-Emir are detailed in the Princeton University's *Archaeological Expedition to Syria in 1904–1905*: H. C. Butler, II, A; Littman, III, A. Also the authors cited in preceding note.
222. For the identification of Hyrcanus Tobias with Messias, son of Joseph, cf. Gressmann, *Tobiaden, loc. cit.*, and Moore, *op. cit.*, II, 370 f.
236. The complicated chronological question of this period is treated in Kugler, *op. cit.*, 338 ff.; W. Kolbe, *Beiträge zur syrischen und jüdischen Geschichte* (Berlin, 1926), 28 f., 34 f.
237. For the site of the Akra, cf. *RB*, 1926, 518 ff.
238. In favor of the reading: "an old Antiochian": cf. Motzo, *op. cit.*, 123 f., who is followed by A. Momigliano, *Prime linee di storia della tradizione maccabaica* (Roma, 1930), 111; the other reading, "an old Athenian" is usually followed, and is defended by Lagrange, *Judaïsme*, 54. Dom De Bruyne and B. Sodar, *Les anciennes traductions latines des Machabées* (Maredsous, 1932), 144 f., give five texts (Latin) which read *senem atheniensem*, whereas only one has *senem antiochenum*.
244 ff. The Sadoqite Document is given in S. Schechter, *Documents of Jewish Sectaries*, I, *Fragments of a Zadoqite work* (English translation) (Cambridge, 1910). Translations and studies: J. Lévi in *Revue des Etudes Juives*, LXI (1910), 213 ff., and later; M. J. Lagrange in *RB*, 1912, 213 ff., and later; R. H. Charles, *The Apocrypha and Pseudepigrapha of the O.T.* (Oxford, 1913), 785–834; Ed. Meyer, *Die Gemeinde des Neuen Bundes im Lande Damaskus, eine jüdische Schrift aus der Seleukidenzeit* (Berlin, 1919); W. Staerk, *Die jüdische Gemeinde des neuen Bundes in Damascus* (Gütersloh, 1922); G. Hölscher, "Zur Frage nach Alter und Herkunft der sogennanten Damaskusschrift" in *ZNTW*, 1929, 21–46; J. B. Frey in *DBS*, I (Paris, 1928), 396–403; *The Zadokite Fragments* (Univ. of Cambridge), 1952; H. R. Rowley, *The Zadokite Fragments and the Dead Sea Scrolls* (Oxford, 1952).
247. The texts relative to the temple at Leontopolis are given in Schürer, *op. cit.*, 144 ff.; cf. Lagrange, *Judaïsme*, 490–493. The foundation of the temple is attributed to Onias III by Motzo, *op. cit.*, 185 f. (cf. 117 f.), and Momigliano, *Prime linee*, 39; *Tobiadi*, 190 f., and they advance a theory (Wellhausen) that Onias III was not murdered by Andronicus.
254 ff. For the geographical side of the story of the Machabees, the studies of Père F. M. Abel, "Topographie des campagnes Maccabéens" in *RB*, 1923, 495, and later, are indispensable, as are his two volumes, *Les livres des Maccabées* (Paris, 1949–1953).
257. The chronology of the events of this period and especially the death of Antiochus IV are dealt with by Motzo, *op. cit.*, 132 ff. (his explanation of the false rumors of Antiochus' death is the most plausible of all, and does justice to the texts), and Momigliano, *Prime linee*, 74 ff. Kolbe, *op. cit.*, 79 ff., holds the contrary view.

259. For the feast of Hanukkah, cf. Höpfl, "Das Chanukafest" in *Biblica*, 1922, 165–179; O. S. Rankin, *The Origin of the Festival of Hanukkah* (Edinburgh, 1931).

279. Momigliano, *op. cit.*, 148 f., 168, denies the sending of a delegation to Rome by Jonathan.

285. R. A. S. Macalister, *The Excavation of Gezer* (London, 1912), I, 211 f.

298. L. Finkelstein, *The Pharisees, the Sociological Background of their Faith* (Philadelphia, 1938); cf. *RB*, 1938, 280–284.

299. V. Aptowitzer, *Parteipolitik der Hasmonäerzeit im rabbin. und pseudepigraph. Schrifttum* (Vienna, 1927), 13 ff., takes up the question of the royal dignity bestowed upon Hyrcanus.

330 ff. For the man Herod, besides Schürer, *op. cit.*, I, 360–418 (and bibliography up to that point), the rigidly technical study of W. Otto, "Herodes I" in Pauly-Wissowa, *Real-Encyclopädie der class. Altertumwiss.*, Supplement II (Stuttgart, 1913), cols. 1–158, is indispensable. More recently, cf. H. Willrich, *Das Haus des Herodes zwischen Jerusalem und Rom* (Heidelberg, 1928), and Lagrange, *Judaïsme*, 164–201.

357. For the oath of the citizenry to Augustus, cf. Schürer, *op. cit.*, I, 399, n. 96.

392. Claudius' letter to the Alexandrians, in H. I. Bell, *Jews and Christians in Egypt* (London, 1924); also by the same author, *Juden und Griechen im römischen Alexandreia* (Leipzig, 1926). Many studies have been written on this letter, cf. S. Lösch, *Epistola Claudiana — Der neuentdeckte Brief das Kaisers Claudius von J. 41 nach Chr. und das Urchristentum* (Rottenburg, 1920); M. J. Lagrange, "La lettre de Claude aux Alexandrins" in *RB*, 1921, 270–276. Concerning the *Acta* of Isidor and Lampon, cf. Schürer, *op. cit.*, I, 67–70.

398. Cf. E. L. Sukenik and L. A. Mayer, *The Third Wall of Jerusalem — An Account of Excavations* (Jerusalem [London], 1930). Vigorously opposed by Père Vincent, "La troisième enceinte de Jérusalem" in *RB*, 1927, 516 ff.; "Encore la troisième enceinte de Jérusalem," *ibid.*, 1947, 90–126; "Jérusalem" in *DBS*, IV (1947), 920–941; and his *Jérusalem de l'Ancien Testament* (Paris, 1954): cf. article "Arma Virumque Cano" in *CBQ*, 1955.

454 (and 471). For the most recent excavation of Masada, cf. A. Schulten, *Masada, die Burg des Herodes und die römischen Lager* (Leipzig, 1933).

477. Concerning the earthquake, see R. Paribeni, *Optimus Princeps — Saggio sulla storia e sui tempi dell'imperatore Traiano* (Messina, 1927), II, 296 f.

478. For this milestone, cf. Paribeni, *op. cit.*, II, 197.

492. Cf. R. Harris, "Hadrian's Decree of Expulsion of the Jews from Jerusalem," in *The Harvard Theological Review*, 1926, 199 ff.

Index

References are to paragraphs, *not* pages.

467